ADVANCED ACCOUNTING

**The Willard J. Graham Series
in Accounting**

Consulting Editor   ROBERT N. ANTHONY   *Harvard University*

ADVANCED ACCOUNTING

CHARLES H. GRIFFIN, Ph.D.
The University of Texas at Austin

THOMAS H. WILLIAMS, Ph.D.
University of Wisconsin—Madison

KERMIT D. LARSON, D.B.A.
The University of Texas at Austin

Third Edition   1977

RICHARD D. IRWIN, INC.   Homewood, Illinois   60430
Irwin-Dorsey Limited   Georgetown, Ontario   L7G 4B3

Third Edition

First Printing, February 1977
Second Printing, August 1977
Third Printing, September 1977
Fourth Printing, November 1977

ISBN 0-256-01899-5
Library of Congress Catalog Card No. 76–47728
Printed in the United States of America

To
Fay Griffin,
Carol Williams,
and
Nancy Larson

Preface

THIS THIRD EDITION of *Advanced Accounting* has been substantially revised to incorporate the many relevant developments that have occurred in financial reporting over the past six years. In addition, the number of short exercises and problems has been expanded in response to the requests of many users of the text. Because cost is an important consideration to students, we have consciously sought to eliminate duplication of illustrations, and have deleted seldom-used chapters. The result is, we believe, a compact, comprehensive coverage of the topics most commonly included in advanced accounting courses.

In recognition of the fact that business combinations and the related consolidated financial statement issues are generally given heavy emphasis in advanced accounting courses, this Third Edition continues to devote a substantial portion of its coverage to these topics (Units One and Two). Also, these units have been more extensively revised than any other single unit.

The two chapters dealing with mergers and acquisitions have been reorganized to provide a more logical and flexible sequence of discussion. A broad introduction to this topic, indicating the historical, economic, and legal implications of business combinations, the alternative methods of classifying combinations, the tax implications of combinations, and the use of pro forma financial statements in planning combinations, is presented in Chapter 1. This is followed by a chapter devoted to accounting analyses that may assist the negotiators of a corporate combination when the combination relates to privately held companies and requires an equitable payment plan, or when the combination involves publicly traded companies for which a negotiation model based on market prices may be useful. Some instructors will believe the negotiations material in Chapter 2 deserves special consideration; others may elect to skip that chapter in which case they may move directly from the introduction to the initial discussion of consolidated statements, in Chapter 3.

The most important change in the treatment of consolidated statements is the shift in emphasis to the equity method. In the prior edition, we observed that *APB Opinion 18* imposed a new, equity method *reporting* requirement for investments in affiliates but did not necessarily require investors to change from the cost method of *recording* in their books. That change, we suggested, was a function of cost and administrative convenience, and only the passage of time would indicate companies' responses to this issue. Based upon our discussions with the technical staffs of public accounting firms and with corporate controllers, we now conclude that most companies have, in fact, changed their method of recording in the books from cost to equity. Additionally, the Uniform CPA examination has, in recent years, emphasized the equity method. Accordingly, we have also elected to emphasize this method.

The change to the equity method has required some major modifications in the schedular form of analysis used in the book, although this Third Edition continues to maintain this schedular emphasis. Working papers are illustrated when they are thought to be helpful to the student's understanding, but we have attempted to avoid repetitive use of them both in the text and the problems. Certain important issues associated with using the equity method for unconsolidated affiliates (for example, elimination of intercompany profits on the investor's books) are also examined, because students are not often exposed to these problems in earlier courses.

Increasingly, financial reporting is influenced by a variety of rules and regulations, as well as by broad principles, and we are persuaded that students should be exposed to the spectrum of currently existing authoritative literature. Correspondingly, the material on business combinations and consolidations reflects the latest pronouncements of the Accounting Principles Board and the Financial Accounting Standards Board. Selected accounting interpretations issued by these policy-setting boards have also been included, as well as important rules promulgated by the Securities and Exchange Commission. Other topics in the book have not been subject to as much environmental change as has the business combinations-consolidated statements area. However, where such changes have occurred, they have been incorporated.

Several additional improvements have been made in this edition. The problems associated with the determination of the cost of an acquired company have been addressed in more detail in Chapter 3, and the treatment of the "differential," or "excess cost," at date of acquisition has been more explicitly linked with *APB Opinion 16*. Accounting for this "differential" subsequent to acquisition—discussed in Chapter 5—has been completely rewritten to achieve what we believe is a significant increase in clarity.

In Chapter 6, the earnings per share discussion has been expanded in its coverage of parent-subsidiary and equity method situations. Also, the section in this chapter on segmental reporting has been extensively revised in light of issuance of *FASB Standard No. 14.* The problem of inter-period tax allocation on intercompany profits is integrated with the discussion of intercompany profits on asset transfers in Chapter 7, rather than leaving it as an isolated topic at the end of the section. Having achieved this coverage, we then eliminate it from the discussion of intercompany bonds in Chapter 8, in order not to further complicate this traditionally difficult topic. A completely new bond elimination schedule has been developed for this revision, which students should find much easier to understand as a summary of the necessary eliminations associated with interaffiliate bondholdings. Chapter 8 also includes a completely revised and expanded discussion of preferred stock issuances by subsidiaries.

In Chapter 9, the issues related to changes in a parent company's ownership interest in affiliates have been organized into a more logical and internally consistent framework. As in Chapter 8, the primary objective of the revision was to provide a sequence of discussion that students will grasp more easily. Multilevel affiliations and bilateral stockholdings are combined in Chapter 10 under the title of special ownership configurations. And Chapter 11 concludes the coverage of consolidated statements with a brief discussion of the "entity theory" of consolidated statements and a digest of the most cogent features of earlier chapters. It also includes a discussion of accounting for branches.

Accounting for international operations (Chapter 12) has been completely rewritten to incorporate *FASB Standard No. 8* and to expand the discussion of accounting for forward exchange contracts. The unit on partnerships (Chapters 13, 14, and 15) has been streamlined, and the fiduciary chapters (Chapters 16, 17, and 18) revised to reflect recent statutory developments. Additionally, the various options available under the bankruptcy statutes have been clarified. The governmental accounting chapter has been expanded to include illustrative journal entries for the more common transactions encountered in all of the various funds. Finally, in Unit Five, the coverage of consignments and installment sales has been compressed into one chapter by eliminating only marginally important illustrations and related narrative; however, recent changes in accounting policy covering installment sales have been incorporated.

The number of short exercises in the text has been expanded significantly, and these exercises have been identified separately from the generally longer problems. The exercises can be used in a variety of different ways, including homework assignments, classroom illustrations, and on quizzes and examinations.

Discussions over the years with numerous instructors clearly indicate a variety of approaches in determining the amount of time which should be devoted to the various topics in an advanced accounting course. We are sympathetic to this diversity of opinion and have sought to provide as much flexibility in the text as possible. However, we do not believe that most topics included in the book, particularly business combinations and consolidated financial statements, can be meaningfully covered in a cursory manner. Accordingly, the text's coverage is intended to be complete, but not redundant, and to provide the student with a rich source of illustrations. Where time constrains the amount of material that can be assigned, we believe that selective omission of topics and techniques is preferable to a more comprehensive, but probably superficial, coverage of the area.

We are indebted to a number of people and organizations for their contributions to this book. The American Institute of Certified Public Accountants has been very generous in granting permission to reproduce selected excerpts from several of its publications, and to use relevant CPA questions and problems. The Financial Accounting Standards Board was equally cooperative in our requests for quotation privileges. We have benefited immeasurably from the comments we have received from the many users of prior editions of this book, and we hope that the Third Edition is as responsive as possible to their needs. We would particularly like to thank Robert Libby of Pennsylvania State University and Wayne Morse of Duke University for their extensive comments on the book, G. Fred Streuling of Brigham Young University for reviewing various sections that have tax implications, and John Jordan of Price Waterhouse & Co. for providing us with some very useful technical material in the consolidation area. Very special thanks are due Anna Fowler of The University of Texas at Austin, Marsha McCarroll Wilson of Babson College, and Russell Anderson of Haskins & Sells, for their assistance during the final stages of the revision, and to Karen Harrison for typing parts of the final manuscript. Finally, we wish to reiterate our continuing appreciation and high regard for Professor Emeritus G. H. Newlove of The University of Texas at Austin, whose pioneering work in this area and life-long example as a scholarly researcher have been an aid and an inspiration to the authors.

January 1977   C.H.G.
                                                           T.H.W.
                                                           K.D.L.

Contents

of Consolidation Policy. Precautions in the Evaluation of Consolidated Statements. Determining Cost of an Acquired Company. Consolidated Balance Sheet. Investment at Book Value of Subsidiary Stock. Investment Cost More than Book Value of Subsidiary Stock. Investment Cost Less than Book Value of Subsidiary Stock. Debit (Credit) Differentials. Other Intercompany Transactions. Unpaid Subsidiary Dividends at Acquisition. Treasury Stock of the Subsidiary. Adjustments. Illustrative Problem.

Working Paper. Refinement of Definition of Consolidated Net Income. INTERCOMPANY PROFIT—PLANT AND EQUIPMENT. INTERCOMPANY PROFITS—RELATED TOPICS: Other Asset Transfers. Transfer Profits before Affiliation. Evolution of Accounting Practice regarding Intercompany Profits.

Appendix: Compound Interest Tables

unit one

ACCOUNTING
FOR
COMBINED
CORPORATE
ENTITIES

1

Mergers and Acquisitions

HISTORICAL, ECONOMIC, AND LEGAL CONSIDERATIONS

"FOR NEARLY a decade, a great corporate merger game has generated more excitement, more glamour—and probably more fortunes—than any other phenomenon in the business scene."[1] That statement was made in 1968 during the peak of the greatest merger movement in the history of modern commerce. The corporate growth objective, which was the driving force underlying this movement, had come to dominate other business goals. One major corporation summarized its objectives in terms of successive three-year plans to double sales and earnings per share.[2] Another corporation began its annual report as follows:

Tenneco Inc. is unique. It is the first and only industrial corporation ever to pass the $3 billion mark in assets while still under 25 years old.

Obviously, this is the result of planned growth, of diligently pursuing a business objective. And purposeful growth, within the confines of good business judgment, remains the goal.[3]

The significance of the growth objective was perhaps stated most clearly in the 1968 annual report of Teledyne, Inc. The following statements were included in the letter to shareholders:

These sustained results reflect our purpose—sound and healthy growth in assets and earnings per share, on both a short-term and a long-term basis, with current gains providing the basis for long-term growth in the future.

---

[1] "Time of Testing for Conglomerates," *Business Week,* March 2, 1968, p. 38.

[2] "Successful People United for Greater Growth," U.S. Industries, Inc., *Annual Report 1968,* p. 3.

[3] Tenneco Inc., *1967 Annual Report,* p. 1.

Teledyne has been systematically organized around a plan designed to produce sustained growth, and its assets are continuously deployed and redeployed with the goal of growth in mind.[4]

During the 1970s, the effects of recession, inflation, and continued uncertainty over the ability of government to control these economic ills have cast dark clouds over those companies known for assuming high risks in the pursuit of more and more growth. The top executives of one large firm publicly acknowledged to the company's shareholders that "the word 'growth' has fallen into disfavor among some social and political observers, especially where it is seen as a process of getting bigger just for the sake of bigness. In light of this antigrowth sentiment, it is important to point out that Pfizer is dedicated to a special kind of growth . . ."[5] Another management reported to its stockholders that "we must be much more selective in identifying and encouraging growth."[6] Apparently, the excessive emphasis on growth in the 1960s has been exposed by the general economic reverses of the 1970s; accordingly, managements are weighing growth much more cautiously in light of myriad other objectives as corporate policy is formulated. In 1976, the *Wall Street Journal* reported that merger-minded companies "appear far more selective than in the 1960s. Wary of spreading themselves too thin, they insist on buying only companies that fit their 'corporate strategy,' " and express concern over the importance of merging only with companies that "fit with the existing business."[7]

The decision to engage in a significant business expansion has an obvious effect on the size of operations. But it also may have a material impact on liquidity, risk, and efficiency, as well as many other management objectives. Further, the form within which the business expansion is accomplished may substantially alter the expansion's effect.

All business expansions can be broadly classified as either internal or external. *Internal* business expansion includes the normal increase in operations arising from increasing demand for a firm's products and services. It also includes the establishment of new product lines and geographic sales areas, so long as these activities are financed through the normal corporate means of earnings retention and issuances of debt and/or residual equities. The primary distinguishing characteristic of internal expansion is that it does not involve the acquisition of preexisting business operations from other business units. *External* business expansion, on the other hand, is achieved by the acquisition of established business operations. Indeed, it frequently involves the acquisition of an *entire* business entity. Subsequent to acquisition, the operations of the acquired firm may be integrated with operating divisions of the purchasing firm; or

---

4 Teledyne, Inc., *1968 Annual Report,* p. 2.

5 Pfizer Inc., *1974 Annual Report,* pp. 2–3.

6 Borg-Warner Corporation, *1974 Annual Report,* p. 5.

7 "Mergers, Acquisitions Come Back Into Style But the Style Is New," *Wall Street Journal,* April 28, 1976, p. 1.

they may be left intact, leaving the acquired unit to operate as a distinct division or subsidiary corporation of the acquiring firm.

"Business combination" is the general term applied to external expansions in which all, or substantially all, of the operations of two or more firms are brought under centralized control. Depending upon the relative sizes of the combining companies it may be somewhat inappropriate to refer to them as "acquiring" or "acquired" firms. The managements of the combining firms may in fact continue with the combined unit in positions of responsibility similar to their roles previous to the combination. The stockholders of both companies may be stockholders in the combined unit. A new corporation may even be formed to replace the legal structures of the combining entities. Nonetheless, such combinations have similar attributes as does the more typical external business expansion, in which one dominant enterprise *acquires* another. All business combinations, whether between relatively equally sized firms or between one dominant company and one small company, are similar in their relationship to the variety of business objectives mentioned earlier. Even a company that anticipates being acquired and losing its corporate identity must relate the prospect of business combination to objectives such as growth, diversification, and minimization of risk.

Historical Significance of Business Combinations

Business combinations are not a recent phenomenon, notwithstanding the widespread significance they have attained in recent years. The formal combination of established business operations under centralized control has undoubtedly existed since the earliest days of organized commercial activity. However, since the first great wave of combination activity in the United States, which took place at the turn of the 20th century, business combinations have gone through cyclical periods of greater and lesser importance. Table 1–1 indicates the sharply varying number of firms that

Table 1–1

Time Period	Firm Disappearances by Merger or Acquisitions
1895–96	69
1897–98	372
1899–1900	1,548
1901–2	802
1903–4	221
1905–6	354
1907–8	137

Source: Ralph L. Nelson, *Merger Movements in American Industry 1895–1956* (Princeton, N.J.: Princeton University Press for the National Bureau of Economic Research, 1959), Table B-7, pp. 153–54.

disappeared as a result of mergers during the years 1895 to 1908. The total number of firms disappearing in any year as a result of mergers or acquisitions did not again reach 200 until 1920.

Table 1–2 discloses the number of business combinations in manufac-

Table 1–2

Time Period	Mergers and Acquisitions in Mining and Manufacturing
1920–24	2,235
1925–29	4,583
1930–34	1,687
1935–39	577
1940–44	906
1945–49	1,505
1950–54	1,424
1955–59	3,365
1960–64	4,366
1965–69	8,213
1970	1,351
1971	1,011
1972	911
1973	874

Source: U.S. Department of Commerce, Bureau of the Census, *Statistical Abstract of the United States 1975*, 96th ed. (Washington, D.C.: U.S. Government Printing Office, 1975), Table No. 834, p. 506.

turing and mining during the period 1920–72. Two additional peaks of business combination activity are clearly evidenced during 1925–29 and during 1955–69. In comparison with the 1965–69 high mark of merger activity, the number of mergers continued to decline through 1975, primarily due to the poor economic conditions of the early 1970s. Nevertheless, the level of merger activity during the early 1970s was very high relative to long-run historical norms, and many informed observers continued to anticipate a rebound in the number of mergers. Writing in the *Financial Executive,* one person observed that "the financial community is watching with mounting interest signs of another round of mergers and takeovers reminiscent of, but totally unlike, the '60s."[8]

In a similar vein, *Business Week* reported in August, 1974, that large, conservative companies with strong cash positions are replacing the conglomerate oriented entrepreneurs of the 1960s as the big source of mergers and acquisitions. "Ironically," they state, "it is now conservative companies with pots of cash . . . that are emerging as the new takeover

[8] William J. Gaskill, "Are You Ready for the New Merger Boom?" *Financial Executive,* September 1974, p. 38.

artists. Wall Street's investment bankers are calling it the rise of the blue-chip raiders."[9] More recently, the *Wall Street Journal* reported that merger activity once again began to increase in 1976. Although buying companies are apparently much more concerned with the importance of having the acquired company fit into the existing operations of the buying company, and "diversification is out of style," the stock market recovery has provided acquisition-minded companies with the best climate in years.[10]

The two early periods of high-combination activity were characterized by the formation of industrial giants representing important and continuing industries in the United States economy. By comparison, the merger boom during the late 1950s and 1960s suggested a desire on the part of management to overcome the risk and general attributes of being limited to any specific industry. Many of these later business combinations resulted in the widest possible diversification of business operations being centrally controlled by one corporate parent. For example, operations during 1968 that were controlled by Ling-Temco-Vought, Inc., included aerospace, electronics, meat products, cable and wire, sporting goods, chemicals, airlines, services, banking, and insurance. Tenneco Inc. classifies its diverse operations as natural gas pipelines, oil production and refining, marketing, chemicals, packaging, manufacturing, land use, and investments (in insurance, banking, etc.).

The problems of accounting for combined business units have become increasingly *significant* to the business community, investors, and government. The student will intuitively recognize that the problems of accounting for such combined units are also becoming more *complex*. Much of the discussion in this and several following chapters relates directly to such accounting problems.

The significance of business combinations to the financial and investing community is highlighted most dramatically in terms of its effect upon particular corporations. In 1958, Ling Electronics reported consolidated operating revenue of less than $8,000,000. Ling-Temco-Vought, Inc., the firm resulting from many business combinations between Ling Electronics and other firms, reported 1968 consolidated sales as $2,769,700,000. It must be understood, of course, that Ling Electronic sales did not grow from $8 million to $2.7 billion in 10 years. The 1968 sales represent the operations of *many* business units that operated separately in 1958. It is the unusual concentration of control over what was once a large variety of separate business entities that is indicated by comparing 1958 sales of Ling Electronics with 1968 sales of Ling-Temco-Vought, Inc. Similar statistics depict the histories of several other corporate giants, e.g., Litton Industries, Inc., and Gulf & Western Industries.

A proper conception of the accounting problems associated with com-

---

9 Rise of the Blue-chip Raiders," *Business Week,* August 1974, p. 65.

10 *Wall Street Journal,* April 28, 1976, p. 1.

bined business units requires, in part, an appreciation for the tremendous alterations in economic characteristics of firms that can result from business combinations. Understanding these accounting problems is also facilitated by a recognition of the motives which underlie business combinations and the constraints associated therewith. These subjects are examined in the following discussion.

Impetus for Business Combinations

Many of the motives underlying business combinations also tend to induce internal business expansion. Thus, it is important to recognize the forces that lead to business combination as a unique form of expansion. Presuming a preexisting desire of management to begin or enlarge a particular set of operations in a given market area, the approach of business combination may have several advantages over internal expansion.

1. Business combination provides the management of the acquiring company the opportunity of utilizing the acquired company's historical data on operations and sales effectiveness. Thus, projections concerning profitability, cash requirements, and many other significant operating factors can be based upon the reality of historical operations. Internal expansion into new product lines, by comparison, is similar to establishing an entirely new business. An adequate historical basis for planning projections *may* be derived from other operations of the firm. But they are, at best, only analogous to the proposed expansion.

2. Combination provides the expanding company the immediate availability of suppliers, productive facilities (including operating management), and an established channel of distribution. Internal expansion provides few or none of these resources, thereby requiring a lengthy start-up period before the new operations evidence an adequate return on investment. This necessary start-up period not only defers the expected return on investment but also increases the risk associated with expansion.

3. Internal expansion into a particular market nearly always involves the interjection of an additional competitor (the expanding firm) into the market, thereby tending to enhance price and service competition. It may also tend to increase production costs by increasing competition in factor markets. Combination, on the other hand, merely alters the organizational structure and the control of an existing competitor, leaving the market's competing forces essentially unchanged.

4. Tax considerations, as in most major business decisions, are significant in evaluating alternative forms of business expansion. Special tax characteristics of a firm, such as the existence of unused operating loss carry forwards, may be transferable to an acquiring firm. One of the important conditions for this to occur, however, is that there must be sound business purpose for the combination other than tax benefits. Nevertheless, such tax benefits may provide a significant impetus for busi-

ness combination. Alternatively, internal expansion may have preferential tax implications in certain instances. Even so, tax factors have frequently led to combinations. Evidence in many situations suggests that the crucial decision in management's election to expand was not between alternative *forms* of expansion (internal versus external); rather, it was whether or not a combination with a *specific* company should be pursued, the dominant benefit of which would be the effect on the tax status of the constituent firms.

The student should not infer that business combination always provides a superior means of expansion. There may be no existing firms that are willing to combine. Also, those which are available may not be suitable from the acquiring firm's point of view. While business combination provides numerous advantages, it also burdens the expansion effort with any inefficiencies that are characteristic of the acquired firm, such as an old plant, ineffective management, and marketing deficiencies.

Other factors which give rise to business combinations also tend to support internal expansion.

1. A traditional motive underlying business expansion is to develop a fully integrated operation in a particular product line. Acquisition of supplier and customer entities, or internal expansion into their fields of operation, leads to centralized control over the productive and distributive channel of a product. This type of expansion reduces the risk of dependence upon particular suppliers and customers; it also provides the firm an opportunity to earn a profit associated with the new operations.

2. Another traditional motive for expansion is to broaden the market area covered by the firm. While this typically implies geographical expansion, it may also involve the addition of related product lines. The expected result is a reduction in the risk associated with the economic vagaries of a narrow product line or limited market area.

3. A more general motive for expansion is to afford the firm economies of large scale. Financial economies are at least as significant in this regard as are the possibilities of increased productive efficiencies. The variety of financing methods, as well as the expense of financing, are usually more favorable for large firms than for small firms. Service or overhead functions such as are provided by corporate management and computer installations are also subject to economies of scale. Thus, expansion may accomplish the employment of what were previously idle resources.

4. The desire to increase the earnings growth rate is an additional stimulus for business combinations. The effect of increasing earnings growth through business combination is frequently referred to as "synergism." To the extent such growth derives from improvements in efficiency or other factors mentioned in this discussion, the synergistic motive is redundant. However, later discussion will disclose how certain business combinations can result in significant increases in reported earn-

ings per share without any real gains in efficiency. Managerial motives for growth of the latter nature may be of questionable propriety, although their existence should be recognized.

5. Business operations that are especially sensitive to cyclical profit patterns frequently lead to expansion in the attempt to stabilize profits. Successful expansion, in these terms, requires that the historical profit pattern of the expanding company be countercyclical to that of the new operations. A noncyclical or relatively stable profit pattern is generally evaluated by the investing community as being less risky.

6. Another impetus to expansion and business combination might be referred to as the "psychology of scale." Aside from consequences of economic efficiencies or inefficiencies, there is an apparent desire on the part of many managements for bigness per se. Management prestige and realm of authority tend to be enhanced as a firm becomes larger. Without rendering a judgment on the appropriateness or quality of such goals, it is important to recognize their existence.

Constraints upon Business Combinations

Various branches of the United States government have exhibited a concern with the movement toward economic concentration that results from business combinations. The Sherman Act and the Clayton Act (as amended) provide the statutory framework with which the Department of Justice and Federal Trade Commission have prevented the formation or continuation of numerous combinations. The Clayton Act was enacted to strengthen the Sherman Act, and it allows government to challenge some mergers that are not yet in violation of the Sherman Act. In general, Section 7 of the Clayton Act disallows any corporate combination the effect of which may be substantially to lessen competition or tend to create a monopoly. The thrust of Section 7 is to deal with monopolistic tendencies before significant injury has been incurred.

Horizontal Combinations. Three general types of combinations have been interpreted by the courts. Firms that perform similar functions in the production or sale of comparable products are horizontal in relationship.[11] Thus, if the acquiring firm and the acquired firm have been competitors or are potential competitors, the combination is referred to as "horizontal." In the process of analyzing horizontal mergers to determine whether they may substantially lessen competition or tend to create monopoly, the courts have considered several factors of varying significance, depending upon the case. After designating the "relevant market" within which the firms in question have influence, courts have considered: (1) the level of concentration in that market; (2) the rank of the acquiring and acquired firms in the market and their shares of the mar-

---

[11] *Brown Shoe Co.* v. *United States,* 370 U.S. 294, p. 334 (1962).

ket; (3) any change in the number of companies operating in the market; (4) any changes in barriers to entering the market; and (5) the elimination of a large independent firm from an oligopolistic market. In general, horizontal mergers are vulnerable ". . . if the acquiring company is a major company and if the acquired company is a strong competitor in its own right and concentration in the relevant market is high; nor can a viable independent with relatively low market shares be acquired if concentration in the relevant market is high, the number of companies is declining in the face of expanding demand, and the acquiring company is a dominant one in the market affected."[12]

Vertical Combinations.   The second general (economic) type of business combination may be referred to as "vertical." In a vertical merger, the combining firms have a supplier-customer relationship. Vertical mergers are especially sensitive to challenge if as a result of the merger, a substantial share of the relevant market will be foreclosed from other firms. In terms of more specific tests, such a combination is likely to be litigated if the market of either constituent is concentrated and if there is a history of similar combinations that have increased the risk of independent firms, making it difficult for them to find suppliers or customers that are not competitors.[13]

Conglomerate Combinations.   A third category of business combinations that has received congressional and judiciary attention is referred to as "conglomerate." Notwithstanding the widespread use of the term "conglomerate" to describe certain combination processes as well as the resulting business entities, there remains considerable disagreement as to what constitutes a conglomerate combination. Part of the confusion stems from somewhat differing usage of the term in the worlds of finance vis-à-vis antitrust law. In a financial context, conglomerate combination tends to imply a union of business units which have little if any production or market similarities. Translated into terms of antitrust significance, this would mean that the products of the combining firms are unrelated and therefore do not compete—for buyers or for raw materials. Given the present antitrust laws and court interpretations thereof, such a definition of conglomerate combination would essentially exclude such mergers from possible prosecution.

However, in framing the 1950 amendments to Section 7 of the Clayton Act, Congress notes that the law applies to all types of combinations, including conglomerates.[14] Apparently, the legislative intent was to include combinations that do not evidence traditional competing patterns in terms

---

[12] Betty Bock, *Mergers and Markets, An Economic Analysis of Developments in the Mid-1960's under the Merger Act of 1950* (New York: National Industrial Conference Board, Inc., 1968), p. 7.

[13] Ibid., p. 7.

[14] U.S. House, 81st Cong. 1st sess. (1949), H. R. 1191, p. 11.

of suppliers, products, or customers.[15] The propriety of a conglomerate combination depends largely upon its effect on *potential* competition. Thus, if the acquiring and acquired firms probably would have become competitors (through internal expansion of either one or both), the combination may be viewed as an arrangement which may eliminate a potential competitor. Even if probable *internal* expansion into a competitive position is unsupported by the evidence, it is possible for the combination to be challenged. Some combinations could discourage further entry into a market even though a potential entrant is not in sight.[16]

The basic antitrust laws affecting contemporary business activity were enacted prior to the emergence of conglomerate combinations as a prevalent type of business expansion. Correspondingly, combinations that exhibit vertical or horizontal characteristics are less likely to succeed than are conglomerate mergers. Many lawmakers have expressed opposition to the long-term trend toward increasing concentration of control in business. But it has been difficult to structure laws that would forestall this trend (in its conglomerate form) and remain within the traditional bounds of attacking monopolistic tendencies and competitive restraining forces. Conglomerate entities have been subjected to increased scrutiny by Congress, the Department of Justice, and the Federal Trade Commission. On another front, the Securities and Exchange Commission, the Accounting Principles Board, and now the Financial Accounting Standards Board have cast a critical eye on the reporting practices of conglomerates, many of which relate to the problems of accounting for highly diversified operations. Currently, however, the amount and types of constraints that should be appropriately placed upon conglomerate combination activity remain unsettled questions.

METHODS OF CLASSIFYING BUSINESS COMBINATIONS

An examination of business combinations is generally facilitated by an attempt to devise classes or categories of combinations. The scheme of classification selected necessarily depends on the purpose of the examination. One of the most frequently used methods of classifying combinations has already been discussed; horizontal, vertical, and conglomerate are expressions which convey certain economic characteristics of the combination classes in question. This economic perspective of business combinations finds significance in studies of the legal implications of combinations.

---

[15] Robert A. Bicks, "Corporate Mergers and the Antitrust Laws: Clayton Act, Section 7" in William W. Alberts and Joel E. Segall, *The Corporate Merger* (Chicago, Ill.: The University of Chicago Press, 1960), p. 85.

[16] Betty Bock "Conglomerate Mergers, Joint Ventures and Potential Competition," *The Conference Board Record* (February 1968), p. 6.

It is also relevant to economists' investigations relating to economic trends and federal policies.

Legal Perspective

A traditional method of classifying business combinations focuses upon the corporate structures involved. Thus, combinations are labeled as mergers, consolidations, or acquisitions. If the only surviving company is one of the original group of companies, the union is termed a *merger;* if a new corporate enterprise is organized for the purpose of acquiring the net assets of other companies, the combination is termed a *consolidation.* In both forms of combination, the legal entity status of each of the controlled companies is normally terminated. The term *acquisition* is applied to a combination in which one firm exchanges its ownership securities for the ownership securities of another firm, and both continue their legal existence. A parent-subsidiary relationship results from this form of combination.

Notwithstanding the distinctions that can be drawn between the terms merger, consolidation, and acquisition, contemporary usage of the terms frequently disregards these definitional refinements. One may expect to find *merger, consolidation, acquisition,* and *business combination* used interchangeably in normal business discourse unless, of course, the objective is to concentrate on the distinctions outlined above.

Tax Perspective

According to the "tax-free reorganization" provisions of the Internal Revenue Code, certain business combinations can be accomplished without requiring that new valuations be determined and income taxes assessed. Business combinations can therefore be classified as taxable exchanges or tax-free reorganizations. The criteria and attributes of both categories will be examined in later discussion.

Financial Perspective

The method of financing used by an acquiring firm to accomplish a combination is significant in several types of analyses. The selection of a financing method, for example, may determine the tax status of the combination. It may also determine the method of accounting for the combination, a selection that can have material effects upon operating reports for future periods. Without attempting to specify all of the problems and analyses for which a financing method has relevance, alternative financing arrangements should be recognized as a means of classifying corporate combinations. Payment methods include the transfer of cash or other assets as well as the issuance of common stock, preferred stock, bonds, and convertible securities. Classifying combinations by financing method does not allow the determination of mutually exclusive and collectively exhaustive classes. Business combinations often involve a mixing of payment methods. Further, the use of treasury stock, or payment by cash shortly following a stock issuance, allows management to accomplish one particular payment form while giving the impression of another. If an acquiring company has available cash with which to make payment but wishes to have the combination classified as an "exchange of stock," it can use the cash to buy treasury stock and then issue the treasury stock to consummate the combination. Conversely, a company can issue stock for cash and use the cash in settlement. Such transactions may allow the firm to benefit from some of the desirable attributes of both payment methods.

An added complexity in financing combinations is sometimes evidenced by firms that have a history of successful acquisitions. Paradoxically, this complexity involves the use of *divisive* reorganizations as a means of financing combinations. A controlling interest in the acquired firm is established by any one of the payment methods mentioned earlier. Assume, for example, that an acquiring corporation issues notes payable and uses the cash proceeds to buy the stock of the acquired firm. The acquired firm is then merged into the acquiring firm, which eliminates the separate corporate existence of the subsidiary, thereby also eliminating any minority (outside) interest in the subsidiary. Outsiders are forced to accept cash in exchange for the fair value of their minority interest in the liquidated subsidiary corporation. Next, the controlling firm organizes a new corporation, the stock of which is issued to the controlling firm in exchange for the assets of the acquired (and now liquidated) firm. Generally, the name selected for the *new* subsidiary corporation will identify it with the successful history of the parent firm. Finally, the parent offers to the public approximately 20 percent of the new corporation's stock. Cash proceeds can be used either to repay the original notes payable issued by the parent or to make unrelated acquisitions.

If the divisive reorganization method of financing is successful, the "new image" of the acquired corporation will substantially increase its market value. As a consequence, the proceeds from issuing a small portion of the new stock to the public will be large enough to defray a substantial portion of the original outlay to acquire the company. In a few actual examples, the proceeds were almost equal to the original expenditure. Thus, the parent acquired a controlling interest in another firm at a net cost that was relatively insignificant.

Case 1. Glammer Company issued $50,000,000 of three-year, 9 percent, notes payable on January 1, 19X1. During January 15–30, it acquired 920,000 shares of Slow Company at an average per share cost of $50. During May, 19X1, Slow Company was merged into Glammer Company. The 80,000 shares held by minority interests were surrendered for $54 per share. Additional costs associated with the merger were $180,000. In October, 19X1, a new corporation, Shimmer, Inc., issued 3,500,000 of its 4,000,000 authorized common shares to Glammer Company in exchange for the operating assets originally belonging to Slow Company. On November 1, 19X1, Glammer Company sold 875,000 shares of Shimmer, Inc., for $30 per share.

Net Cash Outlay of Glammer Company
As of November 1, 19X1

Purchases of stock	$920,000 \times 50 =$	$46,000,000
	$80,000 \times 54 =$	4,320,000
Costs of merger	$=$	180,000
Interest on debt . . $(50,000,000 \times .09 \times 10/12) =$		3,750,000
Total		$54,250,000
Proceeds from stock sale	$875,000 \times 30 =$	26,250,000
Net cash outlay on November 1, 19X1		$28,000,000

Shares owned:		
By Glammer Company	2,625,000	75%
By minority interest	875,000	25
	3,500,000	100%

Current value of Glammer Company's investment:
$$2,625,000 \times 30 = \$78,750,000$$

Accounting Perspective

There are two strikingly different sets of accounting procedures which are used to record business combinations on the books of the combined business entity; these differing accounting procedures are referred to as the *purchase* method and the *pooling of interests* method. In the case of any specific business combination, the question of which method of accounting will be utilized is resolved by analyzing the provisions of the combination agreement and the factual characteristics of the combining companies. In the event a business combination and the combining companies exhibit 12 specific factual conditions, the pooling of interests method of accounting is used to record the combination. Correspondingly, such a combination is referred to as a *pooling of interests* combination. In the event the business combination fails to satisfy any one of the specified 12 conditions, the purchase method of accounting is employed and the combination is referred to as a *purchase* combination. Chapter 6 includes a detailed examination of the criteria that are used to classify business combinations as purchases or poolings of interests and the corresponding sets of procedures that are used to account for these classes. As a consequence, the present discussion is intended only to emphasize the general characteristics of each class.

In general, a business combination is classified as a purchase if the facts of the combination agreement suggest that one of the combining companies, especially its stockholder group, emerges as the dominant, controlling interest; the combining agreement is in substance a purchase-sale transaction in which the dominant company acquires the assets and assumes the liabilities of the other combining firm(s). In contrast to a purchase, a business combination is classified as a pooling of interests if none of the combining companies, especially their stockholder groups, assume a position of dominance in the combined entity; the common stockholders of each combining company become common stockholders in the combined entity, thereby retaining their relative ownership positions.

TAX FACTORS AFFECTING CORPORATE COMBINATIONS

Various business objectives which may lead to expansion through combination have been discussed. The provisions of the Internal Revenue Code were recognized as significant factors in the decision as to whether a contemplated combination should be pursued. Tax consequences are equally significant in determining the methods to be used to pay for the acquired firm. In fact, the influence of taxes on one aspect of a combination often has a simultaneous impact on other aspects of the combination. For example, the tax implications of available payment methods may dominate the final decision as to whether a combination will be completed or abandoned. Furthermore, potential income tax benefits, such as operating loss carryovers, may be a principal motivation underlying a proposed merger; and the transaction must therefore be carefully formulated to conform with relevant tax provisions.

Tax-Free Reorganizations

A critical tax factor in planning a corporate combination involves the taxable or tax-free status of the transaction between the acquiring corporation and the acquired corporation and/or its stockholders. In general, exchanges of assets (including securities such as stock) are recognized by the Code as the appropriate point in time at which to assign new bases to the transferred items and to assess tax. However, corporate combinations may be either taxable or tax-free, depending upon the nature of the agreement and the payments made to the combination participants (or their shareholders).

If a combination qualifies as a tax-free "reorganization," the acquired corporation may, in whole or in part, escape recognition of gain or loss on the transfer of its property to the acquiring corporation; and the existing bases of the assets are carried forward without change in amount to the acquiring corporation. The shareholders of the acquired corporation also may exchange their shares for stock of the acquiring corporation without the recognition of gain or loss. On the other hand, in a taxable combination, gain or loss is recognized by the selling party, and the acquiring corporation usually establishes new (current) bases in the assets acquired.[17]

Criteria for Assessing Tax Status

Tax-free acquisitions are usually effected under one of three basic forms of reorganization defined in Section 368 of the Internal Revenue Code. In general terms, the following alternatives are available:

1. Statutory mergers and consolidations, i.e., a merger or consolidation consummated in accordance with a state statute (type A).
2. Acquisition of stock in exchange for *voting* shares of stock, subject to the requirement that the acquiring corporation must then hold a controlling interest (a minimum of 80 percent) in the acquired corporation (type B).
3. Acquisition of assets in exchange for *voting* stock where "substantially all" of the assets of the selling corporation are transferred to the purchasing corporation (type C).

The type A business combination refers to situations in which the acquiring and the acquired corporations are combined into one corporation (the acquiring, the acquired, or a new corporation) and the combination is effected in compliance with state statutes which specify the procedures to be followed. Such a transaction may qualify as a tax-free reorganization even if preferred stock and nonvoting stock are issued in payment for the acquired corporation. Depending on the relevant state statutes, the use of some limited amounts of cash and debt securities may also be permitted. However, an additional requirement imposed by the courts is that continuity of equity interests be maintained. For example, if debt regarded as excessive in amount is used as part payment, the courts may rule that a continuity of equity interests has not been maintained and accordingly refuse to accord tax-free status to the combination. Thus, it is possible for a combination to comply fully with the appropriate state

---

[17] Boris I. Bittker and James E. Eustice, *Federal Income Taxation of Corporations and Shareholders,* 3d. ed. (Boston, Mass.: Warren, Gorham & Lamont, Inc., 1971), chap. 14. See also James S. Eustice, *1976 Cumulative Supplement, No. 2* (Boston, Mass.: Warren, Gorham, & Lamont, Inc., 1976), chap. 14.

merger laws and with the mechanics of the Code, and yet be disallowed as a tax-free reorganization.

To qualify as a type B reorganization, the means of payment is limited to voting stock of the acquiring corporation. However, past cash purchases of stock by the acquiring corporation of a minority interest in the acquired corporation do not necessarily disqualify the eventual tax-free status of the combination. Moreover, the *acquired* corporation may purchase (for cash) the shares of those stockholders who are unwilling to accept voting stock in the acquiring corporation.

Under a type C reorganization, the question as to what constitutes "substantially all" of the selling corporation's properties is subject to varied interpretation. Final determination depends on the nature of the assets retained, the purposes of retention, and the dollar amount of such assets (measured in terms of fair market value). In general, if the assets retained by the seller are not essential to the past operations of the seller, if retention is not for the purposes of continuing operations or for sales to another purchaser, and if the amount does not exceed the retained liabilities of the seller, the acquisition will satisfy type C requirements.

The type C requirement that payment be made with voting shares is not absolute. If at least 80 percent of the selling firm's assets are acquired in this manner, cash or other forms of consideration may be used to acquire the remaining 20 percent. Finally, the voting shares issued in payment may be shares in the acquiring firm's parent corporation.

Although the voting stock requirements of type B or C combinations are not absolute, it may be observed that the continuity of equity interests problem that may arise under a type A combination is always overcome as a natural consequence by the high voting stock requirements of types B and C reorganizations.

It should be noted that the distinguishable characteristics of the three reorganization types are difficult to isolate in many combination arrangements. What first appears as a type B reorganization may, if the acquired subsidiary is liquidated, have the substance of a type A or type C reorganization. This can be accomplished because the liquidation of a subsidiary into a parent is also tax free. Also, types A and C reorganizations may be essentially equivalent in terms of their final equity arrangements.

Motives for Planning Tax Status

Whether a corporate combination will be deemed a taxable exchange or a tax-free reorganization is obviously susceptible to planning by combination participants. In this regard, a major concern of the acquiring corporation is the bases of the assets to be acquired. If the assets' current fair market values exceed their bases to the acquired firm, a taxable transaction is desirable (other things being equal). Establishing a taxable status to the combination would assign the current fair market values of the assets as the acquiring corporation's bases, thus increasing future periods' tax deductions. Conversely, if current fair market values are less than the acquired corporation's bases in assets, the acquiring corporation should prefer a tax-free combination.

The acquired firm and/or its stockholders will generally prefer a tax-free combination status so long as the fair market value of securities received exceeds their bases in properties and/or shares given up. The general motive is, of course, to defer tax payments. Conversely, should the bases of properties and/or securities given up exceed their fair market value, a taxable exchange status would facilitate early recognition of losses.

Tax Attribute Carryovers

When a tax-free reorganization is accomplished as a type A or type C (as defined in Section 368), certain tax benefits, rights, and obligations of the acquired corporation may carry over to the surviving firm. Subject to specified conditions and limitations, the accounting methods employed by the acquired firm, net operating losses, unused investment credits, unexhausted capital loss carryovers, and other tax attributes generally are applicable to the calculation of income tax for the surviving firm. However, numerous additional restrictions are imposed (e.g., Sections 269, 381, and 382) to prevent special advantages from carrying over if the combination serves no sound business purpose other than to gain the benefit of the acquired corporation's favorable tax attributes.

If a combination involves the establishment of a parent-subsidiary re-relationship (type B), the tax attributes of the acquired-subsidiary corporation typically remain with the subsidiary corporation. Should the constituents of the combination qualify for, and elect to file, a consolidated return, the subsidiary's unique attributes are generally applicable to that return only to the extent that they would be effective on a separate return. If the subsidiary is subsequently liquidated into the parent corporation, the same provisions which provide a carryover (of tax attributes) in a type A or type C reorganization provide a carryover of the liquidated subsidiary's attributes.

PRO FORMA FINANCIAL STATEMENTS

The previous analysis has exposed a variety of factors that must be evaluated and/or negotiated before a corporate combination is completed. Several additional factors will be treated in subsequent chapters. Yet, it should already be apparent that the *combined* effects of each constituent's unique characteristics as well as the alternative means by which a combination might be completed and accounted for are not easily perceived. To overcome this problem, it is often useful to prepare financial statements which assume the completion of specific business transactions that have not yet been executed. Such statements which "give effect to" anticipated or contemplated transactions are commonly referred to as *pro forma* statements.

Pro forma statements may be especially informative in the preliminary negotiations of combination agreements. For example, in devising equitable settlement arrangements with several combination participants, it may be useful to construct a series of pro forma statements, each reflecting the effect of an alternative stock distribution plan. The financial implications of each proposed course of action are then exposed in a similar comparative format for the consideration of management.

Pro forma financial statements are frequently used *after* the combination agreement has been tentatively accepted by the corporate officers of the combining firms. After the agreement between corporate officers, it is frequently necessary to obtain the approval of a specified majority of the stockholders of one or both of the combining firms before a combination can be finalized. Pro forma statements, which portray the tentatively accepted combination conditions, are typically included in the report to stockholders. Further, if the combination involves the issuance of new securities which must be approved by the Securities and Exchange Commission, pro forma statements are generally a required inclusion in the registration statement.[18]

In preparing a pro forma statement, the hypothetical nature of the statement should be clearly disclosed. The title of the statement should carry a reference to its pro forma character and should clearly state the proposed or assumed condition. Furthermore, elaboration of the types of adjustments embodied in the statement should be provided, either in the body or in related footnotes.

A typical pro forma balance sheet is represented in columnar format with entries for the hypothetical transactions juxtaposed against audited balance sheet classifications. Of course, this basic format may also be utilized for pro forma income statement presentations.

Case 2 includes a pro forma balance sheet that was extracted from a prospectus issued by Ling-Temco-Vought, Inc. The case is an illustration of the usefulness of pro forma statements in circumstances where the anticipated transactions are very complex, thereby making it difficult to perceive their financial statement implications.

Case 2. Ling-Temco-Vought, Inc., offered the holders of certain LTV securities the opportunity to exchange those securities for a "package" of different securities. The "package" was defined in terms of *Units,* as follows:

---

[18] It should be clear that pro forma statements can be used in a wide variety of situations other than in anticipation of a business combination. Wherever it is desirable to observe the financial statement effects of hypothetical transactions, pro forma statements may be prepared.

Illustration 1–1

LING-TEMCO-VOUGHT, INC. AND SUBSIDIARIES

Pro Forma Balance Sheet

The following pro forma balance sheet at June 30, 19X3, gives effect to (1) the issuance of debentures and warrants of Ling-Temco-Vought, Inc. in the acquisition of the assets of Greatamerica, (2) the assumption of liabilities of Greatamerica, and (3) certain other transactions described in Note (1) below. The statement should be read in conjunction with the financial statements and related notes of Ling-Temco-Vought, Inc. included elsewhere herein.

		In Thousands		
Assets	*LTV*	*Pro Forma Adjustments*(2)	*Great-america*	*As Adjusted before Exchange Offer*
Current assets	$1,047,151	$ ...	$ 18,695	$1,065,846
Investment in Greatamerica(1)	475,145	25,166	(500,311)	...
Investment in Braniff Airways(1)	...	...	338,736	338,736
Investment in National Car Rental(1)	...	...	134,756	134,756
Other assets	41,151	15,476	37,353	93,980
Fixed assets	960,505	...	455	960,960
Intangibles	48,051	1,500	...	49,551
	$2,572,003	$42,142	$ 29,684	$2,643,829
Liabilities and Stockholders' Equity				
Current liabilities	$ 627,333	$ ...	$ 77,876	$ 705,209
Long-term debt	1,194,001	{25,166 / 16,976	40,005	1,276,148
Due Greatamerica Corporation	88,500	...	(88,500)	...
Deferrals	46,293	...	303	46,596
Minority interests	350,681	...	...	350,681
Stockholders' equity:				
Series A preferred stock	2,962	...	...	2,962
Special stock, class AA	786	...	...	786
Common stock	1,991	...	...	1,991
Capital surplus	168,014	...	...	168,014
Earned surplus	91,442	...	...	91,442
Total Stockholders' Equity	265,195	...	...	265,195
	$2,572,003	$42,142	$ 29,684	$2,643,829

(1) The acquisition of the capital stock of Braniff and National through the purchase of assets of Greatamerica will be carried on the books of LTV as investments in an unconsolidated subsidiary or affiliate. Reference is made to the balance sheets of Braniff and National included elsewhere herein. Paragraphs 8 and 9 of *Opinion No. 10* of the Accounting Principles Board of the American Institute of Certified Public Accountants, which recommends that a portion of the proceeds received for debentures issued with warrants to purchase stock be attributed to such warrants, have been temporarily suspended for further study by the Board. In the event the accounting principles set out in these paragraphs are made effective retroactively to cover transactions in fiscal years beginning after December 31, 19X1 and if accounting principles as there stated are applicable to the issuance of securities with conversion rights or warrants in an acquisition of this type, the Company will establish an amount representing the value of the warrants as deferred debt discount to be amortized over the life of the debentures. This value is estimated at approximately $50,000,000 which, if amortized on a straight line basis, would amount to $2,500,000 annually (subject to adjustment for retirements and use of such debentures in the exercise of warrants), equal after tax reduction to $0.23 per share based on the average number of shares outstanding (including residual securities) during the six month period ended June 30, 19X3.

See also Note B—Long-Term Debt in Notes to Financial Statements of LTV included elsewhere herein.

(2) The following transactions are reflected in the pro forma adjustments:

   (a) The sale by LTV International, N.V. in July, 19X3, of $77,380,000 of 5% guaranteed (subordinated) debentures, less discount of $1,500,000, the borrowing by LTV of $15,476,000 from a foreign bank and contribution of such amount to the capital of LTV International, the deposit by LTV International of such $15,476,000 in a foreign bank, the repurchase by LTV of $17,380,000 of 6½% notes payable June 1, 19X8, and the partial prepayment by LTV of $58,500,000 of bank loans due July 31, 19X4, borrowed in connection with the acquisition of Jones & Laughlin.

   (b) The issuance by LTV of $25,166,000 of its 5% debentures due 20 years hence, in the purchase of the assets of Greatamerica.

Illustration 1-2

The following sets forth the effects of the Exchange Offer on the above pro forma balance sheet assuming (1) the exchange of 100% of the Eligible Securities in the Exchange Offer, and (2) the exchange of 50% of the Eligible Securities in the Exchange Offer.

In Thousands

	Pro Forma	100% Exchange — Effect on Accounts	100% Exchange — Balances after Exchange	50% Exchange — Effect on Accounts	50% Exchange — Balances after Exchange
Assets					
Current assets	$1,065,846	$ (7,836)(3) / 6,260 (4)	$1,064,270	$ (4,305)(3) / 3,192 (4)	$1,064,733
Investment in Braniff	338,736	(103,321)(1)	235,415	(51,660)(1)	287,076
Investment in National Car Rental	134,756	(128,961)(1)	5,795	(64,480)(1)	70,276
Other assets	93,980	…	93,980	…	93,980
Fixed assets	960,960	…	960,960	…	960,960
Intangibles	49,551	(936)(2)	48,615	(468)(2)	49,083
	2,643,829	(234,794)	2,409,035	(117,721)	2,526,108
Liabilities and Stockholders' equity:					
Current liabilities	$ 705,209	$ …	$ 705,209	$ …	$ 705,209
Long-term debt	1,276,148	(248,361)(6)	1,027,787	(124,180)(6)	1,151,968
Deferrals	46,596	3,573 (5)	50,169	1,770 (5)	48,366
Minority interests	350,681	1,830 (7)	352,511	915 (7)	351,596
Stockholders' equity:					
Series A preferred stock	2,962	…	2,962	…	2,962
Special stock, class AA	786	…	786	…	786
Common stock	1,991	(1,000)(8)	991	(500)(8)	1,491
Capital surplus	168,014	(3,989)(3) / 34,722 (9)	198,747	(2,191)(3) / 17,361 (9)	183,184

Earned surplus	91,442	(3,847)(3) (20,409)(10) 6,260 (4) (3,573)(5)	69,873	(2,114)(3) (10,204)(10) 3,192 (4) (1,770)(5)	80,546
	265,195	8,164	273,359	3,774	268,969
Total Stockholders' Equity	$2,643,829	($234,794)	$2,409,035	($117,721)	$2,526,108

The effects of the Exchange Offer on the accounts as reflected in the above statement are explained below:

(1) Reduction in carrying value of investments in Braniff and National applicable to shares exchanged.

(2) Write-off of unamortized discount and expense on debt reduced.

(3) Estimated expenses in connection with Exchange Offer ($7,836,000 in 100% exchange and $4,305,000 in 50% exchange), allocated to capital surplus with respect to common stock reacquired and to gain on debt retired with respect to debt retired.

(4) Estimated current income taxes refundable resulting from loss on retirement of 6½%, 6¾%, and 5¾% debt issues.

(5) Estimated deferred income tax applicable to gain on retirement of 5% debentures.

(6) Face value of debt retired.

(7) Minority interest in CT applicable to shares to be issued.

(8) Par value of common stock to be reacquired.

(9) Capital surplus credit for market value of warrants issued in connection with debt retired ($117,162,000 in 100% exchange and $58,581,000 in 50% exchange), less capital surplus applicable to shares reacquired ($82,440,000 on 2,000,000 shares and $41,220,000 on 1,000,000 shares).

(10) Earned surplus credit for excess of face value of debt retired over carrying value of securities and market value of warrants issued in debt retirement ($15,390,000 in 100% exchange and $7,696,000 in 50% exchange), less retained earnings applicable to shares reacquired ($35,799,000 on 2,000,000 shares and $17,900,000 on 1,000,000 shares).

Each Unit will consist of 1.0 share of Braniff Special Stock, Class A, 0.6 share of National Common Stock, 1.0 share of National Special Stock, Class A, 0.33 share of Computer Technology Common Stock and 1.1 LTV Common Stock Purchase Warrants.

The corporations mentioned in the package, other than LTV, were subsidiaries of LTV. The exchange offer was extended to the holders of the following LTV securities:

1.10 Units for 1 share of LTV Common Stock
9.75 Units for $1,000 principal amount of 6½ % Notes
10.00 Units for $1,000 principal amount of 6¾ % Debentures
6.70 Units for $1,000 principal amount of 5% Debentures
9.50 Units for $1,000 principal amount of 5¾ % Debentures

In preparing pro forma financial statements to show the effects of the exchange offer, LTV first had to prepare a pro forma statement to record the consequences of certain transactions which had actually taken place at the date the prospectus was issued (October 31, 19X3) but had not taken place in time to be included in the June 30, 19X3, balance sheet. These transactions included the acquisition of Greatamerica Corporation. Illustration 1–1 presents this portion of the complete pro forma balance sheet. Illustration 1–2 continues the pro forma presentation by showing the effects of the securities exchange offer, assuming 100 percent and 50 percent acceptances of the exchange offer.

QUESTIONS

1. Distinguish between internal and external expansion in business enterprises.
2. Enumerate and briefly discuss several cogent reasons why a company might wish to acquire control of another company. Additionally, suggest reasons an enterprise might wish to be acquired.
3. What is "synergism" in the context of corporate combination?
4. Describe three general types of business combinations as they have been interpreted by the courts. Give an example of each.
5. What factors do the courts cite as relevant considerations in determining whether horizontal mergers violate antitrust laws?
6. Distinguish between "merger," "consolidation," and "acquisition."
7. Describe briefly the technique involved in financing corporate combinations through divisive reorganizations.
8. What are *pro forma* statements and how do they assist corporate managements in deciding on the provisions of a combination agreement?
9. Briefly describe what is meant by type A, type B, and type C reorganizations under Section 368 of the Internal Revenue Code.
10. Under a type B reorganization, is it possible for minority interests to be purchased for cash and yet preserve a tax-free status?
11. Under a type C reorganization, would it be possible to exchange some

security other than *voting* shares? If so, is there any practical limit to the use of other types of securities?

12. Would a type B or type C reorganization impose limits on the type of "equitable" distribution plan used for a combination?

EXERCISES

Exercise 1–1

Identify the appropriate terms that are used in reference to the following descriptions:

a. The combining of two, or more, previously independent business enterprises in such a manner that the stockholder interests in the combining companies are maintained in the surviving company and none of the participants emerges as a dominant party.

b. A business combination in which the participants perform similar functions in the production or sale of comparable products.

c. An increase in business operations, derived from increasing demand for a firm's products and services and the establishment of new product lines and geographic sales areas, so long as these expansions are financed through the normal corporate means of earnings retention and issuances of debt and/or equity securities and the expansion does not involve the acquisition of preexisting business operations from another business unit.

d. A combination between two business enterprises in which one of the companies, especially its common stockholder group, emerges as the dominant, controlling interest in the combined enterprise.

e. A business combination in which the surviving corporation is one of the original group of combining companies.

f. A business combination which results in a parent-subsidiary relationship between the combining companies.

g. A business combination in which the combining firms have a supplier-customer relationship.

h. An expansion in business operations that is accomplished by acquiring a preexisting business unit.

i. A business combination in which a new corporate enterprise is organized for the purpose of acquiring the net assets of the combining companies.

j. A business combination in which the combining companies have little if any production or market similarities.

Exercise 1–2

Syndicate A controls B Company through the ownership of 75,600 shares of the latter's capital stock out of a total of 96,000 shares outstanding at June 30, 1977. The authorized capital stock of B Company is 150,000 shares, all of one class.

B Company controls C Company through the ownership of 6,250 shares of the latter's capital stock out of a total of 10,000 shares outstanding at June 30, 1977.

The sum of the capital stock and surplus of B Company at June 30, 1977, is $5,894,706, and of C Company, $2,132,470.

B Company wishes to acquire the minority interest in C Company through the issuance of shares of its capital stock at a value equal to its book value at June 30, 1977, taking into account the book value of capital stock of C Company, B Company's investment in which is carried on B Company's books at a total cost of $687,500.

Required:

a. You are to determine the number of shares to be issued by B Company, ignoring fractional shares.
b. You are to compute the percentage of control held by Syndicate A after such shares have been issued.

(AICPA adapted)

Exercise 1–3

The Never-Fail Company had been in operation for the past 10 years making circuit boards. Feeling the need to diversify, the board of directors decided to gain control of the Ever-Brite Plastics Company. Thus, on February 1, 1977, Never-Fail issued $3,000,000 in two-year, 9 percent notes payable. In March the company purchased in the open market 72,000 shares (90 percent) of Ever-Brite at an average per share cost of $35. During June, 1977, Ever-Brite was merged into Never-Fail. At this time the 10 percent (8,000 shares) minority interest in Ever-Brite was purchased for $40 per share. Miscellaneous legal and other costs associated with the merger were $60,000. In September, 1977, a new corporation, Never-Ever, Inc., issued 300,000 of its 350,000 authorized shares to Never-Fail Company in exchange for the operating assets originally belonging to Ever-Brite. On December 1, 1977, Never-Fail Company sold 80,000 shares of Never-Ever, Inc., for $25 per share.

Required:

a. Prepare a schedule showing the net cash outlay for Never-Fail as of December 1, 1977, resulting from the above transactions.
b. What is the implied value of Never-Fail's interest in Never-Ever?

Exercise 1–4

As a merger expert for a large conglomerate which has extensive interests in the meat-packing, insurance, finance, baking, auto rental, and glass industries, you are considering a wide range of possible acquisitions and are concerned about the possible response of the Justice Department.

Required:

a. Explain briefly the difference between horizontal, vertical, and conglomerate mergers.
b. What economic argument could the Justice Department make against your merger with another glass manufacturer? With a flour manufacturer?
c. Summarize the general stance of the Justice Department with respect to horizontal, vertical, and conglomerate mergers. That is, does the Justice

Department appear to react in the same manner to all three types of mergers?

(CMA adapted)

PROBLEMS

Problem 1

The balance sheets for Yachts, Inc. and Sailmaker Company appear as follows as of December 31, 1977.

Assets	Yachts, Inc.	Sailmaker Company
Cash	$ 250,000	$ 400,000
Receivables	350,000	575,000
Inventories	450,000	625,000
Total Current Assets	$1,050,000	$1,600,000
Fixed assets (net)	2,000,000	3,000,000
Total Assets	$3,050,000	$4,600,000
Liabilities and Stockholders' Equity		
Current liabilities	$ 500,000	$ 650,000
Long-term debt	375,000	450,000
Total Liabilities	$ 875,000	$1,100,000
Capital stock ($10 par)	$1,000,000	$2,000,000
Other contributed capital	550,000	750,000
Retained earnings	625,000	750,000
Total Stockholders' Equity	$2,175,000	$3,500,000
Total Liabilities and Stockholders' Equity	$3,050,000	$4,600,000

Yachts, Inc. plans to issue 400,000 shares ($10 par) which can be sold for $15 per share less commissions and other legal costs of $2 per share. It then proposes to acquire the assets and liabilities of Sailmaker Company in exchange for $3,000,000 cash and the balance of the $4,000,000 selling price in long-term notes payable. Yachts, Inc. receivables include $200,000 owed by Sailmaker. The difference between the $4,000,000 price and the book value of Sailmaker Company's net assets is associated with fixed assets, which are undervalued on the books of Sailmaker.

Required:

Prepare a pro forma balance sheet that shows the effect of these transactions.

Problem 2

The Ecton Company proposes to sell all of its assets except cash and receivables to the Jones Company on July 31, 1977. The sales price shall be $10,000,000, adjusted by the change in book value from December 31, 1976, to May 31, 1977, for inventories and property. The May 31 book values of prepaid expenses and other assets are to be added to the sales price.

The settlement shall be:

a. Jones Company 4 percent note for $3,000,000 payable in semiannual installments of $150,000 commencing January 31, 1978.
b. Assumption of all liabilities except the estimated federal income taxes payable and long-term debt.
c. Balance payable in cash immediately.

The company intends to retire the preferred stock and establish a $300,000 reserve for contingencies. The net profit for June and July is estimated at $150,000 before taxes (assume that a 50 percent tax rate has been in effect since 1972).

The last preferred stock dividend was declared on December 31, 1976. The regular common stock dividend was paid on June 15, 1977.

Taxable income for the past four years follows:

1973....................	$1,481,000
1974....................	412,400
1975....................	639,600
1976....................	842,500

ECTON COMPANY

Balance Sheets

Assets	December 31, 1976	May 31, 1977
Cash	$ 1,038,000	$ 472,000
Receivables	2,550,000	3,105,000
Inventories	5,592,000	6,028,000
Prepaid expenses	308,000	297,000
Total Current Assets	$ 9,488,000	$ 9,902,000
Property (net)	6,927,000	6,804,000
Other assets	635,000	604,000
Total Assets	$17,050,000	$17,310,000

Liabilities and Capital		
Accounts payable	$ 2,427,000	$ 3,052,500
Current maturities—long-term debt	600,000	600,000
Accrued liabilities	1,096,000	922,000
Dividends payable—preferred stock	63,000	
Estimated federal income taxes	417,000	333,500
Total Current Liabilities	$ 4,603,000	$ 4,908,000
Long-term debt	4,200,000	4,050,000
Stockholders' equity:		
Preferred cumulative stock— 21,000 shares of $100 par 3%, outstanding, redeemable at $102	2,100,000	2,100,000
Common stock—100,000 shares of $10 par outstanding	1,000,000	1,000,000
Capital contributed in excess of par value of common stock	587,000	587,000
Retained earnings	4,560,000	4,665,000
Total Liabilities and Capital	$17,050,000	$17,310,000

Note: The increase in retained earnings is net of a dividend of $.20 per share paid March 15, 1977, on common stock.

Required:

a. Compute the total sales price and settlement to be made.
b. Compute Ecton Company's gain or loss on the sale, giving effect to income taxes.
c. Prepare a working paper with column headings "Per Books," "Adjustments," and "Estimated Balance Sheet, July 31, 1977" giving effect to the proposed sale and other information given. Support your adjustments with schedules or computations you deem necessary.

(AICPA adapted)

Problem 3

You have just commenced your audit of Shaky Company for the year ended December 31, 1977. The president advises you that the company is insolvent and must declare bankruptcy unless a large loan can be obtained immediately. A lender who is willing to advance $450,000 to the company has been located, but he will only make the loan subject to the following conditions:

a. A $600,000 6 percent mortgage payable on the company's land and buildings held by a major stockholder will be canceled along with four months' accrued interest. The mortgage will be replaced by 5,000 shares of $100 par value, 10 percent, cumulative if earned, nonparticipating, preferred stock.
b. A $450,000 8 percent mortgage payable over 15 years on the land and buildings will be given as security on the new loan.
c. On May 1, 1976, the company's trade creditors accepted $360,000 in notes payable on demand at 6 percent interest in settlement of all past-due accounts. No payment has been made to date. The company will offer to settle these liabilities at $.75 per $1 owed or to replace the notes payable on demand with new notes payable for full indebtedness over five years at 8 percent interest. It is estimated that $200,000 of the demand notes will be exchanged for the longer term notes and that the remaining creditors which hold notes will accept the offer of a reduced cash settlement.
d. A new issue of 500 shares of $100 par value, 9 percent, noncumulative, nonparticipating, preferred stock will replace 500 outstanding shares of $100 par value, 7 percent, cumulative, participating preferred stock. Preferred stockholders will repudiate all claims to $21,000 of dividends in arrears. The company has never formally declared the dividends.
e. A new issue of 600 shares of $50 par value, class A common stock will replace 600 outstanding shares of $100 par value, class A common stock.
f. A new issue of 650 shares of $40 par value, class B common stock will replace 650 outstanding shares of $100 par value, class B common stock.
g. The deficit in retained earnings should be eliminated, if possible, as a result of the entire plan.

The president of the Shaky Company requests that you determine the effect of the foregoing on the company and furnishes the following condensed account balances, which you believe are fairly presented:

Bank overdraft	....	$ 15,000
Other current assets	....	410,000
Fixed assets	....	840,000
Trade accounts payable	....	235,000
Other current liabilities	....	85,000
Contributed capital in excess of par value	...	125,000
Retained earnings deficit	....	345,000

Required:

Prepare a pro forma balance sheet for the Shaky Company at January 1, 1978, as if the recapitalization plan had taken affect. The statement should have one column for the balance sheet prior to the assumed events, two columns in which to journalize the changes, and one column in which to present the pro forma results.

(AICPA adapted)

2

Merger Negotiations:
Prices and Methods
of Payment

A BUSINESS COMBINATION is often one of the most dramatic events in the life of a company. Changes in management, changes in stockholders, new boards of directors, changes in the debt equity structure, new operating procedures, new product relationships in promotion and marketing, and expanded sales areas are a few examples of the way a combination can impact on a company. Some of these changes will be negotiated as part of the combination agreement and some will be unnegotiated "after-effects" of the agreement. Those factors which are deemed to be the most important matters of concern undoubtedly will be given explicit treatment in the negotiation discussions.

Of all the factors which may be negotiated in a business combination, the two which are usually of greatest importance are: (1) the *price* to be paid for the company to be acquired; and (2) the *methods of payment*. This chapter discusses these two topics in the belief that the accountant can provide many negotiators with valuable information and analytical support for their decisions in these areas.

The student should realize that no amount of information and analytical support will replace the subjective assessments and bargaining processes which are the unique responsibility of the negotiator. Indeed, if the negotiator has substantial experience in business combination deliberations, the analytical consultation of the accountant may be of very limited value. But most combinations involve one party who is negotiating a combination for the first (and generally the last) time. The accountant's analyses may provide this party with: (1) some initial ways to structure his or her thoughts on price and method of payment negotiations; (2) some specific factors involving price and methods of payment that should be recognized as limitations on the negotiating alternatives; and (3) some insight as to the objectives, expectations, and limitations which the opposing negotiator may perceive.

It should be reemphasized that none of the analysis in this chapter is offered as a substitute for the subjective value judgments of the negotiators. The analysis may provide general background that will help the negotiators structure their thought processes. But the analysis does *not* comprehend the value systems of the negotiators and it does *not* include a wide variety of pricing considerations and payment methods that may be available. For example, the analysis of publicly traded companies incorporates only the possibility of exchanging common stock for common stock. Many alternative payment packages are obviously possible. Yet, the negotiators may benefit from the analysis in the process of negotiating a price stated in terms of the number of common shares to be issued, whereafter a variety of alternative payment methods could be calculated which are equivalent in total value.

PUBLICLY TRADED COMPANIES: A MARKET APPROACH

One frequently used method of paying for a business combination involves exchanging common stock. In this case, one corporation, generally the acquiring company, issues additional shares of stock to the stockholders of the other combining company (the acquired firm). In return, those stockholders transfer their shares in the acquired company to the issuing corporation.

Determination of Stock Exchange Ratios

Given a business combination which involves a stock-for-stock exchange, the price to be paid is obviously a matter of determining how many of the acquiring company's shares should be issued in exchange for the acquired firm's outstanding stock. This price is usually expressed in terms of a *stock exchange ratio,* which may be defined as the number of shares of the acquiring firm to be given in exchange for one share of the acquired entity.

The stock exchange ratio is, of course, a *negotiated* price. However, that does not mean its determination is beyond analysis. If the common stock securities of both combining companies are publicly traded, the market prices of their shares provide the primary values upon which the negotiation must be based. The accountant may be able to develop an analysis based on these values which will assist the negotiator in the determination or evaluation of a stock exchange ratio.

Assuming that neither party to a combination agreement is willing to accept a reduction in the total market value of its stockholdings as a result of combination, the accountant can provide information which incorporates the negotiator's expectations and which approximates the range of potential exchange ratios within which negotiation should take place. In the present discussion, a common for common stock exchange is assumed. However, if the transfer plan includes other means of payment, the information regarding common stock (only) can often be adjusted so as to retain its relevance.

Significance of Price/Earnings Ratios

The stock exchange ratio is directly related to the expected price/earnings ratio[1] of the combined entity. To understand this relationship, it should prove beneficial to consider first the general significance of price/earnings ratios within the context of business combinations.

Case 1. The following data relate to the constituents in a proposed combination which will involve a common for common stock exchange:

	Acquiring Firm A	*Acquired Firm B*
Net income	$2,000,000	$1,000,000
Common shares outstanding	2,000,000	1,000,000
Earnings per share	$ 1	$ 1
Common stock market price	$40	$10
Price/earnings ratio	40:1	10:1

Given no additional information, the most intuitively obvious exchange ratio to effect this combination is ¼:1, the ratio of current stock prices. Thus, a person holding one share of B stock, worth $10, would exchange it for one-fourth share of A stock, worth $10. If the combination is consummated under these conditions, the combined entity will exhibit the following characteristics:

	Combined Firm AB
Net income	$3,000,000
Common shares outstanding	2,250,000
Earnings per share	$1.33

Assuming that no special efficiencies, inefficiencies, or risk changes are wrought by the combination, the price/earnings ratio of the combined entity should be the average of the constituents' ratios, weighted by the

---

[1] Price/earnings ratio is defined as the market price per common share divided by the earnings per common share. Refinements in the earnings per share calculation which result from complex capital structures (including convertible securities) are analyzed in Chapter 6.

earnings streams they represent. This calculation is presented in Illustration 2–1.

A price/earnings ratio of 30 for the combined firm would result in a market price of $40, which is equal to the old market price of firm A. This

Illustration 2–1

	(1) Price/ Earnings Ratio	(2) Earnings Stream	(1) × (2) Weighted Factors
Firm A	40	$2,000,000	80,000,000
Firm B	10	1,000,000	10,000,000
Total		$3,000,000	90,000,000
Firm AB	30 = 90,000,000 ÷ 3,000,000		

price confirms the reasonableness of a ¼:1 stock exchange ratio. The total market value of AB shares held by former stockholders of A is $80,000,000 which is equal to the value of their former holdings in firm A. Similarly, the market value of the shares held by the former stockholders of firm B remains the same. Neither group enjoys an advantage over the other as a consequence of the combination.

Given an exchange ratio of ¼:1, consider the effect of a change in the expected price/earnings ratio of AB from the weighted average (30) to the level of old firm A (40).

	Combined Firm AB
Price/earnings ratio	40
Net income	$3,000,000
Common shares outstanding	2,250,000
Earnings per share	$ 1.33
Common stock price will be	$53.33

Should these facts occur, a holder of four shares of B Company stock (worth $40) would now gain possession of one share of AB stock (worth $53.33). Similarly, a holder of one share of A Company stock (worth $40) would now find his share[2] worth $53.33.

---

[2] The new combined entity, which has been referred to as AB, may exist in several alternative forms. B may continue to exist as a separate corporate subsidiary to A. Or, a new legal corporation may be formed which replaces both A and B. Also, B may cease to exist, leaving A as the surviving corporation. In any case, and regardless of the surviving corporate name, the combined entity includes the operations of A and B. Thus it is described as AB.

Several conclusions may be drawn from the foregoing discussion. First, if the price/earnings ratio of the combined entity equals a weighted average of the constituents' ratios, total wealth is not altered as a result of the combination. However, if the combined entity's price/earnings ratio exceeds the constituents' ratios' weighted average, total stockholders' wealth will be enhanced by the combination.

Second, given an increase in total stockholders' wealth resulting from a business combination, the allocation of this increment between the stockholder groups representing each combining firm is determined by the stock exchange ratio. As the ratio increases (in Case 1, for example, if the ratio were 1:1 instead of ¼:1), the amount of wealth increment allocated to the former stockholders of the acquired firm will also increase. Conversely, as the ratio decreases, more of the wealth increment is allocated to the former stockholders of the acquiring firm.

Third, any wealth increment will be shared in proportion to the relative precombination stock values of the constituent firms if the exchange ratio equals the inverse of the ratio of the constituents' precombination share prices. In Case 1, when the price/earnings ratio of the combined firm was assumed to be 40, the total market value of the combined firm was $120,000,000 ([$3,000,000 × 40] or [2,250,000 shares × $53.33]). This constituted a total wealth increment of 33⅓ percent. Given the exchange ratio of ¼:1, which is the inverse of the precombination stock prices of $40 and $10, the wealth increment of each constituent stockholder group was 33⅓ percent. Thus the total wealth increment was shared in the same proportion as the relative precombination stock values of the constituents.

Fourth, it may be noted that earnings per share of the combined entity is not the same as it was for either of the precombination constituents. In Case 1, the combined entity's earnings per share is $1.33, whereas it was $1 for each constituent firm. The earnings per share change only occurs if the combining firms have different price/earnings ratios, as reflected by the negotiated stock exchange ratio. Alternatively, if the combining firms' price/earnings ratios are equal, as reflected by the negotiated stock exchange ratio, the earnings per share of the combined entity will be equal to the earnings per share of each combining firm.[3]

For example, each combining firm in Case 1 had earnings per share of $1. Suppose that the price/earnings ratio of each firm was 40:1. The market price of each company's stock would therefore be $40 per share. The negotiated exchange ratio would reflect these facts if it were 1:1. If this exchange ratio were used, the combined entity would have earnings per share of $1, the same as each of the combining firms. These

---

[3] This generalization refers only to common for common stock exchanges and assumes that total combined earnings in the period immediately following combination is equal to the sum of the constituents' total earnings in the period immediately preceding combination.

facts are depicted in Illustration 2–2, Situation II. Compare this situation with Situation I, which discloses the original Case 1 data. Additional examples of this relationship can be observed by comparing Situations III and IV with Situations I and II (Illustration 2–2).

If the combining companies have different price/earnings ratios, then the amount of the earnings per share change will depend on the relative size of the two constituents. More specifically, it will depend on the relative size of their net incomes and number of shares outstanding. This factor can be observed by comparing Situation I with Situation V in Illustration 2–2.

The problem of evaluating earnings per share when it has been materially affected by a business combination is part of the more general problem category of interpretive accounting. Several aspects of this accounting function will be analyzed in Chapter 6.

Exchange Ratio Negotiating Range

A reasonable assumption underlying combination negotiations is that neither negotiating party would accept terms which would result in that party having to incur a loss of wealth. One can point to several factors which might promote a combination even if reasonable expectations did not include a wealth increment. But it is unlikely that any stockholder group would accept a loss of wealth as an appropriate price for participating in a corporate combination. As discussed earlier, the total stockholders' wealth (market value) of the combined entity will equal the sum of the constituent firms' stockholders' wealth *if* the combined entity's price/earnings ratio equals a weighted average of the combining firms' price/earnings ratios.[4] This sets a minimum expected price/earnings ratio for the combined entity, below which the combination will probably not be consummated. If the expected price/earnings ratio of the combined entity were lower, at least one of the constituent firms would be forced by the combination to incur a loss of stockholder wealth.

Case 2. The analysis of Case 1 showed that the combined entity's expected price/earnings ratio of 30 equaled the weighted average of the constituents' price/earnings ratios. Utilizing the expected price/earnings ratio of AB (30) and a stock exchange ratio of ¼:1, the wealth of all stockholders remained unchanged. Assume now that AB's expected price/earnings ratio is only 20. Illustration 2–3 depicts a $30,000,000 reduction in total stockholders' wealth when the expected price/earnings ratio falls from the weighted average (30) to 20. Having established the minimum acceptable combined entity price/earnings ratio, it is important

---

[4] This assumes that total earnings of the combined entity is equal to the sum of the combining companies' total earnings at the time of the combination, i.e., there are no immediate synergistic effects on earnings as a result of the combination.

Illustration 2-2

	(1) Net Income	(2) Shares Outstanding	(3) Stock Market Price	(4) Price/ Earnings Ratio	(5) Exchange Ratio Implied by (3) and (4)	(6) Earnings per Share	Compared to Case A, the Variables Altered Were—
Situation I							
Acquiring firm A	2,000,000	2,000,000	$40	40:1		$1.00	
Acquired firm B	1,000,000	1,000,000	10	10:1	1/4:1	1.00	
Combined firm AB	3,000,000	2,250,000				1.33	
Situation II							Price/earnings ratio of B, altered so that it would equal A's price/ earnings ratio
Acquiring firm A	2,000,000	2,000,000	40	40:1		$1.00	
Acquired firm B	1,000,000	1,000,000	*40*	*40:1*	*1:1*	1.00	
Combined firm AB	3,000,000	3,000,000				*1.00*	
Situation III							Price/earnings ratio of A (and, there- fore, the exchange ratio)
Acquiring firm A	2,000,000	2,000,000	*20*	*20:1*		$1.00	
Acquired firm B	1,000,000	1,000,000	10	10:1	*1/2:1*	1.00	
Combined firm AB	3,000,000	2,500,000				*1.20*	
Situation IV							Price/earnings ratio of B (and, there- fore, the exchange ratio)
Acquiring firm A	2,000,000	2,000,000	40	40:1		$1.00	
Acquired firm B	1,000,000	1,000,000	*80*	*80:1*	*2:1*	1.00	
Combined firm AB	3,000,000	4,000,000				*.75*	
Situation V							Total earnings and shares of B
Acquiring firm A	2,000,000	2,000,000	40	40:1		$1.00	
Acquired firm B	*500,000*	*500,000*	10	10:1	1/4:1	1.00	
Combined firm AB	2,500,000	2,125,000				*1.18*	

Illustration 2–3

	Total Earnings	×	Price/ Earnings Ratio	=	Total Stockholder Wealth
Firm A	$2,000,000		40:1		$80,000,000
Firm B	1,000,000		10:1		10,000,000
Total					$90,000,000
Firm AB	3,000,000		20:1		60,000,000
Loss of wealth					$30,000,000

to note that given this price/earnings ratio, only one exchange ratio is acceptable. It is the inverse of the ratio of the constituent firms' stock prices. Case 3 discloses the effects of assuming exchange ratios that are either equal to, greater than, or less than the unique ratio which leaves the wealth positions of each stockholder group unchanged.

Illustration 2–4

	Combined Firm AB	Number and Total Value of Firm AB Shares Held by—	
		Stockholders from Firm A	Stockholders from Firm B
Net income	$ 3,000,000		
Shares outstanding	2,250,000	2,000,000	250,000
Earnings/share	$ 1.33		
Price/earnings ratio	30:1		
Stock price	$40	$40	$40
Total stock value	$90,000,000	$80,000,000	$10,000,000
Wealth positions prior to combination		$80,000,000	$10,000,000
Gain or [loss] on combination		$ 0	$ 0

Case 3. Given the data of Case 1, consider the effects of alternative stock exchange ratios.

Assumption 1. Given a stock exchange ratio of ¼:1, the equities in firm AB are displayed in Illustration 2–4.

Assumption 2. Given a stock exchange ratio of ½:1, the equities in firm AB are presented in Illustration 2–5.

Assumption 3. Given a stock exchange ratio of ⅛:1, the equities in firm AB are presented in Illustration 2–6.

In Case 3, it is important to recognize that the price/earnings ratio of the combined firm was held constant at 30:1, the weighted average of the

Illustration 2–5

	Combined Firm AB	Number and Total Value of Firm AB Shares Held by—	
		Stockholders from Firm A	Stockholders from Firm B
Net income	$ 3,000,000		
Shares outstanding	2,500,000	2,000,000	500,000
Earnings/share	$ 1.20		
Price/earnings ratio	30:1		
Stock price	$36	$36	$36
Total stock value	$90,000,000	$72,000,000	$18,000,000
Wealth positions prior to combination		$80,000,000	$10,000,000
Gain or [loss] on combination		[$ 8,000,000]	$ 8,000,000

Illustration 2–6

	Combined Firm AB	Number and Total Value of Firm AB Shares Held by—	
		Stockholders from Firm A	Stockholders from Firm B
Net income	$ 3,000,000		
Shares outstanding	2,125,000	2,000,000	125,000
Earnings/share	$ 1.41		
Price/earnings ratio	30:1		
Stock price	$42.35*	$42.35*	$ 42.35*
Total stock value	$90,000,000	$84,705,882	$ 5,294,118
Wealth positions prior to combination		$80,000,000	$10,000,000
Gain or [loss] on combination		$ 4,705,882	[$ 4,705,882]

* Rounded from $42.352941.

constituents' price/earnings ratios. Thus, the total stock value of AB was equal to the sum of the stock values of A and B. The assumed changes in the exchange ratio resulted in differing allocations of this value between the stockholder groups. Since the total wealth did not change as a result of the combination, the allocations on the basis of exchange ratios other than ¼:1 resulted in the two stockholder groups realizing counterbalancing gains and losses. It should be apparent that if the expected price/earnings ratio of AB increases (above the minimum level), total stockholders' wealth also increases (above the precombination level). Correspondingly, as the expected price/earnings ratio increases, the exchange ratio is subject to increasing variability without forcing a loss on either stockholder group.

General Formulation of the Model

Consider the limit on the exchange ratio that would be imposed by an acquiring firm (A). This limit is the maximum exchange ratio that is acceptable to A, given a specific expected price/earnings ratio of the combined entity (AB). In other words, it is the exchange ratio that will leave the wealth positions of firm A stockholders undiminished. Assume the following notation:

W_A = total wealth (market value) of firm A stock.

S_A = firm A outstanding shares.

S_B = firm B outstanding shares.

W_{AB} = total wealth (market value) of firm AB stock.

ER = common stock exchange ratio, i.e., the number of shares of firm A (the acquiring firm) given in exchange for 1 share of (acquired) firm B.

ER_A = maximum exchange ratio acceptable to firm A stockholders.

NI_{AB} = total earnings of firm AB in the first postcombination period. It is assumed that these earnings equal the sum of A's and B's total earnings in the last precombination period.

PE_{AB} = expected price/earnings ratio of firm AB.

From the definitions given above, it may be noted that—

$$\frac{S_A}{S_A + ER(S_B)}$$

equals the equity percentage of firm A stockholders in firm AB. Further, $W_{AB} = NI_{AB} (PE_{AB})$. Thus, to equate the firm A stockholders' precombination wealth with the value of their equity in firm AB:

$$W_A = \frac{S_A}{S_A + ER_A(S_B)} [NI_{AB}(PE_{AB})].$$

To solve for the maximum exchange ratio acceptable to firm A stockholders:

(1) $$ER_A = \frac{(SA/W_A)NI_{AB}(PE_{AB}) - S_A}{S_B}.$$

Within the context of a particular business combination, the values of all terms in equation (1) are constant, except for ER_A and PE_{AB}. Thus, it can be demonstrated that as the expected price/earnings ratio of the combined entity increases, the maximum exchange ratio acceptable to acquiring firm stockholders also increases. Illustration 2–7 depicts the nature of this relationship.

Illustration 2–7

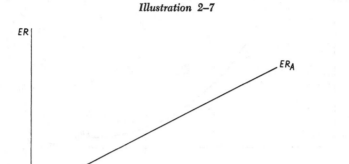

Next, consider the limit on the exchange ratio that would be imposed by an acquired firm B. This limit takes the form of a minimum exchange ratio. It is the ratio that will leave the wealth positions of firm B stockholders undiminished. Assume the notation presented previously and the following:

W_B = total wealth (market value) of firm B stock.

ER_B = minimum exchange ratio acceptable to firm B stockholders.

The equity percentage of firm B stockholders in firm AB is

$$\frac{ER(S_B)}{S_A + ER(S_B)}.$$

Firm B stockholders' precombination wealth is equated with the value of their equity in firm AB as follows:

$$W_B = \frac{ER_B(S_B)}{S_A + ER_B(S_B)} [NI_{AB}(PE_{AB})].$$

Substituting appropriate values in equation (2) which follows, will yield the minimum exchange ratio acceptable to firm B stockholders.

(2) $$ER_B = \frac{S_A}{(S_B/W_B)NI_{AB}(PE_{AB}) - S_B}.$$

Within the context of a particular corporate combination, the values of all terms in equation (2) are constant, except for ER_B and PE_{AB}. Thus, as the expected price/earnings ratio of the combined entity increases, the mimimum exchange ratio acceptable to the acquired firm's stockholders decreases (at a decreasing rate). Illustration 2–8 graphically indicates the nature of this relationship.

Illustration 2–8

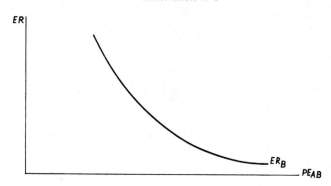

The negotiated exchange ratio of a business combination must be consistent with the boundary conditions (equations 1 and 2) imposed by both negotiating parties. The field of exchange ratios that are consistent with both limits can be portrayed by superimposing the minimum exchange ratio acceptable to the acquired firm (ER_B) on the maximum exchange ratio acceptable to the acquiring firm (ER_A). This field is shown in Illustration 2–9. Thus, the exchange ratio used to execute the combination must fall within the shaded area of the illustration. Upon specifying an expected price/earnings ratio of the combined entity, a negotiator can use the above analysis to assess a reasonable bargaining range. The unique point of intersection between ER_A and ER_B (Illustration 2–9) specifies

Illustration 2–9

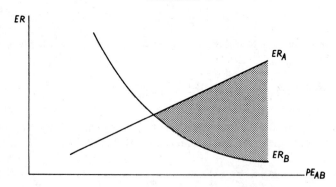

the only acceptable exchange ratio in the event that the expected price/earnings ratio of AB equals the weighted average of the constituent firms' price/earnings ratios. As previously discussed, this unique exchange ratio is equal to the inverse of the ratio of the constituent firms' stock prices.

Case 4. Utilizing the data of Case 1, the stock exchange ratio negotiating ranges are as follows:

Expected Price/Earnings Ratio of Firm AB	(1) ER_A Maximum Exchange Ratio	(2) ER_B Minimum Exchange Ratio
26.67.............	0 :1	.2857:1
30.0	.2500:1	.2500:1
32.5	.4375:1	.2286:1
35.0	.6250:1	.2105:1
37.5	.8125:1	.1951:1
40.0	1.0000:1	.1818:1

(1)
$$ER_A = \frac{(S_A/W_A)NI_{AB}(PE_{AB}) - S_A}{S_B}$$

$$ER_A = \frac{(1/40)3{,}000{,}000(PE_{AB}) - 2{,}000{,}000}{1{,}000{,}000}$$

(2)
$$ER_B = \frac{S_A}{(S_B/W_B)NI_{AB}(PE_{AB}) - S_B}$$

$$ER_B = \frac{2{,}000{,}000}{(1/10)3{,}000{,}000(PE_{AB}) - 1{,}000{,}000}$$

The negotiating field is presented graphically in Illustration 2–10 on the following page.

It must be emphasized that the exchange ratio to be used in a specific combination remains a negotiated price; it is not subject to precise determination through logical analysis. The agreed-upon ratio will depend on the relative bargaining powers of the combination participants as well as the estimated contributions of each constituent to the profitability of the combined entity. The above analysis can only provide information which may facilitate the negotiating process.

Parameter Changes

A firm that exhibits an interest in expansion via the process of acquisition may wish to compare alternative prospective combination participants. By inspecting the general form of the equation for determining its maximum acceptable exchange ratio, an acquiring firm can note the effects (upon ER_A) of firms being considered for combination which have different net income levels or different amounts of outstanding stock.

The income of a potential combination participant, for example, naturally affects the income of the potential combined entity (NI). Given the position of NI_{AB} (in the numerator), it is obvious that the ER_A is directly related to changes in NI. Thus, if firm A is considering three alternative firms to acquire (B, C, D) and if $NI_B > NI_C > NI_D$, the comparative ER curves will have relationships as shown in Illustration 2–11.

Illustration 2–10

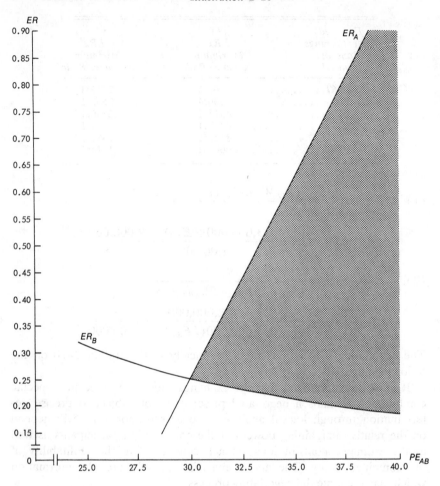

Illustration 2–11

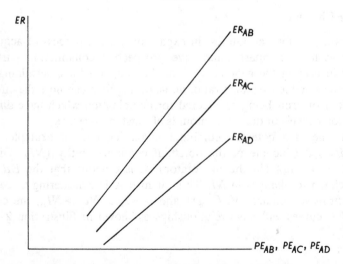

A similar kind of analysis can be made to show the effects of considering alternative firms that have differing amounts of common stock outstanding. By the same token a firm to be acquired can analyze the difference in its boundary condition that results from differing characteristics of alternative combination participants.[5]

CLOSELY HELD COMPANIES: A NORMATIVE APPROACH

Determination of Price

If either of the firms involved in a business combination is not publicly held, so that an observable market price for its stock is not available, the previously discussed market approach to negotiating a price cannot be used. Many combinations involve a large, publicly held, acquiring company and a smaller, closely held company that is being acquired. As a consequence, the determination of an appropriate price to be paid for the closely held company is inherently more difficult; a current market value is probably not available. Even in those cases where a current market price for the acquired company's stock can be reasonably approximated, the potential gain to be realized by refusing a specific offer, in expectation of rising stock prices, usually provokes the acquiring company to offer a premium over the current price. Thus, the determination of an exchange price demands a careful analysis of relevant accounting and statistical data, current market circumstances, and business expectations. The book values of recorded assets seldom provide an equitable basis for settlement; at best, these amounts, together with the earnings history of each company, merely provide a convenient point of departure for a more refined evaluation.

It is important that the accounts of constituent companies be free of significant accounting errors and omissions, and that they reflect comparable underlying measurement processes; accordingly, adjustment should be made, where appropriate, to provide uniform valuation. There are often significant accounting differences between companies regarding inventory pricing, depreciation policies, criteria for distinguishing between capital and revenue expenditures, appraisal of long-lived assets, recognition of contingent liabilities and losses, and policies for deferral and accrual of revenues and expenses. The accountant may offer valuable counsel in reconciling such differences and in translating the accounting data to comparable bases.

While uniform accounting data may be helpful, they are not sufficient to provide a complete basis for an equitable settlement value. The adjusted

---

[5] For further consideration of the exchange ratio model, see Kermit D. Larson and Nicholas J. Gonedes, "Business Combinations: An Exchange Ratio Determination Model," *The Accounting Review,* October 1969, pp. 720–28.

net asset book values are usually inadequate indexes of the earning power of the contributing companies. Replacement costs of individual assets, or their fair appraised values, frequently indicate the earnings prospects of the assets more accurately than do acquisition costs less amortization. But even replacement values of the individual assets may fail to reflect a value increment associated with the established market position and organizational maturity of the company. A *collection* of functionally related assets which exists in the context of an already organized, profitable company often has a present value (from discounting future expected cash flows) which is greater than the sum of the market values of the individual assets in the collection. Thus, an estimate of the future earnings of the constituent companies frequently suggests the existence of unidentified intangibles, or "goodwill."

In projecting the future earnings of each combining company, care should be taken to evaluate any effects the combination may have on the future earnings of the companies. An acquiring company should expect to pay a fair price for the anticipated earnings of the firm to be acquired, based upon its historical performance as an independent entity; but the acquiring company would often hope to reap the full amount of any additional value that may result from economies of scale or other efficiencies attaching uniquely to the combination.

Taking into account all of the available information regarding the financial status and future potential of the combining firms, the price negotiations must finally be focused on the value of the net assets contributed by a company and any additional amount of goodwill associated with the capitalized value of projected earnings.

Methods of Payment

Once the exchange price is established, an acceptable *method* of payment must be determined. A number of alternatives are available. The acquiring corporation may either issue its own securities directly to the individual shareholders of the acquired company *or* to the corporation for distribution as a liquidating settlement with its shareholders. The shares to be issued may be either common or preferred stock, or a combination of the two security types. Payment may also be made in cash, other assets, or bonds. Clearly, the method of payment which is chosen is subject to negotiation and will normally reflect the underlying motivations of those who have initiated the proposal for consolidation.

A factor of special significance in negotiating with a closely held company is the uniquely personal involvement of the owners. The company to be acquired may well represent the cumulative life's work of the owners, and their personal identification with the company may overshadow the underlying economic factors so that the behavioral issues of dealing with the owners/sellers necessarily become of dominant importance.

Many business combinations are predicated upon the desire of the constituents to merge their controlling and ownership interests so that the control and ownership of the new combined entity will reflect the relative positions of the constituent firms' ownership interests. Voting stock must be a primary method of payment in these situations. However, the preservation of interests may also require the distribution of senior securities as well as common stock. The idea of preserving the interests of the various shareholder groups in the new or surviving company is essentially an attempt to make the stock distribution plan *equitable*.

Equitable Stock Distribution Plans

Although equity is in the final analysis a subjective concept, a negotiator may benefit from considering the general meaning of equity in the context of a plan for paying the shareholders whose companies are to be combined. The following two criteria are proposed as essential elements of an *equitable stock distribution plan*. Both criteria must be satisfied if the stock distribution is to be equitable.

1. *Equity requires that the expected income to be generated by any one constituent in a combination should be allocated to those who held shares in that constituent.* Thus, if 60 percent of the combined entity's income will be generated by the assets and operations contributed by constituent firm A, the stock distribution plan should allocate approximately 60 percent of the combined entity's income to shares held by those who were precombination firm A stockholders. As a matter of practicality, the percentage of profits contributed by each constituent is usually approximated by comparing the recent historical earnings records of the combining firms.

2. *Equity requires that the stockholders in a combined entity be given a preference position, as to liquidation and income distribution, for the net severable assets*[6] *contributed by their respective firms.* By agreeing to the combination, the stockholders forego the alternative of selling the assets of the firms piecemeal. Further, the cash receipts from such sales could have been re-invested in relatively safe securities, e.g., preferred stock. Thus, the contribution of severable assets is, in a sense, a more significant commitment than is the "investment" of goodwill; correspondingly, a preference position in return for the investment of severable assets seems equitable. By contributing goodwill, i.e., anticipated earnings that are

---

[6] "Severable" assets include all tangible assets as well as intangibles which can be separately identified and offered for sale. It excludes goodwill, since goodwill cannot be disassociated from the collection of other assets. By implication, a "severable" asset can be individually offered for sale.

above normal, given the amount of severable assets contributed, the share-holders do not forego an alternative of separately selling that goodwill. Thus, they are adequately compensated for the goodwill as the above-normal earnings are allocated to them. This is the essence of the first equity requirement cited above.

To summarize, a contribution of individually severable assets warrants a preference position in liquidation because those assets might have been liquidated whereas goodwill cannot be separately sold. Also, a preference position as to a conservative return on severable assets is warranted, because the alternative of liquidating the assets would have allowed reinvestment of the cash proceeds with high confidence of receiving a conservative return. A typical preferred stock dividend rate (for the type of firm in question) is suggested as a reasonable approximation of this conservative rate of return.[7]

Under certain restrictive conditions, both equity criteria can be satisfied by the issuance of common stock only. Specifically, if each combining firm contributes the same proportion of total severable assets as it does of total combined earnings, then no special preference position is necessary. For example, assume that J Company and K Company plan to combine; J Company will contribute 40 percent of the total severable assets and K Company will contribute 60 percent. Coincidentally, J Company is also expected to contribute 40 percent of the future earnings with K Company contributing 60 percent. In this case, the requirements of equity are fully satisfied if the combined JK Company issues only common stock, so that J Company shareholders receive 40 percent of the outstanding stock and K Company shareholders receive 60 percent.

The issuance of only common stock in a more typical situation would not satisfy the equity criteria. The inequity which may result from issuing common stock only is illustrated as follows.

Case 5.   R Corporation is organized for the purpose of consolidating the operations and resources of companies X, Y, and Z. R Corporation is authorized to issue $100 par, common stock. A summary of selected net severable assets and earnings data for the combination participants is given in Illustration 2–12.

---

[7] Although recognizing preferred stock to be the normal method of satisfying this equity requirement, a strong case can nonetheless be made for the use of *convertible* bonds or *convertible* preferred stock. As the combined entity's life begins to extend beyond the remaining useful lives of net severable assets existing at acquisition, internally financed new investments will derive from *actual* earnings (before depreciation)—not from *normal* earnings. If actual earnings include a return associated with goodwill at acquisition, this goodwill eventually becomes transformed into tangible or severable assets. This transformation is no less real than is the transformation of net severable assets at acquisition into *new* severable assets. Therefore, the preference position associated with severable assets contributed should eventually relate to the total historical earnings of the combined entity. As the proportion of severable assets contributed and the proportion of total earnings contributed approach equality, equity requirements can be fulfilled with common stock. The conversion of senior securities would facilitate this objective.

Illustration 2–12

| Company | Net Severable Assets | | Expected Earnings* | | Percentage Return on Assets |
	Amount Contributed	Percent of Total	Amount Contributed	Percent of Total	
X	$150,000	18.75%	$15,000	15.79%	10%
Y	250,000	31.25	20,000	21.05	8
Z	400,000	50.00	60,000	63.16	15
	$800,000	100.00%	$95,000	100.00%	

* Approximated by averaging past years' earnings.

The R Corporation stock may be allocated among the three companies on the basis of the net severable assets contributed by each. In this case the equitable interests of the former shareholders of the constituent companies in net assets are preserved; yet, the interests of each shareholder group in the earnings of the consolidation are altered in the following respects:

| | Percentage Interest in Earnings | | |
Company	Before Consolidation	After Consolidation	Advantage [Disadvantage]
X	15.79%	18.75%	2.96%
Y	21.05	31.25	10.20
Z	63.16	50.00	[13.16]
	100.00%	100.00%	

Alternatively, the shares of R Corporation may be issued to each company on the basis of the relative interest of each in their combined average earnings. If this plan of stock distribution were adopted, the interest in earnings before and after consolidation necessarily would remain unchanged; yet, the relative interest of each company in the combined net assets of the affiliation would be modified in the following respects:

| | Percentage Interest in Net Assets | | |
Company	Before Consolidation	After Consolidation	Advantage [Disadvantage]
X	18.75%	15.79%	[2.96%]
Y	31.25	21.05	[10.20]
Z	50.00	63.16	13.16
	100.00%	100.00%	

These alternative methods of payment demonstrate that where only shares of common stock of the new enterprise are issued to the several combination participants, the equitable interest of each in either the net assets or the future earnings of the consolidation may be altered from previous interests. Such an alteration occurs whenever the ratios of assets and earnings contributions are orginally unequal. This condition of inequity will persist even when the capitalized values of average earnings are used as the basis for stock distribution, since the capitalized values will necessarily be in the same ratio as the average earnings of the constituents.

Distribution Formula

It is apparent from the previous discussion that protection of the equitable interests of the various shareholder groups frequently requires the new or surviving enterprise to issue preferred stock or other senior securities as well as common stock. The following formula is recommended as a mechanism to determine an appropriate combination of security values:

1. The total amount of stock to be issued to each firm's shareholders is calculated by capitalizing the expected annual earnings contribution of each firm at an appropriate capitalization rate.
2. Preferred stock (cumulative, fully participating) should be issued in exchange for the existing net severable assets contributed by each of the constituents.
3. Common stock should be issued to each constituent's shareholders such that the amount of common stock issued plus the amount of preferred stock issued will equal the total amount of stock to be issued as calculated in 1 above.

This formula requires that the same capitalization rate be applied to the expected earnings of each constituent firm. As a consequence, the allocation of total stock between the shareholder groups will be in the same proportion as are their contributions of expected earnings.

Case 6. In Case 5, R Corporation was authorized to issue $100 par, common stock for the purpose of consolidating companies X, Y, and Z. The data for those companies were presented in Illustration 2–12, page 49. Using the same data, assume that R Corporation is also authorized to issue 5 percent, cumulative, fully participating, preferred stock. Further, the earnings of each constituent are to be capitalized using a capitalization rate of 6 percent. The allocation of total stock would be illustrated as follows:

Company	Earnings	Percent of Total	Capital- ization Rate	Allocation of Total Stock	Percent of Total
X	$15,000	15.79%	6%	$ 250,000	15.79%
Y	20,000	21.05	6	333,333	21.05
Z	60,000	63.16	6	1,000,000	63.16

Refer to the first criterion of an equitable stock distribution plan (page 47). According to that criterion, the distribution of postcombination earnings must be in the same proportions as were the expected contributions of earnings. Thus, to meet that criterion in the present case, the earnings of R Corporation must be allocated to the three shareholder groups as follows:

Former X Company shareholders should be allocated 15.79%.
Former Y Company shareholders should be allocated 21.05%.
Former Z Company shareholders should be allocated 63.16%.

Note that this criterion will be satisfied so long as all of the outstanding stock receives the same percentage of earnings. Since the stock is distributed in the correct ratios, the allocation of earnings will also be in the correct ratios if each dollar (par) of stock is allocated an equal amount of earnings.

The complete stock distribution plan is presented below.

	Company			
	X	Y	Z	Totals
Expected earnings	$ 15,000	$ 20,000	$ 60,000	$ 95,000
Capitalization rate	÷ .06	÷ .06	÷ .06	÷ .06
Total stock to be issued	$250,000	$333,333	$1,000,000	$1,583,333
Less Preferred stock to be issued	150,000	250,000	400,000	800,000
Common stock to be issued	$100,000	$ 83,333	$ 600,000	$ 783,333

Note that preferred stock is issued to each of the shareholder groups in exchange for their contributions of net severable assets. Of the total amount of preferred stock issued, 18.75 percent was issued to X Company shareholders, 31.25 percent was issued to Y Company shareholders, and 50 percent was issued to Z Company shareholders. Since earnings will be distributed first to preferred shares in accordance with the 5 percent preference rate, the first allocation of earnings to the three shareholder groups will be in the same ratio as was the distribution of preferred stock.

Illustration 2–13

Earnings after Consolidation	Allocations of Earnings to Former Shareholders of			Earnings Allocated	
	X Company	Y Company	Z Company	Total Dollars	As a % of Par
$40,000					
Preferred	$ 7,500	$12,500	$20,000	$40,000	5.00%
Common	—	—	—	—	—
Total	$ 7,500	$12,500	$20,000	$40,000	
Percent	18.75%	31.25%	50.00%	100%	
$50,000					
Preferred	$ 7,500	$12,500	$20,000	$40,000	5.00%
Common	1,277	1,064	7,659	10,000	1.28%
Total	$ 8,777	$13,564	$27,659	$50,000	
Percent	17.55%	27.13%	55.32%	100%	
$60,000					
Preferred	$ 7,500	$12,500	$20,000	$40,000	5.00%
Common	2,553	2,128	15,319	20,000	2.55%
Total	$10,053	$14,628	$35,319	$60,000	
Percent	16.75%	24.38%	58.87%	100%	
$70,000					
Preferred	$ 7,500	$12,500	$20,000	$40,000	5.00%
Common	3,830	3,191	22,979	30,000	3.83%
Total	$11,330	$15,691	$42,979	$70,000	
Percent	16.19%	22.41%	61.40%	100%	
$79,167					
Preferred	$ 7,500	$12,500	$20,000	$40,000	5.00%
Common	5,000	4,167	30,000	39,167	5.00%
Total	$12,500	$16,667	$50,000	$79,167	
Percent	15.79%	21.05%	63.16%	100%	
$95,000					
Preferred	$ 9,000	$15,000	$24,000	$58,000	6.00%
Common	6,000	5,000	36,000	47,000	6.00%
Total	$15,000	$20,000	$60,000	$95,000	
Percent	15.79%	21.05%	63.16%	100%	

After the preferred stock has received its 5 percent preference, the next allocation of earnings will be to common shares until those shares have also received 5 percent. At that point, all outstanding shares have been allocated the same rate, and the allocation of earnings has satisfied the first equity criterion. Because the preferred stock is fully participating, any additional earnings will be allocated pro rata among all the shares. Thus, the first equity criterion will be satisfied at all income levels above that which provides the preferred dividend rate to all outstanding shares. In the present case, income allocations in the amount of $79,167 (.05 × 1,588,-333) or greater will result in an equitable allocation.

Illustration 2–13 displays the allocation of earnings to each shareholder group, given six different postconsolidation earnings levels ranging from $40,000 to $95,000. At the $40,000 earnings level, observe that the allocation is entirely to preferred shares. As a consequence, the allocation of earnings to the three shareholder groups is in the same proportions as are their holdings of preferred stock. As earnings increase above $40,000, the percentage allocated to each shareholder group approaches the equitable level. At an earnings level of $79,167, all outstanding shares receive a 5 percent portion and the distribution plan conforms to the equity criterion.

Importantly, the stock distribution plan is equitable even when earnings fail to reach the expected $95,000 level. If earnings do reach $95,000, all shares are allocated earnings amounting to 6 percent of par. But equity prevails when earnings amount to only 5 percent of par.

Illustration 2–14 discloses graphically the earnings distribution patterns calculated in Illustration 2–13. Readers are encouraged to confirm one or more of the earnings distributions shown in these illustrations by calculating the amounts which would accrue to each class of stock and each shareholder group.

Selecting a Capitalization Rate

The expected earnings of each constituent are divided by the capitalization rate to determine the total amount of stock to be issued to the respective shareholder groups. Thus, the capitalization rate effectively specifies the price to be paid for the combining companies. Selection of the capitalization rate is, therefore, a crucial step in the development of an equitable stock distribution plan. All of the subjective considerations previously mentioned as important in negotiating a price are applicable to the selection of a capitalization rate. In addition, the rate which is chosen must fall within two important limits if the resultant stock distribution plan is to be consistent with the equity definition.

1. The rate to be used cannot be greater than the lowest rate of return earned by any of the participants on their contributed net severable assets. If the capitalization rate exceeds any one of the firms' expected return on net severable assets, the resulting total value to be paid for the firm will be less than net severable assets contributed. Thus, the equitable preference position for net severable assets contributed would require more stated value of stock than the entire value to be paid for the firm.

Illustration 2–14

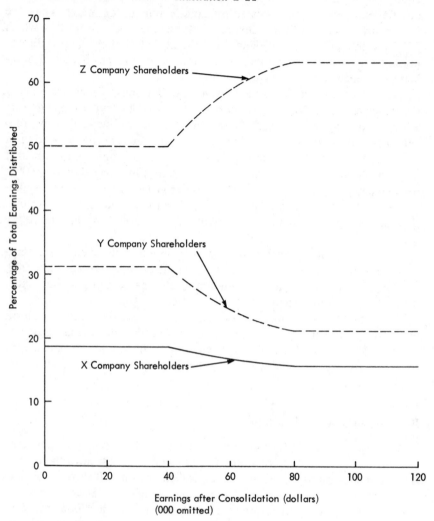

Earnings after Consolidation (dollars)
(000 omitted)

For example, assume the same data for Case 6 except that the capitalization rate to be used is 10 percent. The impossibility of developing an equitable stock distribution plan is disclosed below. Observe that Y Company shareholders should receive $250,000 of preferred stock but the total amount of stock they should receive is only $200,000. Obviously, an equitable stock distribution plan cannot be developed unless the capitalization rate to be used is 8 percent or less.

2. The second limit upon the selection of a capitalization rate is that the rate should not be less than the preferred dividend rate on the preferred stock to be issued. If the selected rate is less than the preferred

	Company			
	X	Y	Z	Totals
Expected earnings	$ 15,000	$ 20,000	$ 60,000	$ 95,000
Net severable assets	150,000	250,000	400,000	800,000
Expected rate of return	10%	8%	15%	
Expected earnings	$ 15,000	$ 20,000	$ 60,000	$ 95,000
Capitalization rate	÷ .10	÷ .10	÷ .10	÷ .10
Total stock to be issued	$150,000	$200,000	$600,000	$950,000
Less preferred stock to be issued	150,000	250,000	400,000	800,000
Common stock to be issued	–0–	?	$200,000	?

dividend rate, an inequitable allocation of earnings will probably result. An equitable earnings allocation demands that *all* outstanding shares receive the same rate of return. Given the existence of some preferred stock, the lowest postcombination income level at which equity occurs is that which provides the preferred rate to all outstanding shares. If a capitalization rate (e.g., 4 percent) that is less than the preferred dividend rate (e.g., 5 percent) is applied to expected postcombination earnings to determine the total stock outstanding, the minimum equitable earnings level (5 percent × par or stated value of outstanding stock) will exceed *expected* earnings (4 percent × par or stated value of outstanding stock).

Case 7. Earnings Capitalized at 4 Percent. The data for this case are the same as for Case 6 except that a 4 percent capitalization rate is used to determine the total amount of stock to be issued to each shareholder group. R Corporation is organized for the purpose of consolidating com-

Illustration 2–15

	Company			
	X	Y	Z	Totals
Expected earnings	$ 15,000	$ 20,000	$ 60,000	$ 95,000
Net severable assets	150,000	250,000	400,000	800,000
Expected rate of return	10%	8%	15%	
Ratio of earnings distribution	15.79%	21.05%	63.16%	100%
Expected earnings	$ 15,000	$ 20,000	$ 60,000	$ 95,000
Capitalization rate	÷ .04	÷ .04	÷ .04	÷ .04
Total stock to be issued	$375,000	$500,000	$1,500,000	$2,375,000
Less preferred stock to be issued	150,000	250,000	400,000	800,000
Common stock to be issued	$225,000	$250,000	$1,100,000	$1,575,000

panies X, Y, and Z. R Corporation is authorized to issue $100 par, common stock and $100 par, 5 percent, cumulative, fully participating, preferred stock. The relevant data for the combining companies and the stock distribution plan are presented in Illustration 2–15 shown on page 55.

The above proposed plan of distribution is tested for its equitable consequence on each combination participant assuming two levels of postconsolidation earnings.

Assumption 1. If the first year's earnings subsequent to consolidation are $95,000, the allocation to shareholders would be made as follows:

	Company		
	X	Y	Z
Preferred shares:			
5% of $150,000	$ 7,500		
5% of $250,000		$12,500	
5% of $400,000			$20,000
Common shares:*			
3.492% of $225,000	7,857		
3.492% of $250,000		8,730	
3.492% of $1,100,000			38,413
Total	$15,357	$21,230	$58,413
Ratio of earnings distribution before consolidation	15.79%	21.05%	63.16%
Ratio of earnings distribution after consolidation	16.16	22.35	61.49
Earnings advantage [disadvantage] after consolidation	.37%	1.30%	[1.67%]

* The return to common stock is calculated as follows: $(95,000 - 40,000)/1,575,000 = .03492$.

It is evident that an inequitable condition results even though postconsolidation earnings are equal to the projected net incomes. This derives from the use of a capitalization rate (4 percent) less than the preferred dividend rate. The condition of inequity, however, does not obtain for all levels of net incomes, as demonstrated in Assumption 2 which follows.

Assumption 2. If the first year's earnings subsequent to consolidation are $118,750 (5 percent return on total shares outstanding), the allocation to shareholders would be made as shown in the accompanying table.

Thus, if the net income reflects a rate of return on all shares equal to the preferred dividend rate, equity is restored. Furthermore, any net income level in excess of this amount will preserve the equitable relationship.

	Company		
	X	Y	Z
Preferred shares:			
5% of $150,000 .... $ 7,500			
5% of $250,000		$12,500	
5% of $400,000			$20,000
Common shares:*			
5% of $225,000 11,250			
5% of $250,000		12,500	
5% of $1,100,000			55,000
Total	$18,750	$25,000	$75,000
Ratio of earnings distribution			
before consolidation	15.79%	21.05%	63.16%
Ratio of earnings distribution			
after consolidation	15.79%	21.05%	63.16%

* The return to common stock is calculated as follows: $(118,750 - 40,000)/1,575,000 = .05$.

These illustrations confirm that the equity consequences of the stock distribution formula are dependent upon the postconsolidation level of earnings *and* the rate used to capitalize the earnings of the constituent companies. Given a capitalization rate equal to, or larger than, the preferred stock dividend rate, but less than the aforementioned upper constraint, an equitable distribution will always exist when consolidation earnings are equal to, or greater than, the preference rate multiplied times the par amount of total stock outstanding. Where the preferred stock dividend rate is greater than the capitalization rate, the required earnings level for an equitable allocation will be greater than the expected earnings level.

In evaluating the appropriateness of a stock distribution plan that has been developed in accordance with the equity definition, one significant characteristic of that definition must be clearly recognized. The definition of equity requires that the expected earnings contributed by each company must be allocated to the former shareholders of that company. This means that the same capitalization rate (which is simply the reciprocal of a price/earnings ratio) must be applied to all of the combining firms' expected earnings. Actually, the use of a single capitalization rate is appropriate only if the weighted risk and growth characteristics of all the firms are equal. In other words, the equity definition assumes that the price/earnings ratios which are appropriate for the constituents are equal.

Suppose that two combining firms, companies A and B, have similar expected growth rates in earnings, but that the expected earnings of A are less certain (more risky) than are the expected earnings of B. One would expect the price/earnings ratio for B to be higher than the price/earnings ratio for A. In situations such as these, the equity definition must be modified to allow for these differences in the characteristics of the combining firms. In essence, the modification would involve increasing B Company shareholders' portion of future earnings to compensate for the fact that the earnings contributed by B are less risky. Similar modifications could be made to reflect differences in expected growth rates.

QUESTIONS

1. In respect to a corporate combination, how is a "stock exchange ratio" generally expressed?

2. If the price/earnings ratio of the combined entity is equivalent to a weighted average of the constituent companies' ratios, is the total wealth of the several companies (increased, decreased, or not altered) as a direct result of the combination?

3. Consider a combination which is accomplished via a common for common stock exchange and which is not expected to result in economies or diseconomies of scale. If the combined entity's price/earnings ratio exceeds a weighted average of the constituent companies' ratios, total shareholders' wealth will be (increased, decreased, or not altered) by the combination?

4. J. R. Wilson compiles the following information concerning companies A and B:

	A Company	B Company
Net income	$2,000,000	$1,500,000
Common shares outstanding ..	1,000,000	750,000
Earnings per share	$ 2	$ 2
Common stock price	$40	$20
P/E ratio	20:1	10:1

Wilson concludes: "If A Company and B Company are combined to form AB Company, the restated earnings per share will be $2. Since it is $2 for A and for B, it obviously will not change." Is Wilson correct? If not, what factors determine the deviation of the earnings per share for the combined entity from the earnings per share of each participant?

5. "If the expected price/earnings ratio of a proposed combined entity were lower than a weighted average of the combining firms' price/earnings ratios, the combination probably would not take place." Comment on the validity of this statement.

6. Two companies, A and B, are contemplating a combination. A Company's corporate management projects a price/earnings ratio for the combined entity of 20. However, B Company's officials are somewhat more op-

timistic and project a ratio of 30. Which forecast would allow the greatest flexibility in establishing a specific stock exchange ratio? Why?

7. In general, there are two classes of financial contributions made by the parties to a combination. What are they?

8. Discuss the problems of measuring the financial contributions made by the parties to a combination, indicating the role of the accountant in resolving these problems.

9. Are there equitable limitations imposed by the issuance of a single class of stock to the parties in a consolidation? If so, what are they? Under what circumstances would the issuance of a single class of stock be as equitable as the issuance of several classes?

10. Describe the procedure involved in issuing securities to the several participants in a consolidation if both the relative net severable assets and the relative earnings contributions are to be preserved.

11. "The degree of inequity associated with a stock distribution plan is determinant only in the context of a specific postconsolidation level of earnings of the new or surviving enterprise." Discuss.

12. What is the meaning of "net severable assets?"

13. Explain why an equitable stock distribution plan might provide a preference position in exchange for the contribution of net severable assets.

14. Why might an accountant have difficulty calculating a range of price negotiation for a combination involving a closely held company?

15. In developing an equitable stock distribution plan, what constraints must be observed in selecting a capitalization rate? Explain the reasons for these constraints.

EXERCISES

Exercise 2–1

L Corporation plans to acquire a television manufacturing company (abbreviated TV). The president of L Corporation wants to calculate the earnings per share and the expected P/E ratio of the proposed combination. He believes that no special efficiencies or inefficiencies will accrue to the new entity as a result of the combination.

Required:

a. Using the notation below, present *general* formulas for calculating E/S_{LTV} and P/E_{LTV} ratio for the new combination.

Let S_L = L Corporation outstanding shares (common),
S_{TV} = firm TV outstanding shares (common),
P_L = current market price of L Corporation stock,
P_{TV} = current market price of firm TV stock,
NI_L = average net income of L Corporation,
NI_{TV} = average net income of firm TV, and
E/R = the exchange ratio determined by taking the inverse of the constituent firms' stock prices.

b. After the combination, the earnings of the new firm equal the combined average precombination earnings of the separate firms; however, the market reacts favorably to the new combination and the price per share increases to P_{LTV}. Present a general formula for computing the P/E ratio at the new price. Use the same notation as above.

Exercise 2–2

The following information is for Eastern, Inc., Western Company and the proposed merger between the two. According to the merger agreement, Eastern, Inc. will issue additional shares in exchange for the outstanding stock of Western.

	Eastern	Western	EW
Net income	$1,000,000	$2,000,000	$3,000,000
Common shares outstanding	1,000,000	1,000,000	1,333,333
Earnings per share	$ 1	$ 2	$ 2.25
Common stock market price	$40	$20	$45
P/E ratio	40:1	10:1	20:1
Stock exchange ratio, 1/3:1			

	Number and Total Value of Firm EW Shares Held by—	
	Eastern Shareholders	Western Shareholders
Number of shares held	1,000,000	333,333
Price per share	$45	$45
Total stock value	$45,000,000	$15,000,000
Value prior to combination	40,000,000	20,000,000
Gain or [loss] on combination	$ 5,000,000	$ [5,000,000]

Required:
Prepare schedules to illustrate the value of EW (Eastern after the merger) shares issued to the shareholders of Eastern and Western if the stock exchange ratio were (a) 1/2:1 and (b) if the ratio were 1:1. Assume the P/E ratio of EW to be 20:1 in both cases.

Exercise 2–3

Assume the same facts as in Exercise 2–2 where the stock exchange ratio is 1/3:1.

Required:

Prepare schedules similar to the one in Exercise 2–2 where the stock exchange ratio remains at 1/3:1 if the expected P/E ratio for the combined entity were instead (a) 30:1 and (b) 15:1.

Exercise 2–4

Swing, Inc., a new corporation, is authorized to issue 100,000 shares of 5 percent, fully participating, $100 par, preferred stock and 100,000 shares of common stock, $10 par. Swing, Inc., was organized for the purpose of combining High Company and Low Company, about which you have determined the following:

	High Company	Low Company
Net severable assets	$100,000	$90,000
Expected annual earnings	15,000	9,000

Required:

a. Utilizing a 6 percent capitalization rate, determine an equitable allocation of Swing, Inc.'s preferred stock and common stock to the shareholders of High Company and Low Company.
b. Determine the minimum annual net income of Swing, Inc., that would allow an equitable distribution of earnings under the conditions outlined above (including the data provided in requirement a).
c. Determine the maximum capitalization rate that could be utilized to provide an equitable allocation of stock. Disregard any facts given in requirements a and b.
d. Given the 5 percent preference rate on preferred stock, could a 4 percent capitalization rate ever result in an equitable allocation of earnings? If yes, at what income level?

Exercise 2–5

Cindy Industries and T. D. Company plan to merge, with Cindy being the only surviving corporation. Their respective contributions to the merger are:

	Cindy Industries	T. D. Company
Net severable assets	$200,000	$300,000
Expected net income	25,000	30,000

In developing an equitable plan of stock distribution, Cindy will issue $50 par, common stock and 4 percent, cumulative, fully participating, preferred stock ($100 par).

Required:

a. If an equitable plan of stock distribution is to be developed, what is the maximum rate of capitalization that can be used?
b. What is the minimum rate of capitalization that can be used?
c. Assuming a capitalization rate of 6 percent, what is the minimum annual net income (combined) that will permit a distribution of earnings which is proportionate to the combining firms' previously anticipated contributions of net income?
d. Assuming a capitalization rate of 6 percent, what is the maximum annual net income (combined) that will permit an equitable distribution of earnings?
e. Develop an equitable plan of stock distribution (if possible) using a capitalization rate of 8 percent.

Exercise 2–6

S Company wishes to purchase the net severable assets of X Company and Y Company, which total $600,000. In exchange for these assets, S Company is willing to give 6,000 shares of its common stock ($100 par). X Company will contribute twice as much in asset value as Y Company. For the last five years, the average percentage return on assets of the individual companies has been 15 percent for X Company and 20 percent for Y Company.

Required:

a. Assume that the earnings streams of X Company and Y Company are not expected to change, and that S Company wishes to distribute the 6,000 shares on the basis of each firm's relative percentage in the combined earnings before consolidation. How much stock will each company receive?
b. If, after the consolidation, Y Company's earnings are expected to increase by 50 percent while X Company's earnings are not expected to change, how would the 6,000 shares of S Company's stock be distributed if the distribution is to be based on each company's relative interest in combined anticipated earnings.
c. Refer to requirement *a,* in which the earnings of each company do not change. Stated in terms of the percentage return on assets of each constituent company, what condition must exist for the relative net incomes of the constituents to be a fully equitable basis of stock distribution?

PROBLEMS

Problem 1

The R Corporation is organized with authorized capital stock of 30,000 shares of $100 par value common stock and 20,000 shares of $100 par value, 5 percent, fully participating, preferred stock. The R Corporation proposes to consolidate companies A, B, and C to which the following information relates:

	Company			
	A	B	C	Total
Net severable assets	$200,000	$100,000	$500,000	$800,000
Expected annual earnings	30,000	20,000	50,000	100,000
Rate of return on net severable assets	15%	20%	10%	
Ratio of earnings distribution before consolidation	——	——	——	——
Stock distribution (earnings capitalized at 8%):				
Preferred stock (5%, fully participating, $100 par)	——	——	——	——
Common stock ($100 par)	——	——	——	——
Earnings distribution:				
Preferred .... (a)	——	——	——	——
(b)	——	——	——	——
(c)	——	——	——	——
Common .... (a)	——	——	——	——
(b)	——	——	——	——
(c)	——	——	——	——
Total .... (a)	——	——	——	——
(b)	——	——	——	——
(c)	——	——	——	——
Ratio of earnings distribution after consolidation .... (a)	——	——	——	——
(b)	——	——	——	——
(c)	——	——	——	——

Required:

Fill in the blanks for the following postcombination earnings levels:

a. $50,000.
b. $62,500.
c. $100,000.

Problem 2

Misiewicz Company is planning to negotiate a stock for stock purchase of Kramer, Inc. The following information is available about the two firms:

	Market Price	No. Shares Outstanding	Average Net Income
Misiewicz	$20	6,000,000	$7,500,000
Kramer	25	4,000,000	5,000,000

Required:

a. Determine the values for minimum and maximum exchange ratios as the expected P/E_{HS} varies from 10 to 40 using increments of 5.

b. Graph the minimum and maximum curves obtained from the calculation in part *a* and shade the area within which negotiations between Misiewicz Company and Kramer, Inc. will take place.

Problem 3

M Corporation plans to acquire one of three firms: O, P, or Q. The possible resulting combinations would be MO, MP, or MQ. In each case, it is believed that first postcombination period earnings will equal the combined precombination earnings of the two constituent firms. (For example, the first period expected net income of firm MO would be the average precombination net income of M plus the average precombination net income of O.)

The following data have been collected during negotiations with each firm:

	Earnings/ Share	Price/ Earnings	No. Shares Outstanding	Par Value	Negotiated ER
Firm M	$4.00	15	2,000,000	$100	
Firm O	.75	20	8,000,000	50	1/4:1
Firm P	2.40	20	5,000,000	100	1/2:1
Firm Q	1.50	18	4,000,000	25	1:1

Required:

Present all answers in good form with supporting calculations.

a. Which combination will produce the largest postcombination P/E ratio, assuming the market attributes no special advantages or disadvantages to the combination?

b. Which combination will result in the largest postcombination net income?

c. Which combination(s) will result in a loss to M Corporation stockholders?

d. Which of the three firms would you recommend M Corporation purchase? What was the basis of your evaluation?

Problem 4

Firm G plans to acquire firm H. The following data are available regarding the companies and the negotiations before combination:

$$P/E_G = \text{Price earnings ratio of firm G} \quad = \quad 15$$
$$P/E_H = \text{Price earnings ratio of firm H} \quad = \quad 20$$
$$S_G \quad = \text{Number of G shares outstanding} = 4,500,000$$
$$S_H \quad = \text{Number of H shares outstanding} = 2,000,000$$
$$NI_G \quad = \text{Average net income of firm G} \quad = \$9,000,000$$
$$NI_H \quad = \text{Average net income of firm H} \quad = \$3,000,000$$
$$E/R \quad = \text{Negotiated exchange ratio} \quad = 1\frac{1}{2}:1$$

Required:

a. If the E/R of $1\frac{1}{2}$ to 1 is the maximum price that firm G was willing to pay, what is the implied P/E_{GH} expected by firm G?

b. If the E/R of 1½ to 1 was the minimum price acceptable to firm H, what is the implied P/E_{GH} expected by firm H?

c. Assume that the combination does not increase or decrease the aggregate wealth of firms G and H. Will either firm incur a diminution in stockholder wealth, given an E/R of 1½ to 1? If so, which firm and in what amount?

Problem 5

Silver Company and Gold Company plan to combine, with Silver to be the resultant parent and Gold to be a wholly owned subsidiary. No growth or synergism is expected from the combination. Information regarding the two firms is as follows:

	Silver Company	Gold Company
Shares outstanding	800,000	600,000
Earnings	$1,200,000	$600,000
Price/earnings ratio	20:1	10:1

Required:

a. Suppose that the negotiated exchange ratio is 1/3:1 and that the resultant price/earnings ratio attributed to the combined firm is 15:1. What will be the gains or losses incurred by the shareholders of each combining company?

b. Given the information provided in requirement a, what stock exchange ratio would eliminate the undesirable result of having one of the negotiating parties incur a loss?

c. Disregard the information in requirement a. If the price/earnings ratio attributed to the combined firm is expected to be 30:1, what is the range of exchange ratios within which negotiation can be expected to occur?

Problem 6

Companies J and K agree to consolidate their assets and liabilities into newly formed L Company. At the time of the proposed consolidation, the following data are relevant.

	J Company	K Company
Net severable assets	$90,000	$60,000
Average net income	7,000	7,000

Required:

a. Demonstrate the inequity of L Company's issuing shares of $100 par value, common stock to companies J and K in the ratio of their contributions of—
    (1) Net assets.

(2) Average net income.
b. If L Company's 6 percent fully participating, $100 par value, preferred stock is issued for the net assets contributed, and $100 par value, common stock is issued for the difference between each company's average earnings capitalized at 7 percent and the net assets contributed, demonstrate the equity of this distribution. Additionally, indicate the inequitable consequence of using the following capitalization rates:
  (1) Five percent.
  (2) Ten percent.

Problem 7

The W Corporation was chartered on July 1, 1977, for the purpose of consolidating the resources and operations of companies X, Y, and Z.

The balance sheets of the affiliates on June 30, 1977, are as follows:

	Company		
	X	Y	Z
Tangible fixed assets—at cost	$500,000	$400,000	$300,000
Goodwill		60,000	
Other severable assets	200,000	280,000	85,000
	$700,000	$740,000	$385,000
Liabilities	$ 80,000	$130,000	$ 35,000
Capital stock (par, $100)	400,000	500,000	250,000
Other contributed capital	70,000		40,000
Retained earnings	150,000	110,000	60,000
	$700,000	$740,000	$385,000
Average profits (7/1/72–6/30/77 inclusive)	$ 90,000	$120,000	$ 50,000
Appraised sale values of tangible fixed assets on June 15, 1977	$620,000	$480,000	$360,000

Conferees to consolidation negotiations are agreed that the recorded goodwill of Y Company is valueless and that the "Other assets" of X Company are inflated to the extent of $50,000. The appraisal report of June 15 in respect to tangible fixed assets is accepted. These adjustments are to be made preliminary to the completion of formal consolidation. The recorded amounts of liabilities are accepted as representing current market values.

The consolidation agreement calls for the exchange of W Corporation's 6 percent, $100 par value, cumulative and fully participating preferred stock for the net assets of companies X, Y, and Z, and for the issuance of its $50 par value common stock for the capitalized average earnings of each acquired company in excess of net severable assets contributed. The capitalization rate is established at 10 percent.

Required:

a. Calculate the amounts of W Corporation's preferred and common shares to be issued to companies X, Y, and Z.

b. Indicate the equity or inequity of this plan of stock distribution if the earnings of W Corporation for the year ended June 30, 1977, are—
   (1) $520,000.
   (2) $130,000.

Problem 8

The stockholders of companies Alpha, Beta, and Gamma have decided to consolidate. The net severable assets and average earnings (for the past five years) are given below:

	Alpha	Beta	Gamma	Total
		Company		
Net severable assets	$1,200,000	$600,000	$1,200,000	$3,000,000
Average earnings	100,000	100,000	100,000	300,000

Companies Alpha and Gamma suggest the issuance of a single class of stock based upon net asset contributions. Beta, however, suggests basing any stock issuance on average earnings.

Required:
a. Discuss these two proposals as to the fairness for all three parties.
b. Can you suggest a plan using more than one class of stock which would be more equitable than either of the two proposed plans?

3

Consolidated Financial Reports—Date of Acquisition

Corporate Affiliations

IN CHAPTER 1, corporate combinations were categorized as *mergers, consolidations,* and *acquisitions.* In the present chapter (and chapters 4 and 5), attention is focused on the financial reports of the economic entity which results from the *acquisition form* of combination. Following an acquisition, the acquiring company owns a majority of the acquired firm's voting stock. The acquiring company is frequently identified as the *parent;* the acquired company is described as a *subsidiary.* Their joint status is called a corporate *affiliation.* Of course, a corporate affiliation may include more than two corporations. The parent may hold a majority of the voting shares of many subsidiaries. Additionally, a chain of majority ownership may be established in which a parent (P) owns a majority interest in the stock of a subsidiary (S_1) which, in turn, owns a majority interest in another subsidiary (S_2), etc. Such multilevel affiliations commonly extend from three to five levels. In fact, the history of United States business evidences some multilevel affiliations which included up to 60 levels in the parent-subsidiary chain. It is not uncommon for some corporations at each level to engage in separate business operations in addition to holding stock in subsidiaries. Alternatively, other corporations are organized for the sole purpose of holding stock in subsidiaries, in which case the parent may be referred to as a *holding company.*

Reasons for Corporate Affiliations

There are numerous reasons why a corporate enterprise may select *acquisition* as a form of corporate combination, in contrast to mergers and consolidations. Stock acquisition is relatively simple, and it usually provides financial control with minimal difficulty. The continuity of legal life of each of the affiliated companies also serves to protect the group assets from possible attachment by creditors of individual subsidiaries. Acquisition may be achieved at substantially less cost than the processes of merger and consolidation. The latter forms of combination require 100 percent ownership by the acquiring firm, whereas the former permits the execution of control with any amount of voting stock in excess of 50 percent. Also, the legal and processing costs of mergers or consolidations are typically avoided by the acquisition method. Further, the asset acquired by the parent—subsidiary stock—may provide collateral to support additional debt financing above the traditionally acceptable levels that would apply to the combined entity existing in the form of one corporate structure. After a formal merger or consolidation, the subsidiary corporation stock that is acquired by the parent is retired or canceled, and therefore is not available for use as collateral. For these and other reasons, control achieved by stock acquisition may produce significant rewards for the parent company, frequently at less cost than would be possible through other forms of business amalgamation.

Consolidated Statements

The primary financial reports of corporate affiliations are described as *consolidated* financial statements. These statements are essentially summations of the assets, liabilities, revenues, and expenses of the individual affiliates, calculated on the basis of transactions with nonaffiliates; the statement formats and the account classifications parallel those of a single corporation. Consolidated statements are prepared because the *unconsolidated* reports of a parent do not provide sufficient information on the financial position and operations under the parent's control. Indeed, the published financial reports of a parent corporation typically do not include the unconsolidated statements of the parent company.

Consolidated statements reflect a single entity perspective of the affiliated companies, from which many of the legal distinctions between the affiliates are ignored as being a matter of form rather than of substance. The overriding objective in consolidated statement preparation is to reflect the operations and financial position of the single *economic* entity. In the event that a minority portion of the subsidiary's stock is owned by parties that are unrelated to the parent, a special equity position must be established in the consolidated statements so that the unique interest of these outside parties will be appropriately disclosed.

While consolidated statements constitute the primary source of financial information regarding corporate affiliations, they should not be viewed as the only source of such information. Some parties, such as minority interest stockholders in a subsidiary and the outside creditors of a subsidiary, are primarily concerned with the separate financial reports of the subsidiary. Thus, the need for separate financial statements of each individual subsidiary corporation is not necessarily eliminated by the preparation of consolidated statements.

Parties whose primary interest is in the parent corporation may find that consolidated statements are not an adequate basis for making detailed analyses of operations. Thus, it is becoming increasingly common to provide, in addition to consolidated statements, supplementary reports which relate to defined segments of the consolidated entity. Such reports may consist of statements for each subsidiary or they may be prepared on other bases, such as product lines. Further consideration of these segmental reports is deferred until Chapter 6.

Criteria for Inclusion in Consolidated Statements

The criteria for including a subsidiary in consolidated statements are typically stated in terms of the degree of control the parent exercises over the subsidiary. There are two essential attributes of this concept of control, neither of which alone provides sufficient ground for inclusion in the consolidated statement. (1) The parent corporation must have the ability to govern, or effectively regulate, the subsidiary corporation's managerial decisions. (2) The parent corporation must be so related to the susbidiary that the economic results of subsidiary operations will accrue to the parent, allowing, of course, for the necessity of making appropriate allocations to reflect the interests of minority (outside, noncontrolling) parties.

Reference has been made to the necessity for owning more than 50 percent of the voting stock of a subsidiary—either directly or indirectly—in order to justify inclusion in consolidated financial statements. Yet, in point of fact, effective *managerial* control may well exist short of this critical percentage. Accountants are generally agreed, however, that it is usually unwise to include in consolidated financial statements those corporations for which this majority ownership condition is not satisfied. On occasions, effective managerial control may exist without the ownership of *any* voting shares. For example, the presence of a lease arrangement, whereby the lessor retains control of leased property, may indicate effective managerial control. Normally, however, situations of this kind do not evidence sufficient control in terms of the second attribute stated above.[1]

Other factors which merit attention in determining the admissibility of a subsidiary in consolidated statements are (1) the expectation of continuity in control; (2) the degree of existing restrictions upon the availability of

---

[1] The SEC specifically prohibits a registrant from consolidating any subsidiary which is not majority owned in filings with the Commission (*Regulation S-X, Part 210—Form and Content of Financial Statements,* Article 4).

assets and earnings of a subsidiary (an item of special importance regarding foreign subsidiaries); and (3) the general coincidence of accounting periods.

In those cases where significant subsidiaries are not consolidated, separate statements for the excluded subsidiaries are normally included as a supplement to the consolidated financial statements.

Disclosure of Consolidation Policy

The consolidation policy adopted by the parent company is important to a complete understanding of consolidated statements and it should be disclosed in the financial reports. A statement of policy normally refers to such matters as the degree of stock control required of the parent company, the accounting methods that were used to record the acquisition of subsidiary stock (alternative methods are examined in Chapter 6), and the status of a subsidiary as either a domestic or a foreign corporate entity. Since the adoption in 1972 of *APB Opinion 22,* "Disclosure of Accounting Policies," companies normally include their consolidation policy in the Summary of Significant Accounting Policies. An example from the 1975 General Motors annual report follows:

Principles of Consolidation
The consolidated financial statements include the accounts of the Corporation and all domestic and foreign subsidiaries which are more than 50% owned and engaged principally in manufacturing or wholesale marketing of General Motors products. General Motors' share of earnings or losses of nonconsolidated subsidiaries and of associates in which at least 20% of the voting securities is owned is generally included in consolidated income under the equity method of accounting. Intercompany items and transactions between companies included in the consolidation are eliminated and unrealized intercompany profits on sales to nonconsolidated subsidiaries and to associates are deferred.

Precautions in the Evaluation of Consolidated Statements

The summarizing character of consolidated statements provides them with special qualities of strength and usefulness; however, this attribute demands that special precautions be taken in evaluting these statements. Among the factors which require special care in the evaluation process are the following:

1. Consolidated statements create numerous and complex problems in statistical analyses, the apparent solutions to which may be misleading. For example, ratios prepared from consolidated account information are weighted averages. As such, their reliability is dependent upon the degree of variability among the account balances of the individual affiliates. A weak position of one company may be balanced, in the process of sum-

mation, by an especially strong position of an affiliate. In such an instance, an average may be an inaccurate descriptive index.

2. Differences in the bases of classification and valuation of accounts of the constituent companies may distort the meaning of composite statements. The unique accounting systems of the affiliates cannot easily be transformed so that the classifications and valuations of each affiliate will be entirely consistent. Further, the differing industry identifications of the affiliates limit the meaning that can be attributed to the aggregated account balances.

3. The monetary equities assigned to both creditors and owners may be misinterpreted in the evaluation of consolidated statements. This is particularly true in respect to the seeming availability of retained earnings for dividend distributions. The earnings of subsidiaries may not actually be available for parent company distributions until formally declared as dividends by the subsidiaries. In regard to liabilities, the result of summation often is to obscure the special legal status of those individual creditors having liens on specific assets. Additionally, minority stockholders must continue to look to the subsidiary's separate financial statements to determine accurately the status of their investment. Their shareholder status relates *only* to the legal entity to which they have committed resources.

4. Consolidated statements involving foreign subsidiaries may be misleading if foreign exchange rates are subject to unusual fluctuations, or if foreign assets are unduly restricted as to their availability to a domestic parent company.

Notwithstanding these limitations, consolidated statements continue to grow in significance and number. Accumulating evidence suggests that they now assume a role of *primary* importance, with the separate statements of affiliates and other segmental reports relegated to a secondary or supplementary position.

Determining Cost of an Acquired Company

The valuation principles used to record the investment in an acquired company depend upon whether the combination is treated as a purchase or a pooling of interests (see Acounting Perspective, Chapter 1). The specific criteria that control this choice and some important financial statement consequences of using one method vis-à-vis the other are discussed in Chapter 6. *At this point and throughout Chapters 3–5, we will treat all acquisitions as purchases.*

General Principle. Under the purchase method, the acquisition of the stock of the subsidiary company is accounted for in accordance with the traditional principles of accounting for the acquisition of assets. The value of the stock acquired is measured by the fair value of the consideration given or the consideration received, whichever is more clearly evident.

Note that the consideration given by the acquiring company may include cash, noncash assets, debt, and/or stock of the acquiring company.

Direct and Indirect Costs. Only the direct, incremental costs of an acquisition are included in the cost of the investment. Indirect and general expenses related to acquisitions (for example, the costs of an "acquisitions" department)[2] are expensed as incurred.

Registration Costs. When costs of registering and issuing equity securities used in an acquisition are incurred, the otherwise determinable fair market value of the securities should be reduced by the amount of these costs. The value assigned to the investment account then is the sum of these registration costs and the net value of the equity securities.[3] If unregistered equity securities are issued in an acquisition with an agreement for subsequent registration, the estimated amount of these registration costs is accrued as a liability, and the net fair value of the shares issued is determined as above.[4]

Contingent Consideration. The terms of a business combination may provide for additional consideration contingent on the occurrence of specified events or transactions in the future. When this situation exists, the following general measurement guidelines are applied:

> Contingent consideration should usually be recorded when the contingency is resolved and consideration is issued or becomes issuable. In general, the issue of additional securities or distribution of other consideration at resolution of contingencies *based on earnings* should result in an additional element of cost of an acquired company. In contrast, the issue of additional securities or distribution of other consideration at resolution of contingencies *based on security prices* should not change the recorded cost of an acquired company.[5]

Elaboration of these general guidelines is contained in paragraphs 77–86 of *APB Opinion 16.*

Acquisition Date. The cost of an acquired company (and the values assigned to assets acquired and liabilities assumed) is determined as of the date of acquisition. Normally, the date of acquisition is the date on which assets are received and other assets are given or securities are issued. However, the parties to the combination transaction may for convenience designate the effective date of the combination to be the end of an accounting period between the dates on which the combination is initiated and consummated. When this occurs, the cost of the investment should be reduced (and interest expense recognized) by the imputed interest on assets given, liabilities incurred, or preferred stock distributed from the acquisition date to the transfer date.[6]

---

[2] *Accounting Interpretation No. 33, APB Opinion 16* ("Business Combinations").

[3] *APB Opinion 16,* paragraph 76.

[4] *Accounting Interpretation No. 35, APB Opinion 16.*

[5] *APB Opinion 16,* paragraph 79. (Emphasis supplied.)

[6] *APB Opinion 16,* paragraphs 93–94.

Consolidated Balance Sheet

Where the dates of investment in subsidiary stock and consolidated statement preparation coincide, attention may be confined to the consolidated balance sheet only. This financial report is a summary enumeration of the assets and liabilities of the various affiliates, calculated without regard to their separate corporate identities. Because majority stock ownership is tantamount to control over the assets of a subsidiary, it is meaningful to substitute the subsidiary's net assets for the stock investment account of the parent company. Traditionally, this substitution is accomplished in consolidated statement working papers by eliminating the parent company's investment account against its equity in the stockholders' equity accounts of the subsidiary. Following this elimination, it is then appropriate to combine the assets and liabilities of the affiliate companies. It is, of course, important that the amounts of other accounts resulting from intercompany transactions, e.g., intercompany receivable-payable balances, also be eliminated, in order that the consolidated balance sheet reflect the assets and equities of the affiliation perceived as a single economic entity.

It may be observed that the *total* net assets of the subsidiary are substituted for the contra investment account, notwithstanding the existence of minority shareholders. This accords with the accounting view that each group of shareholders has a fractional interest in the undivided net assets of the subsidiary. Accordingly, it is appropriate to indicate the value of minority interests in terms of the aggregate net assets rather than in terms of a fractional equity in specific assets and liabilities of a subsidiary.

The form and arrangement of these accumulated data follow the usual statement classifications. Where minority shareholders exist, their rights must be clearly disclosed together with those of other claimants. Since consolidated statements are generally presumed to be oriented toward the dominant shareholders (those of the parent company), the rights and equities of minority interests assume—at least partially—the character of liabilities. Yet, significantly, because the evidences of this type of equity are ownership certificates, they also have a certain quality of proprietorship. Accountants are not generally agreed as to the most appropriate balance sheet disposition of this category; often a compromise position is that of a separate identification between liabilities and stockholders' equity.

Procedural details for the preparation of consolidated balance sheet working papers are described and illustrated in the pages which follow.

Investment at Book Value of Subsidiary Stock

In the cases which follow, it is assumed that concurrent with the acquisition of a subsidiary's capital stock, a consolidated balance sheet is prepared. The stockholders' equity accounts of the subsidiary are reflected in the working paper accompanying each case, and it is assumed that the parent company's investment cost is equal to the book value of the subsidiary stock acquired.

Case 1. Total (100 Percent) Acquisition of Subsidiary Stock. In this first case, it is assumed that P Company acquires 100 percent of the outstanding stock of S Company for $50,000, and that the stockholders' equity account balances of S Company at the date of acquisition are capital stock, $40,000 (Cr.) and retained earnings, $10,000 (Cr.). Thus, the recorded value of the net assets of S Company on this date is equal to P Company's investment cost.

The substitution of S Company's net assets for the investment account of P Company is accomplished in the consolidated balance sheet working paper (Illustration 3–1) by "eliminating" P Company's investment account against its equity in S Company's stockholders' equity accounts and then combining (summing) the remaining account balances of the two companies. The amount of the elimination against each element (account) of the subsidiary company's stockholders' equity is determined by multiplying the parent company's percentage interest in the subsidiary (in this case, 100 percent) by the recorded balance in the account. The summation process relies upon the debit/credit properties of various account balances, and thus the eliminating entry, which is referred to as the *investment elimination entry,* is also expressed in a debit/credit format. For the data of this case, the investment elimination entry is as follows:

```
Capital Stock—S Company (100% × $40,000) ........ 40,000
Retained earnings—S Company (100% × $10,000) .... 10,000
    Investment in S Company .....................        50,000
```

Although the investment elimination entry is traditionally expressed in the format of a "journal entry," it is an "entry" only on the consolidated working paper. *No entry is made on the books of either the parent or the subsidiary.*

In the consolidated working paper (Illustration 3–1), it is useful to relate the contra elements of eliminating entries with some connective notation; in this instance, arabic numerals are used.

An examination of this consolidated working paper will confirm that the net assets of S Company have, in fact, been substituted for the investment account of P Company, and that the amounts extended to the "consolidated" column are merely a result of a summation process. It may also be noted that consolidated capital stock and retained earnings at date of acquisition are the balances in the parent company's accounts, the total amount of the subsidiary's capital stock and retained earnings having been eliminated. Since none of the subsidiary's stock is held by outside parties, this result for consolidated capital stock is obviously appropriate. In respect to retained earnings, the result is in accord with the long established accounting tenet that none of the preacquisition retained earnings (or deficit) of a

Illustration 3–1

P COMPANY AND SUBSIDIARY S COMPANY

Consolidated Balance Sheet Working Paper
(Acquisition Date)

	P Company	S Company	Eliminations Dr.	Eliminations Cr.	Con-solidated
Assets					
Cash	15,000	4,000			19,000
Receivables	30,000	16,000			46,000
Inventory	25,000	35,000			60,000
Investment in S					
Company	50,000			(1) 50,000	
	120,000	55,000			125,000
Equities					
Payables	10,000	5,000			15,000
Capital stock:					
P Company	90,000				90,000
S Company		40,000	(1) 40,000		
Retained earnings:					
P Company	20,000				20,000
S Company		10,000	(1) 10,000		
	120,000	55,000	50,000	50,000	125,000

purchased subsidiary should be included in consolidated retained earnings.[7]

Although the stockholders' equity of S Company in this illustration was limited to capital stock and retained earnings accounts, no special problems would have arisen had there been other elements of stockholders' equity attributable to common shareholders (e.g., amounts of contributed capital in excess of par value and appropriations of retained earnings). Each of these elements would have been additional determinants in the calculation of book value, and subsequently eliminated in the investment elimination entry in the consolidation process. The existence of treasury stock does introduce several minor complications, and these are discussed in a subsequent section of this chapter. The more complex issues associated with the presence of more than one class of stock are however deferred to Chapter 8.

Case 2. Acquisition of a Majority (90 Percent) of Subsidiary Stock (Subsidiary Deficit). This case illustrates the elimination procedures to be followed in the event the parent acquires a controlling interest in the voting shares of a subsidiary by purchasing less than 100 percent of the outstanding stock. Additionally, the case indicates the elimination when the subsidiary has a retained earnings deficit at the acquisition date. It is assumed that 90 percent of a subsidiary's capital stock is acquired at a cost

---

[7] Section 2051.08, *APB Accounting Principles—Current Text.* See however Chapter 6 for a different result when the combination is treated as a pooling of interests.

of $45,000. The stockholders' equity account balances of the subsidiary at the acquisition date are capital stock, $60,000 (Cr.); and retained earnings, $10,000 (Dr.). The investment elimination entry is as follows:

```
Capital stock—S Company (90% × $60,000) .......... 54,000
    Retained earnings—S Company (90% × $10,000) ...        9,000
    Investment in S Company .......................       45,000
```

The deficit is eliminated by a credit to the retained earnings of S Company. It may be noted in Illustration 3–2 that the extended amounts of capital stock and retained earnings of S Company are marked with the letter "M" denoting that these amounts represent the value interests of minority shareholders. Such a notation serves as an appropriate reminder concerning the classification of these amounts in the preparation of formal statements. This working paper illustrates the importance of substituting the *total* net assets of the subsidiary for the investment account of the parent company, even where there exist minority shareholders, and extending the interest of these minority shareholders on the basis of their fractional interest in the recorded stockholders' equity accounts of the subsidiary company. Calculation of the minority interest is made in the same manner, whether the subsidiary has an accumulated earnings balance or a deficit. Manifestly, there is no dilution in minority interests in the consolidation process, as the equity of this group (10 percent of $50,000) is clearly indicated in the enumeration of the various equities.

Illustration 3–2

P COMPANY AND SUBSIDIARY S COMPANY

Consolidated Balance Sheet Working Paper

(Acquisition Date)

	P Company	S Company	Eliminations Dr.	Eliminations Cr.	Consolidated
Assets					
Cash	15,000	4,000			19,000
Receivables	30,000	16,000			46,000
Inventory	25,000	35,000			60,000
Investment in S Company	45,000			(1) 45,000	
	115,000	55,000			125,000
Equities					
Payables	5,000	5,000			10,000
Capital stock:					
P Company	90,000				90,000
S Company		60,000	(1) 54,000		6,000 M
Retained earnings:					
P Company	20,000				20,000
S Company		[10,000]		(1) 9,000	[1,000]M
	115,000	55,000	54,000	54,000	125,000

Investment Cost More than Book Value of Subsidiary Stock

Frequently, it will be necessary for the investing company to pay more than the book value of the subsidiary's capital stock. Costs of investment in excess of book value may be defended with the argument that there is an understatement of a subsidiary's assets, that there exist unrecorded subsidiary assets, or for other less apparent reasons. In such instances it is necessary to recognize and identify this variation, or *differential,* in the consolidated statements.

Case 3. The data of the previous case are repeated here, with the exception that the cost of P Company's 90 percent investment in the capital stock of S Company is assumed to be $50,000. In this instance, the investment elimination entry indicates the presence of a *debit differential.*

```
Capital stock—S Company .......................  54,000
Differential .....................................   5,000
        Retained earnings—S Company .................           9,000
        Investment in S Company .....................          50,000
```

At this point the differential does not require more complete identification; it is sufficient to note that it represents the excess of the cost of the investment over the parent's interest in the book value of subsidiary stock at

Illustration 3–3
P COMPANY AND SUBSIDIARY S COMPANY
Consolidated Balance Sheet Working Paper
(Acquisition Date)

	P Company	S Company	Eliminations Dr.	Eliminations Cr.	Consolidated
Assets					
Cash	15,000	4,000			19,000
Receivables	30,000	16,000			46,000
Inventory	25,000	35,000			60,000
Investment in S Company	50,000			(1) 50,000	
Differential			(1) 5,000		5,000
	120,000	55,000			130,000
Equities					
Payables	10,000	5,000			15,000
Capital stock:					
P Company	90,000				90,000
S Company		60,000	(1) 54,000		6,000 M
Retained earnings:					
P Company	20,000				20,000
S Company		[10,000]		(1) 9,000	[1,000]M
	120,000	55,000	59,000	59,000	130,000

date of acquisition. The working paper treatment of a debit differential is given in Illustration 3–3.

Investment Cost Less than Book Value of Subsidiary Stock

In the event that the investment cost is less than the book value of a subsidiary's capital stock at acquisition, there exists a *credit* differential. This circumstance is illustrated in Case 4. The sources of debit and credit differentials will be developed more completely following this case illustration.

Case 4. Using the basic data of Case 2, it is assumed that P Company acquires 90 percent of the capital stock of S Company at a cost of $40,000. The investment elimination entry follows:

Capital stock—S Company	54,000	
Retained earnings—S Company		9,000
Differential		5,000
Investment in S Company		40,000

These data confirm that there exists a credit differential, and that its amount is measured by the amount of the parent's interest in the book value of subsidiary stock at date of acquisition which is in excess of the cost of the investment (see Illustration 3–4).

Illustration 3–4

P COMPANY AND SUBSIDIARY S COMPANY

Consolidated Balance Sheet Working Paper
(Acquisition Date)

	P Company	S Company	Eliminations Dr.	Eliminations Cr.	Consoli- dated
Assets					
Cash	25,000	4,000			29,000
Receivables	30,000	16,000			46,000
Inventory	25,000	35,000			60,000
Investment in S Company	40,000			(1) 40,000	
Differential				(1) 5,000	[5,000]
	120,000	55,000			130,000
Equities					
Payables	10,000	5,000			15,000
Capital stock:					
P Company	90,000				90,000
S Company		60,000	(1) 54,000		6,000 M
Retained earn- ings:					
P Company	20,000				20,000
S Company		[10,000]		(1) 9,000	[1,000]M
	120,000	55,000	54,000	54,000	130,000

Debit (Credit) Differentials

In the previous two cases, we have seen that the investment cost may exceed, or be less than, the parent's acquired interest in the book value of a subsidiary's capital stock at date of acquisition. This difference occurs because the investment cost normally reflects the current economic values of the subsidiary's assets, and the recorded book values usually do not. In the investment elimination entry, the difference may simply be identified as a debit (or credit) differential, and recorded on the consolidated statement working paper in that fashion. However, it is then necessary to allocate this differential to the individual assets acquired in accordance with the valuation principles established in *APB Opinion 16,* "Business Combinations":

First, all identifiable assets acquired, either individually or by type, and liabilities assumed in a business combination, whether or not shown in the financial statements of the acquired company, should be assigned a portion of the cost of the acquired company, *normally equal to their fair values at date of acquisition.* Second, the excess of the cost of the acquired company over the sum of the amounts assigned to identifiable assets acquired less liabilities assumed should be recorded as goodwill.[8]

Normally, the amount of the differential to be allocated to each asset (or liability) on the subsidiary's balance sheet will equal the parent company's proportionate interest in the difference between the fair value[9] and the recorded value of the asset (or liability). After these allocations have been made to identifiable assets and liabilities, any remaining unallocated *debit* differential is classified as goodwill.[10]

Case 5. Referring to the data of Case 3 (and Illustration 3–3), assume that a study of S Company's assets and liabilities produced the following estimates of fair values:

	Book Value	Fair Value	Excess of Fair Value over Book Value	P Company's 90% Interest in Excess
Receivables	$16,000	$16,000	$ —	$ —
Inventory	35,000	38,000	3,000	2,700
Payables	5,000	5,000	—	—

[8] *APB Opinion 16,* paragraph 87. (Emphasis supplied.)

[9] See *APB Opinion 16,* paragraph 88 for general guidelines to be used in determining "fair value."

[10] In our discussion of the "entity theory of consolidated statements" in Chapter 11, a procedure for recording the *total* difference between fair and recorded values of identifiable assets and the *total* goodwill implicit in the purchase price, with concurrent recognition of the minority interest therein, will be explained. Although sound theoretically, this procedure is seldom applied in current practice. Additionally, paragraph 17 of *APB Opinion 6* would seem to preclude the subsidiary from recognizing the total difference in values by means of an entry on its books to write up its assets to their fair values.

Given this information, the following additional elimination entry would be made to allocate the debit differential:

```
Inventory  ........................  2,700
Goodwill ........................  2,300
    Differential  ...................          5,000
```

Where the allocation of the differential to identifiable assets and liabilities results in a residual (unallocated) *credit,* additional steps are required. In particular, this residual credit is reallocated among the subsidiary's noncurrent assets (except long-term investments in marketable securities) in proportion to the fair values of these assets. If the residual credit should exceed the sum of the fair values of these assets, then the assets are reduced to zero values and the remaining credit would be classified as a "deferred credit."[11]

In view of the current interest in "fair value accounting," it is interesting to note that by means of these procedures for allocating the differential, the fair values of the assets and liabilities of a newly acquired subsidiary must be ascertained at the date of acquisition, and in consolidation these accounts are adjusted to values closely approximating their fair values (depending on the magnitude of the parent's percentage interest). The accounts of the parent company, of course, remain unadjusted for changes in values. Nonetheless, with the adoption of *APB Opinion 16* in 1970, accounting practice moved, albeit on an irregular and limited basis, into the realm of fair value accounting.

Other Intercompany Transactions

Emphasis has thus far been directed to the intercompany transaction establishing the parent-subsidiary relationship. However, other intercompany transactions may be reflected in the accounts of the various affiliates, and their effects also must be eliminated in the consolidated statement working papers. All accounts classified as assets on one affiliate's books for which the originating transaction created a liability on the books of a second affiliate must be totally eliminated. The amount of the elimination is not dependent upon the percentage of stock control. Intercompany accounts receivable are eliminated against related accounts payable; intercompany notes receivable are eliminated against the related notes payable; and the intercompany portion of accrued expenses are eliminated against the corresponding accrued incomes. It is only necessary to establish the intercompany character of the originating transaction. Failure to eliminate the total amount of these accounts—whatever the percentage of stock ownership—will result in a type of transaction circularity in which there are included in the consolidated balance sheet claims to and from the same

---

11 *APB Opinion 16,* paragraph 87.

entity—the economic entity for which the consolidated balance sheet is prepared.

Unpaid Subsidiary Dividends at Acquisition

Should the parent become a stockholder of record after the declaration of subsidiary dividends but before the record date for payment, such dividends merely serve to reduce the cost of the investment shares. As such, they are classified as Dividends Receivable; the remainder of the investment outlay is debited to the Investment account. Subsequent collection of this receivable balance by the parent is recorded in the conventional manner. In the preparation of a consolidated balance sheet at the date of acquisition, Dividends Payable must be eliminated against Dividends Receivable to the extent that the subsidiary's declared dividend will accrue to the shares held by the parent. If the parent failed to record the dividend receivable upon making the investment, an adjustment is necessary to correct this omission.

In the case that a subsidiary declares dividends prior to the parent's purchase of shares and the record date also occurs prior to acquisition of subsidiary stock by the parent, Dividends Payable represents a liability to outside interests. Thus, no adjustment to the investment elimination is necessary and there exists no payable-receivable relationship to be eliminated in the consolidated working paper.

Treasury Stock of the Subsidiary

On some occasions there may exist treasury stock on the books of a subsidiary when its outstanding shares are acquired by a parent company. In such instances, the presence of these shares must be appropriately accounted for in the investment elimination schedule. Consider the following example.

Case 6. P Company acquired 800 shares of the capital stock of S Company on January 1, 19X1, for $115,000 when the latter's net worth consisted of:

Capital stock (par, $100)	120,000
Treasury stock (recorded at par)	(20,000)
Retained earnings	40,000

Before considering the investment elimination entry details, two general observations are important. First, since P Company acquired 80 percent of S Company's *outstanding* shares (800/1,000), the calculation of the purchased interest in S Company's net assets will be based upon this percentage. Second, the treasury stock of the subsidiary is not a meaningful item in the consolidated balance sheet (which is prepared from the point of view of the majority shareholders), and therefore it seems appropriate to treat these shares as having been constructively retired.

Given this perspective, a first elimination in the consolidated statement working paper is:

Capital stock	20,000	
Treasury stock		20,000

The investment elimination entry which follows is based upon the resulting account balances and takes the form:

Capital stock	80,000	
Retained earnings	32,000	
Differential	3,000	
Investment in S Company		115,000

Where the subsidiary's treasury shares are recorded at cost, and such cost is other than par value, an adjustment of its retained earnings accumulation and/or other contributed capital accounts is required before calculating the elimination elements. For example, if the treasury stock is carried at cost—$25,000—in the previous illustration, the first elimination is:

Capital stock	20,000	
Retained earnings	5,000	
Treasury stock		25,000

The investment elimination necessarily relates to the adjusted balances *after* this entry and is calculated in the same manner as before.

The reader is referred to *Intermediate Accounting* in this series for a detailed discussion of accounting for treasury shares.

Adjustments

On occasion, it may be necessary to adjust the account data after the preparation of consolidated working papers has begun. In such cases, adjusting entries may be entered in the "eliminations" column of the working paper. To distinguish adjusting and eliminating entries, it is desirable to adopt an appropriate system of notation. The authors prefer to use numeral prefixes to identify eliminating entries, with lowercase letters used to indicate adjustments. The consolidated working paper in Case 7 uses this notation. Frequently, confusion may be avoided if the statements of the constituent companies are adjusted previous to entering the account information in the consolidated working paper.

Illustrative Problem

It may now be useful to illustrate the preparation of a consolidated balance sheet working paper involving several subsidiaries, where there is a necessity for recording both adjusting and eliminating entries.

Case 7. Assume the following data with respect to affiliate companies P, Y, and Z:

	January 1, 19X1		
	P Company	Y Company	Z Company
Capital stock (par, $100)	$100,000	$50,000	$40,000
Retained earnings	54,000	5,000	4,000

On January 1, 19X1, P Company purchased 90 percent of the capital stock of Y Company for $70,000, and 80 percent of the capital stock of Z Company for $50,000. The notes receivable listed among the assets of Y Company are the result of a loan to Z Company, on which the January 1, 19X1, accrued interest is $60. The interest is as yet unrecorded by Z Company.

The process of constructing a consolidated balance sheet should begin with the preparation of an affiliation diagram indicating percentages and directions of share ownership.

Affiliation Diagram

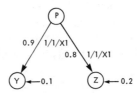

The investment elimination entries based upon the data given are:

Capital stock—Y Company.	45,000	
Retained earnings—Y Company	4,500	
Differential—Y Company	20,500	
Investment in Y Company		70,000

Capital stock—Z Company	32,000	
Retained earnings—Z Company	3,152	
Differential—Z Company	14,848	
Investment in Z Company		50,000

It may be noted that the retained earnings of Z Company on January 1, 19X1, are overstated by the amount of the omission of accrued interest expense. Accordingly, the 80 percent elimination is made against the balance of this account *as adjusted* [80 percent of ($4,000 − $60), or $3,152].

Assume that an examination of the two subsidiaries indicated that all assets and liabilities were stated at their fair values except the inventories and the fixed assets, for which the following values were calculated:

	Book Value	Fair Value	Excess of Fair Value over Book Value	P Company's Interest in Excess
Company Y:				
Inventory	$15,000	$18,000	$ 3,000	$ 2,700
Plant and equipment (net) ..	25,000	35,000	10,000	9,000
Company Z:				
Inventory	10,000	12,000	2,000	1,600
Plant and equipment (net) ..	21,000	36,000	15,000	12,000

Based upon this information, the following allocations of the differentials are made:

Inventory	2,700	
Plant and equipment (net)	9,000	
Goodwill	8,800	
Differential—Y Company		20,500
Inventory	1,600	
Plant and equipment (net)	12,000	
Goodwill	1,248	
Differential—Z Company		14,848

The consolidated working paper is shown in Illustration 3–5, page 86.
The preparation of the formal consolidated balance sheet is completed by recasting the account information from the "consolidated" column of the working paper in traditional statement form (see Illustration 3–6). As mentioned earlier, these data are classified according to usual balance sheet arrangements, with the minority interest typically given separate status between the liability and owners' equity classifications. The equity of minority shareholders is sometimes presented together with that of the controlling interest; more frequently, however, it is interposed between the liabilities and the majority stockholders' equity. The traditional emphasis of consolidated statements on the dominant shareholder group would appear to support this latter position. Those who favor the "entity theory" of consolidated statements, about which more will be said later, would prefer to cite only one category of shareholders' equity, consisting of both majority and minority interest groups.

Illustration 3–5

P COMPANY AND SUBSIDIARIES

Consolidated Balance Sheet Working Paper
January 1, 19X1

	P Company	Y Company	Z Company	Eliminations Dr.		Eliminations Cr.		Consolidated
Assets								
Cash	4,000	4,940	3,000					11,940
Accounts receivable	5,000	19,000	15,000					39,000
Notes receivable		1,000				(5)	1,000	
Inventory	25,000	15,000	10,000	(3)	2,700			54,300
				(4)	1,600			
Interest receivable		60				(6)	60	
Investment in Y Company	70,000					(1)	70,000	
Investment in Z Company	50,000					(2)	50,000	
Plant and equipment (net)	15,000	25,000	21,000	(3)	9,000			
				(4)	12,000			82,000
Differential—Y Company				(1)	20,500	(3)	20,500	
Differential—Z Company				(2)	14,848	(4)	14,848	
Goodwill				(3)	8,800			10,048
				(4)	1,248			
	169,000	65,000	49,000					197,288
Equities								
Accounts payable	5,000	10,000	4,000					19,000
Notes payable	10,000		1,000	(5)	1,000			10,000
Accrued interest payable				(6)	60	(a)	60	
Capital stock:								
X Company	100,000							100,000
Y Company		50,000		(1)	45,000			5,000 M
Z Company			40,000	(2)	32,000			8,000 M
Retained earnings:								
X Company	54,000							54,000
Y Company		5,000		(1)	4,500			500 M
Z Company			4,000	(a)	60			788 M
				(2)	3,152			
	169,000	65,000	49,000		156,468		156,468	197,288

Explanations of adjustments and eliminations:

(a) Adjustment to record the accrual of interest expense by Z Company.
(1) Elimination of investment in Y Company.
(2) Elimination of investment in Z Company.
(3) Allocation of Y Company differential.
(4) Allocation of Z Company differential.
(5) Elimination of intercompany notes.
(6) Elimination of intercompany accrued interest.

Illustration 3–6

P COMPANY AND SUBSIDIARY COMPANIES Y AND Z

Consolidated Balance Sheet
January 1, 19X1

Assets		*Equities*		
Cash	$ 11,940	Accounts payable		$ 19,000
Accounts receivable	39,000	Notes payable		10,000
		Minority interest in—		
Inventory	54,300	Subsidiary Y		
Plant and equipment (net)	82,000	Company	$ 5,500	
		Subsidiary Z		
Goodwill*	10,048	Company	8,788	14,288
		Stockholders' equity:		
		Capital stock	$100,000	
		Retained earn-		
		ings	54,000	154,000
	$197,288			$197,288

* Terminology other than "goodwill" may be used in a company's formal financial statements. For example, one company labeled this item "Unamortized excess of cost of investment in subsidiary over net assets acquired." Other companies combine this asset with other assets into a class labeled "Intangible Assets" or perhaps just "Other Assets."

QUESTIONS

1. What is the appropriate designation of a company that is organized for the sole purpose of holding shares of stock in subsidiaries?
2. Why might a corporation prefer to use the acquisition form of corporate combination as opposed to the merger or consolidation forms?
3. What is the principal motivation in preparing consolidated financial statements of affiliated companies?
4. What are the essential elements of parental control over a subsidiary which must exist if consolidated statements are to be prepared?
5. Is it necessary to own 50 percent of a company's voting stock in order to maintain effective control over the company? Explain.
6. What factors (other than voting control) are important determinants in electing whether or not to include a specific subsidiary in consolidated statements?
7. Interpretation of consolidated statements requires careful consideration of the inherent limitations of these statements. What are some of these inherent limitations?
8. What is the general rule for determining the date of acquisition of a newly acquired subsidiary? Are there any exceptions to this general rule?
9. Given a situation in which a parent owns less than 100 percent of a subsidiary's stock, the consolidated balance sheet nevertheless includes 100 percent of the subsidiary's assets. Explain the reasoning which supports this method of presentation.
10. After the differential has been allocated to identifiable assets and liabilities, any remaining unallocated debit differential is classified as goodwill. How would you justify this classification?

11. In the event a subsidiary has acquired treasury stock before its shares are acquired by a parent company, should the parent company's equity percentage in the subsidiary relate to the number of shares outstanding or to the total number of shares issued?

EXERCISES

Exercise 3–1

On January 1, 19X1, Lincoln Corporation exchanged 10,000 shares of its own $20 par value common stock for 90 percent of the capital stock of the Juilliard Company.

Required:

a. The principal limitation of consolidated financial statements is their lack of separate information about the assets, liabilities, revenues, and expenses of the individual companies included in the consolidation. List the problems which the reader of consolidated financial statements encounters as a result of the limitation.
b. The minority interest in Juilliard Company can be presented several ways on the consolidated balance sheet. Discuss the propriety of reporting the minority interest on the consoliadted balance sheet—
(1) As a liability.
(2) As a part of stockholders' equity.
(3) In a separate classification between liabilities and the equity of the Lincoln Corporation.

(AICPA adapted)

Exercise 3–2

P Company acquired a majority interest in S Company on April 1, 19X1, by issuing 500,000 shares of unregistered P Company no-par, common stock and $1,500,000 cash in exchange for S Company shares. Additionally, P Company agreed to register these shares sometime within the next three months.

It is estimated that the fair value of the P Company shares on the date of exchange is $5 per share, and that total registration costs will amount to $200,000. Additionally, P Company maintains an "acquisitions" department, and P Company management estimates that this department devoted approximately 60 percent of its efforts during the first three months of 19X1 to the acquisition of S Company. This department incurs average monthly expenses of $10,000.

Required:

Prepare the journal entry on April 1, 19X1, to record P Company's investment in S Company. (Ignore the issue of discounting the liability for future registration costs.)

Exercise 3–3

In the preparation of the consolidated balance sheet of a parent corporation and its subsidiaries, a decision must be reached concerning the inclusion or exclusion of each of them as a member of the consolidated group. A common criterion is the percentage of voting stock owned by the parent company.

Required:

a. What is the significance of the percentage of voting stock ownership in justifying the inclusion of a subsidiary company in a consolidated statement?
b. List other criteria upon which the decision to consolidate or not may also rest.

(AICPA adapted)

Exercise 3–4

Prepare investment elimination entries for the Texton Company and its subsidiary, Valley-View Company, for each of the conditions listed below:

	Acquired Interest	Amount Paid	Valley-View Capital Balances		
			Capital Stock	Other Contributed Capital	Retained Earnings [Deficit]
a.	100%	1,450,000	1,000,000	250,000	300,000
b.	90	1,125,000	1,000,000	325,000	[100,000]
c.	75	1,000,000	1,000,000	200,000	120,000

Exercise 3–5

An examination of the December 31, 19X1, balance sheet of S Company revealed the following account balances:

Capital stock (100,000 shares, $10 par) $1,000,000
Other contributed capital 275,000
Donated capital 125,000
Reserve for future inventory losses 100,000
Retained earnings 300,000
Estimated 19X1 federal income tax liability 200,000

Prepare an investment elimination entry immediately following the December 31, 19X1, open-market purchases of S Company's capital stock by P Company in each of the following independent conditions:

a. 100,000 shares; per share cost, $20.
b. 100,000 shares; per share cost, $18.
c. 80,000 shares; total cost, $1,540,000.
d. 80,000 shares; total cost, $1,400,000.
e. 40,000 shares; per share cost, $20⅝.
f. 300,000 shares (authorized, but previously unissued) purchased *directly* from S Company; per share cost, $20.

Exercise 3–6

On December 1, 19X1, B Company declares a dividend of $2.50 per share on its outstanding 100,000 shares for shareholders of record, January 10, 19X2. On December 31, 19X1, A Company acquires 90,000 shares of B Company for a cash outlay of $2,000,000. B Company has the following balances in its capital accounts:

Capital stock ($10 par)	$1,020,000
Treasury stock (recorded at par)	20,000
Other contributed capital	500,000
Retained earnings	400,000

Required:

a. Prepare an investment elimination entry for A Company as of December 31, 19X1.
b. Give the journal entry A Company would make to record the acquisition.

Exercise 3–7

On January 1, 19X1, P Company purchased 90 percent of S Company for $124,000. At the time of the investment, the book values of S Company's assets and liabilities were equal to their fair values. S Company's balance sheet on January 1, 19X1, was as follows:

	S Company
Cash	$ 10,000
Accounts receivable	5,000
Inventory	50,000
Long-term investments in marketable securities	15,000
Plant and equipment (net)	50,000
Land	60,000
	$190,000
Accounts payable	$ 15,000
Notes payable	25,000
Capital stock	50,000
Retained earnings	100,000
	$190,000

Required:

a. Prepare an investment elimination entry for P Company as of January 1, 19X1.
b. Give the elimination entry (entries) necessary to allocate the differential.

Exercise 3–8

P Company purchased an 80 percent interest in S Company for $84,800 on July 1, 19X1. S Company's balance sheet on that date was as follows:

	S Company
Cash	$15,000
Receivables	20,000
Inventory	30,000
Long-term investments in marketable securities	12,000
Plant and equipment (net)	11,000
Patents	4,000
	$92,000
Payables	$12,000
Capital stock	30,000
Retained earnings	50,000
	$92,000

A study of S Company's assets and liabilities revealed the following information:

	Fair Value
Inventory	$40,000
Long-term investments in marketable securities	15,000
Plant and equipment (net)	20,000
Patents	12,000

The fair values of the remainder of the assets and liabilities were equal to their book values.

Required:

a. Prepare the investment elimination entry for July 1, 19X1.
b. Give the elimination entry (entries) necessary to allocate the differential.

Exercise 3–9

P Company acquired a majority interest in S Company on December 31, 19X0 by issuing 500,000 shares of P Company $1 par, common stock in exchange for S Company shares. The current market price of the P Company common stock is $40 per share. Additionally, P Company guaranteed that the market price of its shares will be at least $60 at the end of the second year succeeding the acquisition date. If, at the end of the second year, the market price of P Company stock is less than $60 per share, P Company will issue additional shares with a current market value equal to the difference between the total guaranteed value and the current market value of the shares previously issued.

Required:

Assuming the market value of the P Company shares was $45 on December 31, 19X1, and $50 on December 31, 19X2, prepare the journal entries that P Company must make for this transaction on:

a. December 31, 19X0.
b. December 31, 19X1.
c. December 31, 19X2.

(Hint: It may be helpful to review paragraphs 77–86 of *APB Opinion 16*.)

Exercise 3–10

P Company acquired a majority interest in S Company on December 31, 19X0, by issuing 2,000,000 shares of P Company no-par, common stock in exchange for S Company shares. The current market price of the P Company common stock is $20 per share. Additionally, P Company guaranteed that, if the market price of its shares has fallen below $20 at the end of four years, it will issue additional shares to restore the total market value of consideration given to $40,000,000 as of that date. P Company further guaranteed to pay a total purchase price equal to eight times S Company's average annual earnings for the next four years (S Company's average annual earnings during the past four years were $5,000,000). If the guaranteed price, as calculated on December 31, 19X4, exceeds the December 31, 19X4, market value of shares previously issued, additional shares will be issued to make up the difference. In no case, however, can the total purchase price exceed $60,000,000.

Required:

a. Determine the cost of the investment on the date of acquisition.
b. Explain the economic and accounting implications of the various possible contingent outcomes on December 31, 19X4.

(Hint: It may be helpful to review paragraphs 77–86 of *APB Opinion 16.*)

Exercise 3–11

The annual report for the McLean Trucking Company for the year ended June 30, 19X2 included the following footnote:

Effective October 1, 19X1, all of the common stock of the Forth Worth Refining Company was purchased at an aggregate cost of $8,713,561 composed of cash of $2,000,000, notes in the amount of $5,988,452 and other costs of $725,109. Contingency payments representing 50% of cash profits above a certain amount, as defined in the agreement, are required to be paid to the sellers. A reduction in the purchase price results if certain cash profit levels are not attained. It is the Company's intention to charge contingency payments to operations and net contingency refunds (excess refunds over payments), should they arise, will be applied against the original purchase price. At June 30, 19X2, liability for estimated contingency payments under the Agreement amounted to approximately $209,000.

Required:

Comment on the propriety of this treatment of the contingent consideration. (Hint: It may be helpful to review paragraphs 77–86 of *APB Opinion 16.*)

Exercise 3–12

P Company acquired an 80 percent interest in S Company by issuing cash and other stock valued at $925,000. The investment elimination entry for this investment in P Company's consolidated statement working paper on the date of acquisition was:

Capital stock—S Company	80,000
Retained earnings—S Company	320,000
Differential	575,000
Investment in S Company	975,000

An analysis of the identifiable assets and liabilities of S Company produced the following data:

	Book Value	Fair Value
Cash	$ 50,000	$ 50,000
Receivables (net)	150,000	130,000
Inventory	250,000	310,000
Plant and equipment (net)	350,000	500,000
Patents	–0–	100,000
Land	100,000	150,000
Goodwill	50,000	–0–
	$950,000	$1,240,000
Accounts and notes payable	$300,000	$ 280,000
Accruals	50,000	40,000
Deferred income tax liability	100,000	–0–
	$450,000	$ 320,000
Net assets	$500,000	$ 920,000

Required:

a. Prepare the eliminating entry to allocate the differential to specific assets and liabilities.

b. The determination of "fair value" requires the application of different valuation bases (models) to different categories of assets and liabilities. Based upon the general guidelines established in paragraphs 88–89 of *APB Opinion 16*, indicate the probable valuation basis that was used to estimate the fair value for each asset and liability.

PROBLEMS

Problem 1

The following data relate to companies X, Y, and Z on February 1, 19X1:

	X Company	Y Company	Z Company
Capital stock (par, $100)	$10,000	$10,000	$10,000
Retained earnings [deficit]	4,000	[2,000]	–0–

Prepare an investment elimination entry on February 2, 19X1, following the purchase of stock *from the subsidiary* as indicated in the following independent cases.

Case A: P Company purchased 800 shares of X Company stock; 100 shares were issued concurrently to minority shareholders. Sales price per share for each stockholder group in the following independent examples, was—
   (1) $140.
   (2) $160.
   (3) $120.

Case B: P Company purchased 800 shares of Y Company stock; 100 shares were issued concurrently to minority shareholders. Sales price per share for each stockholder group in the following independent examples, was—
   (1) $80 to P Company.
          $74 to minority shareholders.
   (2) $82 to P Company.
          $84 to minority shareholders.

Case C: P Company purchased 700 shares of Z Company stock; 200 shares were issued concurrently to minority shareholders. Sales price per share for each stockholder group in the following independent examples, was—
   (1) $102 to P Company.
          $105 to minority shareholders.
   (2) $ 93 to P Company.
          $ 91 to minority shareholders.

Problem 2

Given the following data, prepare an investment elimination entry for each of the following independent, open-market, investment transactions:

	January 1, 19X1 Balances				
	Capital Stock (Par Value, $100)	Retained Earnings [Deficit]	Other Contributed Capital	19X1 Net Income [Loss]	19X1 Cash Dividends
M Company	$50,000	$10,000	$6,000	$20,000	$8,000
W Company	40,000	[5,000]		15,000	5,000
Z Company	30,000	12,000	2,000	[5,000]	

For Consolidated Balance Sheet
January 1, 19X1

P Company purchased on January 1, 19X1:
   Case A: 400 shares of M Company capital stock at book value.
   Case B: 300 shares of W Company capital stock at 90.
   Case C: 300 shares of M Company capital stock at 125.
   Case D: 200 shares of M Company capital stock at 130.

**For Consolidated Balance Sheet
January 1, 19X2**

P Company purchased on January 1, 19X2:

Case E: 400 shares of M Company capital stock at 157.
Case F: 300 shares of M Company capital stock at 150.
Case G: 200 shares of Z Company capital stock at 125.
Case H: 300 shares of W Company capital stock at book value and 200 shares of Z
Company capital stock at $3 per share less than book value.

Problem 3

On November 1, 19X0, the Moore Company entered into negotiations with
the Sydney Corporation to purchase a controlling interest in its capital stock.
On December 1, it was mutually agreed that the assets of the Sydney Corporation should be appraised as a condition of final price determination. On December 31, the following data were available:

Long-lived assets:
Cost $100,000
Accumulated depreciation (based upon a 20-year life) 50,000
Reproduction cost—new 200,000
Estimated remaining life .... 15 years
Straight-line depreciation is used

Capital stock (par, $100) .... $ 50,000
Retained earnings (deficit) .... (5,000)
Other contributed capital 10,000

Based on the above information, the Sydney Corporation recorded the appraisal on January 1, 19X1, after which the Moore Company purchased 1,500
shares of Sydney Corporation's unissued capital stock at $300 per share.

Required:

a. Record the appraisal on the books of the Sydney Corporation on January 1,
    19X1.
b. Prepare an investment elimination entry for a consolidated balance sheet
    working paper as of January 1, 19X1.
c. Assuming that Sydney Corporation did *not* record the new appraised value
    of its long-lived assets, as would normally be the case under current account-
    ing policy, prepare the investment elimination entry and the differential
    allocation entry (using the appraised values) for a consolidated balance
    sheet working paper as of January 1, 19X1.
d. Calculate the values that would be shown in the consolidated balance sheet
    for the subsidiary's long-lived assets, accumulated depreciation, and total
    minority interest under *b* and *c*.

Problem 4

On April 1, 19X1, the Pratt Company purchased a controlling interest in
both the Trine Company and the Briski Corporation, after which the following
balance sheet information was prepared:

Assets	Pratt	Trine	Briski
Cash	$ 4,000	$ 1,500	$ 3,500
Accounts receivable	11,000	9,000	12,500
Other current assets	8,000	4,500	10,000
Investments:			
320 shares in Trine Company	50,000		
540 shares in Briski Corporation	51,000		
Long-lived assets (net)	30,000	41,000	54,000
Other assets	26,000	24,000	10,000
	$180,000	$80,000	$90,000

Equities			
Accounts payable	$ 14,000	$ 5,000	$15,000
Other current liabilities	6,000	12,000	8,000
Fixed liabilities	15,000	3,000	11,000
Capital stock (par, $100)	100,000	40,000	60,000
Retained earnings [deficit]	41,000	18,000	[4,000]
Other contributed capital	4,000	2,000	
	$180,000	$80,000	$90,000

Required:

Prepare a consolidated balance sheet working paper as of April 1, 19X1. Assume any differential is allocated to goodwill.

Problem 5

On October 1, 19X1, the Dunhill Company purchased 960 shares of the King Company stock for $160,000 and $50,000 of King Company bonds at par plus accrued interest. Immediately after these transactions, the following trial balances were prepared:

Assets	Dunhill Company	King Company
Cash	$ 19,250	$ 10,000
Accrued interest receivable	750	
Inventory	120,000	100,000
Accounts receivable	80,000	50,000
Long-lived assets (net)	100,000	160,000
Other assets	20,000	10,000
Investment in King Company (stock)	160,000	
Investment in King Company (bonds)	50,000	
	$550,000	$330,000

Equities		
Accounts payable	$ 60,000	$ 21,500
Accrued interest payable		1,500
Accrued expenses	10,000	7,000
Bonds payable, 6%, payable January 1 and July 1 ..		100,000
Capital stock ($100 par)	300,000	150,000
Treasury stock (recorded at par)		[30,000]
Retained earnings	80,000	50,000
Other contributed capital	100,000	30,000
	$550,000	$330,000

Additionally, a $4,000 balance remains in the respective trade accounts receivable and payable from previous trading between the two companies.

Required:

a. Prepare an investment elimination entry on October 1, 19X1.
b. Prepare a consolidated balance sheet working paper on October 1, 19X1.

Problem 6

The December 31, 19X1, trial balances of X Company, a petroleum refinery, and companies Y and Z, two of its crude oil suppliers, are as follows:

Assets	*X Company*	*Y Company*	*Z Company*
Cash	$ 10,400,000	$ 570,000	$ 1,100,000
Marketable securities	27,300,000		
Accounts receivable	29,000,000	1,200,000	3,200,000
Notes receivable			1,500,000
Inventory	55,900,000	2,240,000	10,800,000
Long-lived assets (net)	187,000,000	3,900,000	14,600,000
Other assets	4,320,000	100,000	200,000
	$313,920,000	$8,010,000	$31,400,000

Equities			
Accounts payable	$ 36,900,000	$1,200,000	$ 1,800,000
Notes payable, Z Company		1,500,000	
Dividends payable (Note 1)		100,000	
Accrued expenses	1,820,000	570,000	700,000
Bonds payable	100,000,000		10,000,000
Capital stock:			
$100 par	100,000,000		
$ 10 par		2,000,000	
No par (100,000)			17,400,000
Other contributed capital	47,800,000	1,800,000	
Retained earnings	27,400,000	840,000	1,500,000
	$313,920,000	$8,010,000	$31,400,000

Note 1: Cash dividends were declared December 28, 19X1, payable on January 25, 19X2, to stockholders of record, January 5, 19X2.

On January 1, 19X2, X company purchased a controlling interest in the capital stock of companies Y and Z to assure continuity of supply of crude oil. The acquisition of stock was as follows:

1. 160,000 shares of Y Company's capital stock purchased in the open market for $25⅝.
2. 90,000 shares of Z Company's capital stock acquired by issuing 80,000 shares of X Company's stock to the individual stockholders of Z Company. On January 1, 19X2, the capital stock of X Company was quoted at $250.

Required:

Prepare a consolidated balance sheet working paper as of January 1, 19X2. Assume any differential is allocated to goodwill.

Problem 7

The June 1, 19X1, balance sheets for A Company and B Company are as follows:

Assets	A Company	B Company
Cash	$ 100,000	$ 52,000
Accounts receivable	200,000	125,000
Notes receivable	300,000	100,000
Merchandise inventory	375,000	225,000
Investment in B Company	700,000	
Long-lived assets (net)	825,000	700,000
Total Assets	$2,500,000	$1,202,000

Equities		
Accounts payable	$ 100,000	$ 150,000
Accrued interest payable		2,000
Notes payable	500,000	300,000
Capital stock ($10, par)	1,500,000	500,000
Retained earnings	400,000	250,000
Total Equities	$2,500,000	$1,202,000

All of B Company's assets are recorded at their fair values except for the following:

	Book Value	Fair Value
Merchandise inventory	$225,000	$ 265,000
Long-lived assets (net)	700,000	750,000
	$925,000	$1,015,000

On June 1, 19X1, A Company purchased 80 percent of the capital stock of B Company for $700,000. Included in the accounts receivable for B Company is an account for $25,000 due from A Company. The notes receivable for A Company include a loan to B Company for $50,000 on which the June 1 accrued interest is $2,000. The interest is unrecorded by A Company.

Required:

Prepare a consolidated balance sheet for A Company and its subsidiary as of June 1, 19X1.

Problem 8

The Northern Company purchased 100 percent of the capital stock of the Atlantic Company on January 1, 19X1, for $61,000. Immediately following the investment, the statements of financial position for the constituent companies are as follows:

Assets	Northern Company	Atlantic Company
Cash	$ 8,000	$ 5,000
Accounts receivable	16,000	15,000
Advances to Atlantic	5,000	
Investment in Atlantic Company	61,000	
Inventory	20,000	10,000
Other assets	53,000	40,000
	$163,000	$70,000

Equities		
Liabilities	$ 8,000	$ 5,000
Due to Northern		5,000
Capital stock ($100 par)	100,000	50,000
Retained earnings	55,000	10,000
	$163,000	$70,000

Required:

Prepare a consolidated balance sheet working paper as of January 1, 19X1. Assume that the book values of all of Atlantic Company's assets and liabilities are equal to their fair values.

Problem 9

At December 31, 19X1, the balance sheet of A Company was as follows:

Assets		Equities	
Cash	$ 50,000	Payables	$1,750,000
Receivables (net)	300,000	Accruals	450,000
Inventories	1,600,000	Common stock, 10,000	
Current prepayments	47,000	shares	1,000,000
Long-lived assets (net)	2,003,000	Retained earnings	800,000
	$4,000,000		$4,000,000

An appraisal as of that date, which was carefully considered and approved by the boards of directors of A Company and B Company, placed a total replacement value, less sustained depreciation, of $3,203,000 on the long-lived assets of A Company.

B Company offered to purchase all the assets of A Company, subject to its liabilities, as of December 31, 19X1, for $3,000,000. However, 40 percent of the stockholders of A Company objected to the price on the ground that it did not include a consideration for goodwill, which they believed to be worth at least $500,000. A counterproposal was made, and final agreement was reached on the basis that B Company acquired 60 percent of the common stock of A Company at a price of $300 per share.

B Company's condensed balance sheet at December 31, 19X1, following the acquisition of A Company's stock, showed:

Assets		Equities	
Cash and investments (including stock of A) ...	$ 7,000,000	Payables	$ 7,872,000
Receivables (net)	2,400,000	Accruals	1,615,000
Inventories	11,200,000	Common stock, 100,000	
Current prepayments	422,000	shares	10,000,000
Long-lived assets (net) ...	18,978,000	Retained earnings	20,513,000
	$40,000,000		$40,000,000

Required:

Prepare a consolidated balance sheet working paper as of December 31, 19X1, for the two companies.

(AICPA adapted)

4

Consolidated Financial Reports— Postacquisition

THE PREPARATION of consolidated statements following a period of subsidiary operations is complicated, at least in part, by the introduction of two new variables: the elapsed time since the acquisition of subsidiary shares *and* the parent company's method of accounting for the investment. At date of acquisition, the investment is recorded at total purchase cost; subsequently, an election must be made by the parent as to whether this measurement should be preserved without change *or* periodically adjusted to reflect the activities and operations of the subsidiary. The former, more traditional, approach is the cost, or legal-basis, method. The latter approach is referred to as the equity method. These two alternative methods of accounting for the parent company's investment have been covered in *Intermediate Accounting,* and are summarized below. However, it may be noted at this point that regardless of which method is employed by the parent to account for its investment *in a subsidiary that is to be included in the consolidation,* the formal consolidated statements will remain unaffected. The working paper eliminations are designed to compensate for the differences between the two methods.

The Cost Method

The cost method of accounting for stock investments presumes that cost is an accurate reflection of the market value of the investment at date of acquisition, and that this valuation should remain undisturbed in most instances by the influence of subsequent operations of the company whose stock is held. Accordingly, under the cost method, subsidiary profits are not recorded by the parent when they are reported by the subsidiary.

Similarly, the losses sustained by a subsidiary are not recorded by the parent *unless* there is convincing evidence which indicates the incurrence of a material and apparently permanent impairment of the value of the investment. Income is recognized by the parent company only when the subsidiary declares a cash dividend. At this time, the parent company debits Dividends Receivable and credits Dividend Income for its share of the subsidiary dividends.

The Equity Method

Under the equity method, the parent company's equity in the post-acquisition earnings of a subsidiary is recorded by debiting the investment account and crediting a suitably named account, such as Equity in Subsidiary Earnings. All or part of this "equity" may be in "undistributed" earnings, which emphasizes the unique *realization* criterion underlying the recognition of a subsidiary's contribution to the parent's net income. Historically, when the realization concept was applied to stock investments, it was interpreted as a requirement that income not be recognized by the stockholder until declared as dividends by the issuing company. To the contrary, the equity method involves a significant relaxation of this traditional criterion. In essence, the equity method is based on the argument that the economic impact of a corporation's reported profits and losses immediately accrues to its stockholders, regardless of the timing of dividend declarations.

Postacquisition losses sustained by a subsidiary affiliate are recorded in a similar manner by the parent, i.e., by a debit to Equity in Subsidiary Earnings with a corresponding credit to the investment account. Such losses result from a decrease in the underlying subsidiary net assets; consequently, the parent's entry is an effort to formally recognize the unfavorable economic circumstance.

The parent company's receipt of a subsidiary cash dividend is recorded by debiting Cash and crediting the investment account. Such an entry reflects the financial realization of the parent's equity in subsidiary profits in the amount of the assets transferred; accordingly, the receipt of dividends is treated as a reduction in the reciprocal investment account balance. Since an antecedent entry has been made increasing the investment account for subsidiary profits, the parent's collection of subsidiary cash dividends is simply an act of conversion, or a partial recovery of the adjusted cost of the investment. The effect produced on the parent company's books is merely a transformation in asset form.

Entry Comparison

A comparison of the entries made by the parent company using both the cost and equity methods should expose some of their principal differences.

Illustration 4–1

Cost Method	Equity Method

A 90 percent investment in subsidiary stock is acquired for $50,000.

Cost Method			Equity Method		
Investment in sub- sidiary stock	50,000		Investment in sub- sidiary stock	50,000	
Cash		50,000	Cash		50,000

$4,000 cash dividends are paid by the subsidiary during the first year of its operations.

Cash	3,600		Cash	3,600	
Dividend in- come		3,600	Investment in subsidiary stock		3,600

The subsidiary reports net income of $10,000 for the first year's operations.

No entry.			Investment in sub- sidiary stock	9,000	
			Equity in sub- sidiary earn- ings		9,000

$3,000 cash dividends are paid by the subsidiary during the second year.

Cash	2,700		Cash	2,700	
Dividend in- come		2,700	Investment in subsidiary stock		2,700

The subsidiary reports a net loss of $2,000 for the second year.

No entry.			Equity in subsidiary earnings	1,800	
			Investment in subsidiary stock		1,800

Please note that the entries shown in Illustration 4–1 are those recorded on the books of the parent company. They should not be confused with eliminating entries required for consolidated statement working papers.

The entries shown in Illustration 4–1 to record the parent's equity in subsidiary income under the equity method are based on the assumptions that (1) the cost of the parent's investment at date of acquisition is equal to its acquired equity in the subsidiary's recorded net assets; and (2) there are no transactions between the parent and the subsidiary which involve the recognition of gains or losses. In the event either, or both, of these assumptions are not valid, the calculations would be modified. Since these modifications are also necessary in preparing consolidated statements, they will be examined in subsequent sections of the book. The procedure for giving effect to amortization of the difference between investment cost and the equity in net assets is described in Chapter 5, and elimination of inter-company gains and losses is treated in Chapters 7 and 8.

Although either method of accounting for the investment in the stock of the subsidiary may be used, many companies shifted to the equity method following the issuance in 1971 of *APB Opinion 18,* "The Equity Method of Accounting for Investments in Common Stock." Strictly speaking, this *Opinion* imposes a financial reporting requirement, not an accounting re-quirement, and it has substantive significance only for investments in un-consolidated affiliates. As was mentioned above, the formal consolidated statements are unaffected by the choice of accounting method (cost or equity) for investments in subsidiaries that are consolidated. But the mechanics of consolidation are affected by the accounting method used, and since many, if not most companies are now using the equity method, the illustrations in this text will be based upon the assumption that the equity method has been employed to account for the investment. A simple illustration of the mechanics of consolidation under the cost method is provided in the Appendix to this chapter for reference purposes.[1]

Statements of Consolidated Income and Retained Earnings

Following a period of subsidiary operations, it is important that con-solidated statements of income and retained earnings be prepared in addi-tion to the consolidated balance sheet. A consolidated income statement is essentially a summary enumeration of the revenues, expenses, gains, and losses of the allied companies after elimination of those account balances which result from transactions between the affiliates. The process of com-bination includes a deduction from the combined net incomes of all the affiliated companies, after eliminations, for the amounts of minority in-terests in the net incomes of the subsidiary affiliates. The residual, so de-termined, is then assignable to the majority shareholders and is designated *consolidated net income.*

An alternative definition of consolidated net income is based on the argument that the amount of income allocated to minority interests should be treated as a *distribution* of consolidated net income rather than a *de-duction necessary to determine* consolidated net income. This view empha-sizes the single entity concept of a corporate affiliation. It rests on the be-lief that the *determinants* of an entity's net income should not include allo-cations to any of the stockholders of the entity, notwithstanding the unique character of minority stockholders.

---

[1] The reader may refer to Griffin, Williams, and Larson, *Advanced Accounting,* Rev. Ed. (Homewood, Ill.: Richard D. Irwin, Inc., 1971) for an expanded coverage of special consolidation techniques required under the cost method.

It should be emphasized that the nature of consolidated net income is essentially a definitional problem. The authors support the first definition presented above primarily because it emphasizes the equity of parent company stockholders. The significance of consolidated statements clearly stems from the informational needs of parties that have interests in the parent company, i.e., parent company creditors and stockholders. Defining consolidated net income as the portion of combined net income accruing to the parent is fully consistent with this dominant statement function. Thus, the preferred definition reflects the orientation of the users of consolidated statements. Subsequent development is based on this interpretation unless otherwise noted.

The consolidated statement of retained earnings is simply a sequential ordering of the consolidated retained earnings at the beginning of an accounting period, increased by consolidated net income, and reduced by the parent company's dividends declared; the algebraic sum of these amounts is the balance of consolidated retained earnings at the end of the accounting period.

In the preparation of a consolidated income statement, consolidated statement of retained earnings, and consolidated balance sheet, it is useful to select a working paper, the organization of which accommodates the preparation of all three statements in the series.

The Three-Division Working Paper—First Year Subsequent to Acquisition

Frequently, the source information for consolidated reports is to be found in the financial statements of the separate affiliates. Where the account data are thus conveniently prearranged in statement form, the three-division horizontal working paper is especially suitable for the preparation of the entire complement of consolidated reports. On other occasions, however, the trial balances of the affiliates are more accessible. In these instances, the trial balances must be reclassified in financial statement form to accommodate the three-division working paper format. In the remaining discussion of consolidated statements, trial balances of affiliated companies are given as the source information for consolidated working papers in order to minimize the space devoted to underlying detail; nonetheless, the three-division working paper format will usually be employed because it provides a logical framework for analysis.

Case 1.   It is assumed that P Company acquired 90 percent of the capital stock of S Company on January 1, 19X1, at a cost of $54,000. The trial balances for the two affiliates at December 31, 19X1, are as follows:

	P Company		S Company	
Cash	$ 29,500		$ 8,000	
Accounts receivable	18,000		3,000	
Inventory (1/1)	16,000		4,000	
Investment in S Company	67,500			
Other assets	73,000		62,000	
Accounts payable		$ 22,000		$ 5,000
Other liabilities		6,000		
Capital stock		100,000		50,000
Retained earnings (1/1)		40,000		10,000
Dividends declared	10,000		5,000	
Sales		78,000		40,000
Equity in subsidiary earnings		18,000		
Purchases	42,000		20,000	
Expenses	8,000		3,000	
	$264,000	$264,000	$105,000	$105,000
Inventory (12/31)	$ 10,000		$ 7,000	

The Dividends Declared account is a special classificational refinement that facilitates the analysis in the retained earnings statement division of the consolidated statement working paper. The account has the following properties: it is debited when dividends are declared (rather than Retained Earnings), and at the end of the period, it is closed (along with other nominal accounts) to Retained Earnings. If the accounting system of a company does not actually incorporate this refinement, the trial balance section of the consolidated working paper can nonetheless be set up as if the account existed. Should one choose not to identify dividends declared separately in the consolidated statement working paper, then all consolidation entries that otherwise would affect this account would be made directly against Retained Earnings.

Investment Elimination Entries. Where the investment is carried on an equity basis and a consolidated income statement, statement of retained earnings, and balance sheet are prepared, it is necessary first to eliminate, or reverse, the effects of the parent company's entries for subsidiary profits or losses and dividends for the current year. Such an elimination, or reversal, in the consolidated statement working paper removes the measures of intercompany activities during the current year, and restores the investment account to that balance which prevailed at the *beginning* of the year (which, in this case, is the date of acquisition). A second eliminating entry is then necessary to eliminate the parent company's investment account (as adjusted by the preceding entry) against its equity in the balances of the stockholders' equity accounts of the subsidiary *as of the beginning of the year.*

During 19X1, the parent company made entries to reflect its interest in the activities and operations of the subsidiary and to record the receipt of dividends from the subsidiary, the effects of which are compounded as follows:

```
Cash ...............................................  4,500
Investment in S Company ...........................  13,500
     Equity in subsidiary earnings .....................         18,000
```

Consequently, the first investment elimination entry in the consolidated statement working paper (Illustration 4–2) should reverse the effect of this entry. The account, Dividends Declared, is substituted for Cash in the original entry. The eliminating entry is then of the form:

```
Equity in subsidiary earnings .........................  18,000
     Dividends declared—S Company ...................          4,500
     Investment in S Company ........................         13,500
```

With the investment account restored to its beginning-of-year balance, the second of the two required investment elimination entries then follows:

```
Capital stock—S Company ...........................  45,000
Retained earnings—S Company .......................   9,000
     Investment in S Company .......................         54,000
```

If the investment cost had *not* been equal to the parent company's equity in subsidiary net assets at the date of acquisition, a differential would of course have been recognized in this second of the two required investment elimination entries. The recognition and related adjustments of differentials in consolidated statement working papers subsequent to the date of acquisition are explained in Chapter 5.

Each division of the consolidated working paper (Illustration 4–2) provides the requisite data for the preparation of one of the series of consolidated statements. While the working paper is subdivided for this purpose, the links which unite the various divisions are also clearly evident. All items on the "net income" line of the income statement division, including elimination debits and credits, are carried forward to the same line description in the retained earnings statement division. Similarly, the several totals on the line of the final balance of retained earnings in this division are carried forward to the identical line description in the balance sheet division. These divisions, each representing a formal consolidated statement, articulate with each other. It may be observed that equality of amounts of elimination debits and credits is not preserved in respect to a specific division of the working paper; yet total elimination debits and credits for the three divisions are necessarily balanced. It is additionally important to note that consolidated dividends declared are the parent company's dividend declarations; to the extent that subsidiary dividends are intercompany, they are eliminated; remaining amounts of subsidiary dividends are distributed to nonaffiliate minority shareholders. Accordingly, the consolidated dividends declared represent the earnings distribution of the parent company. In this illustration, subsidiary dividends of $5,000 are distributed $4,500 to the parent and $500 to minority shareholders. The $4,500 payment to P Company is an intercompany transaction and is eliminated in the first of the two investment elimination entries; the $500 payment to nonaffiliate shareholders is extended in the

Illustration 4-2

P COMPANY AND SUBSIDIARY S COMPANY

Consolidated Statement Working Paper
For Year Ended December 31, 19X1

	P Company	S Company	Eliminations Dr.	Eliminations Cr.	Minority Interest	Consolidated
Income Statement:						
Sales	78,000	40,000				118,000
Equity in subsidiary earnings	18,000		(1) 18,000			
Inventory (12/31)	10,000	7,000				17,000
Total credits	106,000	47,000				135,000
Inventory (1/1)	16,000	4,000				20,000
Purchases	42,000	20,000				62,000
Expenses	8,000	3,000				11,000
Total debits	66,000	27,000				93,000
Minority interest in net income—S Company					2,000*	42,000
Net income—carried forward	40,000	20,000	18,000	–0–	2,000	40,000
Retained Earnings Statement:						
Retained earnings, January 1, 19X1:						
P Company	40,000					40,000
S Company		10,000	(2) 9,000		1,000†	
Net income—brought forward	40,000	20,000	18,000	–0–	2,000	40,000
	80,000	30,000			3,000	80,000
Dividends declared:						
P Company	10,000					10,000
S Company		5,000		(1) 4,500	500‡	
Retained earnings, December 31, 19X1—carried forward	70,000	25,000	27,000	4,500	2,500	70,000

Balance Sheet:

	P Company	S Company	Eliminations Dr.	Eliminations Cr.	Minority interest in S Company	Consolidated
Cash	29,500	8,000				37,500
Accounts receivable	18,000	3,000				21,000
Inventory	10,000	7,000				17,000
Investment in S Company	67,500			(1) 13,500		
				(2) 54,000		
Other assets	73,000	62,000				135,000
	198,000	80,000				210,500
Accounts payable	22,000	5,000				27,000
Other liabilities	6,000					6,000
Capital stock:						
P Company	100,000					100,000
S Company		50,000	(2) 45,000		5,000§	
Retained earnings—brought forward	70,000	25,000	27,000	4,500	2,500	70,000
Minority interest in S Company					7,500	7,500 M
	198,000	80,000	72,000	72,000	7,500	210,500

Explanation of eliminations:
 (1) To reverse the parent company's entries during 19X1 for subsidiary dividends and its interest in subsidiary earnings.
 (2) To eliminate the January 1, 19X1, investment account balance against 90 percent of the corresponding stockholders' equity accounts of the subsidiary.

Explanation of minority interest calculations:
  * 10% × $20,000.
  † 10% × $10,000.
  ‡ 10% × $5,000.
  § 10% × $50,000.

working papers as the minority interest in subsidiary dividends and is therefore deducted.

Observe that the minority interest is given separate column identification in each division of the consolidated working paper. *The amount of the minority interest in subsidiary net income is calculated on the basis of the subsidiary's recorded net income, without regard to eliminated revenue and expense items.* This amount is deducted from the combined net incomes of the affiliates, after eliminations, in arriving at consolidated net income. The working paper also discloses how the equity of minority shareholders in retained earnings and capital stock is calculated in the normal progression from one working paper division to another. Note that the *total* minority interest, $7,500, is equal to the minority shareholders' percentage shareholding in the subsidiary (10%) multiplied by the total *recorded* shareholders' equity of the subsidiary ($75,000). This relationship will always hold unless there are intercompany profits to be dealt with, a topic which is covered in Chapters 7 and 8.

Study of the working paper for this illustration will disclose that *the parent company's net income is equal to consolidated net income; also, the parent company's retained earnings are equal to the consolidated retained earnings.* Necessarily, this condition of equivalence will prevail where the investment account is periodically adjusted to reflect the parent's equity in subsidiary net asset changes.

The presence of minority shareholders requires special disclosure in the formal consolidated statements. Their equity in subsidiary net income is indicated in the consolidated income statement as a deduction from the combined net incomes, after eliminations, in arriving at consolidated net income. This is consistent with the usual interpretation of consolidated net income as an amount accruing to the majority shareholders. No explicit disclosure of minority interest is required in the consolidated retained earnings statement, and reference has previously been made to the alternative forms of disclosure for minority interests frequently found in consolidated balance sheets.

The formal consolidated statements for this case are shown in Illustration 4–3.

Consolidated Statement Working Paper—Second Year Subsequent to Acquisition

The consolidated statement working paper for periods subsequent to the first year after acquisition of subsidiary stock is essentially the same, in respect to details of format, eliminations, and extensions, as in the working paper for the year of acquisition. Nonetheless, it is useful to review the mechanics of the investment elimination entries for a second (or later) year to emphasize the specific steps that are followed.

In the previous illustration, only one period of subsidiary operations

Illustration 4–3

P COMPANY AND SUBSIDIARY S COMPANY

Consolidated Income Statement
For Year Ended December 31, 19X1

Sales		$118,000
Cost of sales:		
Inventory, January 1, 19X1	$20,000	
Purchases	62,000	
Total	$82,000	
Inventory, December 31, 19X1	17,000	65,000
Gross profit		$ 53,000
Expenses		11,000
Combined net income		$ 42,000
Minority interest in subsidiary net income		2,000
Consolidated net income		$ 40,000

P COMPANY AND SUBSIDIARY S COMPANY

Consolidated Statement of Retained Earnings
For Year Ended December 31, 19X1

Retained earnings, January 1, 19X1	$40,000
Consolidated net income	40,000
Total	$80,000
Dividends declared	10,000
Retained earnings, December 31, 19X1	$70,000

P COMPANY AND SUBSIDIARY S COMPANY

Consolidated Balance Sheet
December 31, 19X1

Assets			*Equities*		
Cash	$ 37,500		Liabilities:		
Accounts receivable	21,000		Accounts payable		$ 27,000
Inventory	17,000		Other liabilities		6,000
Other assets	135,000		Minority interest:		
			Capital stock	$5,000	
			Retained earnings	2,500	7,500
			Shareholders' equity:		
			Capital stock		100,000
			Retained earnings		70,000
	$210,500				$210,500

separated the preparation of the consolidated statements from the date of the acquisition of subsidiary shares. In such a circumstance, the first eliminating entry, which adjusts the investment account to its beginning-of-year balance, also restores the account to the original investment cost.

The second eliminating entry—to eliminate the investment account (as adjusted by the preceding entry) against the parent's equity in the balances of the stockholders' equity accounts of the subsidiary *as of the beginning of the year*—is then identical (in respect to amounts) to the investment elimination entry made at date of acquisition. However, this equivalence of amounts persists for but one year under the equity method.[2] In the second (or later) year after acquisition, this eliminating entry will usually be different from what it was in the first (or prior) year, and its elements must be calculated in accordance with the specified procedure: viz., multiply the parent's percentage ownership interest times the balances of each of the stockholders' equity accounts of the subsidiary *as of the beginning of the year*.

Case 2. Preparation of a consolidated statement working paper for the second year after acquisition is illustrated by modifying the data for Case I to include the following 19X2 activities:

	P Company	S Company
Net income for 19X2	$44,900	$28,000
Dividends declared, 19X2	15,000	10,000

The investment account at December 31, 19X2, accordingly has a balance of $83,700, as reflected below:

Investment in S Company

Investment cost,			Dividends received from	
January 1, 19X1	54,000		S in 19X1	4,500
Equity in S's 19X1 earnings	18,000		Balance, December 31, 19X1	67,500
	72,000			72,000
Balance, December 31, 19X1	67,500		Dividends received from	
Equity in S's 19X2 earnings	25,200		S in 19X2	9,000
			Balance, December 31, 19X2	83,700
	92,700			92,700
Balance, December 31, 19X2	83,700			

The investment elimination entries for this example are as follows:

1. To reverse the effects of parent company entries in 19X2 reflecting its interest in the activities and operations of, and the receipt of dividends from, the subsidiary:

Equity in subsidiary earnings	25,200	
Dividends declared—S Company		9,000
Investment in S Company		16,200

---

[2] The equivalence generally continues indefinitely under the cost method, which is illustrated in the Appendix to this Chapter.

2. To eliminate the investment account (as adjusted by the preceding entry) against the parent's equity in the balances of the stockholders' equity accounts of the subsidiary as of the beginning of 19X2:

Capital stock—S Company	45,000	
Retained earnings—S Company	22,500	
Investment in S Company		67,500

In calculating the amounts to be eliminated in the second entry, P Company's percentage ownership in S Company (90%) is multiplied times the balances of S Company's Capital Stock and Retained Earnings accounts *as of January 1, 19X2* ($50,000 and $25,000, respectively).

The consolidated statement working paper for this case is shown in Illustration 4–4. The reader may again note in this illustration that the balances accumulated in the parent company's accounts for retained earnings, net income for the year, and dividends declared are identical in amount to their consolidated statement equivalents. Further, the total minority interest ($9,300) is again equal to the minority shareholders' percentage interest in the total shareholders' equity of the subsidiary (10% × $93,000).

Relationship between Investment Account Balance and Net Assets of the Subsidiary. The equity method of accounting for an investment in the common stock of an affiliate increases the investment account as the affiliate's net assets are increased by operations and decreases it when the affiliate's net assets are decreased by cash dividends. The increases and decreases in the investment account balance are of course in proportion to the investor company's percentage interest in the affiliate. Since we have assumed in this chapter that the original investment cost was equal to the investor's acquired monetary interest in the affiliate, it follows that the investment account (adjusted in accordance with the equity method) will maintain this proportional relationship at all future points in time. Thus, for our example, the investment account balance of $83,700 on December 31, 19X2, continues to reflect P Company's equity in S Company's recorded net assets (90% × $93,000 = $83,700).

Other Intercompany Transactions

Discussion has heretofore centered on those intercompany transactions involving the purchase of subsidiary stock, reciprocal debtor-creditor relationships among affiliate companies, and the declaration of subsidiary dividends. If there are other intercompany transactions completed during a period of affiliation, their effects must also be eliminated. One such transaction, which occurs with relative frequency, is the sale of merchandise by one affiliate to another. Since the consolidated income statement should exhibit only those revenues and expenses which result from transactions with nonaffiliates, it is appropriate to eliminate the total

Illustration 4–4

P COMPANY AND SUBSIDIARY S COMPANY

Consolidated Statement Working Paper
For Year Ended December 31, 19X2

	P Company	S Company	Eliminations Dr.	Eliminations Cr.	Minority Interest	Consolidated
Income Statement:						
Sales	96,000	63,000				159,000
Equity in subsidiary earnings	25,200		(1) 25,200			
Inventory (12/31)	14,200	9,200				23,400
Total credits	135,400	72,200				182,400
Inventory (1/1)	10,000	7,000				17,000
Purchases	58,000	29,100				87,100
Expenses	22,500	8,100				30,600
Total debits	90,500	44,200				134,700
Minority interest in net income—S Company					2,800*	47,700
						2,800
Net income—carried forward	44,900	28,000	25,200	–0–	2,800	44,900
Retained Earnings Statement:						
Retained earnings, January 1, 19X2:						
P Company	70,000					70,000
S Company		25,000	(2) 22,500		2,500†	
Net income—brought forward	44,900	28,000	25,200		2,800	44,900
	114,900	53,000			5,300	114,900
Dividends declared:						
P Company	15,000					15,000
S Company		10,000		(1) 9,000	1,000‡	
Retained earnings, December 31, 19X2—carried forward	99,900	43,000	47,700	9,000	4,300	99,900

Balance Sheet:	P Company	S Company	Eliminations Dr.	Eliminations Cr.	Minority Interest	Consolidated
Cash	31,000	12,000				43,000
Accounts receivable	22,000	19,000				41,000
Inventory	14,200	9,200				23,400
Investment in S Company	83,700			(1) 16,200 (2) 67,500		
Other assets	83,000	64,300				147,300
	233,900	104,500				254,700
Accounts payable	30,000	9,000				39,000
Other liabilities	4,000	2,500				6,500
Capital stock:						
P Company	100,000					100,000
S Company		50,000	(2) 45,000		5,000§	-0-
Retained earnings—brought forward	99,900	43,000	47,700		4,300	99,900
Minority interest in S Company				9,000	9,300	9,300 M
	233,900	104,500	92,700	92,700		254,700

Explanation of eliminations:

  (1) To reverse the parent company's entries for subsidiary dividends and its interest in subsidiary earnings.

  (2) To eliminate the January 1, 19X2, investment account balance against 90 percent of the stockholders' equity account balances of the subsidiary.

Explanation of minority interest calculations:

  * 10% × $28,000.

  † 10% × $25,000.

  ‡ 10% × $10,000.

  § 10% × $50,000.

amount of intercompany sales by a debit to Sales and a credit to Purchases (or Cost of Sales) in the consolidated working paper. Special elimination problems arise if some of the items in the intercompany merchandise shipments are not subsequently resold by the purchasing affiliate during the current period and are accordingly included in its final inventory. The complications created by the profit residue in the final inventory are dealt with in detail in Chapter 7.

Other types of intercompany revenue-expense transactions which must be similarly eliminated in the consolidated working papers include transactions arising from intercorporate financing, or the rendering of services by one affiliate to another. All evidences of these transactions must be removed from the consolidated statements to avoid duplicate measurement. Reciprocal accounts, for which eliminating entries must be made in the consolidated statement working paper, include interest income-interest expense, management fee income-management expense, commissions earned-commissions expense, and various others.

Multicompany Affiliations

Our examples to this point have assumed two-party affiliations, a parent company and a single subsidiary. We now will consider the case of a three-party affiliation. It should be noted that an increase in the number of subsidiaries only increases the number of accounts to be dealt with and the eliminations to be made. The principles of consolidated statement preparation developed in the context of two-party affiliations remain unchanged.

Case 3. The affiliation diagram for this example is shown following.

Affiliation Diagram

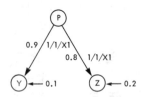

The December 31, 19X1, trial balances for companies, P, Y, and Z are given in Illustration 4–5. The reader should note carefully the additional information included at the foot of the trial balances, because this information provides the basis for several adjustments and/or eliminations in the consolidated statement working paper (See Illustration 4–6).

One may observe in Illustration 4–6 that again the parent company's net income and retained earnings are equal in amount to consolidated net income and retained earnings. Further, the investment elimination entries for the two subsidiaries are dealt with separately, and are determined for each subsidiary in the same manner previously illustrated for single sub-

Illustration 4–5

	P Company		Y Company		Z Company	
Cash	$ 34,300		$ 8,000		$ 4,000	
Accounts receivable ...	18,000		3,000		6,000	
Inventory (1/1)	16,000		4,000		3,000	
Investment in Y Company	67,500					
Investment in Z Company	43,200					
Other assets	35,700		62,000		44,000	
Accounts payable		$ 22,000		$ 5,000		$ 4,000
Other liabilities		6,000				1,000
Capital stock		100,000		50,000		40,000
Retained earnings (1/1)		40,000		10,000		5,000
Dividends declared	10,000		5,000		6,000	
Sales		78,000		40,000		30,000
Equity in subsidiary earnings		30,000				
Purchases	42,000		20,000		12,000	
Expenses	9,300		3,000		5,000	
	$276,000	$276,000	$105,000	$105,000	$80,000	$80,000
Inventory (12/31)	$ 10,000		$ 7,000		$ 5,000	

Additional Information:
1. P Company acquired 90 percent of the capital stock of Y Company on January 1, 19X1, for $54,000. On the same date, P Company acquired 80 percent of the capital stock of Z Company for $36,000.
2. On December 30, 19X1, P Company transferred $1,000 cash to Z Company in partial settlement of a $3,000 obligation, classified by P Company as "other liabilities." As of December 31, this transfer was not yet recorded by Z Company.
3. The sales of merchandise by Y Company to Z Company during 19X1 were $5,000 (ignore the question of unconfirmed, or unrealized, inventory profit).

sidiary cases. The elimination of intercompany sales is handled in accordance with the discussion in the preceding section, and produces amounts for consolidated sales and purchases that reflect transactions with outside parties. Finally, the "adjustment" is necessary to record on the books of Z Company the transfer of cash from P Company. Unlike eliminating "entries" which are not recorded on the books of any affiliate, but merely on the consolidated statement working paper, this adjustment would be recorded on the books of Z Company.

Reconsideration of Basic Definitions

In grappling with the various consolidated statement working paper techniques, one must be careful not to lose touch with the objectives of the process and the underlying definitions that guide our efforts. The objective is to combine the assets, liabilities, revenues and expenses of the affiliates such that the resulting consolidated financial statements reflect the activities and financial position of the group as if it were a single (economic) entity. In pursuit of this objective, the definitions of consolidated net income and consolidated retained earnings (see pp. 104–5) guide our pro-

Illustration 4-6

P COMPANY AND SUBSIDIARIES

Consolidated Statement Working Paper
For Year Ended December 31, 19X1

	P Company	Y Company	Z Company	Adjustments and Eliminations Dr.	Adjustments and Eliminations Cr.	Minority Interest Y Company	Minority Interest Z Company	Consolidated
Income Statement:								
Sales	78,000	40,000	30,000	(6) 5,000				143,000
Equity in subsidiary earnings	30,000			(1) 18,000 (3) 12,000				
Inventory (12/31)	10,000	7,000	5,000					22,000
Total credits	118,000	47,000	35,000					165,000
Inventory (1/1)	16,000	4,000	3,000					23,000
Purchases	42,000	20,000	12,000		(6) 5,000			69,000
Expenses	9,300	3,000	5,000					17,300
Total debits	67,300	27,000	20,000					109,300
	50,700	20,000	15,000					55,700
Minority interest in net income of:								
Y Company—10% of $20,000						2,000		[2,000]
Z Company—20% of $15,000							3,000	[3,000]
Net income—carried forward	50,700	20,000	15,000	35,000	5,000	2,000	3,000	50,700
Retained Earnings Statement:								
Retained earnings, January 1, 19X1								
P Company	40,000							40,000
Y Company		10,000		(2) 9,000		1,000		
Z Company			5,000	(4) 4,000			1,000	
Net income—brought forward	50,700	20,000	15,000	35,000	5,000	2,000	3,000	50,700
	90,700	30,000	20,000			3,000	4,000	90,700
Dividends declared:								
P Company	10,000							10,000
Y Company		5,000			(1) 4,500	500		
Z Company			6,000		(3) 4,800		1,200	
Retained earnings, December 31, 19X1—carried forward	80,700	25,000	14,000	48,000	14,300	2,500	2,800	80,700

Balance Sheet:

	P Company	Y Company	Z Company	Adjustments & Eliminations (Dr.)	Adjustments & Eliminations (Cr.)	Minority Interest	Consolidated
Cash	34,300	8,000	4,000	(a) 1,000			47,300
Accounts receivable	18,000	3,000	6,000		(a) 1,000 (5) 2,000		24,000
Inventory	10,000	7,000	5,000				22,000
Investment in Y Company	67,500				(1) 13,500 (2) 54,000		
Investment in Z Company	43,200				(3) 7,200 (4) 36,000		
Other assets	35,700	62,000	44,000				141,700
	208,700	80,000	59,000				235,000
Accounts payable	22,000	5,000	4,000				31,000
Other liabilities	6,000		1,000	(5) 2,000			5,000
Capital stock:							
P Company	100,000						100,000
Y Company		50,000		(2) 45,000		5,000	
Z Company		25,000	40,000	(4) 32,000		8,000	
Retained earnings—brought forward	80,700	25,000	14,000	14,300		2,500 / 2,800	80,700
Minority interest in Y Company						7,500	7,500 M
Minority interest in Z Company						10,800	10,800 M
	208,700	80,000	59,000	128,000	128,000		235,000

[deduction]

Explanation of adjustments and eliminations:

(a) Adjustment for unrecorded cash receipt by Z Company. (The obligation from P Company is assumed to be reflected in the accounts receivable of Z Company.)

(1) To reverse the parent company's entries during 19X1 for Y Company dividends and its interest in Y Company earnings.

(2) To eliminate the January 1, 19X1, investment (in Y Company) account balance against 90 percent of the corresponding stockholders' equity accounts of Y Company.

(3) To reverse the parent company's entries during 19X1 for Z Company dividends and its interest in Z Company earnings.

(4) To eliminate the January 1, 19X1, investment (in Z Company) account balance against 80 percent of the corresponding stockholders' equity accounts of Z Company.

(5) Elimination of intercompany debt.

(6) Elimination of intercompany sales.

cedural efforts. It is perhaps useful at this point to reconsider and elaborate upon these basic definitions in the context of the numerical data of Case 3.

Consolidated Net Income. Consolidated net income was previously defined as a residual value accruing to the majority shareholders, i.e., the shareholders of the parent company. This residual value is produced in the consolidated working paper by combining the revenues, expenses, gains, and losses of the affiliated companies after eliminating intercompany transactions and the parent's recorded equity in subsidiary earnings, and then deducting the amounts of minority interests in the net incomes of the subsidiaries. But consolidated net income can also be determined independent of the consolidated working paper by working only with the net income figures for the affiliates and certain key figures from the eliminating entries. This independent determination can be made using either of two schedular methods, which are labeled the *incremental approach* and the *residual approach.* Since these two methods embody in summary fashion the basic concepts underlying consolidated statement preparation, the authors believe special attention should be devoted to the discussion which follows. Additionally, frequent references to these analyses will be found in subsequent chapters.

Incremental Approach to Consolidated Net Income. Under this approach, consolidated net income is defined as the parent company's net income (loss) from its own operations, increased (decreased) by its equity in subsidiary net income (loss) for the period. In this definition, "net income from its own operations" should be interpreted to include all revenue and expense elements recognized by the parent company during the period *except* the recognition of its equity in subsidiary earnings. Using the data in Case 3, consolidated net income is determined under this approach as follows:

Parent company's net income from its own operations for 19X1 ($50,700 − $30,000)		$20,700
Increased by—		
Parent company's equity in subsidiaries' net income for 19X1:		
Equity in Y Company's net income (90% × $20,000)	$18,000	
Equity in Z Company's net income (80% × $15,000)	12,000	30,000
Consolidated net income for 19X1		$50,700

As expected, our schedular calculation of consolidated net income yields an amount that is equal to the parent's reported net income (under the equity method of accounting). Indeed, the schedule reveals why this equivalence must always result. The two components of the incremental definition of consolidated net income—(1) the parent's income from its own operations, and (2) the parent's equity in subsidiary net income— embody exactly all of the elements of revenue and expense that are recognized under the equity method of accounting. This particular schedular calculation is especially useful when the effects of confirmed and unconfirmed profits from certain types of intercompany transactions are examined in Chapters 7 and 8.

Residual Approach to Consolidated Net Income.   This method employs the same arithmetic processes found in the previously illustrated working papers. Yet attention in this schedule focuses only on those data which relate to the calculation of consolidated net income. The calculation begins with the addition of the *reported* net incomes of the several affiliates. From this sum of net incomes is deducted the *net* elimination in the income statement division of the consolidated working paper, i.e., the excess of debit eliminations over credit eliminations. The combined net income *remainder* represents the value of the total equity of all shareholders —both majority and minority. The separation of their interests is accomplished by first calculating the value claim of the minority shareholders. After deducting this value from the total equity, there remains the residual claim of the majority shareholders, or consolidated net income.

Using again the data in Case 3, consolidated net income is determined under this approach as follows:

P Company's net income for 19X1		$50,700
Y Company's net income for 19X1		20,000
Z Company's net income for 19X1		15,000
		$85,700
Less net debit elimination—P Company's recorded interest in subsidiary earnings		30,000
Total equity		$55,700
Less minority interest in subsidiary net income:		
Y Company (10% × $20,000)	$2,000	
Z Company (20% × $15,000)	3,000	5,000
Consolidated net income		$50,700

It should be noted that since the elimination of intercompany sales in Case 3 did not result in a *net* debit (or credit) elimination in the income statement division of the consolidated statement working paper, it is not included in this summary calculation of consolidated net income.

Consolidated Retained Earnings.   Consolidated retained earnings may be analyzed in a manner similar to that used to analyze consolidated net income. However, when the parent company uses the equity method of accounting, this analysis is generally not a productive venture. Therefore, we merely note again for possible computational convenience that consolidated retained earnings may be simply viewed as consolidated retained earnings at the beginning of the period, increased by consolidated net income, and reduced by the parent company's dividends declared. Applying this definition to the data of Case 3, and recalling that consolidated retained earnings at date of acquisition is equal to the parent company's retained earnings, the December 31, 19X1, consolidated retained earnings balance is calculated as follows:

Consolidated retained earnings, January 1, 19X1	$40,000
Consolidated net income for 19X1	50,700
	90,700
P Company dividends declared in 19X1	10,000
Consolidated retained earnings, December 31, 19X1	$80,700

APPENDIX: ILLUSTRATION OF CONSOLIDATED STATEMENT WORKING PAPER TECHNIQUES WHEN THE INVESTMENT ACCOUNT IS CARRIED UNDER THE COST METHOD

The consolidated statement techniques described in this and succeeding chapters *are based on the assumption that the investment account is carried under the equity method.* However, the following paragraphs illustrate briefly the mechanics of consolidation under the cost method. Recall that regardless which method is used by the parent company to account for its investment in the subsidiary, the consolidated financial statements will be the same in all respects. To emphasize this point, the data used for our two illustrations will reflect the same economic events as are assumed in Cases 1 and 2 in the main body of the chapter.

Consolidated Statement Working Paper—First Year Subsequent to Acquisition

Case A–1. It is assumed, as in Case 1, that P Company acquired 90 percent of the capital stock of S Company on January 1, 19X1, at a cost of $54,000. The trial balances for the two affiliates at December 31, 19X1, are as follows:

	P Company		S Company	
Cash	$ 29,500		$ 8,000	
Accounts receivable	18,000		3,000	
Inventory (1/1)	16,000		4,000	
Investment in S Company	54,000			
Other assets	73,000		62,000	
Accounts payable		$ 22,000		$ 5,000
Other liabilities		6,000		
Capital stock		100,000		50,000
Retained earnings (1/1)		40,000		10,000
Dividends declared	10,000		5,000	
Sales		78,000		40,000
Dividend income		4,500		
Purchases	42,000		20,000	
Expenses	8,000		3,000	
	$250,500	$250,500	$105,000	$105,000
Inventory (12/31)	$ 10,000		$ 7,000	

The account balances in this trial balance correspond exactly with the balances in Case 1 in the chapter, except for the income that has been recognized under the two different methods and the balance of the investment account.

Under the cost method, the parent company does not give formal accounting recognition to its equity in subsidiary earnings, and the balance of the investment account remains equal to the original cost of the investment. Therefore, the investment elimination entry at the end of the first year of operations is the same as it was at date of acquisition, i.e., it continues to relate to subsidiary net worth balances existing at date of acquisition. Thus, for our data, the investment elimination entry at December 31, 19X1, is:

Capital stock—S Company	45,000	
Retained earnings—S Company	9,000	
Investment in S Company		54,000

The parent company has recognized dividends declared by the subsidiary during the year as dividend income. Since the intercompany dividends are not properly included in a summation of the two companies' revenues, expenses, gains and losses arising from transactions *with outside parties* (as if the two companies were a single economic entity), the dividend income of the parent company must be eliminated against the dividends declared by the subsidiary. Thus, the second eliminating entry is:

Dividend income	4,500	
Dividends declared—S Company		4,500

The consolidated statement working paper for this case is shown in Illustration 4–7. A comparision of this working paper with the consolidated statement working paper in Illustration 4–2 will confirm the *identity of all amounts in the "consolidated" column.* Thus as was previously asserted, the choice between the cost and the equity methods of accounting for the investment on the books of the parent company does not affect th_____ in the consolidated statements. The choice does affect _____unts of income as well as the balance of the invest-_____parent company's books and in the *unconsolidated* _____f the parent company; this may be confirmed by _____mns of the two working papers.

Working Paper—Second Year
_____

_____or Case A–1 are modified to include the follow-

	P Company	S Company
....	$28,700	$28,000
....	15,000	10,000

Illustration 4–7

P COMPANY AND SUBSIDIARY S COMPANY
Consolidated Statement Working Paper
For Year Ended December 31, 19X1

	P Company	S Company	Eliminations Dr.	Eliminations Cr.	Minority Interest	Consolidated
Income Statement:						
Sales	78,000	40,000				118,000
Dividend income	4,500		(2) 4,500			
Inventory 12/31	10,000	7,000				17,000
Total credits	92,500	47,000				135,000
Inventory (1/1)	16,000	4,000				20,000
Purchases	42,000	20,000				62,000
Expenses	8,000	3,000				11,000
Total debits	66,000	27,000				93,000
	26,500	20,000				42,000
Minority interest in net income—S Company					2,000*	2,000
Net income—carried forward	26,500	20,000	4,500	–0–	2,000	40,000
Retained Earnings Statement						
Retained earnings, January 1, 19X1:						
P Company	40,000					40,000
S Company		10,000	(1) 9,000		1,000†	
Net income—brought forward	26,500	20,000	4,500		2,000	40,000
	66,500	30,000			3,000	80,000
Dividends declared:						
P Company	10,000					10,000
S Company		5,000		(2) 4,500	500‡	
Retained earnings, December 31, 19X1—carried forward	56,500	25,000	13,500	4,500	2,500	70,000

Balance Sheet:

	P Company	S Company	Eliminations Dr.	Eliminations Cr.	Minority Interest	Consolidated
Cash	29,500	8,000				37,500
Accounts receivable	18,000	3,000				21,000
Merchandise inventory	10,000	7,000				17,000
Investment in S Company	54,000			(1) 54,000		
Other assets	73,000	62,000				135,000
	184,500	80,000				210,500
Accounts payable	22,000	5,000				27,000
Other liabilities	6,000					6,000
Capital stock:						
P Company	100,000					100,000
S Company		50,000	(1) 45,000		5,000§	
Retained earnings—brought forward	56,500	25,000	13,500	4,500	2,500	70,000
Minority interest in S Company					7,500	7,500 M
	184,500	80,000	65,500	65,500		210,500

Explanation of eliminations:

  (1) Elimination of investment in subsidiary stock.

  (2) Elimination of intercompany dividends.

Explanation of minority interest calculations:

  * 10% × $20,000.

  † 10% × $10,000.

  ‡ 10% × $5,000.

  § 10% × $50,000.

Note that P Company's net income again differs from that shown in Case 2 in the chapter because the parent company is recognizing income from S Company's operations on the basis of dividends declared by S Company during 19X2, not income reported by S Company for 19X2.

The eliminating entries for this example are as follows:

1. To eliminate the investment account against the parent's equity in the balances of the stockholders' equity accounts of the subsidiary *as of the date of acquisition:*

    Capital stock—S Company 45,000
    Retained earnings—S Company 9,000
        Investment in S Company   54,000

2. To eliminate intercompany dividend income of the parent against dividends declared by the subsidiary:

    Dividend income 9,000
        Dividends declared—S Company   9,000

Note that again the investment elimination entry relates to subsidiary net worth balances existing at date of acquisition. This relationship will continue to hold in succeeding years as long as the investment account balance remains equal to the original acquisition cost and there are no realignments of the subsidiary's equity components. The interested reader is referred to the prior edition of this book for illustrations of necessary modifications when such changes occur.[3]

The consolidated statement working paper for this case is shown in Illustration 4–8. Note that the income statement and balance sheet divisions of the consolidated statement working paper for periods subsequent to the first year after acquisition of subsidiary stock are essentially the same in respect to details of format, eliminations, and extensions, as in the working paper for the year of acquisition. However, one significant difference should be noted in respect to the retained earnings division. The previous illustration clearly indicated that the amount of subsidiary retained earnings at acquisition is partially eliminated with the residual amount extended to the minority interest column. In the consolidated statement working papers of subsequent years, however, it is necessary to recognize the parent company's equity in the *changes* in a subsidiary's retained earnings from the date of acquistion to the beginning of the current year. Under the equity method, this equity is reflected in the retained earnings of the parent company as a consequence of the entries to record it in prior years. Under the cost method, recognition of the equity in the "changes" (undistributed earnings from date of acquisition to the beginning of the current year) is accomplished by extending to the "con-

---

[3] Griffin, Williams, and Larson, *Advanced Accounting,* rev. ed. (Richard D. Irwin, Inc., 1971) chapters 11 and 14.

Illustration 4–8

P COMPANY AND SUBSIDIARY S COMPANY

Consolidated Statement Working Paper
For Year Ended December 31, 19X2

	P Company	S Company	Eliminations Dr.	Eliminations Cr.	Minority Interest	Consolidated
Income Statement:						
Sales	96,000	63,000				159,000
Dividend income	9,000		(2) 9,000			–0–
Inventory (12/31)	14,200	9,200				23,400
Total credits	119,200	72,200				182,400
Inventory (1/1)	10,000	7,000				17,000
Purchases	58,000	29,100				87,100
Expenses	22,500	8,100				30,600
Total debits	90,500	44,200				134,700
	28,700	28,000				47,700
Minority interest in net income—S Company					2,800*	2,800
Net income—carried forward	28,700	28,000	9,000	–0–	2,800	44,900
Retained Earnings Statement:						
Retained earnings, January 1, 19X2:						
P Company	56,500					56,500
S Company		25,000	(1) 9,000		2,500†	13,500
Net income—brought forward	28,700	28,000	9,000	–0–	2,800	44,900
	85,200	53,000			5,300	114,900
Dividends declared:						
P Company	15,000					15,000
S Company		10,000		(2) 9,000	1,000‡	
Retained earnings, December 31, 19X2— carried forward	70,200	43,000	18,000	9,000	4,300	99,900
Balance Sheet:						
Cash	31,000	12,000				43,000
Accounts receivable	22,000	19,000				41,000
Inventory	14,200	9,200				23,400
Investment in S Company	54,000			(1) 54,000		–0–
Other assets	83,000	64,300				147,300
	204,200	104,500				254,700
Accounts payable	30,000	9,000				39,000
Other liabilities	4,000	2,500				6,500
Capital stock:						
P Company	100,000					100,000
S Company		50,000	(1) 45,000		5,000§	
Retained earnings— brought forward	70,200	43,000	18,000	9,000	4,300	99,900
Minority interest in S Company					9,300	9,300 M
	204,200	104,500	63,000	63,000		254,700

Explanation of eliminations:
(1) Elimination of investment in subsidiary stock.
(2) Elimination of intercompany dividends.

Explanation of minority interest calculations:
* 10% × $28,000. ‡ 10% × $10,000.
† 10% × $25,000. § 10% × $50,000.

solidated" column of the retained earnings working paper division that part of a subsidiary's retained earnings at the beginning of the year which is neither eliminated as "purchased" retained earnings nor extended to the "minority interest" column. Thus, the amount of retained earnings of S Company on January 1, 19X2, to be extended, $16,000 ($25,000 balance less $9,000 eliminated as "purchased" retained earnings), is allocated $2,500 to minority shareholders and $13,500 to the majority shareholders. The minority interest is 10 percent of the subsidiary's January 1, 19X2, retained earnings balance, i.e., 10 percent of $25,000, or $2,500; the majority interest is 90 percent of the *undistributed* subsidiary earnings from the date of acquisition to the *beginning* of the current period, i.e., 90 percent of ($25,000 − $10,000), or $13,500.

With these minor modifications in working paper techniques, the resulting balances in the "consolidated" column of Illustration 4–8 are again identical to the amounts reflected in the "consolidated" column in Illustration 4–4.

QUESTIONS

1. Suggest two variables which complicate the preparation of consolidated financial statements when the statements are prepared subsequent to the date of a subsidiary's acquisition by a parent.

2. In respect to subsidiary shareholdings, what are the basic accounting differences between a parent company which uses the equity method and one which uses the cost method?

3. How does the realization criterion underlying the equity method differ from that underlying the cost method?

4. What differences exist in the consolidated financial statements where the equity method is used instead of the cost method?

5. Is the cost or equity method preferred as a method of accounting for investments in subsidiaries?

6. What statements are generally included in the "family" of consolidated reports?

7. Indicate two alternative approaches to defining "consolidated net income."

8. What is the composition of the consolidated retained earnings statement?

9. When using the three-division horizontal working paper, do the "debits equal the credits" in *each* of the three sections of the "eliminations" columns? If so, why? If not, why not?

10. How is the minority interest in a subsidiary's net income calculated? Is this amount added to or subtracted from the combined net incomes of the affiliates in order to determine "consolidated net income"?

11. For a company using the equity method, describe the relationship between the parent company's net income and the consolidated net income; and between the parent company's retained earnings balance and the consolidated retained earnings balance.

12. How are the elements of the investment elimination entry, eliminating the investment account against the stockholders' equity accounts of the subsidiary, determined under the equity method?

13. For an investment carried under the equity method, what is the relationship between the investment account balance and the net assets of the subsidiary at any point in time?

14. Enumerate five types of intercompany transactions which generate elimination entries in the consolidation process.

15. Define consolidated net income using the incremental approach.

EXERCISES

Exercise 4–1

On January 1, 19X1, Elizabeth Company acquired an 80 percent interest in Thomas Company at a cost of $72,000. On this date, Thomas Company had capital stock of $50,000 and retained earnings of $40,000.

During 19X1, Thomas Company reported net income of $20,000, and paid cash dividends of $5,000.

Required:

a. Prepare all entries on the books of Elizabeth Company in 19X1 related to its investment in Thomas Company under (1) the cost method and (2) the equity method.

b. Assuming Elizabeth Company uses the equity method of accounting for its investment, prepare the investment elimination entries for a consolidated statement working paper on December 31, 19X1.

Exercise 4–2

Little Bit Company acquired a 70 percent interest in Crunch Company on January 1, 19X1 at a cost of $35,000. On this date, Crunch Company had capital stock of $10,000 and retained earnings of $40,000.

During 19X1 and 19X2, Crunch Company reports net income of $20,000 per year, and pays cash dividends of $5,000 each year.

Little Bit Company uses the equity method of accounting for its investment in Crunch Company.

Required:

a. Determine the balance of the investment account on December 31, 19X1, and December 31, 19X2.

b. Prepare the investment elimination entries for a consolidated statement working paper on December 31, 19X1, and December 31, 19X2.

Exercise 4–3

On January 1, 19X1, Quittmeyer Company acquired a 90 percent interest in Todd Company at a cost of $90,000. On this date, Todd Company had capital stock of $30,000 and retained earnings of $70,000.

During 19X1, Todd Company reports net income of $40,000 and pays a cash dividend of $10,000. During 19X2, Todd Company reports a net loss of $10,000 and pays a cash dividend of $5,000.

Quittmeyer Company uses the equity method of accounting for its investment in Todd Company.

Required:

a. Prepare the entries on Quittmeyer Company's books in 19X1 and 19X2 related to its investment in Todd Company.
b. Prepare the investment elimination entries for a consolidated statement working paper on December 31, 19X1, and December 31, 19X2.

Exercise 4–4

On January 1, 19X1, Vashik Company acquired a 60 percent interest in CPW Company at a cost of $24,000. On this date, CPW Company had capital stock of $10,000 and retained earnings of $30,000.

During 19X1 and 19X2, CPW Company reports net income of $15,000 each year, and pays cash dividends of $10,000 each year.

Vashik Company uses the equity method of accounting for its investment in CPW Company.

Required:

a. Determine the balance of the investment account on December 31, 19X1, and December 31, 19X2.
b. Prepare the investment elimination entries for a consolidated statement working paper on December 31, 19X1, and December 31, 19X2.
c. Calculate the value of the minority interest in CPW Company on December 31, 19X1, and December 31, 19X2.

Exercise 4–5

Snyder Company has an 80 percent interest in Holland Company, purchased in 19X1 at a cost equal to 80 percent of the book value of Holland's recorded net assets.

During 19X5, Snyder Company recorded the following entries:

(1) Investment in Holland Company 16,000
          Equity in subsidiary earnings   16,000

(2) Cash 4,000
          Investment in Holland Company   4,000

At December 31, 19X5, Holland Company reported capital stock of $50,000 and retained earnings of $100,000 (including 19X5 income and dividends).

Snyder Company uses the equity method of accounting for its investment in Holland Company.

Required:

a. Determine the balance of the investment account on December 31, 19X5.
b. Calculate the value of the minority interest in net income for 19X5, and the total value of the minority interest in Holland Company at December 31, 19X5.

c. Prepare the investment elimination entries for a consolidated statement working paper on December 31, 19X5.

Exercise 4-6

P Company purchased the following investments on January 1, 19X1:

90 percent of the capital stock of Y Company, cost $135,000
80 percent of the capital stock of Z Company, cost $56,000
60 percent of the capital stock of W Company, cost $30,000

Additional data concerning these companies are:

	P Company	Y Company	Z Company	W Company
Capital stock (par value, $100)	$200,000	$100,000	$50,000	$40,000
Retained earnings, January 1, 19X1	100,000	50,000	20,000	10,000
Net income [loss], 19X1	79,000	40,000	20,000	[5,000]
Cash dividends, 19X1	10,000	5,000	4,000	

P Company carries its investment in subsidiaries on an equity basis; it reported a profit from its own operations in 19X1 of $30,000.

Required:

a. Prepare journal entries for 19X1 on the books of P Company reflecting its transactions with, or interest in, subsidiary companies.
b. Calculate the amount of consolidated net income for 19X1 and the balance of consolidated retained earnings as of December 31, 19X1.
c. Calculate the amount of minority interest in the 19X1 net income [loss] and the December 31, 19X1, retained earnings of subsidiary companies.

Exercise 4-7

The following data relate to companies M, G, and R for the two-year period ending December 31, 19X1:

	M Company	G Company	R Company
Capital stock ($100 par)	$200,000	$100,000	$50,000
Other contributed capital	20,000	3,500	1,000
Retained earnings [deficit], January 1, 19X0	250,000	40,000	[20,000]
Net income (excluding equity in subsidiary profits):			
19X0	90,000	60,000	30,000
19X1	75,000	40,000	40,000
Dividends paid:			
19X0	20,000	4,000	
19X1	20,000	10,000	5,000

In each of the following independent cases, investments in subsidiary stock are carried by the parent on an equity basis. Assume any resulting differential is allocated to land.

Case 1:   M Company purchased 90 percent of the capital stock of G Company on January 1, 19X0, for $130,000.

Case 2:   G Company purchased 60 percent of the capital stock of R Company on January 1, 19X0, for $20,000.

Case 3:   M Company purchased 80 percent of the capital stock of G Company on January 1, 19X1, for $164,000.

Case 4:   M Company purchased 70 percent of the capital stock of R Company on January 1, 19X0, for $20,000 and 60 percent of the capital stock of G Company on January 1, 19X1, for $125,000.

Required:

In each of the above cases:
a.   Calculate the balance of the investment account on December 31, 19X1.
b.   Calculate the amount of consolidated net income for 19X0 and 19X1, and the balance of consolidated retained earnings on December 31, 19X1.

Exercise 4–8

Clark Motor Transit purchased in the open market 75 percent of the capital stock of Sachs and Ward, Inc., on January 1, 19X1, at $14,000 more than 75 percent of its book value. The entire differential is allocable to land. During the following five years, Sachs and Ward, Inc., reported cumulative earnings of $235,000 and paid $45,000 in dividends. On January 1, 19X6, minority share-holders in Sachs and Ward, Inc., have an equity of $57,500 in the net assets of the company.

Required:

If the parent company carries its investment in subsidiary stock on an equity basis—
a.   Determine the January 1, 19X1, cost of the investment, and
b.   Calculate the investment carrying value on December 31, 19X5.

Exercise 4–9

Ashton Corporation has an 80 percent interest in Hubbard Household Equipment Company. During 19X1, Hubbard reported net income of $20,000, and in 19X2, Hubbard reported a loss of $10,000. Ashton had net income from its own operations of $50,000 each year.

Required:

Calculate consolidated net income for 19X1 and 19X2.

Exercise 4–10

P Company purchased a 90 percent interest in S Company on January 1, 19X1. You are given the following information regarding the companies' earnings and dividends:

	P Company	S Company
Retained earnings, December 31, 19X0	$100,000	$50,000
Net incomes from own operations:		
19X1	20,000	15,000
19X2	30,000	20,000
Dividends declared and paid:		
19X1	10,000	5,000
19X2	15,000	5,000

Required:

a. Using the incremental approach, calculate consolidated net income for 19X1 and 19X2.
b. Using the residual approach, calculate consolidated net income for 19X1 and 19X2.
c. Compute consolidated retained earnings as of December 31, 19X1, and December 31, 19X2.

Exercise 4–11

A Company purchased 80 percent of the capital stock of B Company on January 1, 19X0, and 90 percent of the capital stock of C Company on January 1, 19X1.

The following two-year operating summary relates to the affiliated companies:

	A Company	B Company	C Company
Retained earnings, January 1, 19X0	$70,000	$40,000	$35,000
19X0 net income from own			
operations	40,000	20,000	30,000
19X0 cash dividends		10,000	5,000
19X1 net income from own			
operations	10,000	15,000	20,000
19X1 cash dividends	4,000	6,000	10,000

Required:

a. Using the incremental approach, calculate consolidated net income for 19X0 and 19X1.
b. Using the residual approach, calculate consolidated net income for 19X0 and 19X1.
c. Calculate consolidated retained earnings as of December 31, 19X0, and December 31, 19X1.

Exercise 4–12

P Company acquired a 90 percent interest in the capital stock of Y Company on January 1, 19X1, and an 80 percent interest in the capital stock of Z Company on the same day. You are given the following information regarding the companies' earnings and dividends:

	P Company	Y Company	Z Company
Retained earnings, January 1, 19X1	$40,000	$30,000	$15,000
Net incomes (loss) from own operations:			
19X1	13,200	8,000	(5,000)
19X2	8,400	4,000	7,000
Dividends declared and paid:			
19X1	5,000	2,000	
19X2			2,000

Required:

a. Calculate consolidated net income for 19X1 and 19X2.
b. Calculate consolidated retained earnings on December 31, 19X1, and December 31, 19X2.

PROBLEMS

Problem 1

The Hanna Company purchased 80 percent of the capital stock of the Taylor Corporation on January 1, 19X1, for $48,000, when the latter's capital stock and retained earnings were $50,000 and $10,000 respectively. Trial balances prepared on December 31, 19X1, disclose the following:

	December 31, 19X1	
	Hanna Company	*Taylor Corporation*
Cash	$ 8,000	$ 5,000
Accounts receivable	21,000	17,000
Inventory—January 1	15,000	8,000
Investment in Taylor Corporation stock	56,000	
Other assets	57,000	48,000
Dividends declared	10,000	5,000
Purchases	90,000	20,000
Expenses	10,000	7,000
	$267,000	$110,000
Accounts payable	$ 5,000	$ 6,000
Advances from Hanna		4,000
Other liabilities	5,000	
Capital stock (par $100)	100,000	50,000
Retained earnings	40,000	10,000
Sales	105,000	40,000
Equity in subsidiary earnings	12,000	
	$267,000	$110,000
Inventory—December 31	$ 20,000	$ 10,000

Required:

a. Prepare a consolidated statement working paper for the year ended December 31, 19X1.
b. Prepare formal consolidated statements.

Problem 2

The Parnelli Company purchased 750 shares of the capital stock of the Foyt Company on January 1, 19X1, for $90,000. One year later, the following trial balances are prepared:

	Parnelli Company	Foyt Company
Cash	$ 14,000	$ 23,000
Inventory, December 31	45,000	30,000
Investment in Foyt Company	97,500	
Other assets	122,500	80,000
Cost of goods sold	87,000	65,000
Expenses	14,000	16,000
Dividends declared	20,000	10,000
	$400,000	$224,000
Accounts payable	$ 9,000	
Dividends payable		$ 10,000
Other liabilities	1,500	3,000
Capital stock ($100 par)	200,000	100,000
Retained earnings	64,000	20,000
Sales	118,000	91,000
Equity in subsidiary earnings	7,500	
	$400,000	$224,000

Required:

Prepare a consolidated statement working paper for the year ended December 31, 19X1.

Problem 3

The Cruse Company purchased 80 percent of the capital stock of Summers, Inc., on January 1, 19X1, for $49,600. One year thereafter trial balances of the respective companies were:

	December 31, 19X1	
	Cruse Company	Summers, Inc.
Cash	$ 22,000	$ 12,500
Accounts receivable	5,000	2,000
Inventory, January 1	28,000	11,000
Investment in Summers, Inc.	68,000	
Other assets	59,400	80,500
Dividends declared	8,500	5,000
Purchases	161,000	83,000
Freight-in	1,000	200
Selling expenses	18,000	11,100
Administrative expenses	9,300	5,700
	$380,200	$211,000

	December 31, 19X1	
	Cruse Company	Summers, Inc.
Accounts payable	$ 18,000	$ 12,000
Other liabilities	3,000	16,000
Capital stock (par, $100)	100,000	50,000
Retained earnings	31,000	12,000
Sales	205,000	121,000
Equity in subdiary earnings	22,400	
Interest income	800	
	$380,200	$211,000
Inventory, December 31	$ 41,000	$ 18,000

The accounts payable of Summers, Inc. include $3,000 payable to Cruse Company.

Required:

Prepare a three-division consolidated statement working paper for the year ended December 31, 19X1.

Problem 4

The Bransford Company purchased an 80 percent interest in the Strandberg Company in 19X1 at a cost equal to the acquired interest in Strandberg's net assets. On December 31, 19X5, the companies prepare the following trial balances:

	Bransford Company	Strandberg Company
Cash	$ 14,000	$ 23,000
Inventory, December 31	45,000	30,000
Investment in Strandberg Company	104,000	
Other assets	127,500	80,000
Cost of goods sold	87,000	65,000
Expenses	14,000	16,000
Dividends declared	20,000	10,000
	$411,500	$224,000
Accounts payable	$ 13,500	$ 3,000
Capital stock ($100 par)	200,000	100,000
Retained earnings	64,000	20,000
Sales	118,000	101,000
Equity in subsidiary earnings	16,000	
	$411,500	$224,000

Required:

Prepare a three-division consolidated statement working paper for the year ended December 31, 19X5.

PROBLEMS FOR APPENDIX

Problem 5–A

On January 1, 19X1, the Central Company purchased 80 percent of the capital stock of the Western Company for $48,000. On December 31, 19X1, their trial balances are as follows:

	Central Company	Western Company
Cash	$ 8,000	$ 5,000
Accounts receivable	21,000	17,000
Inventory—January 1	15,000	8,000
Investment in Western Company capital stock	48,000	
Other assets	57,000	48,000
Dividends declared	10,000	5,000
Purchases	90,000	20,000
Expenses	10,000	7,000
	$259,000	$110,000
Accounts payable	$ 5,000	$ 6,000
Other liabilities	5,000	
Advances from Central		4,000
Capital stock (par, $100)	100,000	50,000
Retained earnings	40,000	10,000
Sales	105,000	40,000
Dividend income	4,000	
	$259,000	$110,000
Inventory—December 31	$ 20,000	$ 10,000

Central Company uses the *cost* method of accounting for its investment in Western Company.

Required:

On December 31, 19X1, prepare consolidated statements supported by a three-division working paper.

Problem 6–A

The Cruse Company purchased 80 percent of the capital stock of Summers, Inc., on January 1, 19X1, for $49,600. One year thereafter trial balances of the respective companies were:

| | December 31, 19X1 | |
	Cruse Company	Summers, Inc.
Cash	$ 22,000	$ 12,500
Accounts receivable	5,000	2,000
Inventory, January 1	28,000	11,000
Investment in Summers, Inc.	49,600	
Other assets	59,400	80,500
Dividends declared	8,500	5,000
Purchases	161,000	83,000
Freight-in	1,000	200
Selling expenses	18,000	11,100
Administrative expenses	9,300	5,700
	$361,800	$211,000
Accounts payable	$ 18,000	$ 12,000
Other liabilities	3,000	16,000
Capital stock (par, $100)	100,000	50,000
Retained earnings	31,000	12,000
Sales	205,000	121,000
Dividend income	4,000	
Interest income	800	
	$361,800	$211,000
Inventory, December 31	$ 41,000	$ 18,000

The accounts payable of Summers, Inc., include $3,000 payable to the Cruse Company.

The Cruse Company uses the *cost* method of accounting for its investment in Summers, Inc.

Required:

Prepare a three-division consolidated statement working paper for the year ended December 31, 19X1.

Problem 7–A

On January 1, 19X0, the Belt Company purchased in the open market 90 percent of the capital stock of the Kaplan Company for $135,000 *and* 70 percent of the capital stock of the Baxter Company for $28,000. On this date the following account balances of Kaplan and Baxter were:

	Kaplan	Baxter
Capital stock (par, $100)	$100,000	$50,000
Retained earnings [deficit]	50,000	[10,000]

A summary of changes in retained earnings for 19X1 is as follows:

	Belt	Kaplan	Baxter
Retained earnings, January 1	$100,000	$60,000	$20,000
Net income, 19X1	40,000	25,000	10,000
Dividends paid, 19X1	5,000	8,000	4,000

Required:

If the investments in subsidiary stock are carried at cost—

a. Prepare on December 31, 19X1, an investment elimination entry for a consolidated statement working paper.

b. Prepare a consolidated retained earnings working paper for the year ended December 31, 19X1.

Problem 8–A

A summary of the changes in the stockholders' equity of the Dial Company and the Landry Company for the two-year period ending December 31, 19X1, is given following:

	Dial Company	Landry Company
Capital stock (no-par value), January 1, 19X0:		
Dial Company (20,000 shares)	$120,000	
Landry Company (10,000 shares)		$80,000
Retained earnings, January 1, 19X0	$ 60,000	$40,000
Net income, 19X0	30,000	24,000
	$ 90,000	$64,000
Dividends paid (cash), November 15, 19X0	10,000	8,000
Retained earnings, December 31, 19X0	$ 80,000	$56,000
Net income [loss], 19X1	18,000	[4,000]
	$ 98,000	$52,000
Dividends paid (cash), December 15, 19X1	6,000	10,000
Retained earnings, December 31, 19X1	$ 92,000	$42,000

Dunham, Inc., purchased in the open market the following:

a. 8,000 shares of Landry Company stock on January 1, 19X0, at a cost of $96,000.

b. 18,000 shares of Dial Company stock on January 1, 19X1, at a cost of $180,000.

Dunham uses the cost method of accounting for its investment in Landry and Dial. During 19X0 and 19X1, the only source of income for Dunham was subsidiary dividends. On December 31, 19X1, Dunham had retained earnings, exclusive of dividend income, of $50,000.

Required:

a. Prepare an investment elimination entry for a consolidated statement working paper, December 31, 19X1.

b. Prepare a consolidated retained earnings statement working paper for the year ended December 31, 19X1.

5

Consolidated Financial Reports—Postacquisition (continued)

Treatment of Differentials Subsequent to Date of Acquisition

THE PRINCIPLES underlying the allocation of the differential to specific assets and liabilities at the date of acquisition were described in Chapter 3. Once allocated, however, there remains the problem of the differential's subsequent disposition.

The basic principle applicable to the allocated differential amounts is to account for them consistent with the accounting for the particular asset (or liability) to which they were assigned. Thus, amounts allocated to accounts whose balances are not normally subject to systematic amortization (e.g., land) will continue to be reported at the same, originally allocated values. Amounts allocated to accounts whose balances are expensed or periodically amortized will be accorded similar treatment in consolidated financial statements.

The reader will recall that an unallocated debit differential is classified as goodwill. This value, like the values of all intangible assets, should be amortized on the basis of the estimated life of the specific asset (in this case, goodwill). It should not be written off in the period of acquisition. Admittedly, it is often difficult to estimate the life of goodwill. But the value of the goodwill will almost inevitably become zero at some future date. In view of this potential dilemma, the Accounting Principles Board set an arbitrary maximum life of 40 years for the amortization of goodwill. Generally, straight-line amortization should be applied. It might be noted that this amortization of goodwill does not create a timing difference for income tax allocation purposes, and thus tax allocation is inappropriate.[1]

---

[1] *APB Opinion 17,* "Intangible Assets," paragraphs 23–30.

An unallocated credit differential (after the specified reallocation to noncurrent assets) should similarly be amortized systematically to income over the period of time estimated to benefit therefrom, but not to exceed 40 years. No part of this deferred credit should be added directly to stockholders' equity at the date of acquisition.[2]

Application of these principles at the end of an accounting period will generally result in a set of expense adjustments, the total of which is referred to as the *amortization of the differential for the period* (or sometimes simply *differential amortization*).

Since a differential is part of the cost incurred by the parent company, the amortization of this cost is allocated wholly to the majority shareholders. The values of the interests of minority shareholders are calculated, as before, on the basis of accumulations recorded in the subsidiary's equity accounts.

In addition to recognizing the differential amortization in the consolidated statement working paper, the parent company must also recognize this expense on its books. *APB Opinion 18* states in this regard: "The difference between consolidation and the equity method lies in the details reported in the financial statements. Thus, an investor's net income for the period and its stockholders' equity at the end of the period are the same whether an investment in a subsidiary is accounted for under the equity method or the subsidiary is consolidated. . . ."[3] Accordingly, at the same time that the parent records its equity in subsidiary earnings for the period, an additional entry must be made to record the amortization of the differential for the period.

The specific accounting procedures that are employed to reflect the differential amortization are illustrated in two integrated case examples which follow. The first case deals with the period of acquisition, and the second case considers the period subsequent to acquisition. Each example illustrates both the eliminating entries required for the preparation of a consolidated statement working paper and the formal journal entries recorded on the books of the parent company.

Case 1.   Amortization of Differential—Period of Acquisition.   On January 1, 19X1, P Company purchased an 80 percent interest in S Company for $300,000. On this date, S Company had capital stock of $50,000 and retained earnings of $120,000.

Assume that an examination of S Company's identifiable assets and liabilities revealed that all were recorded at amounts which approximated their fair values except the following assets which are shown in the accompanying illustration.

---

[2] *APB Opinion 16*, "Business Combinations," paragraphs 91–92.

[3] *APB Opinion 18*, "The Equity Method of Accounting for Investments in Common Stock," paragraph 19.

	Book Value	Fair Value	Excess of Fair Value over Book Value	P Company's 80% Interest in Excess
Inventory	$ 20,000	$ 25,000	$ 5,000	$ 4,000
Plant and equipment (net)	80,000	155,000	75,000	60,000
Land	40,000	65,000	25,000	20,000
	$140,000	$245,000	$105,000	$84,000

The inventory on hand on January 1, 19X1, is sold during the current year, and the plant and equipment has an expected remaining life of 10 years. The land is not amortized. P Company plans to amortize any goodwill acquired in the combination over the maximum period of 40 years.

Assume further that S Company reported net income of $50,000 for the year ended December 31, 19X1, and paid $12,500 cash dividends during the year.

The differential generated by this acquisition may be easily determined:

Investment cost	$300,000
P Company's equity in recorded net assets of S Company (80% × $170,000)	136,000
Differential	$164,000

Since the investment cost exceeds the parent's quity in recorded net assets of the subsidiary, the differential is a debit differential. Based upon the examination of the identifiable assets and liabilities of S Company, $84,000 of the differential will be allocated to the three specific assets. The remaining unallocated debit differential of $80,000 will be classified as goodwill in the consolidated statements.

Each allocated portion of the differential is amortized in accordance with the accounting for the asset to which it is assigned. The goodwill requires, of course, an independent assessment of expected useful life. A schedule of differential amortization is presented in Illustration 5–1.

Illustration 5–1

SCHEDULE OF DIFFERENTIAL AMORTIZATION

	Allocated Amount	Annual Amortization		
		Year 1	Years 2–10	Years 11–40
Inventory	$ 4,000	$ 4,000	$ –0–	$ –0–
Plant and equipment (net)	60,000	6,000	6,000	–0–
Land	20,000	–0–	–0–	–0–
Goodwill	80,000	2,000	2,000	2,000
	$164,000	$12,000	$8,000	$2,000

Parent Company Entries—Year 1. Based upon the information presented in the case and the schedule of differential amortization developed in Illustration 5–1, the parent company would make the following entries during 19X1:

1. To record receipt of dividends from S Company:

Cash (80% × $12,500) 10,000
  Investment in S Company 10,000

2. To recognize equity in S Company's reported earnings:

Investment in S Company 40,000
  Equity in subsidiary earnings (80% × $50,000) 40,000

3. To recognize differential amortization for the period (see Illustration 5–1):

Equity in subsidiary earnings 12,000
  Investment in S Company 12,000

Amortization of the differential for the period is charged against the parent company's equity in reported subsidiary earnings because the differential represents the portion of the total investment cost that has not (implicitly) been taken into account in the calculation of subsidiary net income. On the other hand, the remaining portion of the investment cost (i.e., total cost less the differential) corresponds to the parent's equity in the subsidiary's reported net assets at date of acquisition, and is (implicitly) given recognition in the measurement of subsidiary net income through the subsidiary's normal expense recognition procedures.

Eliminating Entries—Year 1. The investment elimination entries for the consolidated statement working paper at the end of 19X1 are:

1. To reverse the entries recorded by the parent company during 19X1 (substituting, as before, Dividends Declared for Cash):

(*a*) Investment in S Company 10,000
      Dividends declared—S Company 10,000

(*b*) Equity in subsidiary earnings 40,000
      Investment in S Company 40,000

(*c*) Investment in S Company 12,000
      Equity in subsidiary earnings 12,000

2. To eliminate January 1, 19X1, investment account balance of P Company against the January 1, 19X1, balances of the stockholders' equity accounts of S Company:

Capital stock—S Company (80% × $50,000) 40,000
Retained earnings—S Company (80% × $120,000) 96,000
Differential 164,000
  Investment in S Company 300,000

Eliminating entries (1*a*), (1*b*), and (1*c*) restore the investment account to its balance at the start of the period. Then this investment account balance is eliminated against the balances in S Company's stockholders' equity accounts at the beginning of the period. As one acquires more proficiency in making these eliminations, it is of course more efficient to compound the three "reversal" entries into a single entry.

As a consequence of these investment elimination entries, the differential as of January1, 19X1, is set up in the consolidated statement working paper. This differential amount must be allocated as appropriate on January 1, 19X1, and the allocated amounts then amortized for the year. The eliminating entries for these two steps are presented following:

3. To allocate the differential as of January 1, 19X1 (see Illustration 5–1):

        Inventory (1/1) 4,000
        Plant and equipment (net) 60,000
        Land 20,000
        Goodwill 80,000
            Differential   164,000

4. To amortize the allocated amounts for 19X1 (see Illustration 5–1):

        Expenses 8,000
            Plant and equipment (net)   6,000
            Goodwill   2,000

Note that it is not necessary to make a specific amortization entry for the amount of the differential allocated to inventory because the beginning inventory is included in the income statement section of the consolidated statement working paper. Additionally, if a more detailed breakdown of expenses is desired, eliminating entry (4) may be modified to separately identify Depreciation Expense ($6,000) and Amortization of Goodwill ($2,000) in lieu of the single charge of $8,000 to Expenses.

These eliminating entries are reflected in the consolidated statement working paper for the year ended December 31, 19X1, in Illustration 5–2. The balances in the working paper are arbitrarily chosen, except where it is required that they correspond with data previously presented in this example.

Inspection of the working paper in Illustration 5–2 reveals that consolidated net income (and retained earnings) equals the parent company's net income (and retained earnings). Since the differential amortization was consistently applied both in the working paper and on the parent company's books, we would expect this equivalence to continue. Indeed, as previously noted, *APB Opinion 18* defines the equity method so as to achieve equivalence.

Refinement of Definitions of Consolidated Net Income. Recognition of differential amortization necessitates a refinement of the definition of consolidated net income. Under the incremental approach, consolidated net income is redefined as follows: *Parent company's net income from its own operations, increased (decreased) by its equity in the sub-*

Illustration 5–2

P COMPANY AND SUBSIDIARY S COMPANY

Consolidated Statement Working Paper
For Year Ended December 31, 19X1

	P Company	S Company	Eliminations		Minority Interest	Consolidated
			Dr.	Cr.		
Income Statement:						
Sales	520,000	290,000				810,000
Equity in subsidiary earnings	28,000		(1b) 40,000	(1c) 12,000		—
Inventory (12/31)	82,000	30,000				112,000
Total credits	630,000	320,000				922,000
Inventory (1/1)	90,000	20,000	(3) 4,000			114,000
Purchases	250,000	150,000				400,000
Expenses	160,000	100,000	(4) 8,000			268,000
Total debits	500,000	270,000				782,000
Net income	130,000	50,000				140,000
Minority interest in net income—S Company					10,000	10,000
Net income—carried forward	130,000	50,000	52,000	12,000	10,000	130,000
Retained Earnings Statement:						
Retained earnings, January 1, 19X1:						
P Company	410,000					410,000
S Company		120,000	(2) 96,000		24,000	—
Net income—brought forward	130,000	50,000	52,000	12,000	10,000	130,000
	540,000	170,000			34,000	540,000
Dividends declared:						
P Company	40,000					40,000
S Company		12,500		(1a) 10,000	2,500	—
Retained earnings, December 31, 19X1—carried forward	500,000	157,500	148,000	22,000	31,500	500,000

Balance Sheet:

	P Company	S Company	Eliminations Dr.	Eliminations Cr.	Minority Interest	Consolidated
Cash	50,000	28,000				78,000
Accounts receivable	100,000	60,000				160,000
Inventory	82,000	30,000				112,000
Investment in S Company	318,000		(1a) 10,000 (1c) 12,000	(1b) 40,000 (2) 300,000		—
Land	50,000	40,000	(3) 20,000			110,000
Plant and equipment (net)	150,000	72,000	(3) 60,000	(4) 6,000		276,000
Differential			(2) 164,000	(3) 164,000		—
Goodwill			(3) 80,000	(4) 2,000		78,000
	750,000	230,000				814,000
Accounts payable	50,000	22,500				72,500
Capital stock:						
P Company	200,000					200,000
S Company		50,000	(2) 40,000		10,000	
Retained earnings—brought forward	500,000	157,500	(2) 148,000	22,000	31,500	500,000
Minority interest in S Company					41,500	41,500 M
	750,000	230,000	534,000	534,000		814,000

Explanation of eliminations:

(1a, 1b, 1c) To reverse the parent company's entries for subsidiary dividends and its interest in subsidiary earnings.

(2) To eliminate the January 1, 19X1, investment account balance against 80 percent of the January 1, 19X1, balances of the stockholders' equity accounts of the subsidiary.

(3) To allocate the differential as of January 1, 19X1.

(4) To amortize the allocated amounts for 19X1.

sidiary's reported net income (loss) for the period, and decreased (increased for a credit differential) by the differential amortization for the period. Applying this revised definition to the data of the example, consolidated net income is determined as follows:

P Company's net income from its own operations for 19X1 ($130,000 − $28,000)	$102,000
Increased by P Company's equity in S Company's reported net income for 19X1 (80% × $50,000)	40,000
Decreased by differential amortization for 19X1	(12,000)
Consolidated net income for 19X1	$130,000

In a similar manner, the "residual" approach gives recognition to the differential amortization by adjusting the sum of the companies' incomes for the "net eliminations" in the income statement section of the consolidated statement working paper. Thus, applying this approach to the data, we obtain:

P Company's net income for 19X1		$130,000
S Company's net income for 19X1		50,000
		$180,000
Less (plus)—net debit (credit) eliminations:		
P Company's recorded interest in S Company's earnings	$28,000	
Amortization of differential	12,000	40,000
Total equity		$140,000
Less (plus)—minority interest in S Company's net income (loss) [20% × $50,000]		10,000
Consolidated net income for 19X1		$130,000

A comparison of the figures in this schedular calculation with the corresponding figures in the income statement section of Illustration 5–2 may be informative to the reader.

Case 2. Amortization of Differential—Period Subsequent to Acquisition. In the second year after acquisition, assume that S Company reported net income of $40,000 for the year ended December 31, 19X2, and again paid $12,500 cash dividends during the year.

Parent Company Entries—Year 2. Based upon the assumed income and dividend figures of Case 2 and again referencing Illustration 5–1 for the differential amortization for 19X2, P Company would make the following entries during 19X2:

1. To record receipt of dividends from S Company:

Cash (80% × $12,500)	10,000	
Investment in S Company		10,000

2. To recognize equity in S Company's reported earnings:

Investment in S Company	32,000	
Equity in subsidiary earnings (80% × $40,000)		32,000

3. To recognize differential amortization for the period (from Illustration 5–1):

Equity in subsidiary earnings	8,000	
Investment in S Company		8,000

Eliminating Entries—Year 2. The investment elimination entries for the consolidated statement working paper at the end of 19X2 are:

1. To reverse the entries recorded by the parent company during 19X2:

   (a) Investment in S Company 10,000
       Dividends declared—S Company 10,000

   (b) Equity in subsidiary earnings 32,000
       Investment in S Company 32,000

   (c) Investment in S Company 8,000
       Equity in subsidiary earnings 8,000

2. To eliminate the January 1, 19X2, investment account balance of P Company against the January 1, 19X2, balances of the stockholders' equity accounts of S Company:

   Capital stock—S Company (80% × $50,000) 40,000
   Retained earnings—S Company (80% × $157,500) 126,000
   Differential 152,000
       Investment in S Company 318,000

As a consequence of these investment elimination entries, the *un-amortized* differential as of January 1, 19X2, is set up in the consolidated statement working paper. This amount is verified in Illustration 5–3.

Illustration 5–3

SCHEDULE OF UNAMORTIZED DIFFERENTIAL
Allocations as of January 1, 19X2

	Original Amounts Allocated— January 1, 19X1	Amortization for 19X1	Unamortized Amounts— January 1, 19X2
Inventory	$ 4,000	$ 4,000	$ –0–
Plant and equipment (net)	60,000	6,000	54,000
Land	20,000	–0–	20,000
Goodwill	80,000	2,000	78,000
	$164,000	$12,000	$152,000

The eliminating entries to allocate these unamortized differentials as of January 1, 19X2, and to recognize the differential amortization for 19X2 are presented following:

3. To allocate the unamortized differential as of January 19X2 (see Illustration 5–3):

   Plant and equipment (net) 54,000
   Land 20,000
   Goodwill 78,000
       Differential 152,000

4.   To amortize the allocated amounts for 19X2 (see Illustration 5–1):

Expenses	8,000	
Plant and equipment (net)		6,000
Goodwill		2,000

Although the differential amortization in elimination entry (4) appears to be the same as it was in 19X1, recall that in 19X1 there was an additional $4,000 amortization of the amount allocated to inventory. Thus, since none of the unamortized differential as of January 1, 19X2, was allocated to inventory, the total differential amortization reflected in the consolidated statement working paper in 19X2 is $8,000, as compared to $12,000 in 19X1.

These elimination entries are reflected in the consolidated statement working paper for the year ended December 31, 19X2, in Illustration 5–4. As before, the balances in the working paper are arbitrarily chosen, except where it is required that they correspond with the data assumed in this example or the figures included in the 19X1 working paper (e.g., December 31, 19X1, inventories are reflected as January 1, 19X2, inventories).

Inspection of the working paper in Illustration 5–4 again reveals that consolidated net income (and retained earnings) equals the parent company's net income (and retained earnings). It is left as an exercise for the reader to make definitional calculations of consolidated net income for 19X2.

Relationship between Investment Account Balance and Net Assets of Subsidiary.   In Chapter 4, it was pointed out that the balance of an investment account carried on the equity method reflects at any point in time the parent company's monetary interest in the recorded net assets of the subsidiary. But this constant relationship holds only when the original cost of the investment at the date of acquisition is equal to the parent's purchased interest in the subsidiary's recorded net assets, i.e., when there is no differential. If a differential exists, the investment account balance will reflect at any point in time the parent's monetary interest in the subsidiary's recorded net assets plus (minus) the unamortized balance of the debit (credit) differential. Thus, in the example, the investment account balance at December 31, 19X2, can be analyzed as follows:

P Company's monetary interest in S Company's recorded net assets [80% × ($50,000 + $185,000)]	$188,000
Unamortized differential at December 31, 19X2 ($152,000 − $8,000)	144,000
Investment account balance, December 31, 19X2	$332,000

Treatment of Separate Accumulated Depreciation Account.   In most of our examples, plant and equipment is depicted net of accumulated depreciation. This treatment facilitates the comparison between book and fair values required for the initial allocation of the differential, and simplifies the eliminating entries in the consolidated statement working paper. The analysis remains the same even if a separate accumulated depreciation account is included in the working paper. However, the eliminating entries must be modified to reflect the two separate components. For example, assume that the plant and equipment in our example was disaggregated as follows:

	Book Value, January 1, 19X1	Fair Value, January 1, 19X1	Difference	P Company's 80% Interest Therein
Plant and equipment (gross)	$240,000	$465,000	$225,000	$180,000
Accumulated depreciation	(160,000)	(310,000)	(150,000)	(120,000)
Plant and equipment (net)	$ 80,000	$155,000	$ 75,000	$ 60,000

The amount of the differential to be allocated to plant and equipment remains $60,000 (P Company's proportionate interest in the difference between fair value and book value), but the eliminating entry at December 31, 19X1, would be modified in the following manner:

Inventory (1/1)	4,000	
Plant and equipment	180,000	
Land	20,000	
Goodwill	80,000	
Accumulated depreciation—plant and		
equipment		120,000
Differential		164,000

The eliminating entry to recognize the amortization of the differential for 19X1 would then be:

Expenses	8,000	
Accumulated depreciation—plant and equipment ...		6,000
Goodwill		2,000

In future periods, the allocation to plant and equipment will remain unchanged, and the effect of prior periods amortization of the differential will be included in the amount assigned to accumulated depreciation. Thus, the eliminating entries at December 31, 19X2, would assume the following form:

(1) Plant and equipment	180,000	
Land	20,000	
Goodwill	78,000	
Accumulated depreciation—plant		
and equipment		126,000
Differential		152,000
(2) Expenses	8,000	
Accumulated depreciation—plant		
and equipment		6,000
Goodwill		2,000

Illustration 5–4

P COMPANY AND SUBSIDIARY S COMPANY

Consolidated Statement Working Paper
For Year Ended December 31, 19X2

	P Company	S Company	Eliminations Dr.	Eliminations Cr.	Minority Interest	Consolidated
Income Statement:						
Sales	586,000	250,000				836,000
Equity in subsidiary earnings	24,000		(1b) 32,000			—
Inventory (12/31)	110,000	50,000		(1c) 8,000		160,000
Total credits	720,000	300,000				996,000
Inventory (1/1)	82,000	30,000				112,000
Purchases	280,000	120,000				400,000
Expenses	198,000	110,000	(4) 8,000			316,000
Total debits	560,000	260,000				828,000
Minority interest in net income—S Company					8,000	168,000
Net income—carried forward	160,000	40,000	40,000	8,000	8,000	160,000
Retained Earnings Statement:						
Retained earnings, January 1, 19X2:						
P Company	500,000					500,000
S Company		157,500	(2) 126,000		31,500	—
Net income—brought forward	160,000	40,000	40,000	8,000	8,000	160,000
	660,000	197,500			39,500	660,000
Dividends declared:						
P Company	50,000					50,000
S Company		12,500		(1a) 10,000	2,500	—
Retained earnings, December 31, 19X2—carried forward	610,000	185,000	166,000	18,000	37,000	610,000

Balance Sheet:

			Eliminations			
			Debit	Credit	Minority Interest	Consolidated
Cash	130,000	36,000				166,000
Accounts receivable	150,000	80,000				230,000
Inventory	110,000	50,000				160,000
Investment in S Company	332,000		(1a) 10,000 (1c) 8,000	(1b) 32,000 (2) 318,000		—
Land	50,000	40,000	(3) 20,000			110,000
Plant and equipment (net)	128,000	64,000	(3) 54,000	(4) 6,000		240,000
Differential			(2) 152,000	(3) 152,000		—
Goodwill			(3) 78,000	(4) 2,000		76,000
	900,000	270,000				982,000
Accounts payable	90,000	35,000				125,000
Capital stock:						
P Company	200,000					200,000
S Company		50,000	(2) 40,000		10,000	
Retained earnings—brought forward	610,000	185,000	(2) 166,000	(4) 18,000	37,000	610,000
Minority interest in S Company					47,000	47,000 M
	900,000	270,000	528,000	528,000		982,000

Explanation of eliminations:

(1a, 1b, 1c) To reverse the parent company's entries for subsidiary dividends and its interest in subsidiary earnings.

(2) To eliminate the January 1, 19X2, investment account balance against 80 percent of the January 1, 19X2, balances of the stockholders' equity accounts of the subsidiary.

(3) To allocate the unamortized differential as of January 1, 19X2.

(4) To amortize the allocated amounts for 19X2.

Note that there is no substantive change in the values assigned to assets or expenses. Only the form of the entries has been modified to correspond with the assumed change in the working paper accounts associated with plant and equipment.

Preparation of Consolidated Balance Sheet Only. On some occasions the objective of the consolidation process may be a consolidated balance sheet only. In these circumstances, the consolidated statement working paper is greatly simplified. Only the balance sheet section of the working paper is relevant, and the eliminating entries are made solely in terms of *end-of-period balances.*

Thus, the eliminating entries for Case 2 for a consolidated balance sheet working paper at December 31, 19X2, are:

1. To eliminate the December 31, 19X2, investment account balance of P Company against the December 31, 19X2, balances of the stockholders' equity accounts of S Company:

Capital stock—S Company (80% × $50,000)	40,000	
Retained earnings—S Company (80% × $185,000)	148,000	
Differential	144,000	
Investment in S Company		332,000

2. To allocate the unamortized differential as of December 31, 19X2:

Plant and equipment (net) ($60,000 − $12,000)	48,000	
Land	20,000	
Goodwill ($80,000 − $4,000)	76,000	
Differential		144,000

Note that the differential allocations are based upon the unamortized balances at the *end* of December 31, 19X2, whereas the beginning of the year balances are used when a complete three-division consolidated statement working paper is prepared.

The consolidated balance sheet working paper is presented in Illustration 5–5. The reader may wish to confirm the equivalence of the values in this working paper with the corresponding values in the balance sheet section of the three-division working paper in Illustration 5–4.

Realignment of Subsidiary's Shareholders' Equity

Among the more common ways of altering a corporation's capital structure are the declaration of stock dividends, changing the par value of outstanding stock, and appropriations of retained earnings. Such actions by a subsidiary do not affect consolidated net income or retained earnings, but in the year of their occurrence they do require special attention in the consolidated statement working paper.

Stock Dividends. The parent company, like any investor, records the receipt of dividend shares of stock only by a memorandum entry. The entry made by the issuing company depends upon the size of the stock dividend, but in any case it will decrease retained earnings and increase the subsidiary's paid-in capital. Therefore, in the year a stock dividend is

Illustration 5–5

P COMPANY AND SUBSIDIARY S COMPANY

Consolidated Balance Sheet Working Paper
For Year Ended December 31, 19X2

	P Company	S Company	Eliminations Dr.	Eliminations Cr.	Minority Interest	Consolidated
Cash	130,000	36,000				166,000
Accounts receivable	150,000	80,000				230,000
Inventory	110,000	50,000				160,000
Investment in S Company	332,000			(1) 332,000		—
Land	50,000	40,000	(2) 20,000			110,000
Plant and equipment (net)	128,000	64,000	(2) 48,000			240,000
Differential			(1) 144,000	(2) 144,000		—
Goodwill			(2) 76,000			76,000
	900,000	270,000				982,000
Accounts payable	90,000	35,000				125,000
Capital stock:						
P Company	200,000					200,000
S Company		50,000	(1) 40,000		10,000	
Retained earnings:						
P Company	610,000					610,000
S Company		185,000	(1) 148,000		37,000	
Minority interest in S Company					47,000	47,000 M
	900,000	270,000	476,000	476,000		982,000

Explanation of eliminations:
(1) To eliminate the December 31, 19X2, investment account balance against 80 percent of December 31, 19X2, balances of the stockholders' equity accounts of the subsidiary.
(2) To allocate the unamortized differential as of December 31, 19X2.

distributed by a subsidiary, an additional eliminating entry must be made in the consolidated statement working paper to restore the subsidiary's equity accounts to their beginning of the year balances and to eliminate the parent's share of (stock) dividends declared. The eliminating entry would be of the following general form:

```
Capital stock—Subsidiary Company ..........................  xx
Additional paid-in capital—Subsidiary Company .................  xx
        Dividends declared—Subsidiary Company .................        xx
```

Of course if no additional paid-in capital is created in the subsidiary's entry recording the stock dividend, that element of the eliminating entry would be deleted. In years subsequent to the distribution of the stock dividend, no special modifications of the standard eliminating entries are required.

There is an accounting convention that the sources of cash dividends are the most recently accumulated earnings and the sources of stock dividends are the earliest accumulated earnings. Therefore, most subsidiary stock dividends effectively capitalize a portion of the subsidiary's retained earnings that is either eliminated or allocated to the minority interest. But what happens when the stock dividends are large enough to capitalize earnings accumulated subsequent to acquisition? The parent's share of these earnings is included in consolidated retained earnings. Yet, the capitalized amount is clearly unavailable for dividend distribution by the parent. One position on this circumstance is to recommend disclosure (parenthetically or by footnote) of this permanent limitation on dividend availability in the formal consolidated statements. Another position is that the restriction imposed by the capitalization of postacquisition subsidiary earnings warrants classification of this amount as additional paid-in capital in the consolidated balance sheet. In this respect, the following official commentary is relevant:

> Occasionally, subsidiary companies capitalize earned surplus [retained earnings] arising since acquisition, by means of a stock dividend or otherwise. This does not require a transfer to capital surplus [additional paid-in capital] on consolidation, inasmuch as the retained earnings in the consolidated financial statements should reflect the accumulated earnings of the consolidated group not distributed to the shareholders of, or capitalized by, the parent company.[4]

Changes in Par Value of Subsidiary Stock.   A subsidiary may change the legal status of its capital stock, either in the amount of the par value, from par value to no-par value, or no-par value to par value. Such an action has no effect on the investment account of the parent company or on consolidated net income and retained earnings. In the consolidated statement working paper for the year of the change, either the original journal entry can be reversed with an eliminating entry to restore the subsidiary's equity accounts to their beginning of the year balances, or the investment elimination entry may be made against end of the year balances in the contributed capital accounts. The latter alternative is usually simpler if there have been no other transactions during the year affecting the subsidiary's contributed capital.

Appropriation of Retained Earnings.   In the event the subsidiary has an appropriation of retained earnings, this balance should merely be included with the unappropriated retained earnings in the consolidated statement working paper. No special disclosure is necessary in the consolidated statements unless the amount of appropriated retained earnings exceeds the retained earnings existing at date of acquisition, in which case this temporary limitation on dividend availability may be disclosed.

Interim Purchases

Attention has thus far focused on the preparation of consolidated statements where the date of acquisition of subsidiary shares and the beginning

---

[4] Section 2051.17, *APB Accounting Principles—Current Text.*

of the affiliates' accounting periods are the same. Unfortunately, the accounting convenience provided by this coincidence of dates occurs infrequently. Since a subsidiary's shares are perhaps more often acquired at interim dates, we must consider how the revenue and expenses of the subsidiary from the beginning of the period to the date of acquisition are to be reflected in the consolidated income statement. Current accounting policy prescribes two alternative methods:

When a subsidiary is purchased during the year, there are alternative ways of dealing with the results of its operations in the consolidated income statement. One method, which usually is preferable, especially where there are several dates of acquisition of blocks of shares, is to include the subsidiary in the consolidation as though it had been acquired at the beginning of the year, and to deduct at the bottom of the consolidated income statement the preacquisition earnings applicable to each block of stock. This method presents results which are more indicative of the current status of the group, and facilitates future comparison with subsequent years. Another method of prorating income is to include in the consolidated statement only the subsidiary's revenue and expenses subsequent to the date of acquisition.[5]

Under either method, preacquisition earnings of the subsidiary do not affect consolidated net income. The methods differ only in the amounts of the subsidiary's revenue and expenses that will be included in consolidated revenue and expenses.

Case 3. To illustrate the alternative impacts of the two methods on the consolidated income statement, assume that P Company acquired 80 percent of the capital stock of S Company on April 1, 19X1, for $124,000. Assume further that on January 1, 19X1, S Company had outstanding capital stock of $100,000 and retained earnings of $50,000, and that the two companies reported the following operating information for the year ended December 31, 19X1:

		S Company		
	P Company*	Total	4/1–12/31 (Estimated)	1/1–3/31 (Estimated)
Sales	$200,000	$100,000	$75,000	$25,000
Cost of sales	$ 90,000	$ 60,000	$45,000	$15,000
Other expenses	50,000	20,000	15,000	5,000
	$140,000	$ 80,000	$60,000	$20,000
Net income	$ 60,000	$ 20,000	$15,000	$ 5,000

* Excluding P Company's interest in S Company's earnings.

[5] Section 2051.10, *APB Accounting Principles—Current Text.* (The problem of dealing with the acquisition of blocks of shares at several different dates is covered in Chapter 9.)

Illustration 5–6

ALTERNATIVE CONSOLIDATED INCOME STATEMENTS

Statements for Interim Purchase of Case 3

	Method A:		Method B:	
	Include Revenue and Expenses of Subsidiary for the Entire Year		*Include only Revenue and Expenses of Subsidiary Subsequent to Date of Acquisition*	
Consolidated sales		$300,000		$275,000
Consolidated expenses:				
Cost of sales	$150,000		$135,000	
Other expenses	70,000	220,000	65,000	200,000
		$80,000		$75,000
Less:				
Minority interest	$4,000†		$3,000‡	
Purchased preacquisition				
earnings	4,000*	8,000	–0–	3,000
Consolidated net income ...		$ 72,000		$ 72,000

Verification of consolidated net income by definition (increment approach):

P Company's income from
   its own operations $60,000
Increased by P Company's equity
   in S Company's postacquisition
   earnings (80% × $15,000) 12,000
   Consolidated net income $72,000

* 80% × $ 5,000.
† 20% × 20,000.
‡ 20% × 15,000.

The consolidated income statements that would be reported under each of the two alternative methods are reflected in Illustration 5–6, and the investment elimination entries are shown in Illustration 5–7.

Whichever method is used, we must estimate the subsidiary's net income from the beginning of the year to the date of acquisition. In the data given for S Company, it is implicitly assumed that income is earned uniformly throughout the year; where there is evidence of pronounced seasonality, however, the allocation of revenue and expenses to preacquisition and postacquisition periods should reflect this nonuniformity.

Under what has been labeled Method A, the subsidiary's total revenue and expenses for the entire year are included in consolidated revenue and expenses. Therefore, the parent company's acquired interest in the preacquisition earnings of the subsidiary must be recognized as a deduction in the consolidated income statement. In this case, preacquisition earnings were estimated to be $5,000, and the parent's purchased interest was 80 percent thereof, or $4,000. The minority interest in net income is determined by multiplying the minority's fractional interest at the end of the

Illustration 5–7

ALTERNATIVE INVESTMENT ELIMINATION ENTRIES

Entries for Interim Purchase of Case 3

Method A—Include revenue and expenses of subsidiary for the entire year:

(1) Equity in subsidiary earnings 12,000
     Investment in S Company   12,000

(2) Capital stock—S Company 80,000
     Retained earnings—S Company (80% × $50,000)   40,000
     Purchased preacquisition earnings (80% × $5,000)   4,000
     Investment in S Company   124,000

Method B—Include only revenue and expenses of subsidiary subsequent to
date of acquisition:

(1) Equity in subsidiary earnings 12,000
     Investment in S Company   12,000

(2) Capital stock—S Company 80,000
     Retained earnings—S Company (80% × $55,000) 44,000
     Investment in S Company   124,000

Note: In eliminating entry (1) under both methods, it is assumed that S Company did
not declare any dividends *subsequent* to acquisition. If dividends had been declared,
the investment account balance would of course be lower and the entry would be
modified to incorporate the elimination of the intercompany dividends.

year (20 percent) by the amount of subsidiary net income ($20,000).
This calculation of minority interest may be confirmed by considering the
different equities of the minority shareholders for the period of time *before*
and *after* P Company's acquisition:

January 1 to March 31:   100% of $ 5,000 .... $5,000
April 1 to December 31:   20% of $15,000 3,000
                                      $8,000

Subsidiary net income purchased by majority
    shareholders: 80% of $5,000 4,000

Interest in net income accruing to year-end
    minority shareholders $4,000

Under Method B, the subsidiary's revenue and expenses have been included only from the date of acquisition. In effect, this method is implemented *as if* the subsidiary closed its books on the date of acquisition.
That is, in the consolidated working paper, S Company's income statement
for nine months (April 1–December 31) would be combined with P
Company's income statement for the year 19X1 to produce 19X1 consolidated income statement figures. Since no preacquisition earnings are
included in the consolidated figures, no adjustment for purchased preacquisition earnings is made under this alternative. Minority interest in net
income is calculated as before: end-of-year fractional interest (20 percent) multiplied by subsidiary net income ($15,000). Finally, consistent
with the "as if closed" approach, the elimination of S Company's retained

earnings is based upon the estimated April 1 balance ($50,000 plus $5,000 estimated earnings), not the January 1 balance as in Method A.

In the event the subsidiary had declared cash dividends in the current period *prior* to acquisition, the investment elimination entries under Method A would be modified slightly. However, since the "as if the books were closed" approach of Method B uses the estimated retained earnings balance on the date of acquisition, the effect of the dividend declaration would be included in that estimate.

Case 4.   To illustrate the effect of preacquisition dividends, assume S Company's retained earnings balance was $60,000 on January 1, 19X1, and that S Company declared a cash dividend of $10,000 on March 15, 19X1. The net effect of these two assumptions is to leave S Company's book value the same as it was in Case 3, but with modified balances in the shareholders' equity accounts. Drawing upon the rest of the data in Case 3, investment elimination entry (2) for the Method A example in Illustration 5–7 would be changed to the following:

```
Capital stock — S Company .......................... 80,000
Retained earnings—S Company (80% × $60,000) ........ 48,000
Purchased preacquisition earnings (80% × $5,000 ........  4,000
    Dividends declared—S Company (80% × $10,000) ..........  8,000
    Investment in S Company ..............................        124,000
```

Note that the *net* effect of the retained earnings and dividends declared elements of this entry is the same as the retained earnings elimination in the entry in Illustration 5–7, and all other elements of the two entries are the same. Entry (1) would be unaffected by these assumptions.

In summary, when a subsidiary is acquired during the year, there are two alternative ways of reporting the subsidiary's operating data in the consolidated income statement. One method includes the subsidiary's revenue and expenses for the entire year, with a corresponding deduction for preacquisition earnings purchased by the parent company. The alternative method includes only the subsidiary's revenue and expenses subsequent to the date of acquisition. Consolidated net income will, however, be the same under both methods.[6]

Income Tax Considerations

Consolidated Income Tax Returns.   Technical rules respecting the preparation of consolidated income tax returns are usually complex and are clearly beyond the scope of this text. Yet, a few summary comments seem appropriate.

---

[6] When the subsidiary is acquired by a single purchase of stock (rather than several blocks), and the combination is accounted for as a purchase, consideration of the general spirit of *APB Opinion 16,* "Business Combinations," would suggest a preference for the alternative of including only the subsidiary's revenue and expenses subsequent to the date of acquisition.

An election to file either a separate or consolidated tax return is available to member corporations of an "affiliated group." To qualify as an "affiliated group," there must exist a corporate ownership chain in which a major parent corporation owns at least 80 percent of the voting power of all classes of stock of the several affiliates; additionally, at least 80 percent of each class of nonvoting stock of at least one affiliate must also be held by the major parent company. The election to file a consolidated return relates to all domestic affiliates; foreign corporations are not normally includible.

Among the advantages of filing consolidated income tax returns are the following: (1) intercompany dividends are not includible in consolidated taxable income; (2) gains on the sale or exchange of property between members of the affiliated group are usually not recognized; and (3) current year's losses of one affiliate may be offset against the current year's net income of another.

The following disadvantages should also be noted: (1) an election to file a consolidated return applies to all future years unless specified qualifying conditions are met; (2) each affiliate is required to use the same taxable year and to adopt a generally uniform method of accounting; and (3) losses in transactions with affiliate members are not recognized in determining consolidated taxable income.

Provision of Deferred Taxes on Undistributed Earnings of Subsidiaries not Included in Consolidated Tax Returns. If a subsidiary is not included in a consolidated tax return (perhaps because it is less than 80 percent-owned or it is a foreign subsidiary), the parent company may have to pay income tax on a portion of its recognized interest in the subsidiary's undistributed earnings at some future date. The tax on currently distributed earnings will of course have been paid and recognized by the parent company. The potential tax on the subsidiary's undistributed earnings may be levied upon a future distribution of cash dividends by the subsidiary (usually subject to an 85 percent dividends received deduction), or perhaps on the proceeds of sale upon disposition of all or part of the stock interest.

In view of this potential tax liability of the parent, *APB Opinion 23* requires the parent to make a deferred income tax provision on the subsidiary's undistributed earnings *unless* there is strong evidence that the earnings will be permanently invested or that eventual remittance will be in the form of a tax-free liquidation. If either of these conditions exists, a footnote should be added to the consolidated statements indicating the reason why deferred taxes were not provided and the cumulative amount of undistributed earnings on which the parent company has not recognized income taxes. If the conditions are not satisfied, the parent company should debit Income Tax Expense and credit Deferred Tax Liability for the deferred income tax on the subsidiary's undistributed earnings of the current period (taking into account the dividends received deduction or other special income tax provisions that might be applicable). It might be noted that when the equity method is applied to a less than 50 percent-owned investee, *APB Opinion 24 requires* tax allocation; no potential "escape" conditions are specified for this type of investment. The deferred tax would be calculated and recorded in the same manner as for a subsidiary.

When a subsidiary files a separate income tax return (federal or state), the tax paid is a determinant of its net income for the period. Thus, the parent's equity is based upon the subsidiary's reported net income after taxes—as it normally should be. However, when the subsidiary pays income tax in the current period on profits that are considered unrealized on a consolidated basis (unconfirmed intercompany profits), these taxes must be deferred. The procedures applicable to these circumstances are explained in Chapter 7.

In subsequent chapters, we will assume that the affiliates have filed consolidated tax returns and/or deferral of income taxes is inappropriate, unless otherwise indicated.

Combined and Parent Company Financial Statements

In addition to its consolidated statements, a parent company will under certain circumstances include supplemental financial statements in its financial reports to shareholders or regulatory commissions. Two such statements most frequently encountered are combined (or group) financial statements and separate (unconsolidated) parent company statements.

Combined (Group) Financial Statements. Some controlled or related companies are excluded from consolidation because they do not meet all of the requisite tests (see Chapter 3). If there are several of these companies, it is often informative to combine their financial statements into one or more groups. The SEC takes the following position on this matter:

> There may be filed financial statements in which majority-owned subsidiaries not consolidated with the parent are consolidated or combined in one or more groups, and 50 percent or less owned persons the investments in which are accounted for by the equity method are consolidated or combined in one or more groups, pursuant to principles of inclusion or exclusion which will clearly exhibit the financial position and results of operations of the group or groups.[7]

Combined statements are also used to present the financial position and results of operations of two or more companies owned by one individual (the so-called brother-sister corporations) or under common management.

The general principles followed in this combining process are similar to those used in consolidating two or more companies. The accounts of the companies are additively combined, with appropriate elimination of intercompany transactions. However, there usually is no investor/investee

---

[7] *Regulation S–X, Part 210—Form and Content of Financial Statements,* Article 4-04.

relationship between companies included in the group, and thus no investment elimination entry.[8]

Parent Company Statements. Under certain circumstances, a parent company may elect to include its separate financial statements with the consolidated statements in order "to indicate adequately the position of bondholders and other creditors or preferred stockholders of the parent."[9] These statements are encountered more frequently however in filings with the SEC. Most SEC registration and report forms require the filing of separate parent company statements. Since it is generally acknowledged that these statements provide little additional information, the SEC usually allows this requirement to be satisfied by including condensed parent company statements in a note to the consolidated statements.[10]

Statement of Changes in Financial Position

In 1963, the Accounting Principles Board issued *Opinion No. 3* encouraging the presentation of a statement of source and application of funds as supplementary information in financial reports. Subsequently, this recommendation was strongly supported by the principal stock exchanges, several regulatory agencies, and the business community at large, resulting in a significant increase in the number of companies presenting the statement. In view of this widespread acceptance, the Board decided in 1971 to require inclusion of this statement in most circumstances:

The Board concludes that information concerning the financing and investing activities of a business enterprise and the changes in its financial position for a period is essential for financial statement users, particularly owners and creditors, in making economic decisions. When financial statements purporting to present both financial position (balance sheet) and results of operations (statement of income and retained earnings) are issued, a statement summarizing changes in financial position should also be presented as a basic financial statement for each period for which an income statement is presented.[11]

Consistent with its earlier opinion, the Board adopted a broadly based disclosure concept and changed the title of the statement to reflect this concept:

The Board also concludes that the statement summarizing changes in financial position should be based on a broad concept embracing all changes in financial position and that the title of the statement should reflect this broad concept.

---

[8] Section 2051.21–.22, *APB Accounting Principles—Current Text.*

[9] Section 2051.23, *APB Accounting Principles—Current Text.*

[10] The parent company statements may be omitted from SEC filings if consolidated statements are filed *and* the registrant is an "operating company" or certain "size" tests are satisfied. (For example, see "Instructions as to Financial Statements," *Form 10-K.*)

[11] *APB Opinion 19,* "Reporting Changes in Financial Position," paragraph 7. This statement is also required in SEC filings.

The Board therefore recommends that the title be Satement of Changes in Financial Position (referred to below as "the Statement"). The Statement of each reporting entity should disclose all important aspects of its financing and investing activities regardless of whether cash or other elements of working capital are directly affected.[12]

The opinion is generally permissive with regard to format, allowing presentation in a balanced form or in a form expressing the changes in terms of cash, cash and temporary assets, quick assets, or working capital. However, one section of the statement must disclose working capital or cash provided by operations for the period.

If the financial reports presented by a company are consolidated statements, the statement of changes in financial position must also be on a consolidated basis. The elements of this statement that are unique to the consolidation process are discussed in the following paragraphs.

Typically, the amount of "funds" (cash or working capital) provided by operations is calculated as the reported net income plus nonfund-using expenses minus nonfund-providing credits. These nonfund adjustments include such items as depreciation expense, amortization of intangibles, and equity in affiliates earnings (in excess of dividends received). Since consolidation often establishes goodwill that is subsequently amortized, this adjustment will frequently appear in the "operations" section of the consolidated statement of changes in financial position. Additionally, the income statement deduction for minority interests is not a fund-using item and must be added to consolidated net income to derive "funds provided by operations." The fact that the minority interest deduction in the income statement does not use funds is evidenced by the carry forward of this item to the retained earnings section of the working paper, and finally to the balance sheet as a long-term equity.

Subsidiary dividend payments to minority shareholders must be disclosed as an application of funds, since the income statement allocation to minority interests is treated as a nonfund-using item. Adequate disclosure in the statement requires that these payments, if material, be shown separately from parent company dividends paid to majority stockholders.

Transactions between affiliates are eliminated in the normal course of preparing a consolidated income statement, statement of retained earnings, and balance sheet. These eliminations are equally applicable to the statement of sources and applications of funds, since interaffiliate transactions do not affect the amount of cash or working capital associated with the consolidated entity.

In the event the parent acquires additional shares of an existing subsidiary, the cost of the acquisition may or may not represent a use of funds. If the shares were purchased directly from the subsidiary corporation, the interaffiliate character of the transaction would eliminate any

---

[12] Ibid., paragraph 8.

effect on consolidated funds. If the shares are purchased from outside (minority) interests, the acquisition represents an application of funds.

Case 5. The consolidated income statement and comparative balance sheets for **P** Company and its 80 percent owned subsidiary S Company are shown in Illustration 5–8. The following additional data is provided:

Illustration 5–8

P COMPANY AND SUBSIDIARY S COMPANY

Consolidated Income Statement
For the Year Ended December 31, 19X1

Sales		$171,000
Expenses:		
Cost of goods sold	$ 60,000	
Depreciation	15,000	
Other operating expenses	75,000	150,000
Income from operations		$ 21,000
Equity in earnings of unconsolidated affiliates		4,000
Combined net income		$ 25,000
Minority interest in net income		2,000
Consolidated net income		$ 23,000

P COMPANY AND SUBSIDIARY S COMPANY

Consolidated Balance Sheets
December 31, 19X1, and 19X0

Assets

	19X1	19X0
Cash	$ 24,000	$ 25,000
Receivables	52,000	60,000
Inventory	84,000	49,000
Equipment (net of depreciation)	155,000	150,000
Investment in unconsolidated affiliates	27,000	26,000
Goodwill	37,000	40,000
Total Assets	$379,000	$350,000

Equities

	19X1	19X0
Liabilities:		
Accounts payable	$ 65,000	$ 55,000
Bonds	80,000	100,000
Total	$145,000	$155,000
Minority interest	$ 21,000	$ 20,000
Stockholders' equity:		
Common stock	$125,000	$100,000
Retained earnings	88,000	75,000
Total	$213,000	$175,000
Total Equities	$379,000	$350,000

1. The amortization of goodwill recognized in the consolidation amounted to $3,000 for the year 19X1. This amount is included in other operating expenses.

Illustration 5–9

P COMPANY AND SUBSIDIARY S COMPANY

Consolidated Statement of Changes in Financial Position
For the Year Ended December 31, 19X1

Working capital was provided by:
Operations:

Net income	$ 23,000	
Charges (credits) not affecting working capital:		
Depreciation expense	15,000	
Amortization of goodwill	3,000	
Minority interest in net income	2,000	
Equity in undistributed earnings of unconsolidated		
affiliates	(1,000)	$ 42,000
Proceeds from sale of common stock		25,000
		$ 67,000

Working capital was used for:
Dividends to:

P company shareholders	$ 10,000
Minority shareholders	1,000
Purchase of equipment	20,000
Retirement of debt	20,000
	$ 51,000
Increase in Working Capital	$ 16,000

Changes in working capital:

Cash	$(1,000)
Receivables	(8,000)
Inventory	35,000
Accounts payable	(10,000)
Increase in Working Capital	$ 16,000

2. Equipment (net of depreciation) increased by $5,000. This increase was the net result of a $20,000 purchase of equipment and depreciation expense of $15,000.

3. P Company recognized income of $4,000 from its equity in unconsolidated affiliates, and received dividend distributions from them of $3,000. Therefore, the investment (on an equity basis) increased by $1,000.

4. Minority interest in net income was $2,000; however, minority interest in the consolidated balance sheet increased by only $1,000. The $1,000 difference represents dividends paid by the subsidiary to minority shareholders. It may be noted that the subsidiary paid dividends of $4,000 to P Company, which amount was appropriately eliminated as an interaffiliate transaction.

5. P Company common stock was increased by $25,000 during 19X1, which represents a stock issuance to outside parties.

6. Consolidated retained earnings increased by $13,000, although consolidated net income was $23,000. The difference of $10,000 reflects dividends paid to P Company stockholders.

The formal consolidated statement of changes in financial position is presented in Illustration 5–9. This statement is designed (arbitrarily) to analyze changes in terms of working capital.

QUESTIONS

1. State the basic principle of accounting for differentials subsequent to the date of acquisition.
2. How does differential amortization affect the value of the minority interest?
3. Define consolidated net income using the incremental approach, and giving recognition to differential amortization.
4. For an investment carried under the equity method, what is the relationship between the investment account balance and the net assets of the subsidiary at any point in time?
5. If the objective of the consolidation process is the preparation of a consolidated balance sheet only, what simplifications are achieved in the consolidated statement working paper?
6. If a stock dividend is declared by a subsidiary, what special steps must be taken in the consolidated statement working paper in the year the dividend is declared? In subsequent years?
7. When a subsidiary is purchased during the year, what are the two alternative ways of reflecting its results of operations for the year in the consolidated income statement?
8. Should deferred taxes be provided on the parent's share of undistributed earnings of subsidiaries not included in consolidated tax returns? On the investor's share of undistributed earnings of an investee?
9. When are combined (group) financial statements prepared?
10. What general principles are used in preparing combined (group) financial statements?
11. When are separate parent company financial statements prepared?
12. Enumerate three "nonfund-using expenses or nonfund-providing credits" that may arise as a result of investments in affiliates.
13. How are subsidiary dividend payments disclosed in the consolidated statement of changes in financial position?

EXERCISES

Exercise 5–1

On January 1, 19X1, P Company purchased an 80 percent interest in S Company for $100,000. On this date, S Company had capital stock of $25,000 and retained earnings of $50,000.

An examination of S Company's assets and liabilities revealed that book values were equal to fair values for all except plant and equipment (net) which had a book value of $50,000 and a fair value of $75,000. The plant and equipment had an expected remaining life of 5 years. P Company planned to amortize any goodwill acquired in the combination over 20 years.

During 19X1 and 19X2, P Company reported net income from its own operations of $20,000, and S Company's income was $10,000 per year. S Company did not pay dividends either year.

Required:

a. Prepare the entries that P Company would have made in 19X1 and 19X2 in respect to its investment in S Company.
b. Prepare the eliminating entries for consolidated statement working papers on December 31, 19X1, and December 31, 19X2.
c. Prepare a schedular calculation of consolidated net income for 19X1 and 19X2.

Exercise 5–2

On January 1, 19X1, P Company purchased a 60 percent interest in S Company for $180,000. On this date, S Company had capital stock of $60,000 and retained earnings of $40,000.

An examination of S Company's assets and liabilities revealed that book values were equal to fair values. P Company planned to amortize any goodwill acquired in the combination over the maximum period of 40 years.

During 19X1 and 19X2, P Company's net income from its own operations was $30,000 per year, and S Company's net income amounted to $20,000 per year.

Required:

a. Prepare the entries that P Company would have made in 19X1 and 19X2 in respect to its investment in S Company.
b. Prepare the eliminating entries for consolidated statement working papers on December 31, 19X1, and December 31, 19X2.
c. Prepare a schedular calculation of consolidated net income for 19X1 and 19X2.

Exercise 5–3

Assume that General Motors acquired all of the outstanding common stock of IBM in an exchange of shares on December 31, 1975. The combination was accounted for as a purchase, and on this date the fair market value of the shares exchanged was determined to be approximately $37,000,000,000.

The following information was taken from the financial statements of the (assumed) combination participants:

	General Motors	IBM
Recorded net assets:		
December 31, 1975	$13,000,000,000	$11,000,000,000
Net income for 1975	1,250,000,000	2,000,000,000

Assume that all of the differential is allocated to goodwill, and that it will be amortized over the maximum time period.

Required:

a. Assuming that the two companies had earnings from their own operations in 1976 equal to the 1975 amounts, and that there were no intercompany transactions during the year, calculate consolidated net income for 1976.
b. Assuming that the December 31, 1976, investment elimination entries have already been prepared, prepare the eliminating entries to allocate the differential and to recognize differential amortization for 1976.
c. If consolidated statements were prepared on January 1, 1976, what percentage of consolidated net assets was represented by the "purchased" goodwill?
d. Assuming that General Motors had 290 million common shares outstanding in 1975 and that it issued 610 million additional common shares to acquire IBM, calculate consolidated earnings per share for 1976. How does this compare to General Motors' earnings per share in 1975.

Exercise 5–4

On January 1, 19X1, P Company purchased an 80 percent interest in S Company for $140,000. On this date, S Company had capital stock of $25,000 and retained earnings of $50,000.

An examination of S Company's assets and liabilities revealed that book values were equal to fair values for all except plant and equipment (net) which had a book value of $30,000 and a fair value of $75,000. The plant and equipment had an expected remaining life of 10 years. P Company planned to amortize any goodwill acquired in the combination over 40 years.

During 19X1 and 19X2, P Company reported net income from its own operations of $20,000, and S Company's income was $20,000 in 19X1 and $15,000 in 19X2. S Company did not pay dividends either year.

Required:

a. Prepare the entries that P Company would have made in 19X1 and 19X2 in respect to its investment in S Company.
b. Prepare the eliminating entries for consolidated statement working papers on December 31, 19X1, and December 31, 19X2.
c. Prepare a schedular calculation of consolidated net income for 19X1 and 19X2.

Exercise 5–5

On January 1, 19X1, P Company purchased a 60 percent interest in S Company for $220,000. On this date, S Company had capital stock of $60,000 and retained earnings of $40,000.

An examination of S Company's assets and liabilities revealed that book values were equal to fair values. P Company planned to amortize any goodwill acquired in the combination over the maximum period of 40 years.

During 19X1 and 19X2, P Company's net income from its own operations was $30,000 per year, and S Company's net income amounted to $10,000 in 19X1 and $15,000 in 19X2.

Required:

a. Prepare the entries that P Company would have made in 19X1 and 19X2 in respect to its investment in S Company.
b. Prepare the eliminating entries for consolidated statement working papers on December 31, 19X1, and December 31, 19X2.
c. Prepare a schedular calculation of consolidated net income for 19X1 and 19X2.

Exercise 5–6

Jones Company purchased in the open market 80 percent of the capital stock of Irwin, Inc. on January 1, 19X1, at $50,000 more than 80 percent of its book value. The differential was allocated totally to goodwill, with an estimated life of 20 years. During the following five years, Irwin, Inc. reported cumulative earnings of $200,000 and paid $50,000 in dividends. On January 1, 19X6, minority shareholders in Irwin, Inc. had an equity of $70,000 in the net assets of the company.

Required:

If the parent company carries its investment in subsidiary stock on an equity basis—
a. Determine the January 1, 19X1, cost of the investment, and
b. Calculate the investment carrying value on December 31, 19X5.

Exercise 5–7

Smith Company purchased in the open market 60 percent of the capital stock of Mori Company on January 1, 19X1, at $100,000 more than 60 percent of its book value. The differential was allocated $40,000 to plant and equipment (net) and $60,000 to goodwill. The plant and equipment had an estimated remaining life of 5 years, and the goodwill was estimated to have a life of 10 years.

On January 1, 19X4, minority shareholders in Mori Company have an equity of $96,000 in the net assets of the company.

Required:

If the parent company carries its investment in subsidiary stock on an equity basis—
a. Determine the net assets of Mori Company on January 1, 19X4.
b. Calculate the investment carrying value on January 1, 19X4.

Exercise 5–8

On January 1, 19X1, P Company purchased an 80 percent interest in S Company for $140,000. On this date, S Company had capital stock of $50,000 and retained earnings of $25,000.

An examination of S Company's assets and liabilities revealed that book values were equal to fair values for all except plant and equipment (net) which had a book value of $100,000 and a fair value of $125,000, and inventory which had a book value of $30,000 and a fair value of $40,000. The plant and equipment had an expected remaining life of 5 years, and the inventory should all be sold in 19X1. P Company planned to amortize any goodwill acquired in the combination over 20 years.

P Company's income from its own operations was $35,000 in 19X1 and $40,000 in 19X2. S Company's income was $30,000 in 19X1 and $25,000 in 19X2. S Company did not pay any dividends either year.

Required:

a. Prepare the entries that P Company would have made in 19X1 and 19X2 in respect to its investment in S Company.
b. Prepare the eliminating entries for consolidated statement working papers on December 31, 19X2, and December 31, 19X2.
c. Prepare a schedular calculation of consolidated net income for 19X1 and 19X2.

Exercise 5–9

On January 1, 19X1, P Company purchased a 60 percent interest in S Company for $113,000. On this date, S Company had capital stock of $10,000 and retained earnings of $20,000.

An examination of S Company's assets and liabilities revealed that book values were equal to fair values for all except plant and equipment (net) which had a book value of $100,000 and a fair value of $150,000, and inventory which had a book value of $25,000 and a fair value of $30,000. The plant and equipment had an expected remaining life of 5 years, and the inventory should all be sold in 19X1. P Company planned to amortize any goodwill acquired in the combination over 40 years.

P Company's income from its own operations was $50,000 in 19X1 and $40,000 in 19X2. S Company's income was $35,000 in 19X1 and $30,000 in 19X2. S Company paid cash dividends of $10,000 each year.

Required:

a. Prepare the entries that P Company would have made in 19X1 and 19X2 in respect to its investment in S Company.
b. Prepare the eliminating entries for consolidated statement working papers on December 31, 19X1, and December 31, 19X2.
c. Prepare a schedular calculation of consolidated net income for 19X1 and 19X2.

Exercise 5–10

P Company purchased an 80 percent interest in S Company on January 1, 19X1, for $40,000, when S Company had capital stock of $20,000 and retained earnings of $30,000.

During 19X1, S Company reported net income of $10,000, and paid cash dividends of $5,000. Additionally, S Company paid a 10 percent stock dividend on October 15, 19X1, on which it made the following entry:

Dividends declared	7,000	
Additional paid-in capital		5,000
Capital stock		2,000

Required:

a. Prepare the entries that P Company would have made in 19X1 in respect to its investment in S Company.

b. Prepare the investment elimination entries for a consolidated statement working paper for the year ended December 31, 19X1.

Exercise 5–11

P Company purchased an 80 percent interest in S Company on March 1, 19X1, for $38,400. On January 1, 19X1, S Company had capital stock of $20,000 and retained earnings of $25,000.

The companies' operating data for 19X1 is as follows:

	P Company*	S Company
Sales	$300,000	$60,000
Cost of sales	$180,000	$30,000
Other expenses	40,000	12,000
	$220,000	$42,000
Net income	$ 80,000	$18,000

* Excluding P Company's interest in S Company earnings.

It is assumed that S Company's net income is earned uniformly throughout the year. Neither company paid any dividends in 19X1.

Required:

a. Prepare a consolidated income statement for 19X1 under each of the two alternative methods of dealing with the subsidiary's operating results for the year.

b. Prepare investment elimination entries for a consolidated statement working paper for the year ended December 31, 19X1, for each of the two alternatives.

Exercise 5–12

P Company purchased a 70 percent interest in S Company on September 1, 19X1, for $70,000. On January 1, 19X1, S Company had capital stock of $50,000 and retained earnings of $30,000.

The companies' operating data of 19X1 is as follows:

	P Company*	S Company
Sales	$140,000	$90,000
Cost of sales	$ 60,000	$45,000
Other expenses	30,000	15,000
	$ 90,000	$60,000
Net income	$ 50,000	$30,000

* Excluding P Company's interest in S Company earnings.

It is assumed that S Company's net income is earned uniformly throughout the year. Neither company paid any dividends in 19X1.

Required:

a. Prepare a consolidated income statement for 19X1 under each of the two alternative methods of dealing with the subsidiary's operating results for the year.
b. Prepare investment elimination entries for a consolidated statement working paper for the year ended December 31, 19X1, for each of the two alternatives.

Exercise 5–13

P Company purchased 90 shares of S Company capital stock on May 1, 19X1, in the open market for $16,200. A partial trial balance as of December 31, 19X1, discloses the following balances:

	P Company	S Company
Capital stock ($100 par)	$100,000	$10,000
Retained earnings (1/1)	40,000	5,000
Dividends declared	5,000	2,000
Sales	200,000	40,000
Cost of goods sold	130,000	20,000
Operating expenses	40,000	8,000
Equity in subsidiary earnings	?	

S Company declared a $10 dividend per share on February 1 and July 1.

It is assumed that subsidiary net income is earned uniformly throughout the year.

P Company elects to include S Company's operating results for all of 19X1 in the 19X1 consolidated income statement.

Required:

a. Prepare the entries made by P Company in 19X1 for its investment in S Company.
b. Prepare the investment elimination entries for a consolidated statement working paper for the year ended December 31, 19X1.
c. Prepare the consolidated income statement for the year ended December 31, 19X1.

Exercise 5–14

Allen, Inc., earned $36,000 during 19X1 without significant seasonal fluctuation. The company declared and paid dividends of $3,000 on March 1 and again on August 1. On January 1, 19X1, Allen's stockholders' equity appeared as follows:

Common stock ($10 par)	$300,000
Other contributed capital	50,000
Retained earnings	100,000

On May 1, 19X1, Shores Enterprises purchased a 90 percent interest in Allen, Inc. in the open market at a cost of $503,100. Any differential arising from the combination is to be allocated to goodwill, and amortized over 10 years (including a pro rata allocation to 19X1).

Shores Enterprises reported net income from its own operations in 19X1 of $50,000.

Required:

a. Prepare the entries made by Shores Enterprises in 19X1 for its investment in Allen, Inc.
b. Prepare the eliminating entries for a consolidated statement working paper for the year ended December 31, 19X1, assuming Shores Enterprises elected to include Allen's operating results for all of 19X1 in the 19X1 consolidated income statement.
c. Prepare a schedular calculation of consolidated net income for 19X1, using (a) the incremental approach and (b) the residual approach.

Exercise 5–15

The consolidated income statement for 19X1 of Clark Corporation and its 90 percent owned subsidiary is as follows:

Sales	$85,000
Cost of goods sold	30,000
Gross profit	$55,000
Operating expenses	25,000
Combined income	$30,000
Minority interest	1,000
Consolidated net income	$29,000

Required:

a. Is it possible to determine the amount of net income contributed by the parent's own operations? If so, how much was contributed by Clark in 19X1?
b. Assuming that none of the reported expenses represent noncash expenses (e.g., depreciation), what is your best estimate of the net amount of working capital generated by operations during 19X1 and therefore available for use by the consolidated entity?

Exercise 5–16

Using the symbols presented below indicate how each of the following items should be disclosed in the consolidated statement of changes in financial position of the Panozzo Company and its subsidiaries when the format is designed to show changes in *working capital*. There may be more than one answer; if so, indicate all answers.

A = Add in determining funds provided by operations.
S = Subtract in determining funds provided by operations.
OS = Other source of working capital.
OU = Other use of working capital.
WC = Included in schedule of changes in elements of working capital.
N = Not separately disclosed or not included.

1._____ Consolidated net income was $90,000.
2._____ Consolidated accounts receivable decreased $5,000.
3._____ The Panozzo Company declared and paid a 5 percent stock dividend.
4._____ The minority interest in combined earnings totaled $4,000.
5._____ Bonds were issued to an unaffiliated company in exchange for equipment valued at $20,000.
6._____ The Panozzo Company declared and paid a cash dividend of $4,000.
7._____ Long-term debt of the Panozzo Company was converted to common stock.
8._____ Consolidated accounts payable increased $3,000.
9._____ Amortization of a premium on bonds payable to an unaffiliated company totaled $500.
10._____ Equipment, with a book value of zero dollars, was sold to an unaffiliated company for $15,000.
11._____ Equipment costing $8,000 was purchased for cash from an unaffiliated company for cash.
12._____ The Panozzo Company issued 5,000 shares of stock in exchange for 80 percent of the stock of the ABC Company.
13._____ Panozzo's share of the earnings of an unconsolidated subsidiary totaled $4,000. The subsidiary did not pay any cash dividends during the year.
14._____ Consolidated depreciation expense totaled $10,000.
15._____ Panozzo's share of a cash dividend declared and paid by a consolidated subsidiary totaled $4,000.
16._____ The minority interest in a cash dividend declared and paid by a consolidated subsidiary totaled $1,000.
17._____ Amortization of goodwill recognized in the consolidation process totaled $8,000.
18._____ Panozzo's share of the cash dividends of an unconsolidated subsidiary exceeded Panozzo's share of the subsidiary's earnings by $3,000.

PROBLEMS

Problem 1

The Bunker Company purchased 80 percent of the capital stock of the Hampton Corporation on January 1, 19X1, for $71,200, when the latter's capital stock and retained earnings were $50,000 and $10,000 respectively. Book values were equal to fair values for all assets and liabilities of Hampton Corporation except inventory which had a fair value of $12,000 on January 1, 19X1. Bunker planned to amortize any goodwill over 10 years.

Trial balances prepared on December 31, 19X1, disclose the following:

	Bunker Company	Hampton Corporation
Cash	$ 8,000	$ 5,000
Accounts receivable	21,000	17,000
Inventory—January 1	15,000	8,000
Investment in Hampton	74,000	
Other assets	33,800	48,000
Dividends declared	10,000	5,000
Purchases	90,000	20,000
Expenses	10,000	7,000
	$261,800	$110,000
Accounts payable	$ 5,000	$ 10,000
Other liabilities	5,000	
Capital stock (par $100)	100,000	50,000
Retained earnings	40,000	10,000
Sales	105,000	40,000
Equity in subsidiary earnings	6,800	
	$261,800	$110,000
Inventory—December 31	$ 20,000	$ 10,000

Required:

a. Prepare the eliminating entries for a consolidated statement working paper for the year ended December 31, 19X1.
b. Prepare a consolidated statement working paper for the year ended December 31, 19X1.

Problem 2

P Company purchased 60 percent of the capital stock of S Company on January 1, 19X1, for $46,000 when the latter's capital stock and retained earnings were $30,000 and $10,000 respectively. Book values were equal to fair values for all assets and liabilities of S Company except plant and equipment (net) which had a fair value $20,000 in excess of book value. The plant and equipment had an estimated remaining life of 5 years, and any goodwill arising from the combination should be amortized over 10 years.

Trial balances for the companies on December 31, 19X2, are shown in this illustration.

	P Company	S Company
Cash	$ 28,800	$ 30,000
Inventory—January 1	30,000	15,000
Investment in S Company ...	51,200	
Plant and equipment (net) ..	80,000	40,000
Dividends declared	20,000	5,000
Purchases	48,000	23,000
Expenses	12,000	7,000
	$270,000	$120,000
Accounts payable	$ 24,400	$ 20,000
Capital stock	100,000	30,000
Retained earnings	50,000	20,000
Sales	90,000	50,000
Equity in subsidiary earnings ..	5,600	
	$270,000	$120,000
Inventory—December 31	$ 20,000	$ 10,000

Required:

a. Prepare the eliminating entries for a consolidated statement working paper for the year ended December 31, 19X2.

b. Prepare a consolidated statement working paper for the year ended December 31, 19X2.

Problem 3

On January 1, 19X1, United Distributors purchased 1,200 shares of Texas Wholesalers, Inc. capital stock for $200,000 when its accumulated retained earnings were $50,000. Book values were equal to fair values for all assets and liabilities of the subsidiary except land and building. Information provided by an appraisal survey completed shortly after the investment indicated the following:

	Replacement Cost New	Sound Value
Land	$50,000	$ 50,000
Building	280,000	140,000

The original estimate of service life in respect to the building remained unchanged by the appraisal, i.e., original estimate, 20 years; remaining life, 10 years.

The December 31, 19X2, trial balances were as shown in the accompanying example (page 178).

	United Distributors	Texas Wholesalers, Inc.
Inventory, January 1	$ 50,000	$ 20,000
Land	100,000	40,000
Building	400,000	200,000
Other assets	790,000	135,000
Investment in Texas Wholesalers, Inc. ...	229,600	
Dividends declared	10,000	5,000
Purchases	200,000	70,000
Expenses	50,000	10,000
	$1,829,600	$480,000
Liabilities	$ 296,000	$ 20,000
Accumulated depreciation—Building	100,000	120,000
Sales	300,000	120,000
Equity in subsidiary earnings	20,800	
Capital stock ($100 par)	742,000	150,000
Retained earnings	370,800	70,000
	$1,829,600	$480,000
Inventory, December 31	$ 75,000	$ 10,000

Required:

a. Prepare the eliminating entries for a consolidated statement working paper for the year ended December 31, 19X2.

b. Prepare a consolidated statement working paper for the year ended December 31, 19X2.

Problem 4

M Company purchased 80 percent of the capital stock of R Company on January 1, 19X1, for $48,000. The balance sheets of the affiliates on this date were:

	M Company	R Company
Cash	$ 62,000	$10,000
Receivables	61,000	36,000
Merchandise	8,000	9,000
Other assets	2,000	10,000
Goodwill	2,000	5,000
	$135,000	$70,000
Liabilities	$ 10,000	$ 5,000
Capital stock (par, $100)	100,000	50,000
Retained earnings	25,000	10,000
Other contributed capital		5,000
	$135,000	$70,000

The book values of R's assets and liabilities were equal to their fair values on January 1, 19X1, except the recorded goodwill which was (according to *APB Opinion 16,* paragraph 88) arbitrarily assigned a fair value of zero.

During 19X1, the affiliates' earnings from their own operations were: M Company, $8,000; R Company, $5,000. On December 31, 19X1, R Company paid a cash dividend of $6,000. Assume that these profits and dividends are reflected in increased cash balances; also, assume other account balances remain the same.

Required:

Prepare a consolidated balance sheet working paper as of December 31, 19X1.

Problem 5

The following are the balance sheets of Barton Company and Casey, Inc., as of December 31, 19X0:

Assets	Barton Company	Casey, Inc.
Cash	$ 432,576	$ 32,569
Accounts receivable	825,620	225,627
Inventories	1,628,429	625,375
Prepaid expenses	36,475	5,648
Total	$2,923,100	$889,219
Equities		
Accounts payable	$ 325,647	$437,989
Federal income tax payable	250,000	15,000
Capital stock	300,000	50,000
Retained earnings	2,047,453	386,230
Total	$2,923,100	$889,219

As of December 31, 19X0, Barton Company acquired from the stockholders all of the shares of stock of Casey, Inc., in exchange for $550,000 of Barton's 4 percent 10-year debentures. The excess cost of acquisition (excess of the purchase price over the net assets of Casey) is to be amortized on Barton's books by charges to income over a 10-year period.

For the years 19X1 and 19X2, operations of Casey, Inc., resulted in *losses* of $52,376 and $15,226, respectively, and operations of Barton Company resulted in *profits* of $387,465 and $420,009, respectively. The profits shown above for Barton are *before* provision for amortization of the excess cost of acquisition and for the losses of its subsidiary, Casey. Dividends of $150,000 were paid by Barton in each of the years 19X1 and 19X2.

The remaining assets and liabilities of Barton and Casey on December 31, 19X1, and 19X2, were as shown in the illustration which follows.

Assets and Liabilities of Barton and Casey

	Barton		Casey	
Assets	19X1	19X2	19X1	19X2
Cash	$ 426,879	$ 490,327	$ 30,194	$ 31,187
Accounts receivable	897,426	940,227	200,525	203,287
Inventories	1,826,162	1,952,173	600,476	535,711
Advances to Casey, Inc.	165,000	180,000		
Prepaid expenses	32,879	34,327	5,347	4,621
Liabilities				
Accounts payable	357,428	298,627	287,688	226,178
Federal income taxes payable	406,000	443,500		
Advances from Barton Company			165,000	180,000

Required:

Prepare a consolidated balance sheet working paper as of December 31, 19X2.

(AICPA adapted)

Problem 6

Hondo Nelson is the sole stockholder of two corporations: Luckenbach Taverns, Inc. and Luckenbach Long Neck Distributors. Financial statements for these companies are presented below:

	Statements of Financial Position December 31, 19X1	
	Luckenbach Taverns, Inc.	Luckenbach Long Neck Distributors
Cash	$ 10,000	$ 25,000
Receivables	35,000	5,000
Inventory	125,000	100,000
Due from Luckenbach Taverns, Inc.		50,000
Long-lived assets	20,000	150,000
	$190,000	$330,000
Current liabilities	$ 20,000	$ 50,000
Long-term debt	100,000	80,000
Stockholders equity:		
Capital stock	10,000	10,000
Retained earnings	60,000	190,000
	$190,000	$330,000

	Income Statements *For Year Ended December 31, 19X1*	
	Luckenbach *Taverns, Inc.*	*Luckenbach Long* *Neck Distributors*
Sales	$300,000	$500,000
Cost of sales	$160,000	$200,000
Other expenses	100,000	150,000
Total expenses	$260,000	$350,000
Net income	$ 40,000	$150,000

Mr. Nelson wishes to make an application for a large bank loan in January, 19X2, and his accountant suggests that he prepare combined financial statements for his two separate business interests. Mr. Nelson agrees, and the accountant develops the following additional data in his review of the records:

1. During 19X1, Luckenbach Long Neck Distributors made sales of $100,000 to Luckenbach Taverns, Inc. None of these goods remained in the December 31, 19X1, inventory to Luckenbach Taverns, Inc.
2. On December 31, 19X1, Luckenbach Taverns, Inc. owed $50,000 to Luckenbach Long Neck Distributors. This debt was included with a note payable to the bank in "long-term debt." No interest was payable on the debt on December 31, 19X1.

Required:

Prepare a combined statement of financial position on December 31, 19X1, and a combined income statement for 19X1 for Mr. Nelson's two businesses. It is not necessary to prepare a working paper.

Problem 7

The consolidated income statement and comparative balance sheets for P Company and its 90 percent owned subsidiary S Company are provided below:

P COMPANY AND SUBSIDIARY S COMPANY
Consolidated Income Statement
For the Year Ended December 31, 19X1

Sales		$150,000
Expenses:		
Cost of goods sold	$ 50,000	
Depreciation	10,000	
Other operating expenses	60,000	120,000
Income from operations		$ 30,000
Equity in earnings of unconsolidated affiliates		3,000
Combined net income		$ 33,000
Minority interest in net income		1,000
Consolidated net income		$ 32,000

P COMPANY AND SUBSIDIARY S COMPANY
Consolidated Balance Sheets
December 31, 19X1, and 19X0

Assets

	19X1	19X0
Cash	$ 23,000	$ 12,000
Receivables	50,000	40,000
Inventory	30,000	50,000
Equipment (net of depreciation)	140,000	130,000
Investment in unconsolidated affiliates (Equity basis)	7,000	8,000
Goodwill	45,000	50,000
Total Assets	$295,000	$290,000

Equities

	19X1	19X0
Liabilities:		
Accounts payable	$ 25,000	$ 30,000
Bonds	50,000	100,000
Total	$ 75,000	$130,000
Minority interest	$ 8,000	$ 10,000
Stockholders' equity:		
Common stock (no par)	$150,000	$100,000
Retained earnings	62,000	50,000
Total	$212,000	$150,000
Total Equities	$295,000	$290,000

The following additional data is provided:

(1) The amortization of goodwill recognized in the consolidation amounted to $5,000 in 19X1. This amount is included in other operating expenses.

(2) P Company received $4,000 in dividend distributions from unconsolidated affiliates in 19X1.

(3) New equipment in the amount of $20,000 was purchased in 19X1.

(4) Dividends of $27,000 were received from S Company during 19X1.

(5) P Company issued additional stock during 19X1 to nonaffiliates in the amount of $50,000.

Required:

Prepare a consolidated statement of changes in financial position for 19X1, with changes analyzed in terms of working capital. Make any inferences that are required.

Problem 8

The consolidated income statement and comparative balance sheets for P Company and its 60 percent owned subsidiary S Company are provided as shown.

P COMPANY AND SUBSIDIARY S COMPANY

Consolidated Income Statement
For the Year Ended December 31, 19X1

Sales		$100,000
Expenses:		
Cost of goods sold	$ 40,000	
Depreciation	5,000	
Other operating expenses	15,000	60,000
Income from operations		$ 40,000
Equity in earnings of unconsolidated affiliates		10,000
Combined net income		$ 50,000
Minority interest in net income		4,000
Consolidated net income		$ 46,000

P COMPANY AND SUBSIDIARY S COMPANY

Consolidated Balance Sheets
December 31, 19X1, and 19X0

Assets

	19X1	19X0
Cash	$ 20,000	$ 10,000
Receivables	35,000	40,000
Inventory	41,000	50,000
Equipment (net of depreciation)	100,000	80,000
Investment in unconsolidated affiliates (Equity basis)	106,000	100,000
Goodwill	18,000	20,000
Total Assets	$320,000	$300,000

Equities

	19X1	19X0
Liabilities:		
Accounts payable	$ 27,000	$ 50,000
Bonds	75,000	50,000
Total	$102,000	$100,000
Minority interest	$ 42,000	$ 40,000
Stockholders' equity:		
Common stock (no par)	$100,000	$100,000
Retained earnings	76,000	60,000
Total	$176,000	$160,000
Total Equities	$320,000	$300,000

The following additional data is provided:

(1) The amortization of goodwill recognized in the consolidation amounted to $2,000 in 19X1. This amount is included in other operating expenses.
(2) P Company received $4,000 in dividend distributions from unconsolidated affiliates in 19X1.
(3) New equipment in the amount of $25,000 was purchased in 19X1.
(4) Dividends in the amount of $3,000 were received from S Company in 19X1.
(5) S Company issued additional bonds during 19X1 to nonaffiliates in the amount of $25,000.

(6)   Neither P Company nor S Company engaged in any stock transactions during 19X1.

Required:

Prepare a consolidated statement of changes in financial position for 19X1, with changes analyzed in terms of working capital. Make any inferences that are required.

6

Interpretive Problems
of Accounting for
Business Combinations

THE TRANSACTIONS which give rise to business combinations and the subsequent operations of the resultant complex economic entities have generated numerous accounting problems. Several of these issues have been analyzed in Chapters 1 through 5. In the current chapter, which concludes this unit of special focus on the varied accounting aspects of business combinations, several interpretive and reporting problems of special significance are considered.

PURCHASE VERSUS POOLING OF INTERESTS ACCOUNTING

In Chapter 1, several different bases for classifying business combinations were discussed. One of these bases, labeled the "accounting perspective," divided business combinations into "purchases" and "poolings of interests." The purpose of this classification scheme derives from the fact that there exist two uniquely different sets of accounting procedures which may be used to record business combinations. One of these sets of procedures, the "purchase method," is utilized in the event a particular business combination is classified as a *purchase* combination. Contrariwise, the "pooling of interests method" is used to account for those combinations which are classified as *pooling of interests* combinations. The process of deciding the appropriate classification of a particular combination involves a careful analysis of the conditions which surround the combination and the nature of the agreement between the combining companies.

The remainder of this section will include an examination of (1) the taxonomic criteria by which business combinations are identified as either purchases or poolings of interests; (2) the purchase method of accounting; (3) the pooling of interests method of accounting; and (4) the financial statement consequences produced by the two accounting methods. Throughout the discussion, the reader should recognize that the problem of classifying business combinations as purchases or poolings of interests exists regardless of the legal form taken by the combined entity. Thus, whether the combination results in a new corporation which replaces all of the constituents (a consolidation), or one of the constituents remains as the surviving corporation (a merger), or a parent-subsidiary relationships results (an acquisition), a combination must be classified (and accounted for) as either a purchase or a pooling of interests.

Criteria for Classifying Business Combinations

Prior to the issuance of *APB Opinion No. 16,* the distinction between a purchase and a pooling of interests was based primarily upon the question of whether the ownership interests in the *combining* companies were preserved and continued in the *combined* business entity.[1] Where the net assets of one or more of the combining companies were acquired by the payment of cash, other assets, or the issuance of debt securities, the common shareholders of the acquired companies would not maintain their ownership interests in the combined firm. Such a combination was classified necessarily as a *purchase.* In substance, the combining agreement was viewed as a purchase-sale transaction between the acquiring corporation and the stockholders of the acquired corporation. Alternatively, if the combination agreement involved an exchange of common stock for common stock, the common shareholders of the combining companies would maintain their positions as owners of the combined company. Such a combination was classified as a *pooling of interests.*

The relatively simple classification criterion described above would be satisfactory if all combination agreements involved either common stock exchanges or payment with cash, other assets, or debt. However, more complex payment methods render the classification process more difficult. The use of convertible stocks and/or bonds, stock warrants, and partial payments with cash, raises the serious question of whether a combination more nearly approximates the purchase or the pooling of interests characteristics. Additionally, the issuance of stock for cash, the proceeds of which are used as payment for an acquired enterprise, raises serious doubts as to the validity of the purchase versus pooling of interests distinction. The same doubt is generated by transactions involving the purchase

---

[1] The phrases "combining companies" and "constituents or participants in the combination" are used in reference to the companies which exist prior to a combination and are combined as a result of the combination. The phrase "combined company" is used in reference to the single business entity which results from and exists after a combination, regardless of its particular legal form(s).

of treasury stock for cash and the subsequent issuance of this stock to consummate a combination.

In the attempt to clarify the classification process, the Committee on Accounting Procedure suggested several aspects or attendant circumstances of a combination that should be evaluated.[2] Examples of these are the relative size of the combining firms, the extent to which assets of a combining company were abandoned, and the continuity of the combining enterprises' managements. However, since none of these circumstances were viewed as controlling or dominating influences, the ultimate classification of any specific combination became increasingly susceptible to managerial determination. Adequate planning of the transactions leading up to and finalizing a combination could frequently result in the emergence of sufficiently conflicting evidence to place the decision within the realm of management choice. Since the classification criteria did not provide a basis for a clear-cut distinction, the election between purchase or pooling of interests often reflected management's motivation to select the accounting treatment which would result in the most favorable financial reports.

A major objective of the Accounting Principles Board pronouncement on business combinations was to establish a more precise set of classification criteria for making the distinction between those combinations which are purchases and those which are poolings of interests. To accomplish this objective, 12 specific conditions were enumerated, *all* of which must be met if a combination is to be classified as a pooling of interests. Where these conditions are satisfied, the pooling of interests accounting method *must* be employed. In the event one (or more) of the 12 conditions is not met, the combination must be accounted for as a purchase. The 12 necessary and sufficient conditions for a pooling of interests are summarized, as follows.[3]

1. Each of the combining companies must be autonomous and must not have been a subsidiary or division of another corporation during the two-year period prior to the initiation of the combination plan. However, this does not exclude companies that were newly incorporated within the preceding two years, unless they were successors to part or all of a company which was not autonomous.

2. At the dates the plan of combination is initiated and consummated, none of the combining companies can hold as intercorporate investments more than 10 percent of the outstanding voting common stock of any combining company, unless the shares held were exchanged for shares that are issued to effect the combination plan. In other

---

[2] Committee on Accounting Procedure, American Institute of Certified Public Accountants, "Business Combinations," *Accounting Research Bulletin No. 48* (1957), paragraph 7.

[3] *APB Opinion 16*, paragraphs 45–48.

words, each of the combining companies must be independent of the other combining companies.[4]

3. The combination must be effected by a single transaction, or in accordance with a specific plan within one year after the plan is initiated.

4. The surviving (or resultant parent) corporation must issue *only* common stock with rights identical to those of the majority of its outstanding voting common stock, in exchange for "substantially all" of the voting common stock of the other (combining) companies outstanding at the date the plan of combination is consummated. *Opinion No. 16* specifies a detailed set of procedures for determining whether the requirement is satisfied that "substantially all" of the voting common stock be exchanged. The essence of the requirement is that 90 percent or more of the outstanding common stock of a combining company must be exchanged (between the dates the plan of combination is initiated and consummated) for the voting common stock issued by the surviving or parent (issuing) corporation.

5. Each of the combining companies must maintain substantially the same voting common stock interest; that is, none of the companies may change those interests by exchanges, retirements, or distributions to stockholders in contemplation of effecting the combination.

6. The combining companies may reacquire shares of voting common stock *only* for purposes other than business combinations, and no company may reacquire more than a normal number of shares after the date the plan of combination is initiated.

7. The ratio of the interest of an individual common stockholder to those of other common stockholders in a combining company must remain the same as a result of the exchange of stock to effect the combination.

8. The voting rights of the common stock interests in the resultant combined corporation must be exercisable by the stockholders; no mechanisms such as a voting trust can be used to deprive or restrict the common stockholders from exercising their voting rights.

9. The combination must be resolved at the date the plan is consummated, with no pending provision of the plan relating to the issue of securities or other consideration. As a consequence, the combined corporation cannot agree to contingent issuances of additional shares

---

[4] However, *FASB Statement 10*, "Extension of 'Grandfather' Provisions for Business Combinations," provides a permanent exception for companies which held a minority interest in other companies on October 31, 1970 (the date *APB Opinion 16* became effective), if the stockholder corporations eventually increase their investments to establish control. In these cases, the stockholder companies may have owned up to 50 percent of the investee's outstanding stock on October 31, 1970, and still qualify for a pooling of interests, so long as the other pooling of interest conditions are satisfied.

or other consideration to the former stockholders of a combining company.

10. The combined corporation must not agree directly or indirectly to retire or reacquire all or part of the common stock issued to effect the combination.

11. The combined corporation must not enter into other financial arrangements for the benefit of the former stockholders of a combining company, such as a guaranty of loans secured by stock issued in the combination.

12. The combined corporation must not intend to dispose of a significant part of the assets of the combining companies within two years after the combination, except to eliminate duplicate facilities or excess capacity and those assets that would have been disposed of in the ordinary course of business of the separate company.

The Purchase Method of Accounting

A business combination which does not meet all of the 12 conditions summarized in the previous paragraphs is deemed to be a purchase. The purchase method of accounting for business combinations is but a specific application of the more general principles of accounting for purchases of all assets. Conventional accounting stipulates that purchased assets should be recorded at cost, which is established by the purchase transaction. This rule is complicated in the case of a business combination by the fact that *many* assets and liabilities are acquired rather than one asset or a single class of assets. Therefore, the total cost of the purchase must be allocated among the individual assets received and liabilities assumed. If cash is rendered in payment, the total cost of the purchased net assets is easily determinable. However, if the consideration given includes noncash items such as equity securities, the purchase price (total cost) must be determined by referring to conventional procedures for noncash acquisitions, i.e., by assessing the fair market value of the consideration given or the consideration received, whichever is most clearly evident or objectively determinable.

To provide the basis for a subsequent comparison with the pooling of interests method of accounting, three significant characteristics of the purchase method should be recognized. First, the total cost of acquiring a company typically *is not* equal to the algebraic sum of the fair market values of the company's identifiable assets and liabilities. In the context of consolidated statement prepartion for parent-subsidiary relationships, appropriate methods of treating such unallocated debit or credit differentials were discussed in Chapter 5. Where the combination takes the form of a merger or consolidation, the procedures for treating differentials would be expressed in terms of entries made by the surviving corporation. Second, the fair market values of the purchased assets and liabilities (separately considered), which are recorded on the books of the combined entity, frequently differ by substantial amounts from their book values, as previously recorded by the *acquired* company. Third, the retained earnings balance of the acquired company does not carry forward to the combined entity. This is, of course, consistent with conventional practice with respect to recording purchase transactions, viz., that the purchase of an income producing asset from a previous user does not result in an increase in the acquiring firm's retained earnings. The previous *earnings* of the asset identify with the selling company and not with the transferred asset. A corollary to this proposition is that balances in the acquired company's revenue and expense accounts at the date of acquisition (i.e., its net income) do not carry forward and are thus accounted for as are retained earnings of the seller.

As previously indicated, the purchase method entries to record a combination yield equivalent results whatever may be the particular legal form taken by the combination (merger, consolidation, or acquisition). If the sole surviving corporation is one of the combining companies (merger) or is a newly created corporation (consolidation), the entries to record the combining transactions, including the valuation of purchased assets and assumed liabilities at their fair market values, are made on the books of the relevant (new or surviving) corporation. Where a parent-subsidiary relationship is created (acquisition), the investment elimination entries on the consolidated working papers provide the basis for reporting appropriate asset and equity valuations. The reader will recall that the investment elimination entries discussed in Chapters 3, 4, and 5 consistently adhered to the precepts of the purchase method of accounting. Preacquisition revenues and expenses (or net income), and retained earnings were either eliminated or were allocated to minority interests; and purchased assets and liabilities were revalued through the allocation of debit or credit differentials, with residual (unallocated) differentials recognized and treated as appropriate under the circumstances.

The Pooling of Interests Method of Accounting

In contrast to the accounting treatment associated with purchase combinations, the pooling of interests method is supported by the argument that some combinations are not best described by a purchase-sale transaction. Proponents of pooling of interests would argue that given the pooling conditions previously described, neither company can be said to *acquire* the other. The history of each combining company can be traced from precombination periods through the act of combining to the continued operations of the combined company. The distinct characteristics and operations of the combining firms are simply commingled in the combined company.

The accounting consequences of this view generally result in a retention and aggregation of the accounting valuations of the combining companies.

Assets and liabilities are carried forward at the valuations reflected in the books of the predecessor companies; and in most instances, the stockholders' equity accounts of the transferors, excluding common stock retired, are accorded similar treatment. The retained earnings of the new enterprise may be less, but never more, than the sum of the separate retained earnings of the constituents. In the event that the stated capital of the new entity is greater than the aggregate stated capitals of the combining companies, the retained earnings of the new enterprise may be less than the sum of the amounts recorded on the books of the combining companies. In this instance, the debit difference is first applied in reduction of the amount of any other contributed capital on the books of the constituents, after which any debit residue is applied in reduction of retained earnings. Where the stated capital of the new enterprise is less than the aggregate stated capitals of its predecessors, the credit difference is reported as an addition to the contributed capital in excess of stated value of the new enterprise.

The following case illustrates accounting values assigned to the stockholders' equity accounts under each of these two pooling of interests conditions.

Case 1. Consolidation Accounted for as a Pooling of Interests. The R Corporation is organized on January 1, 19X1, to consolidate companies X and Y; balance sheets of the constituents on this date are:

	X Company	Y Company
Assets	$310,000	$690,000
Liabilities	$ 10,000	$ 30,000
Capital stock (par, $100)	200,000	500,000
Other contributed capital	40,000	60,000
Retained earnings	60,000	100,000
	$310,000	$690,000

Assumption A. The R Corporation issues one share of its $50 par value common stock for each $80 of net assets contributed by companies X and Y. The initial entry on the books of R Corporation is as follows:

```
Assets ....................................... 1,000,000
    Liabilities ..............................           40,000
    Capital stock (12,000 shares) ..............          600,000
    Other contributed capital ..................          200,000
    Retained earnings ........................          160,000
```

Distribution of R Corporation shares:
$300,000 ÷ $80 = 3,750 shares to X Company
$660,000 ÷ $80 = 8,250 shares to Y Company

In this situation, the $600,000 par value of R Corporation shares is $100,000 less than the outstanding par amount of X Company and Y Company shares. This $100,000 credit difference is added to the Other

Contributed Capital balances of X Company and Y Company to determine the $200,000 R Corporation balance. The sum of the retained earnings of companies X and Y is carried forward to the R Corporation without dilution.

Assumption B. The R Corporation issues one share of its $50 par value common stock for each $60 of net assets contributed by companies X and Y. The initial entry on the books of R Corporation is as follows:

Books of R Corporation

Assets	1,000,000	
Liabilities		40,000
Capital stock (16,000 shares)		800,000
Retained earnings		160,000

Distribution of R Corporation shares:
$300,000 ÷ $60 = 5,000 shares to X Company.
$660,000 ÷ $60 = 11,000 shares to Y Company.

The stated capital of R Corporation exceeds the aggregate stated capitals of X Company and Y Company; accordingly, the difference of $100,000 is applied in reduction of the total amounts of other contributed capital of these companies. The sum of the retained earnings is then carried forward without adjustment. It should be noted that the total stockholders' equity remains the same under both assumptions, as the net assets are recorded at their prior book values.

Case 2. Merger Accounted for as a Pooling of Interests. Suppose that the combining companies described in Case 1, X Company and Y Company, agree to combine through a process of merger, whereby X Company will issue 2,400 additional shares of its $100 par, common stock in exchange for the assets and liabilities of Y Company; thereafter, Y Company will distribute the shares to its stockholders in exchange for the outstanding Y Company stock, and Y Company will be terminated. The entry made by X Company to record the combination is as follows:

Books of X Company

Assets	690,000	
Liabilities		30,000
Capital stock (2,400 shares)		240,000
Other contributed capital		320,000
Retained earnings		100,000

As a consequence of this entry, X Company's accounts will disclose total assets of $1,000,000; liabilities of $40,000; capital stock of $440,000; other contributed capital of $360,000; and retained earnings of $160,000.

If a pooling of interests takes the acquisition form in which a parent-subsidiary relationship is established between the combining companies, the investment account on the parent company's books is debited with the *book value of the subsidiary's net assets.* The amount of this debit represents an important difference between the pooling of interests method and the purchase method; under the purchase method, the investment account on the parent company's books is debited with the fair market value of the consideration (net assets) received, which is frequently most objectively approximated by using the total market value of the shares issued.

In recording the issuance of shares on the books of the parent, where the combination is accounted for as a pooling of interests, it is important to remember that the at-acquisition retained earnings of the subsidiary company are generally carried forward, without deduction, to augment the retained earnings accumulation of the parent company. Accordingly, the parent's retained earnings at the date of acquisition may be equal to the sum of the precombination retained earnings of both parent and subsidiary affiliates. It will be less than this amount, however, in the event the stated value of the parent's newly issued shares is greater than the sum of the parent's equity in the contributed capital of the subsidiary plus any Other Contributed Capital of the parent which is eliminated in the process of recording the issuance of new shares. Where the stated value of the parent's newly issued shares is less than the corresponding equity in the subsidiary's contributed capital, the credit difference is treated as an increment to Other Contributed Capital.

Case 3. Acquisition Accounted for as a Pooling of Interests. The stockholders' equity accounts of A Company and B Company at the date of their combination are as follows:

	A Company	B Company
Common stock (par, $100)	$60,000	$40,000
Other contributed capital	6,000	5,000
Retained earnings	44,000	30,000

The stockholders of B Company exchanged 100 percent of their shares for newly issued shares of A Company common stock in the following amounts:

Assumption 1	300 shares
Assumption 2	400 shares
Assumption 3	500 shares
Assumption 4	600 shares

The entry on the books of A Company to record the issuance of shares, for each of the stated assumptions, is presented in Illustration 6–1.

The investment elimination entry for a consolidated statement working paper at date of acquisition is the same for all of the assumptions. The entry is:

Common stock—B Company	40,000	
Other contributed capital—B Company	5,000	
Retained earnings—B Company	30,000	
Investment in B common stock		75,000

It should be noted that the investment elimination entries do not include debit or credit differentials. The entries to record the issuance were constructed so that the balance in the Investment in B Common Stock ac-

Illustration 6–1

	Assumption							
	1		*2*		*3*		*4*	
	Dr.	*Cr.*	*Dr.*	*Cr.*	*Dr.*	*Cr.*	*Dr.*	*Cr.*
Investment in B common stock	75,000		75,000		75,000		75,000	
Other contributed capital	—		—		5,000		6,000	
Common stock		30,000		40,000		50,000		60,000
Other contributed capital		15,000		5,000		—		—
Retained earnings ..		30,000		30,000		30,000		21,000

count is exactly equal to the parent's 100 percent equity in the stockholders' equity accounts of the subsidiary. Thus, the pooling of interests method does not involve a revaluation of the assets and liabilities of the affiliates. Based upon this investment elimination entry, the consolidated statement working paper for a pooling of interests is then prepared in the same manner as for a purchase.

Financial Statement Differences between Purchases and Poolings of Interests

The classificational scheme that is used to distinguish between purchase combinations and pooling of interests combinations was previously discussed. The purpose of that distinction is to obviate the possibility of applying different accounting methods in situations that are essentially similar. Therefore, the purchase and pooling of interests methods *are not alternative* sets of procedures. Nevertheless, an examination of the 12 conditions which lead to the use of the pooling of interests method will disclose that two given combinations may be similar in *many* respects and yet be accounted for by different methods. Consequently, an understanding of the financial statement differences between the two methods is an important factor in the interpretation of the statements. The following discussion, which focuses on these differences, pertains to those situations where combinations are similar in important particulars but are nonetheless sufficiently different to result in the use of different methods.

Consider the difference between the two methods in respect to asset and liability valuation. In the event that an acquired company's net assets have a fair market value in excess of book value, which amount is recorded as the cost of the parent's investment, the purchase method of accounting results in a debit differential.[5] To the extent this differential is allocated

---

[5] In the current discussion, it will be assumed that the combination takes the form of a parent-subsidiary relationship. Manifestly, the same arguments apply to mergers and consolidations.

to amortizable assets, future reported expenses will be increased and earnings correspondingly reduced. Further, the unallocated residual amount of differential must also be amortized (see Chapter 5), an expense that is not deductible for income tax purposes. It thereby has a magnified negative influence on future reported earnings. Should the combination be treated as a tax-free reorganization (see Chapter 1), not even the portion that is allocated to specific assets would qualify as a deductible expense. Under these circumstances, a similar business combination, although sufficiently different to require the pooling of interests method, would report smaller asset valuations and higher future earnings. Carrying forward the combined companies' assets at their book values eliminates the future expenses associated with the differential amortization (which is unrecognized). Correspondingly, future net incomes, earnings per share, and rates of return will be larger.

If the acquired firm's net assets have a fair market value (reflected in the parent's investment account) that is less than book value, the purchase method of accounting results in a credit differential. In accordance with the analysis of differentials presented in Chapter 5, this differential would be allocated to individual assets and liabilities. Thus, conversely to the debit differential illustration, the purchase method of accounting would result in smaller reported expenses and larger future net incomes, earnings per share, and rates of return.

Case 4 illustrates the effects of purchase accounting relative to pooling of interests accounting, given a situation in which the fair market value of the acquired company's net assets exceeds their total book value.

Case 4. On January 1, 19X1, the R Company issued 20,000 common shares in exchange for 100 percent of the S Company's outstanding stock. The balance sheets of R Company and S Company on January 1, 19X1, immediately prior to the combination, are as follows:

	R Company	S Company
Total Assets	$2,000,000	$1,000,000
Liabilities	$ 600,000	$ 300,000
Common stock ($10 par)	400,000	200,000
Retained earnings	1,000,000	500,000
Total Equities	$2,000,000	$1,000,000

R Company's common stock had a well-established market price of $120 on January 1, 19X1; because the shares were closely held, S Company's stock had no readily attainable market price. The balance sheet of R Company immediately after the common for common stock exchange will vary depending on which method of accounting is appropriate. In the illustrations of pooling of interests accounting to follow, it is assumed that the combination has met all of the 12 conditions specified earlier in this chapter. In the illustrations of purchase accounting, the assumption is made that one of the 12 conditions was not satisfied, e.g., at the date of the combination, the combined management expressly stated the intent of selling a significant portion of S Company's assets within two years after the combination and reinvesting the proceeds in a new line of operations. Immediately after the acquisition, R Company's balance sheet would appear as follows:

R COMPANY
Balance Sheet

Assets	Assuming Purchase Accounting	Assuming Pooling of Interests Accounting
Other assets	$2,000,000	$2,000,000
Investment in S stock	2,400,000	700,000
Total Assets	$4,400,000	$2,700,000
Equities		
Liabilities	$ 600,000	$ 600,000
Common stock	600,000	600,000
Other contributed capital	2,200,000	
Retained earnings	1,000,000	1,500,000
Total Equities	$4,400,000	$2,700,000

The consolidated working papers under each of the accounting treatments are presented in Illustrations 6–2 and 6–3. The consolidated net income of R Company and its subsidiary during the years 19X1–X3 was $300,000, $360,000, and $420,000, excluding any deductions for the amortization of a differential. The combination was treated as a "tax-free" reorganization (see Chapter 1). Thus, none of the differential amortizations are tax deductible.

Assume that the entire differential (arising only under the purchase method) was allocated to assets having remaining estimated useful lives of 17 years. The comparative net incomes and earnings per share under each method are as follows:

		Assuming Pooling of Interests Accounting	Less Differential Amortization	Assuming Purchase Accounting
19X1:	Net income	$300,000	$100,000	$200,000
	Earnings per share	$5.00		$3.33
19X2:	Net income	360,000	100,000	260,000
	Earnings per share	$6.00		$4.33
19X3:	Net income	420,000	100,000	320,000
	Earnings per share	$7.00		$5.33

Illustration 6–2

R COMPANY AND SUBSIDIARY S COMPANY

Consolidated Statement Working Paper
Combination Accounted for as a Purchase
January 1, 19X1

	R Company	S Company	Eliminations Dr.	Eliminations Cr.	Con-solidated
Other assets	2,000,000	1,000,000			3,000,000
Investment in S	2,400,000			(1) 2,400,000	
Differential			(1) 1,700,000		1,700,000
	4,400,000	1,000,000			4,700,000
Liabilities	600,000	300,000			900,000
Common stock:					
R	600,000				600,000
S		200,000	(1) 200,000		
Other contributed capital	2,200,000				2,200,000
Retained earnings:					
R	1,000,000				1,000,000
S		500,000	(1) 500,000		
	4,400,000	1,000,000	2,400,000	2,400,000	4,700,000

Illustration 6–3

R COMPANY AND SUBSIDIARY S COMPANY

Consolidated Statement Working Paper
Combination Accounted for as a Pooling of Interests
January 1, 19X1

	R Company	S Company	Eliminations Dr.	Eliminations Cr.	Con-solidated
Other assets	2,000,000	1,000,000			3,000,000
Investment in S	700,000			(1) 700,000	
	2,700,000	1,000,000			3,000,000
Liabilities	600,000	300,000			900,000
Common stock:					
R	600,000				600,000
S		200,000	(1) 200,000		
Retained earnings:					
R	1,500,000				1,500,000
S		500,000	(1) 500,000		
	2,700,000	1,000,000	700,000	700,000	3,000,000

The essential facts of Case 4 are not atypical. The price paid for S Company, stated in terms of the market value of R Company's common stock, was $2,400,000, while the book value of S Company's stock was $700,000. A market value to book value ratio of 3.4:1 is not unusual. Furthermore, the assumed net incomes exhibit realistic relationships to total assets. Thus, the relative effect on the financial statements of the two accounting methods is easily observable.

The assumptions of Case 4 can be adapted to display the relative effect on the financial statements of the two accounting methods when the book value of S Company's net assets exceeds fair market value. For example, it may be assumed that only 5,000 shares of R Company's stock are issued in payment for S Company. The comparative consolidated financial statements in this case are left as an exercise for the reader.

HISTORICAL SUMMARIES AND FINANCIAL ANALYSES OF COMBINED BUSINESS ENTITIES

Trend Analysis

One method of evaluating the current position and future expectations of a business entity involves a careful examination of the financial trends that have been established by the firm's past history. To facilitate this type of analysis, published financial reports usually include comparative financial statements which typically extend from the past two to five years. Additionally, financial summaries (which focus upon such items as sales, earnings, earnings per share, and selected ratios) are frequently provided for as many as the past 10 or 15 years. The preparation of these comparative statements and financial summaries, as well as interpretive analysis of these data, impose unique difficulties if the period covered by the analysis includes one or more business combinations.

Participation in a business combination is usually a critical event in the history of a business entity. Managerial identity, ownership positions, legal structure, the nature of operations and resources as well as their magnitudes, and many other significant aspects of the entity may undergo dramatic change as the result of a combination. Indeed, it can be argued that many business combinations involve such sweeping changes that meaningful comparisons between the combined entity and its precombination constituents are virtually impossible. Nevertheless, there persists a compelling desire for information that may be relevant to future decisions, which has accented the importance of trend analysis extending over periods that include business combinations.

The most basic problem involved in trend analysis of combined business entities relates to the precombination operating periods; the accountant must decide what data of these periods are comparable to the postcombination financial statements. Two alternative approaches to resolving the data selection problem are utilized by accountants. One method is to select the reported precombination financial statements of the *acquiring* firm as the relevant data to compare with the postcombination financial statements of the combined entity. This approach is essentially consistent with the purchase method of accounting. If a combination is interpreted as an acquisition of assets and assumption of liabilities (which is the view implied by purchase accounting), *adjustments* of precombination statements would not appear to be warranted. Thus, historical financial summaries and comparative financial statements prepared in accordance with the purchase method do not involve retroactive combining of precombination financial data. The past financial statements of the *acquiring* firm as originally reported are the comparative base.

An alternative approach to historical trend analysis involves restatement of the precombination financial statements to retroactively reflect the combination. This method is a natural counterpart to pooling of interests accounting. Under the pooling perspective, a combined (pooled) entity involves nothing more substantive than the merging of two businesses into a single enterprise. Both continue to exist as one combined entity. Given this perspective, it is consistent to argue for the retroactive combining of precombination financial statements. Such recast statements should be comparable to postcombination statements; therefore, after a pooling of interests combination, any financial reference to precombination periods should be expressed in terms of combined data. For example, where a pooling of interests combination occurs after a balance sheet date but before statements are prepared, the subsequently prepared statements should be prepared on a combined basis.

The decision of whether or not precombination financial data are restated has a significant impact upon the trends displayed by historical comparisons. Case 5 exhibits the differences between the two methods.

Case 5. For several years, G Company and H Company have enjoyed 10 percent growth rates in their sales, earnings, and earnings per share. For 1976, these firms reported the following data:

	G Company	H Company
Sales	$1,000,000	$750,000
Earnings	100,000	75,000
Outstanding shares	100,000	75,000
Earnings per share	$1.00	$1.00

G Company acquired 100 percent of H Company's stock on January 1, 1977, in a common for common stock exchange. The exchange ratio was set at .6 to 1. During 1977, G Company and its subsidiary maintained their historical 10 percent growth rates. Financial data for 1977 were as follows:

	G Company	H Company	Consolidated
Sales	$1,100,000	$825,000	$1,925,000
Earnings (excluding parent's equity in subsidiary earnings) ..	110,000	82,500	192,500
Outstanding shares			145,000*
Earnings per share			$1.33

* 100,000 + .6(75,000) = 145,000.

Illustration 6–4

HISTORICAL COMPARISONS OF FINANCIAL DATA

	1976 Data		1977 Data	
	Absolute Amounts	As a Percentage of 1975 Amounts*	Absolute Amounts	As a Percentage of 1976 Amounts
With retroactive adjustments:				
Sales	$1,750,000	110	$1,925,000	110
Earnings	175,000	110	192,500	110
Earnings per share	$1.21	110	$1.33	110
Without retroactive adjustments:				
Sales	$1,000,000	110	$1,925,000	192.5
Earnings	100,000	110	192,500	192.5
Earnings per share	$1.00	110	$1.33	133

* The annual growth rate for sales, earnings, and earnings per share was assumed to be 10 percent for years prior to 1977.

The historical comparisons under both alternative methods are presented in Illustration 6–4. Significantly, the restatement of precombination data results in the 10 percent growth rate being maintained. Thus, if growth rates in sales, earnings, and other operating data are important variables in the decision makers' predictions of future success, restatement would seem appropriate. The large growth rates displayed by comparisons with the unadjusted base are primarily caused by the combination itself; thus, they are not likely to be maintained over several future periods. Maintaining such growth rates requires increasingly large business combinations. Indeed, the size of the firms to be acquired would have to increase at a geometrical rate.

It must be reemphasized that the restatement method is employed only when combinations are accounted for as poolings of interests. The unadjusted method is used if the purchase method is followed.[6] Case 5 was based on the implicit assumption of unique circumstances in which the differences between the purchase and pooling of interests methods did not affect 1977 combined net income. Consequently, the difference in the reported trends was attributable entirely to the restatement or nonrestatement of the data of precombination periods.

---

[6] However, under the purchase method, *APB Opinion 16* (paragraph 96) requires additional, one-time disclosure in the first financial statements issued after the combination. Specifically, the requirement is for footnote disclosure of the current and immediately preceding periods' results of operations based on a pro forma restatement as if the combination had taken place at the beginning of the preceding period.

Earnings per Share Analysis

One of the most critical items of information that is drawn from accounting reports is the earnings per share indicant. As a summary indicator of current success and future expectations of success, the absolute size, periodic variation, and growth rate of earnings per share probably have more informational significance than any other data that can be extracted from financial statements. Nonetheless, accountants frequently warn against the dangers of placing an exaggerated emphasis on earnings per share analysis. This summary indicator should always be interpreted in light of all of the other information obtainable from financial statements and other sources. Prudent accountants would acknowledge that proper analysis of all available data is superior to undue reliance on the preliminary indications of any single item such as earnings per share. Nevertheless, earnings per share continues to be of signal importance to the investing community.

The large number of business combinations in recent years was accompanied by an increasing variety of financing methods. Many of these methods have an immediate or potential impact on earnings per share calculations. Even with the employment of more traditional financing methods, the act of combination often causes a sharp discontinuity in the historical trend of earnings per share. As a result, the meaning and reliability of earnings per share calculations must be viewed circumspectly. Understanding these problems and recent attempts to resolve them is a requisite part of comprehending the broader subject of accounting for business combinations.

In addition to this relationship between earnings per share issues and business combinations, the calculations of earnings per share for consolidated financial statements and for investor companies that use the equity method must be made in accordance with special procedures. Further, unique problems can occur if the securities of one affiliate are convertible into a security of the other affiliate. These factors require a careful consideration of earnings per share calculations in the context of explaining the accounting issues associated with the preparation of consolidated financial statements.

Case 5 displayed the sharp discontinuities that can occur in historical earnings per share trends when combinations involve traditional common for common stock exchanges. This problem was also considered in Chapter 2. The critical factor which causes this phenomenon is the relative size of the combining firms' price/earnings ratios. Retroactive adjustments (used primarily with pooling of interests accounting) are an attempt to report growth trends that are consistent with internal operations. However, it must be recognized that data once reported are probably never completely overturned in the minds of investors, no matter how forcefully the retroactive adjustments may be emphasized.

Traditional Calculations.   Earnings per share is a financial statistic of long standing. Traditionally, it was calculated as a quotient, the numerator of which was net income less preferred dividends declared (including current arrearages) and the denominator of which was the weighted average number of common shares outstanding. The significance of this calculation as a basic success indicator was implicitly accepted for many years. However, increasing usage of convertible securities, common stock warrants, and stock option plans rendered this traditional calculation misleading and inadequate. As a substitute for this summary statistic, accountants developed two calculations: primary earnings per share and fully diluted earnings per share. Sharp controversy continues to exist as to the significance and dependability of these measures as indicants of future business success. Nevertheless, they represent the only evident means of providing the information that was once supplied by the traditional earnings per share calculation.

Primary Earnings per Share.   Primary earnings per share is based on a concept of "common stock equivalents" which are added to common stock presently outstanding[7] to determine the denominator in the calculation. In fact, the primary earnings per share statistic is frequently reported in financial statements as "earnings per common share and common equivalent share." The Accounting Principles Board has defined the concept of "common stock equivalent" as follows:

A common stock equivalent is a security which is not, in form, a common stock but which usually contains provisions to enable its holder to become a common stockholder and which, because of its terms and the circumstances under which it was issued, is in substance equivalent to a common stock. The holders of these securities can expect to participate in the appreciation of the value of the common stock resulting principally from the earnings and earnings potential of the issuing corporation. This participation is essentially the same as that of a common stockholder except that the security may carry a specified dividend or interest rate yielding a return different from that received by a common stockholder.[8]

The most prominent types of securities that are, or may be, common stock equivalents are (1) those which are convertible into common stock and (2) common stock options and warrants which allow the holder to purchase common shares at specified prices.

It should be apparent that the definition of common stock equivalents requires some more specific operational criteria that may be used to decide whether a specific security should be classified as a common stock equivalent or as a senior security. Without such a definitive standard, the

---

[7] The amount to be added is the number of common shares that could be issued through conversion or exercise of the common stock equivalents less the number the company could repurchase using the cash proceeds from the exercise of the common stock equivalents.

[8] *APB Opinion 15,* "Earnings per Share," paragraph 25.

earnings per share calculations of business firms would probably not be based on comparable classifications. With respect to all convertible securities, the Accounting Principles Board stated the following classification criterion:

. . . a convertible security should be considered as a common stock equivalent at the time of issuance if, based on its market price, it has a cash yield of less than 66⅔% of the then current bank prime interest rate. For any convertible security which has a change in its cash interest rate or cash dividend rate scheduled within the first five years after issuance, the lowest scheduled rate during such five years should be used in determining the cash yield of the security at issuance.[9]

An important implication of this criterion is that the common stock equivalent or senior status of a security is determined *only* at the time of issuance, and this status remains unchanged so long as the security remains outstanding.

With respect to common stock options, warrants, and similar obligations, the established criterion is that they be included in the common stock equivalent class at all times. This inclusion is consistent with the fact that such securities generally have no cash yield and therefore derive their value "from their right to obtain common stock at specified prices for an extended period."[10]

In respect to the calculation of primary earnings per share, it should be recognized that the assumed conversion or exercise of a common stock equivalent may be either *dilutive* or *antidilutive;* that is, the effect of the assumed conversion may be either to decrease or to increase the earnings per share figure. However, the underlying purpose of the development of the primary earnings per share statistic was to recognize that some securities (other than common stock) are likely to participate in the value increments of common stock that result from growth in earnings. If earnings are not maintained at a level which would eventually make it profitable for security holders to convert or exercise their securities, it can be assumed that such conversions may not take place. As a consequence, the calculation of primary earnings per share is based on the assumed conversion and exercise of common stock equivalents, *only if the effects of the assumed conversions or exercises are dilutive.* Given several different common stock equivalents, there are obviously several different possible earnings per share amounts, depending upon how each common stock equivalent is treated—conversion assumed, or not. The correct treatment of the common stock equivalents is that which results in the lowest earnings per share amount.

Special consideration must be given to the treatment of common stock

---

[9] Ibid., paragraph 33. If no market price is available at the time of issuance, this test is based on the fair value of the security.

[10] Ibid., paragraph 35.

warrants (and stock options, etc.) in the calculation of primary earnings per share. So long as the number of common shares that are issuable upon the exercise of warrants is 20 percent or less of the total number of common shares outstanding at the end of the period, the treatment of warrants in this calculation is described as the "treasury stock" method. The cash proceeds from the anticipated exercise of warrants are assumed to be used to repurchase shares of common stock at the average market price during the period. If the exercise price of the warrants is less than the average market price of common stock, more common shares will have been issued than will have been repurchased; thus, the net number of common shares outstanding is increased and the warrants are *dilutive* in effect. However, if the exercise price of the warrants is greater than the average price of common stock, the cash proceeds from the assumed exercise of the warrants would provide for repurchasing more common shares than were issued when the warrants were exercised; thus, the net number of common shares outstanding is decreased and the warrants are *antidilutive*. In the latter situation, the warrants should be disregarded in calculating primary earnings per share, notwithstanding the fact that they are classified as common stock equivalents.

In the event that the number of common shares issuable upon the exercise of warrants (and stock options, etc.) exceeds 20 percent of the number of common shares outstanding at the end of the period, the previously described "treasury stock" method is rejected in the belief that it may not provide an adequate reflection of the potential dilution associated with warrants. The Accounting Principles Board described the alternative method to be utilized, as follows:

. . . all the options and warrants should be assumed to have been exercised and the aggregate proceeds therefrom to have been applied in two steps:

a.   As if the funds were first applied to the repurchase of outstanding common shares at the average market price during the period (treasury stock method) but not to exceed 20% of the outstanding shares; and then

b.   As if the balance of the funds were applied first to reduce any short-term or long-term borrowings and any remaining funds were invested in U.S. government securities or commercial paper, with appropriate recognition of any income tax effect.

The results of steps (a) and (b) of the computation (whether dilutive or antidilutive) should be aggregated and, if the net effect is dilutive, should enter into the earnings per share computation.[11]

To summarize, the denominator in primary earnings per share calculations includes the weighted average of the number of common shares outstanding plus the number of common shares that would have been issued if each dilutive common stock equivalent were converted or exercised. In

---

[11] Ibid., paragraph 38.

general, the numerator includes (1) net income, less dividend declarations (including current arrearages) to preferred shares that are classified as senior securities; and (2) the interest charges, less tax effect, on convertible bonds that are classified as dilutive common stock equivalents and on debt that would have been retired with the proceeds from the exercise of dilutive warrants.

Case 6. Primary Earnings per Share. Western Calculations, Inc., reported net income for 1977 of $8,000,000. The firm's common stock is traded actively on the NYSE and had an average market price of $50 during the year; the December 31, 1977, price was $80. The following securities of Western Calculations were outstanding throughout 1977:

Long-term debt:
Six percent bonds, due 1986 .... $ 5,000,000
Four percent 30-year bonds, due 1996 and convertible into common stock at the rate of three shares per $100; at issuance, the prime interest rate was 7 percent; the bonds were issued at par 10,000,000

Outstanding Shares

Stockholders' equity:
Preferred stock, issued January 1, 1977, cumulative as to dividends of $4.50, callable at $100, and convertible into common stock at the rate of two shares for each share of preferred; at issuance, the prime interest rate was 7 percent; issue price, $100 150,000
Preferred stock, cumulative as to dividends of $2.50, callable at $60, and convertible into common stock at the rate of one share for each share of preferred; at issuance, the prime interest rate was 4 percent; issue price was $50 400,000
Common stock 1,500,000
Warrants to purchase common stock:
100,000 shares at $20.
200,000 shares at $52.

Primary earnings per share calculations require a determination of which securities should be classified as common stock equivalents. Applying the rules of the Accounting Principles Board, the classification process is summarized in Illustration 6–5.

Based on the analysis of Illustration 6–5, the computation of primary earnings per share is presented in Illustration 6–6.

Fully Diluted Earnings per Share. Primary earnings per share calculations provide no indication of the potential impact upon common stockholders of possible future conversions or exercises of *senior* securities. To communicate the estimated effect of such contingencies, increasing attention is being given to fully diluted earnings per share. The fully diluted calculation "reflects the dilution of earnings per share that would have occurred if *all* contingent issuances of common stock that would individually reduce earnings per share had taken place at the beginning of the

Illustration 6–5

WESTERN CALCULATIONS, INC.

Classification of Securities
Common Stock Equivalent or Senior

Security	Cash Yield Based on Market Price at Issuance	Prime Interest Rate at Issuance	Common Stock Equivalent/Senior Classification	Criterion
Six percent bonds			Senior	No common stock characteristics
Four percent bonds	4.0%	7.0%	C/S equivalent	Yield is less than ⅔ of prime rate
$4.50 preferred stock	4.5	7.0	C/S equivalent	Yield is less than ⅔ of prime rate
$2.50 preferred stock	5.0	4.0	Senior	Yield is greater than or equal to ⅔ of prime rate
Warrants at $20			C/S equivalent	Always C/S equivalent
Warrants at $52			C/S equivalent	Always C/S equivalent

Illustration 6–6

WESTERN CALCULATIONS, INC.

Primary Earnings per Share

	Shares	Earnings
Reported net income		$8,000,000
Common shares outstanding	1,500,000	
Dividend requirements on $2.50 preferred stock ($2.50 × 400,000)		−1,000,000
		$7,000,000
Effect of assumed conversion or exercise of dilutive common stock equivalents:*		
4 percent convertible bonds:		
[3(10,000,000 ÷ 100)]	300,000	
[.52(.04 × 10,000,000)]		208,000
$4.50 convertible preferred stock (2 × 150,000)	300,000	
Warrants for 100,000 at $20 100,000		
(100,000 × 20) ÷ 50 .... −40,000	60,000	
Warrants for 200,000 at $52 200,000		
(200,000 × 52) ÷ 50 .... −208,000		
	2,160,000	$7,208,000
Primary earnings per share		$3.34

* It should be noted that each of the common stock equivalent securities for which conversion or exercise was assumed had the effect of diluting earnings per share. The warrants for 200,000 common shares at $52 were not included in the calculation since the effect of including them would have been to increase earnings per share. The earnings effect of the 4 percent bond conversion is after taxes (assuming a 48 percent rate).

period (or time of issuance of the convertible security, etc., if later)."[12] Fully diluted earnings per share should be reported concurrently with primary earnings per share whenever present contingencies may result in future common stock issuances that would materially dilute primary earnings per share. It should also be reported if conversions taking place during the current period would have materially diluted primary earnings per share had they taken place at the beginning of the period (or date of issuance, if later).

The fully diluted calculation closely parallels the calculations for primary earnings per share. The principal difference between the two statistics is that fully diluted calculations include the assumed conversion and exercise of *all* potentially dilutive securities; alternatively, the primary calculations assume the conversion and exercise only of dilutive common stock equivalents. Since the essential purpose of the fully diluted statistic is to show the maximum potential dilution, "the computations of fully diluted earnings per share for each period should exclude those securities whose conversion, exercise or other contingent issuance would have the effect of increasing the earnings per share amount or decreasing the loss per share amount for such period."[13] Regarding the fully diluted calculations, one important modification in the previously described primary earnings per share calculations relates to the assumed exercise of warrants and options. In the primary calculations, it is assumed (under the treasury stock method) that the cash proceeds are used to repurchase common stock at the *average* market price during the period. In fully diluted calculations, "the market price at the close of the period reported upon should be used to determine the number of shares which would be assumed to be repurchased . . . if such market price is higher than the average price used in computing primary earnings per share."[14]

Case 7. Fully Diluted Earnings per Share.   Case 7 assumes the same data as presented in Case 6. The calculation of fully diluted earnings per share requires the assumed conversion of all dilutive securities including those designated as senior securities in Illustration 6–5. The computation of fully diluted earnings per share is presented in Illustration 6–7.

Earnings per Share Calculations Involving Affiliates.   Any corporation may have outstanding common stock equivalents or senior securities which involve potential dilution of earnings per share. Additionally, where companies have intercorporate stock investments and the investor corporation uses the equity method or prepares consolidated statements, earnings per share calculations for the investor corporation may be affected by the nature of the securities issued by the investee corporation. In

---

[12] Ibid., paragraph 15. A reduction of less than 3 percent in primary earnings per share is not considered by the Board to be significant enough to warrant the presentation of fully diluted earnings per share.

[13] Ibid., paragraph 40.

[14] Ibid., paragraph 42.

Illustration 6–7
WESTERN CALCULATIONS, INC.
Fully Diluted Earnings per Share

		Shares	*Earnings*
Recorded net income			$8,000,000
Common shares outstanding		1,500,000	
Effect of assumed conversion of dilutive common stock equivalents and senior securities:			
4 percent convertible bonds:			
3(10,000,000/100)		300,000	
.52(.04 × 10,000,000)			208,000
$4.50 convertible preferred stock (2 × 150,000)		300,000	
$2.50 convertible preferred stock (1 × 400,000)		400,000	
Warrants for 100,000 at $20:			
Shares issued	100,000		
(100,000 × 20)/80	−25,000	75,000	
Warrants for 200,000 at $52:*			
Shares issued	200,000		
(200,000 × 52)/80	−130,000	70,000	
		2,645,000	$8,208,000
Fully diluted earnings per share			$3.10

* Note that the warrants for 200,000 common shares at $52 are defined as a common stock equivalent, not as a senior security. Nevertheless, they become dilutive only in the fully diluted earnings per share calculations. This was caused by the increase in the common stock market price from the $50 average price during the year to $80 at the end of the year.

other words, if a corporation's net income includes equity method earnings from holding stock of another corporation, the earnings per share calculations for the stockholder corporation must give explicit consideration to potential dilution associated with the investee corporation's earnings. This is also true regarding earnings per share calculations for consolidated financial statements.

To accomplish this objective, primary and fully diluted earnings per share for the investee corporation must first be calculated. Next, in the calculations for the investor corporation, the net income derived from use of the equity method is excluded from the numerator and is replaced by the investor's equity in the earnings per share of the investee. For example, assuming a parent (P) which holds 900 shares of a subsidiary's (S's) outstanding stock, the general form of the parent's primary earnings per share calculations is as follows:

$$\text{P's Primary EPS} = \frac{\begin{array}{c}\text{P's primary earnings,}\\ \textit{excluding}\text{ P's equity} \\ \text{in S's earnings}\end{array} + 900\left(\begin{array}{c}\text{S's primary}\\ \text{earnings per share}\end{array}\right)}{\begin{array}{c}\text{P's common shares}\\ \text{outstanding}\end{array} + \begin{array}{c}\text{Additional P common shares}\\ \text{issued if P's dilutive common}\\ \text{stock equivalents were converted}\end{array}}$$

In a similar manner, the general form of the parent's fully diluted earnings per share calculations is as follows:

$$\text{P's fully diluted EPS} = \frac{\begin{array}{c}\text{P's fully diluted earnings,}\\ \textit{excluding} \text{ P's equity}\\ \text{in S's earnings}\end{array} + 900 \left(\begin{array}{c}\text{S's fully diluted}\\ \text{earnings per share}\end{array}\right)}{\begin{array}{c}\text{P's common}\\ \text{shares}\\ \text{outstanding}\end{array} + \begin{array}{c}\text{Additional P common}\\ \text{shares issued if P's}\\ \text{dilutive common stock}\\ \text{equivalents were}\\ \text{converted}\end{array} + \begin{array}{c}\text{Additional P common}\\ \text{shares issued if P's}\\ \text{dilutive senior}\\ \text{securities were}\\ \text{converted}\end{array}}$$

These calculational formats are consistent with the *APB Opinion 15* requirements that parent company or consolidated primary [fully diluted] earnings per share "should include the portion of the subsidiary's income that would be applicable to the consolidated group based on its holdings and the subsidiary's primary [fully diluted] earnings per share."[15] However, attention must be given to what is meant by the parent's "holdings." Specifically, it is necessary to decide whether a parent's "holdings" should include assumed conversions and exercises of any of the subsidiary's dilutive common stock equivalents or senior securities held by the parent. An assumption of conversion or exercise would be consistent with the logic inherent in the subsidiary's earnings per share calculations. Thus, the conversions or exercises should be assumed, thereby increasing the number of subsidiary shares held by the parent. If the parent must pay to the subsidiary an exercise price associated with the assumed exercise of subsidiary warrants held by the parent, the cash proceeds are applied to repurchase shares from the parent.

Case 8. Western Calculations, Inc., which was analyzed in cases 5 and 6, is now assumed to be a subsidiary of Northern Computers Corporation. Northern has a simple capital structure with no securities outstanding other than 2,000,000 shares of common stock. The following data is drawn from the records of Northern:

Investments in Western Calculations, Inc.:	
Common stock, acquired at book value	1,000,000 shares
Warrants to purchase common stock at $20	80,000 warrants
Warrants to purchase common stock at $52	40,000 warrants
Net income for 1977, excluding subsidiary earnings	$10,000,000
Equity in subsidiary earnings:	
Subsidiary net income	$8,000,000
Preferred dividends:	
$2.50 preferred	−1,000,000
$4.50 preferred	− 675,000
Earnings allocated to common stock	$6,325,000
Northern's equity therein:	
1,000,000/1,500,000 × $6,325,000	4,216,667
Reported net income (equals consolidated net income)	$14,216,667

---

[15] Ibid., paragraphs 67–68.

Northern does not have any potential dilution in its capital structure. Nevertheless, it should be emphasized that earnings per share for Northern is *not* determined by dividing Northern's reported net income ($14,216,-667) by the number of common shares outstanding (2,000,000). Instead, primary earnings per share is calculated as indicated in Illustration 6–8. Since the $52 warrants were antidilutive in the calculation of primary earnings per share for Western (See Illustration 6–6), they are ignored in the comparable calculation for Western's parent (Illustration 6–8). However, Northern's ownership of $20 warrants must be incorporated in the calculation since they had a dilutive effect on the subsidiary's earnings per share. In Illustration 6–6, the assumed exercise of these $20 warrants had a net result of 60,000 additional common shares outstanding. Since Northern owns 80 percent of the $20 warrants, Northern would have received 48,000 additional shares (net). Each of these additional shares is allocated $3.34 according to Western's primary earnings per share calculation. This amount ($3.34 × 48,000) must be included in the numerator of Northern's primary earnings per share calculation.

Fully diluted earnings per share for Northern Computers Corporation amounts $6.66, which is not materially less than primary earnings per share. The calculations to confirm this $6.66 amount are left for the reader's exercise.

During the 1960s, some subsidiaries began to issue securities (or warrants) which were convertible (or exercisable) into common stock of the parent. Obviously, the conversion or exercise of these securities would not dilute the subsidiary's earnings per share. Therefore, subsidiary calculations need only reflect the appropriate deductions for current cash payments (e.g., dividends) to holders of such securities.

Illustration 6–8
NORTHERN COMPUTERS CORPORATION
Primary Earnings per Share Calculation
Parent Company or Consolidated Statements

Primary earnings of Northern, excluding Northern's equity in subsidiary earnings		$10,000,000
Number of Western common shares held by Northern	1,000,000	
Primary earnings per share of Western	× $3.34	3,340,000
Net number of additional common shares which would have been issued by Western in satisfaction of the exercise of $20 warrants (See Illustration 6–6)	60,000	
Percent of $20 warrants held by Northern (80,000/100,000)	80%	
Number of additional shares which would have been issued to Northern	48,000	
Primary earnings per share of Western	× $3.34	160,320
Total "primary" earnings of Northern		$13,500,320
Number of Northern common shares outstanding		2,000,000
Primary earnings per share, Northern		$6.75

In calculations for the parent, however, such securities must be classified as common stock equivalents or as senior securities. If their effects are dilutive, the assumed conversion or exercise of these securities must be incorporated in parent calculations. In so doing, consideration must be given to the fact that the subsidiary's earnings per share calculations may have involved deductions for payments to the holders of the securities which are convertible into the parent's stock. Thus, if conversion of those securities is assumed in parent calculations, the subsidiary's deductions for payments to the security holders must be restored to earnings, since no payments to outsiders would have been made if the securities had been converted.[16]

Changing Conversion Rates or Exercise Prices. There are several types of corporate securities and transactions that may cause particular difficulty in earnings per share calculations. For example, a convertible security may stipulate a changing rate of conversion with the passage of time. Similarly, the price to exercise stock warrants may change. The obvious difficulty in such cases is to determine which conversion rate or exercise price should be used in computations of primary and fully diluted earnings per share. With respect to *fully diluted* earnings per share, it is reasonable to utilize the rate or price that will be most favorable to the security holders. Such a rate is consistent with the basic implication of the fully diluted statistic—the implication of portraying the maximum dilution that can occur, given current contingencies. However, conversion rates or exercise prices that are effective only in the distant future probably have little relevance to current security holders. Thus, the Accounting Principles Board has concluded that the most attractive rate or price during *only* the 10 years following the latest fiscal period should be used.[17]

Selecting an appropriate conversion rate or exercise price for primary earnings per share calculations is somewhat more arbitrary. As a general rule, it seems appropriate to use the rate or price that is in effect during the period covered by the calculation. The Board provides for the following specific exceptions to this general rule:

If options, warrants or other common stock equivalents are not immediately exercisable or convertible, the earliest effective exercise price or conversion rate if any during the succeeding five years should be used. If a convertible security having an increasing conversion rate is issued in exchange for another class of security of the issuing company and is convertible back into the same or a similar security, and if a conversion rate equal to or greater than the original rate becomes effective during the period of convertibility, the conversion rate

---

[16] In *Accounting Interpretation No. 93, APB Opinion 15,* 100 percent of the restored subsidiary payments is allocated to the parent. This method is followed even when the parent owns less than 100 percent of the subsidiary. There is no obvious rationale for such a treatment. A more logical method would restore the subsidiary's payments to the subsidiary's earnings per share, which are multiplied times the number of shares held by the parent to determine the parent's equity in subsidiary earnings.

[17] *APB Opinion 15,* paragraph 58.

used in the computation should not result in a reduction in the number of common shares (or common share equivalents) existing before the original exchange took place until a greater rate becomes effective.[18]

Contingent Stock Issuances. Contingent stock issuances have been frequently used as part of the financing methods employed in business combinations. They generally involve deferred payments of an indeterminate number of common shares, with the amount to be issued depending on future earnings of the acquired firm. Additionally, the amount to be issued may depend on the market value of the stock at the future date of issuance. Both primary and fully diluted computations of earnings per share may require special refinements when such contingent stock issuances are outstanding.

In an attempt to resolve the difficulties imposed by contingent stock issuances, the Accounting Principles Board has recommended specific rules to follow. With respect to primary earnings per share, stock issuances which depend on future earnings levels should be included to the extent that shares will be issued if earnings are maintained at current levels. Further, if the number of shares to be issued depends on the future market price of the stock, the market price at the most recent balance sheet date should be used to estimate the assumed number of shares to be issued.

Fully diluted earnings per share calculations should also reflect (by inclusion in the denominator) contingent stock issuances that relate to future earnings and/or to future stock prices. But they should not be constrained by the primary calculation requirement that limits the issuance to an amount satisfied by the maintenance of current earnings. Thus, fully diluted calculations should assume the highest reasonable dilution level that can occur. Manifestly, the required increase in earnings (to attain the highest dilution level) should also be added to current earnings in the numerator of the statistic. As in the case of primary calculations, the stock price at the close of the period being reported should be used if the contingent issuances are dependent on future stock prices.[19]

Restatement of Prior Period's Earnings per Share. Several conditions may justify restating the earnings per share statistics which relate to prior periods. Such restatements would be disclosed in the presentation of comparative statements and in historical financial summaries. Among the events that would lead to restatement of prior periods' earnings per share are the following: (1) if the number of common shares outstanding changes due to stock dividends, stock splits, or reverse stock splits; (2) if prior period adjustments of net income are made; (3) if a business combination has occurred and was accounted for as a pooling of interests; (4) if the prior periods' statistics included contingent stock issuances, and at the termination of the contingency agreement the conditions have not

---

[18] Ibid., paragraph 57.
[19] Ibid., paragraphs 62–64.

been met; and (5) if contingent stock issuances, which were included in the statistics of prior periods and remain contingently effective, are dependent on future earnings and/or stock prices, and the current (end-of-period) price and/or earnings level indicate that the assumptions which were previously used in reporting earnings per share should be modified. However, "previously reported earnings per share data should not be restated to give retroactive effect to shares subsequently issued as a result of attainment of specified increased earnings levels."[20]

Other Problem Areas. The previous discussion of earnings per share analysis clearly displays the variety of problems that have been encountered in recent years. A majority of these problems (and others, some of which are summarized below) have gained significance through the transactions, new financing methods, and internal structures of various combined corporate entities. Frequently, the problem conditions have arisen as a direct result of the combination transactions. Additional characteristics of the problems and recommendations regarding earnings per share analysis are outlined below.

Some of the procedures that have been developed for earnings per share calculations can be interpreted as having definite implications for other parts of the financial statements. For example, if convertible bonds are deemed to be common stock equivalents, should those bonds be classified as liabilities or as a special type of stockholders' equity? Furthermore, should the interest on those bonds be reported as an expense or as a special distribution of income? Arguments can be advanced in support of both sides of this and other similar issues arising from the earnings per share discussion. The most widely held position is that these specialized earnings per share methods should not affect the traditional methods of measurement and reporting which apply to other parts of the financial statements.[21]

Some corporations have different classes of stock outstanding which are not convertible into common stock but which participate in specified ratios with common stock as to dividends. A variety of conditions of this general nature may require an entirely different approach to earnings per share calculations. The alternative approach, referred to as the "two-class method," does not assume conversion of these securities. Instead, it recognizes the distributions made to each class of stock and computes a per share figure for the remaining amount retained. This figure is based on outstanding common shares and common stock equivalents. Finally, the retained earnings per share is added to dividends per common share to determine primary earnings per share.[22]

---

[20] Ibid., paragraph 62.

[21] This position is consistent with the conclusion of the Accounting Principles Board, Ibid., paragraph 39.

[22] Ibid., paragraph 55.

SEGMENTAL REPORTING

The various advantages and risks associated with diversified business operations have been subjects of discussion in the business community throughout the 20th century. The natural growth of prospering firms has often led to internally generated diversification. Complementing these *internal* processes of widening product lines, expanding geographical sales coverage, and vertical assumption of supplier and seller functions, have been periodic surges of diversification by the *external* process of business combination. For example, the merger activity of 1955–70 dramatically enhanced the diversified character of individual business firms.

It should be recognized that the unique accounting problems of reporting the operations of highly diversified businesses are not confined to combined corporate entities. Nevertheless, the processes of combining business enterprises frequently give rise to special accounting problems associated with reporting the results of diversified business activity. An obvious objective of many, perhaps most, of the combinations during the 1960s was diversification. As a consequence, a rounded examination of accounting for combined business entities must include reference to the special problems of accounting for diversified business entities.

The Need for Segmental Reports

The basic advantages and limitations associated with consolidated statements were outlined in Chapter 3. Compared with the alternative of presenting only the parent's financial statements, consolidated statements have uniquely important informational significance. These reports clearly are a primary source of information for persons concerned with the operations and financial position of the parent's sphere of control. It should be understood that the interest in, and need for, more detailed reporting on diversified companies does not negate the need for consolidated reports. The movement toward more detailed reporting is rather an *expansion* of the basic consolidated information. Reports which cover significant segments of a diversified firm should be perceived, therefore, as complementary to the consolidated statements. In fact, the method of reporting on segments may involve simply expanding the consolidated statements to include more detail within these statements.

Taken alone, consolidated financial statements do not provide sufficient information regarding the various types of business activity undertaken by the consolidated entity. Revenues, expenses, and assets may be associated with vastly disparate operations; and yet they are aggregated and reported in total. It should be apparent that decisions which relate to widely diversified firms can often be facilitated by the availability of information as to the relative significance to the firm of distinct subunit operations. R. K. Mautz defined a diversified company in a manner that emphasized these informational needs.

A diversified company is . . . a company which either is so managerially decentralized, so lacks operational integration, or has such diversified markets that it may experience rates of profitability, degrees of risk, and opportunities for growth which vary within the company to such an extent that an investor requires information about these variations in order to make informed decisions.[23]

As is true for most informational inputs to human decision processes, it is not possible to specify clearly the precise role played by segmental reports in the decision processes of investors. Nevertheless, the need for such information on diversified firms is becoming widely recognized. This recognition is, however, of fairly recent origin. Although some firms have provided segmented data for a number of years, authoritative pronouncements of generally accepted principles of accounting in this reporting area are of very recent origin.

Identifying Significant Segments of a Firm

Selecting the Basis for Segmenting a Firm.   Several alternative ways of segmenting a diversified firm may result in reports that have informational significance to investors. Three important alternatives that have been seriously considered are (1) geographical division, (2) product line or industrial divisions, and (3) divisions that conform to the internal structure of managerial control. Of course, other possible bases for segmenting a firm's operations may have significance, particularly in specific industries. For example, a division between government and private operations might provide especially relevant information for firms such as those engaged in air-frame construction.

Arguments can be marshaled in support of each of the three primary alternatives mentioned above. As a general rule, the necessary data can probably be accumulated most accurately and at the smallest additional cost when the basis for division conforms to the internal structure of managerial control. On the other hand, segmentation that meaningfully reflects differences in profitability, degrees of risk, and growth opportunities frequently follows the product lines or industrial categories in which a firm is active. Of course, for some enterprises the industrial classification would conform fairly close to the above mentioned managerial units of control. A geographical basis of segmentation may be highly informative for some companies, particularly in its ability to accent important distinctions between domestic and foreign operations.

---

[23] R. K. Mautz, *Financial Reporting by Diversified Companies* (New York: Financial Executives Research Foundation, 1968), pp. 7–8.

The most recent publication on the matter of segmental reporting, by the FASB, calls for information to be presented on each of three items:

a. The enterprise's operations in different industries.
b. Its foreign operations and export sales.
c. Its major customers.[24]

In respect to export sales, *FASB Standard No. 14* requires that if the export sales of the domestic operations are significant in amount, they should be reported in the aggregate and by appropriate geographical areas. Such sales are considered significant if they amount to 10 percent or more of the company's consolidated sales.[25]

Regarding major customers, the *Standard* requires that the fact and the amount of revenue to each major customer be reported. A major customer is one to whom sales equal 10 percent or more of the company's total sales. The customers need not be individually identified by name.[26]

Foreign operations are identified in *Standard No. 14* as operations that are located in foreign countries *and* that generate revenue from sales to unaffiliated customers or from intraenterprise sales or simply from transfers between geographical areas. Without specifying the criteria by which foreign operations in different countries should be grouped, the *Standard* indicates that foreign geographical areas may consist of one or more countries, and requires that certain information be presented separately for each significant geographical area and in the aggregate for those geographical areas which are not individually significant. A geographical area is deemed to be significant if its revenues from unaffiliated customers or its identifiable assets are 10 percent or more of the related consolidated amounts.[27]

Given these definitions, *Standard No. 14* requires that for domestic operations and for each foreign geographical area, the following information be reported: (1) sales to unaffiliated customers; (2) intraenterprise sales and transfers between geographical areas; (3) operating profit (loss) or net income or some other measure of profitability between operating profit (loss) and net income; and (4) identifiable assets.[28]

In addition to the above types of information *FASB Standard No. 14* calls for a system of segmental reporting based upon an industrial segmentation of the entity. The process of identifying the industrial segments of a firm requires that its products and services be grouped by industry lines. The definition of an "industry segment" requires that its sales be

---

[24] *FASB Standard No. 14*, "Financial Reporting for Segments of a Business Enterprise" (December 1976), paragraph 3.

[25] Ibid., paragraph 36.

[26] Ibid., paragraph 39.

[27] Ibid., paragraphs 31–34.

[28] Ibid., paragraph 35.

primarily to unaffiliated customers, and in identifying the segments, attention should be given to the nature of the products produced, the nature of the production processes involved, and the markets and marketing methods employed to sell the products. Differences in these factors help to identify different segments.[29]

Determining How Finely a Firm Should Be Segmented. A problem that relates to the selection of a basis for segmentation is the determination of how finely segmented the reports should be. Mautz argued that the selection of reporting units is essentially a management responsibility.[30] However, in 1969, the Securities and Exchange Commission listed the following requirements for certain reports that are filed with the SEC:

. . . [state] the approximate amount or percentage of (i) total sales and revenues, and (ii) income (or loss) before income taxes and extraordinary items, attributable to each line of business which during either of the last two fiscal years accounted for—

(A) 10 percent or more of the total of sales and revenues.
(B) 10 percent or more of income before income taxes and extraordinary items computed without deduction of loss resulting from operations of any line of business, or
(C) a loss which equalled or exceeded 10 percent of the amount of income specified in (B) above;

provided, that if the total sales and revenues did not exceed $50,000,000 during either of the last two years, the percentages specified in (A), (B) and (C) above shall be 15 percent, instead of 10 percent.[31]

More recently, the FASB stated that an entity should present reports on each industry segment for which one or more of the following tests is satisfied during the year for which financial statements are to be presented:

(A) Its revenue (including both sales to unaffiliated customers and intersegment sales or transfers) is 10 percent or more of the combined revenue (sales to unaffiliated customers and intersegment sales or transfers) of all of the enterprise's industry segments.
(B) The absolute amount of its operating profit or operating loss is 10 percent or more of the greater, in absolute amount, of:
  (i)   The combined operating profit of all industry segments that did not incur an operating loss, or
  (ii) The combined operating loss of all industry segments that did incur an operating loss.
(C) Its identifiable assets are 10 percent or more of the combined identifiable assets of all industry segments.[32]

---

29 Ibid., paragraphs 10–14, 100.

30 Mautz, *Financial Reporting by Diversified Companies,* p. 158.

31 Securities and Exchange Commission, "Adoption of Amendments to Forms S-1, S-7 and 10," *Securities Act Release No. 4988, Securities Exchange Act Release No. 8650* (Washington, D.C., July 14, 1969).

32 *FASB Standard No. 14,* paragraph 15.

In applying the above tests, however, the FASB recognized that abnormal results for a single period may result in a segment meeting one of the 10 percent tests when past periods and future expectations do not support separate reporting of the segment. In such a case, the segment need not be reported. Alternatively, a normally significant segment may happen to fail the tests in a single year, in which case it should be treated as a reportable segment. Also, if a single segment accounts for 90 percent or more of the firm's revenue, operating profit or loss, and identifiable assets, and no other industry segment meets any of the 10 percent tests previously mentioned, reports for that segment need not be presented separate from the consolidated statements for the firm as a whole.[33]

On the other hand, some firms consist of many small segments, most of which may not meet the 10 percent tests listed above. To assure that a substantial portion of a firm's operations be presented in segmental reports, *Standard No. 14* requires that the reports on specific segments should disclose at least 75 percent of the combined revenue from sales to unaffiliated customers. Otherwise, additional industry segments should be identified as reportable segments until the 75 percent test is met.[34]

Intersegmental Transfer Pricing

An important problem that must be resolved for the purposes of segmental reporting is the pricing of intrafirm transfers of goods and services between reporting segments. Some segments may exist entirely for the purpose of providing goods or services to outside customers. Others may be concerned with outside sales *and* intrafirm transfers. To the extent that transfers are made between segments, the reported profits of both the "selling" and "purchasing" segments are directly affected by the prices at which the transfers are recorded.

An ideal basis for setting transfer prices would be the independent market prices for the same goods and services, given a perfectly competitive market. However, good approximations of these conditions rarely exist. One is more likely to discover highly imperfect markets for goods or services that are transferred between segments within an enterprise. Independent market prices for similar goods (given a sensitivity to the quantities being sold) would, however, be a reasonable basis for recording transfer prices whenever such information is available.

As a practical matter, it is perhaps impossible to select a single basis for transfer pricing that would be best in all situations. The *FASB Standard* apparently recognizes this difficulty, and simply concludes that the transfer prices used should be those which are used by the company to price the intersegment sales or transfers.[35]

---

[33] Ibid., paragraphs 16, 20.

[34] Ibid., paragraphs 17–18.

[35] Ibid., paragraph 10.

Allocating Common Costs and Measuring Segmental Profitability

Regardless of the means by which a firm is divided into subunits for reporting purposes, some expenses will be common to two or more of the reporting segments. Typical examples of such expenses would include interest, income taxes, top-management compensation, and general corporate administrative expenses. Depending on the nature of the company's operations, many of the noninventoried expenses may be at times common to more than one subunit.

The allocation of common costs to reporting segments is constrained by two conflicting objectives. On the one hand, the bases of allocation should not be arbitrary. Given this single objective, the accountant would be led to leave many common costs unallocated. Allocations that are patently arbitrary may result in the data being more misleading than informative. Contrariwise, one of the primary objectives of segmental reporting is to provide information concerning each segment's contribution to the profitability of the firm. Where common costs remain unallocated, this objective is only partially fulfilled.

The ability to allocate most common costs depends largely upon the organization and operating procedures of each firm. Consequently, *general rules* of allocation are very difficult to prescribe. And, there exist some common expenses (and revenues) for which reasonable allocations between segments are virtually impossible.

In regard to calculating the *operating profit or loss* of each segment, the *FASB Standard* concludes that nine specific items should not be allocated to segments. They are: (1) revenue earned at the corporate level and not from the operations of an industry segment; (2) general corporate expenses; (3) interest expense, unless it refers to a segment whose operations are essentially financial in nature; (4) income taxes; (5) equity in income or loss from unconsolidated subsidiaries and other unconsolidated investees; (6) gain or loss on discontinued operations; (7) extraordinary items; (8) minority interest; and (9) the cumulative effect of a change in an accounting principle.[36] On the other hand, the *Standard* does not preclude the possibility of presenting additional measures of segmental profitability (other than operating profit) which would involve allocating some or all of the nine items listed above.

Identifying Segmental Assets

Adequate evaluation of segmental performance requires that the operating profit of each segment be related to the investment of resources in segmental operations. However, a complete balance sheet for each segment obviously cannot be prepared. Corporate equities (including liabilities)

---

[36] Ibid., paragraph 10.

generally represent undivided interests in the entire net assets of the business, notwithstanding the fact that some may enjoy special rights in the event of insolvency. The measurement of segmental investment is therefore limited to an allocation of assets between the reporting segments.

Some assets are easily identified with a specific segment because they are used exclusively by that segment. Other assets are shared by more than one segment, and a reasonable basis of determining each segment's usage must be identified and used to allocate the assets between the segments.

A few assets such as cash, marketable securities, and other assets that are used at the company's central office should not be allocated to industry segments. Also, the assets identified with a segment should not include investments accounted for by the equity method. This is consistent with the requirement that earnings from equity method investments not be included in the revenues or operating profits of a segment. However, if an unconsolidated subsidiary or other equity method investee is vertically integrated into the operations of a segment, separate disclosure must be made of the enterprise's equity in the net income from the investment and in the net assets of the investee.[37]

An Example of Segmental Reporting

Illustration 6–9 presents an example of segmental reports and related footnotes for a broadly diversified firm. Operations of the firm include activities other than those disclosed as electronics, chemicals, and machine manufacturing. However, none of these other activities satisfied the 10 percent tests of a reportable segment proposed by the FASB (page 217).

The procedures necessary to prepare such reports depend in large part on the nature of the internal accounting system employed by the firm. Segmental reports may be virtually complete as a consequence of maintaining administrative and budgetary control within the firm. A major factor necessarily is the degree of similarity between reporting segments and the internal structure of control.

QUESTIONS

1. Summarize the essential differences between business combinations that are classified as purchases and those that are deemed to be poolings of interests.

2. Contrast the purchase and pooling of interests methods of accounting with respect to (*a*) the valuation of net assets, (*b*) the valuation of individual assets and liabilities, and (*c*) the amount of retained earnings reported by the combined company.

---

[37] Ibid., paragraphs 7, 10, 27.

3. In the event a business combination results in a parent-subsidiary relationship between the combining companies, what is the amount recorded in the parent's investment account—
   a) If the purchase method of accounting is employed?
   b) If the pooling of interests method is employed?

4. In postcombination periods the method of presenting financial data that relates to precombination periods is dependent upon how the combination is classified. Explain the difference between the purchase and pooling of interests methods with respect to the presentation of precombination financial information.

5. Define the concept "common stock equivalents" and suggest several reasons for including such items in calculations of primary earnings per share.

6. What is the essential distinction between *primary* earnings per share and *fully diluted* earnings per share?

7. Describe the "treasury stock" method of treating common stock warrants in earnings per share calculations.

8. In respect to the earnings per share calculations of a parent company, what is the potential significance of common stock equivalents and dilutive senior securities issued by a subsidiary?

9. Describe the type of company for which segmental financial reports would appear to have the greatest significance.

10. List three alternative bases for segmenting a diversified firm. Which of the three is preferred?

11. In respect to segmental reports, the allocation of common costs between segments is constrained by two conflicting objectives. What are they?

12. List five situations in which previously reported earnings per share data for past years should be restated in financial presentations referring to prior periods.

13. List four major problems the accountant faces in preparing segmental financial statements for a diversified company.

14. What tests are required by the FASB to determine whether or not an industry segment is significant enough to warrant separate financial disclosure?

15. In deciding upon an appropriate basis for pricing goods and services that are transferred between industry segments, what conclusions were reached by the FASB?

16. Should the income from an investment accounted for by the equity method be included in the operating profit of an industry segment? Under what conditions do equity method investments require separate disclosure in the industrially segmented reports?

EXERCISES

Exercise 6–1

The stockholders of Tristar Company and Cycle Corporation agreed to combine their companies in a single transaction. According to the agreement,

Illustration 6–9

INFORMATION ABOUT THE COMPANY'S OPERATIONS IN DIFFERENT INDUSTRIES

Year Ended December 31, 19X1

(in thousands of dollars)

	Electronics	Chemicals	Machine Manu-facturing	Other Industries	Eliminations	Consolidated
Sales to unaffiliated customers	$1,000	$2,000	$1,500	$ 200		$ 4,700
Intersegment sales	200		500		$(700)	
Total revenue	$1,200	$2,000	$2,000	$ 200	$(700)	$ 4,700
Operating profit	$ 200	$ 250	$ 600	$ 50	$ —	$ 1,100
Equity in net income of Electro Company						100
General corporate expenses						(100)
Interest expense						(200)
Income from continuing operations before income taxes						$ 900
Identifiable assets on December 31, 19X1	$2,000	$4,000	$6,000	$1,000	$ —	$13,000
Investment in net assets of Electro Company						400
Corporate assets						1,600
Total Assets at December 31, 19X1						$15,000

Notes: The Company operates principally in three industries, electronics, chemicals, and machine manufacturing. The electronics operations involve the development and manufacture of microcircuitry. Chemical operations involve the manufacture of a variety of petroleum based chemicals for industrial usage. Machine manufacturing operations involve the development and manufacture of precision measuring and cutting instruments for industrial usage. Intersegment sales are accounted for at market values.

Operating profit is total revenue less operating expenses. In computing operating profit, none of the following items has been added or deducted: general corporate expenses, interest expense, income taxes, equity in income from unconsolidated investee, loss from discontinued operations of the Ray-chem division (which was part of the Company's operations in the chemical industry), and an extraordinary gain that occurred in the Machine Manufacturing segment of the Company's operations. Operations in the electronics industry had depreciation of $80 and capital expenditures of $100. In the chemical industry they were $100 and $200, respectively, and in machine manufacturing they were $150 and $400, respectively.

The Company has a 40 percent interest in Electro Company, whose operations are in the United States and are vertically integrated with the Company's operations in electronics.

Identifiable assets by industry are those assets of the Company that are used exclusively in or are reasonably allocable to operations in each industry. Assets employed at the Company's central administrative office are principally cash and marketable securities.

To reconcile industry information to consolidated amounts, $700 of intersegment sales were eliminated. None of the gross profit on these sales remains unrealized at December 31, 19X1, since the transferred goods were used and resold prior to the end of the year.

Source: Adapted from *FASB Standard No. 14*, "Financial Reporting for Segments of a Business Enterprise" (December 1976), Appendix F.

Tristar Company issued common stock in exchange for 100 percent of the outstanding shares of Cycle Corporation. At the date of the combination, which complies with the criteria for a pooling of interests, the stockholders' equity accounts of the companies were as follows:

	Cycle Corporation	Tristar Company
Common stock ($50 par)	$50,000	
Common stock ($100 par)		$ 80,000
Other contributed capital	50,000	
Retained earnings	30,000	100,000

Required:

Prepare the entry on the books of Tristar Company to record the issuance of stock for each of the following independent situations. Also show the investment elimination entry at date of combination and calculate consolidated retained earnings in each case.

	Number of Tristar Company Shares Issued
Case I	1,100
Case II	800
Case III	400

Exercise 6–2

Two companies, X and Y, are planning to combine, with the result that Y will be a wholly owned subsidiary. X will issue 50,000 common shares in exchange for all of the outstanding stock of Y. Data for the two companies follows:

	X	Y
Common stock	$100,000	$ 50,000
Other contributed capital		20,000
Retained earnings	400,000	40,000
Last year's net income	50,000	25,000
Last year's sales	300,000	200,000

Required:

a. From the facts given, can you see any reason why this combination should not be accounted for as a pooling of interests? If yes, what reasons?
b. Suppose the combination is accounted for as a pooling of interests and that the internal growth rate in earnings is zero.
   1. What earnings figure would be reported for the first postcombination year?

2. What rate of earnings growth would be displayed in comparing the first postcombination year's earnings with the previous year's amount, as presented in comparative financial statements?

c. Suppose the combination is accounted for as a purchase and that any differential arising from the combination is allocated to land. In two year comparative financial statements presented after the first postcombination year:
   1. What would be the indicated growth rate in sales?
   2. What would be the indicated growth rate in earnings?

d. Suppose X's shares are $2 par value and that they had a $5 market value at the time of combination. Show X's entry to record the issuance of stock and the investment elimination entry at date of combination, assuming a pooling of interests.

Exercise 6-3

Effective December 31, 1977, Alpha proposes to issue additional shares of its common stock in exchange for all of the assets and liabilities of Bravo and Echo, after which the latter two corporations will distribute the Alpha shares to their shareholders in complete liquidation and dissolution. The plan complies with all of the criteria for a pooling of interests. Balance sheets for each of the three companies immediately prior to the merger are given below. The common stock exchange ratios were each negotiated to be 1:1.

	Alpha	Bravo	Echo
Current assets	$ 2,000,000	$ 500,000	$ 25,000
Fixed assets (net)	10,000,000	4,000,000	200,000
Total	$12,000,000	$4,500,000	$225,000
Current liabilities	$ 1,000,000	$ 300,000	$ 20,000
Long-term debt	3,000,000	1,000,000	105,000
Common stock ($10 par)	3,000,000	1,000,000	50,000
Retained earnings	5,000,000	2,200,000	50,000
Total	$12,000,000	$4,500,000	$225,000

Required:

a. Prepare Alpha's journal entries to record the combination of Alpha, Bravo, and Echo.

b. Assume that the combination fails to meet the criteria for a pooling of interests because Bravo and Echo have not been autonomous entities for two years prior to the combination. The identifiable assets and liabilities of Bravo and Echo are all reflected in the balance sheets (above), and their recorded amounts are equal to their current fair market values. Alpha's common stock is traded actively and has a current market price of $45. Prepare Alpha's journal entries to record the combination.

(AICPA adapted)

Exercise 6–4

On January 1, 1977, Fox, Inc., issued 100,000 common shares in exchange for all of the outstanding common stock of Weber Company. Fox, Inc., employs the equity method of accounting for its investment in Weber Company; Weber Company has never declared dividends. The combination between Fox, Inc., and Weber Company complied with all of the criteria for a pooling of interests. During 1977 and 1978, Weber Company sold merchandise to Fox, Inc., at prices equal to Weber Company's cost. These sales amounted to $50,000 each year. Selected financial data for each of the two companies are presented below:

	1975	1976	1977	1978
Sales:				
Fox	$400,000	$440,000	$450,000	$500,000
Weber	350,000	400,000	360,000	400,000
Net income:				
Fox (includes subsidiary				
earnings)	100,000	150,000	200,000	280,000
Weber	80,000	100,000	80,000	120,000
Earnings per share:				
Fox	$1.00	$1.50	$1.00	$1.40
Weber	.40	.50	.40	.60

Required:

a. Prepare a four-year financial summary of sales, net income, and earnings per share for Fox, Inc., and its subsidiary, to be included in the 1978 annual report of Fox, Inc.

b. Assume that the combination did not comply with all of the criteria for a pooling of interests because some of the shares issued by Fox, Inc., to effect the combination were placed in a voting trust which restricted the voting rights of the stockholders. Fox, Inc.'s common stock is actively traded, and its market price at the date of combination was $40. The book value of Weber Company's common stock was $2,250,000 at the date of the combination. As a result of an analysis of Weber Company's assets and liabilities, the difference between the fair market value of Fox, Inc.'s investment and its equity in Weber Company's recorded net assets was allocated as follows: one half of the difference to fixed assets which have 10 years estimated remaining useful life; and one half of the difference to goodwill, which management decided to amortize over 40 years. Prepare a four-year financial summary similar to that required in (a).

Exercise 6–5

Accounting Principles Board *Opinion No. 15* discusses the concept of common stock equivalents and prescribes methods to be used for reporting primary earnings per share and fully diluted earnings per share.

Required:

a. Discuss the reasons why securities other than common stock may be considered common stock equivalents for the computation of primary earnings per share.

b. Define the term "sénior security" and explain how senior securities which are not convertible enter into the determination of earnings per share data.

c. Explain how convertible securities are determined to be common stock equivalents and how those convertible (senior) securities which are not considered to be common stock equivalents enter into the determination of earnings per share data.

(AICPA adapted)

Exercise 6–6

Sam's Pet Shops had the following securities outstanding throughout 1977:

Common stock, $10 par, average market price during 1977 was $60, ending market price was $60 .... 20,000 shares

Warrants to purchase 7,000 common shares at $50 per share.

Bonds payable, 7 percent, issued at par, market price throughout 1977 was approximately par $200,000

Sam's Pet Shops earned $50,000 net income during 1977. The effective income tax rate is 48 percent.

Required:

Calculate primary and fully diluted earnings per share for 1977.

Exercise 6–7

On December 31, 1977, the following data were taken from the records of Movie Company and its 80 percent owned subsidiary Camera Company:

	Movie Company	Camera Company
Net income, excluding earnings from subsidiary	$50,000	$20,000
Common stock outstanding	10,000	10,000
Earnings per share:		
Primary		$1.50
Fully diluted		$1.25

Movie Company had no securities outstanding other than common stock. Also, Movie Company had no investment in Camera Company other than the shares of common stock.

Required:

a. Calculate consolidated primary earnings per share for 1977.

b. Calculate consolidated fully diluted earnings per share for 1977.

c. Calculate consolidated net income for 1977.

Exercise 6–8

Statements 1–8 below are made in reference to accounting for business combinations. Select from the phrases (*a*)–(*d*) the one which is consistent with each statement: (*a*) pooling of interests, (*b*) purchase, (*c*) neither pooling of interests nor purchase, and (*d*) either pooling of interests or purchase.

(1) If an acquisition results in a debit differential, the assets of the acquired firm will be valued at less than their book value on the books of the acquired firm.

(2) Given credit balances in the retained earnings of the combining companies, consolidated retained earnings are generally greatest under this method.

(3) The existence of a credit differential due to an overvalued building on the books of the acquired firm would result in consolidated earnings per share for the next year being least under this method.

(4) The combination was finalized nine months after the plan for combination was initiated.

(5) The difference between book value and investment cost is recognized under this method.

(6) Consolidated retained earnings are always equal to the sum of the retained earnings of the constituents under this method.

(7) If investment cost is greater than book value of net assets of the acquired firm, it is possible that goodwill resulting from the combination will appear in the consolidated statements.

(8) Several years after the combination, consolidated financial summaries pertaining to pre-combination periods will depict the historical data of only the acquired firm.

Exercise 6–9

Jason Company's operations involve four industry segments: A, B, C, and D. During the most recent year, the operating profits or losses of the segments were as follows:

Industry Segment	Operating Profit [Loss]
A	$[200]
B	400
C	50
D	[400]

Required:

Apply the "operating profit or loss" test required by the FASB to determine which of the four industry segments should be treated as reportable segments.

PROBLEMS

Problem 1

In addition to common stock, a company has three different securities outstanding, each of which is a common stock equivalent. The following data show the effects on earnings and common shares outstanding which would result from the assumed conversion of these securities:

	Common Shares Outstanding	Earnings
Common shares outstanding	1,000	
Earnings prior to assumed conversions ..		$5,000
Impact of assumed conversions of common stock equivalents:		
A.	+1,000	+4,000
B.	+2,000	+3,000
C.	+1,000	+2,000

Required:

Calculate primary earnings per share.

Problem 2

The most recently published statement of consolidated income of National Industries, Inc., a highly diversified "conglomerate" company, appears as follows:

NATIONAL INDUSTRIES, INC.

Statement of Consolidated Income
For the Year Ended July 31, 1977

Net sales	$38,041,200
Other revenue	407,400
Total revenue	$38,448,600
Cost of products sold	$27,173,300
Selling and administrative expenses	8,687,500
Interest expense	296,900
Total cost and expenses	$36,157,700
Income before income taxes	$ 2,290,900
Provision for income taxes	1,005,200
Net income	$ 1,285,700

Charles Norton, a representative of a firm of security analysts, visited the central headquarters of National Industries for the purpose of obtaining more information about the company's operations. In the annual report National's president stated that National was engaged in the pharmaceutical, food processing, toy manufacturing, and metal-working industries. Mr. Norton complained that the published income statement was of limited utility in his analysis of the firm's operations. He said National should have disclosed separately the profit earned in each of its component industries.

Required:

a. Explain what is meant by the term "conglomerate" company.
b. Discuss the accounting problems involved in measuring net profit by industry segments within a company.
c. With reference to National Industries' statement of consolidated income identify the specific items where difficulty might be encountered in measuring the profit earned by each of its industry segments and explain the nature of the difficulty.

(AICPA adapted)

Problem 3

Several years ago, Walker Transportation Company purchased 80 percent of Bonanza, Inc.'s outstanding common stock; the total cost of the investment was equal to Walker's equity in Bonanza's recorded net assets. For 1977, selected financial information for the two companies is presented below. The effective income tax rate is 48 percent.

	Walker	*Bonanza*
Net income (excluding earnings from subsidiary)	$ 51,000	$ 30,000
Common stock market prices during 1977:		
Average	90	80
Ending	135	80
Outstanding securities:		
Bonds payable, 6 percent, due 1996, convertible into common stock at the rate of two shares per $100; bonds issued at par; at the date of issuance, prime interest rate was 8 percent		100,000
Preferred stock, $100 par, 5 percent, cumulative as to dividends	100,000	
Common stock, $50 par	500,000	300,000
Warrants to purchase common:		
1,000 Bonanza shares at $40		
1,500 Walker shares at $90		

Required:

In respect to the 1977 consolidated income statement of Walker Transportation Company and its subsidiary, calculate—

a. Primary earnings per share.
b. Fully diluted earnings per share.

Problem 4

On January 1, 1977, Hawkeye, Inc., issued convertible bonds which have a total par value of $100,000 and mature on January 1, 2007. The bond indenture requires interest payments during 1977 equal to 5 percent of par; the rate of interest increases each year for 20 years by .2 percent. Thus, the rate of interest in the 21st year will be 9.0 percent; it will remain at that rate until the bonds mature. The rate at which the bonds may be converted into common stock also changes. Conversions cannot be made prior to 1980, during which year the conversion rate is one share of common stock per $100 of bond par value. Thereafter, the conversion rate increases each year for 10 years at the rate of .1 share per year. Thus, in 1990, the conversion rate will be 2.0 shares of common stock per $100 par value; after 1990, the conversion rate remains unchanged.

The bonds were issued at par (assume there are no transfer costs). The effective income tax rate is 48 percent. During 1977, Hawkeye, Inc., reported net income of $60,000, which included a deduction of $5,000 for interest expense. The company has 10,000 common shares outstanding and no other common stock equivalents or senior securities. The prime rate of interest on January 1, 1977, was 8 percent.

Required:

a. Determine whether Hawkeye, Inc.'s bonds payable should be classified as common stock equivalents or senior securities and explain the reasoning underlying your decision.
b. Calculate primary earnings per share for 1977.
c. Calculate fully diluted earnings per share for 1977 *or* explain why fully diluted calculations are unnecessary.

Problem 5

Toy, Inc. owns 900 shares of Ball Company's outstanding common stock and 360 warrants to purchase Ball Company common stock at $50 per share. The following information pertains to these companies' financial operations and status during 1977:

	Toy, Inc.	Ball Company
Net income, excluding subsidiary earnings	$20,000	$ 5,000
Common shares outstanding	5,600	1,000
Preferred stock, 7 percent, cumulative, issued at par ($100), convertible into common at $20 (i.e., 5 shares of common for 1 share of preferred). Prime rate at issuance was 12 percent. Shares outstanding	800	
Average price of common stock during 1977	$ 100	$ 300
6 percent, 30 year bonds, issued at par, convertible into common stock at $200 (a $1,000 bond can be exchanged for 5 common shares). Prime rate at issuance was 10 percent. The corporate income tax rate is 48 percent. Bonds outstanding		$200,000

In addition to the above, Ball Company has issued and outstanding 600 warrants to purchase Ball Company common stock at $50 per share. Ball Company also issued warrants to purchase 500 common shares of Toy, Inc. at $20 per share. All of the warrants are outstanding.

Required:

a. Calculate primary earnings per share for Ball Company.
b. Calculate primary earnings per share for Toy, Inc. and its consolidated subsidiary.
c. Calculate consolidated net income.

Problem 6

The operations of Cedar Falls Corporation involve eight different industries. Information on these eight industrial segments for the most recent year is as follows:

Industry Segment	Revenue from Unaffiliated Customers	Intersegment Sales	Operating Profit [Loss]	Identifiable Assets
1	$ 300	$ 100	$ [50]	$ 800
2	800	200	200	1,200
3	5,000	1,000	200	5,000
4	8,000	—	1,100	6,500
5	9,500	—	500	8,500
6	1,200	400	400	1,500
7	1,000	500	[600]	2,000
8	2,000	—	[100]	3,000

An investigation of the operations of recent years suggests that the most recent data are not unusual.

Required:

In anticipation of the need to prepare financial reports on the important segments in which Cedar Falls Corporation operates, and using the criteria required by the FASB, determine which of the eight industry segments should be treated as reportable segments. In other words, for which of the eight should separate financial information be presented?

Problem 7

Jamestown Company is a broadly diversified company whose operations involve five major industries: A, B, C, D, and E. Management of Jamestown Company plans to include in the annual report for 19X1 a segmented financial report prepared in accordance with *FASB Standard No. 14.* Financial data relating to segmental operations during 19X1 are presented below:

	A	B	C	D	E
Sales	$7,000	$19,000	$150,000	$ 6,000	$12,000
Cost of goods sold	$3,000	$12,000	$ 80,000	$ 1,400	$ 7,000
Administrative expenses	1,000	4,000	24,000	1,000	1,000
Selling expenses	1,000	7,000	29,000	1,600	3,000
Total operating expenses	$5,000	$23,000	$133,000	$ 4,000	$11,000
Operating profit	$2,000	$ [4,000]	$ 17,000	$ 2,000	$ 1,000
Identifiable assets	$8,000	$15,000	$ 95,000	$16,000	$35,000

Additional Information:

a. Included in the sales of segment E are $4,000 which were sales to segment
    C. None of items sold to C remain in the December 31, 19X1, assets of C.
b. In addition to the assets identified with industrial segments, the corporate
    offices have assets of $18,000 on December 31, 19X1.
c. Income taxes amount to 30 percent of net operating profits.

Required:

a. Determine which of the industry segments should be reported separately in
    segmental reports and state the basis for your decision in each case.
b. Prepare a summarized financial report by segments which is reconciled
    with summarized consolidated data. Model your report after the one
    presented in Illustration 6–9.

unit two

CONSOLIDATED STATEMENTS: AN EXPANDED ANALYSIS

7

Consolidated Statements— Intercompany Profit on Asset Transfers

SALES OF MERCHANDISE, plant and equipment, and other assets or services often take place between affiliated companies. As a consequence of these asset transfers, a profit is normally reported by the selling company in the period in which the intercompany sale occurs. However, if the merchandise transferred remains in the inventory of the purchasing affiliate, or if the assets or services have been capitalized by this purchaser, the profit should not be recognized *from a consolidated point of view* until confirmed by resale to outside interests.

Since *APB Opinion 18* prescribes recognition of an interest in the earnings of an affiliate in consonance with a consolidated point of view, the existence of unconfirmed intercompany profits requires an adjustment on the books of the parent (or investor) company. Additionally, the effects of the unconfirmed profit on the accounts of the affiliates must be eliminated in the preparation of consolidated financial statements.

INTERCOMPANY PROFIT—MERCHANDISE

We first consider the case of unconfirmed profits arising from the intercompany transfers of merchandise. Then, the concepts and procedures applicable to unconfirmed profits on plant and equipment transfers are described. These two classes of asset transfers provide the methodology for dealing with cases involving transfers of other assets or capitalized services.

Determination of Amount of Intercompany Profit

Seller's Gross or Net Profit. The first step in the measurement of intercompany profit on merchandise transfers is the identification of the amount of profit recognized by the selling affiliate. This amount is usually determined on the basis of the selling affiliate's *gross profit rate*. It has occasionally been proposed that the *net profit rate* is the more appropriate multiplier. The use of this rate, however, would result in a smaller profit elimination, thereby enlarging the consolidated inventory by operating expense elements of the selling affiliate. Such expenses are, however, generally inadmissible as inventoriable costs. Consequently, the gross profit rate is recommended.

Having determined the profit recognized by the seller, we must consider whether any adjustments to this value are appropriate. Three relatively common circumstances which may stimulate the need for such an adjustment are described: (1) transporation costs on merchandise transfers, (2) inventory market adjustments, and (3) income tax effects.

Transportation Costs on Merchandise Transfers. The sale of merchandise by one affiliate to another usually entails costs incident to the conveyance which are valid inventory costs to the consolidated entity. If these transportation costs are paid for by the purchasing affiliate and included in its inventory valuation, no special adjustment is required. However, if the selling affiliate pays for the transportation costs, or if the purchasing affiliate has not capitalized them, the amount of the seller's profit on the intercompany transaction should be reduced by these transportation costs in determining the intercompany profit subject to elimination.

Inventory Market Adjustments. The purchasing affiliate may have applied the "lower of cost or market" rule to the intercompany merchandise in its ending inventory. In this event, where "market" values are currently below the transfer price, the market adjustments recorded by the purchasing affiliate should be considered in determining the amount of the unconfirmed inventory profit. The additional reduction in the inventory of the purchaser attributable to the elimination of inventory profit should be based upon cost after the adjustment for market decline. Since the market adjustment has reduced the inventory value below the original transfer price, the amount of this reduction should be used in abatement of the selling affiliate's reported trading profit in determining the unconfirmed profit to be eliminated. If the market adjustment exceeds the trading profit, no elimination is required.

Income Tax Effects. If the affiliates do not file a consolidated tax return, income tax will be paid and recorded by the selling affiliate on unconfirmed profits. However, since these profits are to be deferred to a future period, the related income tax should also be deferred. Prior to *APB Opinion 11,* this tax deferral was often accomplished by measuring unconfirmed profits "net of taxes," both in the investor's equity "pickup" and in the consolidated statements. *Opinion 11,* however, rejected the net of tax presentation in favor of the deferral method.[1] As a consequence, the income tax effect, if any, is no longer an adjustment to the amount of un-

---

[1] *APB Opinion 11,* "Accounting for Income Taxes," paragraph 35.

confirmed profit to be eliminated *in the consolidated statements*. Rather, the tax deferral is treated as a separate elimination item in the working paper. It is still considered appropriate, however, to record the equity "pickup" net of taxes.[2] If a consolidated tax return is filed, reported and taxable income are synchronized with respect to the unconfirmed profit, and thus there is no income tax effect to be considered.

Amount of Unconfirmed Intercompany Profit to Be Eliminated

Knowing now the amount of the intercompany profit, the next step is the determination of the portion of this profit that should be regarded as unconfirmed and thus subject to elimination. Two basic alternatives exist: (1) Total (100 Percent) Elimination, and (2) Fractional Elimination.

Total (100 Percent) Elimination. One position is that all of the intercompany profit should be eliminated. This treatment was recommended in 1959 in *Accounting Research Bulletin No. 51,* "Consolidated Statements," and still remains part of the authoritative literature:

> The amount of intercompany profit or loss to be eliminated . . . is not affected by the existence of a minority interest. The complete elimination of the intercompany profit or loss is consistent with the underlying assumption that consolidated statements represent the financial position and operating results of a single business enterprise. The elimination of the intercompany profit or loss *may* be allocated proportionately between the majority and minority interests.[3]

Application of this method in the consolidation process results in a reduction of the inventory value to the selling affiliate's cost (perhaps adjusted for transportation cost supplements, if material). Allocation of this eliminated amount to the majority and minority shareholder groups in proportion to their interests in the selling affiliate is optional according to *ARB No. 51,* but we shall treat it as a logical and necessary part of what we have labeled the basic total elimination approach. Later in this chapter, we discuss the rationale for allocating the eliminated amount solely against the majority shareholders, and some of the developments that have occurred recently in accounting practice. Note, however, that an allocation between the groups is required only when a subsidiary is the selling affiliate. If the parent company were the seller, there would be no minority interest in the recorded intercompany profit.

Fractional Elimination. A second position is that only the parent company's equity in the intercompany profit should be regarded as unconfirmed and eliminated. The amount of the elimination is calculated in terms of the parent company's fractional interest in the profit reported by the *selling* affiliate. The effect of this treatment is to emphasize the legal equity of minority shareholders in such profit, as the dollar interest of this

---

[2] See, for example, *Accounting Interpretation No. 1, APB Opinion 18.*

[3] Section 2051.13, *APB Accounting Principles—Current Text.* (Emphasis supplied.)

group remains unaffected by eliminating entries requisite to the preparation of consolidated reports. The inventory value reported in the consolidated balance sheet will accordingly include both the cost of the merchandise to the selling affiliate and the interest of the minority shareholders in the intercompany profits.

It should be observed that the fractional elimination method differs from the total elimination method only when a partially owned subsidiary is the selling affiliate. If the parent or a wholly owned subsidiary is the selling affiliate, then by definition the "parent company's fractional interest in the profit reported by the selling affiliate" is 100 percent. An important modification of this basic definitional element of the fractional method that has developed recently in practice is discussed later in the chapter.

Effect of Alternatives on Consolidated Net Income. Even in those circumstances when the methods differ with respect to the amount of intercompany profit to be eliminated, consolidated net income nonetheless remains equivalent under both methods. This result follows because the amount of unconfirmed (eliminated) profit assigned to the majority shareholders is the same under each method—the parent company's (and thus the majority shareholders) interest in the reported profit. The higher inventory value that results from the application of the fractional method is exactly offset by the assignment of a greater value to the minority interest.

Evaluation of the Alternatives. The arguments which support total (100 percent) elimination of intercompany profits rest heavily on the single entity concept of the affiliation of companies. Notwithstanding the existence of legally separate business enterprises, this position observes that the concept of consolidated financial statements is based upon an assumed extra-corporate economic entity, and essentially affirms consistent application of this notion. Additionally, it might be noted that 100 percent elimination produces more conservative asset valuations.

Support for the fractional elimination of intercompany profits is based upon the perspective of the majority shareholders. It views the minority shareholders not as a complementary ownership group, but as an outside interest in a special fiduciary relationship.

. . . a majority of the holders of stock owe to the minority the duty to exercise good faith, care, and diligence to make the property of the corporation in their charge produce the largest possible amount, to protect the interests of the holders of the minority of the stock and to secure and deliver to them their just proportion of the income and of the proceeds of the property. Any sale of the corporate property to themselves, and disposition by them of the corporation or its property to deprive the minority holders of their just share of it or to get gain for themselves at the expense of the holders of the minority of the stock, becomes a breach of duty and of trust. . . .[4]

---

[4] *Jones* v. *Missouri-Edison Electric Company* (1906), 114 F. 765, 771.

It can be argued that the position of trust which vests in the controlling shareholders logically should extend to the preparation of consolidated financial statements, wherein profit increments due minority shareholders should not be compromised by the elimination process.

Additional support for fractional elimination relates specifically to the parent company's decision to purchase assets from subsidiary affiliates. In the parent's election to purchase from a subsidiary rather than a non-affiliate, it is assumed that the parent anticipates a recoupment of the subsidiary's transfer profit. If operating efficiencies are comparable, this compels the parent to incur only a minimal additional cost, in the amount of the minority interest in subsidiary profit, in preference to purchasing from a nonaffiliate under its full profit margin conditions. This increment may be described as an "adjunct" cost to the majority.

Thus, the intercompany profit may be perceived as consisting of two distinct segments. Edward J. Smolinski describes these elements in the following terms:

The first, the parent's share is an item the parent will, or has already, recovered by way of the subsidiary's profit distributions—a noncost. The other, the minority's share, is likewise one which will, or has already enjoyed recovery in this manner, but by the minority—not the majority. The fact of consolidation changes nothing. Intercompany profit consists of two different and distinct elements and each is evaluated on its merits. This does not suggest that homogenous units of inventory are valued on different bases. Nor is consolidated inventory valued on two different bases. Inventory is valued on the basis of cost, or, the lower of cost or market, but the minority's share of intercompany profit is added as an adjunct cost.[5]

The equity of minority shareholders is clearly a unique stock interest. It relates only to the net assets of a specific subsidiary. As such, it may be realistically viewed as an "outside" interest. Consequently, proponents of fractional elimination argue that profits earned by a subsidiary which appertain to the minority interest should be protected as a cost to the majority.[6]

As a final observation, it might be noted that consolidated net income is defined and calculated in terms of the interest of the majority (parent company) shareholders, and thus the fractional elimination concept is not inconsistent with the process of consolidation (as presently practiced).

The authors believe that the arguments offered in support of both methods have merit. Additionally, both methods (or modifications thereof) are currently applied in practice; the fractional method, although enjoying limited application in the past, is attaining increasing support with the adoption of the equity method of accounting in *APB Opinion 18* and the

---

[5] Edward J. Smolinski, "The Adjunct Method in Consolidations," *Journal of Accounting Research,* Autumn 1963, p. 168.

[6] Ibid., pp. 166–69.

growing practice of consolidating companies with substantial minority interests. Accordingly, we have included illustrations and problems in this and the following chapter that cover both alternatives.

Parent Company Entries for Unconfirmed Inventory Profits

Case 1. P Company has an 80 percent interest in S Company. During 19X1, S Company reports profits after taxes of $100,000, and there is an unconfirmed inventory profit of $5,000 at the end of the year to be eliminated. The companies file separate income tax returns, and thus income tax (40% rate) is paid in 19X1 on the intercompany profit.

Entries in 19X1. The parent company would of course recognize its equity in the *reported* income of the subsidiary as follows:

(*a*) Investment in S Company 80,000
      Equity in subsidiary earnings   80,000

The entry to record the deferral of the unconfirmed intercompany profit is at present subject to several variations. However, the simplest method, regardless of which company is the selling affiliate, is to eliminate the parent's equity in the intercompany profit (net of taxes) against the recorded equity in the affiliate and the parent's investment account. Thus, for our example, the unconfirmed profit of $5,000, less the related income taxes of $2,000 (40% × $5,000), would be deferred as follows:

(*b*)   If subsidiary is seller:

Equity in subsidiary earnings (80% × $3,000) 2,400
      Investment in S Company   2,400

(*c*)   If parent is seller:

Equity in subsidiary earnings (100% × $3,000) 3,000
      Investment in S Company   3,000

When the subsidiary is the selling affiliate, entries (*a*) and (*b*) recognize the parent's equity in confirmed subsidiary earnings. On the other hand, when the parent is the seller, the subsidiary's reported earnings are unaffected by the intercompany transaction. In this case, the rationale for entry (*c*) is that the intercompany profit (included in the parent's operating results) occurs as a consequence of the ownership affiliation, and thus it is appropriate to match the deferral of this item against the income generated by the relationship and recognized in entry (*a*).

The principal alternatives to this method of eliminating unconfirmed intercompany profits on the books of the parent relate to the case when the parent is the selling affiliate. When the amount to be eliminated in such a case is a substantial portion of the parent's equity in reported subsidiary earnings *or* of the parent's income from operations, the following alternative entry has substantial merit:

Intercompany profit deferred to future periods [a deduction from gross profit]	5,000		
Prepaid income taxes	2,000		
Deferred credit for intercompany profit		5,000	
Income tax expense		2,000	

In the illustrations to follow, for reasons of simplicity we assume the parent company has recorded the deferral of intercompany profit (net of taxes, if any) in the manner illustrated in entries (b) and (c) above.

Entry in 19X2. An intercompany inventory profit that is deferred at the end of one period is assumed to be confirmed during the following period. For our example, the following entry would be made in 19X2 (in addition to recognizing the equity in the subsidiary's reported income for 19X2):

(a)   If subsidiary is seller:

Investment in S Company	2,400	
Equity in subsidiary earnings		2,400

(b)   If parent is seller:

Investment in S Company	3,000	
Equity in subsidiary earnings		3,000

If the intercompany profit were not in fact confirmed in 19X2 through resale to outside parties, its continued existence in the 19X2 ending inventory of the purchasing affiliate would usually be detected by the accounting system procedures established to identify intercompany profits (i.e., the procedures that first identified the existence of the intercompany profit at the end of 19X1). The entry to again defer this profit, or any portion thereof, would merely reverse the effect of the above entry. Therefore, the assumption we make about confirmation of intercompany profits in the beginning inventory is essentially a procedural, not a substantive, assumption.

Eliminating Intercompany Inventory Profits in the Consolidated Statement Working Paper

The techniques for eliminating unconfirmed intercompany inventory profits are illustrated following in an integrated set of three case examples involving P Company and its 80 percent owned subsidiary S Company. In the first two cases, the total elimination method is illustrated for the year in which the intercompany profit arises and the subsequent year in which it is assumed to be confirmed. In the third case, the fractional elimination method is illustrated for the same time periods. Additionally, for the purpose of illustrating more clearly the effects of the eliminating entries, accounts reflecting the effects of intercompany transactions are separately labeled. (In the absence of this classificational refinement, as is frequently the case, eliminations are merely made against the single account aggregating transactions with both affiliates and nonaffiliates.) The companies are assumed to file separate income tax returns, and the relevant tax rate is 25 percent. Finally, we employ a minimum number of accounts in the consolidated statement working paper to focus attention on the inventory profit eliminations (including the assumption that no differential exists).

Case 2. Total Elimination—First Year. It is assumed that P Company acquired its 80 percent equity interest in S Company on January 1, 19X1 at a cost of $60,000, when S Company had Capital Stock of $50,000 and Retained Earnings of $25,000. During 19X1, S Company sold merchandise to P Company for $20,000, on which the recorded gross profit was $8,000 (i.e., a gross profit rate of 40 percent). On December 31, 19X1, the inventory of P Company includes $5,000 of the merchandise purchased from S Company. S Company reported net income of $15,000 for 19X1.

The unconfirmed intercompany profit in P Company's ending inventory that was acquired from S Company is calculated by multiplying this value ($5,000) by the selling affiliate's gross profit rate (40 percent), or $2,000. Since income taxes were paid by the subsidiary on this profit on its separate income tax return, the unconfirmed profit net of taxes is $1,500 [$2,000 − (25% × $2,000)].

In accordance with the procedures described in the preceding section, the parent company entries to record its equity in the subsidiary's earnings and to defer the intercompany inventory profit are:

(1)   To record equity in S Company's 19X1 reported income (80% × $15,000):

Investment in S Company	12,000	
Equity in subsidiary earnings		12,000

(2)   To record deferral of parent's interest in intercompany profit, net of taxes (80% × $1,500):

Equity in subsidiary earnings	1,200	
Investment in S Company		1,200

The working paper eliminating entries for this example are presented following:

(1)   To reverse P Company entries during 19X1:

Equity in subsidiary earnings	10,800	
Investment in S Company		10,800

(2)   To eliminate the investment account balance at the beginning of the year against the beginning-of-year balances in the stockholders' equity accounts of S Company:

Capital stock—S Company	40,000	
Retained earnings—S Company	20,000	
Investment in S Company		60,000

(3)   To eliminate 100% (*total elimination method*) of the unconfirmed profit in the ending inventory of P Company ($2,000), and recognize the related deferral of income taxes ($500):

Inventory, 12/31 (Income Statement)	2,000	
Prepaid income taxes	500	
Inventory, 12/31 (Balance Sheet)		2,000
Income tax expense		500

(4)   To eliminate intercompany sales:

Sales	20,000	
Purchases		20,000

The consolidated statement working paper for this example is presented in Illustration 7–1. In accordance with our previous practice, the balances in this (and subsequent) working papers are arbitrarily chosen, except where it is required that they correspond with data previously presented in the example.

In the working paper (and the eliminating entries above), the full amount of the intercompany inventory profit is eliminated (under the total elimination method) by a debit to the ending inventory as it appears in the income statement division, and a credit to the ending inventory as it appears in the balance sheet division. Since income taxes were paid on this intercompany profit, they too are deferred in accordance with the deferral method prescribed in *APB Opinion 11*. These two related operations are combined in eliminating entry (3). Intercompany sales and purchases are eliminated in entry (4) in the same manner as originally illustrated in Chapter 4. As a consequence of these entries, all recorded effects of intercompany activities are deleted, and the consolidated column reflects transactions with nonaffiliates. Accounts for intercompany purchases and sales are reduced to zero balances, and the ending inventory that P Company acquired from S Company is reduced to S Company's cost. Note also that the adjusted consolidated income tax expense, $10,500, is 25 percent of the total equity in combined income before income taxes [25% × ($31,500 + $10,500) = $10,500)].

As prescribed by *APB Opinion 18,* the parent company's net income and retained earnings are equal to consolidated net income and retained earnings. One may wonder how this equivalence was obtained when the parent company's entry to record the deferral of intercompany profits was based on its equity in these unconfirmed profits (i.e., 80 percent of $1,500, or $1,200), but the working paper eliminating entry deferred the total intercompany profit ($2,000) net of the related income taxes ($500). The answer resides in the calculation of minority interest in net income. The total elimination method (as defined here) prescribes deferral of the total intercompany profit and related income taxes, *and* allocation of the eliminated amounts to the majority and minority shareholder groups in proportion to their interests in the selling affiliate. Thus, from a consolidated

Illustration 7-1

P COMPANY AND SUBSIDIARY S COMPANY

Consolidated Statement Working Paper (Total Elimination)
For Year Ended December 31, 19X1

	P Company	S Company	Eliminations Dr.	Eliminations Cr.	Minority Interest	Consolidated
Income Statement:						
Sales:						
To nonaffiliates	100,000	40,000				140,000
Intercompany	-0-	20,000	(4) 20,000			-0-
Equity in subsidiary earnings	10,800		(1) 10,800			-0-
Inventory (12/31):						
Acquired from nonaffiliates	15,000	10,000				25,000
Acquired from affiliates	5,000	-0-	(3) 2,000			3,000
Total credits	130,800	70,000				168,000
Inventory (1/1):						
Acquired from nonaffiliates	10,000	8,000				18,000
Acquired from affiliates	-0-	-0-				-0-
Purchases:						
From nonaffiliates	60,000	38,000				98,000
Intercompany	20,000	-0-		(4) 20,000		-0-
Expenses	6,000	4,000				10,000
Income tax expense	6,000	5,000		(3) 500		10,500
Total debits	102,000	55,000				136,500
Net income	28,800	15,000				31,500
Minority interest in net income—S Company [20% of ($15,000 − $1,500)]					2,700	2,700
Net income—carried forward	28,800	15,000	32,800	20,500	2,700	28,800

Retained Earnings Statement:

	P Company	S Company	Elim. Dr	Elim. Cr	Minority Interest	Consolidated
Retained earnings, January 1, 19X1:						
P Company	40,000					40,000
S Company		25,000	(2) 20,000		5,000	–0–
Net income—brought forward	28.800	15,000	32.800	20,500	2,700	28,800
Retained earnings, December 31, 19X1—carried forward	68.800	40,000	52.800	20,500	7,700	68,800

Balance Sheet:

	P Company	S Company	Elim. Dr	Elim. Cr	Minority Interest	Consolidated
Other assets	89,200	90,000				179,200
Inventory:						
Acquired from nonaffiliates	15,000	10,000				25,000
Acquired from affiliates	5,000	–0–		(3) 2,000		3,000
Investment in S Company	70,800			(1) 10,800 (2) 60,000		–0–
Prepaid income taxes			(3) 500			500
	180.000	100.000				207,700
Other liabilities	11,200	10,000				21,200
Capital stock:						
P Company	100,000					100,000
S Company		50,000	(2) 40,000		10,000	–0–
Retained earnings—brought forward	68,800	40,000	52.800	20,500	7,700	68,800
Minority interest in S Company					17,700	17,700 M
	180,000	100,000	93,300	93,300	17,700	207,700

Explanation of eliminations:
(1) To reverse P Company entries during 19X1.
(2) To eliminate the investment account balance at the beginning of the year against the beginning-of-year balances in the stockholders' equity accounts of S Company.
(3) To eliminate the intercompany profit in P Company's ending inventory, and recognize the related deferral of income taxes.
(4) To eliminate intercompany sales.

point of view, S Company's confirmed income is $13,500 ($15,000 reported income less $1,500 unconfirmed intercompany profit), and the minority shareholders' interest in this is $2,700 (20% × $13,500). This calculation has the effect of allocating 20 percent of the deferred intercompany profit to the minority shareholders, leaving the remaining 80 percent to be borne by the majority shareholders (consistent with the entry on the parent company books).

Case 3. Total Elimination—Second Year. In continuation of Case 2, we assume that during 19X2 S Company sold merchandise to P Company for $10,000, recognizing a transfer profit of $4,000 (again a gross profit rate of 40 percent). Additionally, P Company sold merchandise to S Company for $15,000, on which the profit amounted to $4,500 (i.e., a gross profit rate of 30 percent). On December 31, 19X2, the inventory of P Company contained $2,500 of merchandise purchased from S Company, and the inventory of S Company contained $6,000 of merchandise purchased from P Company. S Company reported net income of $12,000 for 19X2.

The 19X2 intercompany sales and the unconfirmed intercompany profits in the beginning and ending inventories of the affiliates are summarized in Illustration 7–2.

Based upon these data and S Company's reported income, P Company would make the following entries in 19X2:

(1)   To record equity in S Company's 19X2 reported income (80% × $12,000):

Investment in S Company 9,600
    Equity in subsidiary earnings 9,600

(2)   To record confirmation of parent's interest in intercompany profit, net of taxes, in the beginning inventory (see Illustration 7–2):

Illustration 7–2

INTERCOMPANY SALES AND PROFITS IN INVENTORIES—19X2

	Ending Inventory			*Beginning Inventory (from Case 2)*
	P Company	*S Company*	*Total*	*S Company*
Sales during 19X2	$15,000	$10,000	$25,000	—
Amount left in purchaser's ending inventory	$ 6,000	$ 2,500		$5,000
Seller's gross profit rate	30%	40%		40%
Intercompany profit	$ 1,800	$ 1,000	$ 2,800	$2,000
Related income taxes	$ 450	$ 250	$ 700	$ 500
Intercompany profit, net of taxes	$ 1,350	$ 750	$ 2,100	$1,500
Parent's interest in intercompany profit, net of taxes	$ 1,350	$ 600	$ 1,950	$1,200

Investment in S Company	1,200	
Equity in subsidiary earnings		1,200

(3) To record deferral of parent's interest in intercompany profit, net of taxes, in ending inventories of the affiliates (see Illustration 7–2):

Equity in subsidiary earnings	1,950	
Investment in S Company		1,950

The working paper eliminating entries for this example are presented following:

(1) To reverse P Company entries during 19X2:

Equity in subsidiary earnings	8,850	
Investment in S Company		8,850

(2) To recognize confirmation of 100 percent (*total elimination method*) of intercompany profit in the beginning inventory and related income taxes (see Illustration 7–2):

Retained earnings—S Company	1,500	
Income tax expense	500	
Inventory, 1/1 (Income Statement)		2,000

(3) To eliminate the investment account balance at the beginning of the year against the beginning-of-year balances in the stockholders' equity accounts of S Company (where the beginning retained earnings balance of S Company is *adjusted* for the preceding eliminating entry):

Capital stock—S Company	40,000	
Retained earnings—S Company [80% × ($40,000 − $1,500)]	30,800	
Investment in S Company		70,800

(4) To eliminate 100 percent (*total elimination method*) of the unconfirmed profits in the ending inventories of the affiliates ($2,800), and recognize the related deferral of income taxes ($700) (see Illustration 7–2):

Inventory, 12/31 (Income Statement)	2,800	
Prepaid income taxes	700	
Inventory, 12/31 (Balance Sheet)		2,800
Income tax expense		700

(5) To eliminate intercompany sales (see Illustration 7–2):

Sales	25,000	
Purchases		25,000

The consolidated statement working paper for this example is presented in Illustration 7–3. Again, consolidated net income and retained earnings are equal to P Company's corresponding measures.

In eliminating entry (2), the intercompany profit in the beginning inventory ($2,000) is eliminated (confirmed on a consolidated basis), the related income tax expense ($500) recognized, and the beginning retained

Illustration 7–3

P COMPANY AND SUBSIDIARY S COMPANY
Consolidated Statement Working Paper (Total Elimination)
For Year Ended December 31, 19X2

	P Company	S Company	Eliminations Dr.	Eliminations Cr.	Minority Interest	Consolidated
Income Statement:						
Sales:						
To nonaffiliates	95,000	40,000				135,000
Intercompany	15,000	10,000	(5) 25,000			-0-
Equity in subsidiary earnings	8,850		(1) 8,850			-0-
Inventory (12/31):						
Acquired from nonaffiliates	22,500	8,000				30,500
Acquired from affiliates	2,500	6,000	(4) 2,800			5,700
Total credits	143,850	64,000				171,200
Inventory (1/1):						
Acquired from nonaffiliates	15,000	10,000				25,000
Acquired from affiliates	5,000	-0-		(2) 2,000		3,000
Purchases:						
From nonaffiliates	72,000	19,000				91,000
Intercompany	10,000	15,000		(5) 25,000		-0-
Expenses	5,000	4,000				9,000
Income tax expense	7,000	4,000	(2) 500	(4) 700		10,800
Total debits	114,000	52,000				138,800
Minority interest in net income—S Company [20% of ($12,000 + $1,500 − $750)]	29,850	12,000			2,550	32,400
Net income—carried forward	29,850	12,000	37,150	27,700	2,550	29,850

Retained Earnings Statement:

	P Company	S Company	Eliminations Dr.	Eliminations Cr.	Minority Interest	Consolidated
Retained earnings, January 1, 19X2:						
P Company	68,800				7,700†	68,800
S Company		40,000	(2) 1,500 / (3) 30,800*			-0-
Net income—brought forward	29,850	12,000	37,150	27,700	2,550	29,850
Retained earnings, December 31, 19X2—carried forward	98,650	52,000	69,450	27,700	10,250	98,650

Balance Sheet:

	P Company	S Company	Eliminations Dr.	Eliminations Cr.	Minority Interest	Consolidated
Other assets	102,350	101,000				203,350
Inventory:						
Acquired from nonaffiliates	22,500	8,000		(4) 2,800		30,500
Acquired from affiliates	2,500	6,000		(1) 8,850		5,700
Investment in S Company	79,650			(3) 70,800		-0-
Prepaid income taxes			(4) 700			700
	207,000	115,000				240,250
Other liabilities	8,350	13,000				21,350
Capital stock:						
P Company	100,000					100,000
S Company		50,000	(3) 40,000		10,000	-0-
Retained earnings—brought forward	98,650	52,000	69,450	27,700	10,250	98,650
Minority interest in S Company					20,250	20,250 M
	207,000	115,000	110,150	110,150	20,250	240,250

* Elimination of S Company's January 1 retained earnings = 80% × ($40,000 − $1,500).

† Minority interest in S Company's January 1 retained earnings = 20% × ($40,000 − $1,500).

Explanation of eliminations:

(1) To reverse P Company entries during 19X2.

(2) To recognize confirmation of intercompany profit in the beginning inventory and related income taxes.

(3) To eliminate the investment account balance at the beginning of the year against the beginning-of-year balances in the stockholders equity accounts of S Company.

(4) To eliminate intercompany profit in ending inventories of affiliates, and recognize the related deferral of income taxes.

(5) To eliminate intercompany sales.

earnings of S Company adjusted for the net amount ($1,500). S Company's beginning retained earnings are adjusted because this company (the selling affiliate in the 19X1 transaction producing the unconfirmed profit) recognized the intercompany profit, net of taxes, in 19X1 and thus it was transferred to retained earnings in the closing process. As a consequence of eliminating entry (2), the elimination of the subsidiary's retained earnings in the investment elimination entry (entry no. 3) must be based upon the beginning-of-year *confirmed* retained earnings (i.e., $40,000 − $1,500). When the parent company is the selling affiliate, the elimination of intercompany profit in the beginning inventory is changed only to debit the profit net of taxes *to the parent's investment account* (instead of the subsidiary's beginning retained earnings).[7] In this case, the investment elimination entry is based upon the adjusted investment account, which, as a result of the beginning inventory elimination, is restored to the proper proportional correspondence with the stockholders' equity accounts of the subsidiary.

The elimination of intercompany profit in the ending inventories of the affiliates and the deferral of the related income taxes are accomplished in the same manner as in 19X1, as is the elimination of intercompany sales. Note further that these entries combine the intercompany values of the two affiliates into aggregate values (see Illustration 7–2).

We observed in the previous case that when the total elimination method is used, the minority interest calculations must be adjusted for the minority shareholders' equity in unconfirmed profits. In this case, we must adjust both the minority interest in net income and in S Company's beginning retained earnings for the intercompany profits, net of taxes, for which S Company was the selling affiliate. Thus, S Company's confirmed net income for 19X2 ($12,750) is its reported net income ($12,000) plus intercompany profit, net of taxes, in the beginning inventory of P Company ($1,500), less intercompany profit, net of taxes, in ending inventory of P Company ($750). The minority interest in 19X2 net income ($2,550) is then calculated to be 20 percent of S Company's confirmed net income of $12,750 for 19X2 (see income statement division of Illustration 7–3). Similarly, the minority interest in S Company's January 1, 19X2 retained earnings is based upon the confirmed retained earnings at the beginning of the year. Since the $1,500 intercompany profit, net of taxes, at the end of 19X1 was unconfirmed at that time, S Company's beginning retained earnings must be reduced by this amount (see retained earnings division of Illustration 7–3). Thus, the minority's share in the $1,500 intercompany profit at the beginning of the year is deducted from the minority interest in the January 1, 19X2 retained earnings calculation and added in the minority interest in net income calculation. These two

---

[7] If for reasons of clerical convenience the parent does not adjust the investment account for intercompany profits, the elimination would be made against the January 1 balance of the parent's retained earnings.

adjustments are offsetting in end-of-year values, and thus the minority interest in end-of-year retained earnings is affected only by its share in end-of-year intercompany profits. This observation may be confirmed in Illustration 7–3 where the minority interest in December 31, 19X2 retained earnings ($10,250) is 20 percent of S Company's confirmed retained earnings at December 31, 19X2 [20% × ($52,000 − $750) = $10,250].

We again observe in the income statement division of Illustration 7–3 that consolidated income taxes, $10,800, as adjusted for taxes on confirmed and unconfirmed intercompany profits, is 25 percent (the assumed tax rate) of the total equity in consolidated income before income taxes [25% × ($32,400 + $10,800) = $10,800].

The previous two cases have dealt with the effects of intercompany profits in inventories on the parent company's entries to record its equity in affiliate's earnings and the preparation of consolidated statements, assuming total (100 percent) elimination of these unconfirmed profits. The following case, using the same source information, illustrates the procedures for applying the fractional elimination method to the two years. Since the parent company entries are based upon the parent's share in the unconfirmed profits, they are unchanged by the choice of the elimination method. *Only the eliminating entries in the consolidated statement working paper and certain balances in the consolidated statements are affected by the choice of elimination methods.* Recall however, that consolidated net income and retained earnings will remain unchanged.

Case 4. Fractional Elimination—Both Years. In Illustration 7–2, the intercompany profits in the inventories of the affiliates were summarized for use in Case 3. These data are presented in a modified form in Illustration 7–4. It may be noted that the parent's interest in intercompany profits,

Illustration 7–4

INTERCOMPANY PROFITS IN INVENTORIES

For Application of Fractional Elimination Method

	Ending Inventory (19X1) Beginning Inventory (19X2)	Ending Inventory (19X2)		
	S Company	P Company	S Company	Total
Total amount				
Intercompany profit	$2,000	$1,800	$1,000	$2,800
Related income taxes	500	450	250	700
Intercompany profit, net of taxes	1,500	1,350	750	2,100
Parent's share*				
Intercompany profit	1,600	1,800	800	2,600
Related income taxes	400	450	200	650
Intercompany profit, net of taxes	1,200	1,350	600	1,950

* 100 percent when P Company is selling affiliate, and 80 percent when S Company is selling affiliate.

net of taxes, is unchanged from Illustration 7–2. This equivalence produces the same parent company entries and the same values for consolidated net income and retained earnings, regardless of which elimination method is used. However, in Illustration 7–4, we have incorporated columns for the parent's share in gross intercompany profits in inventories and the related income taxes. These amounts, rather than the gross figures, are used in the application of the fractional elimination method to the consolidated statement working papers. The form of the eliminating entries, of course, remains unchanged. Thus, eliminating entry (3) to defer the unconfirmed profit in the 19X1 ending inventory would take the following alternative values depending upon the elimination method chosen:

	Total Elimination (Illustration 7–1)		Fractional Elimination (Illustration 7–5)	
Inventory, 12/31 (I.S.)	2,000		1,600	
Prepaid income taxes	500		400	
Inventory, 12/31 (B.S.) ..		2,000		1,600
Income tax expense		500		400

Similarly, eliminating entries (2) and (4) in the 19X2 consolidated statement working papers would use the following alternative values:

	Total Elimination (Illustration 7–3)		Fractional Elimination (Illustration 7–6)	
Elimination (2)—19X2 beginning inventory: Retained earnings—				
S Company	1,500		1,200	
Income tax expense .	500		400	
Inventory, 1/1 (I.S.) ...		2,000		1,600
Elimination (4)—19X2 ending inventory:				
Inventory, 12/31 (I.S.)	2,800		2,600	
Prepaid incomes taxes	700		650	
Inventory, 12/31 (B.S.)		2,800		2,600
Income tax expense		700		650

In accordance with the concept of fractional elimination previously explained, the elimination of only the parent company's share of intercompany profits from the inventory values and the related income tax expense is accompanied by the *calculation of the minority interest based upon S Company's recorded values for net income and retained earnings.*

The investment elimination entry, the entry to reverse the parent's entries to its investment account during the year, and the entry to eliminate intercompany sales are unaffected by the choice of total or fractional elimination, and thus they do not change in this example.

The consolidated statement working papers for 19X1 and 19X2 are presented in Illustrations 7–5 and 7–6. The reader may confirm that consolidated net income and retained earnings are the same for these illustrations employing fractional elimination as they were when total elimination was used (Illustrations 7–1 and 7–3). The accounts with different consolidated values under the two elimination methods are compared following:

		Dr (Cr)				
		19X1			19X2	
	Total Elimination	Fractional Elimination	Dr (Cr) Difference	Total Elimination	Fractional Elimination	Dr (Cr) Difference
Income statement:						
Inventory, 12/31 (Cost of sales)	$(3,000)	$(3,400)	$(400)	$(5,700)	$(5,900)	$(200)
Inventory, 1/1 (Cost of sales)	18,000	18,000	–0–	28,000	28,400	400
Income tax expense	10,500	10,600	100	10,800	10,750	(50)
Minority interest in net income	2,700	3,000	300	2,550	2,400	(150)
			–0–			–0–
Balance Sheet:						
Assets:						
Inventory, 12/31	3,000	3,400	400	5,700	5,900	200
Prepaid income taxes	500	400	(100)	700	650	(50)
			300			150
Equities:						
Minority interest	(17,700)	(18,000)	(300)	(20,250)	(20,400)	(150)

The differences in the values of income statement accounts completely offset, and the net difference in values assigned to assets (inventory and prepaid income taxes) is equal to the change in minority interest. Thus, the major impact on the end of period consolidated financial statements is the capitalization in the ending inventory of the minority's share of intercompany profits, net of taxes (the so-called adjunct cost to the majority shareholders) and the offsetting increase in the recognized equity of the minority interest.

Examination of the two fractional elimination working papers also reveals that all minority interest calculations are based upon the subsidiary's recorded values, and that consolidated income tax expense for the period

Illustration 7-5

P COMPANY AND SUBSIDIARY S COMPANY

Consolidated Statement Working Paper—Fractional Elimination
For Year Ended December 31, 19X1

	P Company	S Company	Eliminations Dr.	Eliminations Cr.	Minority Interest	Consolidated
Income Statement:						
Sales:						
To nonaffiliates	100,000	40,000				140,000
Intercompany	-0-	20,000	(4) 20,000			-0-
Equity in subsidiary earnings	10,800		(1) 10,800			-0-
Inventory (12/31):						
Acquired from nonaffiliates	15,000	10,000				25,000
Acquired from affiliates	5,000	-0-	(3) 1,600			3,400
Total credits	130,800	70,000				168,400
Inventory (1/):						
Acquired from nonaffiliates	10,000	8,000				18,000
Acquired from affiliates	-0-	-0-				-0-
Purchases:						
From nonaffiliates	60,000	38,000				98,000
Intercompany	20,000	-0-		(4) 20,000		-0-
Expenses	6,000	4,000				10,000
Income tax expense	6,000	5,000		(3) 400		10,600
Total debits	102,000	55,000				136,600
Minority interest in net income—S Company (20% × $15,000)					3,000	31,800
Net income—carried forward	28,800	15,000	32,400	20,400	3,000	28,800

Retained Earnings Statement:

	P Company	S Company	Eliminations Dr	Eliminations Cr	Minority Interest	Consolidated
Retained earnings, January 1, 19X1:						
P Company	40,000					40,000
S Company		25,000	(2) 20,000		5,000	-0-
Net income—brought forward	28,800	15,000	32,400	20,400	3,000	28,800
Retained earnings, December 31, 19X1—carried forward	68,800	40,000	52,400	20,400	8,000	68,800

Balance Sheet:

	P Company	S Company	Eliminations Dr	Eliminations Cr	Minority Interest	Consolidated
Other assets	89,200	90,000				179,200
Inventory:						
Acquired from nonaffiliates	15,000	10,000				25,000
Acquired from affiliates	5,000	-0-		(3) 1,600		3,400
Investment in S Company	70,800	-0-		(1) 10,800 (2) 60,000		-0-
Prepaid income taxes			(3) 400			400
	180,000	100,000				208,000
Other liabilities	11,200	10,000				21,200
Capital stock:						
P Company	100,000					100,000
S Company		50,000	(2) 40,000		10,000	-0-
Retained earnings—brought forward	68,800	40,000	52,400	20,400	8,000	68,800
Minority interest in S Company					18,000	18,000 M
	180,000	100,000	92,800	92,800	18,000	208,000

Explanation of eliminations:

(1) To reverse P Company entries during 19X1.

(2) To eliminate the investment account balance at the beginning of the year against the beginning-of-year balances in the stockholders' equity accounts of S Company.

(3) To eliminate the parent's fractional interest in the intercompany profit in P Company's ending inventory, and recognize the related deferral of income taxes.

(4) To eliminate intercompany sales.

Illustration 7-6

P COMPANY AND SUBSIDIARY S COMPANY

Consolidated Statement Working Paper—Fractional Elimination
For Year Ended December 31, 19X2

	P Company	S Company	Eliminations Dr.	Eliminations Cr.	Minority Interest	Consolidated
Income Statement:						
Sales:						
To nonaffiliates	95,000	40,000				135,000
Intercompany	15,000	10,000	(5) 25,000			–0–
Equity in subsidiary earnings	8,850		(1) 8,850			–0–
Inventory (12/31):						
Acquired from nonaffiliates	22,500	8,000				30,500
Acquired from affiliates	2,500	6,000	(4) 2,600			5,900
Total credits	143,850	64,000				171,400
Inventory (1/1):						
Acquired from nonaffiliates	15,000	10,000				25,000
Acquired from affiliates	5,000	–0–		(2) 1,600		3,400
Purchases:						
From nonaffiliates	72,000	19,000				91,000
Intercompany	10,000	15,000		(5) 25,000		–0–
Expenses	5,000	4,000				9,000
Income tax expense	7,000	4,000	(2) 400	(4) 650		10,750
Total debits	114,000	52,000				139,150
						32,250
Minority interest in net income— S Company (20% × $12,000)					2,400	2,400
Net income—carried forward	29,850	12,000	36,850	27,250	2,400	29,850

Retained Earnings Statement:

	P Company	S Company	Eliminations Dr.	Eliminations Cr.	Minority Interest	Consolidated
Retained earnings, January 1, 19X2:						
P Company	68,800				8,000†	68,800
S Company		40,000	(2) 1,200 / (3) 30,800*		8,000†	–0–
Net income—brought forward	29,850	12,000	(3) 36,850	27,250	2,400	29,850
Retained earnings, December 31, 19X2—carried forward	98,650	52,000	68,850	27,250	10,400	98,650

Balance Sheet:

	P Company	S Company	Eliminations Dr.	Eliminations Cr.	Minority Interest	Consolidated
Other assets	102,350	101,000				203,350
Inventory:						
Acquired from nonaffiliates	22,500	8,000				30,500
Acquired from affiliates	2,500	6,000		(4) 2,600		5,900
Investment in S Company	79,650			(1) 8,850 / (3) 70,800		–0–
Prepaid income taxes			(4) 650			650
	207,000	115,000				240,400
Other liabilities	8,350	13,000				21,350
Capital stock:						
P Company	100,000					100,000
S Company		50,000	(3) 40,000		10,000	–0–
Retained earnings—brought forward	98,650	52,000	68,850	27,250	10,400	98,650
Minority interest in S Company					20,400	20,400 M
	207,000	115,000	109,500	109,500	20,400	240,400

* Elimination of S Company's January 1 retained earnings = 80% × ($40,000 − $1,500).
† Minority interest in S Company's January 1 retained earnings = 20% × $40,000.
Explanation of eliminations:
(1) To reverse P Company entries during 19X2.
(2) To recognize confirmation of the parent's fractional interest in the intercompany profit in the beginning inventory and related income taxes.
(3) To eliminate the investment account balance at the beginning of the year against the beginning-of-year balances in the stockholders' equity accounts of S Company.
(4) To eliminate the parent's fractional interest in the intercompany profit in ending inventories of affiliates, and recognize the related deferral of income taxes.
(5) To eliminate intercompany sales.

is still 25 percent of the total equity in consolidated income before income taxes.

Refinement of Definition of Consolidated Net Income

The last refinement of our definition of consolidated net income (Chapter 5) did not provide for unconfirmed profits on the transfer of assets between affiliates. The definition must therefore be modified in terms sufficiently general to accommodate this intercompany profit element. Under the incremental approach, consolidated net income is now redefined as follows:

Parent company's net income from its own operations that has been confirmed or realized in transactions with nonaffiliates, increased (decreased) by its equity in the subsidiary's net income (loss) that has been confirmed or realized in transactions with nonaffiliates, and decreased (increased for a credit differential) by the differential amortization for the period.

The reader will notice that this rendering is not substantially different from the earlier definition in Chapter 5. It does, however, emphasize the importance of confirmation or realization of intercompany profit before it may be included in the calculation of consolidated net income (and thus, by extension, consolidated retained earnings). Because of its generality, it is applicable to all situations involving intercompany profits.

Using the data for 19X2 in our examples above, consolidated net income is determined as follows:

P Company's *confirmed* net income from its own operations for 19X2 ($29,850 − $8,850 − $1,350)	$19,650
Increased by P Company's equity in S Company's *confirmed* net income for 19X2 [80% × ($12,000 + $1,500 − $750)]	10,200
Consolidated Net Income for 19X2	$29,850

It should be observed that this definition of consolidated net income does not depend upon the elimination method chosen. The same conclusion was reached in our analysis of the parent company entries for unconfirmed profits, but this schedular calculation illustrates more clearly the separate compenents of consolidated net income.

In a similar manner, the "residual" approach must also recognize the existence of intercompany profits. Although consolidated net income must of course be equal under both elimination methods, the details of the calculation under the residual approach will differ somewhat because working paper entries are included therein. Applying the residual approach to our data, we obtain (see Illustrations 7–3 and 7–6):

	Total (100 Percent) Elimination	Fractional Elimination
P Company's net income for 19X2	$29,850	$29,850
S Company's net income for 19X2	12,000	12,000
	$41,850	$41,850
Less (plus)—net debit (credit) eliminations:		
P Company's recorded interest in S Company's net income	$ 8,850	$ 8,850
Confirmation of intercompany profit in beginning inventory, net of taxes	(1,500)	(1,200)
Deferral of intercompany profit in ending inventory, net of taxes	2,100	1,950
	$ 9,450	$ 9,600
Total equity	$32,400	$32,250
Less (plus)—minority interest in S Company's income (loss):		
100 percent basis [20% × ($12,000 + $1.500 − $750)]	2,550	
Fractional basis (20% × $12,000)		2,400
Consolidated Net Income for 19X2	$29,850	$29,850

INTERCOMPANY PROFIT—PLANT AND EQUIPMENT

As in the case of intercompany sales of merchandise, profit elimination is also required where there are transfers of plant and equipment between affiliates, to the extent that the exchange price exceeds the recorded book value of the transferred asset. Upon the sale of plant and equipment to an affiliate, there is, however, the additional problem of measuring and accounting for the effects of depreciation upon consolidated statements. In respect to the affiliation, profit on the sale of depreciable property remains unrealized, or unconfirmed, until the relevant property is depreciated. *Confirmation or validation is accomplished through the recognition of depreciation.* In this sense, the process of depreciation is comparable to the transaction of resale by the purchasing affiliate in the case of intercompany inventories. The current depreciation expense measures the economic value consumed in generating revenues from nonaffiliates. Of course, if the purchasing affiliate is a manufacturer, that part of periodic depreciation which relates to the cost of finished production remains unconfirmed until sale of the manufactured product. However, a precise determination of this amount is often difficult, and unless material, may often be ignored.

The following two case examples illustrate the treatment of intercompany profits arising from the transfer of plant and equipment between affiliates for the year of sale and the subsequent year. It is assumed that 100 percent elimination of intercompany profit is used in consolidated statement working paper preparation. As was previously demonstrated for intercompany inventory profits, this working paper is easily reconciled with one which provides for fractional elimination.

Case 5. Total Elimination—First Year. As in Case 2, we assume that
P Company acquired an 80 percent equity interest in S Company on January 1, 19X1 at a cost of $60,000. Additionally, the same beginning-of-
year shareholders' equity account balances will be used. We now assume
that there are no intercompany transfers of merchandise, but on January
2, 19X1, S Company sold plant and equipment having a cost of $20,000
and accumulated depreciation of $10,000 to P Company for $15,000. The
gain of $5,000 is reported separately by S Company as Profit on Sale of
Plant and Equipment. The assets are estimated to have a remaining service
life to the purchasing affiliate (P Company) of five years. As before, it is
assumed that S Company paid income tax on this intercompany profit at
a 25 percent rate. S Company reported net income of $24,000 for 19X1.

The parent company entries to record its equity in the subsidary's earnings and to recognize the intercompany profit on the transfer of plant and
equipment are:

(1)   To record equity in S Company's 19X1 reported income (80% ×
      $24,000):

Investment in S Company	19,200	
Equity in subsidiary earnings		19,200

(2)   To record deferral of parent's interest in the intercompany profit
      ($5,000), net of applicable income taxes ($1,250), or 80% ×
      $3,750:

Equity in subsidiary earnings	3,000	
Investment in S Company		3,000

(3)   To record confirmation of parent's interest in one-fifth of the inter-
      company profit, net of taxes, due to the recognition of depreciation
      expense during 19X1 (80% × $750):

Investment in S Company	600	
Equity in subsidiary earnings		600

Since the subsidiary was the selling affiliate, the parent's interest in the
intercompany profit, net of taxes, is based upon the parent's equity interest
in the subsidiary (80%). Note that entry (2) defers the parent's share of
the intercompany profit, net of taxes, as of the date of transfer. In recognition of one year's depreciation subsequent to transfer, entry (3) recognizes
validation of this portion of the profit, net of taxes, journalized by S
Company [80% × (one-fifth of $3,750)].

The working paper eliminating entries for this example are presented
following:

(1)   To reverse P Company entries during 19X1:

Equity in subsidiary earnings	16,800	
Investment in S Company		16,800

(2)   To eliminate the intercompany profit on the transfer of plant and
      equipment, restore the asset and related accumulated depreciation

Illustration 7-7

RECORDED AND CONSOLIDATED BASIS VALUES

For Asset Transferred between Affiliates in Case 5

	January 2, 19X1	December 31, 19X1	December 31, 19X2
Plant and Equipment:			
On consolidated basis	$20,000	$20,000	$20,000
Recorded by purchasing affiliate ..	15,000	15,000	15,000
	$ 5,000	$ 5,000	$ 5,000
Accumulated Depreciation:			
On consolidated basis	($10,000)	($12,000)	($14,000)
Recorded by purchasing affiliate ..	–0–	(3,000)	(6,000)
	($10,000)	($ 9,000)	($ 8,000)
Unconfirmed intercompany profit, before income taxes	$ 5,000	$ 4,000	$ 3,000
Applicable income taxes	$ 1,250	$ 1,000	$ 750
Unconfirmed intercompany profit, net of income taxes	$ 3,750	$ 3,000	$ 2,250

accounts to their original cost basis, and defer the applicable income taxes (see Illustration 7–7):

Gain on sale of plant and equipment	5,000	
Prepaid income taxes	1,250	
Plant and equipment	5,000	
Accumulated depreciation		10,000
Income tax expense		1,250

(3) To eliminate depreciation expense on the intercompany profit, and recognize the applicable income tax on this confirmed profit:

Accumulated depreciation	1,000	
Income tax expense	250	
Depreciation expense		1,000
Prepaid income taxes		250

(4) To eliminate the investment account balance at the beginning of the year against the beginning-of-year balances in the stockholders' equity accounts of S Company:

Capital stock—S Company	40,000	
Retained earnings—S Company	20,000	
Investment in S Company		60,000

The consolidated statement working paper for this example is presented in Illustration 7–8.

On a consolidated basis, the transferred asset should be reflected in term's of the selling affiliate's original transaction cost and related accumulated depreciation. Illustration 7–7 reveals that the intercompany profit before taxes of $5,000 is composed of an understatement of the asset account of $5,000 and an understatement of accumulated deprecia-

Illustration 7-8

P COMPANY AND SUBSIDIARY S COMPANY

Consolidated Statement Working Paper
For Year Ended December 31, 19X1

	P Company	S Company	Eliminations Dr.	Eliminations Cr.	Minority Interest	Consolidated
Income Statement:						
Sales	120,000	80,000	(1) 16,800			200,000
Equity in subsidiary earnings	16,800					–0–
Gain on sale of plant and equipment	–0–	5,000	(2) 5,000			–0–
Inventory (12/31)	30,000	12,000				42,000
Total credits	166,800	97,000				242,000
Inventory (1/1)	40,000	10,000				50,000
Purchases	74,000	50,000				124,000
Expenses	8,000	5,000		(3) 1,000		12,000
Income tax expense	7,000	8,000	(3) 250	(2) 1,250		14,000
Total debits	129,000	73,000				200,000
Minority interest in net income—S Company [20% × ($24,000 − $3,750 + $750)]					4,200	42,000
Net income—carried forward	37,800	24,000	22,050	2,250	4,200	37,800
Retained Earnings Statement:						
Retained earnings, January 1, 19X1:						
P Company	40,000					40,000
S Company		25,000	(4) 20,000		5,000	–0–
Net income—brought forward	37,800	24,000	22,050	2,250	4,200	37,800
Retained earnings, December 31, 19X1—carried forward	77,800	49,000	42,050	2,250	9,200	77,800

Balance Sheet:

	P Company	S Company	Eliminations Dr.	Eliminations Cr.	Minority	Consolidated
Other assets	128,200	108,000				236,200
Inventory	30,000	12,000				42,000
Investment in S Company	76,800	–0–		(1) 16,800 (4) 60,000		–0–
Plant and equipment (intercompany)	15,000	–0–	(2) 5,000			20,000
Prepaid income taxes			(2) 1,250	(3) 250		1,000
	250,000	120,000				299,200
Accumulated depreciation (intercompany)	3,000	–0–	(3) 1,000	(2) 10,000		12,000
Other liabilities	69,200	21,000				90,200
Capital stock:						
P Company	100,000					100,000
S Company		50,000	(4) 40,000			–0–
Retained earnings—brought forward	77,800	49,000	(4) 42,050	2,250		77,800
Minority interest in S Company					10,000 9,200	77,800
					19,200	19,200 M
	250,000	120,000	89,300	89,300		299,200

Explanation of eliminations:

(1) To reverse P Company entries during 19X1.
(2) To eliminate the intercompany profit on the transfer of plant and equipment.
(3) To eliminate depreciation expense on the intercompany profit.
(4) To eliminate the investment account balance at the beginning of the year against the beginning-of-year balances in the stock-holders' equity accounts of S Company.

tion of $10,000. Eliminating entry (2) adjusts these accounts to their proper consolidated basis at the date of transfer (the combined effect is, of course, a $5,000 credit to plant and equipment—net of accumulated depreciation), and defers the income tax paid by the subsidiary on this intercompany profit.

The adjusted asset account continues to be properly stated at the end of the year. However, the accumulated depreciation account must be additionally adjusted for the difference between depreciation recorded by P Company (the purchasing affiliate) for 19X1 and depreciation for the year on the basis of S Company's (the selling affiliate) original transaction cost. Annual depreciation recorded by P Company (classified in the statements merely as Expenses) on the basis of a five-year service life and a $15,000 purchase price amounts of $3,000. The depreciation on the basis of original transaction cost would, however, amount to only $2,000 ($10,000 book value allocated over the remaining five-year life). Accordingly, P Company has recognized $1,000 *depreciation on the intercompany profit*—an overstatement of expenses and accumulated depreciation on a consolidated basis. Eliminating entry (3) adjusts for this overstatement, including the recognition of $250 of the prepaid income taxes as income tax expense on the $1,000 confirmed profit. Note that the net credit in the income statement division of the consolidated statement working paper is $750, or one-fifth of the intercompany profit net of taxes of $3,750.

Since 100 percent of the intercompany profit is eliminated, the calculation of minority interest in net income is based upon the subsidiary's confirmed net income. For 19X1, S Company's confirmed net income of $21,000 is its reported net income ($24,000), less the unconfirmed profit on the intercompany transfer of plant and equipment ($3,750), plus the portion of this intercompany profit confirmed by the recognition of depreciation expense during the year (one-fifth of $3,750, or $750). The minority shareholders' interest in this confirmed net income is 20 percent, or $4,200. This amount is entered in the income statement division of the consolidated statement working paper in Illustration 7–8. Note also in Illustration 7–8 that consolidated income tax expense, $14,000, is 25 percent of the total equity in combined income before income taxes [25% × ($42,000 + $14,000) = $14,000].

As a consequence of these working paper eliminations, consolidated net income (and retained earnings) are again equal to the parent company's net income (and retained earnings).

Case 6. Total Elimination—Second Year. In continuation of Case 5, we assume that S Company reported net income for 19X2 of $15,000, and that there were no transfers of assets between the affiliates in 19X2.

The parent company entries to record its equity in the subsidiary's earnings and to recognize the confirmation of an additional portion of the intercompany profit arising from the 19X1 transfer of assets between the affiliates are:

(1)   To record equity in S Company's 19X2 reported income (80% × $15,000):

Investment in S Company	12,000	
Equity in subsidiary earnings		12,000

(2)   To record confirmation of parent's interest in one-fifth of the 19X1 intercompany profit, net of taxes, due to the recognition of depreciation expense during 19X2 (80% × $750):

Investment in S Company	600	
Equity in subsidiary earnings		600

Since there were no asset transfers between the companies in 19X2, there is no unconfirmed intercompany profit to be deferred. Recall that the entire intercompany profit in 19X1 was deferred in the parent company's entries at the end of 19X1, and thus the investment account reflects the residual effect of that transaction. As this intercompany profit is confirmed through the recognition of depreciation expense, however, the parent company must continue to reflect this fact in its accounts. Accordingly, entry (2) above will be continued throughout the next three years, or the remaining service life of the transferred asset.

The working paper eliminating entries for 19X2 are presented following:

(1)   To reverse P Company entries during 19X2:

Equity in subsidiary earnings	12,600	
Investment in S Company		12,600

(2)   To eliminate the unconfirmed profit in the January 1 retained earnings of S Company, and adjust the plant and equipment, accumulated depreciation, and prepaid income taxes to their proper balances as of that date (see Illustration 7–7):

Retained earnings—S Company	3,000	
Prepaid income taxes	1,000	
Plant and equipment	5,000	
Accumulated depreciation		9,000

(3)   To eliminate depreciation expense on the intercompany profit, and recognize the applicable income tax on this confirmed profit:

Accumulated depreciation	1,000	
Income tax expense	250	
Depreciation expense		1,000
Prepaid income taxes		250

(4)   To eliminate the investment account balance at the beginning of the year against the beginning-of-year balances in the stockholders' equity accounts of S Company (where the beginning retained earnings balance of S Company is *adjusted* for eliminating entry (2) above):

Capital stock—S Company	40,000	
Retained earnings—S Company		
[80% × ($49,000 − $3,000)]	36,800	
Investment in S Company		76,800

Illustration 7-9

P COMPANY AND SUBSIDIARY S COMPANY

Consolidated Statement Working Paper
For Year Ended December 31, 19X2

	P Company	S Company	Eliminations Dr.	Eliminations Cr.	Minority Interest	Consolidated
Income Statement:						
Sales	140,000	85,000				225,000
Equity in subsidiary earnings	12,600		(1) 12,600			-0-
Inventory (12/31)	25,000	15,000				40,000
Total credits	177,600	100,000				265,000
Inventory (1/1)	30,000	12,000				42,000
Purchases	93,000	54,000				147,000
Expenses	12,000	14,000		(3) 1,000		25,000
Income tax expense	7,500	5,000	(3) 250			12,750
Total debits	142,500	85,000				226,750
Minority interest in net income—S Company [20% × ($15,000 + $750)]					3,150	3,150
Net income—carried forward	35,100	15,000	12,850	1,000	3,150	35,100
Retained Earnings Statement:						
Retained earnings, January 1, 19X2:						
P Company	77,800					77,800
S Company		49,000	(2) 3,000 (4) 36,800*		9,200†	-0-
Net income—brought forward	35,100	15,000	12,850	1,000	3,150	35,100
Retained earnings, December 31, 19X2—carried forward	112,900	64,000	52,650	1,000	12,350	112,900

Balance Sheet:

	P Company	S Company	Eliminations Dr.	Eliminations Cr.	Minority Interest	Consolidated
Other assets	170,600	125,000				295,600
Inventory	25,000	15,000				40,000
Investment in S Company	89,400	–0–		(1) 12,600 (4) 76,800		–0–
Plant and equipment (intercompany)	15,000	–0–	(2) 5,000			20,000
Prepaid income taxes			(2) 1,000	(3) 250		750
	300,000	140,000				356,350
Accumulated depreciation (intercompany)	6,000	–0–	(3) 1,000	(2) 9,000		14,000
Other liabilities	81,100	26,000				107,100
Capital stock:						
P Company	100,000					100,000
S Company		50,000	(4) 40,000		10,000	–0–
Retained earnings—brought forward	112,900	64,000	52,650	1,000	12,350	112,900
Minority interest in S Company					22,350	22,350 M
	300,000	140,000	99,650	99,650		356,350

* Elimination of S Company's January 1 retained earnings = 80% × ($49,000 − $3,000).

† Minority interest in S Company's January 1 retained earnings = 20% × ($49,000 − $3,000).

Explanation of eliminations:
(1) To reverse P Company entries during 19X1.
(2) To eliminate the unconfirmed profit in the January 1 retained earnings of S Company.
(3) To eliminate depreciation expense on the intercompany profit.
(4) To eliminate the investment account balance at the beginning of the year against the beginning-of-year balances in the stockholders' equity accounts of S Company.

The consolidated statement working paper for this second year of the example is presented in Illustration 7–9.

Since S Company recognized the intercompany profit on its books in 19X1, it now resides in S Company's January 1, 19X2 retained earnings. Accordingly, the unconfirmed portion of this profit, net of taxes, *on this date* ($4,000 − $1,000) must be eliminated from the beginning retained earnings, and the plant and equipment, accumulated depreciation, and prepaid income taxes adjusted to their January 1, 19X2 consolidated basis balances. Drawing on the data in Illustration 7–7, eliminating entry (2) provides for these adjustments. As was the case with inventory transfers, if the parent company had been the selling affiliate, this elimination of unconfirmed profit at the beginning of the year is changed only to debit the profit net of taxes *to the parent's investment account* (instead of the subsidiary's beginning retained earnings).

In the same manner as in 19X1, eliminating entry (3) recognizes the confirmed profit during 19X2 and adjusts for the overstatement of depreciation expense by P Company during 19X2. As a consequence of these two eliminating entries, the elimination of retained earnings (see eliminating entry (4) above) and the calculation of the minority interest therein (see Illustration 7–9) are based upon S Company's January 1, 19X2 confirmed retained earnings ($49,000 − $3,000), and the calculation of minority interest in net income (see Illustration 7–9) is based upon S Company's confirmed 19X2 net income ($15,000 + $750). As we previously observed in the case of total elimination of intercompany inventory profits, note that the minority interest in *ending* retained earnings ($12,350) is 20 percent of S Company's confirmed retained earnings at December 31, 19X2 [20% × ($64,000 − $2,250) = $12,350]. If fractional elimination had been used, all of these calculations would have been based upon S Company's recorded values.

Verification of Consolidated Net Income by Definition. In the refinement of the definition of consolidated net income earlier in this chapter, it was pointed out that the definition applies to all situations involving intercompany profits. Applying this definition to the data of Cases 5 and 6, consolidated net income (and P Company's net income) is verified as follows:

	19X1	19X2
P Company's *confirmed* net income from its own operations:		
19X1: ($37,800 − $16,800)	$21,000	
19X2: ($35,100 − $12,600)		$22,500
Increased by P Company's equity in S Company's *confirmed* net income:		
19X1: [80% × ($24,000 − $3,750 + $750)]	16,800	
19X2: [80% × ($15,000 + $750)]		12,600
Consolidated Net Income	$37,800	$35,100

INTERCOMPANY PROFITS—RELATED TOPICS

Other Asset Transfers

The elimination of the selling company's profit recorded on the intercompany sales of merchandise or plant and equipment illustrated above applies equally to all forms of asset transfers between affiliates. The basic principles which apply are: (1) The acquired asset is adjusted to its original transaction cost to the selling affiliate, and (2) the intercompany profit is confirmed only when the asset is transferred to outside parties (either through sale or use of the asset).

Transfer of Nondepreciable Assets. In the event that the transferred asset is nondepreciable, the consolidated statement elimination for intercompany profit is constant in amount each year. The profit recorded by the selling affiliate (whether the parent or subsidiary) is eliminated against the contra asset account. Assuming the profit to be eliminated is $2,000, the entry in the year of sale is:

Profit on sale of long-lived assets	2,000	
Long-lived assets		2,000

Significantly, when the asset is nondepreciable, the profit will remain unconfirmed, or unrealized, in all succeeding periods; however, the elimination debit in the consolidated working paper in periods following the period of acquisition will be made against either the beginning retained earnings of the subsidiary (if the subsidiary were the seller) or the investment account of the parent (if the parent were the seller):

Retained earnings, 1/1 (or Investment in subsidiary)	2,000	
Long-lived assets		2,000

This entry will be repeated in consolidated working papers for all future periods until disposition of the asset by the purchasing affiliate. Such disposition indicates the point in time at which the transfer profit between affiliates is confirmed.

Transfer of Services. Affiliates of a consolidated entity may engage in intercompany sales of services which are of such a nature that they are capitalized on the books of the purchasing affiliate. For example, the parent may do a management consulting engagement for the subsidiary that is expected to provide benefits for, say, five years. In this case, the profit on the consulting service is initially deferred, and then recognized on a consolidated basis as it is confirmed through the amortization of the intangible asset.

On the other hand, some transfers of services are treated by the purchasing affiliate as period expenses. In these cases, the confirmation of the selling affiliate's profit on the transaction is assumed to occur during the same period as the transfer of services. Like the confirmation of fixed asset profit by depreciation, the expense of acquiring a service is presumed to generate the revenues in the same period in which the expense occurs. As a consequence, no elimination entries are required to remove such "profits" from the consolidated statements. The corresponding revenue and expense items must, of course, be eliminated, as for all other intercompany transactions.

In respect to the calculation of the minority interest in subsidiary net income (assuming 100 percent elimination of unconfirmed profit), the reader is reminded that the equity of minority interests relates to *confirmed* subsidiary net income. Thus, as an extension of the above discussion, it may be noted that the calculation of confirmed subsidiary net income does not involve adjustments to the reported subsidiary net income for such intercompany revenues and expenses transactions, since they do not generate asset valuations which require subsequent confirmation. It should also be recognized that the conventional calculation of the minority interest's equity on the basis of the subsidiary's confirmed *net* income is logically equivalent to a calculation based upon the separate elements of revenue and expense.

Transfer Profits before Affiliation

Accountants are not agreed as to the most desirable treatment to be accorded unrealized, or unconfirmed, profits on assets transferred between companies prior to their affiliation. One position is that the profit element should *not* be eliminated from the relevant asset accounts in consolidated working papers. The argument in general runs as follows. If a newly acquired subsidiary earns a profit on the transfer of assets to the parent, or to another affiliate, prior to the acquisition of the selling subsidiary's stock by the parent, such profit is one of the factors used to determine the book value of the subsidiary's capital stock at date of acquisition, and is accordingly eliminated in the investment elimination entry; necessarily, this profit should not again emerge as an element of consolidated net income, as the profit appropriately relates to the period in which earned.

A second position is one which supports a deduction of the preaffiliation profit existing at date of acquisition, with confirmation of such profit deferred to subsequent periods, to be recognized as a consequence of the elimination process. This treatment was cited several years ago as a prevailing practice, based upon a study of the American Institute of Certified Public Accountants.[8] The strength of this position is to be found primarily in its appeal to conservatism with respect to asset valuation, particularly for long-lived assets, and to the fact that intercompany profit is not, or should not be, solely a function of the affiliation date. The elimination of the preaffiliation profit from the inflated asset and retained earnings of the affiliates, however, merely defers its recognition until disposition is made

---

[8] Research Department, American Institute of Certified Public Accountants, *Survey of Consolidated Financial Statement Practices* (New York, 1956), p. 21.

of the relevant assets (merchandise or fixed assets), and results in its subsequent inclusion in consolidated net income and consolidated retained earnings. Presumably the recognition of profit would follow in the next accounting period, in most instances, for items of merchandise, while its recognition in respect to fixed assets would extend over the period of remaining service life of the transferred assets. Thus, if, *in fact,* the intercompany profit relates to the period prior to acquisition of the selling affiliate, the deferment of profit recognition introduces a measure of distortion in periodic net income reporting. The distortion is short-lived, but more pronounced, in respect to merchandise; the effects are moderate, but more extended, in the case of nonmerchandise items. With respect to consolidated retained earnings, the inclusion is, of course, permanent. Where the intercompany profit arises out of transactions during the period of negotiation for an affiliate's capital stock, the argument for elimination gains additional support.

If the parent is the selling affiliate, these two positions must be interpreted merely as a question of timing of income recognition. Whether eliminated or not prior to subsequent "confirmation," the intercompany profit element will ultimately reside in consolidated retained earnings, if not consolidated net income; inclusion in the investment elimination entry is not a relevant consideration under these circumstances.

Evolution of Accounting Practice regarding Intercompany Profits

Recall that *Accounting Research Bulletin No. 51,* "Consolidated Statements," issued by the AICPA Committee on Accounting Procedure in 1959, recommended 100 percent elimination of intercompany profits, with the *option* of absorbing the eliminated amount totally against the interest of the majority shareholders or allocating it between the majority and minority shareholders in proportion to their interests therein. At the time this bulletin was issued, most consolidated subsidiaries had small, if any, minority shareholder interests. Indeed, some accountants interpreted this bulletin as discouraging consolidation if a significant outside ownership interest existed. Further, there was but limited application of the equity method to unconsolidated subsidiaries. In view of these facts, the predominant practice was, largely as a matter of convenience, to eliminate 100 percent of the intercompany profits, all against the majority shareholders. The measures of consolidated net income and retained earnings that resulted from this practice would not be in harmony with our fundamental definitions, but because of the insignificant outside shareholder interests, the differences would normally be small.

Since the adoption of Bulletin 51, several changes in the business environment and accounting principles have occurred. More subsidiaries with significant minority interests exist, and these subsidiaries are generally consolidated. Further, *APB Opinion 18* imposed the equity method of accounting not only on investments in subsidiaries, but also on investments in less than majority-owned affiliates whose policies can be "significantly influenced" by the investor. These developments have magnified the differences that can result from the application of the two alternative forms of the total elimination method. Additionally, in 1971, the Accounting Principles Board added yet another alternative to the set of "acceptable" practices of eliminating intercompany profits. In *Accounting Interpretation No. 1 to APB Opinion 18*, the Board approved, under specified conditions, the following practice:

. . . [in certain cases], it would be appropriate for the investor to eliminate intercompany profit in relation to the investor's common stock interest in the investee. In these cases, the percentage of intercompany profit to be eliminated *would be the same* regardless of whether the transaction is "downstream" (i.e., a sale by the investor to the investee) or "upstream" (i.e., a sale by the investee to the investor).[9]

This practice was instituted largely in response to situations where a "joint venture" participant engaged in a large construction project for the joint venture, and deferral of all the profit on the project under the equity method would materially affect (distort?) the reported profit of the contractor. However, because of the strong interrelationship between the equity method of accounting and consolidation practices, this interpretation has important implications for the general problem of intercompany profits. Note that if the subsidiary (investee) were the selling affiliate, this new practice would be equivalent to the application of fractional elimination (a practice formerly considered to be inappropriate under *ARB 51*). However, where the parent (investor) is the seller, the fractional elimination method requires elimination of all of the intercompany profit (the majority shareholders' interest in the selling affiliate), and thus a new alternative has been spawned by this interpretation. In general, the conditions required for this new alternative to be justified are: (1) the exchange price specified in the transaction can be objectively verified as a reasonable value; (2) there is reasonable assurance of realization of the selling price; and (3) there is an effective sharing of the risk of ownership (e.g., the outside ownership interests in the investee must have supplied sufficient capital to bear any possible risk of loss). When these conditions are satisfied (and usually one would expect this only when the investee is not a majority-owned company) and this "modified fractional elimination method" is applied to sales by the parent to an affiliate, the parent's net income would be higher than it would be under the fractional elimination method presented in this chapter (because a portion of the intercompany profit is considered to be confirmed upon transfer of the asset to the investee).

---

[9] *Accounting Interpretation No. 1, APB Opinion 18* (Emphasis supplied).

As a consequence of these developments, the treatment of intercompany profits both in consolidation and under the equity method is at the present time subject to a variety of alternative methods. Fractional, or modified fractional, elimination has gained increased acceptance and support during the past decade, and the elimination of 100 percent of intercompany profit totally against the majority shareholders has probably been less frequently elected. Since this variety is the result of a series of largely uncoordinated developments over a 25 year period, it is not unreasonable to expect the Financial Accounting Standards Board to study the question of intercompany profits (perhaps in the context of a broader review of consolidation and equity method principles) in the near future with a view toward bringing more stability to the process.

QUESTIONS

1. Describe the general treatment of profits recognized on asset transfers between affiliates.

2. Indicate the profit rate—net or gross—that should be used in determining the amount of unconfirmed intercompany inventory profit to be eliminated, and explain the reasoning for this choice.

3. How are transportation costs incurred in transferring goods between affiliated companies accounted for in determining the amount of the intercompany profit?

4. Assume that two affiliates with intercompany sales of merchandise utilize the "cost or market, whichever is lower" method of pricing their inventories. What would be the effect upon the intercompany profit elimination, given a situation in which period-end market price is lower than the transfer price?

5. How are income taxes paid by the selling affiliate on intercompany profits treated in the consolidated statements and the equity "pickup"?

6. In the event that profit exists in the inventory (or other assets) purchased from an affiliated company, what elections exist as to the amount of elimination?

7. In regard to the impact on consolidated net income, what is the consequence of the decision as to the amount of intercompany profit to be eliminated?

8. In calculating the interest of minority shareholders (in net income or retained earnings), what difference is produced between the total elimination and the fractional elimination method? Why?

9. In what manner is intercompany profit "confirmed" or "realized"? Your answer should relate to both merchandise and other asset transfers.

10. How is consolidated net income redefined under the incremental approach to give effect to the new variable—intercompany profit?

11. What are the two alternative treatments of intercompany profits on assets transferred between companies prior to their affiliation?

12. What general conditions must be satisfied in order to eliminate only the parent's interest in intercompany profits on asset transfers from the parent to an affiliate?

EXERCISES

Exercise 7–1

Item A: X Corporation manufactures at a finished cost of $20 per unit and sells to Y Corporation @ $25 per unit. Y Corporation leaves its inventory in the warehouse of X Corporation, withdrawing only as needed and pays to X Corporation storage at the rate of 50 cents per unit per month. The quantity in the inventory of Y Corporation at December 31 was purchased six months previously. Y Corporation resells at $40 F.O.B. shipping point which is the same price at which X Corporation sells to others.

Item B: X Corporation owns and operates a mine from which item B is extracted. The average cost of mining item B is $5 per ton. The cost of the mine and development thereof is subject to depletion at the rate of $2.50 per ton. The cost of loading on freight cars averages $1 per ton. Y Corporation purchases from X Corporation at cost F.O.B. the mine and transports to its plant, paying freight of $1.50 per ton. X Corporation sells approximately 75 percent of its mined product to others at a price of $15 per ton, F.O.B. the mine, and Y Corporation sells at a substantial profit after refinement.

Item C: X Corporation buys manufacturing supplies at a price of $50 per unit less trade discounts of 10/10/20. A portion of the supplies purchased by X Corporation are resold to Y Corporation at a price of $41 F.O.B. Y Corporation's plant. The freight, paid by X Corporation, amounts to 50 cents per unit. Y Corporation does not have access to the market from which X Corporation buys.

Item D: X Corporation manufactures this item at the average cost of $29 per unit and sells its total output to Y Corporation @ $35 per unit, F.O.B. X Corporation's plant under terms of a firm contract. The freight amounts to $2 per unit. The amount obtainable from X Corporation is only about 50 percent of the quantity required by Y Corporation. The balance of Y Corporation's requirements are obtained from other sources at a price of $32.50 per unit, F.O.B. Y's plant. Y resells this item at a price which yields $34 per unit after allowing for sales and handling expense.

Item E: X Corporation manufactures at a cost of $6 per unit and sells to Y Corporation and others @ $5 per unit, F.O.B. X Corporation's plant. The freight to Y's plant amounts to 75 cents per unit. Y Corporation processes this item and sells at a profit.

Required:

Consider that there were 10 units of each of the five items in the inventory of *each corporation* at the end of their concurrent fiscal years. You are to show the proper valuation at the lower of cost or market for inventory purposes in the financial statements and to explain in connection with each valuation the reason for using it. Answer for each item separately.

a. In the separate financial statements of X Corporation and Y Corporation.
b. In the consolidated financial statements, assuming Y Corporation is a 90 percent owned subsidiary of X Corporation.

(AICPA adapted)

Exercise 7–2

P Company has a 90 percent interest in S Company. During 19X1, S Company reported net income after taxes of $20,000. Additionally, at the end of the year, S Company's ending inventory includes $15,000 unconfirmed intercompany profit on purchases from P Company. The companies file separate income tax returns, and thus P Company paid income tax (40% rate) in 19X1 on the intercompany profit.

Required:

a. Prepare the entries made by P Company at the end of 19X1 to record its equity in S Company's income, using the method generally applied throughout the chapter.
b. Prepare the entries made by P Company at the end of 19X1 to record its equity in S Company's income and to eliminate the unconfirmed inventory profit against the results of its own operations.

Exercise 7–3

P Company has a 90 percent interest in S Company. During 19X1, S Company reported net income after taxes of $30,000, and there is an unconfirmed inventory profit of $4,000 at the end of the year to be eliminated. The companies file separate income tax returns, and thus income tax (40% rate) is paid in 19X1 on the intercompany profit.

Required:

a. Assuming that S Company was the seller on the transaction producing the intercompany profit:
 (1) Prepare the entries made by P Company at the end of 19X1 to record its equity in S Company's confirmed profits.
 (2) Prepare the eliminating entry for consolidated statement working papers at December 31, 19X1 for the unconfirmed profit for both total and fractional elimination.
 (3) Calculate minority interest in 19X1 net income for both total and fractional elimination.
b. Assuming that P Company was the seller on the transaction producing the intercompany profit:
 (1) Prepare the entries made by P Company at the end of 19X1 to record its equity in S Company's income, using the method generally applied throughout the chapter.
 (2) Prepare the eliminating entry for consolidated statement working

papers on December 31, 19X1 for the unconfirmed profit for both total and fractional elimination.

(3) Calculate minority interest in 19X1 net income for both total and fractional elimination.

Exercise 7–4

Kersbergen owns 80 percent of Algoe Ltd.'s common stock. Algoe sells merchandise to Kersbergen at 50 percent over cost. During 19X0 and 19X1 such sales (at transfer or sales prices) amounted to $90,000 and $60,000. At the end of each year Kersbergen had in inventory one half of the amount purchased from Algoe that year. Assume that each firm reported $50,000 net income from their own operations during 19X1 and that Kersbergen uses 100 percent elimination of intercompany profit on the consolidated statements. The affiliates file consolidated income tax returns.

Required:

Prepare a schedular calculation of consolidated net income for 19X1 using the:

a.   Incremental approach.
b.   Residual approach.

Exercise 7–5

The Hart Company owns 90 percent of the capital stock of the Lake Company. During 19X1 the Hart Company sold merchandise to the Lake Company for $10,000 and purchased $5,000 of merchandise from the Lake Company. Twenty percent of all intercompany sales remains in the ending inventory of the purchasing affiliate. The beginning inventory of the Hart Company included $500 of merchandise purchased in the previous period from the Lake Company. Each company marks merchandise to sell at 25 percent above cost.

The 19X1 net incomes from their own operations of the Hart Company and the Lake Company were $20,000 and $10,000 respectively. The affiliates file consolidated income tax returns.

Required:

a.   Prepare eliminating entries for all eliminations in respect to the intercompany sales. Assume the amount of the elimination of intercompany profit is 100 percent.
b.   Calculate the minority interest in subsidiary net income for 19X1.
c.   Calculate 19X1 consolidated net income.

Exercise 7–6

W Company owns 80 percent of the capital stock of Z Company. For the year ended December 31, 19X1, companies W and Z reported net incomes from their own operations of $24,000 and $5,000 respectively. The January 1, 19X1, inventory of W Company included $1,000 of profit recorded by Z Company on 19X0 sales. During 19X1 companies W and Z made intercompany sales of $5,000 and $10,000 respectively, on which each recorded a markup of 25 percent on cost. The ending inventory of W Company included $1,000 of these goods, while Z Company's ending inventory included $1,500 of goods purchased from W Company.

The affiliates file separate tax returns, and the applicable rate is 25%.

Required:

Prepare eliminating entries in respect to intercompany sales and unconfirmed inventory profit *and* compute the consolidated net income and minority interest in subsidiary net income for 19X1:

a.   If the amount of the elimination is assumed to be 100 percent of intercompany inventory profit.
b.   If the amount of the elimination is assumed to be the majority shareholders' interest in intercompany inventory profit.

Exercise 7–7

P Company purchased in the open market 90 percent of the capital stock of S Company on January 1, 19X1, for $2,200 less than its equity in the book value of S Company stock. The parent uses the equity method. The credit differential relates to land. On December 31, 19X2, the consolidated balance sheet discloses the value of the minority interest to be $8,608. Other summary information for the years 19X1 and 19X2 is as follows:

	19X1	*19X2*
Consolidated net income	$109,200	$116,900
P Company net income from its own operations	80,000	60,000

Additionally, an analysis of intercompany sales revealed the existence of the following unconfirmed inventory profits:

	December 31, 19X1	*December 31, 19X2*
In the inventory of—		
P Company	$2,000	$1,000
S Company	5,000	3,000

In the preparation of consolidated financial statements, 100 percent of intercompany inventory profits is eliminated.

S Company paid cash dividends of $20,000 in both 19X1 and 19X2.

Required:

a.   Compute the cost of the investment in S Company stock at date of acquisition.
b.   What is the carrying value of the investment account on December 31, 19X2?

Exercise 7–8

On January 1, 19X1, P Company purchased 90 percent of S Company's outstanding stock. On January 2, 19X1, S Company sold equipment to P Company for $25,000 that had a cost of $40,000 and accumulated depreciation of $20,000. The equipment has a remaining life of five years. The companies file separate income tax returns, and the applicable rate is 40 percent. During 19X1, both firms reported net income from their own operations of $10,000.

Required:

a. Prepare the entries by P Company on December 31, 19X1, to recognize its equity in S Company's earnings and to eliminate the intercompany profit.
b. Using the total elimination method, prepare the eliminating entries for a consolidated statement working paper on December 31, 19X1.
c. Prepare a schedular calculation of consolidated net income for 19X1 using both the incremental and the residual approaches.

Exercise 7–9

P Company has an 80 percent interest in the capital stock of S Company. On January 1, 19X1, S Company sold equipment, which cost $100,000 ten years ago, to P Company for $80,000. The original estimate of service life was 20 years, and P Company decided that a remaining life of 10 years was reasonable.

During 19X1 and 19X2, the companies' reported incomes from their own operations were: P Company, $50,000, and S Company, $40,000. The companies file a consolidated income tax return, and the total elimination method is used.

Required:

a. Prepare eliminating entries related to the asset transfer for a consolidated statement working paper on December 31, 19X1.
b. Prepare eliminating entries related to the asset transfer for a consolidated statement working paper on December 31, 19X2.
c. Prepare a schedular calculation of consolidated net income for 19X1 and 19X2.
d. Calculate minority interest in net income for 19X1 and 19X2.

Exercise 7–10

On January 1, 19X1, Seydel, Inc., purchased 90 percent of White Corporation's outstanding stock and concurrently White Corporation purchased 80 percent of Hanson Company's outstanding stock. On January 2, 19X1, Hanson sold a truck to White for $15,000. The truck had a book value to Hanson of $10,000 and was expected to be useful for another five years.

The three firms each reported net income from their own operations of $10,000 during 19X1. A consolidated income tax return was filed in 19X1.

Required:

a. Using the total elimination method, prepare the eliminating entries relating to the truck sale that would be necessary on consolidated statement working papers for the year ended December 31, 19X1.

b. Prepare a schedular calculation of consolidated net income for 19X1.

c. Calculate minority interest in net income for 19X1.

Exercise 7–11

Heath Associates, Inc., acquired 90 percent of the capital stock of the Prentice Company on January 1, 1971. On January 1, 1977, equipment originally costing the Prentice Company $60,000 on January 1, 1967, was sold to Heath Associates, Inc., for $70,000. Accumulated depreciation to the date of sale (based upon a 60-year service life) was $10,000. The 1977 net incomes of Heath Associates, Inc., and the Prentice Company from their own operations were $40,000 and $38,000, respectively. The companies file consolidated income tax returns.

Required:

a. Prepare eliminating entries for a consolidated statement working paper for the years ended December 31, 1977, and 1978 in respect to the equipment transfer if—

   (1) The amount of the profit elimination is 100 percent.

   (2) The amount of the profit elimination is based upon the parent company's equity in the selling affiliate.

b. Calculate consolidated net income for 1977, and the minority interest in the subsidiary's net income for 1977 under conditions (1) and (2) above.

Exercise 7–12

During its fiscal year ended October 31, 1977, the S Company, a wholly owned subsidiary of the P Company, sold to the latter, at a profit, materials which it used in constructing a new building for its own use. State (*a*) how the profit on the sale of these materials should be treated in preparing the consolidated financial statements of the P Company and its subsidiary as of October 31, 1977, and for the year then ended respectively, and (*b*) how it should be treated in preparing financial statements in subsequent years.

(AICPA adapted)

Exercise 7–13

P Company had a 60 percent interest in S Company. During 19X1, both companies reported net incomes from their own operations of $20,000. At the end of 19X1, there were unconfirmed inventory profits on which P Company was the seller of $5,000, and unconfirmed inventory profits on which S Company was the seller of $3,000. Ignore income taxes.

Required:

Prepare a schedular calculation of consolidated net income for 19X1 assuming:

a. 100 percent elimination, all against the majority shareholders.

b. 100 percent elimination, allocated pro rata between majority and minority shareholders.

c. Fractional elimination.

d. Modified fractional elimination (Assume the general conditions for the applicability of this method are satisfied).

Exercise 7–14

On January 1, 19X1, DFP Company entered into a joint venture with two other companies to manufacture and sell frisbees. The three companies plan to share profits from the joint venture equally.

During 19X1, DFP Company manufactured equipment for the joint venture. The equipment was delivered on December 31, 19X1 at a price of $225,000; DFP Company's manufacturing cost was $150,000. The equipment has an expected useful life of five years.

The joint venture began operations in 19X2 following the receipt of the equipment. It had no income or loss for 19X1, and $60,000 net income in 19X2.

DFP Company reported net income from its own operations (including the sale of the equipment to the joint venture) in 19X1 of $125,000. In 19X2, DFP Company's income from its own operations amounted to $100,000. Ignore income taxes.

Required:

a. Calculate DFP Company's equity-basis net income for 19X1 and 19X2, assuming that 100 percent of the "intercompany profit" is eliminated.

b. Calculate DFP Company's equity-basis net income for 19X1 and 19X2, assuming that "intercompany profits" are eliminated in accordance with the modified fractional method specified in *APB Opinion 18*.

PROBLEMS

Problem 1

On January 1, 19X0, the Moyer Company purchased 90 percent of the capital stock of Bedford, Inc., when the latter had accumulated retained earnings of $30,000. Two years later, the following information is made available by the affiliate companies:

	December 31, 19X1	
	Moyer Company	*Bedford, Inc.*
Sales	$94,000	$43,000
Purchases	50,000	26,000
Expenses	4,000	2,000
Inventory, January 1	18,000	8,000
Inventory, December 31	24,000	12,000
Retained earnings, January 1	92,000	43,000
Dividends declared	10,000	
Equity in subsidiary earnings	16,830	

During 19X1, Bedford, Inc., sold merchandise to the Moyer Company for $20,000. Bedford, Inc., regularly marks its merchandise to sell for 20 percent above cost. Of this 19X1 shipment, 30 percent remains in the inventory of the Moyer Company on December 31. At the beginning of the year (January 1, 19X1) the Moyer Company's inventory contained goods purchased from Bedford, Inc., in 19X0 for $3,600.

The companies file separate income tax returns, and the applicable income tax rate is 25 percent.

Required:

a. Prepare the income statement and retained earnings statement divisions of a consolidated statement working paper for the year ended December 31, 19X1. Also include at the foot of this partial working paper the following balance sheet accounts: Prepaid income taxes and Inventory, December 31. The total elimination method is to be used.

b. Using the incremental approach, prepare a schedular calculation of consolidated net income for 19X1.

Problem 2

Using the information of Problem 1, prepare a similar partial consolidated statement working paper for the year ended December 31, 19X1, with intercompany profits eliminated under the *fractional method*.

Compare the 100 percent elimination (Problem 1) and the fractional elimination as they affect:

a. Consolidated net income for 19X1.

b. Consolidated retained earnings, as of December 31, 19X1.

c. Minority interest in 19X1 subsidiary net income and retained earnings as of December 31, 19X1.

Problem 3

The Banner Corporation owns 80 percent of the capital stock of the Ribbon Company. On January 1, 1977, the Ribbon Company sold fixed assets to the Banner Corporation for $45,000. These assets were purchased originally by the Ribbon Company for $50,000 on January 1, 1967. Accumulated depreciation to the date of sale (estimated service life of 25 years) amounted to $20,000.

On December 31, 1978, the trial balances of the affiliates were:

	Banner Corporation	Ribbon Company
Inventory, January 1	$ 12,000	$ 10,000
Fixed assets	180,000	64,000
Other assets	115,620	149,700
Investment in Ribbon Company	139,680	
Dividends declared	10,000	8,000
Purchases	80,000	60,000
Expenses	12,000	7,400
	$549,300	$299,100
Liabilities	$ 23,000	$ 8,000
Accumulated depreciation	31,200	24,000
Sales	122,000	89,000
Equity in subsidiary earnings	14,800	
Capital stock	250,000	100,000
Retained earnings	108,300	78,100
	$549,300	$299,100
Inventory, December 31	$ 13,500	$ 5,900

The companies file a consolidated income tax return. Intercompany profits are eliminated using the total elimination method.

Required:

Prepare a consolidated statement working paper for the year ended December 31, 1978.

Problem 4

The Buckley Company purchased 80 percent of the capital stock of the Carson Company and 70 percent of the capital stock of the Diamond Company on January 1, 19X0.

Intercompany sales of merchandising during 19X1 were as follows:

From	To	Sales	December 31 Inventory
Buckley	Carson	$20,000	$2,000
Carson	Buckley	15,000	1,000
Diamond	Carson	30,000	5,000

Intercompany sales of merchandise during 19X0 include the following:

Carson	Buckley	$10,000	$2,000
Diamond	Carson	12,000	3,000

Gross profit rates (based on selling price) for 19X0 and 19X1 were:

Buckley	20%
Carson	25
Diamond	30

During 19X1, the companies reported net income from their own operations as follows:

Buckley	$40,000
Carson	30,000
Diamond	20,000

The companies file separate income tax returns, and the applicable income tax rate is 40 percent. Intercompany profits are eliminated in the consolidated statements using the total elimination method.

Required:

a. Calculate the intercompany profits, gross and net of taxes, in the beginning and ending inventories in 19X1.

b. Using the incremental approach, prepare a schedular calculation of consolidated net income for 19X1.

c. Calculate minority interest in 19X1 net income.

d. Prepare the eliminating entries related to the intercompany merchandise transactions for a consolidated statement working paper at December 31, 19X1.

e. Using the residual approach, prepare a schedular calculation of consolidated net income for 19X1.

Consolidated
Statements—
Preference Interests

INTERCOMPANY BONDS

WHENEVER a corporation issues bonds and subsequently retires some or all of these bonds at a price that is different from the book value of the bonds at the date of retirement, a gain or loss on bond retirement is realized. From the point of view of a consolidated entity, the purchase of an affiliate's bonds by another affiliate constitutes constructive retirement of the bonds. Correspondingly, where the cost to the purchasing affiliate is unequal to the carrying value of the bond liability, there exists a *consolidated basis* "gain or loss on the purchase of affiliate's bonds." Significantly, this gain or loss is *not recorded* by any of the affiliates. The issuing corporation is obliged to continue the payment of interest and to record the expense as well as the amortization of any premium or discount on bonds payable. Also, the purchasing affiliate periodically records the receipt of interest and amortization of any premium or discount on bond investment with corresponding credits to interest revenue.

Eliminations at Date of Purchase

From the discussion above, it is apparent that the existence of intercompany bond holdings must be dealt with in a special manner in the preparation of consolidated statements. Assuming the bonds are purchased on the last day of the accounting period, the first set of consolidated statements to be affected by the purchase would be prepared as of the date of purchase. To remove the intercompany indebtedness, it is conventional to eliminate the *par* value of the bond investment and the *par* value of the bond liability as follows:

Bonds payable .... (par)

Investment in bonds ....   (par)

At the date of the bond acquisition, the above elimination would leave any premium or discount on bonds payable *and* premium or discount on bond investment as amounts yet to be eliminated. Most frequently, the intercompany bonds would have been issued at some previous date to outside parties; the current acquisition of the bonds by the purchasing affiliate would therefore be made from outside parties. As a consequence, the current amount of premium or discount on bonds payable may be substantially different from the amount of discount or premium on bond investment. The algebraic sum of these items determines the consolidated basis gain or loss on the purchase of intercompany bonds. This is, of course, equivalent to the previous statement that the gain or loss is calculated as the difference between the carrying value of the bond liability and the acquisition cost of the bond investment. Elimination entries which remove these premium or discount balances also accomplish the recognition of the gain or loss on the consolidated income statement.

For example, assume that Y Company issued $5,000 (par) bonds payable several years ago at a premium. After several years of amortization, at the current date, the premium on bonds payable account has a remaining balance of $250. At the current date, X Company (Y Company's parent) has acquired these bonds in the open market at a price of $5,140, recording the purchase as follows:

Investment in Y Company bonds 5,000

Premium on bond investment 140

Cash   5,140

The consolidated basis gain on the purchase of these intercompany bonds is calculated as $110 ($5,250 carrying value less $5,140 purchase price). The elimination entries for consolidated working papers at the date of purchase are as follows:

Bonds payable 5,000

Investment in Y Company bonds   5,000

Premium on bonds payable 250

Loss [Gain] on purchase of affiliate's bonds   250

Loss [Gain] on purchase of affiliate's bonds 140

Premium on bond investment   140

Analysis of Gain or Loss

Upon recognition of a gain or loss on the purchase of intercompany bonds, it then becomes necessary to determine an appropriate allocation of the gain or loss between the purchasing and issuing affiliates. In that one or both of the affiliates may have minority interest stockholders, the allocation of gain or loss may affect the calculations of minority interest in combined net income and thus the determination of consolidated net income.

It may be argued that the total gain or loss should be allocated to the company that issued the bonds. The purchasing company would thus be perceived as simply an *agent* for the issuing affiliate; given this interpretation, the act of purchasing is deemed to be in behalf of the issuing firm which is the principal to the transaction. On the other hand, it can be argued that the gain or loss should be allocated entirely to the purchasing affiliate. In this instance, emphasis is placed on the purchase transaction, which is regarded as the critical event giving rise to the gain or loss. This event being undertaken by the purchasing affiliate, it follows that the gain or loss should be attributed to the purchaser.

The authors believe that the most reasonable analysis of gain or loss on purchase of intercompany bonds recognizes that the actions of *both* affiliates are essential to the existence of a gain or loss. As such, both should participate in its effects. A recommended method of allocating the gain or loss that should be followed consistently is to assume that the constructive retirement of the bonds is effected at their par value. Thus, the gain or loss of the issuing affiliate is determined by comparing the carrying value of the bond liability (at the date the bonds are acquired by the purchasing affiliate) with the par value. Similarly, the gain or loss of the purchasing affiliate is determined by comparing its purchase price with par value. In other words, at the date of purchase, any premium on intercompany bonds payable represents gain to the issuing company; similarly, a discount on intercompany bonds payable would represent loss to the issuing company. A premium on bond investment represents a loss to the purchasing company; a discount on bond investment represents a gain. The algebraic sum of gains or losses of both affiliates constitutes the total consolidated basis gain or loss. In the previous example, Y Company would be allocated a $250 gain and X Company would be allocated a $140 loss, which sum to a net gain of $110.

Eliminations after Date of Purchase

After the date of purchase, the issuing and purchasing affiliates will necessarily record cash transfers of interest. At consolidation points, such accumulations of intercompany interest expense and revenue (to the extent of cash transfers) should be eliminated against each other. Additionally, it may be necessary to eliminate contra accounts of interest receivable and interest payable. The par value of bonds payable and bond investment must also be eliminated, as previously discussed.

When a subsidiary issues bonds which are subsequently purchased by an affiliate, and then the subsidiary records the amortization of premium or discount on bonds payable in periods subsequent to their "constructive retirement," the subsidiary is effectively recognizing in its own records a portion of the gain or loss previously attributed to it. If not eliminated, the amount of such periodic amortizations would constitute a *double* recognition of the gain or loss in the consolidated statements. Thus, the subsidiary's current amortization of premium or discount (reflected as an increment or decrement to interest expense) together with the remaining premium or discount balance must be eliminated against the beginning-of-the-period retained earnings balance (or if during the same period as the purchase, against the gain or loss account). Similarly, when a subsidiary purchases intercompany bonds, the eliminations of amortizations of premium or discount on bond investment exactly parallel the elimination entries when the subsidiary is the issuer. The current amortization (evidenced in the interest revenue account) and the remaining balance of premium or discount are eliminated against the beginning-of-the-period retained earnings.

When a parent issues or purchases intercompany bonds, the entries it makes to record its equity in subsidiary earnings include its equity in the gain or loss on constructive retirement of intercompany bonds. Also, the parent records periodic amortization of the premium or discount on the bonds it has issued or purchased. Thus, there is a potential double counting on the parent's books of the gain or loss associated with its recorded premium or discount on intercompany bonds. To avoid this double booking by the parent of this portion of the gain or loss, the periodic entries to record the parent's equity in subsidiary earnings are adjusted to offset the current amount of amortization of premium or discount booked by the parent.

For example, on December 31, 19X1, suppose a parent which owns 90 percent of a subsidiary's stock pays a $300 premium for bonds which were issued by the subsidiary at par. The bonds have two years remaining to maturity and, for simplicity, we will assume amortization of $150 per year. The parent's entries at the end of 19X1, 19X2, and 19X3 to amortize the premium and the related entries to record the parent's equity in subsidiary earnings are as follows:

December 31, 19X1:
    Investment in subsidiary stock .... .9(Y's net income) − $300
        Equity in subsidiary earnings ....   .9(Y's net income) − $300

December 31, 19X2:
    Investment in subsidiary stock .... .9(Y's net income) + $150
        Equity in subsidiary earnings ....   .9(Y's net income) + $150
    Bond interest income 150
        Premium on bond investment   150

December 31, 19X3:
    Investment in subsidiary stock .... .9(Y's net income) + $150
        Equity in subsidiary earnings ....   .9(Y's net income) + $150
    Bond interest income 150
        Premium on bond investment   150

On consolidated working papers, the parent's current amortization of the premium together with the remaining premium balance are eliminated against the Investment in Subsidiary Stock account, thereby reinstating the amount of loss which, as of January 1, had not yet been booked by the parent in the form of amortization of premium. As a consequence, the Investment in Subsidiary Stock balance is restored to its proportional (90 percent) relationship to the total amount of the subsidiary's common stock and confirmed retained earnings.

The similarity between the eliminations for intercompany bond holdings and the eliminations of intercompany profit on depreciable asset transfers should now be apparent. In the case of asset transfers, an unconfirmed profit is recorded by the selling affiliate; it is deferred in the consolidated statements and is given recognition only in future periods as confirmation is accomplished through depreciation. In the case of intercompany bonds, the gain or loss is regarded as confirmed at the date of acquisition and is so recognized in the consolidated statements. The affiliates, however, record their respective elements of the gain or loss over future periods in the form of premium or discount amortizations; accordingly, *double* recognition is avoided by eliminating, in the consolidated working papers, the effects produced by these subsequent amortizations. Consequently, the result of the elimination process is to *defer* recognition of profit (or loss) on asset transfers and to *accelerate* its recognition in respect to intercompany-held bonds. In both instances, there is an evident underlying philosophy of reporting profits or losses only at the time they are confirmed by transactions with nonaffiliate parties. Obviously, this philosophy is just as applicable to the eliminations of intercompany inventory profit as it is to intercompany depreciable asset transfers and bond holdings.

As was true regarding the elimination of profit on asset transfers, accountants are not in complete agreement as to the appropriate *amount* of intercompany unamortized bond discounts or premiums to be eliminated in a consolidated working paper. The prevailing practice is to eliminate 100 percent of these balances; however, some accountants favor the elimination of amounts based upon the parent company's fractional interest in the capital stock of the relevant affiliate. Obviously, the position taken will affect the amount of gain or loss on the purchase of intercompany bonds to be recognized.

The following cases illustrate a number of different conditions of intercompany bondholdings. Case 1 is slightly expanded so that it demonstrates the impact of intercompany bondholdings on the equity method entries made by the parent and the corresponding eliminations. Subsequent cases display only the eliminations which relate directly to the intercompany bond accounts.

Case 1. Subsidiary Company's Bonds Completely Acquired by Parent—100 Percent Elimination. On January 1, 1970, Y Company issued $5,000 (par), 9 percent bonds, due January 1, 1980. Interest is payable semiannually on July 1 and January 1. The cash proceeds from the issue were $6,250, and the $1,250 premium is being amortized at the rate of

$125 per year.[1] On January 1, 1977, at which date Y Company had common stock of $100,000 and zero retained earnings, X Company purchased 80 percent of Y Company's outstanding stock for $80,000. On December 31, 1977, X Company purchased the Y Company bonds at a cost of $5,140 plus $225 accrued interest for six months. The relevant account balances of the two companies on December 31, 1977 are as follows:

	December 31, 1977	
Accounts	X Company Dr. [Cr.]	Y Company Dr. [Cr.]
Bonds payable, 9%		$[5,000]
Premium on bonds payable		[250]
Accrued interest payable		[225]
Investment in Y Company bonds	$5,000	
Premium on bond investment	140	
Accrued interest receivable	225	

A schedule of eliminations in respect to these intercompany bonds is presented in Illustration 8–1. The bond elimination schedule presents a complete summarization of the elimination entries that must be made on successive consolidation dates starting with the date of acquisition and terminating on the day before the bonds mature. The top half of the schedule summarizes each affiliate's account balances related to bonds, the eliminations which must be made in the consolidation process, and the resultant amounts which appear on consolidated financial statements. The bottom half of the schedule presents (in general journal form) the elimination entries which are entered on consolidated working papers to accomplish the results disclosed in the top half of the schedule.

It is evident that the consolidated basis gain (or loss) on the purchase of intercompany bonds should be recognized in the year of acquisition. In Illustration 8–1, this gain of $110 is entered on the consolidated income statement for 1977. The $325 interest expense ($450 cash transfer less $125 amortization of premium on bonds payable) for 1977 is extended

---

[1] In order to simplify the discussion and to focus attention upon the consolidation process and the development of appropriate elimination entries, the examples of this chapter assume that amortization of premium or discount on bonds payable and on bond investments are calculated by the straight-line method. However, the reader should remember that *Accounting Principles Board Opinion No. 21* requires that premium or discount on bonds payable and on bond investments be amortized according to the "interest" method, whereby a constant interest rate (the effective rate) is applied to the beginning-of-the-year carrying value to determine the total interest expense or income for the period. The cash transfer of interest is then subtracted from the expense or income to determine the current year's amortization of premium or discount. Other methods such as straight-line amortization may be used only if the results do not materially differ from those obtained under the interest method.

Illustration 8–1

BOND ELIMINATION SCHEDULE
Dr. [Cr.]

	December 31, 1977			December 31, 1978			December 31, 1979		
	Total Recorded Values	Amounts to be Eliminated	Extended to Consolidated Column	Total Recorded Values	Amounts to be Eliminated	Extended to Consolidated Column	Total Recorded Values	Amounts to be Eliminated	Extended to Consolidated Column
Year-end recorded amounts:									
On the books of X Company:									
Investment in Y Company bonds	$ 5,000	$5,000	$ –0–	$ 5,000	$5,000	$ –0–	$ 5,000	$5,000	$ –0–
Premium on bond investment	140	140	–0–	70	70	–0–	–0–	–0–	–0–
Bond interest income	–0–	–0–	–0–	[380]	380	–0–	[380]	380	–0–
Accrued interest receivable	225	[225]	–0–	225	[225]	–0–	225	[225]	–0–
On the books of Y Company:									
Bonds payable	$[5,000]	$5,000	–0–	$[5,000]	$5,000	–0–	$[5,000]	$5,000	–0–
Premium on bonds payable	[250]	250	–0–	[125]	125	–0–	–0–	–0–	–0–
Bond interest expense	325	–0–	325	325	[325]	–0–	325	[325]	–0–
Accrued interest payable	[225]	225	–0–	[225]	225	–0–	[225]	225	–0–
Account created by elimination entries:									
Loss [Gain] on purchase of bonds	–0–	[110]	[110]	–0–	–0–	–0–	–0–	–0–	–0–

	December 31, 1977		December 31, 1978		December 31, 1979	
	Debit	Credit	Debit	Credit	Debit	Credit
Elimination entries to accomplish the above:						
Bonds payable	5,000		5,000		5,000	
Investment in Y Company bonds		5,000		5,000		5,000
Accrued interest payable	225		225		225	
Accrued interest receivable		225		225		225
Bond interest income	450		450		450	
Bond interest expense				450		450
Loss [Gain] on purchase of bonds	140					
Premium on bond investment		140				
Premium on bonds payable	250					
Loss [Gain] on purchase of bonds		250				
Investment in Y Company stock			140		70	
Premium on bond investment				70		70
Bond interest income				70		
Premium on bonds payable			125		125	
Bond interest expense			125			125
Retained earnings, 1/1, Y Company				250		

to the consolidated column because the bonds were held throughout 1977 by outside parties. Since X Company paid those outside parties the last six months interest ($225) as a part of its purchase price, Accrued Interest Receivable and Accrued Interest Payable are reciprocal accounts between the affiliates and must be eliminated.

In years subsequent to the year of purchase, the consolidated income statement should not include any of the premium amortizations recorded by the affiliates. Since the total amount of those premiums was included in the gain reported in 1977, the inclusion of future premium amortizations would constitute double counting of the gain. Accordingly, the amounts of amortization subsequently recorded by each affiliate should be eliminated to avoid duplicate measurement.

As of December 31, 1978, the $250 credit elimination to the January 1 retained earnings of Y Company (Illustration 8–1) reflects the fact that the recorded retained earnings of Y Company as of January 1 does not include the $250 gain which was allocated to the company in 1977. However, during 1978, Y Company records a $125 amortization of premium on bonds payable with a corresponding credit to interest expense. As a consequence, the recorded retained earnings of Y Company as of December 31, 1978 includes $125 of the gain originally allocated to the company in December of 1977. Thus, as of December 31, 1979, the credit elimination to the January 1 retained earnings of Y Company is for only $125, which is the remaining portion of the $250 gain not yet recorded by Y Company as of January 1, 1979. The elimination of premium on bonds payable which is made each year reflects the total amount of unamortized premium remaining at the end of the year. Finally, the debit elimination of bond interest expense ($125 each year) reflects the annual amortization of premium on bonds payable which was recorded as a credit to interest expense.

The eliminations associated with X Company can be explained in a manner similar to the above discussion of eliminations pertaining to Y Company accounts. However, in Illustration 8–1, note that the December 31, 1978, and 1979, eliminations of premium on bond investment and the related amortization of that premium are charged against the Investment in Y Company Stock account, as follows:

	1978		1979
Investment in Y Company stock	140		70
Premium on bond investment		70	—
Bond interest income		70	70

As the following paragraphs will clarify, when X Company records its 1977 equity in subsidiary earnings, the entry includes X Company's equity in the net gain on purchase of bonds; that is, the entry is for the following amount: [80% (Y's reported net income + $250) − $140]. In respect to the $140 loss associated with the premium on bond investment, the Investment in Y Company Stock account is effectively reduced by that amount. Thus, the $70 premium on bond investment that remains on December 31, 1978, and the 1978 amortization of premium ($70) are eliminated against the Investment in Y Company Stock account, thereby reinstating the $140 which was removed from the account when X Company booked its 1977 equity in subsidiary earnings. Similarly, in making the eliminations for 1979 consolidated working papers, the 1979 amortization of premium ($70) would be eliminated against the Investment in Y Company Stock account to reinstate the $70 which was removed from the account in 1977 and not replaced during 1978. Finally, in each year, after the equity in subsidiary earnings is eliminated against the investment account, the remaining investment account balance is eliminated against the parent's equity in Y Company's common stock and confirmed retained earnings as of January 1.

To illustrate the impact of these intercompany bonds on the consolidated statement working papers, assume the following net incomes for X Company and Y Company. The indicated net income amounts exclude the effects of interest and X Company's net incomes exclude its equity in subsidiary earnings.

	1977	1978
X Company	$30,000	$25,000
Y Company	20,000	10,000

Partial consolidated statement working papers for 1977 and 1978 are presented in Illustration 8–2 and Illustration 8–3. Notice again that the gain or loss on intercompany bonds affects the amount of subsidiary earnings booked by the parent under the equity method. *APB Opinion No. 18* requires that the equity in subsidiary earnings to be booked by the parent must be adjusted for *all* intercompany profit eliminations so that the parent's unconsolidated financial statements constitute, in effect, a "one-line consolidation." Thus, the parent must record its equity in the net income of the subsidiary adjusted for all intercompany profit eliminations; both the intercompany profit items attributable to the subsidiary and the intercompany profit items attributable to the parent must be eliminated in the booking of income. In this case, X Company's equity in 1977 subsidiary earnings is calculated as $[80\% (\$19,675 + \$250) - \$140] = \$15,800$. Thus, X Company's $140 loss on purchase of affiliate's bonds is recognized as is X Company's 80 percent equity in Y Company's $250 gain on purchase of affiliate's bonds. In 1978, X Company's equity in subsidiary earnings is calculated as $.8(\$9,675 - \$125) + \$70 = \$7,710$. These entries are recorded by X Company in the following form:

	1977	1978
Investment in Y Company stock	15,800	7,710
Equity in subsidiary earnings	15,800	7,710

The eliminations of these amounts are disclosed in Illustration 8–2 and in Illustration 8–3.

In the consolidated working paper for 1978 (Illustration 8–3), the investment elimination entry appears as follows:

Common stock—Y Company	80,000	
Retained earnings, January 1, 1978, Y Company	15,940	
Investment in Y Company stock		95,940

The $80,000 elimination of common stock is 80 percent of the $100,000 common stock outstanding. The $15,940 elimination of retained earnings is 80 percent of Y Company's confirmed retained earnings on January 1, i.e., .8($19,675 + $250) = $15,940. The $95,940 elimination of the investment in Y Company stock is the remaining balance in the investment account after eliminating the 1978 equity in subsidiary evenings ($7,710) and the $140 loss associated with premium on bond investment, i.e., $103,510 + $140 − $7,710 = $95,940.

Case 2. Parent Company's Bonds Partially Acquired by Subsidiary Affiliate—100 Percent Elimination. The following data relate to A Company and its 80 percent owned subsidiary, B Company:

	January 1, 1977 Balances	
Accounts	A Company Dr. [Cr.]	B Company Dr. [Cr.]
Bonds payable, 8%	$[20,000]	
Premium on bonds payable	[600]	
Investment in A Company bonds		$5,000
Discount on bond investment		[90]

B Company purchased $5,000 of A Company's bonds on January 1, 1977, for $4,910. The bonds were originally issued several years ago and mature on January 1, 1980. Interest is payable semi-annually on July 1 and January 1.

The bond elimination schedule for A Company and B Company is presented in Illustration 8–4. At the date the bonds were acquired, their carrying value on the books of A Company was $5,150. Since the acquisition cost was $4,910, the purchase of the affiliate's bonds resulted in a total gain of $240, which was allocated $150 to the issuer (A Company) and $90 to the purchaser (B Company). Since the date of acquisition was January 1, 1977, the $240 gain is reported on the consolidated income statement for the year ended December 31, 1977. During 1977, the affiliates recorded amortizations of premium on bonds payable ($50) and discount on bond investment ($30), which, in effect, amount to part of the $240 gain. Nevertheless, these adjustments to interest income and interest

X COMPANY AND SUBSIDIARY Y COMPANY

Partial Consolidated Statement Working Paper
For Year Ended December 31, 1977

	X Company	Y Company	Eliminations Dr.	Eliminations Cr.	Minority Interest	Consolidated
Income Statement:						
Net income, before interest and equity in subsidiary earnings	30,000	20,000				50,000
Equity in subsidiary earnings [.8($19,675 + $250) − $140]	15,800			(5) 15,800		–0–
Interest expense		[325]	(4) 140	(3) 250		[325]
Gain on purchase of affiliate's bonds						110
Net income	45,800	19,675			3,985	49,785 [3,985]
Minority interest .2($19,675 + $250)					3,985	[3,985]
Net income — carried forward	45,800	19,675	15,940	250	3,985	45,800
Retained Earnings Statement:						
Retained earnings, January 1, 1977:						
X Company	–0–					
Y Company		–0–	(6) –0–			
Net income—brought forward	45,800	19,675	15,940	250	3,985	45,800
Retained earnings, December 31, 1977—carried forward	45,800	19,675	15,940	250	3,985	45,800
Balance Sheet:						
Debits:						
Investment in Y Company stock	95,800			(5) 15,800 (6) 80,000		–0–
Investment in Y Company bonds	5,000			(1) 5,000		–0–
Premium on bond investment	140			(4) 140		–0–
Accrued interest receivable	225			(2) 225		–0–
Credits:						
Bonds payable		5,000	(1) 5,000			–0–
Premium on bonds payable		250	(3) 250			–0–
Accrued interest payable		225	(2) 225			–0–
Common stock—Y Company		100,000	(6) 80,000		20,000	–0–

[deduction]

Illustration 8–3

X COMPANY AND SUBSIDIARY Y COMPANY
Partial Consolidated Statement Working Paper
For Year Ended December 31, 1978

	X Company	Y Company	Eliminations Dr.	Eliminations Cr.	Minority Interest	Consolidated
Income Statement:						
Net income, before interest and equity in subsidiary earnings	25,000	10,000				35,000
Equity in subsidiary earnings .8($9,675 − $125) + $70	7,710		(6) 7,710			-0-
Interest income	380		(3) 450	(4) 70		-0-
Interest expense		[325]	(5) 125	(3) 450		-0-
Net income	33,090	9,675				35,000
Minority interest .2($9,675 − $125)					1,910	[1,910]
Net income—carried forward	33,090	9,675	8,285	520	1,910	33,090
Retained Earnings Statement:						
Retained earnings, January 1, 1978:						
X Company	45,800					45,800
Y Company		19,675	(7) 15,940	(5) 250	*3,985	-0-
Net income—brought forward	33,090	9,675	8,285	520	1,910	33,090
Retained earnings, December 31, 1978—carried forward	78,890	29,350	24,225	770	5,895	78,890
Balance Sheet:						
Debits:						
Investment in Y Company stock	103,510		(4) 140	(6) 7,710 / (7) 95,940		-0-
Investment in Y Company bonds	5,000			(1) 5,000		-0-
Premium on bond investment	70			(4) 70		-0-
Accrued interest receivable	225			(2) 225		-0-
Credits:						
Bonds payable		5,000	(1) 5,000			-0-
Premium on bonds payable		125	(5) 125			-0-
Accrued interest payable		225	(2) 225			-0-
Common stock—Y Company		100,000	(7) 80,000		20,000	-0-

[deduction]
* .2($19,675 + $250).

expense are eliminated so that the full $240 will be disclosed as gain rather than partially as adjustments to interest income and expense.

Two significant differences between Case 2 and Case 1 can be observed by comparing Illustration 8–4 with Illustration 8–1. First, Case 1 involved a purchase of the entire amount of bonds which the affiliate had issued. By comparison, in Case 2, only $5,000 of the outstanding bonds ($20,000) was purchased. Thus, the account balances associated with the $15,000 of bonds which remain outstanding must be extended to the consolidated statement column; only the amounts pertaining to the intercompany bonds are eliminated. Second, in Case 1, the parent purchased the subsidiary's bonds whereas, in Case 2, the subsidiary purchased the parent's bonds. A comparison of the two bond elimination schedules indicates that the elimination procedures are the same regardless of which affiliate is the issuer and which is the purchaser.

To continue Case 2 so as to illustrate the consequences of this situation upon the consolidated statement working papers, assume the following net incomes of A Company and B Company. The indicated net income amounts exclude the effects of interest and A Company's net incomes exclude its equity in subsidiary earnings.

	1977	1978
A Company	$40,000	$30,000
B Company	15,000	20,000

Partial consolidated statement working papers for 1977 and 1978 are presented in Illustration 8–5 and Illustration 8–6.

Case 3. Parent Company's Bonds Partially Acquired by Subsidiary Affiliate—Fractional Elimination. Case 3 is based on the same facts that were given for Case 2. However, in the present situation, the intercompany profit is eliminated only to the extent of the parent's percentage interest in the profits. The relevant facts of the case are repeated below.

	January 1, 1977 Balances	
Accounts	*A Company* *Dr. [Cr.]*	*B Company* *Dr. [Cr.]*
Bonds payable, 8%	$[20,000]	
Premium on bonds payable	[600]	
Investment in A Company bonds		$5,000
Discount on bond investment		[90]

B Company purchased $5,000 of A Company bonds on January 1, 1977, for $4,910. The bonds were originally issued several years ago and mature on January 1, 1980. Interest is payable semi-annually on July 1 and January 1.

Illustration 8–4

A COMPANY AND SUBSIDIARY B COMPANY

Bond Elimination Schedule
Dr. [Cr.]

	December 31, 1977			December 31, 1978			December 31, 1979		
	Total Recorded Values	Amounts to be Eliminated	Extended to Consolidated Column	Total Recorded Values	Amounts to be Eliminated	Extended to Consolidated Column	Total Recorded Values	Amounts to be Eliminated	Extended to Consolidated Column
Year-end recorded amounts:									
On the books of A Company:									
Bonds payable	$[20,000]	$ 5,000	$[15,000]	$[20,000]	$ 5,000	$[15,000]	$[20,000]	$ 5,000	$[15,000]
Premium on bonds payable	[400]	100	[300]	[200]	50	[150]	-0-	-0-	-0-
Bond interest expense	1,400	[350]	1,050	1,400	[350]	1,050	1,400	[350]	1,050
Accrued interest payable	[800]	200	[600]	[800]	200	[600]	[800]	200	[600]
On the books of B Company:									
Investment in A Company bonds	$ 5,000	$[15,000]	$ -0-	$ 5,000	$[15,000]	$ -0-	$ 5,000	$[15,000]	$ -0-
Discount on bond investment	[60]	60	-0-	[30]	30	-0-	[430]	430	-0-
Bond interest income	[430]	430	-0-	[430]	430	-0-	200	[200]	-0-
Accrued interest receivable	200	[200]	-0-	200	[200]	-0-	-0-	-0-	-0-
Account created by elimination entries:									
Loss [Gain] on purchase of affiliate's bonds	-0-	[240]	[240]	-0-	-0-	-0-	-0-	-0-	-0-

	December 31, 1977		December 31, 1978		December 31, 1979	
	Debit	Credit	Debit	Credit	Debit	Credit
Elimination entries to accomplish the above:						
Bonds payable	5,000		5,000		5,000	
Investment in A Company bonds		5,000		5,000		5,000
Accrued interest payable	200		200		200	
Accrued interest receivable		200		200		200
Bond interest income	400		400		400	
Bond interest expense		400		400		400
Premium on bonds payable	100		50		—	
Bond interest expense	50		50		50	
Loss [Gain] on purchase of affiliate's bonds		150		—		—
Investment in B Company stock		—		100		50
Discount on bond investment	60		30		—	
Bond interest income	30		30		30	
Loss [Gain] on purchase of affiliate's bonds		90		—		—
Retained earnings, 1/1, B Company		—		60		30

Illustration 8–5

A COMPANY AND SUBSIDIARY B COMPANY
Partial Consolidated Statement Working Paper
For Year Ended December 31, 1977

	A Company	B Company	Eliminations Dr.	Eliminations Cr.	Minority Interest	Consolidated
Income Statement:						
Net income, before interest and parent's equity in subsidiary earnings	40,000	15,000				55,000
Equity in subsidiary earnings [80% (15,430 + 90 − 30) + 150 − 50]	12,492		(6) 12,492			-0-
Interest income		430	(3) 400 (5) 30			-0-
Interest expense	[1,400]			(3) 400		[1,050]
Loss [Gain] on purchase of affiliate's bonds			(4) 50	(4) 150 (5) 90		240
Net income	51,092	15,430				54,190
Minority interest [20% of (15,430 + 90 − 30)]					3,098	[3,098]
Net income—carried forward	51,092	15,430	12,972	640	3,098	51,092
Balance Sheet:						
Debits:						
Investment in B Company stock	xx			(x) xx (6) 12,492		-0-
Investment in A Company bonds		5,000		(1) 5,000		-0-
Accrued interest receivable		200		(2) 200		-0-
Credits:						
Bonds payable	20,000		(1) 5,000			15,000
Premium on bonds payable	400		(4) 100			300
Accrued interest payable	800		(2) 200			600
Discount on bond investment		60	(5) 60			-0-

[deduction]
(x) Partial investment elimination under the equity method.

A COMPANY AND SUBSIDIARY B COMPANY

Partial Consolidated Statement Working Paper
For Year Ended December 31, 1978

	A Company	B Company	Eliminations Dr.	Eliminations Cr.	Minority Interest	Consolidated
Income Statement:						
Net income, before interest and parent's equity in subsidiary earnings	30,000	20,000				50,000
Equity in subsidiary earnings [80% (20,430 − 30) − 50]	16,270		(6) 16,270			-0-
Interest income		430	(3) 400 (5) 30 (4) 50	(3) 400		-0-
Interest expense	[1,400]					[1,050]
Net income	44,870	20,430	16,750	400	4,080	48,950
Minority interest [20% of (20,430 − 30)]					4,080	[4,080]
Net income—carried forward	44,870	20,430	16,750	400	4,080	44,870
Retained Earnings Statement:						
Retained earnings, January 1, 1978:						
A Company	51,092		(x) 12,392	(5) 60	*3,098	51,092
B Company		15,430			-0-	-0-
Net income—brought forward	44,870	20,430	16,750	400	4,080	44,870
Retained earnings, December 31, 1978—carried forward	95,962	35,860	29,142	460	7,178	95,962
Balance Sheet:						
Debits:						
Investment in B Company stock	xx			(x) xx		-0-
Investment in A Company bonds		5,000		(4) 100 (6) 16,270 (1) 5,000		-0-
Accrued interest receivable		200		(2) 200		-0-
Credits:						
Bonds payable	20,000		(1) 5,000			15,000
Premium on bonds payable	200		(4) 50			150
Accrued interest payable	800		(2) 200			600
Discount on bond investment		30	(5) 30			-0-

[deduction] *[20% of (15,430 + 90 − 30)]. (x) Partial investment elimination entry under the equity method.

The bond elimination schedule for A Company and B Company is presented in Illustration 8–7. As in the previous case, the $240 gain on purchase of an affiliate's bonds is allocated $150 to the issuer (A Company) and $90 to the purchaser (B Company). However, only the parent's equity in the gain is eliminated. Thus, of the $150 allocated to A Company, 100 percent is recognized; of the $90 allocated to B Company, only $72 (80% of $90) is recognized. The total amount of gain reported on the consolidated income statement for 1977 is therefore $222.

Since the $90 gain allocated to the subsidiary is only recognized to the extent of the parent's equity in the subsidiary ($72), the corresponding eliminations of Discount on Bond Investment and the annual amortization of the discount (adjustment to Interest Expense) are also limited to the parent's equity therein. For example, at December 31, 1977, $60 of Discount on Bond Investment remains on the books of B Company and $48 of that amount is eliminated. Similarly, B Company's annual amortization of discount is $30 and the elimination is $24 (80% of $30). The reader will note that the minority interest equity in the discount on bond investment and in the amortization of discount are extended to the consolidated column (Illustration 8–7). Unless the consolidated entity has investments in bonds of outside parties which also involve a discount, the minority interest in Discount on Bond Investment will stand alone as a balance sheet item. Similarly, if the consolidated entity does not have other interest income, the minority interest in Interest Income will also stand alone as an income statement item. The apparent anomaly of showing the discount separately when the Investment in A Company Bonds account has been totally eliminated may create some confusion among statement readers. Consequently, since these balances are rarely material in amount, the discount may be added to other deferred charges in the balance sheet. Similar problems are presented with the minority interest's equity in Premium on Bond Investment or, if the subsidiary is the issuer of the intercompany bonds, in Premium or Discount on Bonds Payable.

The consolidated statement working papers for Case 3 are presented in Illustration 8–8 and Illustration 8–9. Continuing to use the same facts that were used in Case 2, the net incomes of A Company and B Company, excluding the effects of interest and excluding A Company's equity in subsidiary earnings, are as follows:

	1977	1978
A Company	$40,000	$30,000
B Company	15,000	20,000

Illustration 8–8 and Illustration 8–9 disclose minority interest calculations which apply the minority interest percentage to the *reported* subsidiary net incomes and retained earnings. For example, in Illustration 8–9, minority interest in net income is calculated as 20% ($20,430) =

$4,086 and minority interest in retained earnings (January 1) is calculated as 20% ($15,430) = $3,086. These calculations are consistent with the fractional elimination of intercompany profits; since only the parent's share of the intercompany profit items was eliminated, the minority interest's share is extended to the consolidated statements and should be allocated to the minority interest. Applying the minority interest percentage to the *reported* subsidiary net income and *reported* retained earnings accomplishes this objective.

Interim Purchases of Intercompany Bonds

Cases 2 and 3 involved purchases of intercompany bonds on the first day of the accounting period. If the purchases are made at some interim date between interest payment dates, *no* conceptual differences are introduced. Proper recognition of the amortizations of discounts or premiums during the remaining months of the first interest period must, of course, be given. But the procedures for doing so parallel completely those which were illustrated in Case 2 and Case 3.

Bonds Payable and Investment in Bonds Recorded Net of Discount or Premium

Some companies may choose to record Bonds Payable net of any premium or discount, thereby omitting the use of a separate Premium or Discount on Bonds Payable. Similarly, companies may debit Investment in Bonds for the net cost of the bonds and omit the use of a separate Premium or Discount on Bond Investment. In these circumstances, the elimination entries to be made on consolidated statement working papers are summarized to conform to the account structure of the affiliates. For example, in Case 3, if A Company and B Company had recorded the bond liability and bond investment net of the premium and discount, the elimination entries which would have been displayed in the bond elimination schedule (Illustration 8–7) would be as follows:

	1977		1978		1979	
	Dr.	*Cr.*	*Dr.*	*Cr.*	*Dr.*	*Cr.*
Accrued interest payable	200		200		200	
Accrued interest receivable		200		200		200
Bond interest income	400		400		400	
Bond interest expense		400		400		400
Bonds payable	5,100		5,050		5,000	
Bond interest income	24		24		24	
Bond interest expense	50		50		50	
Investment in A Company bonds		4,952		4,976		5,000
Gain on purchase of affiliate's bonds		222		—		—
Investment in B Company stock		—		100		50
Retained earnings, 1/1, B Company		—		48		24

Illustration 8–7

A COMPANY AND SUBSIDIARY B COMPANY

Bond Elimination Schedule
Dr. [Cr.]

	December 31, 1977			December 31, 1978			December 31, 1979		
	Total Recorded Values	Amounts to be Eliminated	Extended to Consolidated Column	Total Recorded Values	Amounts to be Eliminated	Extended to Consolidated Column	Total Recorded Values	Amounts to be Eliminated	Extended to Consolidated Column
Year-end recorded amounts:									
On the books of A Company:									
Bonds payable	$[20,000]	$ 5,000	$[15,000]	$[20,000]	$ 5,000	$[15,000]	$[20,000]	$ 5,000	$[15,000]
Premium on bonds payable	[400]	100	[300]	[200]	50	[150]	–0–	–0–	–0–
Bond interest expense	1,400	[350]	1,050	1,400	[350]	1,050	1,400	[350]	1,050
Accrued interest payable	[800]	200	[600]	[800]	200	[600]	[800]	200	[600]
On the books of B Company:									
Investment in A Company bonds	$ 5,000	$[5,000]	$ –0–	$ 5,000	$[5,000]	$ –0–	$ 5,000	$[5,000]	$ –0–
Discount on bonds investment	[60]	48	[12]	[30]	24	[6]	–0–	–0–	–0–
Bond interest income	[430]	424	[6]	[430]	424	[6]	[430]	424	[6]
Accrued interest receivable	200	[200]	–0–	200	[200]	–0–	200	[200]	–0–
Account created by elimination entries:									
Loss [Gain] on purchase of affiliate's bonds	–0–	[222]	[222]	–0–	–0–	–0–	–0–	–0–	–0–

	December 31, 1977		December 31, 1978		December 31, 1979	
	Debit	Credit	Debit	Credit	Debit	Credit
Elimination entries to accomplish the above:						
Bonds payable	5,000		5,000		5,000	
Investment in A Company bonds		5,000		5,000		5,000
Accrued interest payable	200		200		200	
Accrued interest receivable		200		200		200
Bond interest income	400		400		400	
Bond interest expense		400		400		400
Premium on bonds payable	100		50		—	
Bond interest expense	50		50		50	
Loss [Gain] on purchase of affiliate's bonds		150		—		—
Investment in B Company stock		—		100		50
Discount on bond investment	48		24		—	
Bond interest income	24		24		24	
Loss [Gain] on purchase of affiliate's bonds		72		—		—
Retained earnings, 1/1, B Company		—		48		24

Illustration 8-8

A COMPANY AND SUBSIDIARY B COMPANY
Partial Consolidated Statement Working Paper
For Year Ended December 31, 1977

	A Company	B Company	Eliminations Dr.	Eliminations Cr.	Minority Interest	Consolidated
Income Statement:						
Net income, before interest and parent's equity in subsidiary earnings	40,000	15,000				55,000
Equity in subsidiary earnings [80% (15,430 + 90 − 30) + 150 − 50]	12,492		(6) 12,492			–0–
Interest income		430	(3) 400 (5) 24 (4) 50	(3) 400 (4) 150 (5) 72		6
Interest expense	[1,400]					[1,050]
Loss [Gain] on purchase of affiliate's bonds						222
Net income	51,092	15,430				54,178
Minority interest (20% of 15,430)					3,086	[3,086]
Net income—carried forward	51,092	15,430	12,966	622	3,086	51,092
Balance Sheet:						
Debits:						
Investment in B Company stock	xx			(x) xx (6) 12,492		–0–
Investment in A Company bonds		5,000		(1) 5,000		–0–
Accrued interest receivable		200		(2) 200		–0–
Credits:						
Bonds payable	20,000		(1) 5,000			15,000
Premium on bonds payable	400		(4) 100			300
Accrued interest payable	800		(2) 200			600
Discount on bond investment		60	(5) 48			12

[deduction]

(x) Partial investment elimination entry under the equity method.

Illustration 8–9

A COMPANY AND SUBSIDIARY B COMPANY

Partial Consolidated Statement Working Paper

For Year Ended December 31, 1978

	A Company	B Company	Eliminations Dr.	Eliminations Cr.	Minority Interest	Consolidated
Income Statement:						
Net income, before interest and parent's equity in subsidiary earnings	30,000	20,000				50,000
Equity in subsidiary earnings [80% (20,430 − 30) − 50]	16,270		(6) 16,270			–0–
Interest income		430	(3) 400 (5) 24 (4) 50			6
Interest expense	[1,400]			(3) 400		[1,050]
Net income	44,870	20,430				48,956
Minority interest (20% of 20,430)					4,086	[4,086]
Net income—carried forward	44,870	20,430	16,744	400	4,086	44,870
Retained Earnings Statement:						
Retained earnings, January 1, 1978:						
A Company	51,092					51,092
B Company		15,430	(x) 12,392	(5) 48	*3,086	–0–
Net income—brought forward	44,870	20,430	16,744	400	4,086	44,870
Retained earnings, December 31, 1978—carried forward	95,962	35,860	29,136	448	7,172	95,962
Balance Sheet:						
Debits:						
Investment in B Company stock	xx			(x) xx (4) 100 (6) 16,270		–0–
Investment in A Company bonds		5,000		(1) 5,000		–0–
Accrued interest receivable		200		(2) 200		–0–
Credits:						
Bonds payable	20,000		(1) 5,000			15,000
Premium on bonds payable	200		(4) 50			150
Accrued interest payable	800		(2) 200			600
Discount on bond investment		30	(5) 24			6

[deduction] * [20% of (15,430). (x) Partial investment elimination entry under the equity method.

PREFERRED STOCK

Many corporations issue preferred stock as well as common stock. If a subsidiary has both common and preferred stock outstanding, several unique difficulties may arise in the preparation of consolidated statements. The parent may, of course, acquire all, some, or none of the subsidiary's preferred stock. Whether or not the parent holds some of the subsidiary's outstanding preferred stock, the consolidated financial statements must take into account the fact that part of the subsidiary's net income and perhaps retained earnings must be allocated to preferred stock with the residual amount accruing to common stockholders. If the parent holds some of the preferred stock, the parent's investment must be eliminated against the preferred stockholders' equity accounts. To calculate the appropriate amounts to be eliminated as part of the preferred stock investment elimination, and also the amounts to be eliminated as part of the common stock investment elimination, the subsidiary's retained earnings balance at the date of acquisition must first be allocated between the two classes of stock. After the date of acquisition, the postacquisition subsidiary earnings must be allocated between preferred and common shares so that the calculations of majority and minority interests therein will correctly reflect the rights of each security.

Allocation of Earnings

The allocation of net income and retained earnings between preferred and common stock necessarily depends upon the specific preferences which attach to the preferred shares. Since these features are discussed and illustrated in detail in *Intermediate Accounting* in this series, they will be accorded only summary treatment here.

1.   Where the preferred stock is nonparticipating and noncumulative, the accumulated subsidiary retained earnings relate totally to the common shares. Once dividends have been declared, the first distribution is made to preferred stockholders according to the designated preference rate; following this distribution, any residual amount is disbursed to common shareholders.

2.   In the event that the preferred stock is nonparticipating but cumulative, only that portion of retained earnings which is equal to any arrearage in dividends on preferred stock is allocated to preferred shares; the remainder relates to common shares. In calculating the distribution of subsidiary net income between majority and minority interests, the current year's arrearage must be allocated to preferred stock with the residual net income or loss being allocated to common stock. Case 4 illustrates the preparation of consolidated statements in which the subsidiary's preferred stock is cumulative and nonparticipating.

3. Where preferred stock is noncumulative, or cumulative without arrearage in dividends, *and* full participating, subsidiary retained earnings and net income are apportioned ratably to common and preferred shares.

4. In the event that preferred stock is cumulative with dividends in arrears *and* also fully participating, the amount of retained earnings which is equal to any arrearage in dividends is first allocated to preferred shares, after which the remainder is ratably apportioned to common and preferred shares. Only the current year's arrearage must be allocated to preferred stock in the distribution of subsidiary net income, with the residual net income or loss being apportioned ratably between the two securities.

5. Preferred stock which is convertible into common stock is generally treated in accordance with its other preference characteristics (as outlined above) until such time as the conversion takes place. The act of conversion frequently changes the equity of the parent in the subsidiary, which topic is examined in Chapter 9.

Treatment in Consolidated Statements—Nonparticipating, Cumulative, Preferred Stock

Case 4. On December 31, 1977, X Company purchased 90 percent of the common stock of Y Company for $126,000, and 30 percent of its cumulative, nonparticipating, 8 percent preferred stock for $14,000. The preferred stock was not in arrears at the date of acquisition. Account balances for the two companies are:

	December 31, 1977, Dr. [Cr.]	
	X Company	*Y Company*
Investment in Y Company preferred stock	$ 14,000	
Investment in Y Company common stock	126,000	
Other assets	160,000	$ 190,000
Common stock (par, $100)	[200,000]	[100,000]
Preferred stock (par, $100)		[50,000]
Retained earnings	[100,000]	[40,000]

The consolidated balance sheet working paper for December 31, 1977, is presented in Illustration 8–10. Observe that the $14,000 cost of preferred stock is $1,000 less than its book value; this $1,000 differential is credited to Other Contributed Capital. If such a differential applied to common stock, it would be allocated toward the revaluation of Y Company's assets and liabilities. However, under normal circumstances, a preferred stock differential relates to changes in interest rates since the stock was originally issued. Thus, the $1,000 does not imply that the net assets of Y Company require revaluation. From the perspective of the consolidated entity,

Illustration 8–10

X COMPANY AND SUBSIDIARY Y COMPANY

Consolidated Balance Sheet Working Paper
December 31, 1977

	X Company	Y Company	Eliminations		Consolidated
			Dr.	Cr.	
Assets					
Investment in Y Company stock:					
Preferred stock	14,000			(2) 14,000	–0–
Common stock	126,000			(1) 126,000	–0–
Other assets	160,000	190,000			350,000
	300,000	190,000			350,000
Equities					
Preferred stock		50,000	(2) 15,000		35,000 M
Common stock:					
X Company	200,000				200,000
Y Company		100,000	(1) 90,000		10,000 M
Retained earnings:					
X Company	100,000				100,000
Y Company		40,000	(1) 36,000		4,000 M
Other contributed capital				(2) 1,000	1,000
	300,000	190,000	141,000	141,000	350,000

the purchase of preferred stock is comparable to the retirement of preferred stock by a single corporation; as a consequence, similar procedures should be employed. If the preferred stock differential is a credit, it should be added to Other Contributed Capital. If the differential is a debit, it should be subtracted from Other Contributed Capital of the parent or, if none is available, it should be subtracted from the retained earnings balance of the parent.

Illustration 8–10 also shows that the preferred shareholders have *no* equity in the retained earnings of Y Company. Since the preferred stock is nonparticipating and is not in arrears, the equity of preferred shareholders is limited to the par value of the stock. If an arrearage had existed, an amount of retained earnings equal to the arrearage would have been allocated to preferred stock and the elimination entry for the parent's equity in preferred stock would have included a debit to retained earnings equal to 30 percent of the amount allocated to cover the arrearage.

Continuing the example of Case 4, assume that Y Company fails to pay any dividends during 1978. The 1978 net incomes of the two companies, excluding X Company's equity in subsidiary earnings, are: X Company, $20,000; Y Company, $1,000.

The consolidated statement working paper for 1978 is presented in

X COMPANY AND SUBSIDIARY Y COMPANY

Consolidated Statement Working Paper
For Year Ended December 31, 1978

	X Company	Y Company	Eliminations Dr.	Eliminations Cr.	Minority Interest	Consolidated
Income Statement:						
Net income, before equity in subsidiary earnings	20,000	1,000				21,000
Equity in subsidiary earnings [90% (1,000 − 4,000)]	[2,700]			(1) 2,700		−0−
Dividend income (preferred)	−0−					
	17,300	1,000				21,000
Minority interest:						
Preferred stock [70% (4,000)]					2,800	[2,800]
Common stock [10% (1,000 − 4,000)]					[300]	300
Net income—carried forward	17,300	1,000	−0−	2,700	2,500	18,500
Retained Earnings Statement:						
Retained earnings, January 1, 1978:						
X Company	100,000					100,000
Y Company		40,000	(2) 36,000		4,000	−0−
Net income—brought forward	17,300	1,000	−0−	2,700	2,500	18,500
Retaining earnings, Dec. 31, 1978—carried forward	117,300	41,000	36,000	2,700	6,500	118,500
Balance Sheet:						
Investment in Y Company:						
Common stock	123,300		(1) 2,700	(2) 126,000		−0−
Preferred stock	14,000			(3) 14,000		−0−
Other assets	180,000	191,000				371,000
	317,300	191,000				371,000
Preferred stock		50,000	(3) 15,000		35,000	−0−
Common stock:						
X Company	200,000					200,000
Y Company		100,000	(2) 90,000		10,000	−0−
Retained earnings—brought forward	117,300	41,000	36,000	(3) 2,700	6,500	118,500
Other contributed capital				1,000		1,000
Minority interest					51,500	51,500 M
	317,300	191,000	143,700	143,700	51,500	371,000

[deduction]

Illustration 8–11. Observe the equity in subsidiary earnings booked by X Company and the calculations of minority interest in net income. Those items were determined as follows:

	Allocated to X Company	Allocated to Minority Interest	Y Company Net Income
Preferred stock allocation ...	(30%) $ 1,200	(70%) $ 2,800	$ 4,000
Residual loss to common stock	(90%) [2,700]	(10%) [300]	[3,000]
Totals	$[1,500]	$ 2,500	$ 1,000

Although no dividends were paid during 1978, $4,000 must be allocated to preferred stock in recognition of the cumulative feature; otherwise, the residual allocation to common stock would be overstated.

Assume that, in 1979, X Company earned $25,000 excluding dividend income from preferred stock and excluding its equity in subsidiary earnings. Y Company earned $18,000 during 1979 and paid $10,000 in dividends, $8,000 to preferred shares and $2,000 to common shares. The consolidated statement working paper for 1979 is presented in Illustration 8–12.

Y Company's January 1, 1979, retained earnings amount to $41,000, of which $33,300 is eliminated, $6,500 is allocated to the minority interest, and $1,200 is included in consolidated retained earnings. Because preferred dividends were $4,000 in arrears on January 1, preferred shareholders have an equity of $4,000 in the January 1 retained earnings; common shareholders have the remaining $37,000 equity. The $33,300 elimination pertains to X Company's 90 percent equity in Y Company's common stock; thus, 90% ($37,000) = $33,300. The $6,500 minority interest is explained by the minority interest equity in retained earnings allocated to preferred stock [70% ($4,000)] plus the minority interest equity in retained earnings allocated to common stock [10% ($41,000 − $4,000)]. The $1,200 inclusion in consolidated retained earnings represents X Company's 30 percent equity in the $4,000 arrearage as of January 1, 1979.

Note that the recorded retained earnings of X Company at December 31, 1979, is equal to consolidated retained earnings. Remember that Y Company's preferred stock is nonparticipating. Since there is no dividend arrearage as of December 31, 1979, the entire retained earnings balance of Y Company belongs to common shares. Therefore, X Company's use of the equity method of accounting for its common stock investment results in X Company's recorded retained earnings being equal to consolidated retained earnings.

Definitional Calculations

Consolidated net income in Case 4 may be stated definitionally as follows:

	1978	1979
X Company's net income (excluding equity in subsidiary earnings and dividend income)	$20,000	$25,000
X Company's equity in Y Company's net income:		
30 percent of Y Company's net income allocated to preferred stock: 30% ($4,000)	1,200	1,200
90 percent of Y Company's net income allocated to common stock:		
90% ($1,000 − $4,000)	[2,700]	
90% ($18,000 − $4,000)		12,600
Consolidated Net Income	$18,500	$38,800

Similarly, consolidated retained earnings may be calculated definitionally, as follows:

	December 31,	
	1978	1979
X Company's retained earnings, December 31, (excluding equity in subsidiary earnings and dividend income)	$120,000	$145,000
X Company's equity in Y Company's postacquisition earnings:		
30 percent of Y Company's postacquisition net income allocated to preferred stock	1,200	2,400
90 percent of Y Company's postacquisition net income allocated to common stock:		
90% ($1,000 − $4,000)	[2,700]	
90% ($19,000 − $8,000)		9,900
Consolidated Retained Earnings	$118,500	$157,300

QUESTIONS

1. To what extent does the purchase by one affiliate of the bonds of another affiliate parallel the acquisition and retirement by one company of all (or part) of its own outstanding bonds payable?

2. Explain the nature of the "gain or loss" on the acquisition of intercompany bonds. How is this amount determined? To what extent should it be allocated between the participating affiliates?

3. Indicate what the arguments are for assigning the total gain or loss on the purchase of intercompany bonds to the issuing company. To the purchasing company.

Illustration 8–12

X COMPANY AND SUBSIDIARY Y COMPANY

Consolidated Statement Working Paper
For Year Ended December 31, 1979

	X Company	Y Company	Eliminations Dr.	Eliminations Cr.	Minority Interest	Consolidated
Income Statement:						
Net income, before dividend income and equity in subsidiary earnings	25,000	18,000				43,000
Dividend income (preferred) [30% (8,000)]	2,400			(1) 2,400		–0–
Equity in subsidiary earnings [90% (18,000 − 4,000)]	12,600			(2) 12,600		–0–
	40,000	18,000				43,000
Minority interest:						
Preferred stock [70% (4,000)]					2,800	[2,800]
Common stock [10% (18,000 − 4,000)]					1,400	[1,400]
Net income—carried forward	40,000	18,000	15,000	–0–	4,200	38,800
Retained Earnings Statement:						
Retained earnings, January 1, 1979:						
X Company	117,300					117,300
Y Company		41,000	(4) *33,300		†6,500	1,200
Net income—brought forward	40,000	18,000	15,000		4,200	38,800
	157,300	59,000			10,700	157,300
Dividends declared:						
Common		2,000		(2) 1,800	200	
Preferred		8,000		(1) 2,400	5,600	
Retained earnings, December 31, 1979	157,300	49,000	48,300	4,200	4,900	157,300

Balance Sheet:

Investment in Y Company:						
Common stock	134,100			(2) 10,800 (4) 123,300		-0-
Preferred stock	14,000			(3) 14,000		-0-
Other assets	209,200	199,000				408,200
	357,300	199,000				408,200
Preferred stock		50,000	(3) 15,000		35,000	-0-
Common stock:						
X Company	200,000					200,000
Y Company		100,000	(4) 90,000		10,000	-0-
Retained earnings—brought forward	157,300	49,000	48,300	(3) 4,200	4,900	157,300
Other contributed capital				1,000		1,000
Minority interest					49,900	49,900 M
	357,300	199,000	153,300	153,300	49,900	408,200

[deduction]
* [90% (41,000 − 4,000)].
† [10% (41,000 − 4,000) + 70% (4,000)].

4. In respect to intercompany bonds the recorded amortizations of premiums and discounts on the books of the relevant affiliates are eliminated in consolidated statement working papers to avoid "double recognition." Explain this concept of double recognition and indicate why an elimination is necessary.

5. In regard to the elimination of profit on interaffiliate sales of depreciable assets, the effect of the elimination entries is to defer the profit recorded by the selling affiliate and formally recognize it over the remaining life of the relevant assets. Compare this profit *deferral* with the accounting consequence produced by elimination entries for interaffiliate bond holdings.

6. What complexity is introduced in the elimination process if an affiliate's bonds are purchased between interest dates?

7. Describe the accounting problems associated with the elimination process as a result of the subsidiary's having both common and preferred stock outstanding.

8. Assume that a subsidiary has both common and preferred stock outstanding and the preferred stock is noncumulative and nonparticipating. On what basis should the retained earnings of the subsidiary be allocated between preferred and common shares for the purpose of preparing the investment elimination entry? How would your answer differ if the preferred stock were cumulative, in arrears, and fully participating?

9. Suppose a subsidiary has outstanding $100,000 of 9 percent, nonparticipating, cumulative, preferred stock which is owned entirely by minority interests. Since 1970, the parent has owned 100 percent of the subsidiary's common stock. On December 31, 1977, the preferred stock is three years in arrears. On the consolidated income statement for 1977, the minority interest deduction should be either $9,000 or $27,000. Which is correct? Explain why.

10. Refer to question 9. Suppose the retained earnings balance of the subsidiary on December 31, 1977, is $20,000. What amount should be reported on the consolidated balance sheet as minority interest in retained earnings?

11. Refer to question 9. Suppose the subsidiary earns net income of $30,000 and pays dividends of $40,000 during 1978. What is the minority interest deduction on the consolidated income statement for 1978?

12. If dividends are in arrears on the date a parent acquires the outstanding preferred stock of a subsidiary, the parent will typically record the subsequent receipt of the dividend arrearage as Dividend Income. Nevertheless, the consolidated income statement for the year in which the dividends are paid will not disclose the dividend income booked by the parent. Explain why this is true.

EXERCISES

Exercise 8–1

On January 1, 1969, Shelter Company issued $200,000 of 8 percent, 10-year bonds at 105. Interest is payable July 1 and January 1. On January 1, 1977,

Tarp Company, a 90 percent owned subsidiary, acquired $100,000 of these bonds at 102. Assume straight-line amortizations of premiums and discounts are used.

Required:

Prepare the eliminating entries for consolidated statement working papers on December 31, 1977, and December 31, 1978—
a. Assuming the elimination of premium and/or discount on intercompany bonds is based upon the parent company's interest in the relevant affiliate.
b. Assuming 100 percent elimination of premium and/or discount.

Exercise 8–2

The following data relate to the Racket Corporation and its 90 percent owned subsidiary, the Ball Corporation, immediately after the subsidiary acquired $6,000 of the parent company's outstanding bonds at a cost of $5,400. Interest on the bonds is paid January 1 and July 1.

	January 1, 1977	
Accounts	*Racket Corporation Dr. [Cr.]*	*Ball Corporation Dr. [Cr.]*
7 percent bonds payable, due December 31, 1980	$[10,000]	
Discount on bonds payable	500	
Investment in Racket Corporation bonds		$ 6,000
Discount on bond investment		[600]
Net income (excluding the effects of interest) (for 1977 and 1978)	20,000	10,000

Required:

Assume the companies amortize discounts according to the straight-line method. If 100 percent of the unamortized discount on intercompany bonds is to be eliminated for consolidated statement working papers on December 31, 1977, and 1978—
a. Journalize all eliminations in respect to the intercompany bonds.
b. Calculate the minority interest in subsidiary net income.

Exercise 8–3

Weber Company owns 90 percent of Schwab, Inc.'s outstanding stock. On January 1, 1973, Schwab, Inc., issued 9 percent bonds, $100,000 par value, due January 1, 1983. The issue price was 103 (percent of par). Weber Company purchased $25,000 (par value) of these bonds on January 1, 1977, at 101.8 (percent of par). Interest is payable twice each year on January 1 and July 1. Weber uses the 100 percent elimination method in preparing consolidated statements and both companies amortize premiums by the straight-line method.

Required:

a. Journalize all elimination entries relating to Weber's ownership of Schwab's bonds for consolidated working papers prepared on—
    (1) December 31, 1977.
    (2) December 31, 1978.
b. Assume that Schwab, Inc.'s 1977 net income was $20,000, excluding the deduction for interest expense. Compute the minority interest's equity in 1977 net income.

Exercise 8–4

On July 1, 1976, Sports Company purchased $200,000 of Golf Company's 8 percent bonds in the open market at 111½ and accrued interest. These bonds are part of an original issue of $1,000,000 bonds sold on January 1, 1968, at 105. Interest is paid annually on January 1. The bonds mature on January 1, 1988. Periodic straight-line amortization has been recorded by each company on December 31.

Required:

If Sports Company owns a 90 percent interest in the capital stock of Golf Company, prepare journal entries for consolidated statement working papers for the year ended December 31, 1977:
a. If the unamortized premium on intercompany bonds is 100 percent eliminated.
b. If the amount of the premium elimination is based upon the parent company's equity in the subsidiary.
c. In (b) above, what eliminating entries are required in respect to intercompany bonds for a consolidated balance sheet only?

Exercise 8–5

On December 31, 1977, A Company acquired 80 percent of B Company's common stock for $200,000, and 60 percent of B Company's 8 percent, preferred stock for $60,000. Account balances for the companies are:

	A Company	B Company
Preferred stock, $100 par		$ 80,000
Premium on preferred stock		10,000
Common stock, $50 par	$400,000	100,000
Other contributed capital		15,000
Retained earnings	200,000	20,000

Required:

Prepare elimination entries to be used in consolidated working papers on December 31, 1977, under each of the following conditions:

a. The preferred stock is cumulative, nonparticipating, and two years in arrears.
b. The preferred stock is noncumulative and fully participating.
c. The preferred stock is cumulative, fully participating, and one year in arrears.

Exercise 8–6

Bolts, Inc. acquired 90 percent of Washer, Inc.'s common stock and 60 percent of its 9 percent, preferred stock on December 31, 1977, at which date the companies had the following stockholders' equity account balances:

	Bolts, Inc.	Washer, Inc.
Preferred stock, $100 par		100,000
Premium on preferred stock		20,000
Common stock, $50 par	300,000	150,000
Other contributed capital	10,000	30,000
Retained earnings	90,000	40,000

Required:

Prepare elimination entries for the consolidated balance sheet working paper as of December 31, 1977, under each of the following circumstances:
a. The preferred stock is cumulative and nonparticipating, and dividends are not in arrears. Bolts, Inc. paid $100,000 for the preferred stock and $250,000 for the common stock.
b. The preferred stock is cumulative, nonparticipating, and two years in arrears. Bolts, Inc. paid $80,000 for the preferred stock and $250,000 for the common stock.
c. The preferred stock is cumulative, fully participating, and dividends are not in arrears. Bolts, Inc. paid $90,000 for the preferred stock and $200,000 for the common stock.

PROBLEMS

Problem 1

On January 1, 1977, the White Company owns 90 percent of the capital stock of Kaplan Company and 70 percent of the capital stock of the Jensen Company. On January 1, 1971, the Kaplan Company issued $200,000 of 7 percent, 10-year bonds to nonaffiliates at 96. On January 1, 1977, the Jensen Company acquired $60,000 of these bonds at 103. Interest is payable January 1 and July 1.

The following data relate to the period January 1, 1977, through December 31, 1978:

	White Company	Kaplan Company	Jensen Company
Retained earnings (1/1/77)	$415,000	$283,000	$196,000
Net income (exclusive of interest and equity in subsidiary earnings):			
1977	100,000	50,000	60,000
1978	85,000	45,000	38,000

Required:

a. Prepare eliminating entries in respect to intercompany bonds for inclusion on consolidated statement working papers for years ended December 31, 1977, 1978, 1979, and 1980; the elimination of discount/premium on intercompany bonds is to be 100 percent.
b. Calculate consolidated net income, following the definitional approach, for 1977 and 1978.

Problem 2

The South Company has a controlling interest in the North Corporation, having acquired 80 percent of its capital stock in 1971. On January 1, 1977, the North Corporation had outstanding a $300,000 issue of 8 percent bonds payable, interest payable on January 1 and July 1. The unamortized discount on these bonds as of January 1, 1977, amounted to $9,000. The bonds are due January 1, 1980.

On May 1, 1977, the South Company acquired $75,000 of these bonds at 101.6 plus accrued interest. The 1977 net incomes of the affiliates, exclusive of interest and excluding South Company's equity in North Corporation's earnings, are:

> South Company $80,000
> North Corporation 60,000

Required:

a. Prepare the eliminating entries in respect to intercompany bonds, assuming 100 percent elimination, for 1977 through 1979.
b. Prepare a consolidated income statement working paper for the year ended December 31, 1977.

Problem 3

On January 1, 1977, X Company acquired 800 shares of Y Company's common stock for $17,000 and 180 shares of its 5 percent cumulative, nonparticipating preferred stock for $19,000. On this date the proprietary accounts of Y Company were:

> Common stock ($10 par value) $10,000
> Preferred stock ($100 par value) 20,000
> Retained earnings 12,000

On January 1, 1977, there were two years' dividends in arrears on preferred stock.

During 1977, Y Company reported earnings of $10,000 and paid $9,000 in dividends; X Company earned $10,000, exclusive of dividend income and of its equity in subsidiary earnings.

Required:

a. Prepare the investment elimination entries on January 1, 1977.
b. Calculate 1977 consolidated net income and the minority interest in subsidiary net income; prepare elimination entries for December 31, 1977 consolidated statement working papers.
c. If the preferred stock had been cumulative and participating, calculate the consolidated net income for 1977 and the minority interest in the subsidiary's net income.

Problem 4

Part A

The P Corporation bought from its wholly owned subsidiary for $16,000 certain equipment which was carried on the books of the subsidiary at a cost of $31,000 with accumulated depreciation of $17,000.

Required:

State the effect on the consolidated balance sheet of the purchase of equipment from the subsidiary. State specifically what eliminating entries, if any, should be made on the consolidated work paper used for preparation of the consolidated financial statements.

Part B

On January 1, 1973, the S Corporation issued $200,000 of 10-year 8 percent bonds. These were sold at 98, and expenses of issue were $2,400. Interest is payable January 1 and July 1.

In March, 1976, the P Corporation acquired 80 percent of the outstanding stock of S Corporation. On March 31, 1977, the P Corporation purchased on the open market $100,000 face value of S Corporation's 8 percent bonds at 90 and accrued interest.

Required:

State what eliminating entries should be made as a result of the bond transactions on the consolidated work papers used for preparation of the consolidated statements at December 31, 1977, and December 31, 1978 (assume 100 percent elimination).

(AICPA adapted)

Problem 5

	Balances, December 31, 1977			
	P Company		S Company	
	Debit	Credit	Debit	Credit
Cash	$ 23,000		$ 30,000	
Accounts receivable	94,000		60,000	
Inventory, 1/1/77—cost ...	105,000		51,000	
Investment in stock of S ...	166,000			
Investment in bonds of S ..	51,800			
Other assets	445,000		210,000	
Current liabilities		$ 163,000		$ 17,100
Bonds payable—5 percent .				200,000
Deferred bond premium ...				5,400
Sales		630,000		340,000
Purchases	485,000		300,000	
Operating expenses	92,000		70,000	
Other expenses	22,000		15,500	
Interest		3,800		
Dividends paid	20,000		10,000	
Retained earnings, 1/1/77 .		107,000		84,000
Common stock		600,000		100,000
	$1,503,800	$1,503,800	$746,500	$746,500

Additional Information

a.   The investment in stock of S Company represents a 90 percent interest which was acquired January 1, 1977, for $175,000. At the same time $50,000 face amount of bonds of S were acquired for $52,000. These bonds had been issued on January 1, 1967, at 106 and are due January 1, 1987. S Company has recorded the amortization of the bond premium applicable to 1977 as an adjustment of interest expense. The stock and the bonds were purchased in the open market.

b.   Included in the Purchases account of S Company is a total of $180,000 of goods bought from P Company at 120 percent of cost to P Company. The closing inventory of S Company is estimated to include the same proportion of these purchases as of other purchases.

c.   Inventories at December 31, 1977, at cost to each company, were:

P Company....$80,000
S Company.... 45,000

d.   Although P Company uses the equity method, it has not yet recorded its equity in subsidiary earnings.

Required:

Prepare the income statement section of the three division working paper for the year ended December 31, 1977. Use the 100 percent elimination method.

(AICPA adapted)

Problem 6

Four years ago The American Company acquired 50 percent of the preferred stock of the Banner Corporation for $55,000 and 90 percent of that corporation's common stock for $195,000. At acquisition date the Banner Corporation had retained earnings of $60,000, and dividends on the 5 percent, cumulative preferred stock were not in arrears. The investments were recorded by The American Company at the book value shown by the Banner Corporation at date of acquisition. However, the excess of book values over the cost of common stock was known to relate to overvalued land on the books of Banner Corporation.

Consolidated statements are now being prepared as of December 31, 1978, for The American Company and its subsidiary. The financial position of the individual companies was as follows on that date:

THE AMERICAN COMPANY

Miscellaneous assets	$116,000	Liabilities	$ 50,000
Investments:		Preferred stock (4 percent) ..	100,000
Banner preferred	50,000	Common stock	100,000
Banner common	234,000	Retained earnings	150,000
	$400,000		$400,000

BANNER CORPORATION

Miscellaneous assets	$400,000	Liabilities	$ 60,000
		Preferred stock (5 percent)* .	100,000
		Common stock	200,000
		Retained earnings	40,000
	$400,000		$400,000

* Preferred stock dividends are three years in arrears. No dividends have been paid on common since acquisition by The American Company. Profit in 1975 was $8,000, but losses during the past three years have totaled $23,000.

Required:

a. Prepare the investment elimination entry on December 31, 1978.
b. Prepare a consolidated balance sheet working paper as of December 31, 1978.

(AICPA adapted)

9

Consolidated Statements— Changes in Parent Company's Equity

CHANGES in a parent company's equity in an affiliate occur as a result of transactions which increase or decrease the parent's proportionate ownership interest. Transactions of this type include: (1) parent company purchases of additional shares of the affiliate from the public; (2) parent company sales to the public of all or a portion of its shares of the affiliate; and (3) certain transactions by the affiliate of a capital nature (e.g., affiliate sales of additional shares of its common stock to the public). As a consequence of these types of transactions, the parent company's dollar interest in the net assets of the affiliate may increase or decrease more or less than the cash received or paid by the parent company in the transaction (or it may increase or decrease when the parent company was not a party to the transaction). Such changes must be appropriately accounted for both under the equity method of accounting for an investment (including investment in less than 50%-owned companies)[1] and in the consolidation process. This chapter explains the basic principles and techniques that are applicable to this class of transactions.

INCREMENTAL PURCHASES OF SUBSIDIARY STOCK FROM THE PUBLIC

On some occasions, the controlling interest in a subsidiary company may be established by the first purchase of its shares; on other occasions, a succession of purchases are required by the parent company to effectuate control. Where blocks of stock are acquired at different dates, it is im-

---

[1] *APB Opinion 18,* paragraph 19.

326

portant to examine the cost of each block and relate it to the corresponding book value of the subsidiary shares at the date these shares are acquired. Although the preparation of consolidated statements necessarily must be deferred until majority ownership of subsidiary shares exists, it remains important to analyze the cost of each block separately and in terms of the relevant acquisition book value.

Current accounting policy supports this position:

When one company purchases two or more blocks of stock of another company at various dates and eventually obtains control of the other company, the date of acquisition (for the purpose of preparing consolidated statements) depends on the circumstances. If two or more purchases are made over a period of time, the earned surplus of the subsidiary at acquisition should generally be determined on a step-by-step basis.[2]

However, the policy continues:

. . . if small purchases are made over a period of time and then a purchase is made which results in control, the date of the latest purchase, *as a matter of convenience,* may be considered as the date of acquisition.[3]

The latter treatment results in the exclusion from consolidated retained earnings of undistributed subsidiary profit increments which accrue to the partial holdings prior to the establishment of control. This potential exclusion of subsidiary earnings can be defended only in terms of materiality or convenience.

Case 1.   Block Purchases in the Open Market.   P Company acquired shares of S Company's stock according to the following schedule:

Date	Number of Shares	Cost
January 1, 19X1	200	$30,000
January 1, 19X2	100	17,500
January 1, 19X3	100	20,000

On January 1, 19X1, S Company had $50,000 of capital stock (par, $100) outstanding and retained earnings of $20,000. Annual profits for 19X1, 19X2, and 19X3 are assumed to be $10,000 in each year.

Assuming the individual block purchases are eliminated on a step-by-step basis, as is preferred, the purchased equity in the net assets of the subsidiary and the related differential for each block are:

---

[2] Section 2051.09, *APB Accounting Principles—Current Text.* This same position is also endorsed for the application of the equity method in *APB Opinion 18,* paragraph 19m.

[3] Ibid. (Emphasis supplied.)

	First Block (40%)	Second Block (20%)	Third Block (20%)
Investment cost	$30,000	$17,500	$20,000
Purchased equity in subsidiary net assets	(1) 28,000	(2) 16,000	(3) 18,000
Differential	$ 2,000	$ 1,500	$ 2,000

(1) 40 percent of $70,000.
(2) 20 percent of $80,000.
(3) 20 percent of $90,000.

Of course, the investment account will be increased over the three-year period to reflect the parent's equity in the subsidiary's reported earnings. Assuming for the sake of simplicity that the differentials are allocated to nonamortizable assets, the balance of the investment account at the end of 19X3 may be analyzed as follows:

	Acquisition Cost	Equity in Subsidiary Earnings	Carrying Value, December 31, 19X3
First Block	$30,000	(1) $12,000	$42,000
Second Block	17,500	(2) 4,000	21,500
Third Block	20,000	(3) 2,000	22,000
Total	$67,500	$18,000	$85,500

(1) 40 percent of $30,000.
(2) 20 percent of $20,000.
(3) 20 percent of $10,000.

It is usual for the parent company to carry the several blocks of subsidiary shares in a single investment account. Consequently, it is sufficient to make one summary elimination for the total investment. At December 31, 19X3, the investment elimination would be simply accomplished as follows:

Equity in subsidiary earnings (80% × $10,000)	8,000	
Investment in S Company		8,000

Capital stock (80% × $50,000)	40,000	
Retained earnings [80% × ($20,000 + $20,000)]	32,000	
Differential	5,500	
Investment in S Company ($85,500 − $8,000)		77,500

Thus, if the investment account is increased for the parent's equity in subsidiary earnings on a step-by-step basis, the investment elimination at the end of any period may be effected as if only one aggregate block of stock existed. By assuming no amortization of the differential, we can easily see that these entries set up a differential value equal to the sum of the differentials identified in the analysis of the individual blocks. Similarly, minority interest calculations in the consolidated statement working paper are made simply by multiplication of the end-of-period minority interest percentage times the relevant subsidiary values (net income, beginning retained earnings, etc.). Of course, consolidation would not be appropriate in this case until after majority control is established by the January 1, 19X2 purchase.

SALES OF SUBSIDIARY STOCK TO THE PUBLIC

Sales of subsidiary shares to the public are accounted for by the parent company essentially as are other disposals of its corporate assets. The investment account is adjusted up to the date of sale for the parent company's equity in subsidiary earnings to that time, and then this adjusted carrying value is matched against the proceeds of sale to determine the trading gain or loss.

When the parent sells only a portion of its investment in the subsidiary, the carrying value of the shares sold may be determined in several different ways. For federal income tax purposes, either specific identification or the first-in, first-out rule must be used, and these methods are also generally acceptable in practice for financial reporting. However, the strongest conceptual case can be made, in the opinion of the authors, for use of the *average carrying value* of all shares held. All of the shares are interchangeable and of equal economic value, and thus it seems less arbitrary to measure their "adjusted cost" in terms of the overall average than to allow selection of particular stock certificates or an artificial flow assumption determine the amount of profit to be reported. When the average carrying value method is used to determine the gain for financial reporting purposes, the difference between this gain and the taxable gain is a timing difference that requires income tax allocation.

Case 2. Partial (Interim) Sale of Holdings of Subsidiary Stock. Using the data of Case 1 in this example, it is assumed that on March 31, 19X4, P Company sold 100 shares of S Company's stock (representing 20 percent of the outstanding shares) to nonaffiliate interests for $25,000. During 19X4, S Company reported net income of $10,000, earned uniformly throughout the year. P Company uses the average carrying value of the shares to determine the gain or loss on the sale. We continue to assume the allocated differential is not subject to amortization. Income tax allocation is ignored.

We have previously determined that the carrying value of the investment on December 31, 19X3 was $85,500. The investment account would be further adjusted to the date of sale as follows:

Investment in S Company 2,000
    Equity in subsidiary earnings
      [80% × (3/12 × $10,000)]   2,000

After this entry, the average carrying value of the 400 shares of stock held by P Company is $218.75 per share ($87,500 ÷ 400 = $218.75). The entry to record the sale would therefore be:

```
Cash ......................................... 25,000
    Investment in S Company (100 × $218.75) .......    21,875
    Gain on sale of stock ..........................     3,125
```

Following the sale, P Company holds 300 shares of S Company's outstanding stock, or a 60 percent equity interest. Accordingly, at the end of 19X4, P Company would record its interest in S Company's income for the last nine months of the year as follows:

```
Investment in S Company .......................... 4,500
    Equity in subsidiary earnings
        [60% × (9/12 × $10,000)] ....................    4,500
```

The changes in the investment account balance are summarized following:

```
Balance, December 31, 19X3 ...................... $85,500
Equity in subsidiary earnings,
    1/1-3/31 (80% × $2,500) ....................    2,000
Sale of 100 shares (100 × $218.75) ............... (21,875)

Balance, March 31, 19X4 (300 × $218.75) .......... 65,625
Equity in subsidiary earnings,
    4/1-12/31 (60% × $7,500) ....................    4,500

Balance, December 31, 19X4 ...................... $70,125
```

In the preparation of a consolidated statement working paper, the reversal of the parent company's entries to record its interest in subsidiary earnings is based upon the shares *retained* by the parent at the end of the year (i.e., 60% × $10,000 = $6,000). This leaves $500 in the "equity in subsidiary earnings," the portion of the equity applicable to the sold shares. The $500 will be extended to the "consolidated" column, and is analogous to the "purchased preacquisition earnings" that appears in the consolidated statements when there is an interim purchase and operating data for the entire year are combined with calculations based upon end-of-period percentage ownership interests. In this case, also, elimination of the investment account and calculation of minority interests are based upon the *percentage ownership interests held by the majority and minority shareholders at the end of the period*. The balance of the investment account eliminated in the investment elimination entry is the balance at the end of the year, adjusted for the "reversal" entry. Applying these procedures to our example, the following eliminating entries are made:

```
(1) Equity in subsidiary earnings (60% × $10,000) ....    6,000
        Investment in S Company .................            6,000

(2) Capital stock—S Company (60% × $50,000) ......   30,000
    Retained earnings—S Company (60% × $50,000) ..   30,000
    Differential (300/400 × $5,500) ...............    4,125
        Investment in S Company ($70,125 − $6,000) .           64,125
```

In the second eliminating entry, it should be noted that the differential is the proportionate part of the original total differential attributable to the retained shares. Viewed from another perspective, this relationship implies that the portion of the total differential associated with the sold shares (on an *average* basis) has been matched (together with these shares' average equity in the subsidiary's net assets) against the sales proceeds in determining the trading gain on the sale. This is appropriate, as the differential is part of the parent company's total carrying value of the shares.

These data are presented in a partial consolidated statement working paper in Illustration 9–1, in which it is further assumed that P Company's 19X4 net income (exclusive of the gain on the sale of stock and the equity in subsidiary earnings) was $25,000, and its January 1, 19X4 retained earnings amounted to $80,000.

If the differential were subject to amortization (as it normally would be),

Illustration 9–1

P COMPANY AND SUBSIDIARY S COMPANY

Partial Consolidated Statement Working Paper
For Year Ended December 31, 19X4

	P Company	S Company	Eliminations Dr.	Eliminations Cr.	Minority Interest	Consolidated
Income Statement:						
Net income (excluding gain on sale of stock and equity in subsidiary earnings)	25,000	10,000				35,000
Gain on sale of stock	3,125					3,125
Equity in subsidiary earnings	6,500		(1) 6,000			500
	34,625	10,000				38,625
Minority interest in S Company net income—40% of $10,000					4,000	4,000
Net income—carried forward	34,625	10,000	6,000	–0–	4,000	34,625
Retained Earnings Statement:						
Retained earnings, January 1, 19X4:						
P Company	80,000					80,000
S Company		50,000	(2) 30,000		20,000	—
Net income—brought forward	34,625	10,000	6,000	–0–	4,000	34,625
Retained earnings, December 31, 19X4—carried forward	114,625	60,000	36,000	–0–	24,000	114,625

the *unamortized* differential at the date of sale would be allocated between the sold and the retained shares, and amortization for the remainder of the year after the sale would be based upon the portion of the unamortized differential allocated to the retained shares. In this case, the "reversal" entry would be based upon the equity in subsidiary earnings, net of differential amortization, for the retained shares; and the differential set up in the investment elimination entry would be the unamortized differential applicable to the retained shares at the beginning of the year. Differential amortization would then be recorded in the consolidated statement working paper on this unamortized differential balance (as allocated to specific assets), and the equity in subsidiary earnings on the sold shares that is extended to the "consolidated" column would be net of differential amortization to the date of sale on the portion of the beginning-of-year differential applicable to these shares.

The partial consolidated statement working paper in Illustration 9–1 indicates that consolidated net income for 19X4 is $34,625. A calculation by definition confirms this amount:

P Company's income from its own operations:		
Reported income (exclusive of trading gain and equity in subsidiary earnings)	$25,000	
Trading gain on sale of subsidiary stock	3,125	$28,125
Increased by:		
80 percent of three months' 19X4 subsidiary net income (80% × $2,500)	2,000	
60 percent of nine months' 19X4 subsidiary net income (60% × $7,500)	4,500	6,500
Consolidated net income for 19X4		$34,625

SUBSIDIARY TRANSACTIONS OF A CAPITAL NATURE

In the previous two sections of this chapter, we have examined parent company transactions with third parties whereby the parent company's proportionate interest in the subsidiary is increased or decreased. Since the parent controls the policies of the subsidiary, the same effects may be achieved by causing the subsidiary to issue additional shares of stock or repurchase treasury shares on a nonratable basis between majority and minority shareholders. The change in the parent company's equity that results from these types of transactions is a consequence of the exchange price of the shares issued or repurchased, the consideration given or received (if any) by the parent company, *and* the book value of the subsidiary's shares at the date of the transaction.

Because the economic substance of this class of transactions is equivalent from the parent company's point of view to the purchase and sale transactions previously analyzed, the change in equity should be recognized in a consistent manner. Accordingly, when the transaction *increases* the proportionate ownership interest of the parent company, the ownership change is analogous to a purchase from third parties and a net change in equity (in excess of the cost or proceeds, if any) should be treated as an adjustment of the previously existing unamortized differential. When the transaction *decreases* the parent's proportionate ownership interest, it is analogous to a sale to third parties and the net change in equity (in excess of the cost or proceeds, if any) should be recognized as a gain or loss of the period. Some accountants, however, believe that change in equity "gains" properly relate to contributed capital. Their argument rests on the assumption that it is improper to allow a subsidiary's trading in its own stock to be the source of a "profit" element in the calculation of consolidated net income and retained earnings. Accordingly, they support crediting these "gains" to consolidated paid-in capital. This practice has been widely followed, and supported by the SEC. However, there are, we believe, two fallacies in this position. First, under the prevailing philosophy of a majority interest orientation in the consolidated statements, consolidated paid-in capital should reflect transactions between the majority shareholders and the parent company. Subsidiary transactions in its own stock do not. Second, over the life of the investment, the parent company should reflect as income the total of dividends received and the excess of proceeds of disposal over the cost of the investment. If the "gains" on subsidiary stock transactions that reduce the parent company's proportionate ownership interest are credited to consolidated paid-in capital, this goal will not be achieved. Accordingly, we treat both gains and losses on subsidiary stock transactions that decrease the parent's proportionate interest as income determining elements, recognizing that the "paid-in capital treatment" may be encountered (or required) in practice for gains.

Since subsidiary transactions of a capital nature affect the balances in the shareholders' equity accounts of the subsidiary, and usually the parent company's proportionate ownership interest as well, a special analytical procedure is required. First, the parent's equity in the subsidiary's net assets is calculated immediately before and immediately after the subsidiary's stock transaction. Then, the change in the parent company's equity is determined by taking the difference between these two amounts. By isolating the effects of this single transaction in this manner, it follows that the computed change in equity is properly identifiable with the subsidiary's stock transaction.

If the new shares are issued or acquired by the subsidiary at an exchange price equal to their current book value, the change in the parent company's dollar equity in the subsidiary will be equal to the cost incurred or the proceeds received. If the parent is not a party to the transaction, its total dollar equity will not change. However, when the exchange price is more or less than the current book value of the shares, the change in equity will not equal the consideration given or received, if any, and it must be treated as an adjustment of the unamortized differential or as a gain or loss, depending upon whether the transaction increased or decreased the parent's proportionate ownership interest. In the illustrations to follow, we consider examples of subsidiary stock transactions that are executed at an exchange price greater than, equal to, and less than the book value of the subsidiary's shares.

In all illustrations, we assume for simplicity of exposition that the subsidiary stock transactions take place at the beginning of the year. The same principles, together with the principles previously described for interim purchases and sales, apply to interim subsidiary stock transactions.

Issuance of New Subsidiary Shares

For the cases to follow, we will assume that on January 1, 19X1, S Company had outstanding capital stock (par, $100), $100,000, and retained earnings of $150,000. On this date, P Company held 800 of S Company's shares (an 80 percent ownership interest), and the Investment in S Company account had a balance of $260,000. Since P Company's equity in the net assets of S Company is $200,000 (80% × $250,000), the investment account includes an unamortized differential of $60,000. The book value of S Company's outstanding shares is $250 per share ($250,000/1,000).

Case 3. New Shares Totally Subscribed by the Parent. Assume that on January 1, 19X1, S Company issued an additional 200 shares of stock at a price of $340 per share, all of which were purchased by P Company.

As a consequence of this transaction, the subsidiary's net assets increased by $68,000 ($340 × 200), and the parent's proportionate ownership interest increased from 80 percent (800/1000) to 83.3 percent (1000/1200). As indicated earlier, the change in the parent's dollar interest produced by subsidiary transactions of a capital nature must be determined by calculating the parent's equity in the subsidiary's net assets (using here the stockholders' equity accounts of the subsidiary to indicate the composition of the changes) immediately before and immediately after the capital transaction. This analysis is accomplished following:

	S Company's Net Assets		P Company's Equity in S Company's Net Assets		Increase (Decrease) in P Company's Equity
	Before Trans-action	After Trans-action	Before Trans-action (80%)	After Trans-action (10/12)	
Capital stock	$100,000	$120,000	$ 80,000	$100,000	$20,000
Retained earnings	150,000	150,000	120,000	125,000	5,000
Other contributed capital	–0–	48,000	–0–	40,000	40,000
	$250,000	$318,000	$200,000	$265,000	$65,000

Since the parent company's proportionate ownership interest increased, the $3,000 difference between its cost ($68,000) and the increase in its equity in the subsidiary's net assets ($65,000) is treated as an addition to the unamortized differential. This $3,000 would be allocated to specific assets of the subsidiary based upon their current fair values and the parent's proportionate increase in ownership interest (in this case, 3.3%), and amortized over their remaining lives.

Assuming that a consolidated statement working paper were prepared immediately following this transaction, the following investment elimination entry would be made:

```
Capital stock (10/12 × $120,000) .....................  100,000
Retained earnings (10/12 × $150,000) ................  125,000
Other contributed capital (10/12 × $48,000) ............   40,000
Differential .........................................   63,000
     Investment in S Company ($260,000 + $68,000) .....            328,000
```

The $63,000 differential established in this entry is the sum of the previously existing unamortized differential of $60,000 and the $3,000 incurred in the purchase of 200 additional shares from the subsidiary.

In this example, the exchange price ($340) for the sale of new shares was more than the book value of the existing shares ($250). If the exchange price had been equal to the book value, no additional differential would have resulted; if the exchange price had been less than the book value, a negative (credit) differential on this transaction would have resulted. These relationships are illustrated below for exchange prices of (a) $250 and (b) $190, ignoring the component elements of S Company's stockholders' equity:

	S Company's Net Assets		P Company's Equity in S Company's Net Assets		Increase (Decrease) in P Company's Equity	Invest-ment Cost	Differ-ential Dr. (Cr.)
	Before Trans-action	After Trans-action	Before Trans-action (80%)	After Trans-action (10/12)			
Exchange price ($250) equal to book value	$250,000	$300,000	$200,000	$250,000	$50,000	$50,000	$–0–
Exchange price ($190) less than book value	250,000	288,000	200,000	240,000	40,000	38,000	(2,000)

If an investment elimination entry for a consolidated statement working paper were prepared for these two alternative situations, the differential set up for alternative (a) would be $60,000, the preexisting unamortized differential, and for alternative (b), $58,000 ($60,000 − $2,000).

Case 4. New Shares Totally Subscribed by Third Parties. Assume now that on January 1, 19X1, S Company issued the 200 additional shares to third parties (instead of P Company) at the same price of $340 per share (more than book value).

This transaction again increased the net assets of S Company by $68,000, but P Company's proportionate ownership interest *decreased* from 80 percent (800/1000) to 66.67 percent (800/1200). The change in P Company's dollar interest in S Company as a consequence of this transaction is calculated in the same manner as before (again ignoring the components of S Company's stockholders' equity):

P Company's equity in S Company's net assets:
After transaction [8/12 × ($250,000 + $68,000)] $212,000
Before transaction (8/10 × $250,000) 200,000

Increase (Decrease) in equity .... $ 12,000

Thus, the issue of subsidiary shares to third parties at more than book value results in an increase in the parent company's monetary equity in the subsidiary's net assets in the amount of $12,000. Because the parent's percentage ownership interest declined, this change in equity is treated as a gain or loss. To compute the gain or loss, the parent's increase in equity in the subsidiary's net assets must be adjusted for the portion of the pre-existing unamortized differential that relates to the "sold" ownership interest. This amount is calculated by a pro rata allocation of the differential to the retained and "sold" ownership interests as follows:

	Percentage Ownership Interest	Pro Rata Allocation	Unamortized Differential
After subsidiary stock transaction:			
Retained	66.7%	5/6	$50,000
"Sold"	13.3	1/6	10,000
Before subsidiary stock transaction	80.0%	1.0	$60,000

Thus, the net gain (loss) is computed:

Increase in equity in S Company's net assets $12,000
Portion of preexisting differential allocated
  to "sold" interest 10,000

Net gain (loss) on transaction .... $ 2,000

This gain is *recorded by the parent company* with the following entry:

```
Investment in S Company  .........................  2,000
    Gain on subsidiary stock transaction  ..............      2,000
```

Note that this entry is a composite of two adjustments to the investment account: (1) an increase of $12,000 to reflect the parent's increased equity in the subsidiary's net assets, and (2) a decrease of $10,000 to the previously recorded unamortized differential. For purposes of the parent's subsequent differential amortization entries, and in the consolidation process, the $10,000 decrease in the previously recorded unamortized differential of $60,000 would generally be allocated pro ratably to the specific assets to which the $60,000 had been assigned. For example, if the $60,000 unamortized differential before the subsidiary's stock transaction had been allocated $15,000 to plant and equipment and $45,000 to goodwill, then after the transaction the remaining $50,000 would be allocated as follows:

	Unamortized Differential before Transaction	Differential Allocated to "Sold" Interest	Unamortized Differential after Transaction
Plant and Equipment	$15,000	$(2,500)	$12,500
Goodwill	45,000	(7,500)	37,500
	$60,000	$(10,000)	$50,000

If a consolidated statement working paper were prepared immediately after the subsidiary sale of stock, the following investment elimination entry would be made:

```
Capital stock  (8/12 × $120,000)  .................   80,000
Retained Earnings (8/12 × $150,000)  ..............  100,000
Other contributed capital (8/12 × $48,000)  .........   32,000
Differential  ...................................   50,000
    Investment in S Company
        ($260,000 + $2,000)  ....................          262,000
```

The differential set up by this eliminating entry corresponds with the value we previously calculated.

Under the treatment preferred by the authors, the $2,000 "gain on subsidiary stock transaction" recorded by the parent company would be extended to the consolidated column in the income statement division of the working paper (for the year in which the transaction took place). The question of whether or not deferred income taxes are to be concurrently recognized should be resolved in accordance with the principles of *APB Opinion 23*. If the alternative method of treating "gains" of this type is followed, the $2,000 will be extended to consolidated paid-in capital (rather than consolidated net income and retained earnings).

In this example, the sale of subsidiary shares was made at a price in excess of the book value of the shares. In general, if the exchange price exceeds book value, the parent's equity in the subsidiary's net assets will increase. If the exchange price is less than book value, the parent's equity will decrease. Since the parent's percentage ownership interest decreases the same amount regardless of the exchange price, the portion of the differential to be allocated to the "sale transaction" (from the parent company's point of view) remains the same. Thus the adjusted gain or loss will always result in a loss unless the exchange price is at least greater than book value. The effects of two alternative exchange prices, (a) $250 and (b) $190, for the sale of the 200 shares are illustrated below:

	(a) Exchange Price ($250) Equal to Book Value	(b) Exchange Price ($190) Less than Book Value
P Company's equity in S Company's net assets:		
After transaction	$200,000*	$192,000†
Before transaction (8/10 × $250,000)	200,000	200,000
Increase (decrease) in parent's equity	$ –0–	$(8,000)
Differential allocated to "sold" interest	10,000	10,000
Net gain (loss) on transaction	$(10,000)	$(18,000)

* 800/1200 × ($250,000 + $50,000).
† 800/1200 × ($250,000 + $38,000).

New Shares Nonratably Subscribed by Majority and Minority Shareholders.   Cases 3 and 4 illustrate two special instances of a nonratable issue of the new shares—the parent either purchased all of the new shares or none of them. Many other possibilities exist. In all such cases, however, the same principles apply. If the parent company subscribes to more than its preexisting ownership percentage, the transaction is treated analogously to a purchase; the difference between the parent's cost and its change in equity is added to (or substracted from) the unamortized differential. If the parent subscribes to less than its ownership percentage, the transaction is treated analogously to a sale; the difference between the parent's cost and its change in equity, adjusted for the portion of the differential allocable to the ownership percentage that is "sold," is reported as a gain or loss (or perhaps paid-in capital for "gains").

New Shares Ratably Subscribed by Majority and Minority Shareholders.   If the new issue of subsidiary shares is ratably subscribed by the majority and minority shareholders (i.e., the parent purchases the same percentage of these shares as its proportionate ownership interest), the parent company's ownership percentage remains unchanged. Additionally, regardless of the relationship between the exchange price for the new shares and the book value of the old shares, the change in the parent company's equity will equal its cost, and thus there is no "excess" or "difference" to be analyzed.

Interim Subsidiary Stock Issue. If the new issue of subsidiary shares takes place during the year, the principles described above for the treatment of a change in the parent's equity apply in the same manner. Additionally, we must draw upon the previously described principles for interim purchases or sales.

For example, if the parent increased its percentage ownership interest through an interim purchase of all of the new shares (as in Case 3), the analysis of the change in its dollar equity would incorporate the subsidiary's estimated earnings from the beginning of the year to the date of the stock transaction. Assuming a preexisting controlling interest, the interim purchase alternative of presenting operating data for the subsidiary for the entire year would normally be appropriate. Therefore, the investment elimination entry for the year the transaction occurs would include a component for "purchased preacquisition earnings." The amount of this component would be calculated by multiplying the parent's *increase in ownership percentage* by the subsidiary's estimated earnings to the date of the transaction. Otherwise, the transaction would be analyzed in the same manner as in Case 3.

Similarly, if the parent's ownership interest were decreased because third parties purchased all of the new stock issue (as in Case 4), the analysis would again include the subsidiary's estimated earnings to the date of the stock transaction. Additionally, as in the example of interim sales presented earlier in this chapter, the reversal of the parent's entries to record its equity in subsidiary earnings would be based upon the retained ownership percentage, and the consolidated column would include an extension for "equity in subsidiary earnings, net of applicable differential amortization" for the sold interest. The gain or loss on the sold interest would be calculated as in Case 4, where the unamortized differential allocation would now be calculated on the basis of the value as of the date of the stock transaction.

In both types of situations, the parent would record its equity in subsidiary earnings prior to the new stock issue based upon its ownership percentage during that time, and its equity for the remainder of the year based upon the adjusted ownership percentage. Differential amortization would also be recorded for the two time periods based upon the beginning-of-year differential value and the adjusted differential value, respectively.

Subsidiary Repurchase of Treasury Shares

Case 5. Treasury Shares Repurchased Exclusively from Minority Shareholders. Continuing with our basic data for **P** Company and its 80 percent-owned subsidiary S Company, and disregarding the previous two cases dealing with the issuance of new shares, assume that on January 1, 19X1, S Company repurchased all of the 200 shares held by minority shareholders at a price of $300 per share.

As a consequence of this transaction, S Company's net assets decreased by $60,000 ($300 × 200), and P Company's proportionate ownership interest increased from 80 percent to 100 percent. The change in P Company's monetary interest in S Company resulting from this treasury stock transaction by the subsidiary is calculated by means of the same analytical procedure that we employed for new stock issues by the subsidiary:

P Company's equity in S Company's net assets:
After transaction [100% × ($250,000 − $60,000)] $190,000
Before transaction (80% × $250,000) 200,000
Increase (Decrease) in equity .... $(10,000)

Thus, the subsidiary's repurchase of its outstanding shares from minority shareholders at more than book value results in a decrease in the parent company's monetary equity in the subsidiary's net assets in the amount of $10,000. Because the parent's percentage ownership interest increased, this change in equity is treated as an adjustment of the unamortized differential.[4] A decrease in the parent's equity in net assets implies, of course, that the previously recorded unamortized differential will be increased by this amount. Thus in this example, the unamortized differential increases from $60,000 to $70,000. No entry is made on the books of the parent company. However, the adjustment must be taken into account in the parent's subsequent differential amortization entries (with the $10,000 allocated on the basis of current fair values for subsidiary assets and an "acquired" ownership percentage from this transaction of 20 percent). Additionally, the adjusted differential will be picked up in the investment elimination entry.

Assuming that S Company recorded the acquisition of its shares in a Treasury Stock account, the investment elimination entries for a consolidated statement working paper prepared immediately after this transaction are:

(1) Capital stock (200 × $100) 20,000
    Retained earnings 40,000
        Treasury stock (200 × $300) 60,000
(2) Capital stock [100% × ($100,000 − $20,000)] 80,000
    Retained earnings
        [100% × ($150,000 − $40,000)] 110,000
    Differential ($60,000 + $10,000) 70,000
        Investment in S Company 260,000

---

[4] Even if the original combination were treated as a pooling of interests, the acquisition of an additional interest from the minority shareholders at a subsequent date would be accounted for as a purchase (see *APB Opinion 16,* paragraphs 5 and 43, and *Accounting Interpretation No. 26 of APB Opinion 16*).

The exchange price in this example was more than the book value of the subsidiary's shares. If the exchange price had been less than book value, the parent's equity in the net assets of the subsidiary would have increased, resulting in a negative (credit) differential adjustment.

Case 6. Treasury Shares Repurchased Exclusively from Parent Company. Assume now that on January 1, 19X1, S Company repurchased 200 of its outstanding shares from P Company (instead of the minority shareholders) at a price of $300 per share.

This transaction again decreased S Company's net assets by $60,000, and P Company's proportionate ownership interest decreased from 80 percent (800/1000) to 75 percent (600/800). The change in P Company's monetary interest in S Company's net assets is:

```
P Company's equity in S Company's net assets:
  After transaction [75% × ($250,000 − $60,000)] ........ $142,500
  Before transaction (80% × $250,000) ...............   200,000

  Increase (Decrease) in equity ........................ $ (57,500)
```

Because the parent's percentage ownership interest declined, P Company will recognize a gain (loss) in an amount equal to the excess of the sales proceeds over the sum of (1) the decrease in its equity in S Company's net assets, and (2) the proportionate part of the unamortized differential applicable to the "sold" interest.

In this example, a 5 percent interest was sold and 75 percent retained. Thus, P Company will record the following entry for the transaction:

```
Cash (200 × $300) ...............................  60,000
Loss on sale of stock to subsidiary ................   1,250
  Investment in S Company
    [$57,500 + (5/80 × $60,000)] ...............            61,250
```

Assuming again that S Company recorded the acqustion of its shares in a Treasury stock account, the investment elimination entries for a consolidated statement working paper prepared immediately after this transaction are:

```
(1)  Capital stock (200 × $100) ....................  20,000
     Retained earnings ...........................  40,000
       Treasury stock ........................            60,000
(2)  Capital stock [75% × ($100,000 − $20,000)] ....  60,000
     Retained earnings [75% × ($150,000 − $40,000)] .  82,500
     Differential (75/80 × $60,000) ...............  56,250
       Investment in S Company
         ($260,000 − $61,250) ................           198,750
```

If the exchange price had been less than book value, the decrease in the parent company's equity would have exceeded the proceeds of sale, and thus the loss on the sale transaction would have been greater.

Other types of nonratable repurchases of treasury stock by the subsidiary, ratable repurchases, and interim treasury stock transactions by the subsidiary are treated in a manner analogous to that described in the previous section on new stock issues. Accordingly, these discussions are not repeated here.

Effect on Fundamental Definition of Consolidated Net Income

In the case of subsidiary transactions of a capital nature that *decrease* the parent company's proportionate ownership interest, the parent company recognizes a gain or loss on its books. This gain or loss is considered confirmed from a consolidated point of view, and is extended to the "consolidated" column of the working paper. Accordingly, this element of the parent company's reported net income is treated in the same manner as a sale of a portion of the investment to third parties in the schedular calculation of consolidated net income.

Subsidiary transactions of a capital nature that *increase* the parent company's proportionate ownership interest have no income effect. Accordingly, the only effect of these transactions on the schedular calculation of consolidated net income is the need to calculate the parent's share of the subsidiary's reported net income before and after the transaction on the basis of the two different ownership percentages.

UNCONFIRMED PROFIT ON ASSET TRANSFERS

Special consideration should be given to intercompany profit eliminations where there occurs a change (either an increase or decrease) in the parent company's percentage interest in the selling affiliate during the current period. This change of equity relates importantly to the investment elimination and to the intercompany profit elimination—either 100 percent or fractional elimination.

In respect to asset transfers between affiliates, it is important that the process of profit confirmation be identified with specific time periods. The amount of cumulative confirmed profits at the start of the current year necessarily relates to that period between the originating intercompany transaction and this date; the amount of profit confirmation during the current year must identify with the relevant fractional parts of the year *before* and *after* the change of the parent company's equity in the selling subsidiary. Once these broad time intervals have been associated with the relevant confirmed profit elements, two methods of analysis are available to the accountant.

One method, which is preferred by the authors, is to calculate the amount of the investment elimination elements and the change in the parent's monetary equity on the basis of the *confirmed* net income and retained earnings of the subsidiary at the date of change in the parent company's equity percentage. Since an economic entity is preexistent to this transaction, it is plausible that the purchased or sold net assets should be based upon subsidiary earnings which are then confirmed on a consolidated basis. Calculations of consolidated net income and retained earnings of subsequent periods would allocate confirmed profits of these periods on the basis of equity interests then existing. The definitional calculation of consolidated net income, therefore, would continue to accumulate incremental interests of confirmed subsidiary net income based upon the parent's percentage interests during the fractional periods for which the different equity interests prevail. For purposes of consolidated working paper preparation, intercompany profits are eliminated and minority interests calculated on the basis of equity percentages existing at the *end* of the accounting period. These concepts in respect to intercompany profits apply to either increases or decreases in the parent company's percentage interest in subsidiary shares and are consistent with the definitional framework constructed in the previous chapters.

A second basic elimination method calculates the amount of investment elimination elements and the change in the parent's monetary equity on the basis of *reported* net income and retained earnings. This method results in an effective confirmation of that portion of the intercompany profit for those shareholders, either majority or minority, whose percentage interest in the selling affiliate is decreased. In the preparation of consolidated working papers, this method requires that the amount of the unconfirmed profit elimination be based on the percentage interest prevailing at the time of the intercompany profit transaction. In those instances where the change in equity results in a decrease in the parent company's percentage interest, some accountants advocate use of the lower percentage. This essentially is a commitment to report the lowest possible consolidated net income and is analogous to the "lower of cost or market" rule for valuation of inventories.

Since specific identification of items of inventory containing intercompany profit is often difficult to determine accurately, accountants may be justified in applying the rule of first-in, first-out with respect to the flow of inventory costs. If there is evidence to indicate that the refinement introduced by the intraperiod calculation is not materially different from an application of year-end percentages, the latter rates may be used without unusual distortion of consolidated net income.

The above commentary is equally applicable to the analysis of profit confirmation in respect to the gain (or loss) on the acquisition of intercompany bonds.

QUESTIONS

1. Enumerate three types of transactions that change a parent's ownership interest in a subsidiary.

2. When a parent gains control of a subsidiary by acquiring several blocks of stock at different dates, there are two alternative methods of determining the investment elimination of the subsidiary's retained earnings. What is the nature of these alternatives? Which is preferred?

3. How does a parent company account for its sales of subsidiary stock to the public?

4. When the parent company sells a portion of its subsidiary stock to the public, how is the carrying value of the stock determined?

5. Why is it necessary to distinguish between blocks of a subsidiary's stock purchased in the open market and stock acquired directly from the subsidiary?

6. How are subsidiary transactions of a capital nature similar to the parent's purchases or sales of the subsidiary's stock in the open market?

7. In general, how are subsidiary transactions of a capital nature accounted for?

8. Explain the theoretical disagreement over "gains" resulting from a decrease in a parent company's proportionate ownership interest due to a subsidiary's stock transaction.

9. Describe the analytical procedure used to identify the change in the parent's equity from a subsidiary stock transaction.

10. Describe the two alternative methods of calculating the investment elimination elements and the change in the parent's monetary equity at the date of a change in the parent company's equity percentage when unconfirmed intercompany profits exist as a result of prior transactions between the affiliates.

EXERCISES

Exercise 9–1

On January 1, 19X1, S Company had outstanding capital stock (par, $10) of $10,000 and retained earnings of $90,000. P Company made the following purchases of S Company stock in the open market:

February 1, 19X1—600 shares, cost $70,000
October 1, 19X1—200 shares, cost $27,000

During 19X1, S Company reported net income (earned uniformly over the year) of $30,000, and P Company reported net income from its own operations, exclusive of the equity in subsidiary earnings, of $40,000. Assume all differentials are assigned to nonamortizable assets.

Required:

a. Prepare the entry that would be made by the parent company at December 31 to recognize its equity in subsidiary earnings.

b. Prepare the investment elimination entries for a three-division consolidated statement working paper at December 31, 19X1. (Assume P Company includes all of S Company's 19X1 operating data in the consolidated income statement.)

c. Prepare schedular calculations of consolidated net income for 19X1 using (1) the incremental approach and (2) the residual approach.

Exercise 9–2

On January 1, 19X1, S Company had outstanding capital stock (par, $10) of $20,000, and retained earnings of $80,000. P Company held 1,200 of the S Company shares, and the Investment in S Company account had a balance of $90,000. On this date, P Company purchased an additional 600 shares of S Company stock in the open market at a cost of $50,000.

The unamortized differential prior to the acquisition of the new block of shares was allocated $11,000 to plant and equipment (net), and the remainder to goodwill. An appraisal of the subsidiary's assets and liabilities on January 1, 19X1 indicated that the fair value of the plant and equipment (net) was $200,000 and its book value was $170,000; for all other assets and liabilities, book values equaled fair values. The estimated remaining lives of the plant and equipment and the goodwill were five years and twenty years, respectively.

During 19X1, S Company reported net income of $30,000.

Required:

a. Calculate the amounts of the total differential from both blocks to be allocated to plant and equipment and goodwill on January 1, 19X1 after the purchase of S Company stock.
b. Prepare the entries that would be made by P Company on December 31, 19X1 to record its equity in subsidiary earnings and differential amortization.
c. Prepare the investment elimination and differential amortization entries for a three-division consolidated statement working paper on December 31, 19X1.

Exercise 9–3

On January 1, 19X1, S Company had outstanding capital stock (par, $10) of $10,000, and retained earnings of $30,000. P Company held 800 of the S Company shares, and the Investment in S Company account had a balance of $48,000.

On January 1, 19X1, P Company sold 100 of its 800 S Company shares to third parties at a price of $50 per share. P Company uses the average carrying value of the shares to determine the gain or loss on the sale.

The unamortized differential on January 1, 19X1 was allocated wholly to plant and equipment (net), with an estimated remaining life of five years. S Company reported net income of $15,000 for 19X1, and P Company's 19X1 net income, exclusive of its equity in S Company's earnings and the gain or loss on the sale of subsidiary stock, was $25,000.

Required:

a. Prepare the entries that would be made by P Company during 19X1.
b. Reconcile the balance of the investment account at December 31, 19X1 with the sum of the parent's equity in subsidiary net assets and the unamortized differential.
c. Prepare the investment elimination and differential amortization entries for

a three-division consolidated statement working paper on December 31, 19X1.

d. Prepare schedular calculations of consolidated net income for 19X1 using (1) the incremental approach and (2) the residual approach.

Exercise 9–4

On January 1, 19X1, S Company had outstanding capital stock (par, $10) of $20,000 and retained earnings of $80,000. P Company held 1,800 of the S Company shares, and the Investment in S Company account had a balance of $105,000. On this date, S Company issued an additional 1,000 shares of stock at a price of $80 per share, all of which were purchased by third parties.

Required:

a. Determine the gain or loss that P Company realized on this transaction.
b. Prepare any journal entries that would be made by P Company.
c. Assuming a consolidated statement working paper were prepared immediately after this transaction, prepare the investment elimination entry.
d. Assuming that the unamortized differential before this transaction was allocated wholly to goodwill and that its remaining life was estimated to be 20 years, prepare the entry that P Company would make at December 31, 19X1 to record differential amortization.

Exercise 9–5

On January 1, 19X1, S Company had outstanding capital stock (par, $10) of $20,000 and retained earnings of $80,000. P Company held 1,800 of the S Company shares, and the Investment in S Company account had a balance of $105,000. On this date, S Company issued an additional 1,000 shares of stock at a price of $40 per share, all of which were purchased by third parties.

Required:

a. Determine the gain or loss that P Company realized on this transaction.
b. Prepare any journal entries that would be made by P Company.
c. Assuming a consolidated statement working paper were prepared immediately after this transaction, prepare the investment elimination entry.
d. Assuming that the unamortized differential before this transaction was allocated wholly to goodwill and that its remaining life was estimated to be 20 years, prepare the entry that P Company would make at December 31, 19X1 to record differential amortization.

Exercise 9–6

On January 1, 19X1, S Company had outstanding capital stock (par, $10) of $20,000, and retained earnings of $80,000. P Company held 1,800 of the S Company shares, and the Investment in S Company account had a balance of $130,000. On this date, S Company issued an additional 2,000 shares of stock at a price of $80 per share, all of which were purchased by P Company.

Required:

a. Determine the change in P Company's equity and the differential adjustment as a result of the subsidiary stock transaction.

b. Prepare any journal entries that would be made by P Company.

c. Assuming a consolidated statement working paper were prepared immediately after this transaction, prepare the investment elimination entry.

d. Assume that $15,000 of the unamortized differential before the subsidiary stock transaction was allocated to plant and equipment (net) and the remainder to goodwill. Additionally, on this date, the fair value of the plant and equipment (net) was $400,000 and its book value was $360,000; for all other assets, book values equaled fair values. Calculate the amounts of the total adjusted differential allocated to plant and equipment (net) and goodwill after the subsidiary stock transaction.

e. Assuming that on January 1, 19X1 the estimated remaining lives of the plant and equipment and the goodwill were five years and twenty years respectively, prepare the entry that P Company would make at December 31, 19X1 to record differential amortization.

Exercise 9–7

On January 1, 19X1, S Company had outstanding capital stock (par, $10) of $20,000, and retained earnings of $80,000. P Company held 1,800 of the S Company shares, and the Investment in S Company account had a balance of $130,000. On this date, S Company issued an additional 2,000 shares of stock at a price of $40 per share, all of which were purchased by P Company.

Required:

a. Determine the change in P Company's equity and the differential adjustment as a result of the subsidiary stock transaction.

b. Prepare any journal entries that would be made by P Company.

c. Assuming a consolidated statement working paper were prepared immediately after this transaction, prepare the investment elimination entry.

d. Assume that $15,000 of the unamortized differential before the subsidiary stock transaction was allocated to plant and equipment (net) and the remainder to goodwill. Additionally, on this date, the fair value of the plant and equipment (net) was $400,000 and its book value was $360,000; for all other assets, book values equaled fair values. Calculate the amounts of the total adjusted differential allocated to plant and equipment (net) and goodwill after the subsidiary stock transaction.

e. Assuming that on January 1, 19X1 the estimated remaining lives of the plant and equipment and the goodwill were five years and twenty years respectively, prepare the entry that P Company would make at December 31, 19X1 to record differential amortization.

Exercise 9–8

On January 1, 19X1, S Company had outstanding capital stock (par, $10) of $20,000, and retained earnings of $80,000. P Company held 1,800 of the

S Company shares, and the Investment in S Company account had a balance of $110,000. On this date, S Company repurchased all 200 of its shares held by minority shareholders at a price of $100 per share.

Required:

a.   Determine the change in P Company's equity and the differential adjustment as a result of the subsidiary's repurchase of its shares.
b.   Prepare any journal entries that would be made by P Company.
c.   Assuming a consolidated statement working paper were prepared immediately after this transaction, prepare the investment elimination entry (S Company recorded the repurchased shares at cost in a Treasury Stock account).
d.   Assume that $14,000 of the unamortized differential before the subsidiary stock transaction was allocated to plant and equipment (net) and the remainder to goodwill. Additionally, on this date, the fair value of the plant and equipment (net) was $100,000 and its book value was $60,000; for all other assets, book values equaled fair values. Calculate the amounts of the total adjusted differential allocated to plant and equipment (net) and goodwill after the subsidiary stock transaction.
e.   Assuming that on January 1, 19X1 the estimated remaining lives of the plant and equipment and the goodwill were four years and ten years respectively, prepare the entry that P Company would make at December 31, 19X1 to record differential amortization.

Exercise 9–9

On January 1, 19X1, S Company had outstanding capital stock (par, $10) of $20,000, and retained earnings of $80,000. P Company held 1,800 of the S Company shares, and the Investment in S Company account had a balance of $110,000. On this date, S Company repurchased 400 of its shares from P Company at a price of $40 per share.

Required:

a.   Determine the gain or loss that P Company realized on this transaction.
b.   Prepare any journal entries that would be made by P Company.
c.   Assuming a consolidated statement working paper were prepared immediately after this transaction, prepare the investment elimination entries (S Company recorded the repurchased shares at cost in a Treasury Stock account).
d.   Assume that $14,000 of the unamortized differential before the subsidiary stock transaction was allocated to plant and equipment (net) and the remainder to goodwill. Calculate the amounts of the total adjusted differential allocated to plant and equipment (net) and goodwill after the subsidiary stock transaction.
e.   Assuming that on January 1, 19X1 the estimated remaining lives of the plant and equipment and the goodwill were five years and ten years respectively, prepare the entry that P Company would make at December 31, 19X1, to record differential amortization.

Exercise 9–10

On January 1, 19X1, S Company had outstanding capital stock (par, $10) of $10,000, and retained earnings of $40,000. P Company held 700 of the S Company shares, and the Investment in S Company account had a balance of $38,500. On this date, S Company repurchased 400 shares of its outstanding stock at a price of $60 per share. 300 shares were purchased from P Company, and the remaining 100 shares were purchased from minority shareholders.

Required:

a. Determine the gain or loss that P Company realized on this transaction.
b. Prepare any journal entries that would be made by P Company.
c. Assuming a consolidated statement working paper were prepared immediately after this transaction, prepare the investment elimination entries (S Company recorded the repurchased shares at cost in a Treasury Stock account).

Exercise 9–11

On January 1, 19X1, S Company had outstanding capital stock (par, $10) of $10,000, and retained earnings of $40,000. P Company held 700 of the S Company shares, and the Investment in S Company account had a balance of $38,500. On this date, S Company repurchased 400 shares of its outstanding stock at a price of $60 per share. 200 shares were repurchased from P Company, and the remaining 200 shares were purchased from minority shareholders.

Required:

a. Determine the change in P Company's equity and the differential adjustment as a result of the subsidiary's treasury stock transaction.
b. Prepare any journal entries that would be made by P Company.
c. Assuming a consolidated statement working paper were prepared immediately after this transaction, prepare the investment elimination entries (S Company recorded the repurchased shares at cost in a Treasury Stock account).

Exercise 9–12

On January 1, 19X1, S Company had outstanding capital stock (par, $100) of $100,000, and retained earnings of $150,000. P Company held 800 of the S Company shares, and the Investment in S Company account had a balance of $260,000. On this date, S Company issued an additional 200 shares of stock at a price of $340 per share. P Company purchased 100 shares of the stock, and the remaining 100 shares were purchased by third parties.

Required:

a. Determine the gain or loss that P Company realized on this transaction.
b. Prepare any journal entries that would be made by P Company.
c. Assuming a consolidated statement working paper were prepared immediately after this transaction, prepare the investment elimination entry.

d.   Assuming that the unamortized differential before this transaction was allocated $12,000 to plant and equipment and the remainder to goodwill, determine the amounts of the adjusted differential that would be allocated to these assets.

Exercise 9–13

On January 1, 19X1, S Company had capital stock (par, $100) of $100,000 and retained earnings of $100,000. P Company held 600 of S Company's 1,000 outstanding shares, and the Investment in S Company account had a balance of $140,000. On this date, S Company issued an additional 1,000 shares at a price of $250 per share. P Company purchased 800 shares, and the remaining 200 shares were purchased by third parties.

Required:

a.   Determine the change in P Company's equity and the differential adjustment as a result of the subsidiary stock transaction.
b.   Prepare any journal entries that would be made by P Company.
c.   Assuming a consolidated statement working paper were prepared immediately after this transaction, prepare the investment elimination entry.

Exercise 9–14

On January 1, 19X1, S Company had outstanding capital stock (par, $100) of $100,000, and retained earnings of $150,000. P Company held 800 of the S Company shares, and the Investment in S Company account had a balance of $260,000. On this date, S Company issued an additional 200 shares of stock. P Company purchased its ratable share of this new issue, or 160 shares; the remaining 40 shares were purchased by third parties.

Required:

a.   Confirm that the increase in the parent company's equity is equal to its cost regardless of the relationship between the exchange price of the new shares and the book value of the old shares by calculating the parent's increase in equity and its cost for each of the following alternative exchange prices:
(1) $250 per share (equal to book value per share)
(2) $340 per share (greater than book value per share)
(3) $190 per share (less than book value per share)
b.   Prepare the investment elimination entry for a consolidated statement working paper prepared immediately after the new issue of subsidiary shares for each of the three alternative exchange prices.

Exercise 9–15

On January 1, 19X1, S Company had outstanding capital stock (par, $100) of $100,000, and retained earnings of $150,000. P Company held 800 of the S Company shares, and the Investment in S Company account had a balance of $260,000. On this date, S Company issued an additional 200 shares of stock at a price of $190 per share. P Company purchased 100 shares of the stock, and the remaining 100 shares were purchased by third parties.

Required:

a. Determine the gain or loss that P Company realized on this transaction.
b. Prepare any journal entries that would be made by P Company.
c. Assuming a consolidated statement working paper were prepared immediately after this transaction, prepare the investment elimination entry.
d. Assuming that the unamortized differential before this transaction was allocated $12,000 to plant and equipment and the remainder to goodwill, determine the amounts of the adjusted differential that would be allocated to these assets.

Exercise 9–16

On January 1, 19X1, S Company had capital stock (par, $100) of $100,000 and retained earnings of $100,000. P Company held 600 of S Company's 1,000 outstanding shares, and the Investment in S Company account had a balance of $140,000. On this date, S Company issued an additional 1,000 shares at a price of $150 per share. P Company purchased 800 shares, and the remaining 200 shares were purchased by third parties.

Required:

a. Determine the change in P Company's equity and the differential adjustment as a result of the subsidiary stock transaction.
b. Prepare any journal entries that would be made by P Company.
c. Assuming a consolidated statement working paper were prepared immediately after this transaction, prepare the investment elimination entry.

Exercise 9–17

On January 1, 19X1, S Company had outstanding capital stock (par, $10) of $20,000, and retained earnings of $80,000. P Company held 1,800 of the S Company shares, and the Investment in S Company account had a balance of $110,000. On this date, S Company repurchased 500 of its outstanding shares of stock. P Company sold its ratable share, or 450 shares, and the remaining 50 shares were repurchased from the minority shareholders.

Required:

a. Confirm that the decrease in the parent company's equity is equal to its proceeds regardless of the relationship between the exchange price of the repurchased shares and their book value by calculating the parent's decrease in equity and its proceeds for each of the following alternative exchange prices:
   (1) $50 per share (equal to book value per share)
   (2) $60 per share (greater than book value per share)
   (3) $40 per share (less than book value per share)
b. Prepare the investment elimination entries for a consolidated statement working paper prepared immediately after the subsidiary's repurchase of

treasury shares for each of the three alternative exchange prices. (Assume the subsidiary recorded the reacquired shares at cost in a Treasury Stock account).

PROBLEMS

Problem 1

On January 1, 19X1, S Company had outstanding capital stock (par, $10) of $10,000 and retained earnings of $30,000. P Company made the following purchases of S Company stock in the open market:

> January 1, 19X1—50 shares, cost $2,500
> July 1, 19X1—100 shares, cost $5,500
> October 1, 19X1—750 shares, cost $45,000

During 19X1, S Company reported net income (earned uniformly over the year) of $20,000, and P Company reported net income from its own operations, exclusive of the equity in subsidiary earnings, of $50,000. Assume all differentials are assigned to nonamortizable assets.

Required:

a. Assuming the individual block purchases are eliminated on a step-by-step-basis:
   (1) Prepare the entry that would be made by the parent company at December 31 to recognize its equity in subsidiary earnings.
   (2) Prepare the investment elimination entries for a three-division consolidated statement working paper at December 31, 19X1. (Assume that P Company elects to include the results of S Company's operations for all of 19X1 in the 19X1 consolidated income statement.)
   (3) Prepare schedular calculations of consolidated net income for 19X1 using (a) the incremental approach and (b) the residual approach.
b. Assuming that the last purchase is treated as the date of acquisition, repeat the three requirements in (a) above.

Problem 2

On January 1, 19X1, S Company had outstanding capital stock (par, $5) of $10,000, and retained earnings of $50,000. P Company held 1,800 of the S Company shares, and the Investment in S Company account had a balance of $84,000.

On September 30, 19X1, P Company sold 600 of the S Company shares it held to third parties at a price of $25 per share. P Company uses the average carrying value of the shares to determine the gain or loss on the·sale.

The differential is allocated wholly to Land, and thus is not subject to amortization. During 19X1, S Company reported net income (earned uniformly over the year) of $20,000, and P Company's net income, exclusive of its equity in S Company's earnings and the gain or loss on the sale of subsidiary stock, was $50,000.

Required:

a. Prepare the entries that would be made by P Company during 19X1.
b. Reconcile the balance of the investment account at December 31, 19X1 with the sum of the parent's equity in subsidiary net assets and the differential.
c. Prepare the investment elimination entries for a three-division consolidated statement working paper on December 31, 19X1.
d. Prepare schedular calculations of consolidated net income for 19X1 using (1) the incremental approach and (2) the residual approach.

Problem 3

On January 1, 19X1, S Company had outstanding capital stock (par, $10) of $20,000, and retained earnings of $80,000. P Company held 1,800 of the S Company shares, and the Investment in S Company account had a balance of $117,000.

On July 1, 19X1, P Company sold 200 of its S Company shares to third parties at a price of $80 per share. P Company uses the average carrying value of the shares to determine the gain or loss on the sale.

The unamortized differential on January 1, 19X1 was allocated wholly to goodwill, with an estimated remaining life of 10 years. During 19X1, S Company reported net income of $10,000 (earned uniformly throughout the year) and P Company reported net income, exclusive of its equity in S Company's earnings and the gain or loss on the sale of subsidiary stock, of $20,000.

Required:

a. Prepare the entries that would be made by P Company during 19X1.
b. Reconcile the balance of the investment account at December 31, 19X1 with the sum of the parent's equity in subsidiary net assets and the unamortized differential.
c. Prepare the investment elimination and differential amortization entries for a three-division consolidated statement working paper on December 31, 19X1.
d. Prepare schedular calculations of consolidated net income for 19X1 using (1) the incremental approach and (2) the residual approach.

Problem 4

On January 1, 19X1, S Company had outstanding capital stock (par, $5) of $10,000, and retained earnings of $50,000. P Company held 1,800 of the S Company shares, and the Investment in S Company account had a balance of $84,000.

On July 1, 19X1, S Company issued an additional 1,000 shares to third parties at a price of $70 per share.

The differential as of January 1, 19X1, is allocated wholly to goodwill, which has an estimated life of ten years. During 19X1, S Company reported net income (earned uniformly over the year) of $20,000, and P Company's net income, exclusive of its equity in S Company's earnings and the gain or loss on the subsidiary stock transaction, was $50,000.

Required:

a. Determine the gain or loss that P Company realized on the subsidiary's stock transaction.

b. Prepare all investment-related journal entries that would be made by P Company in 19X1.

c. Reconcile the balance of the investment account at December 31, 19X1 with the sum of the parent's equity in subsidiary net assets and the un-amortized differential.

d. Prepare the eliminating entries for a three-division consolidated statement working paper on December 31, 19X1.

e. Assuming that P Company's retained earnings on January 1, 19X1 amounted to $100,000, and that neither company paid any dividends, prepare a partial consolidated statement working paper (income statement and retained earnings statement divisions) for the year.

f. Prepare a schedular calculation of consolidated net income for 19X1 using the incremental approach.

Problem 5

On January 1, 19X1, S Company had outstanding capital stock (par, $10) of $20,000, and retained earnings of $80,000. P Company held 1,800 of the S Company shares, and the Investment in S Company account had a balance of $130,000.

On July 1, 19X1, S Company issued an additional 2,000 shares of stock at a price of $100 per share, all of which were purchased by P Company.

The differential as of January 1, 19X1 is allocated wholly to goodwill, which has an estimated life of ten years. At July 1, 19X1, the book values of S Company's assets and liabilities were equal to their fair values. During 19X1, S Company reported net income (earned uniformly over the year) of $40,000, and P Company's net income, exclusive of its equity in S Company's earnings, was $60,000.

Required:

a. Determine the change in P Company's equity and the differential adjust-ment as a result of the subsidiary stock transaction.

b. Prepare all investment-related journal entries that would be made by P Company in 19X1.

c. Reconcile the balance of the investment account at December 31, 19X1 with the sum of the parent's equity in subsidiary net assets and the un-amortized differential.

d. Prepare the eliminating entries for a three-division consolidated statement working paper on December 31, 19X1. (Assume P Company includes all of S Company's 19X1 operating data in the consolidated income state-ment.)

e. Assuming that P Company's retained earnings on January 1, 19X1 amounted to $150,000, and that neither company paid any dividends, prepare a partial consolidated statement working paper (income statement and retained earn-ings statement divisions) for the year.

f. Prepare a schedular calculation of consolidated net income for 19X1 using the incremental approach.

Problem 6

P Company purchased 800 shares of S Company stock on January 1, 19X1, for $120,000, when S Company had capital stock ($100 par) of $100,000 and retained earnings of $50,000. P Company purchased an additional 100 shares on July 1, 19X2, for $17,700. On July 1, 19X3, S Company issued 200 new shares to minority shareholders for $40,000.

Intercompany profit on asset transfers by S Company to P Company existed as follows:

a. $2,000 unconfirmed inventory profit reported in 19X1, confirmed in the last six months of 19X2.
b. $1,000 unconfirmed inventory profit reported in the first six months of 19X2, confirmed in the first six months of 19X3.
c. $10,000 unconfirmed profit on the transfer of plant and equipment on July 2, 19X2, and this asset has an expected life of 10 years.

P Company had an annual net income of $100,000 (exclusive of its equity in S Company's earnings and the gain or loss on the subsidiary stock transaction), and S Company earned $20,000 uniformly over each year.

Assume calculations of changes in equity are based upon confirmed profits.

Required:

a. Prepare schedular calculations of consolidated net income for *19X2* using both the incremental and the residual approaches. Under the residual approach, both fractional and 100 percent elimination should be considered.
b. Prepare schedular calculations of consolidated net income for *19X3* using both the incremental and the residual approaches. Under the residual approach, both fractional and 100 percent elimination should be considered.

10

Consolidated Statements— Special Ownership Configurations

MULTILEVEL AFFILIATIONS

AFFILIATION DIAGRAMS have heretofore usually been of the following basic form:

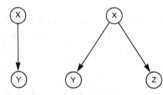

Affiliation diagrams for a parent company and three or more subsidiaries may be depicted by merely extending the second level of the diagram horizontally as necessary. In each of these cases, control is *directly* exercised by the parent company over all members of the affiliation. Yet, on occasions, the intercorporate stock arrangements may indicate one subsidiary's control over other subsidiaries; in this instance, the parent's control over second-level subsidiaries is, at least in part, *indirect* in nature. In such cases, the associations are best described as multilevel affiliations.

In a multilevel affiliation, at least one company other than the parent company will be an "investor company," and each "investor company" will carry its investment in affiliates on an equity basis. Accordingly, the calculation of amounts for the investment elimination entries, minority interests, equities in affiliates' earnings, and so forth, will be based upon the results of applying equity method accounting. Otherwise, parent company entries are made and consolidated statement working paper techniques applied as described in previous chapters.

The following two cases illustrate affiliations that are multilevel in form. The account balances which relate to each of these examples are:

	January 1, 19X1		
	P Company	Y Company	Z Company
Capital stock	$200,000	$100,000	$50,000
Retained earnings	80,000	20,000	10,000

It is assumed that each company reported income, exclusive of any equity in affiliates' earnings, of $10,000 each year. Additionally, for reasons of simplicity, it is assumed that no dividends were declared, and that all differentials relate to nonamortizable assets.

Case 1. Y Company purchased 80 percent of the capital stock of Z Company on January 1, 19X1, for $50,000. One year later, P Company purchased 90 percent of the capital stock of Y Company for $125,000. As a consequence of these transactions, the affiliation diagram for this multi-level affiliation is as follows:

Since both P Company and Y Company hold stock investments in affiliates, each will record an equity in an affiliate's earnings and each will be subject to an investment elimination entry in the consolidated statement working paper. The purchased equity in the net assets of the affiliate and the related differential for each of these two investments are analyzed following:

	P Company in Y Company	Y Company in Z Company
Investment cost	$125,000	$50,000
Purchased equity in affiliate's net assets:		
Capital stock	$ 90,000	$40.000
Retained earnings	34,200*	8,000
	$124,200	$48,000
Differential	$ 800	$ 2,000

* 90% × $38,000.

Y Company's purchased equity in Z Company's net assets is based upon the amounts for capital stock and retained earnings at January 1, 19X1. However, since P Company purchased the shares of Y Company one year later, Y Company's retained earnings must be modified for its 19X1 operations. During 19X1, Y Company's income, *on an equity method basis,* is $18,000 [$10,000 + (80% × $10,000)], and thus its retained earnings balance on January 1, 19X2, when acquired by P Company, is $38,000.

During 19X2, P Company and Y Company would each record their equity in affiliates' earnings. For Y Company, this equity in Z Company's earnings would amount to $8,000 (80% × $10,000), as it was in 19X1. For P Company, the equity in Y Company's 19X2 equity-basis income would amount to $16,200 [90% × ($10,000 + $8,000)].

A partial consolidated statement working paper for this affiliation for the year ended December 31, 19X2 is presented in Illustration 10–1. Note that minority interests are based simply on the subsidiaries' recorded incomes and net assets, which in the case of Y Company reflects its equity interest in Z Company.

Consolidated net income for 19X2 may be confirmed by definition (incremental approach) as follows:

P Company's income from its own operations $10,000
Increased by its equity in Y Company's reported (equity-basis)
     income: 90% × $18,000 16,200
Consolidated net income for 19X1 .... $26,200

Case 2. On January 1, 19X1, P Company purchased 80 percent of the capital stock of Y Company for $100,000, and 70 percent of the capital stock of Z Company for $43,000. One year later, Y Company purchased 20 percent of the capital stock of Z Company for $15,000.

The affiliation diagram and the analysis of the purchased equities in the net assets of affiliates are presented following:

Affiliation Diagram

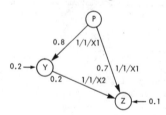

In Case 1, Y Company was, technically, both a "parent" and a subsidiary, and P Company's control over Z Company was indirect through Y Company. In this example, however, P Company exercises direct con-

Illustration 10–1

P COMPANY AND SUBSIDIARY COMPANIES

Partial Consolidated Statement Working Paper
For Year Ended December 31, 19X2

	P Company	Y Company	Z Company	Eliminations Dr.	Eliminations Cr.	Minority Interests Y Company	Minority Interests Z Company	Consolidated
Income Statement:								
Net income (excluding equity in affiliates' earnings)	10,000	10,000	10,000					30,000
Equity in affiliates' earnings	16,200	8,000		(1) 24,200				–0–
Minority interests						1,800	2,000	(3,800)
Net income—carried forward	26,200	18,000	10,000	24,200	–0–	1,800	2,000	26,200
Retained Earnings Statement:								
Retained earnings, January 1, 19X2:								
P Company	90,000							90,000
Y Company		38,000		(3) 34,200		3,800		–0–
Z Company			20,000	(2) 16,000			4,000	–0–
Net income—brought forward	26,200	18,000	10,000	24,200	–0–	1,800	2,000	26,200
Retained earnings, December 31, 19X2—carried forward	116,200	56,000	30,000	74,400	–0–	5,600	6,000	116,200
Balance Sheet:								
Investment in Y Company	141,200				(1) 16,200 (3) 125,000			–0–
Investment in Z Company		66,000			(1) 8,000 (2) 58,000			–0–
Differential—P Company in Y Company				(3) 800				800
Differential—Y Company in Z Company				(2) 2,000				2,000
Capital stock:								
P Company	200,000							200,000
Y Company		100,000		(3) 90,000		10,000		–0–
Z Company			50,000	(2) 40,000			10,000	–0–
Retained earnings—brought forward	116,200	56,000	30,000	74,400	–0–	5,600	6,000	116,200
Minority interest—Y Company					–0–	15,600		15,600 M
Minority interest—Z Company							16,000	16,000 M

Explanation of eliminations:

(1) To reverse 19X2 entries by investor companies recognizing their equities in affiliates' earnings. (2) Investment elimination entry for P Company's investment in Z Company. (3) Investment elimination entry for P Company's investment in Y Company. (2) Investment elimination entry for Y Company's investment in Y Company.

	P Company in Y Company	P Company in Z Company	Y Company in Z Company
Investment cost	$100,000	$43,000	$15,000
Purchased equity in affiliate's net assets:			
Capital stock	$ 80,000	$35,000	$10,000
Retained earnings	16,000	7,000	4,000*
	$ 96,000	$42,000	$14,000
Differential	$ 4,000	$ 1,000	$ 1,000

* 20% × $20,000.

trol over both subsidiaries, and only obtains additional indirect control over Z Company through Y Company's 20 percent equity in Z Company.

Y Company should again carry its investment in Z Company on the equity basis, because "significant influence" is clearly exerted over the financial and operating policies of Z Company. Even if a second-level "investor company" holds less than a 20 percent interest in another affiliate in a multilevel affiliation, the equity method is justified under *APB Opinion 18* when significant influence and/or control is exerted through a combination of direct and indirect shareholdings. Note that if the acquisitions had been reversed in time, that is, if Y Company had first acquired its interest in Z Company and then P Company acquired controlling interests in the two companies, the acquisition of Z Company would be in essence a step-by-step acquisition that would require a retroactive adjustment of Y Company's investment account if it were not previously carried on an equity basis. In the event a second-level "investor company" does not carry its investment on the equity basis, a working paper adjustment would be required to convert it to an equity basis prior to the preparation of eliminating entries.

A partial consolidated statement working paper for this affiliation for the year ended December 31, 19X2 is presented in Illustration 10–2. As in the previous example, the investment accounts are carried under the equity method, and minority interest calculations are based upon the subsidiaries' recorded incomes and net assets.

Consolidated net income for 19X2 may again be confirmed by definition (incremental approach) as follows:

P Company's income from its own operations		$10,000
Increased by its equity in affiliates' reported (equity-basis) incomes:		
Y Company: 80% × $12,000	$9,600	
Z Company: 70% × $10,000	7,000	16,600
Consolidated net income for 19X2		$26,600

Effects of Differential Amortization

In the previous two illustrations, we assumed that all differentials were allocated to nonamortizable assets. If these differentials were allocated to amortizable assets, as they normally would be, differential amortization would have to be taken into account in calculating consolidated net income and the minority interests in subsidiaries with investments in other affiliates. The parent company's differential amortization would be allocated wholly to the majority shareholders, as in previous chapters, and thus poses no new problems. Differential amortization by a subsidiary with an investment in another affiliate must be allocated between the parent company and the subsidiary's minority shareholders. Since differential amortization would be recorded by the subsidiary in calculating its equity-basis net income, the parent company would automatically recognize its proper share of this expense when it records its equity in the subsidiary on the basis of the subsidiary's equity-basis net income. Furthermore, in the preparation of the consolidated statement working paper, the subsidiary's differential amortization is appropriately taken into account in the calculation of minority interests when the subsidiary's equity-basis net income is used. Thus, the procedures we have illustrated above will be appropriate for cases involving amortizable as well as nonamortizable differentials as long as the subsidiary has properly calculated its equity-basis net income. Of course, on the consolidated statement working paper, the differential must be allocated to specific assets (and liabilities), and appropriate amortizations recognized thereon.

Chain Control (Indirect) Less than 50 Percent

On occasion, intercorporate stock ownership arrangements may indicate a chain of interests, the product of which does not represent control of the lower level subsidiary, where control is defined in terms of the 50 percent stock ownership minimum. The following diagram is an example of such an affiliation:

In this instance, the preparation of consolidated statements is warranted, notwithstanding the 42 percent indirect interest of P Company in Z Com-

Illustration 10–2

P COMPANY AND SUBSIDIARY COMPANIES

Partial Consolidated Statement Working Paper
For Year Ended December 31, 19X2

	P Com-pany	Y Com-pany	Z Com-pany	Eliminations Dr.	Eliminations Cr.	Minority Interests Y Com-pany	Minority Interests Z Com-pany	Consoli-dated
Income Statement:								
Net income (excluding equity in affiliates' earnings)	10,000	10,000	10,000					30,000
Equity in affiliates' earnings	16,600	2,000		(1) 18,600				–0–
Minority interest						2,400	1,000	(3,400)
Net income—carried forward	26,600	12,000	10,000	18,600	–0–	2,400	1,000	26,600
Retained Earnings Statement:								
Retained earnings, January 1, 19X2:								
P Company	105,000*							105,000
Y Company		30,000		(2) 24,000		6,000		
Z Company			20,000	(3) 14,000 (4) 4,000			2,000	
Net income—brought forward	26,600	12,000	10,000	18,600	–0–	2,400	1,000	26,600
Retained earnings, December 31, 19X2—carried forward	131,600	42,000	30,000	60,600	–0–	8,400	3,000	131,600

Balance Sheet:

	P Company	Y Company	Z Company	Eliminations Dr.	Eliminations Cr.	Minority Interest—Y	Minority Interest—Z	Consolidated
Investment in Y Company	117,600†				(1) 9,600 (2) 108,000			-0-
Investment in Z Company	57,000‡				(1) 7,000 (3) 50,000			-0-
Investment in Z Company		17,000§			(1) 2,000 (4) 15,000			-0-
Differential—P Company in Y Company				(2) 4,000				4,000
Differential—P Company in Z Company				(3) 1,000				1,000
Differential—Y Company in Z Company				(4) 1,000				1,000
Capital stock:								
P Company	200,000							200,000
Y Company		100,000		(2) 80,000		20,000		-0-
Z Company			50,000	{ (3) 35,000 (4) 10,000			5,000	-0-
Retained earnings—brought forward	131,600	42,000	30,000	60,600	-0-	8,400	3,000	131,600
Minority interest—Y Company						28,400		28,400 M
Minority interest—Z Company							8,000	8,000 M

* $80,000 + [$10,000 + (80% × $10,000) + (70% × $10,000)].
† $100,000 + [(80% × $10,000) + (80% × $12,000)].
‡ $43,000 + [(70% × $10,000) + (70% × $10,000)].
§ $15,000 + (20% × $10,000).

Explanation of eliminations:
(1) To reverse 19X2 entries by investor companies recognizing their equities in affiliates' earnings.
(2) Investment elimination entry for P Company's investment in Y Company.
(3) Investment elimination entry for P Company's investment in Z Company.
(4) Investment elimination entry for Y Company's investment in Z Company.

pany. Clearly the question of control relates to *direct* share ownership. In the illustration depicted above, control is confirmed by the percentages of stock owned independently by P Company and Y Company. Significantly, while the product of equities in the chain are factors in the determination of consolidated net income and consolidated retained earnings, it is not a determinant in establishing a minimal condition for preparation of consolidated financial statements.

Intercompany Profit in Multilevel Affiliations

Previous discussion of the elimination of the intercompany profit on asset transfers has focused on affiliations in which the subsidiary is one level removed from the parent company. The calculation of consolidated net income is not fundamentally altered by the intercompany profit element existing at the second level of a multilevel affiliation. In respect to 100 percent elimination, the minority interest in subsidiary net income (or retained earnings) is calculated in terms of the subsidiary's *confirmed* equity-basis income (or retained earnings). Where the fractional elimination method is used, the amount of the minority interest is determined on the basis of the subsidiary's equity-basis income, *unadjusted* for the intercompany profit, and the amount of the profit eliminated is based upon the parent company's interest (direct and/or indirect) in the selling affiliate.

Consider the following data and affiliation diagram in respect to companies P, Y, and Z:

<table>
<tr><td>Affiliation Diagram</td><td>19X2 Net Incomes, Excluding
Equities in Affiliates' Earnings</td></tr>
</table>

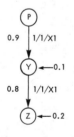

P Company	$20,000
Y Company	10,000
Z Company	5,000

The net income of Z Company is assumed to contain an element of unconfirmed intercompany profit in the amount of $2,000.

Consolidated net income for 19X2 may be determined by residual calculation (together with an indication of the amounts of intercompany profit to be eliminated under the two alternative methods) as follows:

	100 Percent Elimination	Fractional Elimination
P Company	$31,160	$31,160
Y Company	12,400	12,400
Z Company	5,000	5,000
	$48,560	$48,560

Deduct (add)—net debit (credit)eliminations:

Equity in affiliates' earnings ($11,160 + $2,400)	$13,560	$13,560
Elimination of unconfirmed intercompany profit:		
100% of $2,000	2,000	
90% of 80% of $2,000		1,440
	$15,560	$15,000
Total equity	$33,000	$33,560

Minority interests:

Y Company:		
10% of [$10,000 + 80% ($5,000 − $2,000)]	$ 1,240	
10% of [$10,000 + (80% × $5,000)]		$ 1,400
Z Company:		
20% of ($5,000 − $2,000)	600	
20% of $5,000		1,000
	$ 1,840	$ 2,400
Consolidated net income	$31,160	$31,160

Using the incremental approach, consolidated net income would be determined as follows:

Y Company's equity-basis income $= \$10,000 + 80\% (\$5,000 - \$2,000)$
$$= \$12,400$$

Consolidated net income (or P
Company's equity-basis income) $= \$20,000 + 90\% (\$12,400)$
$$= \$31,160$$

BILATERAL STOCKHOLDINGS—TRADITIONAL ALLOCATION METHOD

In all of our previous examples, attention was focused on unilateral ownership by one or more companies of corporate shares of other affiliated companies. Although such ownership configurations are most frequently encountered, on occasions one may find a bilateral stockholding, wherein two or more of the affiliated companies are related through the reciprocal ownership of corporate stock. In the discussion to follow, we consider the problems associated with bilateral stockholdings. First, the traditional method of allocating the affiliates' income between majority and minority shareholders is explained. Thereafter, an alternative method—the treasury stock method—is briefly outlined.

Bilateral Stockholdings Not Involving Parent Company

Case 3.   Consider the following affiliation diagram:

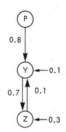

If the net incomes of companies P, Y, and Z *from their own operations* are $50,000, $20,000, and $10,000 respectively, one method of apportioning the total of their net incomes of $80,000 between majority and minority shareholders is by successive iteration, a variate on the trial and error method; a second method is algebraic simplification. Whichever the method chosen, the first step is to determine the net income of each reciprocally related member of the affiliation *on an equity basis*. The equity basis net income is the net income of an affiliate reckoned in terms of its interdependency with other affiliates. In other words, the equity basis net income of a company equals the net income earned on its own operations plus its equity (accruing from its ownership of stock) in the equity basis net incomes of other affiliates. Secondly, the equity basis net incomes of the several affiliates may be directly allocated to the majority and minority interests.

Successive Iteration.   Where the involvements of intercompany stockholdings are not especially complex and where the number of mutually related companies is not unusually large, the successive iteration method may be easily applied. The method presumes that a consolidated basis net income in respect to a given company can be determined by a series of approximations in the manner indicated in Illustration 10–3.

Illustration 10–3 indicates that the successive iteration method proceeds with a progression of successive estimates. Each value total is based upon a sequence of approximations. The sequence of steps in the calculation continues, as illustrated, until solution value totals stabilize. In this illustration no change in the amount of total net incomes for Y Company and Z Company results after step 7. These value totals are the equity basis net incomes of companies Y and Z. Since there is no bilateral affiliation involving the parent company, P Company is not included in the iterative process in Illustration 10–3. Additionally, in general, only those subsidiary

Illustration 10–3

Step	Y Company			Z Company		
	Net Income from Own Operations	70% of Net Income of Z Company	Total	Net Income from Own Operations	10% of Net Income from Y Company	Total
1	$20,000	$7,000.00	$27,000.00	$10,000	$2,700.00	$12,700.00
2	20,000	8,890.00	28,890.00	10,000	2,889.00	12,889.00
3	20,000	9,022.30	29,022.30	10,000	2,902.23	12,902.23
4	20,000	9,031.56	29,031.56	10,000	2,903.16	12,903.16
5	20,000	9,032.21	29,032.21	10,000	2,903.22	12,903.22
6	20,000	9,032.25	29,032.25	10,000	2,903.23	12,903.23
7	20,000	9,032.26	29,032.26	10,000	2,903.23	12,903.23
8	20,000	9,032.26	29,032.26	10,000	2,903.23	12,903.23

affiliates whose equity basis net incomes include an interest, direct or indirect, in bilaterally related affiliates must be included in this type of calculation.

Allocation of net incomes of the affiliate companies *to outside shareholder interests* (majority and minority shareholders) is accomplished in the following manner:

P Company's net income from its own operations	$50,000.00	
80 percent of Y Company's equity basis net income (80% of $29,032.26)	23,225.81	
Consolidated net income		$73,225.81
Minority interest in Y Company:		
10 percent of Y Company's equity basis net income (10% of $29,032.26)		2,903.22
Minority interest in Z Company:		
30 percent of Z Company's equity basis net income (30% of $12,903.23)		3,870.97
Total net incomes of affiliate companies		$80,000.00

Although the aggregated equity basis net incomes exceed the aggregated net incomes of the bilateral affiliates *from their own operations,* it should be observed that the allocation process results in the calculation of majority and minority interests equal in amount to the total operating incomes of the three affiliates. This condition must exist, regardless of the type or complexity of the interdependency relationships. Note that Z Company's equity basis net income does not enter the calculation of consolidated net income; it is utilized only to determine the equity of Z Company's minority interest. This is appropriate since Y Company's equity basis net income includes Y's equity in Z's net income. P Company's equity in Z's net income is, therefore, included in consolidated net income as a part of the calculation which includes P's equity in Y's equity basis net income (80 percent of $29,032.26).

Although the equity basis net incomes determined in the first step are used only as an "intermediate calculation," they are subject to interpretation. One way of viewing these calculations is to assume that each mutually related company paid dividends in the amount of their income from their own operations; then they paid another dividend equal to the amount received from their investments in affiliates; and so forth. When this process stabilizes, in the same manner as it did in the successive iteration calculation, the equity basis net incomes would be equal to the total amount of money handled (or dividends paid) by each affiliate.[1] Another way of viewing the "equity basis net incomes" is to regard them as appropriate equity method accounting for investments in mutually re-

---

[1] This interpretation was suggested in Roman Weil, "Reciprocal or Mutual Holdings: Allocating Earnings and Selecting the Accounting Method," *The Accounting Review,* October 1973, p. 753.

lated companies, from the point of view of each affiliate as a separate legal entity.[2] This latter perspective, while implicit in the terminology and the calculations, results, however, in certain inconsistencies with *APB Opinion 18,* as is discussed subsequently in connection with entries to be made by the affiliates.

Algebraic Solution. The same interdependency structure may be more formally expressed as a system of linear equations. Where such a system is relatively simple, viz., two or three affiliates, algebraic simplification is perhaps the most easily applied solution form. Assume the following notation:

$$Y = \text{Net income of Y Company on an equity basis.}$$
$$Z = \text{Net income of Z Company on an equity basis.}$$

The problem may now be formulated and solved as follows:

$$Y = \$20,000 + .7Z,$$
$$Z = \$10,000 + .1Y.$$

$$Y = \$20,000 + .7(\$10,000 + .1Y),$$
$$Y = \$20,000 + \$7,000 + .07Y,$$
$$.93Y = \$27,000,$$
$$Y = \$29,032.26.$$

$$Z = \$10,000 + .1(\$29,032.26),$$
$$Z = \$10,000 + \$2,903.23,$$
$$Z = \$12,903.23.$$

As noted previously, P Company is not in the interdependency structure and thus is excluded from the system of equations. Given the above consolidated basis net incomes of Y Company and Z Company, the allocation of the total net incomes of the affiliates is made in the same amounts as in the illustration of the successive iteration method.

Bilateral Stockholdings Involving Parent Company

The previous illustration in Case 3 dealt with mutually related subsidiary affiliates. The calculation of equity basis net incomes is not essentially different if the parent is also bilaterally related to one or more affiliates. However, since the majority interest in the parent company is less than 100 percent (because one or more of the affiliates owns stock in the parent), in this circumstance the parent's equity basis net income must be allocated to the majority shareholders in the same way that the subsidiaries' equity basis net incomes were allocated to the minority shareholders in the previous illustration.

---

[2] Ibid., p. 754.

Case 4. Consider now the following affiliation diagram:

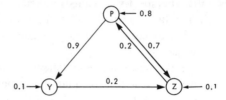

Companies P, Y, and Z are again assumed to have net incomes from their own operations of $50,000, $20,000, and $10,000.

The equity basis net incomes of the affiliates are calculated algebraically as follows:

$$P = \text{Net income of P Company on an equity basis.}$$
$$Y = \text{Net income of Y Company on an equity basis.}$$
$$Z = \text{Net income of Z Company on an equity basis.}$$

$$P = \$50,000 + .9Y + .7Z,$$
$$Y = \$20,000 + .2Z,$$
$$Z = \$10,000 + .2P.$$

$$P = \$50,000 + .9(\$20,000 + .2Z) + .7Z,$$
$$P = \$50,000 + \$18,000 + .18Z + .7Z,$$
$$P = \$68,000 + .88Z.$$

$$P = \$68,000 + .88(\$10,000 + .2P),$$
$$P = \$68,000 + \$8,800 + .176P,$$
$$.824P = \$76,800,$$
$$P = \$93,203.88.$$

$$Z = \$10,000 + .2(\$93,203.88),$$
$$Z = \$10,000 + \$18,640.77,$$
$$Z = \$28,640.77.$$

$$Y = \$20,000 + .2(\$28,640.77),$$
$$Y = \$20,000 + \$5,728.16,$$
$$Y = \$25,728.16.$$

The equity basis net incomes of the three affiliates are allocated to majority and minority shareholder interests as follows:

Consolidated net income:	
80 percent of P Company's equity basis net income	
(80% of $93,203.88)	$74,563.10
Minority interest in Y Company:	
10 percent of Y Company's equity basis net income	
(10% of $25,728.16)	2,572.82
Minority interest in Z Company:	
10 percent of Z Company's equity basis net income	
(10% of $28,640.77)	2,864.08
Total net incomes of affiliates	$80,000.00

In consolidated net income determination, only the nonaffiliate share-holders in the parent company constitute the majority interest. In this case, 20 percent of P Company's stock is held by Z Company; accordingly, the outside interest in P Company of 80 percent is the equity multiplier in calculating consolidated net income.

Intercompany Profit on Asset Transfers

For eliminations of intercompany profit on the transfer of assets be-tween affiliate companies, the same elimination procedures control in re-spect to reciprocally related companies as for unilateral affiliations. The amount of the intercompany profit to be eliminated may be either 100 percent or a fractional amount based upon the parent company's equity in the selling affiliate. As was illustrated in Chapter 7, if the amount of the eliminated profit is 100 percent, the profit elimination results in a rat-able diminution of the interests of both majority and minority shareholders; where the elimination relates only to the parent's equity in the selling affiliate, the amount of the elimination is absorbed totally by the majority shareholders. In the latter case, the equity basis net income of each sub-sidiary, unadjusted for intercompany profit, is the basis used in calculat-ing the equity of minority shareholders.

Case 5. Bilateral Stockholdings Not Involving Parent.   The follow-ing affiliation diagram is assumed:

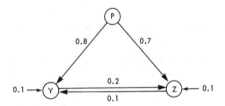

Inventory profit currently recorded by Z Company, which is unconfirmed from a consolidated standpoint, is $9,800.

Assume the following notation:

P_E = Interest of P Company in the unconfirmed inventory
    profit on an equity basis.
Y_E = Interest of Y Company in the unconfirmed inventory
    profit on an equity basis.
Z_E = Interest of Z Company in the unconfirmed inventory
    profit on an equity basis.

The various interests in the unconfirmed inventory profit are reflected as follows:

$$P_E = .8Y_E + .7Z_E,$$
$$Y_E = .2Z_E,$$
$$Z_E = \$9,800 + .1Y_E.$$

372 Advanced Accounting

By substitution and simplification, solution values are determined to be:

$$P_B = \$8,600,$$
$$Y_B = \$2,000,$$
$$Z_B = \$10,000.$$

In the consolidated working paper, the eliminating entry in respect to intercompany inventory profit is as follows:

1. If the amount of the elimination is based upon the parent company's fractional interest in the selling affiliate:

Inventory (Income Statement division)	8,600	
Inventory (Balance Sheet division)		8,600

2. If the amount of the elimination is 100 percent of the unconfirmed profit:

Inventory (Income Statement division)	9,800	
Inventory (Balance Sheet division)		9,800

In the latter case, minority shareholders must absorb a ratable amount of the eliminated inventory profit, calculated as follows:

Minority in Y Company (10% of $2,000)	$ 200	
Minority in Z Company (10% of $10,000)	1,000	
	$1,200	

Thus the total elimination of $9,800 is allocated:

To the majority shareholders	$8,600
To the minority shareholders	1,200
	$9,800

Depending upon the method used, interests in the unconfirmed inventory profits are deducted, as appropriate, from the equity basis net incomes calculated as before.

The algebraic solution may be simplified, however, in the event of a 100 percent elimination of intercompany inventory profit. Given net incomes from their own operations of $50,000, $20,000, and $10,000 for companies P, Y, and Z respectively, the equation system of the mutually related subsidiaries may take the following form:

$$Y = \$20,000 + .2Z,$$
$$Z = \$200 + .1Y.$$

Z Company's net income in the second equation is reduced to $200 by deducting the $9,800 of unconfirmed inventory profit from the recorded net income of $10,000. By substitution and simplification, solution values are determined to be:

$$Y = \$20,448.98,$$
$$Z = \$ \ 2,244.90.$$

Allocation of the net incomes of the affiliate companies is then made as follows:

P Company's net income from its own operations	$50,000.00	
80 percent of Y Company's equity basis net income (80% of $20,448.98)	16,359.18	
70 percent of Z Company's equity basis net income (70% of $2,244.90)	1,571.43	
Consolidated net income		$67,930.61
Minority interest in Y Company: 10 percent of Y Company's equity basis net income (10% of $20,448.98)		2,044.90
Minority interest in Z Company: 10 percent of Z Company's equity basis net income (10% of $2,244.90)		224.49
Total confirmed net incomes of affiliates		$70,200.00

This method implicitly deducts the majority and minority interests in the unconfirmed inventory profit, as calculated above, from the allocated shares of total net income.

Had fractional elimination been applied, the equity basis net incomes of the three affiliates must first be calculated without regard for the intercompany profit. In this case, the equity basis net incomes would be determined as follows (using the same notation as before):

$$P = \$50,000 + .8Y + .7Z$$
$$Y = \$20,000 + .2Z$$
$$Z = \$10,000 + .1Y$$

$$P = \$76,530.61$$
$$Y = \$22,448.98$$
$$Z = \$12,244.90$$

Thereafter, the $8,600 intercompany inventory profit element would be eliminated against the equity basis net income of P Company. In this instance, the allocation of net incomes of the affiliate companies is made in the following manner:

P Company's equity basis net income	$76,530.61	
Less: Unconfirmed inventory profit elimination	8,600.00	
Consolidated net income		$67,930.61
Minority interest in Y Company: 10 percent of Y Company's equity basis net income (10% of $22,448.98)		2,244.90
Minority interest in Z Company: 10 percent of Z Company's equity basis net income (10% of $12,244.90)		1,224.49
Total confirmed net incomes of affiliates		$71,400.00

The variation in the total of the net incomes allocated, $1,200, may be attributed to the different bases for calculating minority interests. Significantly, the amount of consolidated net income in both calculations remains the same.

Case 6. Bilateral Stockholdings Involving Parent. The following is an illustration of an affiliation involving intercompany profit in which the parent is bilaterally related to one subsidiary:

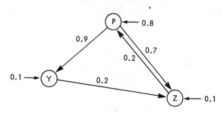

Inventory profit currently recognized by Z Company, although unconfirmed from a consolidated standpoint, is assumed to be $8,240.

Notation:

P_E = Interest of P Company in the unconfirmed inventory profit on an equity basis.

Y_E = Interest of Y Company in the unconfirmed inventory profit on an equity basis.

Z_E = Interest of Z Company in the unconfirmed inventory profit on an equity basis.

The interests in the unconfirmed inventory profit are:

$$P_E = .9Y_E + .7Z_E,$$
$$Y_E = .2Z_E,$$
$$Z_E = \$8,240 + .2P_E.$$

By substitution and simplification, solution values are determined to be:

$$P_E = \$8,800,$$
$$Y_E = \$2,000,$$
$$Z_E = \$10,000.$$

Since consolidated net income is but 80 percent of the parent company's equity basis net income (recall that only the parent company's shares held by nonaffiliate interests are determinants of consolidated net income), the effect of the above unconfirmed profit elimination is a reduction of consolidated net income by $7,040 (80 percent of $8,800).

The eliminating entry for consolidated working papers is:

1. If the amount of the elimination is based upon the parent company's equity in the selling affiliate:

Inventory (Income Statement division) 7,040
    Inventory (Balance Sheet division)   7,040

2. If the amount of the elimination is 100 percent of the unconfirmed profit:

Inventory (Income Statement division) 8,240
Inventory (Balance Sheet division)   8,240

In this instance, the amounts of minority interests in the unconfirmed profit on a consolidated basis are calculated as follows:

Minority interest in Y Company (10% of $2,000) .... $ 200
Minority interest in Z Company (10% of $10,000) 1,000
                                                            $1,200

Thus, the total elimination of $8,240 is allocated:

To the majority shareholders 7,040
To the minority shareholders 1,200
                                                           $8,240

Effects of Differential Amortization

Our illustrations of allocating income between majority and minority shareholders in a bilateral stockholding have ignored the existence of differential amortization. Normally, affiliates with an investment in another affiliate will have a differential that must be allocated and amortized, and thus differential amortization must be incorporated into our calculations.

In the case of multilevel affiliations, it was pointed out that use of a subsidiary's equity basis income will result in a proper allocation of the differential amortization between majority and minority shareholders. In bilateral affiliations, the same effect can be achieved by deducting each affiliate's differential amortization for the period from its income from operations, and then calculating the affiliates' equity basis incomes. Alternatively, the proper allocations of the affiliates' differential amortizations may be separately calculated in the same manner as was illustrated for unconfirmed intercompany profits. Note that if the parent company is bilaterally related to one or more of the subsidiaries, a portion of the parent company's differential amortization will be allocated to the minority shareholders; in all previous circumstances, the parent company's differential amortization was borne wholly by the majority shareholders.

Purchase of Shares in a Mutually Related Subsidiary

Reference has been repeatedly made to the necessity for eliminating the parent company's purchased equity in the accumulated retained earnings of a subsidiary at date of acquisition, assuming the purchase method of accounting for the acquisition is employed. In the event the subsidiary is a preexisting member of a reciprocally related corporate affiliation, it is important that the equity basis retained earnings of the subsidiary on this date be used as a basis for determining the amount of the retained earnings elimination. Similarly, where the parent is a controlling shareholder in a subsidiary prior to the latter's purchase of the parent's stock, it is also important that the parent's equity basis retained earnings be used in calculating the amount of the retained earnings elimination; necessarily, this amount is the at-acquisition equity-basis retained earnings of the parent.

Recording Equity in Affiliates' Earnings

The parent company in an affiliation involving bilateral stockholdings should carry its investment under the equity method, just like any other parent company.[3] There is a problem, however, in determining the proper carrying value for the investment when the parent company is bilaterally related to one or more of its subsidiaries. In particular, should the parent company record (1) its "equity basis" net income as calculated in the examples above, or (2) the majority interest in its "equity basis" net income, i.e., consolidated net income? Although the equity basis net income value seems to reflect the basic equity method concept, recall that *APB Opinion 18* states the following application principle: "The difference between consolidation and the equity method lies in the details reported in the financial statements. Thus, an investor's *net income for the period and its stockholders' equity at the end of the period* are the same whether an investment in a subsidiary is accounted for under the equity method or the subsidiary is consolidated. . . ."[4] In view of this stated principle, the appropriate value to be recorded would appear to be the majority interest in the parent's equity basis net income.

Recording the majority interest in the parent's equity basis net income will achieve equality between the parent company's net income and consolidated net income, as prescribed in *APB Opinion 18*. However, achieving the prescribed equality between the parent company's stockholders' equity and consolidated stockholders' equity is a problem that appears insoluble when the parent company and a subsidiary are bilaterally related. In consolidation, the subsidiary's investment in the parent company will be eliminated against the parent's stockholders' equity accounts. But there is no apparent way of achieving this elimination on the parent company's books that has any economic justification. Thus, in general,

---

[3] It is possible to construct hypothetical mutual stockholdings for which determination of the "parent" company is a moot point—for example, A Company owns 60 percent of B Company, and B Company owns 60 percent of A Company. However, such stockholdings would seldom, if ever, be encountered in practice.

[4] *APB Opinion 18,* paragraph 19. (Emphasis supplied.)

the parent company's stockholders' equity will be greater than consolidated stockholders' equity.[5]

In our consideration of multilevel affiliations earlier in this chapter, it was asserted that subsidiaries with an investment in another affiliate should carry the investment under the equity method. Use of this method provides relevant information to the subsidiary's minority shareholders, facilitates the consolidation process, and seems generally consistent with the "significant influence" criterion of *APB Opinion 18*. It is debatable, however, whether these same arguments can be used to justify the equity method for subsidiaries involved in a mutual stockholding. Particularly is this true when the reciprocal stockholdings exist between a subsidiary and the parent company. Accordingly, no general rule is appropriate for the method of accounting for a subsidiary's investment in an affiliate where mutual stockholdings are involved. Rather, each case must be evaluated on its individual merits.

Investment Elimination Entry

In the preparation of a consolidated statement working paper, all entries on the books of "investor" companies to recognize equities in affiliates' earnings for the period must be reversed, and the investment accounts must be eliminated against the related stockholders' equity accounts. Since one or more of the subsidiaries may not carry their investments on an equity basis, no general rules can be established for the investment elimination entries. In any particular circumstance, one may use the calculated minority (or majority) interest in the subsidiary's (or parent's) equity basis income and the minority (or majority) interest in January 1 retained earnings from the prior year's consolidated statement working paper for the appropriate extensions to the minority interest (or consolidated) column, and the remainder of the subsidiary's (or parent's) January 1 retained earnings is eliminated against the appropriate investment account. In the year of acquisition, of course, the elimination of the retained earnings at acquisition is based upon the supplementary calculation of purchased retained earnings. The eliminations against stockholders' equity accounts other than retained earnings will generally be analogous to eliminations for unilateral ownership configurations.

Matrix Applications for Complex Affiliations

The benefits to be derived from a matrix formulation of "complex" intercorporate stockholdings are especially significant and are illustrated in the paragraphs which follow.

---

[5] Apparently when *Opinion 18* was prepared, the Accounting Principles Board did not consider the special case of mutual stockholdings.

Assume the following affiliation diagram and supporting data for the year 19X1 are given:

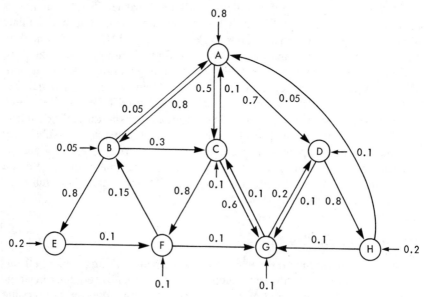

The affiliates' net incomes from their own operations are:

A Company....................................	$ 40,000
B Company....................................	30,000
C Company....................................	30,000
D Company....................................	40,000
E Company....................................	10,000
F Company....................................	20,000
G Company....................................	10,000
H Company....................................	20,000
	$200,000

As illustrated previously, the equity basis net incomes of the individual companies may be defined in algebraic form. Letting $A, B, \ldots, H$ denote net incomes of the respective companies on an equity basis, there results:

$$A = \$40,000 + .80B + .50C + .70D,$$
$$B = \$30,000 + .80E + .30C + .05A,$$
$$C = \$30,000 + .80F + .60G + .10A,$$
$$D = \$40,000 + .80H + .10G,$$
$$E = \$10,000 + .10F,$$
$$F = \$20,000 + .15B + .10G,$$
$$G = \$10,000 + .10C + .20D,$$
$$H = \$20,000 + .05A + .10G.$$

These equations may be rearranged in a form exhibiting the underlying matrix structure as follows:

$$
\begin{array}{llllll}
+ & A & -.80B & -.50C & -.70D & & & & = \$40,000 \\
-.05A & + & B & -.30C & & -.80E & & & = \$30,000 \\
-.10A & & + & C & & & -.80F & -.60G & = \$30,000 \\
& & & + & D & & & -.10G & -.80H = \$40,000 \\
& & & & + & E & -.10F & & = \$10,000 \\
& -.15B & & & & + & F & -.10G & = \$20,000 \\
& & -.10C & -.20D & & & + & G & = \$10,000 \\
-.05A & & & & & & -.10G & + & H = \$20,000.
\end{array}
$$

Based upon this equation system, the problem may be easily expressed in matrix form:

$$
\begin{bmatrix}
1 & -.80 & -.50 & -.70 & 0 & 0 & 0 & 0 \\
-.05 & 1 & -.30 & 0 & -.80 & 0 & 0 & 0 \\
-.10 & 0 & 1 & 0 & 0 & -.80 & -.60 & 0 \\
0 & 0 & 0 & 1 & 0 & 0 & -.10 & -.80 \\
0 & 0 & 0 & 0 & 1 & -.10 & 0 & 0 \\
0 & -.15 & 0 & 0 & 0 & 1 & -.10 & 0 \\
0 & 0 & -.10 & -.20 & 0 & 0 & 1 & 0 \\
-.05 & 0 & 0 & 0 & 0 & 0 & -.10 & 1
\end{bmatrix}
\begin{bmatrix}
A \\ B \\ C \\ D \\ E \\ F \\ G \\ H
\end{bmatrix}
=
\begin{bmatrix}
\$40,000 \\ \$30,000 \\ \$30,000 \\ \$40,000 \\ \$10,000 \\ \$20,000 \\ \$10,000 \\ \$20,000
\end{bmatrix}
$$

There now remains the arithmetical problem of calculating the inverse of this 8 × 8 coefficient matrix. After this inverse is computed, the matrix formulation assumes the form shown in Illustration 10–4.

By the simple process of matrix multiplication, the values for the equity basis net incomes of the eight companies are easily determined:

$$
\begin{bmatrix}
A \\ B \\ C \\ D \\ E \\ F \\ G \\ H
\end{bmatrix}
=
\begin{bmatrix}
\$203,322 \\ \$\ 80,741 \\ \$\ 99,114 \\ \$\ 70,245 \\ \$\ 13,550 \\ \$\ 35,507 \\ \$\ 33,961 \\ \$\ 33,562
\end{bmatrix}.
$$

Consolidated net income for 19X1 and the minority interests in subsidiary net incomes are now calculated as before:

Allocation of net incomes:
Consolidated net income (.80 × $203,322)		$162,658
Minority interests:		
B Company (.05 × $80,741)	$4,037	
C Company (.10 × $99,114)	9,911	
D Company (.10 × $70,245)	7,025	
E Company (.20 × $13,550)	2,710	
F Company (.10 × $35,507)	3,551	
G Company (.10 × $33,961)	3,396	
H Company (.20 × $33,562)	6,712	37,342
Total net incomes of affiliates		$200,000

Illustration 10–4

$$
\begin{bmatrix} A \\ B \\ C \\ D \\ E \\ F \\ G \\ H \end{bmatrix}
=
\begin{bmatrix}
1.19654 & 1.09201 & 1.01394 & 1.01372 & .87361 & .89852 & .88069 & .81097 \\
.10622 & 1.15050 & .43101 & .13985 & .92040 & .43685 & .32746 & .11188 \\
.14971 & .27266 & 1.24678 & .28506 & .21813 & 1.01924 & .90131 & .22805 \\
.05244 & .05040 & .06535 & 1.08473 & .04032 & .05631 & .24009 & .86778 \\
.00185 & .01763 & .00784 & .00455 & 1.01410 & .10768 & .01629 & .00364 \\
.01848 & .17631 & .07843 & .04552 & .14105 & 1.07685 & .16293 & .03642 \\
.02546 & .03735 & .13775 & .24545 & .02988 & .11319 & 1.13815 & .19636 \\
.06237 & .05834 & .06447 & .07523 & .04667 & .05624 & .15785 & 1.06018
\end{bmatrix}
\begin{bmatrix} \$40{,}000 \\ \$30{,}000 \\ \$30{,}000 \\ \$40{,}000 \\ \$10{,}000 \\ \$20{,}000 \\ \$10{,}000 \\ \$20{,}000 \end{bmatrix}
$$

The increased number of affiliates and the additional involvements of the incorporate stockholdings obviously introduce a number of complications in the arithmetic calculations of the equity basis net incomes. However, once these values are determined, the allocation of net incomes is only slightly more tedious than less complex affiliation structures.

A problem such as this may be solved using the iterative (trial and error) method. However, the practical value of the matrix method derives from the *permanence* of the inverse of the coefficient matrix. If there are no changes in the intercorporate shareholdings, the equity basis net incomes are easily determined each period (month, quarter, etc.) with one matrix multiplication. This characteristic of the matrix representation greatly alleviates the arithmetic complexities, as a single calculation of the inverse of the coefficient matrix provides a continuing basis for the relatively simple calculation of the affiliates' equity basis net incomes in subsequent periods. Multiplication of these values by the appropriate majority or minority shareholder interests then gives the desired solutions.[6]

BILATERAL STOCKHOLDINGS—TREASURY
STOCK METHOD

Some accountants take the position that the purchase of a parent company's stock by a subsidiary affiliate is not essentially unlike the parent's acquisition of "treasury shares." Where such stockholdings are thus accorded the status of treasury shares, it is appropriate to deduct the cost of these shares from the amounts of contributed capital and retained earnings of the parent company in the prepartion of consolidated financial statements. In this accounting treatment, the calculation of minority interests (unlike the conventional algebraic solution) is based upon the recorded amounts of a subsidiary's retained earnings arising from its own operations—*calculated without regard to the effects of bilateral share ownership.*

It should be noted that the traditional allocation method, explained above, also removes the parent company's shares held by affiliates from the consolidated balance sheet through the elimination of the affiliate's investment account against the stockholders' equity accounts of the parent. Thus, both methods are in conformity with current accounting policy, which states: "Shares of the parent held by a subsidiary should not be treated as outstanding stock in the consolidated balance sheet."[7] Where

---

[6] Roman Weil, "Reciprocal or Mutual Holdings," has shown that the second step of multiplying by the external shareholder interests may also be incorporated in the matrix solution, thus reducing the calculation to a single matrix multiplication.

[7] Section 2051.12, *APB Accounting Principles—Current Text.*

the methods differ is in their conception of the nature of the transaction. The treasury stock method presumes the subsidiary is acting in behalf of the parent, and thus the acquired shares do not participate in the allocation of earnings of the parent company (as they would not *if* the parent company had directly purchased the shares). The traditional allocation method, on the other hand, recognizes the minority shareholders' interest in this use of the subsidiary's assets by allocating a portion of the parent's income to the shares.[8]

If consolidated statements are prepared on the date reciprocal ownership of shares is established, the traditional allocation and treasury stock methods produce similar results (varying only in the amount of the differential in this transaction). Also, if the *total* amount of the subsidiaries' outstanding shares are held either by the parent or other subsidiaries, the effects produced on consolidated statements are again essentially the same. However, where neither condition prevails, the allocated amounts from applying the two methods will usually continue to diverge, in some instances materially.

In the following example, consolidated balance sheets are prepared both on the date of bilateral affiliation and on a subsequent date.

Case 7. On January 1, 19X1, P Company purchased 80 percent of the capital stock (par, $100) of Y Company concurrent with the latter's purchase of 20 percent of the capital stock (par, $100) of P Company. On this date, the balance sheet of each company is as illustrated in the following table:

	P Company	Y Company
Investments in corporate stock:		
P Company		$ 50,000
Y Company	$120,000	
Other assets	170,000	95,000
	$290,000	$145,000
Liabilities	$ 10,000	$ 5,000
Capital stock	200,000	100,000
Retained earnings	80,000	40,000
	$290,000	$145,000

---

[8] A recent survey of accounting practice suggested that normally the treasury stock method is applied in practice when a subsidiary holds shares of the parent company. Accountants International Study Group, *Consolidated Financial Statements: Current Recommended Practices in Canada, the United Kingdom, and the United States,* 1973, paragraph 67.

A consolidated balance sheet on this date is given following (treasury stock method):

P COMPANY AND SUBSIDIARY
Consolidated Balance Sheet
January 1, 19X1

Assets

Other assets		$265,000
Cost of investment in excess of corresponding book value of subsidiary stock		8,000
		$273,000

Equities

Liabilities		$ 15,000
Minority interest:		
Capital stock, Y Company	$ 20,000	
Retained earnings, Y Company	8,000	28,000
Owners' equity:		
Capital stock, P Company:		
Issued	$200,000	
Held by Y Company	40,000	
Held by nonaffiliates		160,000
Retained earnings:		
Consolidated retained earnings	$ 80,000	
Premium on treasury stock purchased	10,000	70,000
		$273,000

The reader will note that the conventional solution, incorporating the investment elimination of Y Company in P Company (see p. 384), would add to the consolidated balance sheet a $6,000 credit differential (contra to the $8,000 differential), and accordingly reduce consolidated retained earnings to $64,000 ($80,000 − 20 percent of $80,000).

Case 8. In this example, the data of Case 7 are repeated, adjusted for 19X1 earnings. It is assumed that the net income of each affiliate from its own operations for 19X1 is $30,000, with a corresponding increase in the amount of "other assets."

A consolidated balance sheet on December 31, 19X1, is presented as follows (treasury stock method):

P COMPANY AND SUBSIDIARY

Consolidated Balance Sheet
December 31, 19X1

Assets

Other assets		$325,000
Cost of investment in excess of corresponding book value of subsidiary stock		8,000
		$333,000

Equities

Liabilities		$ 15,000
Minority interest:		
Capital stock, Y Company	$ 20,000	
Retained earnings, Y Company	14,000	34,000
Owners' equity:		
Capital stock, P Company:		
Issued	$200,000	
Held by Y Company	40,000	
Held by nonaffiliates		160,000
Retained earnings:		
Consolidated retained earnings	*$134,000	
Premium on treasury stock purchased	10,000	124,000
		$333,000

* $110,000 + 80% of $30,000 = $134,000.

Use of the traditional allocation method in this instance will yield different allocations of retained earnings as between majority and minority shareholders. At acquisition, the following investment eliminations would be made:

	Dr. (Cr.)	
	P Company in Y Company	Y Company in P Company
Capital stock	$ 80,000	$ 40,000
Retained earnings	32,000	16,000
Differential	8,000	(6,000)
Investment	$(120,000)	$(50,000)

The conventional solution provides for the elimination of the "investment" of Y Company in P Company, in addition to the principal investment elimination of P Company in Y Company. The interdependency structure with respect to the allocation of the affiliates' net incomes may be represented as follows:

$$P = \text{Net income of P Company on an equity basis}$$
$$Y = \text{Net income of Y Company on an equity basis}$$

$$P = \$30,000 + .8Y$$
$$Y = \$30,000 + .2P$$

By substitution and simplification, solution values are:

$$P = \$64,285.71; \quad 80\% \quad \text{whereof} = \$51,428.57$$
$$Y = \$42,857.14; \quad 20\% \quad \text{whereof} = \$8,571.43$$

It follows that the allocation of $132,000 of retained earnings of companies P and Y (the combined retained earnings, $180,000, less the sum of the retained earnings eliminations, $48,000) is made:

Consolidated retained earnings ($64,000 + $51,428.57)	$115,428.57
Minority interest ($8,000 + $8,571.43)	16,571.43
Total	$132,000.00

In the illustrated treasury stock treatment, the allocation was made:

Consolidated retained earnings (net of premium on treasury stock purchased)	$124,000.00
Minority interest	14,000.00
Total	$138,000.00

The difference of $6,000 ($138,000 − $132,000) is attributable to the aforementioned alternative of either eliminating 20 percent of the retained earnings of the parent company ($16,000), or charging the premium on the treasury stock ($10,000) against consolidated retained earnings. However, the important difference exhibited in the postacquisition consolidated balance sheets is the disparity in the relative shares of the remaining retained earnings; this difference is a function of the different allocation ratios inherent in each method.

The allocation differences are magnified as the nonaffiliate shareholder interests in the mutually related affiliates increase; additionally, these differences continue to increase in succeeding consolidated financial statements.[9]

QUESTIONS

1. Define "multilevel affiliation," and illustrate by example (diagram) such an affiliation.

---

[9] A technique incorporating the treasury stock method for calculating consolidated net income and the traditional allocation method for calculating, as supplementary information, minority interest is proposed in Enrico Petri and Roland Minch, "The Treasury Stock Method and Conventional Method in Reciprocal Stockholdings—An Amalgamation," *The Accounting Review*, April 1974. Its validity, like the validity of the two methods individually, depends upon one's conception of the nature of a transaction wherein the subsidiary acquires the parent's stock.

2. In a multilevel affiliation, what method of accounting is used for a subsidiary's 30 percent investment in another affiliate? A 10 percent investment?

3. How is differential amortization recorded by a subsidiary with an investment in another affiliate allocated between majority and minority shareholders?

4. When intercompany profit exists at the second level of a multilevel affiliation, how is the minority interest calculated if 100 percent elimination is used? If fractional elimination is used?

5. A Company is the owner of 55 percent of the outstanding stock of B Company, while B Company holds 60 percent of the shares of C Company. Are consolidated statements justified? What is the criterion to apply in making such a decision?

6. Define "bilateral stockholding" and illustrate by example (diagram) such an affiliation.

7. What is meant by "equity basis net incomes" of reciprocally related members of an affiliation?

8. Briefly describe the successive iteration method in the context of a consolidation process involving reciprocal stockholdings.

9. Given a situation in which the affiliates of a consolidated entity have reciprocal stockholdings, explain why the sum of the equity basis net incomes exceeds the sum of the affiliates' net incomes from their own operations, notwithstanding the fact that the ultimate determination of majority and minority interests are equal in total to the summed net incomes from the affiliates' own operations.

10. Explain any additional complications in the calculation of consolidated net income that result from a situation in which the bilateral stockholdings involve the parent.

11. How is the elimination of intercompany profits on the transfer of assets complicated by the existence of reciprocal stockholdings?

12. How is differential amortization allocated between majority and minority shareholders in a bilateral stockholding?

13. When the parent company is bilaterally related to one or more of its subsidiaries, what amount is recorded by the parent company to recognize its equity in affiliates?

14. What do you see as the principal advantage of the matrix method over the other calculation methods in calculating the equity basis net incomes of reciprocally related affiliates?

15. How does the determination of minority interests differ as between the treasury stock method and the traditional allocation method?

EXERCISES

Exercise 10–1

On January 1, 19X1, P Company acquired a 90 percent interest in R Company, R Company acquired an 80 percent interest in S Company, and S Company acquired a 70 percent interest in T Company. Each of the companies earned $5,000 from their own operations during 19X1, except P Company which as a holding company had no income from operations.

No dividends were paid by any of the affiliates during 19X1. Ignore differentials.

Required:

Prepare a schedular calculation of consolidated net income for 19X1 using the incremental approach.

Exercise 10–2

Bravo Company purchased 70 percent of Charlie Company's outstanding stock on January 1, 19X1. Alpha Company purchased 80 percent of Bravo Company's outstanding stock on January 1, 19X2. Each of the three companies earned $10,000 from their own operations during 19X1 and 19X2. Each of the three companies declared annual dividends of $6,000 during 19X1 and 19X2. Each of the three firms had retained earnings of $50,000 on January 1, 19X1.

Assume differentials are allocated to nonamortizable assets.

Required:

a. What is Alpha Company's purchased equity in Bravo Company's retained earnings on January 1, 19X2?
b. Prepare the entries made on the books of Alpha Company and Bravo Company during 19X2 to account for their interests in affiliates.
c. Prepare a schedular calculation of consolidated net income for 19X2 using the incremental approach.
d. Calculate consolidated retained earnings at December 31, 19X2.

Exercise 10–3

On January 1, 19X1, P Company acquired a 90 percent interest in Y Company, and Y Company acquired a 70 percent interest in Z Company. In these purchase transactions, P Company had a debit differential of $25,000 and Y Company had a debit differential of $15,000. Both differentials were allocated wholly to goodwill, which is to be amortized over a ten year period.

During 19X1, the companies reported the following incomes from their own operations:

P Company	$30,000
Y Company	20,000
Z Company	10,000

Required:

a. Prepare the entries made on the books of P Company and Y Company at the end of 19X1 to record their equities in affiliates' earnings and differential amortization.
b. Prepare a schedular calculation of consolidated net income for 19X1 using the incremental approach.

Exercise 10–4

On January 1, 19X1, P Company purchased 80 percent of the outstanding stock of Y Company, and 70 percent of the outstanding stock of Z Company. On the same date, Y Company acquired 20 percent of Z Company's stock.

During 19X1, the companies reported the following incomes from their own operations:

P Company	$40,000
Y Company	30,000
Z Company	20,000

The net income of Z Company for 19X1 contains an element of unconfirmed intercompany profit in the amount of $5,000.

Required:

a. Prepare a schedular calculation of consolidated net income for 19X1 using the incremental approach.
b. Prepare a residual calculation of consolidated net income for 19X1, assuming:
  (1) 100 percent elimination
  (2) Fractional elimination

Exercise 10–5

A Company owns 80 percent of the capital stock of B Company, 70 percent of the capital stock of C Company, 60 percent of the capital stock of D Company, and 70 percent of the capital stock of E Company. Additionally, B Company owns 20 percent of the capital stock of C Company, D Company owns 30 percent of the capital stock of E Company, C Company owns 10 percent of the capital stock of B Company, and E Company owns 20 percent of the capital stock of D Company.

Net incomes from operations were:

Company A	$ 54,000
Company B	30,000
Company C	26,400
Company D	40,000
Company E	39,000
	$189,400

Required:

Using the traditional allocation method, compute consolidated net income for 19X1, and the minority interests in subsidiary net income. (Solution hint: Draw the affiliation diagram)

Exercise 10–6

The financial facts shown below pertain to corporations R and S which had mutual holdings of capital stock during and at the end of the fiscal year.

There has been no change in the mutual holdings during the year.

	Corporation	
	R	S
Of the issued capital stock:		
R owns	10 percent	50 percent
S owns	20 percent	10 percent
Net assets (exclusive of investment accounts),		
December 31, 19X1	$540,000	$590,000

Required:

Compute the dollar equity of outside shareholders in the total net assets of R and S, respectively.

(AICPA adapted)

Exercise 10–7

P Company owns 80 percent of the capital stock of S Company, and S Company owns 10 percent of the capital stock of P Company. During 19X1, the companies net incomes from their own operations were:

P Company	....	$20,000
S Company	....	15,000

Purchase differentials have been amortized in prior years.

Required:

a. Using the traditional allocation method, compute consolidated net income for 19X1, and the minority interest in S Company's net income.
b. Using the treasury stock method, compute consolidated net income for 19X1, and the minority interest in S Company's net income.

Exercise 10–8

A Company owns 90 percent of the capital stock of B Company, 80 percent of the capital stock of C Company, and 80 percent of the capital stock of D Company. Additionally, C Company owns 80 percent of the capital stock of E Company, and E Company holds 5 percent of the outstanding stock of C Company.

Net incomes for the year 19X1 from the companies' own operations were:

A Company	....	$50,000
B Company	....	30,000
C Company	....	32,000
D Company	....	30,000
E Company	....	20,000

Required:

Using the traditional allocation method, compute consolidated net income for 19X1 and the minority interests in subsidiary net income. (Solution hint: Draw the affiliation diagram.)

PROBLEMS

Problem 1

On January 1, 19X1, B Company purchased an 80 percent interest in C Company. A Company purchased a 90 percent interest in B Company on January 1, 19X3. Both A and B utilize the equity method in accounting for their interests in subsidiaries.

Relevant data for 19X3 is as follows:

	A Company	B Company	C Company
Common stock, January 1, 19X3	$200,000	$100,000	$50,000
Retained earnings, January 1, 19X3	100,000	26,000	18,000
Investment in C Company, January 1, 19X3		56,400	
Investment in B Company, January 1, 19X3	120,000		
Net income for 19X3, excluding equity in affiliates' income	20,000	10,000	10,000
Dividends paid in 19X3	10,000	5,000	6,000

Assume both differentials are allocated to Land.

Required:

a. Prepare the investment elimination entries for a consolidated balance sheet on January 1, 19X3.
b. Prepare a *partial* consolidated statement working paper for 19X3.
c. Prepare a schedular calculation of consolidated net income for 19X3 using the incremental approach.

Problem 2

On January 1, 19X1, P Company acquired an 80 percent interest in Y Company at a cost of $78,000, and Y Company acquired a 90 percent interest in Z Company at a cost of $56,000. The stockholders' equity accounts of the affiliates on this date were:

	P Company	Y Company	Z Company
Capital stock	$50,000	$40,000	$20,000
Retained earnings	30,000	20,000	20,000

The differentials are to be allocated wholly to goodwill, and are to be amortized over a ten year period.

Each of the three companies earned $10,000 from their own operations during 19X1 and 19X2. No dividends were paid by any of the affiliates.

Required:

a. Prepare the entries made on the books of P Company and Y Company at the end of 19X2 to record their equities in affiliates' earnings for 19X2 and differential amortization for 19X2.
b. Prepare a *partial* consolidated statement working paper for the year ended

December 31, 19X2. (Hint: Make the income statement division eliminations for differential amortization against "net income, excluding equity in
affiliates' earnings.")

c. Prepare a schedular calculation of consolidated net income for 19X2 using
the incremental approach.

Problem 3

Y Company purchased 80 percent of Z Company's outstanding stock on
January 1, 19X1, and on January 1, 19X2, P Company purchased 80 percent
of Y Company's stock. Each of the three companies earned $20,000 from their
own operations during 19X1 and 19X2, and each had retained earnings of
$30,000 on January 1, 19X1.

The net income of Z Company for 19X1 contains an element of unconfirmed
inventory profit of $5,000, and Z Company's net income for 19X2 contains
unconfirmed inventory profit at the end of that year of $2,000.

Assume no dividends are paid by the affiliates, and ignore differentials.

Required:

a. Prepare a schedular calculation of consolidated net income for 19X2 using
the incremental approach.

b. Prepare a residual calculation of consolidated net income for 19X2, assuming:

(1) 100 percent elimination
(2) Fractional elimination

c. Prepare a *partial* consolidated statement working paper for the year ended
December 31, 19X2, assuming 100 percent elimination of the unconfirmed
inventory profits. (Hint: Make the income statement division eliminations
for beginning and ending inventory against "net income, excluding equity
in affiliates' earnings.")

Problem 4

For the year 19X1, companies X, Y, and Z have net incomes from their own
operations of $30,000, $20,000, and $9,500 respectively.

Required:

Using the traditional allocation method, compute consolidated net income
and the minority interest in subsidiary net income for the year 19X1 in each of
the following independent cases:

Case 1: X Company has an 80 percent interest in Y Company, and Y Company has a 10 percent interest in X Company.

Case 2: X Company owns 80 percent of the stock of Y Company, Y Company owns 80 percent of the stock of Z Company, and Z Company
has a 10 percent interest in Y Company.

Case 3: X Company has a 90 percent interest in Y Company, Y Company has a 60 percent interest in Z Company, and Z Company has a 10 percent interest in X Company.

Problem 5

On January 1, 19X0, the Gregory Company purchased 80 percent of the capital stock of the Morris Company and 60 percent of the capital stock of the Adams Company. On January 1, 19X1, the Morris Company purchased 30 percent of the capital stock of the Adams Company. Also on January 1, 19X1, the Adams Company purchased 20 percent of the capital stock of the Gregory Company.

During 19X1 the net incomes from operations were:

Gregory Company	$42,800
Morris Company	40,000
Adams Company	10,000

Required:

a. Calculate consolidated net income for 19X1.
b. Calculate the interests of the majority and minority shareholders in intercompany profit, assuming that unconfirmed inventory profit is included in the selling affiliates' 19X1 incomes as follows:

Morris Company	$3,000
Adams Company	2,000

c. Specify the amount of unconfirmed inventory profit that would be eliminated in the 19X1 consolidated statement working paper for:

(1) 100 percent elimination
(2) Fractional elimination

d. Still assuming the existence of the unconfirmed inventory profits, calculate consolidated net income for 19X1 and the minority interests in net income for:

(1) 100 percent elimination
(2) Fractional elimination

Problem 6

A diagram depicting the intercompany stock ownership of companies X, Y, and Z on January 1, 19X1, follows:

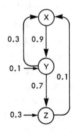

Net incomes from operations for 19X1 were:

X Company	$71,000
Y Company	37,600
Z Company	35,400

Y Company's net income includes $3,000 of unconfirmed profit in the ending inventory of X Company; the originating sale was made during 19X1.

Required:

Prepare the eliminating entry for unconfirmed inventory profit and calculate majority and minority interests in 19X1 net income assuming:

a. One hundred percent elimination of unconfirmed inventory profit.
b. Fractional elimination of unconfirmed inventory profit.

Problem 7

On January 1, 19X1, P Company acquires 90 percent of the capital stock of S Company for $37,000, and S Company acquires 20 percent of the capital stock of P Company for $20,000. The stockholders' equity accounts of the companies on this date were:

	P Company	S Company
Capital stock	$20,000	$10,000
Retained earnings	50,000	20,000

The differentials are to be allocated wholly to goodwill, and are to be amortized over a ten year period.

Both companies earned $10,000 from their own operations during 19X1, and neither paid any dividends.

Required:

a. Using the traditional allocation method, calculate consolidated net income for 19X1 and minority interest in S Company's net income.
b. Using the treasury stock method, calculate consolidated net income for 19X1 and minority interest in S Company's net income.
c. Calculate the values that would be shown for minority interest and stockholders' equity in the December 31, 19X1 consolidated balance sheet under each of the two methods.

11

Consolidated Statements— Miscellaneous; Branch Accounting

THE ENTITY THEORY

THE PREPARATION of consolidated financial statements has heretofore emphasized the unique importance of the controlling shareholders—i.e., those individuals (excluding affiliates) owning voting shares of the parent company. This "parent company" concept is essentially a *proprietary theory* approach—similar in concept to most of the accounting conventions for single enterprises. Notwithstanding this emphasis, special effort has been made to disclose the value of the rights of minority claimants. The separateness of this shareholder interest group is indicated by its classification between the liabilities and stockholders' equity divisions in the consolidated balance sheet.

Theorists have sometimes taken the position, however, that the total resources of any enterprise have a unity or entity status in which the various owner and creditor claimants have an undivided and indistinguishable interest. An extension of this concept to the prepartion of consolidated financial statements was made in 1944 by Professor Maurice Moonitz in a monograph, *The Entity Theory of Consolidated Statements.* This monograph gives expression, in perhaps its most refined form, to the relevance of the entity concept to the reports of corporate affiliations. In respect to equity interests, the entity theory, literally interpreted, denies the primacy of the controlling shareholder group; rather, its interest is fused with those of minority shareholders and is accorded no preferential accounting treatment, either in measurement or classification.

Prevailing practices of consolidated statement preparation cannot be neatly summarized as being wholly consistent with either the "parent company" or "entity" concepts.[1] Of course, these theories do not provide contradictory arguments for all aspects of consolidated statement preparation. Nevertheless, the entity theory has definite implications regarding several computations and forms of presentation in consolidated statements. Specific areas influenced by the principal thrust of the entity theory argument include the calculation of the differential at acquisition, the amount of the unconfirmed (or unrealized) profit elimination on asset transfers among affiliates, the elimination of unamortized discounts or premiums on intercompany bondholdings, and the calculations and disclosure of the equity of minority shareholders.

Debit and Credit Differentials

Where less than 100 percent of a subsidiary company's stock is purchased by a parent company, it is usual to recognize the difference between the acquisition cost and the corresponding purchased equity in the subsidiary's stockholders' equity accounts as a debit or credit differential, which is then allocated to specific assets and liabilities. The entity theorist would insist that the *total* differential implicit in the purchase cost (not merely the excess amount attributable to the majority interest payment) be formally recognized. For example, if 90 percent of a subsidiary's capital stock is acquired at a cost of $8,100 more than the equity in the corresponding book value of the subsidiary's shares, a differential would be recognized under the entity concept in the amount of $9,000 ($8,100 ÷ 90%), appropriate credit therein being given to minority shareholders for $900. Thus, the $8,100 reflects the cost to acquire a 90 percent interest in the undervalued or unrecorded assets—tangible or intangible.

Intercompany Profit on Asset Transfers

Reference has been made previously to the necessity for eliminating unconfirmed intercompany profit on sales of merchandise or other assets between corporate affiliates. The previous dicussion of this matter recognized two alternative procedures: eliminating 100 percent of such profit, or the parent company's fractional interest therein. The entity theorist would argue for a total elimination of the intercompany profit element, proportionally applied to majority and minority shareholders. This view harmonizes with the concept of an integrated proprietary equity; a partial elimination (the controlling interest in unconfirmed intercompany profit) preserves the separate identities of majority and minority share-

---

[1] A recent study suggested that the "parent company" concept is generally applied in practice, although there is some diversity in applying it. Accountants International Study Group, *Consolidated Financial Statements: Current Recommended Practices in Canada, the United Kingdom, and the United States*, 1973, paragraphs 23–27.

holders. Defense of fractional elimination rests heavily on the argument that such intercompany profit is confirmed, or realized, *from the viewpoint of minority shareholders.* The entity theorist would answer that consolidated statements are not presumed to be based upon any distinction, legal or otherwise, between shareholder classes. The reader is encouraged to refer again to Chapter 7 to review the consolidated statement working papers which distinguish between the fractional elimination and the 100 percent elimination of unconfirmed profit on intercompany asset transfers. It is sufficient to note here that neither consolidated net income nor consolidated retained earnings is a function of the amount of the eliminated profit. Reconciliation of the two views in respect to the intercompany profit elimination is explained in terms of the calculation of the amount of minority interests.

Unamortized Discounts/Premiums on Intercompany Bondholdings

It is appropriate to eliminate unamortized discounts or premiums on intercompany-held bonds *as if* such bonds were retired at par value. From the standpoint of the entity, the purchase transaction is not essentially unlike that of a company's purchase of its own bonds, i.e., the acquisition of treasury bonds. For an affiliation of companies, the purchase of intercompany bonds—essentially a constructive bond retirement—may produce "gain" or "loss" to the extent of intercompany unamortized discounts or premiums on the books of the relevant affiliates. The amount of gain or loss given recognition in consolidated statements may be either total or fractional. The 100 percent recognition of the amount of such gain or loss accords with the entity theory; recognition of a partial amount ignores the bond retirement effect in respect to the minority shareholders. In either case, it remains important to eliminate the effects of subsequent amortization of discounts or premiums in order to neutralize any duplicate recognition of gain or loss on acquisition. In regard to intercompany bondholdings, the arguments which were offered in respect to the amount of the confirmed profit recognition are equally valid, whether in defense of, or in rejection of, the entity theory.

Minority Shareholder Interests

The acceptance of the entity notion for consolidated statements carries with it the obligation to regard all shareholders as equal per share claimants to the combined resources of the affiliated companies. The presentation of shareholders' interests should be made in such manner as to clearly indicate the values attributable to controlling and noncontrolling interests, *but without reference to legal preference or implications as to hierarchical status.* Clearly, according to this view, an identification of minority interests as liabilities in consolidated statements is inappropriate; it may also be argued that the compromise consolidated balance sheet position between the liabilities and the controlling stockholders' equity divisions violates the spirit of the entity theory.

Additionally, the measurement of consolidated net income is necessarily independent of assignments of interests therein to the shareholder groups. Thus, consolidated net income must be redefined under the entity theory as the confirmed profits of the parent company from its own operations, plus the confirmed profits of the subsidiary company. In contrast to the conventional calculation technique, this revised definition focuses upon the income aggregates after eliminations but before deduction of "minority interest." The consolidated net income is then allocated between the two shareholder groups in the normal manner. Calculation of consolidated retained earnings, and relative interests therein, proceeds in a similar fashion.

Illustrative Problem—Entity Theory

P Company purchased 90 percent of the capital stock of S Company on January 1, 19X1 for $64,800. Trial balances of the affiliates on December 31, 19X1, are as follows:

	P Company	S Company
Investment in S Company	$ 88,020	
Inventory, January 1	30,000	$ 20,000
Other assets	127,200	89,000
Purchases	90,000	70,000
Expenses	10,000	8,000
	$345,220	$187,000
Liabilities	$ 2,000	$ 7,000
Capital stock (par, $100)	100,000	50,000
Retained earnings	60,000	20,000
Sales	160,000	110,000
Equity in subsidiary earnings	23,220	
	$345,220	$187,000
Inventory, December 31	$ 20,000	$ 15,000

Sales of merchandise by S Company to P Company during 19X1 amounted to $40,000; the cost of these goods to S Company was $32,000; $5,000 of this merchandise remained in the inventory of P Company on December 31, 19X1. The differential is allocated wholly to goodwill, and amortized over a ten-year period.

The differential for this example is calculated as follows:

Investment cost	$64,800
Purchased equity in S Company net assets:	
Capital stock (90% × $50,000)	$45,000
Retained earnings (90% × $20,000)	18,000
	$63,000
Excess of P Company's cost over purchased equity in recorded net assets of S Company	$ 1,800

Under the parent company concept, a differential of $1,800 would be recognized in the consolidated statement working paper, and allocated to specific assets and liabilities based upon the parent's share of the difference between fair value and book value. Under the entity concept, however, the $1,800 is regarded as a measure of 90 percent (the purchased interest) of the *total* differential between the fair value and the book value of S Company. Accordingly, the total differential of $2,000 ($1,800 ÷ 90%)[2] would be recognized in the consolidated statement working paper, with $200 credit therein being given to the minority shareholders for their interest in this unrecorded value (10% × $2,000).

The investment elimination entry at acquisition under the entity concept would be:

```
Capital stock ....................................  45,000
Retained earnings ...............................  18,000
Differential ....................................   2,000
     Minority interest in differential .................          200
     Investment in S Company .....................             64,800
```

Allocation and amortization of the $2,000 differential on the consolidated statement working paper is analogous to the procedure outlined in Chapter 5, except that under the entity concept amortization must be allocated between the majority and minority shareholders. Note that the majority shareholders' interest in the values assigned to assets (and the subsequent amortization thereof) is the same as it is under the parent company concept, i.e., 90 percent of $2,000, or $1,800. Thus, as was observed above, the entity concept results in the recognition of additional values allocable to the minority shareholders, without changing the values attributed to majority shareholders.

On the books of the parent company, differential amortization is based upon the parent's interest in the total differential, or $1,800. Elimination of unconfirmed intercompany profits is also still based upon the parent's interest therein. Hence, parent company accounting for its investment is unaffected by the choice of the entity or parent company concept for the consolidated statements.

The consolidated statement working paper for this example is presented in Illustration 11–1. The modification in format reflects the different orientation of the entity concept. Formal financial statements are presented in Illustration 11–2. Observe that the amounts assigned to majority shareholder interests in these statements are equivalent to the amounts that would be identified as consolidated net income and consolidated stockholders' equity under the parent company concept.

---

[2] Viewed from a different perspective, the parent's investment cost of $64,800 for a 90 percent ownership interest implies a total fair value for S Company's net assets of $72,000 ($64,800 ÷ 90%). Since the total book value of S Company's net assets is $70,000, this calculation yields a total differential of $2,000. The two calculational approaches are equivalent.

THE TRIAL BALANCE WORKING PAPER

The three-division horizontal form of consolidated statement working paper has been consistently used throughout the previous chapters. Consistency of usage has obvious advantages for instructional purposes. There are, however, a wide variety of working paper forms that can be used in the preparation of consolidated statements. Regardless of the particular form used, the fundamental principles of consolidated statement preparation remain the same. Specific forms may have special advantages in differing situations, but the resultant consolidated statements are not dependent on the form selected.

As an alternative to the three-division working paper that utilizes the financial statements of each affiliate as input data, consolidated statements may be prepared by using the trial balances of the constituent companies. Where the account data are summarized in this form, a different working paper construction may be used which avoids the necessity of preclassifying the accounts in financial statement terms. One appropriate format provides vertical columns for the individual statements, arranged in sequence, to which the account balances *net of eliminations* are extended. The reader will recognize that the differences introduced by such a working paper are primarily subtleties of form. For example, the three-division horizontal working paper provides for the collection and summation of account information in respect to a given statement in vertically arranged subdivisions, while the trial balance form simply calls for a series of vertical columns as the organizing framework for statement classification and summation.

For illustrative purposes, assume that P Company acquired 90 percent of the capital stock of S Company on January 1, 19X1, at a cost of $61,000. The December 31, 19X1, trial balances of companies P and S are as follows:

	P Company		S Company	
Cash	$ 29,500		$ 8,000	
Accounts receivable	18,000		3,000	
Merchandise (1/1/X1)	16,000		4,000	
Investment in S Company	74,500			
Other assets	66,000		62,000	
Accounts payable		$ 22,000		$ 5,000
Other liabilities		6,000		
Capital stock		100,000		50,000
Retained earnings (1/1/X1)		40,000		10,000
Dividends declared	10,000		5,000	
Sales		78,000		40,000
Equity in subsidiary earnings		18,000		
Purchases	42,000		20,000	
Expenses	8,000		3,000	
	$264,000	$264,000	$105,000	$105,000
Merchandise (12/31/X1)	$ 10,000		$ 7,000	

Illustration 11-1

P COMPANY AND SUBSIDIARY S COMPANY

Consolidated Statement Working Paper (Entity Concept)
For Year Ended December 31, 19X1

	P Company	S Company	Eliminations Dr.	Eliminations Cr.	Consolidated	Assignable to Minority	Assignable to Majority
Income Statement:							
Sales	160,000	110,000	(5) 40,000		230,000		
Equity in subsidiary earnings	23,220		(1) 23,220		–0–		
Inventory (12/31)	20,000	15,000	(6) 1,000*		34,000		
Total credits	203,220	125,000			264,000		
Inventory (1/1)	30,000	20,000			50,000		
Purchases	90,000	70,000		(5) 40,000	120,000		
Expenses	10,000	8,000	(4) 200		18,200		
Total debits	130,000	98,000			188,200		
Net income	73,220	27,000			75,800		
Assignable to minority shareholders						2,580†	
Assignable to majority shareholders							73,220‡
Net income—carried forward	73,220	27,000	64,420	40,000	75,800	2,580	73,220
Retained Earnings Statement:							
Retained earnings, January 1, 19X1:							
P Company	60,000				60,000		60,000
S Company		20,000	(2) 18,000		2,000	2,000	
Net income—brought forward	73,220	27,000	64,420	40,000	75,800	2,580	73,220
Retained earnings, December 31, 19X1—carried forward	133,220	47,000	82,420	40,000	137,800	4,580	133,220

Balance Sheet:

	P Company	S Company	Eliminations Dr	Eliminations Cr	Consolidated	Minority Interest	Consolidated Balance Sheet
Other assets	127,200	89,000			216,200		
Inventory	20,000	15,000		(6) 1,000	34,000		
Investment in S Company	88,020			(1) 23,220 (2) 64,800	–0–		
Differential			(2) 2,000	(3) 2,000			
Goodwill			(3) 2,000	(4) 200	1,800		
	235,220	104,000			252,000		
Liabilities	2,000	7,000			9,000		
Minority interest in differential				(2) 200	200	200	
Capital stock:							
P Company	100,000				100,000		100,000
S Company		50,000	(2) 45,000		5,000	5,000	
Retained earnings—brought forward	133,220	47,000	(2) 82,420	40,000	137,800	4,580	133,220
	235,220	104,000	131,420	131,420	252,000	9,780	233,220

* Gross profit percentage: $8,000/$40,000 = 20\%$. Unconfirmed inventory profits: 20% of $5,000 = $1,000$.

† 10% ($27,000 − $1,000$) − 10% (200) = $2,580$.

‡ $50,000 + 90% ($27,000 − $1,000$) − 90% (200) = $73,220$.

Illustration 11–2

P COMPANY AND SUBSIDIARY S COMPANY

Consolidated Income Statement (Entity Concept)
For Year Ended December 31, 19X1

Sales		$230,000
Cost of sales:		
Inventory, January 1	$ 50,000	
Purchases	120,000	
	$170,000	
Inventory, December 31	34,000	136,000
Operating margin		$ 94,000
Expenses		18,200
Consolidated net income		$ 75,800
Assignable to minority shareholders		$ 2,580
Assignable to majority shareholders		73,220

P COMPANY AND SUBSIDIARY S COMPANY

Consolidated Balance Sheet (Entity Concept)
December 31, 19X1

Assets		*Equities*	
Inventory	$ 34,000	Liabilities	$ 9,000
Other assets	216,200	Stockholders' equity:	
Unrecorded asset value implicit		Majority shareholders	233,220
in the purchase cost which is		Minority shareholders	9,780
in excess of corresponding			
book value of subsidiary			
stock	1,800		
	$252,000		$252,000

Based on the data provided above, a trial balance working paper is presented in Illustration 11–3. (Allocation of the differential is ignored.)

In a modified form of this trial balance working paper, sometimes encountered on the *Uniform Certified Public Accountant Examination,* one column labeled "consolidated balances" replaces the last four columns in Illustration 11–3. Using this format, a separate "row" must be provided to accumulate the minority interest additions and deductions; otherwise, the working paper operations are similar to those illustrated.

CONSOLIDATED STATEMENTS—A REVIEW

Consolidated financial statements are the summary reports of an affiliation of companies, prepared without regard to the separate legal status of member affiliates. Among the criteria for determining the propriety of including the accounts of a subsidiary in consolidated statements are the parent company's ownership of more than 50 percent of its voting shares, the present exercise and anticipated continuity of effective managerial and financial control by the parent company, a general homogeneity of assets and operations of the affiliates, and a general coincidence of accounting periods. Consolidated statements purport to reflect the results of transactions of the affiliation with nonaffiliate interests; accordingly, to the extent that there are intercompany transactions among the affiliates, their effects must be excluded from the accounts of the consolidated statements. Among the more important types of such eliminations are the following:

1. *Investment elimination.* Of first importance in the sequence of eliminations is the elimination of the investment account of the parent company against the parent's equity in the corresponding book value of the subsidiary's capital stock. Essentially, this elimination results in a substitution of the subsidiary's net assets for the parent company's investment account. The substitution is made in terms of total subsidiary net assets, and the minority shareholders' equity therein is given appropriate recognition in the financial statements. In the event that there exist several classes of subsidiary stock, it is important that an appropriate allocation of the subsidiary's total stockholders' equity be made as between the different classes. If the subsidiary's shares are purchased in blocks at different dates, it is also important to analyze the book value appertaining to each block separately at the relevant acquisition date. Although control may be deferred until a subsequent purchase, the elimination in respect to the first purchase should relate to the at-acquisition book values of subsidiary stock. Where shares are purchased directly from a subsidiary affiliate, it is important to determine the changes produced in the accounts of the subsidiary as a result of the new issue. For this reason, it is desirable to compare the parent's equity in the stockholders' equity accounts of the subsidiary immediately before the new issue with the equity immediately after the issuance. The variation in dollar equity is identified as the increase (decrease) attributable to the new issue.

2. *Asset-liability eliminations.* All assets which arise out of intercompany transactions for which there exist offsetting liabilities on the books of an affiliate must be eliminated. The amount of the elimination is 100 percent, notwithstanding the parent company's less-than-100-percent share ownership in the relevant affiliate.

3. *Revenue-expense eliminations.* Revenues and expenses produced by intercompany transactions must also be totally eliminated. As in the case of asset-liability eliminations, the amount of the elimination is not a function of the parent company's equity in the participating affiliates.

4. *Intercompany profit eliminations.* To the extent that asset transfers between affiliates result in profit recognition by the selling affiliate, a residue of which remains in the assets of the purchasing affiliate, such profit should be eliminated. The amount of the profit, unconfirmed or unrealized from the point of view of the consolidated entity, may be either totally or partially eliminated. Some accountants prefer the fractional elimination, believing that the legal interests of minority shareholders

Illustration 11–3
P COMPANY AND SUBSIDIARY S COMPANY
Trial Balance Consolidated Statement Working Paper
For Year Ended December 31, 19X1

	P Company	S Company	Eliminations Dr.	Eliminations Cr.	Income Statement	Retained Earnings Statement	Minority Interest	Balance Sheet
Debits								
Cash	29,500	8,000						37,500
Accounts receivable	18,000	3,000						21,000
Merchandise inventory (1/1/X1)	16,000	4,000			20,000			–0–
Investment in S Company	74,500			(1) 13,500 (2) 61,000				
Other assets	66,000	62,000						128,000
Dividends declared	10,000	5,000		(1) 4,500		10,000	500	
Purchases	42,000	20,000			62,000			
Expenses	8,000	3,000			11,000			
Differential		3,000	(2) 7,000					7,000
	264,000	105,000						
Merchandise inventory (12/31/X1)	10,000	7,000						17,000
Income statement debits—S Company—deducted contra		27,000						
Total debits—deducted contra					93,000	10,000	500	210,500

Credits

Credits	P Company	S Company	Eliminations			
Accounts payable	22,000	5,000				27,000
Other liabilities	6,000					6,000
Capital stock:						
P Company	100,000					100,000
S Company		50,000	(2) 45,000		5,000	
Retained earnings, January 1, 19X1:						
P Company	40,000			40,000		
S Company		10,000	(2) 9,000		1,000	
Sales	78,000	40,000		118,000		
Equity in subsidiary earnings	18,000		(1) 18,000			
	264,000	105,000				
Merchandise inventory (12/31/X1)	10,000	7,000		17,000		
Total credits				135,000 [93,000]	40,000 [10,000]	6,000 [500]
Total debits				42,000		
Combined net income						
Income statement credits—S Company		47,000				
Income statement debits—S Company		27,000				
Net income—S Company		20,000		[2,000]	40,000	2,000
Minority interest—10% whereof		2,000				
Consolidated net income				40,000	40,000	
Consolidated retained earnings					70,000	70,000
Minority interest in S Company					7,500	7,500 M
		79,000	79,000	79,000	7,500	210,500

[deduction]

should not be diminished, or otherwise compromised, by the elimination process. There is authoritative support, however, for the 100 percent elimination, the results of which are that the eliminated profit is absorbed ratably by both majority and minority shareholders of the selling affiliate.

5. *Intercompany bond eliminations.* As in the case of other intercompany transactions, it is important to eliminate the effects of intercompany-held bonds. No special difficulty is encountered where the carrying value of the bond investment and the book value of the bond liability are both equal to the par value of the bonds. However, where this equivalence does not exist, due to unamortized issuance discount or premium and/or purchase discount or premium, there exists a consolidated basis "gain or loss" on the acquisition (constructive retirement) of these bonds. The amount of such gain or loss to be reported in the consolidated income statement may be either 100 percent, or the majority shareholders' interest therein. This choice of elimination method essentially parallels that for unconfirmed intercompany profit on asset transfers.

It is important to recognize that the accountant's election to eliminate all, or a fractional interest in, these profit elements will affect the reported interests of minority shareholders. The majority interest elimination requires that the amount of minority interests be calculated on the basis of a subsidiary's recorded book net income. The 100 percent elimination requires that the amount of minority interests be calculated on the basis of the subsidiary's *confirmed* net income.

BRANCH ACCOUNTING

Business expansion is achieved by carefully conceived programs for new investment in productive assets or by plans to improve and optimize the use of present facilities. Any substantive enlargement in the scale of business operations, however, entails significant organizational changes. Expansion may take the form of an integration of allied business interests by merger agreements, or by an investment in the corporate stock of affiliate companies. On other occasions, expansion may be accomplished by the creation of new sales—and perhaps production—outlets to exploit heretofore undeveloped geographic areas or to more intensively cultivate existing markets. In the latter instance, agencies or branch offices are often the optimal organizational forms.

Agencies and Branches

While both the agency and the branch office are vehicles for enlarging sales volume, they exhibit a number of significant operational differences. An agency usually carries sample or display merchandise and accepts orders for delivery by the home office only. The credit status of prospective buyers is appraised, and judgments in respect thereto are rendered by the home office; customers' remittances are normally made to the home office. On the other hand, a branch normally carries a full complement of merchandise, makes the usual warranties respecting quality, makes collections of accounts receivable, and functions in many respects as an autonomous and formally structured business unit.

While these characteristics are descriptive in general terms of the typical agency and branch, it is not unusual to find compromise forms of business subdivisions. On occasions, the agency may carry a full line of merchandise, make collections of accounts receivable, or otherwise accept responsibilities normally reserved to the branch. Similarly, a branch may sometimes be denied some of the autonomy of operation previously noted.

The extent of branch self-management is a function of corporate policy in regard to decentralized operating and administrative control. While different branches within the same company may be accorded different degrees of administrative authority, the status of each branch as an operating subdivision will usually be established by general standards which extend company-wide.

The data accumulation process for the operations of agencies does not introduce any new accounting problems, as an agency is essentially little more than an extension of existing sales territories; consequently, the discussion which follows will be confined to accounting for branches.

Branch Accounts

Branch accounting is essentially an application of the controlling account principle in which the subsidiary records are those of a reasonably independent operating unit. In respect to transactions with the branch, it is conventional for the home office to adopt an account terminology which clearly identifies and describes branch operations. The accounts are selected on the basis of expected frequency of use, their relevance to branch operations, and their contribution to overall accounting control. The general ledger controlling account is variously referred to as Branch Current, Branch Account, or Investment in Branch.

Equivalence of debit and credit balances is preserved in the branch ledger by the use of a Home Office Current account, which is reciprocal to the Branch Current account. The Home Office Current account has a number of properties which traditionally characterize a proprietorship account, particularly in respect to the branch closing process; branch profits and losses are periodically closed thereinto. However, viewed more precisely, the account has no special identity, and its balance is perhaps best described as merely the algebraic sum of all other account balances in the branch ledger.

The Branch Current account is normally charged with the cost of assets or services contributed to the branch by the home office and is credited with remittances from the branch. Periodically, the account is adjusted to give effect to branch net income or loss. Where there are numerous branches, the use of separate current accounts for each branch is often desirable. Although there is no evident consensus as to the specific accounts most appropriate for inclusion in the branch records, it is usual to find only those accounts most closely allied with branch operations, such as those which relate to sales, accounts receivables, inventories, expenses incurred by the branch, etc. It is not uncommon to find the accounts of the branch fixed assets in the home office records; yet, depreciation expense in respect thereto may be recorded by the branch making use of the property. In some instances, other expenses incurred by the home office which are in support of branch operations may also be allocated to the benefiting branch. Notice of such expense assignment should be given the relevant branch for purposes of entry in the branch records. Such an identification of expenses with specific branches makes it possible to measure more accurately the operating efficiency of each branch as an independent entity. Those expenses incurred by the home office for the benefit of several branches which do not accommodate to convenient allocation, however, are best reflected in aggregates in combined financial statements of the branches and the home office. If expenses applicable to one or more branches are not formally assigned to, and recorded by, the branches, they are usually charged against the branch net income or loss recorded by the home office in the closing process.

Illustrative Entries

The following transactions relate to the establishment of a branch and its first month's operations:

(1) Cash is transferred to the branch, $1,000.
(2) Merchandise costing $5,000 is shipped to the branch. Billing of home office shipment is made at cost.
(3) Expenses are incurred and paid by the branch, $200.
(4) Additional merchandise, costing $2,500, is acquired by the branch from outside wholesalers.
(5) Branch credit sales are $8,000.
(6) Branch collections on account amount to $4,700.
(7) Cash remitted by the branch to the home office is $1,000.
(8) Closing entries are prepared by the branch; a monthly operating summary is submitted to the home office. The month-end branch inventory is $1,800.

Journal entries for these transactions are recorded on the books of the home office and branch in Illustration 11–4. Additional entries by the home office are necessary to close the revenue and expense accounts from its own operations. It should be noted that the Shipments to Branch account (on the home office books) is a contra account to Purchases or Cost

Illustration 11–4

Home Office Books

(1) Branch current 1,000
    Cash   1,000

(2) Branch current 5,000
    Shipments to branch   5,000

(7) Cash 1,000
    Branch current   1,000

(9) Branch current 2,100
    Branch net income   2,100

Branch Books

(1) Cash 1,000
    Home office current   1,000

(2) Shipments from home office 5,000
    Home office current   5,000

(3) Expenses 200
    Cash   200

(4) Purchases 2,500
    Accounts payable   2,500

(5) Accounts receivable 8,000
    Sales   8,000

(6) Cash 4,700
    Accounts receivable   4,700

(7) Home office current 1,000
    Cash   1,000

(8) Sales 8,000
    Merchandise inventory 1,800
    Purchases   2,500
    Shipments from home office ...   5,000
    Expenses   200
    Income summary   2,100

(9) Income summary 2,100
    Home office current   2,100

of Goods Manufactured on the books of the home office; consequently, it necessarily *always* reflects the *cost* of goods shipped and is closed at the end of the accounting period. Contrariwise, the Shipments from Home Office account (on the branch books) is equivalent to a Purchases account and accordingly reflects the intracompany billing price; it also is closed at the end of the accounting period. These reciprocal accounts are used for the purpose of maintaining accounting control of intracompany merchandise shipments.

At completion of a period of branch operations, it is customary for the branch to render operating and position statements to the home office, supported in most instances by transaction details in respect to branch inventories and the Home Office Current account. The latter information may be especially useful where there exist foreign branches and where there are numerous cash remittances to and from the home office. Once these data are compiled, it is frequently desirable to prepare combined financial statements of the home office and branch.

Combined Financial Statements

While the separate statements of the branch and home office disclose much useful information in respect to the operations of each division, they do not adequately convey important analytical data about the composite business unit. To merely include in the home office operating statement a single figure for branch net income or loss is not fully informative. Summary disclosures concerning total sales, cost of sales, and operating expenses of the business unit as a whole are often more meaningful than data revealed in the separate statements of the affiliate divisions; indeed, they are required in company-wide policy decisions.

Combined statements of the home office and branch are needed to reflect the effects of transactions of the total business entity with outside interests. Accordingly, the effects of transactions between the home office and branches (or between branches) must be eliminated to avoid value overstatement or duplicate measurement in the accounts. Combined statements make use of the *principle of substitution*—the branch's asset, liability, and operating accounts are substituted for the Branch Current account. This is accomplished in a combined statement working paper by *eliminating* the Branch Current account against the Home Office Current account. To the extent that there are evidences in other accounts of intracompany transactions, their effects must also be eliminated. For example, balances found in the reciprocal Shipments to Branch–Shipments from Home Office accounts, and Remittances to Home Office–Remittances from Branch accounts (the latter accounts reflecting periodic cash transfers) must also be eliminated, as they represent only the internal movements of company resources. *The eliminating entries are working paper entries only;* accordingly, they are not entered on the books of either the home office or the branch.

One familiar form of combined statement working paper is given in Illustration 11–5. As a basis for this illustration, the trial balance information for the home office and branch on December 31, 19X1, is provided:

	Home Office	Branch
Cash	$ 40,000	$15,000
Accounts receivable	22,000	20,000
Merchandise, January 1	15,000	
Branch current	17,000	
Other assets	14,000	
Purchases	65,000	9,000
Shipments from home office		12,000
Expenses	7,000	4,000
	$180,000	$60,000
Liabilities	$ 8,000	$12,000
Capital stock	50,000	
Retained earnings	10,000	
Home office current		17,000
Sales	100,000	31,000
Shipments to branch	12,000	
	$180,000	$60,000
Merchandise, December 31	$ 10,000	$ 4,000

The working paper (Illustration 11–5) is divided into three divisions to accommodate the preparation of the income statement, the retained earnings statement, and the balance sheet. The balances in the reciprocal accounts are eliminated as noted. The reader will observe that the working paper in Illustration 11–5 refers to retained earnings balances in respect to both the home office and the branch. As noted earlier, the branch does not ordinarily accumulate branch profits and losses in a retained earnings account; rather, it records such profits and losses as adjustments in the Home Office Current account, and the beginning balance of "retained earnings" of the branch will always necessarily be zero. Accordingly, variation in the balances of the Home Office Current account as found in the combined statement working paper and as reported in the branch's period-end balance sheet may be explained in terms of the branch's periodic profit or loss. However, the working paper format does indicate the total retained earnings for the composite entity at the end of the period, i.e., the accumulated earnings of the home office increased or decreased by the branch net profit or loss for the period.

The formal combined statements are easily prepared using the data found in the "combined" column of the working paper. The combined statements for the affiliate divisions of X Company are presented in Illustration 11–6.

Illustration 11–5

X COMPANY

Combined Statement Working Paper
For Year Ended December 31, 19X1

	Home Office	Branch	Eliminations Dr.	Eliminations Cr.	Combined
Income Statement:					
Sales	100,000	31,000			131,000
Merchandise, December 31	10,000	4,000			14,000
Shipments to branch	12,000		(2) 12,000		–0–
Total credits	122,000	35,000			145,000
Merchandise, January 1	15,000				15,000
Purchases	65,000	9,000			74,000
Shipments from home office		12,000		(2) 12,000	–0–
Expenses	7,000	4,000			11,000
Total debits	87,000	25,000			100,000
Net income—carried forward	35,000	10,000	12,000	12,000	45,000
Retained Earnings Statement:					
Retained earnings, January 1	10,000				10,000
Net income—brought forward	35,000	10,000	12,000	12,000	45,000
Retained earnings, December 31 —carried forward	45,000	10,000	12,000	12,000	55,000
Balance Sheet:					
Cash	40,000	15,000			55,000
Accounts receivable	22,000	20,000			42,000
Merchandise, December 31	10,000	4,000			14,000
Branch current	17,000			(1) 17,000	–0–
Other assets	14,000				14,000
	103,000	39,000			125,000
Liabilities	8,000	12,000			20,000
Capital stock	50,000				50,000
Retained earnings—brought forward	45,000	*10,000	12,000	12,000	55,000
Home office current		17,000	(1) 17,000		–0–
	103,000	39,000	29,000	29,000	125,000

* Increment to Home Office Current due to periodic branch net income.

Branch Billing in Excess of Cost

The home office may elect to bill the branch at a value in excess of cost—either at retail price or at an arbitrary amount above cost. Under either of these conditions, the branch manager frequently is not given complete information concerning the cost of branch shipments; therefore, net profit as reckoned by the branch will necessarily require adjustment by the home office to the extent of realized intracompany profit, i.e., only the intracompany profit in the unsold branch merchandise is deferred. Consider the following transactions which illustrate the accounting consequence of this type of billing:

Illustration 11–6

X COMPANY

Income Statement
For Year Ended December 31, 19X1

Sales		$131,000
Cost of sales:		
Merchandise, January 1	$15,000	
Purchases	74,000	
	$89,000	
Merchandise, December 31	14,000	75,000
Gross Margin		$ 56,000
Expenses		11,000
Net Income		$ 45,000

X COMPANY

Retained Earnings Statement
For Year Ended December 31, 19X1

Retained earnings, January 1	$10,000
Net income, 19X1	45,000
Retained earnings, December 31	$55,000

X COMPANY

Balance Sheet
December 31, 19X1

Assets		Equities	
Cash	$ 55,000	Liabilities	$ 20,000
Accounts receivable	42,000	Capital stock	50,000
Merchandise	14,000	Retained earnings	55,000
Other assets	14,000		
Total Assets	$125,000	Total Equities	$125,000

(1)   Merchandise costing the home office $4,000 is billed to the branch at $5,000. The branch is not informed of the merchandise cost.

(2)   One half of the above shipment is sold by the branch for $3,000.

(3)   The branch closes its books and reports its net income to the home office.

The journal entries for these transactions, or events, are recorded on the books of the home office and branch in Illustration 11–7.

The net income calculation of the branch is based upon the transfer price of the merchandise. The home office, possessed of complete information in respect to intracompany billing, is able to make appropriate adjustment for the intracompany inventory profit. That amount of the profit on the original shipment subsequently *confirmed* by branch sales is appropriately transferred in the home office closing process to branch net income; the amount of profit identified with unsold branch merchandise is reserved as a credit in the Intracompany Inventory Profit account until the relevant units are sold. The balance in the Intracompany Inventory Profit account should be reported as a deduction from the balance in the Branch Current

Illustration 11-7

Home Office Books

(1) Branch current	5,000	
Shipments to branch (at cost)		4,000
Intracompany inventory profit		1,000
(3) Branch current	500	
Branch net income		500
Intracompany inventory profit	500	
Branch net income		500

Branch Books

(1) Shipments from home office	5,000	
Home office current		5,000
(2) Accounts receivable	3,000	
Sales		3,000
(3) Merchandise inventory	2,500	
Sales	3,000	
Shipments from home office		5,000
Income summary		500

account in the balance sheet of the home office. In combined statements prepared before closing, the Intracompany Inventory Profit account is eliminated as a part of the Shipments to Branch–Shipments from Home Office elimination and accordingly does not appear as an extended value in the combined statement working paper. Additionally, the unconfirmed profit in the ending inventory of the branch is eliminated. To the extent that the accountant may favor disclosing the amount of inventory profit, it may be retained in the combined balance sheet as a deduction from the profit-inflated inventory, reducing the latter to cost.

Illustrative Problem

The following illustrative problem introduces a combined statement working paper involving residual intracompany inventory profit. The trial balances of the home office and branch on December 31, 19X1 are:

	Home Office	Branch
Cash	$ 40,000	$ 15,000
Accounts receivable	22,000	20,000
Merchandise, January 1	15,000	12,000
Branch current	53,000	
Other assets	14,000	50,000
Purchases	65,000	9,000
Shipments from home office		36,000
Expenses	7,000	4,000
	$216,000	$146,000
Liabilities	$ 18,000	$ 12,000
Capital stock	50,000	
Retained earnings	10,000	
Home office current		53,000
Sales	100,000	81,000
Shipments to branch	30,000	
Intracompany inventory profit	8,000	
	$216,000	$146,000
Merchandise, December 31	$ 10,000	$ 4,800

The home office bills all shipments to the branch at 20 percent above cost. The branch's beginning and ending inventories consist exclusively of merchandise purchased from the home office.

The combined statement working paper for this problem is shown in Illustration 11–8. It may be observed that the beginning inventory of the branch, $12,000, is profit inflated to the extent of $2,000. This amount must be eliminated from both the Merchandise, January 1 and Intracompany Inventory Profit accounts. Similarly, Shipments from Home Office, $36,000, contains a profit factor of $6,000, which reconciles the contra shipment accounts. It is important that the reciprocal shipment accounts be eliminated, together with the residual $6,000 of intracompany inventory

Illustration 11–8

X COMPANY

Combined Statement Working Paper
For Year Ended December 31, 19X1

	Home Office	Branch	Eliminations Dr.	Eliminations Cr.	Com-bined
Income Statement:					
Sales	100,000	81,000			181,000
Merchandise, December 31	10,000	4,800	(4) 800		14,000
Shipments to branch	30,000		(3) 30,000		–0–
Total credits	140,000	85,800			195,000
Merchandise, January 1	15,000	12,000		(2) 2,000	25,000
Purchases	65,000	9,000			74,000
Shipments from home office		36,000		(3) 36,000	–0–
Expenses	7,000	4,000			11,000
Total debits	87,000	61,000			110,000
Net income—carried forward	53,000	24,800	30,800	38,000	85,000
Retained Earnings Statement:					
Retained earnings, January 1	10,000				10,000
Net income—brought forward	53,000	24,800	30,800	38,000	85,000
Retained earnings, December 31—carried forward	63,000	24,800	30,800	38,000	95,000
Balance Sheet:					
Cash	40,000	15,000			55,000
Accounts receivable	22,000	20,000			42,000
Merchandise, December 31	10,000	4,800		(4) 800	14,000
Branch current	53,000			(1) 53,000	–0–
Other assets	14,000	50,000			64,000
	139,000	89,800			175,000
Liabilities	18,000	12,000			30,000
Capital stock	50,000				50,000
Retained earnings—brought forward	63,000	*24,800	30,800	38,000	95,000
Home office current		53,000	(1) 53,000		–0–
Intracompany inventory profit	8,000		(2) 2,000 (3) 6,000		–0–
	139,000	89,800	91,800	91,800	175,000

* Increment to Home Office Current due to periodic branch net income.

profit. Finally, there remains an elimination in respect to the profit element in the final inventory of the branch. The branch inventory, $4,800, contains $800 of intracompany profit. It is sufficient to make this elimination by merely reducing the inventory value as it appears in the income statement division and also as it appears in the balance sheet division of the combined statement working paper.

The home office may prefer to bill the branch at retail price. Such a billing often serves to improve merchandise control in respect to branch operations. Where the billing is made at an established sales price, necessarily the difference between the value of goods available for sale and the value of goods sold is the retail value of unsold merchandise. Comparison of this amount with a physical inventory permits easy detection of inventory discrepancies. By the simple expedient of applying the relevant gross profit rate, the inventory at retail may be translated to cost. The use of this method obviously results in the calculation of a branch net loss in an amount equal to the branch's operating expenses. Combined statements are prepared in the same manner as illustrated previously for billings at arbitrary values in excess of cost.

Where the branch is billed at an arbitrary value in excess of cost, the billing may nonetheless be competitive with quotations from outside suppliers. To this extent, the branch profit and loss statement is a fairly reliable index of its operating efficiency. Where the billing is at retail price, the branch's operating statement can hardly be more than a statistical summary of revenues and expenses. In this instance, an index of the branch management's efficiency must necessarily relate to the minimization of operating expenses, or more precisely, maximization of sales volume and minimization of the ratio of operating expenses to sales.

Reconciling Adjustments

All intracompany reciprocal account balances must be eliminated in the preparation of a combined financial statement for the branch and home office. Sometimes these accounts will not carry equivalent balances on specified statement dates. The variations can often be explained in terms of inventory shipments or cash remittances in transit. It is accordingly necessary to give effect to these, and other adjustments, in order to establish reciprocity prior to the making of eliminating entries. It is preferable that adjustments be made on the books of the affected division before the preparation of a combined statement working paper is begun; however, they may be entered on the working paper in the same manner as eliminating entries.

Transshipments of Merchandise

On occasions, it may be necessary for one branch to ship merchandise to a second branch. In such a circumstance, it is important that each branch record the transaction so as to give appropriate recognition to the effect produced *on the home office books*. For example, the receiving branch should debit the accounts of the assets received and credit the Home Office Current account; contrariwise, the shipping branch should reduce by appropriate entries both its Home Office Current account and the accounts for the assets transferred. It is unusual for branches to carry current accounts with other branches; rather, interbranch transactions are ordinarily analyzed in terms of accountability to the home office.

Freight on assets transferred by the home office to a branch is properly included as an element of asset cost to the receiving branch. However, where assets are transshipped from one branch to another, it is appropriate to include in the cost of the asset only that amount of freight as would have been paid had the shipment been directed originally from the home office to the ultimate branch recipient. Payments in excess of this amount are normally charged to expense by the home office, the assumption being that the home office is at least nominally responsible for the excess charge resulting from indirect routing.

Freight on branch transshipments is illustrated below. It is assumed that merchandise costing the home office $1,000 is shipped to Branch A. Freight on this shipment, $80, is paid by the home office. Subsequently, these goods are transshipped to Branch B, with the payment of additional freight of $40 by Branch A. It is determined that direct routing from the home office to Branch B would have resulted in an aggregate freight cost of $100. Entries for these transactions are as follows:

Home Office

Branch A current	1,080	
Shipments to Branch A		1,000
Cash		80
Shipments to Branch A	1,000	
Shipments to Branch B		1,000
Branch B current	1,100	
Excess freight on branch transshipment	20	
Branch A current		1,120

Branch A

Shipments from home office	1,000	
Freight-in	80	
Home office current		1,080
Home office current	1,120	
Shipments from home office		1,000
Freight-in		80
Cash		40

Branch B

Shipments from home office	1,000	
Freight-in	100	
Home office current		1,100

Other Accounting Systems

On occasions, the home office may elect to centralize the accounting for all branch operations within the structure of home office records. This may result in the creation of a separate set of accounts to identify the details of branch operations, or these operations may be subsumed in the same system of accounts as are used in nonbranch transactions. In either circumstance, the documentary evidences of all branch transactions must be regularly submitted to the home office for entry. Such a system is not essentially unlike that used for agencies.

On other occasions, the accounting system may take the form of a complete record-keeping by *both* branch and home office in respect to all branch transactions. Necessarily this duplication has disadvantages. Yet, the more complete dissemination of accounting information may, in fact, promote greater operating efficiencies in the administrative decentralization than the added cost of maintaining duplicate records would appear to indicate.

QUESTIONS

1. Describe briefly the parent company and entity concepts of consolidated financial statements.

2. What effect(s) does the adoption of the entity concept of consolidated financial statements have on entries made by the parent company to record its equity in earnings of affiliates and differential amortization?

3. Which concept of consolidated financial statements is generally used in practice?

4. Describe the calculations of debit and credit differentials where the entity theory of consolidated statements is accepted.

5. What is the entity theorist's position regarding the amount of elimination of intercompany profits on asset transfers?

6. What is the relationship between the amounts of consolidated net income and stockholders' equity assignable to majority shareholders under the entity concept and the amounts of consolidated net income and stockholders' equity reported under the parent company concept?

7. What is the relationship between and the function of the accounts "Branch Current" and "Home Office Current"?

8. What is meant by the "principle of substitution" as applied to branch accounting?

9. If the home office elects to bill the branch for merchandise at a price in excess of cost, why would it be preferable to use a price above cost but less than retail?

10. What are "reconciling adjustments" in branch accounting?

EXERCISES

Exercise 11–1

P Company owns 80 percent of S Company. During 19X1, both companies had incomes from their own operations of $25,000.

Required:

a. Under the parent company concept, calculate consolidated net income for 19X1.
b. Under the entity concept, calculate consolidated net income and the amounts assignable to majority and minority shareholders for 19X1.

Exercise 11–2

P Company purchased 80 percent of the capital stock of S Company on January 1, 19X1 for $52,000, when the book value of S Company's net assets was $50,000. The differential is to be allocated wholly to goodwill, which is to be amortized over ten years. P Company uses the entity concept in the preparation of consolidated financial statements. During 19X1, both companies had incomes from their own operations of $20,000.

Required:

a. Calculate the total differential implicit in the purchase price.
b. Prepare P Company's entries at December 31, 19X1 to record its equity in S Company's 19X1 earnings and differential amortization for the year.
c. Calculate the amount of goodwill amortization that would be reported in the 19X1 consolidated income statement.
d. Calculate consolidated net income and the amounts assignable to majority and minority shareholders for 19X1.

Exercise 11–3

P Company owns 70 percent of S Company. During 19X1, both companies had incomes from their own operations of $10,000. P Company's income includes $2,000 of unconfirmed intercompany profit, and S Company's income includes $3,000 of unconfirmed intercompany profit.

P Company uses the entity concept in the preparation of consolidated financial statements. At the date of acquisition, the total differential was determined to be $40,000. This differential was allocated to goodwill, and is being amortized over ten years (including 19X1).

Required:

a. Prepare P Company's entries at December 31, 19X1 to record its equity in S Company's 19X1 earnings and differential amortization for the year.
b. Calculate consolidated net income and the amounts assignable to majority and minority shareholders for 19X1.

Exercise 11–4

P Company purchased 80 percent of the capital stock of S Company on January 1, 19X1 for $70,000, when S Company had capital stock of $10,000 and retained earnings of $40,000. An appraisal of S Company's assets and lia-bilities on this date indicated that plant and equipment (net) had a fair value of $100,000 and a book value of $80,000, and that the book values of all other assets and liabilities were equal to fair values. Assume the plant and equipment has a remaining life of five years, and goodwill is to be amortized over ten years.

P Company's retained earnings on January 1, 19X1 were $60,000. During 19X1, the companies had incomes from their own operations as follows: P Company—$30,000; S Company—$10,000. P Company uses the entity con-cept in the preparation of consolidated financial statements.

Required:

a. Calculate the total differential implicit in the purchase price.
b. Determine the allocation of the *total* differential to specific assets, and the annual amortization for the next ten years.
c. Prepare the entries on P Company's books at December 31, 19X1 to record its equity in S Company's 19X1 earnings and differential amortization for the year.
d. Prepare the investment elimination and differential allocation and amortiza-tion entries for a three-division consolidated statement working paper at December 31, 19X1.
e. Calculate 19X1 consolidated net income and December 31, 19X1 consoli-dated retained earnings, and indicate the amounts assignable to majority and minority shareholders.

Exercise 11–5

On January 1, 1975, A Company acquired 80 percent of the capital stock of B Company and 90 percent of the capital stock of C Company.

The following operating summary relates to the affiliation for the year ended December 31, 1978.

	Companies		
	A	B	C
Income from operations	$65,000	$40,000	$26,000
Recognized intercompany inventory profit, unconfirmed on:			
January 1		6,000	
December 31	4,000	1,000	2,000

A Company acquired on January 1, 1978, machinery and equipment from B Company on which the latter recorded a profit of $10,000. On January 1, 1978, it was estimated that the equipment had a remaining service life of 10 years.

C Company acquired on January 1, 1978, $20,000 of 5 percent bonds of A Company for $23,000. The bonds with 20 years' maturity were issued by A Company on January 1, 1968, at 90.

Required:

Using the parent company concept, calculate consolidated net income for 1978.

Exercise 11–6

Edwards Company opened a Dallas branch in January, 1977. During 1977, Edwards recorded merchandise transfers to the branch and merchandise returns from the branch with the following entries.

Branch current	156,000	
Sales		156,000
Sales returns	3,900	
Branch current		3,900

Transfers to and from the branch were recorded by Edwards at 130 percent of Edwards' cost.

The Dallas branch reported to the home office a net loss of $12,000 for 1977. In addition, the branch reported a closing inventory of $65,000, all of which was acquired from the home office.

Required:

Assume that the home office books have not been closed for 1977. Prepare the journal entries on the books of the home office that are necessary at the end of 1977 to (1) correct the accounts of the home office and (2) recognize the results of branch activities during 1977.

Exercise 11–7

On July 1, the Demaris Company, central distributor for Arlo Metal Castings, Inc., organized a southwest sales outlet in El Paso. Following are the home office–branch transactions for the month of July:

July 1 The Demaris Company transferred $2,500 to its El Paso branch for operating fund purposes.

    2 Merchandise costing the home office $3 per unit was shipped to the branch at an invoice price of $5 per unit. One thousand units were shipped on July 2; a second order was to be filled by local suppliers.

    2 Shipping costs on the above were paid:

By the home office	$150
By the branch	50

    5 Additional merchandise was acquired by the El Paso branch from regional distributors, 500 units @ $3.10.

    7 Display equipment was purchased by the home office, cost $3,600, and delivered to the El Paso branch. Fixed asset accounts are kept by the home office.

  10 Branch sales for the period July 3–10: On account, 800 units @ $5.

  18 Branch collections on account, $3,200.

  25 Branch sales for the period July 11–24: On account, 500 units @ $5.

  29 Cash remittance by branch to home office, $1,000.

  30 Monthly summary of branch cash expenses:

Advertising	$ 40
Sales commissions	650
Miscellaneous	10

July 31   Depreciation recorded by the Demaris Company for July included $150 which related to the display equipment used by the El Paso branch. Insurance on this equipment was amortized by the home office in the amount of $25.

   31   Inventories of merchandise at El Paso on July 31 included:

From the home office	150 units @ $5.00
From local suppliers	50 units @ $3.10

Required:

Journalize the above transactions on the books of the Demaris Company and the El Paso branch office and prepare closing entries for July month-end statements.

PROBLEMS

Problem 1

The Tucker Company acquired an 80 percent interest in the capital stock of the Taylor Corporation on January 1, 19X1, for $90,000. On December 31, 19X1, the trial balances of the affiliated companies are:

	Tucker Company	Taylor Corpora- tion
Cash	$ 40,000	$ 32,000
Receivables	20,000	16,000
Merchandise, January 1	12,000	8,000
Investment in Taylor Corporation common stock	114,000	
Long-lived assets	93,000	41,000
Other assets	17,000	35,000
Dividends declared		10,000
Purchases	50,000	43,000
Expenses	18,000	15,000
	364,000	$200,000
Payables	$ 12,000	$ 10,000
Capital stock:		
Tucker Company	100,000	
Taylor Corporation		60,000
Retained earnings:		
Tucker Company	120,000	
Taylor Corporation		40,000
Sales	100,000	90,000
Equity in subsidiary earnings	32,000	
	364,000	$200,000
Merchandise, December 31	$ 10,000	$ 16,000

Assume the differential is allocated to "other assets," and is *not* subject to amortization.

Required:

Using the "entity theory," prepare:

a. A consolidated statement working paper for the year ended December 31, 19X1.

b. A consolidated balance sheet as of December 31, 19X1, and a consolidated income statement for the year then ended.

Problem 2

On January 1, 19X1, the Irwin Corporation acquired 90 percent of the capital stock of the Prentice Company for $84,000 and 80 percent of the capital stock of Simons, Inc., for $70,000. Accumulated retained earnings of the Prentice Company and Simons, Inc., at acquisition were $40,000 and $20,000 respectively.

Trial balances of the affiliate companies on December 31, 19X2, follow:

	Irwin Corp.	Prentice Co.	Simons, Inc.
Cash	$ 19,000	$ 23,000	$ 7,000
Receivables	41,000	27,000	12,000
Merchandise, January 1	11,000	8,000	7,000
Investment in Prentice Company	119,100		
Investment in Simons, Inc.	86,000		
Other assets	8,000	74,000	86,000
Dividends declared		6,000	4,000
Purchases	57,000	64,000	33,000
Expenses	10,600	5,000	10,000
	$351,700	$207,000	$159,000
Payables	$ 18,000	$ 5,000	$ 12,000
Capital stock (par $100)	100,000	50,000	60,000
Retained earnings	119,000	70,000	35,000
Sales	94,000	82,000	52,000
Equity in subsidiary earnings	20,700		
	$351,700	$207,000	$159,000
Merchandise, December 31	$ 6,000	$ 10,000	$ 8,000

During 19X2 Simons, Inc., made sales to the Irwin Corporation in the amount of $12,000. In respect to these sales $4,000 remain in the December 31 inventory of Irwin. Simons, Inc., regularly marks up goods 25 percent on selling price on sales to both affiliates and nonaffiliates.

Assume the differentials are allocated to "other assets," and are *not* subject to amortization.

Required:

Using the "entity theory," prepare a consolidated statement working paper for the year ended December 31, 19X2.

Problem 3

The Cruse Company purchased 80 percent of the capital stock of Summers, Inc., on January 1, 19X1, for $49,600. One year thereafter, trial balances of the respective companies were:

	December 31, 19X1	
	Cruse Company	Summers, Inc.
Cash	$ 23,400	$ 12,500
Notes receivable	5,000	2,000
Merchandise, January 1	28,000	11,000
Investment in Summers, Inc.	68,000	
Other assets	58,000	80,500
Dividends declared	8,500	5,000
Purchases	161,000	83,000
Freight-in	1,000	200
Selling expenses	18,000	11,100
Administrative expenses	9,300	5,700
	$380,200	$211,000
Accounts payable	$ 18,000	$ 12,000
Other liabilities	3,000	16,000
Capital stock (par, $100)	100,000	50,000
Retained earnings	31,000	12,000
Sales	205,000	121,000
Equity in subsidiary earnings	22,400	
Interest income	800	
	$380,200	$211,000
Merchandise, December 31	$ 41,000	$ 18,000

"Other liabilities" of Summers, Inc., include a $3,000 noninterest-bearing note payable to the Cruse Company.

Required:

Prepare a *trial balance* consolidated statement working paper for the year ended December 31, 19X1.

Problem 4

The individual and consolidated statements of companies X and Y for the year ending December 31, 19X2, are as follows:

	X Company	Y Company	Consoli- dated
Cash and receivables	$ 35,000	$108,000	$ 97,400
Inventories	40,000	90,000	122,000
Plant (net)	460,000	140,000	600,000
Goodwill			50,000
Investment in Y	276,900		
X bonds owned		103,000	
	$811,900	$441,000	$869,400
Current payables	$ 70,000	$ 23,000	$ 53,000
Dividends payable	10,000	8,000	12,400
Mortgage bonds	200,000	50,000	150,000
Capital stock	300,000	200,000	300,000
Retained earnings	231,900	160,000	231,900
Minority interest			122,100
	$811,900	$441,000	$869,400
Sales	$600,000	$400,000	$760,000
Cost of sales	360,000	280,000	403,000
Gross profit	$240,000	$120,000	$357,000
Operating expenses	130,000	54,000	184,000
Operating profit	$110,000	$ 66,000	$173,000
Interest income	1,800	5,000	1,800
Equity in subsidiary earnings	14,325	–0–	–0–
Total	$126,125	$ 71,000	$174,800
Interest expense	$ 10,000	$ 3,000	$ 8,000
Provision for income taxes	56,000	34,000	90,000
Nonrecurring loss			3,000
Amortization of goodwill			6,250
Minority interest			7,425
Net income	$ 60,125	$ 34,000	$ 60,125
Dividends	20,000	16,000	24,800
Transfer to retained earnings	$ 40,125	$ 18,000	$ 35,325

X Company purchased its 70 percent interest in Y Company on January 1, 19X1. X Company sells its product in part to Y Company for further processing, and in part to other firms. The inventories of Y Company included an intercompany markup at both the beginning and end of the year. Cash transfers are made between the companies according to working capital needs.

Early in 19X2, Y Company purchased $100,000 face value of the bonds of X Company as a *temporary* investment. These are carried on Y's books at cost.

X Company uses the 100 percent method for eliminating intercompany profits.

Required:

On the basis of the information you can develop from an analysis of the individual and consolidated statements, answer the nine questions below.

Show clearly all computations necessary to support your answers.

1. Does X Company carry its *Investment in Y* on the cost or equity basis? State the reason for your conclusion.

2. The Goodwill is based upon a revaluation of the *total* (entity concept) of Y Company's net assets on the basis of the price paid by X Company for its interest in Y Company on January 1, 19X1, and it is being amortized over ten years. What was the balance of Goodwill on the date of acquisition?
3. What is the nature of *Nonrecurring Loss* on the consolidated income statement? Show the consolidating elimination entry from which it originated.
4. Show the amounts of intercompany debts, excluding the bonds, and show which company is the debtor and which is the creditor in each instance.
5. Prepare a schedule reconciling the sum of the *Cost of Sales* of X and Y individually with the *Consolidated Cost of Sales*. Show clearly the intercompany markup in the beginning and ending inventories of Y Company and how you determined the amounts.
6. Prepare a schedule reconciling the balance of Minority Interest in the December 31, 19X2 consolidated balance sheet with Y Company's net assets and other appropriate values.
7. Prepare a schedule reconciling the balance of the Investment in Y at December 31, 19X2 with Y Company's net assets and other appropriate values.
8. Prepare a schedular calculation, using the incremental approach, of consolidated net income for 19X2. (Hint: Although X Company used the entity concept in valuing Y Company's assets at acquisition, the parent company concept is used to determine consolidated net income.)
9. Confirm the calculation of minority interest in net income for 19X2.

(AICPA adapted)

Problem 5

The Cincinnati home office of The Geis Company regularly acquires merchandise at a cost of $4 a unit, which is subsequently marked to sell at $6 a unit by both the home office and its Athens branch. During 1977 the home office purchased 4,000 units, sold 3,000 units, and shipped 500 units to the branch. During 1978 the home office purchased an additional 4,500 units, sold 3,200 units, and made a second shipment of 1,000 units to the Athens branch.

Branch sales of units acquired from the home office were: 400 units in 1977 and 900 units in 1978.

Required:

a. Journalize all transactions on the books of The Geis Company and its Athens branch (including closing entries) for the years 1977 and 1978 *if* the home office bills merchandise shipped to the branch at $4 a unit.
b. Same conditions as in (a) except that the home office bills merchandise shipped to the branch at $5 a unit.

Problem 6

Using the data of Problem 5 prepare working papers for a *combined* income statement for The Geis Company and its Athens branch for the years 1977 and 1978 if—

a. The home office bills merchandise shipped to the branch at $4 a unit.
b. The home office bills merchandise shipped to the branch at $5 a unit.

Problem 7

The Longley Company of Indianapolis regularly distributes its products through branch retail outlets. Shipments to its Frankfort branch, which was established at the beginning of the year, are billed as follows: Case A, at cost; Case B, 25 percent above cost; Case C, retail price at date of shipment.

During the year the Frankfort branch received merchandise from the home office, cost, $60,000. Additionally, the branch recorded credit sales of $81,000; made collections on account, $64,000; paid expenses, $14,000; and remitted cash to the Indianapolis home office, $61,200. The December 31 final inventory of the branch was: Case A, $6,000; Case B, $7,500; and Case C, $9,000.

The trial balance of the Indianapolis home office on December 31 was:

	Case A	Case B	Case C
Cash	$ 39,000	$ 39,000	$ 39,000
Accounts receivable	45,000	45,000	45,000
Branch current	[1,200]	13,800	28,800
Purchases	150,000	150,000	150,000
Expenses	17,200	17,200	17,200
	$250,000	$265,000	$280,000
Accounts payable	$ 20,000	$ 20,000	$ 20,000
Shipments to branch	60,000	60,000	60,000
Intracompany inventory profit		15,000	30,000
Capital stock	40,000	40,000	40,000
Sales	130,000	130,000	130,000
	$250,000	$265,000	$280,000
Merchandise, December 31	$ 8,000	$ 8,000	$ 8,000

Required:

a. Journalize the transactions of the branch for the year, as recorded by the Indianapolis home office and the Frankfort branch.

b. Prepare closing entries for the branch and home office.

c. Prepare a combined statement working paper (Case C only).

Problem 8

Sales distribution of the Electronic Transistor Company is principally conducted by its home office and one centrally located branch. Units of merchandise shipped to the branch are uniformly priced at 120 percent of cost. The trial balances of the home office and branch at December 31, 1977, are as follows:

	December 31, 1977	
	Home Office	*Branch*
Cash	$ 125,200	$ 17,600
Marketable securities	229,000	
Accounts receivable (net)	172,700	84,300
Inventory—January 1, 1977	341,000	133,200
Branch current	122,300	
Fixed assets (net)	1,172,600	
Purchases	2,450,000	
Expenses	381,000	78,100
Shipments from home office		811,200
	$4,993,800	$1,124,400
Accounts payable	$ 397,000	$ 12,400
Accrued expenses	14,100	1,700
Capital stock	1,000,000	
Retained earnings	172,300	
Home office current		72,300
Sales	2,547,000	1,038,000
Shipments to branch	701,000	
Intracompany inventory profit	162,400	
	$4,993,800	$1,124,400
Inventory—December 31, 1977	$ 284,000	$ 120,000

An examination of duplicate deposit tickets on January 3, 1978, discloses that the branch made a $20,000 deposit to the credit of the home office on December 31, 1977.

Required:

a. Prepare a working paper for a combined statement for the home office and branch for the year ended December 31, 1977.
b. Journalize adjusting and closing entries for the branch and home office.

Problem 9

You are the accountant for the Johnson Export Company. The trial balance at December 31, 1977, follows:

	Home Office	Branch
Cash	$ 15,000	$ 2,000
Accounts receivable	20,000	17,000
Inventory—December 31, 1977	30,000	8,000
Fixed assets—net	150,000	
Branch office current	44,000	
Cost of sales	220,000	93,000
Expenses	70,000	41,000
Total	$549,000	$161,000
Accounts payable	$ 23,000	
Mortgage payable	50,000	
Capital stock	100,000	
Retained earnings—January 1, 1977	26,000	
Sales	350,000	$150,000
Accrued expenses		2,000
Home office current		9,000
Total	$549,000	$161,000

The following additional information is also brought to your attention:

a. The branch receives all of its merchandise from the home office. The home office bills goods to the branch at 125 percent of cost. During 1977 the branch was billed for $105,000 on shipments from the home office.

b. The home office credits Sales for the invoice price of goods shipped to the branch.

c. On January 1, 1977, the inventory of the home office was $25,000. The branch books showed a $6,000 inventory.

d. The home office billed the branch for $12,000 on December 31, 1977, representing the branch's share of expenses paid at the home office. The branch has not recorded this billing.

e. All cash collections made by the branch are deposited in a local bank to the account of the home office. Deposits of this nature included the following:

Amount	Date Deposited by Branch	Date Recorded by Home Office
$5,000	December 28, 1977	December 31, 1977
3,000	December 30, 1977	January 2, 1978
7,000	December 31, 1977	January 3, 1978
2,000	January 2, 1978	January 5, 1978

f. Expenses incurred locally by the branch are paid from an imprest bank account which is reimbursed periodically by the home office. Just prior to the end of the year the home office forwarded a reimbursement check in the amount of $3,000 which was not received by the branch office until January, 1978.

g. It is not necessary to make provisions for federal income tax.

Required:

a. Prepare a working paper for a combined statement for the home office and branch for the year ended December 31, 1977.
b. Prepare a reconciliation of the Branch Current and Home Office Current accounts showing the correct book balance.

(AICPA adapted)

Problem 10

The Koufax Sporting Goods Company of Los Angeles decided on July 1 to establish sales branches in Chicago and New York as a means of expanding and improving its services to customers in these areas. Transactions with these branches for the month of July are as follows:

July 1   The home office transferred $75,000 cash to the Chicago branch and $100,000 to the New York branch to be used as working funds.
     2   Merchandise costing $310,000 was shipped to the New York branch and was billed at 140 percent of cost. Freight charges, paid by the home office, amounted to $1,400.
     3   Merchandise costing $225,000 was shipped to the Chicago branch and was billed at a 25 percent markup on the invoice price. Freight charges of $888 were paid by the Chicago branch.
    10   Fixed assets costing $400,000 were purchased for the use of the Chicago branch and $500,000 were purchased for the New York branch. General ledger control over fixed assets is maintained by the home office.
    15   Timely reporting is facilitated by the use of electronic data processing equipment; as a consequence, the first semimonthly summary of operating data was received on July 15 and disclosed the following:

	Branches	
	Chicago	New York
Credit sales	$42,000	$57,000
Collections on account	34,000	41,000
Expenses	8,000	12,000
Payments on account	6,400	9,700

    17   Merchandise previously shipped to Chicago was transshipped to New York. These goods, on which freight charges amounted to $147, had been billed to Chicago at $20,000. Additional freight paid by the New York branch for the transshipment amounted to $68. Had the shipment been initially directed to New York, transportation costs would have totaled $175.
    20   The home office shipped additional merchandise to branches as follows: Chicago, $150,000 cost; New York, $200,000 cost. The terms of branch billing remain unchanged. Freight charges, paid by the home office, were $700 on the Chicago shipment and $1,150 on the New York shipment.

July 31   The semimonthly operating summary is as follows:

	Branches	
	Chicago	New York
Credit sales	$122,100	$150,800
Collections on account	97,700	128,100
Expenses	19,000	27,000
Payments on account	19,600	26,300

31   Cash remittances to the home office were:

New York branch $125,000
Chicago branch 100,000

Required:

a.   Prepare journal entries for July for each branch and the home office. (In the home office books, use separate accounts in respect to the transactions of each branch.)

b.   Prepare closing entries, given the following additional information:

(1)   Inventories, July 31:

New York branch $560,000
Chicago branch 360,000

Inventories are determined by physical count; freight charges on merchandise shipments are not allocated to inventory.

(2)   Depreciation on fixed assets is regularly recorded by the home office. Depreciation expense for the month of July is:

Property at New York branch $500
Property at Chicago branch 400

12

Accounting for International Operations

THE ESSENTIALLY uninterrupted expansion of American business activity since World War II has included a significant increase in what may be broadly classified as international operations. For many companies, these operations consist merely of trading activity (imports or exports) with suppliers or customers that are domiciled in other countries. On a larger scale, this growing involvement in foreign operations may take the form of investment in foreign firms, and/or the establishment of foreign branches or subsidiaries, either to carry on productive operations or to serve as sales outlets or both.

Although there are business enterprises whose foreign investments are so extensive and diverse that they might be characterized as international in scope, having no particular identification with a specific country, each firm must necessarily select one country within which its parent corporation has legal recognition and sanctuary. Additionally, the necessity of accumulating financial information about the entire business enterprise compels that one country's currency be identified as the unit of account by which financial information will be aggregated. Yet, the basic financial records of each segment of the firm are generally expressed in terms of the currency of the particular country within which the segment conducts its operations. Thus, a major problem of accounting for foreign operations relates to the translation of each segment's financial data into a common currency unit. Also, transactions between parties that are located in different countries generally require one party to *purchase* the currency of another country. Such actions interject a new variable into the determination of profit; the fluctuations in the value of one country's currency may result in gains or losses to a firm of another country which utilizes the currency of the first country.

This chapter provides an overview of the principal accounting issues related to transactions involving foreign currencies and to the translation (conversion) of monetary expressions stated in terms of one country's curency into that of another country. Additionally, the status of transnational financial reporting is briefly considered.

Currency Exchange Rates

From the perspective of any given country, foreign currencies may be viewed as commodities that have specifiable *prices* in terms of the domestic currency. These prices, or rates of exchange, express the relative values of the two currencies. Historically, these rates purported to equate the gold content of the different currencies. However, this is no longer a significant relationship. Presently, two principal types of exchanges rates are important: (1) *free* rates, which reflect the fluctuating market prices of the currency as an economic good (a function of supply and demand); and (2) *official* rates, which are established by government. A given country may have several official rates, each of which pertains to a designated type of economic and financial activity and which reflects governmental policies in respect to desired economic development. For example, one rate may apply to the conversion of a country's currency for the purpose of importing new capital goods into the country, and a less favorable rate for conversion of its currency in order to make a dividend payment to owners domiciled in another country. The existence of a multiple rate structure requires the choice of a rate for financial accounting purposes by individuals doing business with, or holding ownership interests in, companies located in such a country. The particular choices specified by current accounting policy are covered in connection with the discussion of translating foreign currency transactions and foreign currency financial statements.

Since the currency exchange rate between two countries is merely a ratio, it may be stated in terms of either country's currency. If one unit of foreign currency is expressed in terms of its domestic monetary equivalent, the exchange rate is said to be quoted *directly*. On the other hand, if one unit of domestic currency is set equal to its equivalent in foreign units, the quotation is said to be *indirect*. In the United States at the present time, foreign exchange rates are quoted directly. Thus, for example, exchange quotations are stated as follows:

Country (Currency)	Dollar Equivalent of One Foreign Unit
Britain (pound)	$1.80
France (franc)	.21
Mexico (peso)	.08

If the exchanged currencies are to be delivered immediately, the exchange rate is referred to as the *spot rate*. In addition to immediate delivery, a market also exists for future delivery of exchanged currencies (for example, in 30, 90, or 180 days). *Future, or forward, rates* express the rate of exchange that is presently agreed upon for future delivery or receipt of foreign currency units at a specified future date. The futures market allows a company to hedge against fluctuations in the spot exchange rate.

At present, certain accounting translations are based upon exchange rates in effect at different points in time. For purposes of our discussion, a *"current exchange rate"* is the rate prevailing at a balance sheet date, and an *"historical exchange rate"* is the rate that existed at the time a particular transaction or event took place.

TRANSLATING FOREIGN CURRENCY TRANSACTIONS

One of the important accounting problems of foreign operations relates to transactions between enterprises that are located in two different countries having different currencies. In such instances, one of the parties to the transaction must accept its obligation (or receive its payment) in terms of a foreign currency. The party that undertakes this rather unique function frequently incurs an *exchange gain or loss,* depending upon the direction and amount of the fluctuation in exchange rates between the date of billing and the date of payment. For example, if a domestic importer who purchases merchandise abroad is billed *in a foreign currency,* the invoice amount may be translated into domestic currency through the current rate of exchange (free or official) at the billing date. To extinguish the created debt, however, the domestic importer must, within the time interval between the billing date and the due date, acquire foreign currency. In the event that exchange rates have fluctuated in the period between the date of purchase and the subsequent acquisition of foreign currency, gain or loss clearly results and identifies with the domestic importer. Had the billing been expressed in domestic monetary units, the exchange gain or loss would have been that of the foreign exporter. A parallel may be easily drawn for a domestic exporter and a foreign importer. To guard against the hazards of loss from exchange rate fluctuations, a domestic importer, concurrent with the purchase of merchandise abroad, may also purchase foreign currency for future delivery. Billing and settlement are thereby made in terms of the same rate of exchange. A similar precaution may be taken in respect to a domestic exporter, who may elect to sell foreign currency for future delivery where the settlement of the account receivable is to be made in foreign monetary units.

Illustrative Import/Export Transactions

Case 1. In order to illustrate the accounting for import-export operations, consider the following transactions for the Leader Corporation (alternative billing terms will be considered separately):

1. The Leader Corporation (domiciled in the United States) sold merchandise to the East Indies Company of London when the rate of exchange was $1.80. The billing is expressed in dollars/pounds as follows: (a) $18,000, (b) £10,000.
2. The Leader Corporation purchased merchandise from the Villa Company of Mexico City when the rate of exchange was $.08. The billing is expressed in dollars/pesos as follows: (a) $10,000, (b) 125,000 pesos.
3. Payment of the East Indies Company account with the Leader Corporation was received when the exchange rate was $1.82.
4. Remittance was made to the Villa Company by the Leader Corporation when the exchange rate was $.0808.
5. The Leader Corporation sold merchandise to the Acapulco Company of Mexico for 100,000 pesos when the exchange rate was $.0807 (equivalent to $8,070 at this time). Concurrent with the sale of merchandise, the Leader Corporation also sold 100,000 pesos for future delivery at $.0807.
6. The Leader Corporation received payment from the Acapulco Company when the exchange rate was $.0793; thereupon, the pesos were delivered to the exchange broker in settlement of the futures contract.

Ignoring the effects of commissions and other service charges, the entries on the books of the Leader Corporation for these transactions are shown on page 437.

It should be observed that exchange gains or losses emerge only as a consequence of settlement transactions. Further, when the transaction is "hedged" with a concurrent transaction in the futures market, as was illustrated in transactions (5) and (6), the "net" exchange gain or loss is zero.

When exchange gains or losses are recognized, two principal alternatives have been advocated with respect to disclosure in the operating statement for the period:

1. Offset the exchange gains and/or losses against the related Sales and Purchases accounts of the originating transactions. This method views the purchase (or sale) and the subsequent payment (or collection) as a *single transaction,* and thus recognizes cost (or revenue) from transactions denominated in foreign currency in an amount equal to the consideration in dollars required to settle the indebtedness at the time of payment.

2. Recognize the exchange gains and/or losses with separate disclosure as a "financial" item. The validity of this classification is best illustrated by reexamining the sale transaction which was accompanied by a concurrent transaction in exchange futures. By selling pesos for future delivery, the exporter was able to hedge against possible future reductions in the value of the peso. Had no such collateral transaction been effected, an exchange loss of $140 would have been sustained, as the exchange rate declined from $.0807 at the date of sale to $.0793 at the date of settlement.

	(a) Where Billing Is in Domestic Currency (Dollars)		(b) Where Billing Is in Foreign Currency (Pounds Sterling or Pesos)	
(1) Accounts receivable	18,000		18,000	
Sales		18,000		18,000
(2) Purchases	10,000		10,000	
Accounts payable		10,000		10,000
(3) Cash	18,000		18,200	
Exchange gain				200
Accounts receivable		18,000		18,000
(4) Accounts payable	10,000		10,000	
Exchange loss			100	
Cash		10,000		10,100
(5) Accounts receivable			8,070	
Sales				8,070
Due from exchange broker ..			8,070	
Liability for currency sold				8,070
(6) Foreign currency (100,000 × $.0793)			7,930	
Exchange loss			140	
Accounts receivable				8,070
Cash			8,070*	
Due from exchange broker				8,070
Liability for currency sold ..			8,070	
Exchange gain				140
Foreign currency (100,000 × $.0793)				7,930

* The amount of cash to be received for the future delivery of pesos was fixed in the futures transaction at $.0807 per peso.

Conversely, an importer may *purchase* foreign exchange for future delivery, thereby obviating the possibility of loss should rates of exchange increase. If the billing is thus expressed in foreign currency units, and if it is assumed to accurately reflect a freely negotiated exchange price in equivalent dollars, based upon prevailing rates of exchange at the date of purchase or sale, the originating entry correctly measures the operating cost or revenue. Any resulting exchange gain or loss represents a financial decision to speculate in exchange rates, and accordingly should be disclosed in the operating statement as a financial item.

Although practice varied substantially in the past, with the adoption of *FASB Standard 8* in October, 1975 by the Financial Accounting Standards Board, alternative accounting treatments were eliminated and firms must henceforth recognize these exchange gains or losses in their current income statement as a separate item.

In our illustrative entries, all transactions were assumed to have been settled before a balance sheet date. If there were an intervening balance sheet date, receivables or payables that are denominated in a foreign currency must be assigned a value—either the value established at the date of the transaction or a value reflecting the current exchange rate. In the past, accounting practice varied on this question also. However, *FASB Standard 8* specifically requires that these receivables or payables be valued at the current exchange (spot) rate, and that the resulting exchange gain or loss be recognized in the current income statement as a separate item.

Thus, to recap present accounting policy related to import/export transactions denominated in a foreign currency: [1]

1. At the transaction date, each asset, liability, revenue, or expense should be measured using the current spot rate.
2. At any balance sheet date, recorded receivables or payables from import/export transactions that remain unsettled should be adjusted to reflect the current spot rate.
3. Exchange gains or losses resulting from settlement or valuation of an open account should be recognized in the current income statement as a separate item.

Forward Exchange Contracts—An Elaboration

In our example for Leader Corporation in Case 1 above, a forward exchange contract was included with one transaction to illustrate the *hedging* opportunity available to importers or exporters. We now elaborate on the accounting issues associated with these forward contracts.

A forward exchange contract may be established for the following reasons: [2]

1. To hedge a foreign currency commitment.
2. To hedge a foreign currency exposed net asset or liability position. [3] (The Leader Corporation example was of this type).
3. To speculate in foreign currency exchange price movements.

In general, exchange gains or losses should be measured and included in net income of the current period for each of these situations *except* a hedge of a foreign currency commitment that meets three conditions specified in

---

[1] *Statement of Financial Accounting Standards No. 8*, "Accounting for the Translation of Foreign Currency Transactions and Foreign Currency Financial Statements," paragraphs 7 and 17. Copyright © by the Financial Accounting Standards Board, High Ridge Park, Stamford, Connecticut 06905, U.S.A. Quoted with permission. Copies of the complete document are available from the FASB.

[2] *FASB Standard 8*, paragraph 22.

[3] *FASB Standard 8* defines an *exposed net asset* (*liability*) *position* as an excess of assets (liabilities) that are measured or denominated in a foreign currency and translated at the current rate over similar liabilities (assets) that are also translated at the current rate.

FASB Standard 8. Exchange gains or losses on forward contracts that satisfy these conditions are deferred until the date the related transaction occurs, and are then included as an adjustment of the dollar measure of the transaction. Current spot rates are used to value the forward exchange contracts for all situations except the speculative contracts, which use current forward rates for the remaining life of the contract.

In many cases, the forward rate differs slightly from the current spot rate on tne date the forward exchange contract is executed. This difference, when multiplied by the number of foreign currency units contracted for receipt or delivery, is referred to as the *discount* or *premium* on the forward contract. Although there may be many reasons for the existence of this differential, the Financial Accounting Standards Board concluded that normally it reflects an interest rate differential between the two countries, and thus should be amortized over the life of the forward contract entered into for hedging purposes.[4] For hedges that qualify as a hedge of a foreign currency commitment, the premium or discount may be included together with the exchange gain or loss as an adjustment of the dollar measure of the transaction. Speculative forward contracts are valued using forward rates, and thus the discount or premium does not enter into the calculations.

Case 2. Hedging a Foreign Currency Commitment. In order to illustrate the applicability and rationale of the special provisions of *FASB Standard 8* related to certain foreign currency commitments, the example provided in the *Statement* will be adapted for this case.[5] Assume that on January 1, 19X1, a U.S. firm contracts with a U.S. customer to sell for $200,000 some equipment that will be manufactured by a Swiss supplier and delivered in 18 months. At this date, the spot rate for the Swiss franc is $.40, and the cost of the equipment to the U.S. firm is 400,000 Swiss francs. Thus, the selling price of $200,000 provides a gross margin of $40,000 based upon current exchange rates. In order to insure that this gross margin will be realized, the U.S. firm enters into a forward exchange contract to receive 400,000 Swiss francs in 18 months at the current forward rate of $.41. Since this rate is $.01 greater than the current spot rate of $.40, there is a premium of $4,000 (400,000 × $.01). The following spot rates prevail in the future: December 31, 19X1 −$.45; June 30, 19X2 −$.51.

Because this forward contract qualifies as a hedge of an identifiable foreign currency commitment,[6] the following entries will be made:

---

[4] *FASB Standard 8,* paragraph 212.

[5] *FASB Standard 8,* paragraphs 207–208.

[6] *FASB Standard 8,* paragraph 27, establishes the following conditions, *all* of which must be satisfied: (1) The life of the forward contract extends from the foreign currency commitment date to the anticipated transaction date or a later date; (2) The forward contract is denominated in the same currency as the foreign currency commitment and for an amount that is the same or less than the amount of the foreign currency commitment; and (3) The foreign currency commitment is firm and uncancelable.

(1) At January 1, 19X1:

Receivable for currency purchased (400,000 × $.40)	160,000	
Premium on forward contract	4,000	
Due to exchange broker (400,000 × $.41)		164,000

(2) At December 31, 19X1:

Receivable for currency purchased	20,000	
Deferred exchange gain [400,000 × ($.45 − $.40)]		20,000

(3) At June 30, 19X2:

Receivable for currency purchased	24,000	
Deferred exchange gain [400,000 × ($.51 − $.45)]		24,000
Due to exchange broker	164,000	
Cash		164,000
Inventory	204,000	
Accounts payable (400,000 × $.51)		204,000
Foreign currency (400,000 × $.51)	204,000	
Receivable for currency purchased		204,000
Accounts payable	204,000	
Foreign currency (400,000 × $.51)		204,000
Deferred exchange gain	44,000	
Premium on forward contract		4,000
Inventory		40,000
Accounts receivable	200,000	
Cost of sales	164,000	
Inventory		164,000
Sales		200,000

The net effect of these transactions, as reflected in the above entries, is that the U.S. firm incurs a cash outlay of $164,000 to purchase the equipment from the Swiss supplier, and then bills its U.S. customer the agreed upon contract price of $200,000. The exchange gain and the premium were deferred to the date of the transaction, and then recognized as adjustments of the dollar measure of the transaction.

If the forward contract had not been secured, the cost at the time the commitment materialized in the form of a transaction would have been $204,000 (due to the increase in the exchange price for Swiss francs), and the U.S. importer's gross margin would have been eliminated. Thus, the forward contract enabled the firm to maintain its planned margin, subject to the additional "interest cost" embodied in the premium on the forward contract, and the accounting entries reflect these economic facts. Note that if commitments were recorded in accounting, instead of waiting for a transaction to occur, these special procedures for foreign currency commitments would not be required.

Case 3. Hedging a Foreign Currency Exposed Net Asset or Liability Position. Assume that a U.S. exporter sells goods to a British firm on Dec.

1, 19X1 for 10,000 pounds sterling, payable (in pounds) on March 1, 19X2. On December 1, the spot rate for the pound is $1.80, and the future rate for delivery in 90 days is $1.77. In order to hedge the exposed net asset position, the U.S. exporter on December 1, sells 10,000 pounds for delivery in 90 days.

Assuming the spot rate for the pound is $1.70 on December 31, 19X1, and $1.72 on March 1, 19X2, the exporter would make the following entries:

(1) At December 1, 19X1:

Accounts receivable (10,000 × $1.80)	18,000	
Sales		18,000
Due from exchange broker (10,000 × $1.77)	17,700	
Discount on forward contract	300	
Liability for currency sold (10,000 × $1.80)		18,000

(2) At December 31, 19X1:

Exchange loss [10,000 × ($1.80 − $1.70)]	1,000	
Accounts receivable		1,000
Liability for currency sold	1,000	
Exchange gain [10,000 × ($1.80 − $1.70)]		1,000
Amortization of exchange discount	100	
Discount on forward contract (⅓ × $300)		100

(3) At March 1, 19X2:

Foreign currency (10,000 × $1.72)	17,200	
Exchange gain		200
Accounts receivable		17,000
Cash	17,700	
Due from exchange broker		17,700
Liability for currency sold	17,000	
Exchange loss	200	
Foreign currency (10,000 × $1.72)		17,200
Amortization of exchange discount	200	
Discount on forward contract ($300 − $100)		200

By engaging in the forward contract, the exporter was able to insure collection of the dollar equivalent selling price at the date of sale, less the $300 discount incurred because of the difference between the forward rate and the spot rate. In 19X1, the exchange loss ($1,000) incurred on the open account receivable was exactly offset by the exchange gain ($1,000) on the forward contract, and thus the net expense reported in the exporter's 19X1 income statement would be the $100 amortization of the discount on the forward contract. Although in this simple case it seems unnecessary to value and record the offsetting exchange gains and losses on the open asset account and the forward contract, the two transactions are viewed as independent events that should be separately accounted for. Furthermore, in practice, it may often be difficult to relate specific hedging transactions with specific open accounts. Of course, in order to determine that a particular forward contract is a hedge as opposed to a speculative contract, one must be able to identify at least on an aggregate basis that the contract relates to an exposed foreign currency position (resulting from foreign currency transactions and/or an investment in a foreign subsidiary or branch).

Case 4. Speculation in Foreign Exchange Fluctuations.   Assume that a U.S. firm without any identifiable foreign currency commitments or an exposed foreign currency position decided to speculate in fluctuations in the value of the pound sterling. On December 1, 19X1, the firm purchased 10,000 pounds for delivery in 90 days. On this date, the spot rate for the pound is $1.80 and the 90-day futures rate is $1.77. Assuming on December 31, 19X1 the forward rate for a 60-day delivery (the remaining time on the purchased forward contract) is $1.68, and that on March 1, 19X2 the spot rate is $1.72, the firm would make the following entries:

(1) At December 1, 19X1:

Receivable for currency purchased (10,000 × $1.77)	17,700	
Due to exchange broker		17,700

(2) At December 31, 19X1:

Exchange loss [10,000 × ($1.77 − $1.68)]	900	
Receivable for currency purchased		900

(3) At March 1, 19X2:

Due to exchange broker	17,700	
Cash		17,700
Foreign currency (10,000 × $1.72)	17,200	
Exchange gain		400
Receivable for currency purchased ($17,700 − $900)		16,800

As was indicated previously, a forward contract entered into for speculative purposes is valued at the current forward rate for the remaining life of the contract. Thus, on December 31, 19X1, the forward rate for a 60-day delivery was used, because the original contract matures on March 1, 19X2. This valuation results in an exchange loss of $900 that is recognized in the 19X1 income statement. Final settlement on March 1, 19X2 produces an exchange gain of $400, as the value of the pound strengthened slightly over the period from December 31, 19X1 to March 1, 19X2; this gain will be reported in the 19X2 income statement. Overall, the company incurred an exchange loss of $500, as can be seen by comparing the $17,700 paid to the exchange broker with the $17,200 value of the 10,000 pounds received.

In this example, a speculative forward contract was individually identified. The same treatment would also be given to the amount of foreign currency on forward contracts in excess of identifiable foreign currency commitments and/or exposed net asset or liability positions.

Accounting for forward contracts under the provisions of *FASB Standard 8* may be summarized as follows:

Type	Balance Sheet Valuation	Treatment of Exchange Gain(Loss)	Treatment of Discount or Premium
(1) Hedge of identifiable foreign currency commitment	Current spot rate	Deferred to date of transaction; then an adjustment of dollar measure of transaction.	May treat same as exchange gain or loss, or amortize against operations over contract life.
(2) Other hedge	Current spot rate	Recognized currently in income statement.	Amortize against operations over contract life.
(3) Speculation	Current forward rate	Recognized currently in income statement.	Not separately measured.

Multiple Exchange Rates

If transactions are denominated in a foreign currency that has multiple exchange rates, the following rates should be used:[7]

1. At the transaction date, the transaction should be translated and recorded at the rate at which that particular type of transaction could be then settled.
2. At a subsequent balance sheet date on which the amount owing remains unsettled, the receivable or payable should be translated at the rate at which they then could be settled.

Normally, the applicable rate will remain unchanged between the transaction date and the settlement date.

TRANSLATING FOREIGN CURRENCY FINANCIAL STATEMENTS

A second major problem of accounting for foreign operations is the translation or restatement of account balances expressed in a foreign currency to monetary equivalents expressed in domestic currency. Obviously, this is an essential step if one is to record a domestic firm's equity in the earnings of a foreign subsidiary or investee, or to prepare combined or consolidated financial statements for a domestic firm with one or more foreign branches or subsidiaries. *The primary objective of the translation process is to obtain valuations (in domestic terms) that are essentially consistent with domestic accounting principles which control the valuations of the specific accounts being translated.*[8] For example, if an account balance

---

[7] *FASB Standard 8,* paragraph 30(a).

[8] *FASB Standard 8,* paragraph 6.

refers to fixed tangible assets, generally accepted accounting principles require that the account reflect the unexpired original cost of the asset. Therefore, the procedures for translation should accomplish the conversion of the
cost balance expressed in foreign currency to a domestic monetary expression which also reflects unexpired original cost.

Obviously, if the foreign currency statements were initially prepared
using accounting principles different from those that are generally acceptable in the United States, translation procedures will not remedy this deficiency. Accordingly, in such cases, the foreign currency statements must
first be adjusted so as to conform to U.S. accounting principles, and then
translated and incorporated (through combination, consolidation, or equity
method) into the financial statements of a U.S. firm.[9]

Translating Assets and Liabilities

A number of different methods of translating the assets and liabilities on
foreign currency financial statements have been applied in accounting practice. At one time, the *current-noncurrent* method was widely applied,
whereby all current assets and liabilities were translated at the current rate,
and other assets and liabilities were translated at the historical rate in effect
on the date they were recorded. This method was subject to criticism on
several grounds, including the arbitrariness of the current-noncurrent classification and the resulting dissimilar treatment given to inventory and other
real assets and to short-term and long-term debt. Because of its conceptual
weaknesses, the current-noncurrent method was gradually superseded by
the *monetary-nonmonetary* method. Under this method, all monetary assets
and liabilities are translated at the current rate, and nonmonetary assets
and liabilities are translated at the applicable historical rates. In 1972, a
research study was released by the AICPA in which yet another method
was proposed—the *temporal* method.[10] Under the temporal method, assets
and liabilities are translated in a manner that retains the accounting principles that have been applied to them. For example, if an asset is measured
at original transaction cost, a historical translation rate would be used; if it
were valued at replacement cost, a current translation rate would be appropriate. As long as original transaction costs are used to value nonmonetary
assets and liabilities, as they generally are today, the temporal method produces results essentially equivalent to the monetary-nonmonetary method.

---

[9] *FASB Standard 8,* paragraphs 9–10. Here and throughout the remaining discussion of the translation process, we assume U.S.-based firms operating under accounting principles that are generally acceptable in the United States. Although certain of
the specific rules would change, the accounting issues addressed are the same regardless of the choice of a particular country as an arbitrary focal point.

[10] Leonard Lorensen, *Accounting Research Study No. 12,* "Reporting Foreign
Operations of U.S. Companies in U.S. Dollars" (New York: AICPA, 1972).

However, if accounting principles were to be modified (as seems quite possible), the methods would yield different results.

In *FASB Standard 8,* the Financial Accounting Standards Board opted in large measure for the temporal method:

In preparing foreign statements, balances representing cash and amounts receivable or payable that are denominated in other than the local currency shall be adjusted to reflect the current rate between the local and the foreign currency. Those adjusted balances and other balances representing cash and amounts receivable or payable that are denominated in the local currency shall be translated into dollars at the *current rate.*

For assets and liabilities other than those described [above], the particular measurement basis used shall determine the translation rate. Several measurement bases are used in financial accounting under present generally accepted accounting principles. A measurement may be based on a price in a past exchange (for example, historical cost), a price in a current purchase exchange (for example, replacement cost), or a price in a current sale exchange (for example, market price). Foreign statements may employ various measurement bases. Accordingly, accounts in foreign statements that are carried at exchange prices shall be translated in a manner that retains their measurement bases as follows:

(a) Accounts carried at prices in past exchanges (past prices) shall be translated at *historical rates.*

(b) Accounts carried at prices in current purchase or sale exchanges (current prices) or future exchanges (future prices) shall be translated at the *current rate.*[11]

Application of these general translation principles to a collection of specific assets and liabilities is reflected in Illustration 12–1.

Translating Revenue and Expenses

In the past, revenue and expense items in the foreign currency financial statements were generally translated at the average rate prevailing for the period, except that expenses (and occasionally revenue) that could be directly identified with an asset or liability (for example, depreciation expense) were translated at the same rate as the related asset. This procedure was generally followed whether the current-noncurrent or the monetary-nonmonetary methods were used.

In *FASB Standard 8,* essentially the same principle was prescribed:

Revenue and expense transactions shall be translated in a manner that produces approximately the same dollar amounts that would have resulted had the underlying transactions been translated into dollars on the dates they occurred. Since separate translation of each transaction is usually impractical, the specified

---

[11] *FASB Standard 8,* paragraphs 11–12. (Emphasis supplied.)

Illustration 12–1

RATES USED TO TRANSLATE ASSETS AND LIABILITIES

	Current	Historical
		*Translation Rates*

	Current	Historical
Assets		
Cash on hand and demand and time deposits	x	
Marketable equity securities:		
Carried at cost		x
Carried at current market price	x	
Accounts and notes receivable and related unearned discount	x	
Allowance for doubtful accounts and notes receivable	x	
Inventories:		
Carried at cost		x
Carried at current replacement price or current selling price ...	x	
Carried at net realizable value	x	
Carried at contract price (produced under fixed price contracts)	x	
Prepaid insurance, advertising, and rent		x
Refundable deposits	x	
Advances to unconsolidated subsidiaries	x	
Property, plant, and equipment		x
Accumulated depreciation of property, plant, and equipment		x
Cash surrender value of life insurance	x	
Patents, trademarks, licenses, and formulas		x
Goodwill		x
Other intangible assets		x
Liabilities		
Accounts and notes payable and overdrafts	x	
Accrued expenses payable	x	
Accrued losses on firm purchase commitments	x	
Refundable deposits	x	
Deferred income		x
Bonds payable or other long-term debt	x	
Unamortized premium or discount on bonds or notes payable	x	
Convertible bonds payable	x	
Accrued pension obligations	x	
Obligations under warranties	x	

Source: *Statement of Financial Accounting Standards No. 8*, p. 20.

result can be achieved by using an average rate for the period. However, revenue and expenses that relate to assets and liabilities translated at historical rates shall be translated at the historical rates used to translate the related assets or liabilities.[12]

Exchange Gains and Losses

Exchange gains and losses emerge in the process of translating the account balances of foreign branches, investees, and subsidiaries. These gains

---

[12] *FASB Standard 8*, paragraph 13.

or losses are the consequence of fluctuations in the exchange rates between the beginning and the end of the period for assets and liabilities that are translated at the current rate. In the past, a variety of treatments were accorded exchange gains and losses. However, *FASB Standard 8* prescribed the same treatment for exchange gains and losses arising from account translation as for those arising from credit transactions denominated in a foreign currency, i.e., inclusion in the income statement for the period in which the rate changes.[13]

Foreign Branches

The following two sections of this chapter give special attention to the problems associated with accounting for foreign branches and foreign subsidiaries. In this discussion, it should be apparent that many of the techniques of translating foreign currency financial statements are common to both *branches* and *subsidiaries*. Accordingly, the reader should remain alert to the frequent applicability of the discussion to either type of investment.

Accounting for foreign branches is not essentially unlike that for domestic branches; most of the new accounting problems introduced relate to the translation of foreign currencies to domestic monetary units. Necessarily, the accounts of foreign business subdivisions are expressed in units of the local currency and accordingly must be translated to equivalent domestic units before they are meaningful in the preparation of combined financial statements. Most of the procedures needed for this translation process have been described in the previous discussion. There remains only the special case of branch accounts that have reciprocal balances in home office accounts, and these are translated simply by restating them in domestic currency amounts equal to the balances in the contra home office accounts. This conversion accomplishes the same results that would be obtained if each transaction accumulated in the reciprocal accounts were translated using the historical exchange rate effective at the transaction date.

The journalizing of transactions for a domestic home office and a foreign branch involve few differences from those recorded in the case of a domestic branch. Transactions of the branch are, of course, recorded in foreign monetary units. Additionally, it may be desirable to maintain a separate record of currency movements between the home office and branch. Special "remittance" accounts, which facilitate this objective, are utilized to record the intracompany currency transfers of each period; at the end of the period, the remittance accounts are closed to the relevant Branch Current or Home Office Current accounts.

Consider the following transactions, which are journalized in Illustration 12–2:

---

[13] *FASB Standard 8*, paragraph 17. For a discussion of several alternative proposals that were considered by the Board and rejected, see paragraphs 172–199.

Illustration 12–2

Houston Home Office Books (In Dollars)

(1) Remittance to branch 1,920
    Cash 1,920

(2) Branch current 4,131
    Shipments to branch 4,131

(8) Cash 2,688
    Remittance from branch 2,688

Mexico City–Branch Books (In Pesos)

(1) Cash 24,000
    Remittance from home office 24,000

(2) Shipments from home office 51,000
    Home office current 51,000

(3) Purchases 18,000
    Accounts payable 18,000

(4) Fixed assets 90,000
    Notes payable 90,000

(5) Accounts receivable 62,500
    Sales 62,500

(6) Cash 31,000
    Accounts receivable 31,000

(7) Expenses 7,600
    Cash 7,600

(8) Remittance to home office 32,000
    Cash 32,000

(9) Depreciation expense 850
    Bad debts 525
    Accumulated depreciation 850
    Allowance for doubtful accounts 525

(1)   A Houston home office opened a Mexico City branch, forwarding to it a draft for 24,000 pesos, purchased at $.080, to be used for working fund purposes.

(2)   Merchandise costing the home office $4,131 was shipped to the branch when the current rate of exchange was $.081.

(3)   The branch acquired from regional distributors additional merchandise on account for 18,000 pesos.

(4)   The branch purchased fixed assets locally for 90,000 pesos, giving a 60-day noninterest-bearing note in payment. The accounts in respect to these assets are customarily carried on the books of the branch. The rate of exchange at date of purchase was $.079.

(5)   Sales on account recorded by the branch were 62,500 pesos.

(6)   Collections on account amounted to 31,000 pesos.

(7)   Cash expenses paid by the branch were 7,600 pesos.

(8)   A remittance of 32,000 pesos was made by the branch to the home office; the rate of exchange was $.084.

(9)   Month-end adjustments were recorded by the branch for:

> Depreciation .... 850 pesos
> Provision for doubtful accounts .... 525 pesos

The final inventory of the branch consisted of 24,000 pesos of merchandise received on shipment from the home office; unsold merchandise purchased locally amounted to 5,475 pesos. The average rate of exchange during the period was $.075, while the current rate of exchange at the end of the month was $.085.

The adjusted trial balance of the Mexico City branch at the end of the first month's operations is as follows:

	(*In Pesos*)	
Cash	15,400	
Accounts receivable	31,500	
Allowance for doubtful accounts		525
Fixed assets	90,000	
Accumulated depreciation		850
Accounts payable		18,000
Notes payable		90,000
Remittance from home office		24,000
Remittance to home office	32,000	
Home office current		51,000
Sales		62,500
Shipments from home office	51,000	
Purchases	18,000	
Expenses (cash)	7,600	
Depreciation	850	
Provision for doubtful accounts	525	
	246,875	246,875

The branch closing entries take the following form:

	(In Pesos)	
Inventory	29,475	
Sales	62,500	
Purchases		18,000
Shipments from home office		51,000
Expenses		7,600
Depreciation		850
Bad debts		525
Income summary		14,000
Income summary	14,000	
Home office current		14,000
Remittance from home office	24,000	
Home office current	8,000	
Remittance to home office		32,000

At the end of each period, the branch will provide the home office with copies of its adjusted trial balance, closing entries, financial statements, and a summary of the transaction details of its Home Office Current account. These data, before they are useful to the home office, must be converted into domestic currency. The working paper in Illustration 12–3 provides a convenient vehicle for summarizing these data and translating them into equivalent domestic monetary units. The combined statement working paper may be easily prepared beginning with the final columns of the translation working paper.

When the adjusted trial balance of a foreign branch is translated into equivalent domestic currency units, only infrequently are the sum of the debit and the sum of the credit account balances equal, as may be noted in the working paper in Illustration 12–3. The amount necessary to reconcile these sums is the *exchange adjustment gain or loss*. The gain or loss is stated in terms of domestic currency units and must be recorded by the home office in the closing entry sequence. Referring to the example, the entry to record this loss would be as follows.

Exchange adjustment loss	83.00	
Branch current		83.00

In subsequent accounting periods, double counting of the exchange adjustment loss is prevented by translating (in the working paper) the Home Office Current account into an amount in domestic currency equal to the new balance in Branch Current.

It should be noted that this process of translating the Home Office Current account precludes the possibility of observing equivalent (domestic) balances in the two reciprocal accounts as a test or confirmation that *all* reciprocal transactions have been recorded in both accounts. Such a test was suggested in Chapter 11 as a means of determining whether any reconciling adjustments should be recorded on the books of a domestic branch and/or home office. Since the test cannot be applied to a foreign

Illustration 12–3

MEXICO CITY BRANCH

Translation Working Paper
(Date)

	Adjusted Trial Balance (Pesos)	Exchange Rates Code	Exchange Rates Rate	Adjusted Trial Balance (Dollars)	Income Statement (Dollars)	Balance Sheet (Dollars)
Debits						
Cash	15,400	C	.085	1,309.00		1,309.00
Accounts receivable	31,500	C	.085	2,677.50		2,677.50
Fixed assets	90,000	H	.079	7,110.00		7,110.00
Remittance to home office	32,000	R		2,688.00		2,688.00
Shipments from home office	51,000	R		4,131.00	4,131.00	
Purchases	18,000	A	.075	1,350.00	1,350.00	
Expenses	7,600	A	.075	570.00	570.00	
Depreciation	850	H	.079	67.15	67.15	
Bad debts	525	C	.085	44.63	44.63	
	246,875					
Inventory:						
From home office	24,000	H	.081			1,944.00
From foreign suppliers	5,475	A	.075			410.63
Exchange adjustment loss				83.00	83.00	
Net income—branch					796.35	
				20,030.28	7,042.13	16,139.13
Credits						
Allowance for doubtful accounts	525	C	.085	44.63		44.63
Accumulated depreciation	850	H	.079	67.15		67.15
Accounts payable	18,000	C	.085	1,530.00		1,530.00
Notes payable	90,000	C	.085	7,650.00		7,650.00
Remittance from home office	24,000	R		1,920.00		1,920.00
Home office current	51,000	R		4,131.00		4,131.00
Sales	62,500	A	.075	4,687.50	4,687.50	
	246,875					
Inventory:						
From home office	24,000	H	.081		1,944.00	
From foreign suppliers	5,475	A	.075		410.63	
Net income—branch						796.35
				20,030.28	7,042.13	16,139.13

Code:
  C = current rate of exchange, end of month, $.085.
  H = historical rate of exchange, date of purchase.
  R = balance of reciprocal account, home office books.
  A = average rate of exchange for the month, $.075.

branch, the possible need for reconciling adjustments must be determined by a comparative audit of the entries recorded in each reciprocal account.

Foreign Subsidiaries

In the event that international operations take the form of an investment in foreign subsidiaries, the accounts of the foreign subsidiaries should be included in consolidated statements if the parent exercises sufficient control over the subsidiary. In determining the presence of effective parent control, the same criteria should apply for both foreign and domestic affiliates. Yet, the accountant should be especially alert to the limitations of consolidated financial statements which include foreign subsidiaries. "In view of the uncertain values and availability of the assets and net income of foreign subsidiaries subject to controls and exchange restrictions and the consequent unrealistic statements of income that may result from the translation of many foreign currencies into dollars, careful consideration should be given to the fundamental question of whether it is proper to consolidate the statements of foreign subsidiaries with the statements of United States companies."[14]

Current accounting policy indicates at least four methods of disclosing in financial statements information respecting foreign subsidiaries:

(a)   To exclude foreign subsidiaries from consolidation and to furnish (1) statements in which only domestic subsidiaries are consolidated and (2) as to foreign subsidiaries, a summary in suitable form of their assets and liabilities, their income and losses for the year, and the parent company's equity therein. The total amount of investments in foreign subsidiaries should be shown separately, and the basis on which the amount was arrived at should be stated. If these investments include any surplus [retained earnings] of foreign subsidiaries and such surplus had previously been included in consolidated surplus, the amount should be separately shown or earmarked in stating the consolidated surplus in the statements here suggested. The exclusion of foreign subsidiaries from consolidation does not make it acceptable practice to include intercompany profits which would be eliminated if such subsidiaries were consolidated.

(b)   To consolidate domestic and foreign subsidiaries and to furnish in addition the summary described in (a) (2) above.

---

[14] Section 1081.08, *APB Accounting Principles—Current Text*. The reader should note that the problem of assessing the sufficiency of parental control over a foreign subsidiary may also be relevant to the preparation of combined statements for a domestic home office and a foreign branch. It may occur that foreign governmental restrictions, or similar factors, so inhibit the home office's operational and financial control over a foreign branch that the preparation of combined financial statements should be avoided.

(c)   To furnish (1) complete consolidated statements and also (2) consolidated statements for domestic companies only.

(d)   To consolidate domestic and foreign subsidiaries and to furnish in addition parent company statements showing the investment in and income from foreign subsidiaries separately from those of domestic subsidiaries.[15]

Although information on foreign subsidiaries may be presented in several ways, increasingly they are included in the consolidated statements.

Establishing Values at Acquisition.   On the date that an investment in a foreign subsidiary is made, the assets and liabilities of the subsidiary are adjusted to their fair values, and then *all* assets and liabilities of the subsidiary are translated at the current rate in effect on the date of acquisition. Thereafter, this current rate on the date of acquisition is the relevant rate for assets and liabilities that are to be translated at historical rates in subsequent balance sheets. Note that under this procedure, the differential is wholly allocable to goodwill, which is fixed in dollars at acquisition.[16]

Accounting Subsequent to Acquisition.   The equity method of accounting for investments in affiliates is equally applicable to domestic and foreign affiliates. In order to apply the equity method, the financial statements of the investee must be completely translated, and then the parent's share of the affiliate's net income expressed in dollars can be determined and recorded. It is *not* proper to translate the affiliate's net income expressed in foreign currency, because this single figure is a composite of many values requiring many different exchange rates. Note that this procedure must also be applied to less-than-50-percent-owned affiliates that are accounted for under the equity method.[17]

Translating the Subsidiary's Accounts.   Translation of a subsidiary's assets and liabilities are based upon the same general principles that apply to all foreign currency financial statements, and illustrated for a foreign branch in the preceding section. We now must consider the translation procedures for the capital accounts of the subsidiary and the minority interest.

The subsidiary's capital stock is normally translated at the spot rate prevailing at the date of acquisition. Contributed capital in excess of par value of capital stock is likewise translated at this rate. The retained earnings balance of the subsidiary at the beginning of a statement period is translated on the basis of its *dollar* balance at the end of the previous period, and the current period's increments and decrements are calculated from the translated effects of the income statement and dividend declarations.

---

[15] Section 1081.09, *APB Accounting Principles—Current Text.*

[16] *FASB Standard 8,* paragraph 41. This procedure applies to investments accounted for under the *purchase* method, which has been the main focus of the text. If the investment were recorded as a *pooling of interests,* the assets and liabilities of the subsidiary are not revalued, and applicable historical rates are based upon the dates that assets and liabilities were acquired.

[17] *FASB Standard 8,* paragraph 42.

Finally, minority interest calculations are based upon stockholders' equity values in the translated financial statements.

Multiple Exchange Rates

When multiple exchange rates exist, the rate to be used in translating foreign currency financial statements is subject to debate. *FASB Standard 8* prescribes the rate applicable to conversion of the foreign currency for purposes of dividend remittances. This choice is defended on two grounds. First, it is asserted that the translated operating results are more meaningful because earnings can only be converted into dollars (or the currency of the country in which the parent company is domiciled) at this rate. Second, the dividend rate measures the sacrifice incurred by the foreign company in foregoing remittance to acquire or hold an asset.[18]

Financial Statement Disclosure

In addition to covering the translation of foreign currency transactions and financial statements, *FASB Standard 8* specifies certain disclosures that should be included in the financial statements of U.S. firms. These disclosures include the following:[19]

(1) Disclose the aggregate exchange gains or losses included in the determination of net income for the period.

(2) If the effects of exchange rate changes during the period on the reported revenue and expenses were significant, these effects, if practicable, shall be described and quantified. This disclosure does not relate to the mere mathematical translation of results of operations; rather, it deals with the economic impacts of the exchange rate changes on the foreign affiliate's selling prices, sales volume, cost structures, etc. To a considerable extent, it parallels the current SEC requirement for inclusion of a "management analysis of operations" in domestic financial statements.

(3) If exchange rates change after the date of a foreign affiliate's financial statements, no adjustment shall be made, but if the change is significant, disclosure may be necessary.

TRANSNATIONAL FINANCIAL REPORTING

It should be clear that a listing of potential problem areas associated with accounting for international operations would be virtually limitless. Since accounting reports depend on a wide variety of social, economic, legal, and even political relationships, the potential problem areas of international accounting may emerge from the differences between any of these rela-

---

[18] *FASB Standard 8,* paragraphs 30(b) and 227.

[19] *FASB Standard 8,* paragraphs 32–34 and 223–225.

tionships in the various countries. Perhaps the most important problem area the international accountant must face is the wide variation in countries' "generally accepted" accounting principles. Three alternative schools of thought have been developed or advocated in connection with this issue:[20]

(1) *Develop primary and secondary financial statements.* The Accountants International Study Group (previously referred to) studies accounting, auditing, and financial reporting in Canada, the United Kingdom, and the United States, with the purpose of promoting greater international harmonization. Several studies have been published by this Study Group, including in 1975 *International Financial Reporting.* In this study, the AISG recommends that multiple statements be prepared by companies with interested audiences in several countries. Primary financial statements are prepared from the point of view of investors in the company's country of domicile, and secondary financial statements are prepared to satisfy the requirements of investors in other countries.

(2) *Single domicile reporting.* This school of thought holds that financial statements can only be prepared from the point of view of the country of domicile.

(3) *International reporting standards.* An increasing number of accountants believe that uniform international accounting standards should accompany the growing number of companies involved in international operations. This position has been recently strengthened with the establishment of the International Accounting Standards Committee, with joint representation from professional accounting bodies in nine countries (Australia, Canada, France, Germany, Japan, Mexico, the Netherlands, the United Kingdom and Ireland, and the United States). As of April 1976, the IASC had issued three standards (Disclosure of Accounting Policies, Valuation and Presentation of Inventories, and Consolidated Financial Statements), and several additional topics were in exposure drafts or on the committee's agenda. The AICPA is actively supporting this effort to develop uniform international financial accounting standards, and the prospects seem promising at the present time.

Although individual countries will probably always impose certain constraints on financial reporting standards, the development of uniform standards will greatly assist the necessary translations of foreign currency financial statements.

A second problem is the perceived need for information about the relative profitability, degrees of risk, and growth opportunities of each of the major geographical areas of a multinational firm's operations. This particular set of disaggregated data is of course but one instance of the broader issue of segmental reporting, discussed in Chapter 6. The reader is referred to Chapter 6 for a discussion of proposed FASB guidelines for the presentation of supplementary information on foreign operations.

---

[20] Gerhard G. Mueller and Lauren M. Walker, "The Coming of Age of Transnational Financial Reporting," *The Journal of Accountancy,* July 1976.

QUESTIONS

1. Define currency exchange rates.
2. Distinguish between free and official rates of exchange.
3. Distinguish between quoting an exchange rate for a given currency "directly" and "indirectly."
4. Distinguish between spot and forward rates of exchange.
5. Distinguish between current and historical rates of exchange.
6. When do exchange gains or losses occur in import/export transactions?
7. How should exchange gains or losses arising from import/export transactions be reported?
8. Summarize current accounting policy related to import/export transactions denominated in a foreign currency.
9. Enumerate the three major types of forward contracts.
10. Summarize current accounting policy for forward contracts.
11. When multiple exchange rates exist, what rate should be used in translating foreign currency transactions?
12. What is the objective in translating foreign currency financial statements?
13. How are assets and liabilities in foreign currency financial statements translated?
14. How are revenue and expense items in foreign currency financial statements translated?
15. How are the exchange gains or losses arising from the translation of foreign currency financial statements reported under current accounting policy?
16. What limiting factors affect the decision as to whether or not a foreign subsidiary should be consolidated with a domestic parent?
17. When multiple exchange rates exist, what rate should be used in translating foreign currency financial statements?
18. Indicate three types of disclosure related to foreign operations that are required under *FASB Standard 8*.

EXERCISES

Exercise 12–1

John Weber is planning a trip through several foreign countries, during which he expects to purchase and inspect the products sold in each country that compete with those of his employer. In anticipation of the trip, Weber purchases $300 worth of each country's currency. He received the following amounts:

Country	Currency	Amount Received
Belgium	Franc	14,925
Denmark	Krone	2,256
France	Franc	1,667
Italy	Lira	187,500

Required:

State the exchange rate between U.S. dollars and each foreign currency purchased by Weber. Express each rate:
a. Directly.
b. Indirectly.

Exercise 12–2

Journalize the following transactions of the Black and White Company (a New York corporation) arising from its foreign operations:

June 1 Purchased merchandise from an Edinburgh, Scotland, manufacturer at an invoice cost of £1,000. On this date the exchange rate for pounds was $1.80.

5 Purchased merchandise from a Glasgow, Scotland, manufacturer. The billing is rendered for $2,000. The exchange rate for pounds is $1.82.

7 Sold merchandise to a Toronto wholesaler. Billing price is $4,000 (Canadian dollars), and the exchange rate for Canadian dollars is $1.02.

15 Paid £500 on account to the Edinburgh manufacturer. The exchange rate is $1.75.

20 Paid the amount due the Glasgow manufacturer. The exchange rate is $1.75.

25 Returned merchandise to the Edinburgh manufacturer and received credit for £100. The exchange rate is $1.75.

28 Received full payment on account from the Toronto wholesaler. The exchange rate is $.98.

30 Remitted final payment to the Edinburgh manufacturer. The exchange rate is $1.76.

Exercise 12–3

Prepare the journal entries to record the following transactions on the books of Schwab Corporation.

a. The Schwab Corporation purchased merchandise from the Z Company of Belgium for 50,000 francs when the exchange rate for the franc was $.02. Concurrently, the Schwab Corporation purchased 25,000 francs for future delivery at $.02.

b. The Schwab Corporation paid the Z Company for transaction (a) when the exchange rate for the franc was $.018. The futures purchased in (a) were received from the exchange broker.

c. The Schwab Corporation sold merchandise to the D Company of Finland for 10,000 Markkas when the exchange rate for the Markka was $.25. Concurrently, the Schwab Corporation sold 5,000 Markkas for future delivery at $.25.

d. The Schwab Corporation received payment from the D Company for transaction (c) when the exchange rate for the Markka was $.22. The futures sold in (c) were delivered to the exchange broker.

Exercise 12–4

The X Corporation engaged in the following international transactions during December, 19X1 (all purchase and sales invoices are expressed in foreign currency):

a. The X Corporation sold merchandise to the Y Company of Italy for 1,000,000 lire when the exchange rate for the lira was $.0016. Concurrently, the X Corporation sold 500,000 lire for future delivery at $.0016.

b. The X Corporation received payment from the Y Company in respect to transaction (a) when the exchange rate for the lira was $.0017. The futures sold in (a) were delivered to the exchange broker.

c. The X Corporation purchased merchandise from the A Company of Great Britain for 1,000 pounds when the exchange rate for the pound was $1.80. Concurrently, the X Corporation purchased 500 pounds for future delivery at $1.80.

d. The X Corporation paid the A Company for the merchandise purchased in transaction (c) when the exchange rate for the pound was $1.85. The futures purchased in (c) were received from the exchange broker.

e. The X Corporation sold merchandise to the B Company of Mexico for 10,000 pesos when the exchange rate for the peso was $.08.

f. The X Corporation purchased merchandise from the C Company of Mexico for 20,000 pesos when the exchange rate for the peso was $.08.

Required:

a. Prepare the journal entries to record the above transactions on the books of the X Corporation.

b. If the debts created by the last two transactions remain unpaid on December 31, 19X1, discuss their valuation if the exchange rate is $.10. Would your answer be different if the X Corporation had purchased, or sold, foreign exchange (pesos) for future delivery?

Exercise 12–5

On October 1, 19X1, Advanced Electronics, Inc., secured an order from a company located in West Germany for a new computer, to be delivered on April 1, 19X2. The sales price, which is payable in marks, is 200,000 marks. The 180-day delivery schedule allows for custom manufacture, delivery, and installation. Payment is received on delivery.

The spot rate for West German marks on October 1, 19X1 is $.40. In order to protect itself against foreign exchange fluctuations, Advanced Electronics, Inc., entered into a 180-day forward contract for the delivery of 200,000 marks at a price of $.41.

The following exchange rates prevailed:

(a) December 31, 19X1:
(1) Spot rate—$.37
(2) Forward rate for 90-day delivery—$.38
(b) April 1, 19X2:
Spot rate—$.35

Assume that the forward contract qualifies as a hedge of an identifiable foreign curerncy commitment under *FASB Standard 8*.

Required:

a. Prepare the entries that would be made by Advanced Electronics, Inc., for these transactions on:

(1)   October 1, 19X1
(2)   December 31, 19X1 (when the firm's annual report is prepared)
(3)   April 1, 19X2

b. Indicate the classification and valuation of accounts that would be reported in Advanced Electronics' balance sheet on December 31, 19X1.

Exercise 12–6

Indicate whether the following accounts on the books of a foreign company would be translated into dollars at the current or the historical rate:

(1)   Patents
(2)   Accrued liabilities
(3)   Marketable equity securities carried at cost
(4)   Deferred income
(5)   Inventory carried at cost
(6)   Allowance for doubtful accounts
(7)   Inventory carried at net realizable value
(8)   Property, plant, and equipment
(9)   Accumulated depreciation
(10) Advances to unconsolidated subsidiaries

Exercise 12–7

Dhia Products Company was incorporated in the State of Virginia in 1970 to do business as a manufacturer of medical supplies and equipment. Since incorporating, Dhia has doubled in size about every three years and is now considered one of the leading medical supply companies in the country.

During January 1974, Dhia established a subsidiary, Ban, Ltd., in the emerging nation of Shatha. Dhia owns 90 percent of the outstanding capital stock of Ban; the remaining 10 percent of Ban's outstanding capital stock is held by Shatha citizens, as required by Shatha constitutional law. The investment in Ban, accounted for by Dhia by the equity method, represents about 18% of the total assets of Dhia at December 31, 1977, the close of the accounting period for both companies.

Required:

a. What criteria should Dhia Products Company use in determining whether it would be appropriate to prepare consolidated financial statements with Ban, Ltd., for the year ended December 31, 1977? Explain.

b. Independent of your answer to (*a*), assume it has been appropriate for Dhia and Ban to prepare consolidated financial statements for each year

1974 through 1977. But before consolidated financial statements can be prepared, the individual account balances in Ban's December 31, 1977, adjusted trial balance must be translated into the appropriate number of United States dollars. For each of the ten (10) accounts listed below, taken from Ban's adjusted trial balance, specify what exchange rate (for example, average exchange rate for 1977, current exchange rate at December 31, 1977, etc.) should be used to translate the account balances into dollars and explain why that rate is appropriate. Number your answers to correspond with each account listed below.

1. Cash in Shatha National Bank.
2. Trade accounts receivable (all from 1977 revenues).
3. Supplies inventory (all purchased during the last quarter of 1977).
4. Land (purchased in 1974).
5. Short-term note payable to Shatha National Bank.
6. Capital stock (no par or stated value and all issued in January 1974).
7. Retained earnings, January 1, 1977.
8. Sales revenue.
9. Depreciation expense (on buildings).
10. Salaries expense.

(AICPA adapted)

PROBLEMS

Problem 1

Panozzo, International, a Chicago-based firm, enters into a 90-day forward contract on December 1, 19X1 to deliver 500,000 pounds at a price of $1.75, in order to hedge an exposed net asset position in a British affiliate amounting to 300,000 pounds and to speculate in exchange price fluctuations. The spot rate on this date is $1.77.

The following exchange rates prevailed:
    (a)   December 31, 19X1:
          (1)   Spot rate—$1.82
          (2)   Forward rate for 60-day delivery—$1.80
    (b)   March 1, 19X2:
          Spot rate—$1.85

Required:

a. Prepare the entries that would be made by Panozzo, International, for this forward contract on:
   (1)   December 1, 19X1
   (2)   December 31, 19X1 (when the firm's annual report is prepared)
   (3)   March 1, 19X2
b. Indicate the classification and valuation of accounts related to this forward contract transaction that would be reported in Panozzo, International's 19X1 financial statements.
c. Prepare a reconciliation of the total gain or loss ultimately realized on the maturity of this forward contract with the expense or income recognized in the 19X1 and 19X2 income statements.

Problem 2

The trial balance of Seneque Corporation, a South African corporation, at December 31, 19X1, is presented below (in rands):

Cash	60,000
Accounts receivable	100,000
Airplanes (net)	500,000
Depreciation expense	80,000
Other expenses	160,000
	900,000
Allowance for doubtful accounts	10,000
Notes payable	200,000
Capital stock	100,000
Retained earnings, January 1	290,000
Revenue	300,000
	900,000

The capital stock was issued seven years ago when the company was formed to provide charter air service; at that time, the exchange rate was $.80. The current fleet of airplanes was acquired three years ago when the exchange rate was $.90; the notes were given to a local bank at the same time. Revenue and other expense were realized uniformly over 19X1. The spot rates for rands in 19X1 were:

January 1	—	$1.10
Average for 19X1	—	$1.15
December 31	—	$1.20

Retained earnings in the December 31, 19X0 balance sheet (in dollars) of Seneque Corporation amounted to $233,000.

Required:

a. Prepare a trial balance in dollars for Seneque Corporation at December 31, 19X1.

b. Calculate Seneque Corporation's 19X1 net income in dollars.

c. Prepare a balance sheet for Seneque Corporation at December 31, 19X1 expressed in dollars.

d. Assuming that May Corporation, a Seattle firm, held an 80 percent ownership interest in Seneque Corporation, prepare the entry that May Corporation would make at December 31, 19X1 to record its equity in Seneque's 19X1 earnings (ignore differential amortization).

Problem 3

The trial balance of Mommessin Corporation, a French company, at December 31, 19X1, is presented below (in francs):

Cash	40,000
Accounts receivable	20,000
Inventory, January 1	70,000
Plant and equipment (net)	100,000
Purchases	100,000
Depreciation expense	20,000
Expenses	50,000
	400,000

Notes payable	60,000
Capital stock	100,000
Retained earnings, January 1	60,000
Sales	180,000
	400,000

The capital stock was issued and plant and equipment acquired four years ago when the exchange rate for the French franc was $.30. The inventory at the beginning of the year was acquired during the last quarter of 19X0 when the exchange rate was $.23. Purchases and sales were made and expenses incurred uniformly over 19X1, and the average exchange rate for 19X1 was $.22. Retained earnings in the December 31, 19X0 balance sheet (in dollars) of Mommessin Corporation amounted to $15,200. The spot rate for the French franc at December 31, 19X1 was $.20.

Required:

a. Prepare a trial balance in dollars for Mommessin Corporation at December 31, 19X1.
t. Assuming the December 31, 19X1 inventory amounted to 60,000 francs, and that it was acquired when the exchange rate was $.21, calculate 19X1 net income in dollars.
c. Prepare a balance sheet for Mommessin Corporation at December 31, 19X1 expressed in dollars.
d. Assuming that Faison Importers, Inc., a Virginia firm, held a 70 percent ownership interest in Mommessin Corporation, prepare the entry that Faison Importers, Inc. would make at December 31, 19X1 to record its equity in Mommessin's 19X1 earnings (ignore differential amortization).

Problem 4

Carter Company, an Atlanta-based firm, purchased 100 percent of the outstanding capital stock of Fritz Corporation, a West German firm, on January 1, 19X2 for $380,000. The book and fair values of Fritz Corporation's assets and liabilities on December 31, 19X1 are as follows (in marks):

	Book Value	Fair Value
Cash	100,000	100,000
Accounts receivable	150,000	150,000
Inventory	250,000	300,000
Plant and equipment (net)	400,000	600,000
	900,000	1,150,000
Bank notes and bonds payable ...	300,000	300,000
Net assets	600,000	850,000
Composed of:		
Capital stock	100,000	
Retained earnings	500,000	
	600,000	

The capital stock was issued and plant and equipment acquired five years ago when the exchange rate for marks was $.30, and the inventory was acquired during the last quarter of 19X1 when the exchange rate was $.38. On December 31, 19X1 and January 1, 19X2, the current spot rate for marks is $.40.

Required:

a. Prepare a trial balance for Fritz Corporation in dollars on December 31, 19X1.
b. Prepare the investment elimination and differential allocation entries for a consolidated balance sheet on January 1, 19X2.
c. Assuming that the exchange rate for marks averaged $.43 during the last quarter of 19X2 (when the inventory on hand at December 31, 19X2 was acquired), and that the current spot rate for marks on December 31, 19X2 was $.45, indicate what rates would be used to translate the asset, liability, and stockholders' equity accounts of Fritz Corporation for the purpose of preparing a consolidated balance sheet on December 31, 19X2 (Assume no new categories of assets or liabilities existed, and that no new plant and equipment was acquired).
d. Assuming that the goodwill was amortized over ten years, at what value would goodwill be carried in the December 31, 19X2 consolidated balance sheet?

Problem 5

The adjusted trial balances of the Dallas Company and its Swedish branch on December 31, 1977, were:

	Home Office (Dollars)		Branch (Krona)	
Cash	$ 27,800		18,300	
Accounts receivable	32,000		30,000	
Allowance for doubtful accounts..		$ 400		300
Merchandise inventory (1/1) ...	24,000		9,000	
Plant and equipment	140,000		68,000	
Accumulated depreciation		25,000		12,000
Accounts payable		20,000		7,000
Remittance to home office			20,000	
Remittance from branch		4,200		
Shipments from home office			42,000	
Shipments to branch		7,000		
Branch current	21,560			
Home office current				108,000
Sales		100,000		78,000
Purchases	76,360		10,000	
Expenses	12,000		8,000	
Capital stock		150,000		
Retained earnings		27,120		
	$333,720	$333,720	205,300	205,300
Merchandise inventory (12/31) ..	$ 18,000		12,000	

The plant and equipment carried on the books of the branch were acquired in foreign markets in 1969 when the exchange rate was $.26.

The branch inventory on January 1 included 7,000 krona of merchandise received from the home office, which cost the latter $1,470; the remainder was acquired from local suppliers in Sweden when the exchange rate was $.23.

The December 31 branch inventory consisted of 7,500 krona of merchandise acquired by current shipment from the home office; all other merchandise was purchased locally throughout the year. Annual adjustments for depreciation (5 percent annual rate) and doubtful accounts (1 percent of receivable balance) have been made.

Exchange rates:

        January 1, 1977 .... $.23
        December 31, 1977 .... .20
        Average for 1977 .... .24

Required:

a. Prepare a working paper to convert the branch trial balance to dollars, indicating operating statement and balance sheet extensions.
b. Journalize closing entries for the home office.

Problem 6

The following are the account balances and the amounts at which they were converted into dollars by the home office as of January 1, 1977:

JOHNSON COMPANY
Iraq Branch

	Dinars		Dollars	
Cash	3,300		$13,530	
Accounts receivable	2,000		8,200	
Allowance for bad debts		50		$ 205
Inventory	2,500		10,250	
Fixed assets	1,000		4,200	
Accumulated depreciation		100		420
Accounts payable		1,300		6,530
Current account		7,350		29,025
	8,800	8,800	$36,180	$36,180

The following transactions were completed by the branch during 1977.

a. Home office shipped merchandise costing $48,600 to branch, exchange rate being $4.05.

b. For use at branch, home office shipped equipment costing $8,120; exchange rate, $4.06.

c. Sales made by branch on account 6,000.

d. Remittance by branch to home office, 3,000 draft, sold in New York at $4.08.

e. Purchases by branch, 3,500, on account.

f. Collections by branch on account, 5,200.

g. Branch paid expenses, 1,100.

h. Payments of account payable by branch, 1,300.

i. Cash sales, 3,200.

j. Remittance by branch, 1,000; sold in New York for $4,120.

k. Adjustments for the period ended December 31, 1977, were as follows:

Estimated depreciation, 300; estimated bad debts, 60; accounts receivable written off as uncollectible, 48; final inventory of merchandise, 12,000, which is made up partially of current purchases by the branch and partially of shipments from the home office. Analysis of the final inventory discloses that a translation on the basis of historical exchange rates results in a U.S. equivalent of $49,000; the current rate of exchange at the end of the period, $4.10; the average rate of exchange was computed to be $4.09.

Required:

a. Journal entries on the books of the home office and of the branch to record these transactions.

b. Branch working paper in dollars.

c. Closing entries on the branch books.

d. Entries on the home office books to take up branch profit.

unit three

ACCOUNTING
FOR
PARTNERSHIPS

13

Formation and
Operation
of Partnerships

THE PARTNERSHIP is a form of business affiliation involving two or more individuals associated in a joint profit-making endeavor. A number of problems peculiar to this type of organizational structure have generated unique accounting procedures for reporting on partnership operations and for disclosing the economic and legal equities of various interested parties in partnership assets. These accounting techniques will be the focus of attention in the following three chapters.

NATURE OF A PARTNERSHIP

Although the common law originally provided the legal framework within which partnership operations were generally conducted, most states have now adopted the Uniform Partnership Act, or some variant thereof, as the controlling statutory authority. Emphasis will hereafter be directed toward relevant provisions of this Act.

Aggregative versus Entity Concept

Section 6 of the Uniform Partnership Act defines a partnership as "an association of two or more persons to carry on as co-owners a business for profit."[1] This definition suggests an aggregative, or proprietary, concept of the partnership as the underlying legal philosophy; a partnership is perceived as being nothing more than an aggregation of the rights and respon-

---

[1] Section 2 defines the terms person and business as they are used in the definition of a partnership; Section 6 provides criteria for the legal determination of the *existence* of a partnership.

sibilities of the individual partners. Such a notion was fundamental to the structure of the common law and has been extended in the Uniform Partnership Act in the provision that the individual partners are jointly liable for all debts and obligations of the partnership (Section 15). Yet, the dominant theme of the Act nonetheless appears to rest upon a concept of the partnership as a legal entity, separate and distinct from the individual partners. This point of view is implicit in numerous provisions, among which are the following:

1. In the event of liquidation, partnership creditors have priority in respect to the assets of the partnership and creditors of the individual partners are given priority in respect to the partners' personal assets (Section 40).
2. Title to partnership assets may be vested in the name of the partnership (Section 8).
3. A clear distinction is drawn between the partners' rights to partnership assets and their interests in the partnership (Sections 25 and 26).
4. A continuity of partnership organization may exist under circumstances which formerly, under the common law, would have caused a dissolution of the partnership (see, for example, Section 23, continuation of the partnership beyond a fixed term, and Section 27, assignment of a partner's interest in the partnership).

Notwithstanding this evolving legal conception of the partnership organization, many current accounting practices continue to emphasize the aggregative aspects of the partnership. This is no doubt due in large measure to an inheritance of the proprietary emphasis from both accounting and law, and it derives additional support from current provisions of the Internal Revenue Code. The following two examples illustrate the basic proprietary emphasis of the Code:

1. When individual partners contribute assets to the partnership, the existing tax bases transfer to the partnership, regardless of market values existing at the time of the contribution.
2. The income tax is levied on the individual partners' shares of periodic net income of the partnership and is reported in their separate returns; it is not assessed on the net income of the partnership.

The existence of such tax legislation partially explains the continuing infusion of the aggregative notion in partnership accounting; it does not, however, provide strong theoretical justification for the practice.

Specific examples of the aggregative and entity concepts of the partnership will be referred to subsequently in this chapter.

Partnership Agreement

Before a particular form of organizational structure is selected for a business activity, the various parties at interest should carefully analyze the advantages and disadvantages of alternative types of organizations—the corporation, general partnership, limited partnership, etc. If a general partnership is regarded as the suitable choice, an important first step in the organization sequence is to formulate basic provisions within which the partners elect to operate—from initial formation, through operating routines and realignment of ownership interests, to eventual dissolution of the partnership. Appropriate attention to the details of these provisions at the time the partnership is initially formed will minimize or eliminate the subsequent emergence of possible inequities and legal uncertainties regarding the relationships between partners and their relations with outside parties. The partnership agreement may be either a written or an oral contract. A formal, written agreement between the partners, often called the articles of partnership, or copartnership, is the best method of delineating the desired relationships in respect to individual partners' rights and responsibilities. The importance of this agreement should be emphasized. Although the Uniform Partnership Act imposes certain obligations upon the partnership which may not be avoided or overcome, such as joint liability for all partnership debts, most of the provisions of this act control *only* in the absence of an express agreement to the contrary between the partners. Indeed, judicial remedy is often based upon the court's interpretation of what the partners *intended,* when in fact the partners may not have anticipated a particular problem currently in dispute. Consequently, partners would be wise to seek the counsel of both an accountant and an attorney in formulating a comprehensive, *written* agreement indicating their intentions in various areas of partners' responsibilities and interests which if omitted or ambiguously conceived may subsequently cause dispute and possibly litigation.

Important provisions in the articles of partnership, including the purpose of the partnership, management rights and authority, and causes of dissolution, should reflect clearly the partners' intentions in terms of prevailing legal doctrine. There are also a number of legally unregulated areas of mutual interest to the several partners which have important accounting (and equity) implications. The accountant may offer valuable counsel in these areas. Among these interest areas are the following:

1. The assets which the partners initially are to contribute to the partnership and the monetary value to be ascribed thereto should be itemized.
2. A clear distinction should be drawn between the individual partners' initial interests in partnership capital and their interests in subsequent profits or losses. If the initial interest in capital is not consistent with a summation of the agreed-upon values for the contributed assets, the articles should be specific in regard to the treatment of this difference. For example, if the partners insist upon an equal dollar interest in capital, even though the valuations of their contributed assets are not equal, two different accounting solutions are possible: (*a*) either a bonus, or capital transfer, may be effected between the partners in order to equal-

ize their capital credits; or (*b*) intangible assets, which may derive from unusual managerial ability or widespread customer appeal and which apparently are implicit in such an agreement, may be recognized in the accounts. Although the judgment of the partners should not be the principal criterion for recognizing intangible assets in the partnership books, an explicit indication in the partnership agreement of the purported existence of such intangibles does provide an initial argument for account recognition.

3.   The basis for dividing partnership profits should be expressly stated. In the absence of a contrary agreement, Section 18 of the Uniform Partnership Act provides that the partners shall share equally in profits. If it is desired that individual partners be rewarded for their separate capital contributions and/or services to the partnership before a distribution of the residual profits in the profit-sharing ratios, the basis or monetary value for this distribution should be specified.

4.   If contributed capital is to be a basis for distributing partnership profits, the agreement should normally be responsive to the following questions:

a.   Is the distribution to be based on initial capital contributions, or capital as adjusted by subsequent contributions, profits, and/or withdrawals?

b.   If the distribution is computed upon adjusted capital, is it to be based upon beginning, average, or ending capital balances for the year?

c.   In the event average or ending capital balances are used, what treatment should be accorded current withdrawals? In particular, if it is desired to distinguish between capital withdrawals and withdrawals in anticipation of the current period's profits, the basis for the distinction should be expressly stated. Moreover, where the distinction is made, the accounting treatment of amounts available for withdrawal but permitted to remain in the business must be established.

5.   Section 18 of the Act further provides that losses are to be shared in the profit-sharing ratio. Thus, if it is desired to protect a partner, whose principal contribution is service, from incurring a disproportionate share of possible losses, special loss-sharing ratios should be indicated.

6.   The bases for calculating the monetary equity of a withdrawing partner, either through retirement or death, should be outlined. A withdrawal may involve consideration of such factors as the possible revaluation of tangible assets and the recognition of implicit intangible asset values.

7.   If net income and the partners' drawing accounts are to be closed to the capital accounts at the end of the accounting period, thereby increasing or decreasing the total contributed capital, this closing sequence should be indicated. Such a provision may be important in the

event the partnership is dissolved and assets are distributed to the retiring partners.

Although this list of significant provisions is necessarily incomplete, it does indicate the *type* of accounting considerations which are important in a careful formulation of the partnership agreement.

PARTNERSHIP FORMATION

Recording the Initial Contributions

The initial formation of a partnership presents relatively few difficult accounting problems. In the event that there exists a predecessor business, an election must be made as to whether its records are to be preserved; if not, new books must be opened. In the former case, only those entries necessary to record the contributions of partners not previously affiliated with the predecessor are required; in the latter case, all contributions must be entered in the new records. Based upon the provisions of the articles of partnership, the opening journal entries for the new partnership record the several assets contributed and the liabilities assumed. The partners' respective dollar interests in the initial capital of the organization are entered as credits to their individual capital accounts. The following two cases illustrate typical accounting entries to open the books of a new partnership.

Case 1. The partnership agreement of X and Y lists the following assets which are to constitute the resources of the new XY Partnership:

	Contributed by	
	X	*Y*
Cash	$10,000	$20,000
Merchandise		10,000
Building		30,000
Furniture and equipment	5,000	

The building is subject to a mortgage loan of $25,000, which is to be assumed by the partnership.

The journal entry to open the books of the partnership is as follows:

Cash	30,000	
Inventory	10,000	
Building	30,000	
Furniture and equipment	5,000	
Mortgage payable		25,000
X, capital		15,000
Y, capital		35,000

In this case, the partners' capital credits are based upon the net assets contributed by each partner.

Case 2. Assume that in the previous illustration, the partnership agreement provided that the partners initially should have an equal interest in partnership capital (or partnership net assets).

Two accounting solutions are possible. If it is the intent of the partners that the capital accounts be equalized by means of a bonus—transferring capital equity from Y to X—the assets and liabilities would be recorded as before; however, each partner would receive a capital credit of $25,000 (one half of $50,000 net assets). Under these circumstances, Y essentially pays a bonus of $10,000 to X, in the form of an increased monetary equity in the firm, as an inducement to enter the partnership venture.

A second solution is predicated on the assumption that X contributes to the partnership an additional asset, intangible in character but having value to the partnership. Based upon the requirement of equalizing capital balances, it can be inferred that this asset has a value of approximately $20,-000. The entry under these conditions is:

Cash	30,000	
Inventory	10,000	
Building	30,000	
Furniture and equipment	5,000	
Goodwill (or some other intangible asset)	20,000	
Mortgage payable		25,000
X, capital		35,000
Y, capital		35,000

The net assets of the business with this assumption are $70,000, of which $50,000 are represented by net tangible assets.

If the partners' future interests in partnership profits and losses are also to be equal, the choice of either method (bonus or goodwill) will produce no inequity in the relative monetary interest of the two partners, as they will share equally in the subsequent gain or loss, of whatever amount, on the realization of the intangible asset. However, recording the goodwill in the partnership books will have a significant effect on the balance sheet of the partnership; accordingly, the measurement of goodwill must be carefully determined, as the reported valuation of this intangible asset will make an impression upon the reader of the partnership balance sheet.

The above examples refer to the source of new partnership assets in terms of the contributing partners. On occasions one or more of the new partners may contribute the assets and liabilities of an existing business to the new partnership. In such a circumstance, it is important that the assets be appraised at the time the new partnership is formed; existing book values of the contributed assets may be grossly inadequate as a measure of the relative capital investments of the partners in the new venture.

Income Tax Considerations

Although the problems in income tax accounting are not a principal concern of this text, certain *fundamental* income tax concepts are briefly considered within the context of partnership formation. Basically the Internal Revenue Code adopts the aggregative theory and treats the partnership as a conduit through which net income of the firm is allocated to the partners *as if* they had individually earned it. With this partnership conception, two value bases are particularly relevant to initial formation of the firm:

1. The tax "basis" of the *assets* contributed to the partnership.
2. The tax "basis" of the partners' dollar *interest* in the partnership.

No taxable gain or loss is assumed to result from the contribution of property to a partnership by an individual partner. Rather, the partnership adopts the same *asset* basis, or unamortized cost, for income tax purposes as applied to the individual partner in respect to the calculation of his personal tax liability. It is unlikely that this value will be equivalent to the fair market value of the asset at the date of contribution. Although the market valuation of contributed assets is an important determinant in computing the dollar interest of the partners in the capital of the new firm, the tax-basis valuation will necessarily modify the relative interests of the partners for income tax purposes.

The tax "basis" of a partner's *interest* in the firm is defined as *the sum of the bases of the individual assets he contributes to the firm, increased by any liabilities of other partners which he assumes, and decreased by his personal liabilities, if any, which are assumed by other partners.* Thus, an accounting equation for the tax bases of the partners' interests in the firm takes the following form: the sum of the bases of the contributed assets is equal to the sum of the bases of the partners' separate interests in the partnership. It should be noted that partnership liabilities are excluded from this basic equation, as they are implicitly included in the bases of the partners' separate interests.

The following case illustrates these provisions:

Case 3. Using the data of Case 1 and assuming that the basis of the building to Y is $20,000, that other assets have a tax basis equal to their present market values, and that X agrees to accept joint liability for the mortgage on the building, the income tax implications of the initial formation may be reflected in the following journal entry form:[2]

Cash	30,000	
Merchandise	10,000	
Building	20,000	
Furniture and equipment	5,000	
Basis of X's interest		27,500
Basis of Y's interest		37,500

Significantly, this entry is *not* made in the partnership books; it is simply a convenient way of expressing the tax bases of the contributed assets and

---

[2] This method of analyzing the tax bases of partners' interests is described more completely in Richard H. Homburger, "Tax Basis of Partner's Interest Explained by Double Entry," *The Accounting Review,* January 1960, pp. 132–34.

the partners' tax basis interests in the partnership. The journalizing form of expression may be utilized in supporting tax records or working papers.

In the above entry, it is evident that the basis equation is satisfied, as the sum of the asset bases, $65,000, equals the sum of the bases of the partners' interests. The computation of the interests of X and Y is made as follows:

	X	Y
Bases of assets contributed:		
Cash	$10,000	$20,000
Inventory		10,000
Building		20,000
Furniture and equipment	5,000	
	$15,000	$50,000
Add: Liabilities assumed by X (½ of $25,000 mortgage)	12,500	
Deduct: Personal liability transferred to X		[12,500]
	$27,500	$37,500

The implications of the tax bases associated with the partnership formation are to reduce, for tax purposes, the depreciable cost of partnership assets by $10,000 and to alter the relative monetary interests of the individual partners. The ultimate effect of these changes will be reflected in the periodic determination of taxable net income for the partnership to be allocated to the individual partners, and in the computation of taxable gain or loss in the event one or both partners elect to dispose of their interests in the firm.

PARTNERSHIP OPERATIONS

Accounting for the operations of a partnership is not essentially unlike accounting for other profit-oriented businesses. The primary objective of the accounting process continues to be the determination of periodic net income. To this end, a partnership is perceived as a separate and distinct accounting entity. Net income is calculated in the traditional manner, i.e., by relating periodic revenues and expenses, with only the accounting treatment of salary payments to the partners and interest on capital investments subject to theoretical dispute.

The special problems of accounting for partnership operations are classified for discussion purposes as follows:

1. Establishing the nature and determining the amount of the relative interests of the partners in the firm.
2. Determining the proper distribution of partnership net income between the partners.
3. Preparing financial statements for the partnership: the balance sheet, income statement, and statement of partners' capital.

Nature and Amount of Relative Interests

The partners' interests in, and obligations to, the partnership may be dichotomized initially into (1) debtor-creditor relationships and (2) capital equities and/or deficiencies. In many cases, these divisions are essentially arbitrary in nature, but in light of generally accepted accounting practices, they may materially influence the financial statements of the partnership.

Debtor-Creditor Relationships. If in addition to contributions to the capital of the firm, a partner advances money to the partnership in the form of a loan, with provision that it be repaid within a specified period of time, appropriate recognition of the separateness of the accounting entity and the nature of the transaction requires that such an advance be recorded as a partnership liability. Similarly, advances to individual partners, which are to be repaid subsequently to the partnership, are properly classified as partnership receivables. Interest expense and/or income generated by these explicitly conceived contractual obligations are normally considered in the periodic computation of partnership net income. This treatment is consistent with the classification of the originating transaction as a business loan and with the acceptance of the separate entity status of the partnership.

Capital Equities and/or Deficiencies. The total capital equity of the partnership is, of course, the amount of partnership assets which are in excess of partnership liabilities. It is necessary, however, that the amount of each partner's capital credit in the firm be independently calculated and recorded. Normally, two accounts are maintained for each partner: (1) a drawing, or personal account; and (2) a capital account. The drawing account is debited with the partner's withdrawals of cash or other assets during the period in anticipation of his interest in partnership net income, and is credited subsequently with his equity in the final distribution of partnership net income. The capital account, as previously mentioned, initially reflects the dollar investment of each partner at the date of formation of the partnership. Subsequently, additional investments or withdrawals which are believed to be relatively permanent in character are entered in the account; if the partners should so elect, the balance of the drawing account may be periodically transferred to the capital account. As will be discussed later, it is possible that a more informative statement of financial position may result from segregating capital transactions from those which summarize profits; where the transactions are thus separated, the closing of the drawing accounts to capital accounts may prove undesirable.

Conventionally, interest credits on capital equities are not accounted for as partnership expenses. Interest credits on partners' loans, however, are deducted as a determinant of partnership net income. Thus, the objectivity of net income determination is at least partially compromised if the partners, at their discretion, can control whether additional equity shall be provided by partners' loans or accumulated profits. However, in this connection, a subtlety often overlooked relates to the implicit interest on "excessive" capital contributions. In the absence of a contrary agreement, Section 18 (c) of the Act provides that a partner, who in aid of the partnership makes any payment or advance beyond the amount of capital which he agreed to contribute, shall be paid interest from the date of the payment or advance. An extension of this argument implies that from a legal point of view, profit accumulations of the partnership *may* be the basis of interest payments to individual partners. In point of fact, little substantive difference exists between accumulated profits and loans to the partnership. It would appear that the accounting problem is eliminated only where there is a complete acceptance of the proprietary theory, wherein no expense or income may be generated in transactions with the owners, *or* by a complete acceptance of the entity theory, wherein the expense of total capital (creditors' and owners') is recognized.

Determining Distributive Shares of Net Income

Some of the fundamental problems underlying the distribution of partnership net income were discussed earlier in terms of eliminating unnecessary ambiguity from the partnership agreement. The three most commonly used bases for allocating partnership net income are:

1. Specified ratios.
2. Relative capital investments of the partners.
3. Service contributions of the partners.

Frequently, some combination of these several bases is used to reward the partners, appropriate weight being given each factor contributed by an individual partner in respect to partnership profitability.

Specified Ratios. As noted before, the Uniform Partnership Act provides that in the absence of an explicit contrary agreement, profits are to be allocated equally (equal ratios) among the partners. If the partners prefer some other uniform basis of distribution, negotiated ratios may be specified in the partnership agreement.

Case 4. Assume that X and Y agree to divide profits from their partnership operations in a ratio of 3:1, that is, 75 percent to X and 25 percent to Y. If net income for the year is $60,000, the following journal entry indicates the allocation of profits:

```
Income summary ................................. 60,000
    X, drawing (¾ × $60,000) ....................        45,000
    Y, drawing (¼ × $60,000) ....................        15,000
```

In the absence of this specific profit-sharing agreement, each partner would have received $30,000. In both cases, the allocation of profits is uniform; each partner receives a predetermined percentage of profits, without regard to the magnitude of such profits.

Relative Capital Investments. Because capital is an income-producing factor, it may be important to consider the partners' respective capital investments in allocating partnership net income. If partners are to be rewarded, in part at least, in proportion to the relative magnitudes of their investments of capital, it is imperative that there be an unequivocal statement in the partnership agreement concerning the computation of these capital balances. As indicated earlier, if average or ending capital balances are to be used, the treatment of withdrawals, or amounts available for withdrawal, may pose a problem.

The following data will be used in Cases 5 and 6 to illustrate alternative approaches to the allocation of net income when it is based upon the partners' relative capital investments.

X, Capital

2/1	10,000	1/1 Balance	50,000
		4/1	10,000
		8/1	20,000
		11/1	20,000

X, Drawing

1/1–12/1 ($1,000/month, per agreement)	12,000

Y, Capital

4/1	5,000	1/1 Balance	25,000
7/1	10,000	9/1	15,000

Y, Drawing

1/1–12/1 ($1,000/month, per agreement)	12,000

Income Summary

12/31	50,000

It is assumed that withdrawals *in excess of* the $1,000 monthly allowance (withdrawals in anticipation of profits) are to be accounted for as permanent reductions in capital; accordingly, they are entered as debits to the partners' capital accounts.

Case 5. Interest on Beginning Capital Balances. In this example, it is assumed that each partner is to receive a 6 percent return (interest) on his capital investment, calculated in terms of the capital balances at the beginning of the year, with the remaining profit (or loss) to be distributed in a ratio of 4:6 to X and Y respectively. Computation of the allocated partnership net income is as follows:

	X	Y	Total
Interest:			
6% × $50,000 .... $ 3,000			$ 3,000
6% × $25,000		$ 1,500	1,500
Remainder (in residual profit-sharing ratio):			
4/10 × $45,500	18,200		18,200
6/10 × $45,500		27,300	27,300
	$21,200	$28,800	$50,000

Case 6. Interest on Average Capital Balances. In this example, each partner is assumed to receive a 6 percent return (interest) on his *average* capital investment, utilizing the basis previously described for determining capital withdrawals. Since each partner withdrew the total amount allowable each month, no problem arises concerning amounts available for withdrawal but not actually withdrawn. After interest allowances, the residual profit element is again to be allocated in the ratio 4:6.

The first step in determining profit allocations is to calculate the average capital balance for each partner. This may be accomplished by weighting each new capital balance by the number of months (or other appropriate time interval) that the balance remains unchanged; by adding each of these products and dividing by the sum of weights, an average balance is determined. Calculation for the data in this example is made as follows:

	Capital Balance	Weighting Factor— Number of Months	Weighted Product
X's capital balance:			
January 1–February 1	$50,000	1	$ 50,000
February 1–April 1	40,000	2	80,000
April 1–August 1	50,000	4	200,000
August 1–November 1	70,000	3	210,000
November 1–December 31	90,000	2	180,000
		12	$720,000
Average capital balance ($720,000 ÷ 12)			$ 60,000
Y's capital balance:			
January 1–April 1...................	$25,000	3	$ 75,000
April 1–July 1	20,000	3	60,000
July 1–September 1...............	10,000	2	20,000
September 1–December 31..........	25,000	4	100,000
		12	$255,000
Average capital balance ($255,000 ÷ 12)			$ 21,250

Following the calculation of average capital balances, the several profit elements are allocated as follows:

	X	Y	Total
Interest:			
6% × $60,000	$ 3,600		$ 3,600
6% × $21,250		$ 1,275	1,275
Remainder (in residual profit-sharing ratio):			
4/10 × $45,125	18,050		18,050
6/10 × $45,125		27,075	27,075
	$21,650	$28,350	$50,000

The ending capital balances of the partners may be used also as a basis for interest allowances in net profit distribution. Or, alternatively, the total net profit for the accounting period may be allocated on the basis of relative capital investments. However, it is perhaps more usual for partnership agreements to specify that only a *reasonable* return should accrue from the investment of capital and that additional excess earnings of the partnership should be divided in some specified ratio to compensate the partners for the disproportionate contributions they make to the operation of the business. Furthermore, in determining the base to be used in computing the return on investments, the beginning or average capital balances are frequently preferred—the beginning balance because of the simplicity of interest calculation, or the average capital balance because it provides a more refined measurement of the actual capital available to the firm *during* the accounting period.

Services Rendered. In order to reward the individual partners for their different service contributions to the operation of the partnership, salary allowances are often provided as an additional basis for distributing partnership net income. This basis, as in the case of interest allowances on capital investments, is frequently used in combination with negotiated ratios or other allocation bases. Where the partners contribute a disproportionate amount of time and talent to partnership activities, inclusion of a provision for salaries in the allocation basis may contribute to a more equitable distribution of the net income of the business.

Case 7. Using the data of Case 6, with the additional provision that salaries of $6,000 and $12,000 are to be awarded to X and Y respectively, the net profit is distributed as follows:

	X	Y	Total
Salary allowances	$ 6,000	$12,000	$18,000
Interest credits	3,600	1,275	4,875
Remainder:			
4/10 × $27,125	10,850		10,850
6/10 × $27,125		16,275	16,275
	$20,450	$29,550	$50,000

If the proprietary theory is literally accepted, salary allowances should be considered a *distribution* of net income rather than a *determinant* of net income. Although this position has no effect upon the ultimate capital accumulations of the various partners, it results in an amount of partnership net income which is in excess of that calculated for a corporate enterprise wherein officer-shareholders have a status comparable to that of partners in a partnership. For this reason, the argument is frequently made that if it is desirable to make net income comparisons with other similar types of businesses, some of which may be incorporated, *or if the partners are examining the feasibility of incorporating, partners' salaries should be accounted for as an expense.* Notwithstanding the value of these comparisons, this position would seem to avoid a basic issue. If the salary of an officer-stockholder of a closely held corporation is treated as an expense when it meets the test of reasonableness, why is not the salary of a partner similarly a factor in net income determination if it satisfies the same criterion? If the entity theory is adopted in accounting for one type of transaction between the partners and the firm (debtor-creditor relationships), why is it denied in other types of business transactions which appear to be equally valid? While little theoretical support can be marshalled for this traditional accounting distinction between salaries of corporate officers (expenses) and salaries of partners (distributions of income), it currently remains dominant in accounting practice.

Order of Distribution. If the net income is insufficient to cover the prescribed distributions for salaries and/or interest on capital balances, two alternatives are available. First, the partners may elect that the distribution for salaries and interest on investment be made and that the earnings deficiency produced by these allocations be allocated in the residual profit-and loss-sharing ratio, or loss-sharing ratio if separate ratios exist. Second, a sequence of distributions may be specified, with the provision that available net income is to be distributed to the fullest extent possible. This necessarily requires that the relative ratio of the partners' earned salaries or interest on investment be used to distribute that amount of net income remaining after prior distributions, if any, which is insufficient to make a total distribution for a profit-sharing factor. Consider the following data:

	X	Y	Total
Earned salaries	$10,000	$5,000	$15,000
Earned interest	4,000	6,000	10,000

If X and Y agreed that available earnings are to be distributed first for salaries, then for interest on capital investment, and finally in the residual profit-sharing ratio, this second method yields the following types of distributions of earnings when there are insufficient profits to make total distributions for both salaries and interest:

	X	Y	Total
Case I. (Net income, $9,000):			
Salaries:			
X (10/15 × $9,000)	$ 6,000		$ 6,000
Y (5/15 × $9,000)		$3,000	3,000
	$ 6,000	$3,000	$ 9,000
Case II. (Net income, $20,000):			
Salaries	$10,000	$5,000	$15,000
Interest:			
X (4/10 × $5,000)	2,000		2,000
Y (6/10 × $5,000)		3,000	3,000
	$12,000	$8,000	$20,000

The net income would be distributed differently if the first method were employed, i.e., salaries and interest would be first allocated, after which the resulting deficiency would be distributed.

This situation reflects yet another instance requiring adequate forward planning in the formulation of the partnership agreement. In the absence of such an agreement, or where the agreement is silent as to the order of earnings distribution, the first method discussed is generally followed. It may be observed that this method implicitly treats the salaries and interest on capital investments as a partnership expense, and thus makes but one actual distribution of net income, viz., partnership net income after partners' salaries and interest on their investments. If the entity theory is otherwise adopted, this method further confirms the commitment to the entity concept.

Correction of Prior Years' Net Income.   Whereas the correction of prior years' net income has important reporting implications for virtually all forms of business organization, there exists in respect to the partnership an additional problem of allocating adjustments and corrections of net income among the partners. If the identity of the partners is the same as in the year to which the adjustments or corrections relate and the profit- and loss-sharing ratios remain unchanged, with no special constraints on allocations of salaries and/or interest, no special complication is met in respect to the earnings correction of prior years.

If these rather restrictive conditions are not fully satisfied, however, the accountant must examine more carefully a proposed correction or adjustment of prior years' net income. In determining whether specific items should be treated as prior period adjustments, the principles to be generally followed have been enunciated by the Accounting Principles Board in *Opinion No. 9* and *Opinion No. 20*. In essence, the Board defined prior period adjustments very narrowly so that only a few items fall in that category.[3] However, it must be recognized that the primary focus of the APB was on the preparation of financial statements for public distribution and use. In the case of a partnership, where the income allocation between partners is directly affected by the prior period adjustment decisions, the agreed upon will of the partners should dominate over the pronouncements of the APB, FASB, or other rule-making bodies. For example, partners may feel that a material bad debt which was not adequately allowed for during the period of sale should be treated as a prior period adjustment, notwithstanding the APB conclusion to the contrary.

The accountant may often be called upon to provide consultation as to the appropriate treatment of items which are potentially prior period adjustments. Although the APB pronouncements may be relied upon as an expression of norms, consideration should be given to three basic alternatives:

1. The amount of the adjustment is minor, and it may be absorbed in the current period's net income without material effect on the partners' capital balances.
2. The adjustment is material in amount but is not easily identified with a specific period or periods. An example of such an adjustment may be a correction of the allowance for uncollectible accounts. In this case, the gain or loss resulting from over- or under-allowances in prior periods may be absorbed in the current period, or an arbitrary allocation to prior periods may be made, depending upon the decision of the partners.
3. The adjustment is material in amount and is identifiable with specific accounting periods. This condition may exist where clerical or bookkeeping errors are discovered. In this type of circumstance, equity would seem to call for a recomputation of the allocations of adjusted net incomes for the affected periods.

Of course, corrections of prior periods' net incomes may not be the only, nor the most significant, adjustments which affect an equitable distribution

---

[3] For a more complete discussion of prior period adjustment criteria, see Glenn A. Welsch, Charles T. Zlatkovich and John Arch White, *Intermediate Accounting,* 4th ed. (Homewood, Illinois: Richard D. Irwin, Inc., 1976).

of partnership net income. The existence of material, extraordinary or non-recurring gains or losses raises the question as to the specific period or periods to which they properly relate. Where this problem exists, the traditional realization criterion should be applied until further refinements in accounting methodology permit a more accurate determination of periodic net income.

Financial Statement Presentation

Income Statement. As previously indicated, accounting practice conventionally regards interest on partners' loans as a partnership expense, while it excludes partners' salaries and interest on capital as factors in profit determination. The exclusions are normally cited in an appendage to the income statement, which contains the distribution of the net income elements. The following income statement follows the traditional format:

XY PARTNERSHIP
Income Statement
For Year Ended December 31, 19X1

Sales		$100,000
Cost of goods sold		60,000
Gross profit		$ 40,000
Operating expenses:		
Interest on partners' loans	$ 1,000	
Other expenses	19,000	20,000
Net Income		$ 20,000

Allocated as follows:

	X	Y	Total
Partners' salaries	$ 8,000	$4,000	$12,000
Interest on capital	–0–	2,000	2,000
Remainder equally	3,000	3,000	6,000
	$11,000	$9,000	$20,000

If the position is taken that partners' salaries are "reasonable compensation for services rendered," consistent reporting would require disclosure of the $12,000 as an operating expense, with a corresponding reduction of net income to $8,000.

Statement of Partners' Capital. In the same manner that the activity in respect to changes in corporate retained earnings are excluded from the balance sheet and are reported separately in a statement of retained earnings, so are the changes (both increases and decreases) in the partners' equity reported separately in a statement of partners' capital. This statement typically assumes the following form:

XY PARTNERSHIP

Statement of Partners' Capital
For Year Ended December 31, 19X1

	X	Y	Total
Capital, January 1	$10,000	$20,000	$30,000
Net income for the year	11,000	9,000	20,000
	$21,000	$29,000	$50,000
Withdrawals	12,000	10,000	22,000
Capital, December 31	$ 9,000	$19,000	$28,000

Balance Sheet. The usual partnership balance sheet reflects the proprietary concept in its equity section, as the capital accounts of the partners are separately disclosed. Following is an abbreviated example of this format:

XY PARTNERSHIP

Balance Sheet
December 31, 19X1

Cash	$ 6,000	Current liabilities ...		$30,000
Accounts receivable	12,000	Loans payable		25,000
Inventory	20,000	Capital:		
Fixed assets (net)	40,000	X	$ 9,000	
Other assets	5,000	Y	19,000	28,000
	$83,000			$83,000

Possibly, a more meaningful disclosure may result if the equity section were divided into capital and accumulated profits divisions. In addition to the fact that Section 40 of the Uniform Partnership Act makes such a distinction, albeit a vague one, between partners' capital and accumulated partnership profits, potentially useful information respecting the financial management of the business is provided if this distinction is maintained in the balance sheet. Also, for credit purposes, the balances of the individual partners' accounts are relatively unimportant, as the partners remain jointly liable for partnership obligations, settlement to be made from their personal assets should this be necessary. Additionally, the information relating to the individual partners' equities in the business is reported in detail in the statement of partners' capital. It is to be regretted that the conventional partnership balance sheet fails to show the separate net worth elements—partners' capital and accumulated profits.

QUESTIONS

1. What is the essential nature of a partnership? What distinguishes it from other forms of business organization?

2. Enumerate five important provisions which should be explicitly considered in the partnership agreement.

3. The partnership agreement of the XYZ partnership provides that "profits and losses shall be shared in the ratio of the partners' capital balances." Can you foresee any problems with the language of this profit-sharing arrangement? Should such an agreement be in writing to have full legal effect on the parties?

4. How is the tax "basis" of a partner's interest in the partnership defined? Is this concept different from the tax basis of the assets a partner contributes?

5. What are three commonly used bases for allocating partnership net income to the partners?

6. What is the justification for salary allowances in a partnership agreement? Why is interest on capital balances frequently included in a partnership agreement as a basis for profit distribution?

7. "The pronouncements of the APB and FASB may not always serve as appropriate guidelines for partnership accounting." Explain the basis for this statement.

8. If by agreement the partners wish to begin with equal interests in the partnership net assets yet do not contribute assets of equal value, what methods exist to enable them to accomplish their objective?

9. What alternatives exist for correction of prior years' net income when (a) the amount of the adjustment is minor; (b) the adjustment is material in amount but is not easily identifiable with a specific period or periods; (c) the adjustment is material in amount and is identifiable with specific accounting periods?

10. What advantages may derive from reporting partners' capital accounts on the balance sheet *divided between contributed capital and accumulated profits?* Does present practice more closely approximate the proprietary or entity concept of the partnership?

11. Explain why salaries to partners are typically accounted for as distributions of income rather than as expenses.

12. What advantage would result from reporting the salaries and interest paid on partners' capital balances as *expenses* on the income statement rather than recognizing them as earnings distributions?

EXERCISES

Exercise 13–1 √

The partnership of Wayne and Ellen was formed on February 28, 1977. At that date the following assets were contributed:

	Wayne	Ellen
Cash	$25,000	$ 35,000
Merchandise		55,000
Building		100,000
Furniture and equipment	15,000	

The building is subject to a mortgage loan of $30,000 which is to be assumed by the partnership. The partnership agreement provides that Wayne and Ellen share profits or losses equally.

Required:

a. What are the capital balances of the partners on February 28, 1977?
b. If the partnership agreement states that the initial capital balances of the partners should be equal, and no recognition should be given to any intangible assets contributed, what are the partners' capital balances on February 28, 1977?
c. Given the facts stated in requirement (b) except that any contributed goodwill should be recognized in the accounts, what are the partners' capital balances on February 28, 1977? How much goodwill should be recognized?

(AICPA adapted)

Exercise 13–2√

Partnership contracts usually specify a profit and loss ratio. They may also provide for such additional profit- and loss-sharing features as salaries, bonuses, and interest allowances on invested capital.

Required:

a. What is the objective of profit- and loss-sharing arrangements? Why may there be a need for features in addition to the profit and loss ratio? Discuss.
b. Discuss the arguments for recording salary and bonus allowances to partners as charges to operations.
c. What are the arguments against treating partnership salary and bonus allowances as expenses? Discuss.
d. In addition to its other profit- and loss-sharing features, a partnership agreement may state that "interest is to be allowed on invested capital." List the additional provision that should be included in the partnership agreement so that "interest to be allowed on invested capital" can be computed.

(AICPA adapted)

Exercise 13–3

Ashe and Jones are partners in the AJ Pharmacy. Their capital account balances on January 1, 1977, are $40,000 and $25,000 respectively. They agree that partnership profits are to be distributed as follows:

	Ashe	Jones
Salary	$3,000	$7,000
Interest on beginning capital balances	5%	5%
Bonus	20% of net income *after* salaries and bonus *but before* interest has been deducted	None
Residual profits or losses	40%	60%

Required:

Calculate the distribution of 1977 partnership profits (identifying the profit elements separately) if the partnership net income before salaries, interest, and bonus is $25,000.

Exercise 13–4

Ray and Charles joined in a partnership on January 1, 1977. The partners share equally in profits, losses, and capital. Charles contributed land valued at $10,000 which had a tax basis of $8,000. He also contributed a building valued at $90,000 which had a tax basis of $50,000. The partnership assumes a mortgage loan against the building and land in the amount of $20,000. Ray contributed $50,000 cash, and equipment valued at $30,000 which had a tax basis of $15,000. There was no goodwill contributed.

Required:

a.   Prepare a general journal entry to record the formation of the partnership and the contributions of the partners.
b.   Present in the form of a journal entry the partnership's tax bases in the assets and the partners' tax bases in the partnership.

Exercise 13–5

Krogstad and Harrison share profits 3:4 after annual salary allowances of $10,000 and $18,000 respectively; however, if partnership net income is insufficient to make these distributions in full amount, net income shall be divided equally between the partners. In 1977, the following errors were discovered:

a.   Depreciation for 1976 was understated by $4,200.
b.   Inventory on December 31, 1976 was overvalued by $8,400.

The partnership net income for 1976 was reported to be $35,000.

Required:

Indicate the correcting entry or entries necessary upon discovery of these errors.

Exercise 13–6

Haskins, Mitchell, and Young are partners sharing profits and losses as follows:

Salaries:
Haskins	$10,000
Mitchell	6,000
Young	4,000

Interest (6 percent) on the following average capital balances:
Haskins, capital	30,000
Mitchell, capital	25,000
Young, capital	20,000

Residual profits or residual losses are divided equally.

Required:

If the partnership net income for 1977 is reported to be $20,000, indicate the distribution to each partner. Identify the profit and loss elements separately.

PROBLEMS

Problem 1

Jackson and Smith organized the JS partnership on January 1, 1977. The following entries were made in their capital accounts during 1977.

	Debit	Credit	Balance
Jackson, capital:			
January 1		$30,000	$30,000
April 1	$2,000		28,000
October 1		4,000	32,000
Smith, capital:			
January 1		15,000	15,000
March 1		3,000	18,000
September 1	1,000		17,000
November 1		500	17,500

Required:

If the partnership net income, computed without regard to salaries or interest, is $14,000 for 1977, indicate its division between the partners under the following independent profit-sharing conditions:

a. Interest at 4 percent is allowed on average capital investments, and the remainder is divided equally.

b. A salary of $6,000 is to be credited to Smith; 4 percent interest is allowed each partner on his ending capital balance.

c. Salaries are allowed Jackson and Smith in amounts of $8,500 and $9,500 respectively, and residual profits or residual losses are divided in the ratio of average capital balances.

d. A bonus of 10 percent of partnership net income is credited to Jackson, a salary of $4,000 is allowed to Smith, and residual profits or residual losses are shared equally. (The bonus is regarded as an "expense" for purposes of calculating its amount.)

Problem 2

Ray Winters developed an interesting idea for marketing sport coats in Alaska. He interested Ed Fields in joining him in a partnership. Following is the information you have collected relative to their original contributions.

Ed contributed $50,000 cash, a tract of land, and delivery equipment. Ray contributed $90,000 cash. After giving special consideration to the tax bases of the assets contributed, the relative usefulness of the assets to the partnership versus the problems of finding buyers for the assets and contributing cash, and other such factors, the partners agreed that Ray's contribution was equal to 45 percent of the partnership's tangible assets, measured in terms of the fair value of the assets *to the partnership*. However, in that the marketing idea originated with Ray, it was agreed that he should receive credit for 50 percent of the recorded capital. Recent sales of land similar to that contributed by Ed suggested a market value of $45,000. Likewise, recent sales of delivery equipment similar to that contributed by Ed suggest $45,000 as the market value of the equipment. These sales, of course, were not entirely representative of the particular assets contributed by Ed and therefore may be a better indicator of their *relative* values than their absolute values. In reflecting on their venture, the partners agree that it is a rather risky affair in respect to anticipated profits. Hopefully, however, they will be able to build good customer relations over the long run and establish a permanent business with an attractive long-run rate of return.

Required:

a. Journalize the partners' contributions under the most appropriate method, given the circumstances.
b. Journalize their contributions under another method, probably less appropriate.
c. State why you think method (*a*) is better than (*b*) in this situation.

Problem 3

Crenshaw and Harrington organize the C & H partnership on January 1, 1977, with capital contributions of $40,000 and $55,000 respectively. It is agreed that each will be allowed a salary credit of $4,000 annually plus an additional 5 percent credit for interest on the beginning-of-year capital balances. Residual profits are to be divided equally.

Year	Profits before Interest and Salaries	Cash Withdrawals Crenshaw	Harrington
1977	$22,750	$3,000	$4,750
1978	17,500	4,500	6,250

Required:

a. Prepare a statement of partners' capital accounts for the two years ended December 31, 1978.
b. Prepare closing entries as of December 31, 1978.

Problem 4 √

A, B, and C have been partners throughout the year 1977. The average balances for the year and their balances at the end of the year before closing the nominal accounts are as follows:

		Average Balances		Balances, Dec. 31, 1977	
A	Cr.	$90,000	Cr.	$60,000
B	Cr.	3,000	Dr.	1,000
C	Cr.	7,000	Cr.	10,000

The profit for 1977 is $75,000 before charging partners' drawing allowances (salaries) and before interest on average balances at the agreed rate of 4 percent per annum. A is entitled to a drawing account credit of $10,000, B of $7,000, and C of $5,000 per annum. The balance of the profit is to be distributed at the rate of 60 percent to A, 30 percent to B, and 10 percent to C.

It is intended to distribute amounts of cash to the partners so that after credits and distributions as indicated in the preceding paragraph, the balances in the partners' accounts will be proportionate to their profit-sharing ratio. None of the partners is to pay in any money, but it is desired to distribute the lowest possible amount of cash.

Required:

Prepare a schedule of the partners' capital accounts, showing balances at the end of 1977 before closing, the allocations of the net profit for 1977, the cash distributed, and the closing balances.

(AICPA adapted)

Problem 5

The Fellingham-Russell-McCarroll partnership was formed in 1976, Fellingham contributing a major portion of the capital, with Russell and McCarroll to provide important management skills and experience. The partnership agreement specifies that the accounting records shall be maintained on the accrual basis and that the net income shall be distributed to the partners as follows:

a. Each partner shall receive 5 percent interest on the balance in his capital account at the beginning of the year.
b. Russell and McCarroll shall each receive a commission of 20 percent of an amount representing net income determined under cash basis accounting after deducting the normal allowance for depreciation and the interest on

capital. For this purpose all merchandise purchased is to be regarded as an expense.

c. The net income remaining after deducting the interest on capital and commissions due to Russell and McCarroll shall be distributed equally, except that the total portion of net income to Fellingham must not be less than 50 percent of the net income determined under accrual accounting.

During 1977, $150 of accounts receivable were considered uncollectable and charged off to the allowance for doubtful accounts, and $10 were collected on accounts which had been charged off to the allowance for doubtful accounts in prior years.

There were no changes in the partners' capital accounts during 1977.

FELLINGHAM-RUSSELL-McCARROLL

Comparative Balance Sheet

	December 31, 1976		December 31, 1977	
Assets				
Cash		$ 7,000		$ 11,120
Accounts receivable—customers	$ 5,000		$ 6,000	
Allowance for doubtful accounts	100	4,900	120	5,880
Inventory		26,000		24,000
U.S. government bonds (at cost)				8,000
Fixed assets (at cost)	$120,000		$220,000	
Accumulated depreciation	42,500	77,500	46,300	173,700
Prepaid expenses		1,000		800
Total Assets		$116,400		$223,500
Liabilities and Capital				
Accounts payable—trade		$ 7,000		$ 4,000
Accrued wages		3,000		5,000
Accrued taxes		500		500
Deferred income		5,900		
Bonds payable				100,000
Net income, 1977				14,000
Partners' capitals:				
Fellingham	$ 80,000		$ 80,000	
Russell	12,500		12,500	
McCarroll	7,500	100,000	7,500	100,000
Total Liabilities and Capital ...		$116,400		$223,500

Required:

Given the balance sheets above, prepare—

a. A schedule, supported by computational detail, showing the adjustments necessary to convert the net income for 1977 from an accrual basis to a cash basis.

b. A statement, supported by computational detail, indicating the distribution of 1977 net income to the partners.

(AICPA adapted)

Problem 6

Lynn and Vickrey, architectural designers and interior decorators, combined May 1, 1977, agreeing to share profits: Lynn, 80 percent; Vickrey, 20 percent. Lynn contributed furniture and fixtures, $3,000, and cash, $2,000; Vickrey contributed cash, $500.

They plan to submit monthly bills and make the following arrangements with their clients:

a. The salaries of draftsmen and shoppers, who are paid on an hourly basis, shall be billed to clients at the hourly rate for time spent on each job, plus 125 percent for overhead and profit and plus 4½ percent for all payroll taxes.

b. Partners' time on jobs shall be billed at $10 an hour.

c. A 10 percent service fee shall be charged on purchases of furniture, drapes, etc., installed on the jobs. (Lynn and Vickrey will pay the vendors and charge their clients for these purchases but would like to have their operating statements reflect only revenue from services.)

d. There will be no service fee on taxis, telephone, and other expenses identifiable to jobs and charged to clients.

Voucher register totals for May are given below:

Credits:

Vouchers payable	$3,469
Taxes withheld—federal income	93
Taxes withheld—FICA	27
Income from charges to jobs for partners' time	790
Total	$4,379

Debits:

Purchases and expenses chargeable to clients	$1,615
Partners' drawings (Lynn, $100; Vickrey, $125)	225
General expenses	784
Jobs in process:	
Draftsmen's salaries	940
Partner's time	790
Petty cash fund	25
Total	$4,379

The first debit column is analyzed in the voucher register as follows:

Purchases subject to 10 percent fee:

Client M, Job 51	$1,210	
Client H, Job 52	320	$1,530

Expenses chargeable to clients:

Client M 51	$ 23	
Client M 54	7	
Client H 52	19	
Client L 53	36	85
		$1,615

The client has not yet authorized them to do Job M 54. The partners are confident, however, that the job will be authorized and the above expenses, as well as charges for time spent by Lynn and a draftsman on preliminary designs, will be billed and collected.

The payroll analysis is summarized below. Partners' time on jobs, charged to the jobs at $5 an hour, is summarized in the payroll analysis for convenience in posting costs to job sheets, although the partners are not paid for direct time on jobs.

	Secretary	Draftsmen	Lynn	Vickrey
Job:				
M 51		$ 312	$120	$150
H 52		276	60	115
L 53		304	65	160
M 54		48	120	
		$ 940	$365	$425
General Expenses:				
General office	$160	40		
Idle time		60		
Total payroll	$160	$1,040		

Journal entries recorded depreciation on furniture and fixtures of $25 and the employer's share of federal and state taxes of $54.

There were no cash receipts other than the original investment. The cash disbursements book shows the following totals:

Debit:	Vouchers payable	$2,373
Credit:	Cash	2,358
Credit:	Discount on purchases	15

Required:

a. Compute billings to clients for May.
b. Prepare a work sheet showing the balance sheet, profit and loss general ledger accounts, and the profit allocation at May 31, 1977. Show how you arrive at these balances by entering all May transactions on the work sheet. Use the accounts indicated in the voucher register.

(AICPA adapted)

Problem 7

Thompson-Spray Company is a partnership that has not maintained adequate accounting records because it has been unable to employ a competent bookkeeper. The company sells hardware items to the retail trade and also wholesales to builders and contractors. As the company's CPA, you have been asked to prepare the company's financial statements as of June 30, 1977.

Your work papers provide the following postclosing trial balance at December 31, 1976.

THOMPSON-SPRAY COMPANY

Postclosing Trial Balance
December 31, 1976

	Debit	Credit
Cash	$10,000	
Accounts receivable	8,000	
Allowance for bad debts		$ 600
Merchandise inventory	35,000	
Prepaid insurance	150	
Automobiles	7,800	
Allowance for depreciation—automobiles		4,250
Furniture and fixtures	2,200	
Allowance for depreciation—furniture and fixtures ...		650
Accounts payable		13,800
Bank loan payable		8,000
Accrued expenses		200
Thompson, capital		17,500
Spray, capital		18,150
Total	$63,150	$63,150

You are able to collect the following information at June 30, 1977.

a. Your analysis of cash transactions, derived from the company's bank statements and checkbook stubs, is as follows:

Deposits:

Cash receipts from customers ($40,000 of this amount represents collections on receivables including redeposited protested checks totaling $600)	$65,000
Bank loan, 1/2/77 (due 5/1/77, 5%)	7,867
Bank loan, 5/1/77 (due 9/1/77, 5%)	8,850
Sale of old automobile	20
Total deposits	$81,737

Disbursements:

Payments to merchandise creditors	$45,000
Payments to Internal Revenue Service on Spray's 1977 declaration of estimated income tax	3,000
General expenses	7,000
Bank loan, 1/2/77	8,000
Bank loan, 5/2/77	8,000
Payment for new automobile	2,400
Protested checks	900
Thompson withdrawals	5,000
Spray withdrawals	2,500
Total disbursements	$81,800

b. The protested checks include customers' checks totaling $600 that were redeposited and a $300 check from an employee that is still on hand.

c. Accounts receivable from customers for merchandise sales amount to $18,000 and include accounts totaling $800 that have been placed with an attorney for collection. Correspondence with the client's attorney reveals that one of the accounts for $175 is uncollectible. Experience indicates that 1 percent of credit sales will prove uncollectible.

d. On April 1 a new automobile was purchased. The list price of the automobile was $2,700, and $300 was allowed for the trade-in of an old automobile, even though the dealer stated that its condition was so poor that he did not want it. The client sold the old automobile, which cost $1,800 and was fully depreciated at December 31, 1976, to an auto wrecker for $20. The old automobile was in use up to the date of its sale.

e. Depreciation is recorded by the straight-line method and is computed on acquisitions to the nearest full month. The estimated life for furniture and fixtures is 10 years and for automobiles is three years. (Salvage value is to be ignored in computing depreciation. No asset other than the car in item [d] was fully depreciated prior to June 30, 1977.)

f. Other data as of June 30, 1977, include the following:

Merchandise inventory	$37,500
Prepaid insurance	80
Accrued expenses	166

g. Accounts payable to merchandise vendors total $18,750. There is on hand a $750 credit memorandum from a merchandise vendor for returned merchandise; the company will apply the credit to July merchandise purchases. Neither the credit memorandum nor the return of the merchandise had been recorded on the books.

h. Profits and losses are divided equally between the partners.

Required:

Prepare a work sheet that provides on the accrual basis information regarding transactions for the six months ended June 30, 1977, the results of the partnership operations for the period, and the financial position of the partnership at June 30, 1977.

(AICPA adapted)

Problem 8

The A, B, & C Partnership engaged you to adjust its accounting records and convert them uniformly to the accrual basis in anticipation of admitting D as a new partner. Some accounts are on the accrual basis and others are on the cash basis. The partnership's books were closed at December 31, 1977, by the bookkeeper who prepared the general ledger trial balance that appears below:

A, B, & C PARTNERSHIP

General Ledger Trial Balance
December 31, 1977

	Debit	Credit
Cash	$ 10,000	
Accounts receivable	40,000	
Inventory	26,000	
Land	9,000	
Buildings	50,000	
Allowance for depreciation of buildings		$ 2,000
Equipment	56,000	
Allowance for depreciation of equipment		6,000
Goodwill	5,000	
Accounts payable		55,000
Allowance for future inventory losses		3,000
A, capital		40,000
B, capital		60,000
C, capital		30,000
Total	$196,000	$196,000

Your inquiries disclosed the following:

a.   The partnership was organized on January 1, 1976, with no provision in the partnership agreement for the distribution of partnership profits and losses. During 1976 profits were distributed equally among the partners. The partnership agreement was amended effective January 1, 1977, to provide for the following profit and loss ratio: A, 50 percent; B, 30 percent; and C, 20 percent. The amended partnership agreement also stated that the accounting records were to be maintained on the accrual basis and that any adjustments necessary for 1976 should be allocated according to the 1976 distribution of profits.

b.   The following amounts were not recorded as prepayments or accruals:

	December 31	
	1977	*1976*
Prepaid insurance	$700	$ 650
Advances from customers	200	1,100
Accrued interest expense		450

   The advances from customers were recorded as sales in the year the cash was received.

c.   In 1977 the partnership recorded a provision of $3,000 for anticipated declines in inventory prices. You convinced the partners that the provision was unnecessary and should be removed from the books.

d.   The partnership charged equipment purchased for $4,400 on January 3, 1977, to expense. This equipment has an estimated life of 10 years and an estimated salvage value of $400. The partnership depreciates its capitalized equipment under the income tax declining balance method at twice the straight-line depreciation rate.

e.   The partners agreed to establish an allowance for doubtful accounts at 2 percent of current accounts receivable and 5 percent of past-due accounts. At December 31, 1976, the partnership had $54,000 of accounts receivable, of which only $4,000 was past due. At December 31, 1977, 15 percent of accounts receivable was past due, of which $4,000 represented sales made in 1976 and was generally considered collectible. The partnership had written off uncollectible accounts in the year the accounts became worthless as follows:

	Account Written Off in	
	1977	*1976*
1977 accounts	$ 800	
1976 accounts	1,000	$250

f.   Goodwill was recorded on the books in 1977 and credited to the partners' capital accounts in the profit and loss ratio in recognition of an increase in the value of the business resulting from improved sales volume. The partners agreed to write off the goodwill before admitting the new partner.

Required:

Prepare a work sheet showing the adjustments and the adjusted trial balance for the partnership on the accrual basis at December 31, 1977. All adjustments affecting income should be made directly to partners' capital accounts. Number your adjusting entries. Supporting computations should be in good form.

(AICPA adapted)

Problem 9

You are engaged to assist the J & L Jewelry Company, a partnership, which was organized on January 2, 1977 and has operated one year unsuccessfully. Jensen, who owns Jem Distributors Company, contributed $10,000 in inventory for a 50 percent interest in J & L Jewelry Company. On the same date, January 2, 1977, Lansing, who owns Western Dishes Distributors Company, contributed $2,000 cash and $8,000 in inventory for a 50 percent interest. All profits and losses are shared equally.

While examining the records of J & L Jewelry Company, you determine the following facts:

a. An incompetent part-time bookkeeper had discarded all cash register tapes and invoices for expenses and purchases. He also served as bookkeeper for the Western Dishes Distributors Company.

b. The partners state that the only existing payables are to themselves and are as follows:

Jem Distributors Company	$ 9,740
Western Dishes Distributors Company	5,260
	$15,000

c. You prepare the following summary of cash transactions from bank statements and canceled checks:

Cash balance, January 2, 1977		$ 2,000
Receipts:		
Sales	$70,000	
Inventory liquidation	7,000	77,000
		$79,000
Disbursements:		
Purchases	$36,000	
Operating expenses	26,000	
Leasehold improvements (five year lease)	6,000	
Liquidating expenses	4,000	72,000
Cash balance, December 31, 1977		$ 7,000

d. On December 31, 1977, each partner was paid $3,500 in partial settlement of the $15,000 liability.

e. The partners indicate that the dollar amounts of regular sales of jewelry and dishes were approximately equal, and that the dollar amounts of liquidation sales of jewelry and dishes were also approximately equal. There was a uniform markup of 40 percent on cost of jewelry and 25 percent on cost of dishes. All sales were for cash. The ending inventory of merchandise was liquidated on December 31, 1977, for 50 percent of the retail sales price.

f. The partners believe that some dishes may have been returned to Western Dishes Distributors Company; there is no record of such returns, however, on the books of either company.

Required:

a. Estimate the unrecorded amount of dishes returned to Western Dishes Distributors Company, if any.
b. Prepare an income statement for the partnership for 1977.
c. Prepare a statement of changes in partners' capital accounts in 1977.

(AICPA adapted)

14

Legal Dissolution: Realignment of Ownership Structure

NATURE OF REALIGNMENT

Basic Legal Provisions

UNDER THE COMMON LAW, any change in the ownership structure of a partnership resulted in its dissolution, although concurrently a new partnership was often formed. In many instances the legal dissolution was not a reflection of an overt intention to interrupt the continuity of partnership operations. However, the existence of this common law provision, together with numerous concepts concerning the nature of partnership dissolution, often created problems which disrupted and sometimes terminated the operations of the business. Problems often created by this legal dissolution include, among others, the determination of equitable settlements to the partners and the computation of their taxable net income. Provisions of the Uniform Partnership Act partially ameliorate the dangers of an unexpected dissolution by stating more precisely the nature of a dissolution, and also by reducing the number of conditions under which the partnership may be dissolved.

Section 29 of the Act defines dissolution of a partnership as "the change in the relation of the partners caused by any partner ceasing to be associated in the carrying on as distinguished from the winding up of the business." The following partial enumeration from Sections 31 and 32 indicates the various types of conditions which constitute a legal dissolution of a partnership:

1. By completion of a definite term of existence (or a particular undertaking) specified in the partnership agreement.
2. By the express will of any partner when no definite term of existence is specified in the agreement.

3. By the death of a partner.
4. By decree of a court for various reasons.
5. By the bankruptcy of any partner or the partnership.

It should be noted, however, that conveyance of an interest in the partnership does not of itself constitute a dissolution (Section 27), and although the admission or retirement of a partner by implication dissolves the partnership, according to Section 41 (1), this provision has little *functional* significance if the partnership is immediately reestablished without actually terminating its operations. Furthermore, various states have adapted for their own purposes certain provisions of the Uniform Partnership Act such that the partners are permitted to include in the articles of copartnership further restrictions on dissolution; for example, the Texas Uniform Partnership Act allows a provision to be included in the partnership agreement prescribing that the death of a partner is not a cause of dissolution. In view of this trend toward greater permanency in the partnership structure, the *legal* problems associated with ownership realignment need not be emphasized in the following discussion.

Types of Realignment

In order to facilitate a systematic review of the accounting problems involved in changes in the ownership structure, three general classes of realignment will be considered:

1. Admission of a new partner.
2. Retirement of a partner.
3. Death of a partner.

These classes are obviously not mutually exclusive; for example, a new partner may be admitted to an existing partnership by purchasing the interest, or partial interest, of a retiring partner. Nonetheless, the above classes do provide a framework for analyzing most of the basic accounting problems associated with the realignment of ownership interests.

ADMISSION OF A NEW PARTNER

There are two principal bases upon which a new partner may be admitted to an existing partnership. Either the new partner may invest cash or other assets in the business so that the net assets of the partnership are increased by his contribution, or he may purchase an interest directly from one or more of the existing partners. In the latter case, the consideration merely passes between the partners, acting as individuals, and partnership net assets are usually not altered. The firm's potential need for additional resources is often an important determining factor as to the method elected to admit a new partner; for example, a deficiency in current working capital may be the compelling initial motivation for the admission of a new partner. Once the partners have selected a basis for admitting a new partner, his capital credit must be duly recorded, as well as any necessary adjustments to the capital accounts of the existing partners and/or the assets of the partnership.

Prior to the admission of a new partner, a careful analysis is generally required of the partnership's asset (and liability) values as well as of the asset values to be contributed by the new partner. In this analysis, three types of assets should be considered:

1. Existing assets, tangible and intangible, presently recorded in the books of the partnership should be appraised and their current market values established. Although the accountant may elect not to record appraisal increments, these values should nonetheless be considered in analyzing the basis of the admission "price" to be paid by the new partner.
2. Unrecorded partnership assets, particularly intangible assets, may be inferred from a comparison of the price paid by the new partner for an interest in the partnership and the preexistent capital after adjustment for appraisal increments. Unrecorded assets may include identifiable items and also goodwill attributable to the existing partners.
3. The assets to be contributed by the new partner must be valued. In addition, a comparison of the admission price with the new partner's equity in identifiable assets may suggest that goodwill is being contributed by the new partner.

After these analyses have been completed, the respective partners' capital account values can be derived from the asset and liability values to be recorded.

Admission with Payment to the Partnership

The entries to record the admission of a new partner vary depending upon the results of the analyses described in the previous paragraph. A sequence of three cases will be used to illustrate alternative entries to record the admission of a new partner under varying fact conditions. In each case, the new partner contributes assets to the partnership in payment for being admitted as a partner.

Case 1. Assume that X and Y are partners with capital balances of $7,000 and $3,000 respectively. The profit- and loss-sharing ratio is 60:40. Z invests tangible assets valued at $15,000 for a 50 percent interest in the capital of the partnership. Concurrently, an appraisal of existing partnership net assets reveals a current market valuation of $15,000.

An analysis of these data indicates that Z is investing $15,000 for a one-half interest in partnership net assets, which after the investment total $30,000. The data further imply that additional unrecorded assets do not exist. However, the accountant must elect whether or not to record the appraisal increment for existing partnership assets. The alternative entries to record the admission of Z are as follows:

1. *Appraisal increment recorded:*

Assets	5,000	
X, capital		3,000
Y, capital		2,000
Assets	15,000	
Z, capital		15,000

2. *Appraisal increment not recorded:*

Assets	15,000	
X, capital (60% × $2,500)		1,500
Y, capital (40% × $2,500)		1,000
Z, capital		12,500

In the first entry, the existing assets are restated to reflect the results of the appraisal. Coincidentally, the increment in the value of existing assets is precisely the amount necessary to explain the $30,000 total value of the partnership which is inferred from Z's purchase of a 50 percent interest for $15,000.

Recorded assets prior to Z's admission	$10,000
Value increment per appraisal	5,000
Assets contributed by Z	15,000
Total asset value after Z's admission	$30,000

Since the $30,000 value of identifiable assets fully explains the inferred total value of the partnership, the potential existence of goodwill is denied.

Corresponding to the revaluation of assets, the capital accounts of the old partners are credited by an amount equal to the increment in asset values. The increment is allocated between the partners on the basis of their profit sharing percentages. Note that under this alternative, Z's capital account is credited for the full $15,000 amount of his investment. One argument in favor of this method is that the capital credit in the full amount of the contribution has psychological appeal to the new partner.

In the second entry, Z is merely given a 50 percent interest in the *recorded values* of the net assets (without appraisal increment adjustments) of the new partnership, and X and Y are awarded capital credits as consideration for Z's newly acquired, implicit interest in the *unrecorded values* of these assets. In effect, X and Y transfer to Z $2,500 of their preexisting interests in these unrecorded values ($5,000 appraisal increment) when Z is given a 50 percent interest in partnership assets, and they are accordingly rewarded therefor in their capital accounts. This method is frequently referred to as the *bonus method,* and it yields equivalent results to the first method only under certain restrictive conditions to be considered later. Hereafter, it will be assumed that the recorded assets of the firm are properly valued, or that an adjustment for current market values has previously been recorded in the old partners' capital accounts.

Case 2. X and Y are partners with capital balances of $40,000 and $10,000 respectively. Profits and losses are shared in the ratio of 80:20. Z invests tangible assets valued at $30,000 for a 25 percent interest in the capital of the new partnership.

Analysis of these facts indicates that Z has acquired a $20,000 (25% × $80,000) interest in the tangible net assets of the firm, inclusive of Z's contribution, at a cost of $30,000. Since it is assumed that all tangible assets are properly valued, Z is apparently paying $10,000 for a one-fourth interest in *unrecorded* intangible assets of the partnership. Conventionally, this type of intangible asset is described as partnership "goodwill." The amount of the goodwill can be determined by applying the following rule:

1. Let C equal the total new capital of the firm, including the as yet undetermined goodwill, and solve the following two equations:
   a. (Fractional interest in capital retained by the old partners) $\times$ C = Total recorded capital balances of old partners.
   b. (Fractional interest in capital obtained by the new partner) $\times$ C = Investment of the new partner.
2. Determine the amount of implied goodwill by subtracting the total recorded net assets of the *new* firm (including the tangible assets contributed by the new partner) from the larger amount computed for C in (1) above. If (*a*) is larger, the new partner contributes goodwill; if (*b*) is larger, the goodwill identifies with the old partners.[1]

This technique may be applied to the data of Case 2 in the following manner:

1. Computation of alternative capital balances:

   a. .75 (C) = $ 50,000,
       (C) = $ 66,667.
   b. .25 (C) = $ 30,000,
       (C) = $120,000.

2. Computation of goodwill:

   Goodwill = $120,000 − $80,000
   = $ 40,000.

The $40,000 valuation for goodwill may be explained in different terms by reconsidering the details of the investment transaction. It was noted that Z paid $10,000 more than his acquired capital interest in the net tangible assets of the new firm. It is now evident that this $10,000 was a payment for a one-fourth interest in the unrecorded goodwill of $40,000.

---

[1] See the Note at the end of this chapter.

There are two alternative methods for recording the entry of the new partner into the partnership:

1. *Bonus method:*

Assets	30,000	
X, capital (4/5 × $10,000)		8,000
Y, capital (1/5 × $10,000)		2,000
Z, capital (1/4 × $80,000)		20,000

2. *Goodwill method:*

Goodwill	40,000	
X, capital (4/5 × $40,000)		32,000
Y, capital (1/5 × $40,000)		8,000
Assets	30,000	
Z, capital		30,000

These two methods are, in substance, identical with the alternative methods employed in the previous case. In this illustration, however, the accountant's election relates to the propriety of recording implicit goodwill rather than of recording appraisal increments (or decrements). Generally, the evidence supporting the existence and amount of "goodwill" is less persuasive than that provided by an appraisal which indicates the market replacement values of tangible assets. As indicated before, the motivational impetus provided by giving the new partner credit for his *total* investment often overcomes the disadvantage of the indefiniteness of the amount of goodwill. The equivalance of the two methods with respect to the relative equities of the partners is, as before, subject to certain constraints to be investigated after considering the following case.

Case 3. X and Y are partners with capital balances of $50,000 and $30,000, respectively. Profits and losses are shared in the ratio of 70:30. Z invests tangible assets valued at $15,000 for a 20 percent interest in the capital of the new partnership.

In this instance, Z acquires an interest of $19,000 (⅕ × $95,000) in the net tangible assets of the firm at a cost of $15,000. By implication Z has contributed an additional, undeclared asset to the partnership for which he receives additional capital credit. The undeclared asset is usually described as goodwill (unusual managerial ability, special customer appeal, etc.). The rule cited earlier may again be applied to estimate the amount of the implicit goodwill:

1. Computation of alternative capital balances:

    a.   .80 $(C) = \$ 80,000,$
          $C = \$100,000.$
    b.   .20 $(C) = \$ 15,000,$
          $C = \$ 75,000.$

2. Computation of goodwill:

    Goodwill $= \$100,000 - \$95,000$
           $= \$ 5,000.$

A heuristic argument similar to that offered above may again be cited to justify the appropriateness of this amount. The existing partners have acquired an 80 percent interest in the implicit goodwill contributed by Z when it accrues to the benefit of the partnership. For this interest, they have given to Z a $4,000 interest in partnership assets in excess of the tangible assets he contributed to the firm ($19,000 − $15,000). Therefore, the amount of the goodwill, as measured by the price imposed upon Z for his interest in net tangible assets, is $5,000 ($4,000 ÷ .80).

Either the goodwill or the bonus method may again be used to record this transaction:

1. *Bonus method:*

Assets	15,000	
X, capital (70% × $4,000)	2,800	
Y, capital (30% × $4,000)	1,200	
Z, capital (20% × $95,000)		19,000

2. *Goodwill method:*

Assets	15,000	
Goodwill	5,000	
Z, capital		20,000

In the previous three cases, it may be observed that the profit and loss ratios were used when allocating goodwill among the partners or when a bonus was allocated between the partners. For example, if a bonus was given to the new partner, the old partners were charged with the bonus with each partner sharing the charge in accordance with his profit- and loss-sharing percentage. Similarly, when a bonus was given to the old partners, it was allocated between them on the basis of their profit and loss ratio. The recognition of goodwill can be perceived as a current recognition of the present value of future net income in excess of normal. If goodwill is not recognized, the future net income will be allocated in accordance with the profit-sharing ratio as the net income is realized. The decision to presently book the present value of that income does not alter the fact that it is income from the perspective of the partners. Thus, it should be shared in accordance with the profit and loss ratio.

In a similar manner, a bonus to the old partners increases their capital accounts in apparent reflection of their operating effectiveness and, from the perspective of the old partners, has exactly the same impact as would additional partnership net income; thus, it is also shared in accordance with the profit and loss ratio. If the old partners are charged for a bonus that is given to the new partner, the bonus may be viewed as a cost which is incurred and charged to the old partners. From this perspective, it should be treated like an expense which is chargeable to the old partners.

A Comparison of the Bonus and Goodwill Methods

Acounting problems of recording asset revaluations and/or implicit goodwill have been considered relative to the alternative *bonus* method of recording a new partner's admission with payment to the partnership. However, an understanding of the implications of selecting one method or the other requires further analysis of the conditions under which the two methods are ultimately equivalent in terms of their effects on the relative equities of the individual partners.

Assume that goodwill is recorded and subsequently proves to have been overstated. A condition of equivalence would require that after the write-down adjustment to eliminate the recorded goodwill (loss realization), the individual partners' capital accounts should be equivalent to those balances that would have resulted had the bonus method been originally used. Alternatively, if the bonus method is initially employed and subsequently a determinable amount of goodwill is confirmed by an objective transaction of the partnership, a similar requirement of equality is imposed to establish equivalence.

The conditions necessary to achieve equivalence of these alternative methods will be introduced by means of an example. Using the data of Case 3, the effect of recording the admission of Z with goodwill recognized, and subsequently writing off the total amount of this intangible, is contrasted with the capital balances obtained by initially applying the bonus method (see Illustration 14–1). Interim transactions are ignored in order

Illustration 14–1

	X	Y	Z	Total
Bonus method—				
capital balances	$47,200	$28,800	$19,000	$ 95,000
Goodwill method:				
Situation (1):				
Initial capital balances	$50,000	$30,000	$20,000	$100,000
Write-off of goodwill	[2,800]	[1,200]	[1,000]	[5,000]
Ending capital balances	$47,200	$28,800	$19,000	$ 95,000
Difference between methods				
after writeoff	$ –0–	$ –0–	$ –0–	$ –0–
Situation (2):				
Initial capital balances	$50,000	$30,000	$20,000	$100,000
Write-off of goodwill	[2,450]	[1,050]	[1,500]	[5,000]
Ending capital balances	$47,550	$28,950	$18,500	$ 95,000
Difference between methods				
after write-off	$ 350	$ 150	$ [500]	$ –0–
Situation (3):				
Initial capital balances	$50,000	$30,000	$20,000	$100,000
Write-off of goodwill	[3,000]	[1,000]	[1,000]	[5,000]
Ending capital balances	$47,000	$29,000	$19,000	$ 95,000
Difference between methods				
after write-off	$ [200]	$ 200	$ –0–	$ –0–

to isolate the equity effects of the two methods. Three different profit and loss ratios are assumed:

	Profit and Loss Ratios		
	X	Y	Z
Situation (1)	56%	24%	20%
Situation (2)	49	21	30
Situation (3)	60	20	20

Illustration 14–1 isolates in situation (1) the two conditions necessary for the equivalence of the bonus and goodwill methods, viz.:

1. The percentage interest in profits and losses of the new partner must be the same as his initial fractional interest in the partnership capital; *and*
2. The new (or adjusted) percentage interests in profits and losses of the old partners must be in the same relative proportion as their old percentage interests.

In situation (1), Z has a 20 percent interest in profits and losses, which is equal to his initial fractional interest in partnership capital, and the new percentage interests in profits and losses of X and Y are in the same relative proportion as their prior percentage interests—80 percent of 70 percent for X, and 80 percent of 30 percent for Y, or 70:30 = 56:24. In situation (2), the new percentage interests in profits and losses of the old partners are in the same relative proportion, but the interest of Z in profits and losses exceeds his initial fractional interest in capital; consequently, an advantage accrues to X and Y equivalent in amount to the disadvantage to Z. In situation (3), the new percentage interests of X and Y are in a different proportion than existed prior to the admission of Z, i.e., 70:30 ≠ 60:20; this condition results in an advantage to Y, and a disadvantage to X.

Admission with Payment to the Existing Partner(s)

A second basic method of acquiring an interest in a partnership is to purchase a capital equity directly from one or more of the old partners, without an increase in partnership assets. In this section, two cases will be distinguished:

1. Purchase of a portion of one partner's interest, and
2. Purchase of a partial interest uniformly from all of the existing partners.

In both instances, the ownership structure is numerically enlarged by the conveyance of an interest in the existing partnership to a new member. In the discussion of retirement of partners, the sale by one partner of his *total* interest in the partnership will be described briefly.

If an existing partner sells a portion of his interest in capital and profits to another individual, the only entry *required* on the books of the partnership is one which establishes the new partner's capital credit by a transfer of the amount of the purchased interest from the capital account of the selling partner. For example, if X and Y are partners, with capital balances of $60,000 and $40,000 respectively, and Y sells one fourth of his interest to Z for $12,000, the only entry required on the partnership books is:

Y, capital (1/4 × $40,000) 10,000
    Z, capital   10,000

The cash consideration which passes between the old and new partner is established independently by Y and Z and need not be reflected in the above entry on the partnership books. From the point of view of the partnership entity, Y has merely transferred a personal asset to a new partner, viz., one fourth of his *recorded* interest in partnership capital; only this fact need be recognized in the partnership accounts.

If in the preceding illustration Z had purchased a one-fourth interest in the partnership by means of a direct purchase from *both* X and Y for $30,000 (a ratable transfer of one fourth of the monetary interest of each in the partnership), the accounting entry to record the capital transfer is essentially the same. Each partner conveys to Z one fourth of his interest in the *recorded* capital of the firm.

X, capital (1/4 × $60,000) 15,000
Y, capital (1/4 × $40,000) 10,000
    Z, capital   25,000

Again, the cash price for the purchased interests is not a compelling factor affecting the partnership accounts, as the sale represents an *independent* transaction between the existing partners and the incoming partner. The transaction may be compared to the sale of shares of corporate stock in the open market subsequent to their original issuance; the total stockholders' equity of the corporate entity remains unaffected by the sale—only the identity and the relative interests of the various owners are changed.

Two problems intrude upon this relatively simple accounting framework for recording the purchase of a partnership interest directly from one or more partners. First, an argument can be made that the cash price established in the sale of an interest should be used as an independent index of the current value of the partnership net assets. If this premise is accepted and if the recorded net assets of the partnership are assumed to reflect current market values, the purchase price may be used to estimate the amount of goodwill possessed by the preexistent partnership. Returning to the previous example in which Z purchased a one-fourth ratable interest from X and Y for $30,000, there is an indication that the total value of the partnership net assets may be $120,000 (one fourth of the total value = $30,000). Since the recorded net worth presently is only $100,000, implicit goodwill of $20,000 may be inferred from this purchase. If the goodwill

were recorded, and assuming X and Y share profits and losses equally, the
entries to record the admission of Z are:

Goodwill	20,000	
X capital		10,000
Y, capital		10,000
X, capital (1/4 × $70,000)	17,500	
Y, capital (1/4 × $50,000)	12,500	
Z, capital		30,000

In an analogous manner, goodwill identified with the new partner may be
computed. The advantages and disadvantages of recording the implicit
goodwill in either case, and the requisite conditions for the equivalence of
this and the preceding method, are the same as those discussed earlier in
this chapter.

A second problem arising from the purchase of an interest from more
than one existing partner concerns the distribution settlement of cash to the
selling partners. This is ultimately a matter of negotiation between the new
partner and each of the old partners or between the old partners. Frequently, however, the accountant is consulted and asked to suggest a basis
for distributing the cash contributed by the new partner. Using the above
data, the following tabulation is the conventional approach:

	X	Y	Total
Capital balances, as recorded	$60,000	$40,000	$100,000
Implicit goodwill—allocated in profit and loss ratio ..	10,000	10,000	20,000
Adjusted capital balances	$70,000	$50,000	$120,000
Retained capital—three fourths of adjusted balances ..	52,500	37,500	90,000
Capital transferred to Z—basis for allocation of cash ..	$17,500	$12,500	$ 30,000

An analysis of this schedule of cash distribution raises several questions
concerning its general validity. Since the sale was assumed to be independent
of the partnership entity, one may take the position that it is inappropriate
to utilize present partners' capital balances and provisions of the partnership agreement (i.e., the profit and loss ratios of X and Y) as a basis for
determining the cash allocations. In this case, the capital balances are not in
the profit- and loss-sharing ratios; consequently, X and Y are surrendering
an interest in recorded partnership capital according to one ratio, 60:40,
and they are forsaking an interest in future profits in yet another ratio,
50:50. The above schedule indicates the accepted method of recording, on
the partnership books, the existence of implicit goodwill, and the resulting
transfers of capital from X and Y to Z. The schedule, however, may not
represent the most appropriate allocation of the $30,000 as between the
amount paid for an interest in present partnership capital and that amount
which is paid for an interest in future profits and losses. Clearly, the ultimate decision in respect to cash distributions remains with the old partners.

The above solution may or may not represent an acceptable settlement; their preferences should and will control.

One may also appropriately question the basic premise underlying the conventional computation of implicit goodwill. It is tacitly assumed that the capital balances of the old partners and the purchase price of the new partner may serve as a basis for inferring the existence of unrecorded goodwill. However, as noted above, the new partner is, in fact, buying an interest in both present capital *and* future profits; accordingly, it is questionable whether only one of these components should be used in computing the amount of goodwill. For example, the price paid for a partnership interest which is in excess of identifiable net assets acquired may be a payment for the excess earning capacity of the business (goodwill); or, it may represent the purchase of a greater interest in profits than in capital. If the latter interpretation prevails, the existence and amount of goodwill is an indeterminate element and should be recorded only when supporting evidence is compelling.

Legal Status of a New Partner

Section 27 of the Uniform Partnership Act confers upon any partner the right to convey by assignment to a third party his interest in the partnership —which is, as previously noted, personal property. This assignment does not, however, give the assignee authority to participate in the management of the business. Rather, it entitles him merely to receive the profits and in the case of dissolution to receive an interest in net assets which would normally accrue to the assignor.

If the existing partners agree to admit by assignment a new partner to the ownership structure, as is implicitly done when a prospective partner invests assets in the business, the new partner assumes the same rights and obligations as the old partners; this assumption is modified somewhat in Section 17 of the Act, in which it is provided that the new partner is personally liable for only those liabilities created subsequent to his admission to the firm. Thus, if dissolution should occur shortly after the admission of a new partner, it is necessary to distinguish between "old" and "new" liabilities of the partnership. The reader will note that the accounting treatment previously discussed for the "purchase of an interest" implicitly assumes that the assignee is admitted to the partnership with the status of a new partner, i.e., no special equity status is identified.

Tax Basis of a New Partner

The tax basis of a new partner admitted by investing assets in the business is determined in the same manner as was outlined in the preceding chapter, viz., his basis is the sum of the bases of the contributed assets plus the amount of any partnership liabilities assumed by the new partner, and less the amount of any personal liabilities of the new partner which is assumed by the existing partners.

Case 4. Assume the following data for the XY Partnership:

	Tax Basis	Book Value
Assets	$50,000	$60,000
Liabilities	18,000	18,000
Capital (interest) of partners:		
X	30,000	25,000
Y	20,000	17,000

Z is admitted to a one-fourth interest in the capital, profits, and losses of XY Partnership by contributing $14,000 (one fourth of the net assets of the new firm), and he assumes a one-fourth responsibility for present partnership obligations.

Assuming X and Y have equal interests in profits and losses, the tax bases of the contributed assets and relevant capital adjustments are given as follows:

Basis of assets	14,000	
Basis of X's interest	2,250	
Basis of Y's interest	2,250	
Basis of Z's interest		18,500

The basis of Z's interest can be proved:

Basis of assets contributed	$14,000
Partnership liabilities assumed (¼ × $18,000)	4,500
	$18,500

Although Z acquired a one-fourth interest in future profits and losses of the partnership, he also assumed responsibility for one fourth of the existing partnership liabilities. This is recognized in the reduction of X's and Y's tax bases by $2,250 each, the amount of partnership liabilities transferred to Z. Importantly, the sum of the asset tax bases, $64,000 ($50,000 + $14,000), is equal to the sum of the bases of the partners' capital interests in the firm, $64,000 ($27,750 + $17,750 + $18,500).

When a new partner purchases an interest *directly* from one or more of the existing partners, Section 742 of the Internal Revenue Code states that the basis of the new partner's interest in the firm is determined in a manner similar to Case 4. In essence, his basis is the price paid to acquire the interest, adjusted for liabilities which he assumes and/or liabilities which the other partners assume. Obviously, the tax basis of the new partner's interest can be different from the tax basis of the old partners' interests. This difference is subject to alternative tax treatments. The following case illustrates this point.

Case 5. Z purchases one half of Y's interest in the XY Partnership for $10,000 when the tax basis of Y's total interest is $16,000.

The tax basis of the interest transferred to Z is $8,000; and subject to certain specified conditions, Y must recognize a capital gain on the sale. Based upon the provision that the tax basis of Z's interest is the cost of acquisition, or $10,000, an examination of the separate tax bases of Y and Z indicates the following:

Basis of Y's interest	8,000	
Differential	2,000	
Basis of Z's interest		10,000

If additional adjustments are not made, this differential measures the extent to which the sum of the partners' interests in the firm exceeds the sum of the bases of the assets. The differential will remain until either Z transfers his interest to some new partner (at which time it may simply be confirmed by that transaction and continue to exist) or until the partnership is liquidated. However, Section 754 of the Code provides that the partnership may *elect* to increase the bases of its assets by an amount equal to this excess payment (differential), as it is assumed that it measures and confirms an increase in the market value of partnership assets over their tax bases. If this election is made, the differential is allocated to the various partnership assets in relation to the relative increase in fair market value over the tax basis of each asset category.[2] Importantly, however, the adjustment of the assets' bases only affects the subsequent tax position of the new partner Z. If the assets are subsequently sold, the taxable gain is then allocated to the partners, with the increased basis of $2,000 in the partnership assets being applied to reduce Z's portion of the gain. In other words, the taxable gain allocated to Z at the time of sale will be *less* than if the adjustment had not been made.

RETIREMENT OR DEATH OF A PARTNER

Retirement of a Partner

If one of the partners desires to withdraw from the partnership and he is not in violation of the agreement between the partners (Section 31),[3] two sections of the Uniform Partnership Act are relevant. As noted previously, Section 27 permits a partner to convey his interest in the partnership either to the existing partners or to a third party. If sold to a third party, the assignee is admitted to the partnership and is accorded the status of partner, *only* with the consent of the continuing partners; if they should disapprove, the assignee is entitled to receive the profits which would have accrued to the assignor; he is not otherwise entitled to management privileges.

---

[2] If goodwill is revealed by this transaction, the allocation must include this partnership asset.

[3] If the withdrawal and the resulting partnership dissolution is in contravention of the articles of copartnership, the retiring partner is liable for damages suffered by the innocent partners (Section 38).

If there is no express agreement in respect to settlement of accounts with a retiring partner, Section 42 provides that the retiring partner is entitled to have the value of his equity at the date of retirement ascertained, and to receive, as an ordinary creditor, an amount equal to this value plus an interest credit on this amount. However, at his option, he may retain a passive interest in the firm and receive, in lieu of interest, the "profits attributable to the use of his right in the property of the dissolved partnership." Determining the value of a retiring partners' equity is often a basic issue in the settlement arrangement. The accounting problems of reclassifying the retiring partner's capital equity as a liability and the treatment of any assigned value increment in excess of recorded capital will be considered in the following discussion.

Sale of an Interest to a New Partner

The sale of a retiring partner's interest to a new partner introduces no special problems other than those which relate to a conveyance of a partial interest. The admission of the new partner is recorded merely by transferring the recorded capital interest of the retiring partner to the new partner; however, the conditions of admission may indicate the presence of partnership goodwill. If goodwill is to be formally recognized in the accounts, the recorded amount is normally the *total* amount of goodwill attaching to the partnership entity, not merely the amount which relates to the retiring partner. However, in the event goodwill previously existed in the partnership books and is reduced as a consequence of the retirement of a partner, i.e., the goodwill attaches primarily to the retiring partner as a separate individual, the purchase transaction may indicate the amount of "lost" goodwill.

Sale of an Interest to Continuing Partners

If the continuing partners acquire the interest of a retiring partner, whether negotiating jointly or separately *outside* the partnership or jointly *within* and *through* the partnership entity, the essence of the accounting problem remains substantially unchanged. If the purchase is completed independently of the partnership, the transaction is analogous to the sale of an interest to a third party; if the retiring partner sells his interest to the partnership entity, the substance of the transaction is unchanged but the partnership assumes the obligation to make payment to the retiring partner —essentially a liquidating distribution. As before, partnership goodwill may be inferred if the purchase price (or the computed amount of a liquidating settlement) exceeds the recorded capital of the retiring partner. In this case, however, the evaluation of goodwill is subject to greater question, as the parties to the transaction are not mutually independent. The accountant, therefore, should be especially circumspect in recording partnership goodwill in this instance. The following case illustrates the sale to the partnership of a retiring partner's interest.

Case 6. Z elects to retire from the XYZ Partnership, and the remaining partners agree to purchase his interest for and through the partnership. The partners share profits and losses equally. On this date the balance sheet of the partnership is as follows:

XYZ PARTNERSHIP

Balance Sheet
Date of Proposed Retirement

Assets		*Equities*	
Assets	$110,000	Liabilities	$ 10,000
		X, capital	30,000
		Y, capital	30,000
		Z, capital	40,000
	$110,000		$110,000

An examination of the values of existing assets and an estimate of prospective earnings for future years indicate that Z's interest is worth considerably more than his recorded capital credit. It is determined that the current market value of the partnership assets is $140,000. After negotiation with Z and in consideration of the demonstrated excess earnings potential of the partnership, it is agreed that Z shall receive $60,000 for his capital interest, payment to be made in four annual installments, with interest of 4 percent accruing annually on the unpaid balance.

As a consequence of Z's retirement, the partnership is legally dissolved; the first accounting objective, therefore, is to determine and record the status of the retiring partner and to establish a proper basis of accounting for the partnership as a continuing entity. From this point of view, it is appropriate to adjust the assets to their current market values. Accordingly, the entry to record the value adjustments is as follows (assuming profits and losses are shared equally):

Assets	30,000	
X, capital		10,000
Y, capital		10,000
Z, capital		10,000

The entry to adjust the equity of the retiring partner in the continuing partnership may be made in either of two ways. Using a method similar to the bonus method previously discussed, the entry may take the following form:

Method 1:

Z, capital	50,000	
X, capital	5,000	
Y, capital	5,000	
Notes payable to Z		60,000

Since Z received $10,000 more than his recorded capital interest after adjustments were made for asset revaluations, there is evidence that the partnership has unrecorded goodwill. Should the partners elect to recognize a value for goodwill, it may be recorded in the following manner:

Method 2:

Z, capital	50,000	
Goodwill	10,000	
Notes payable to Z		60,000

The entry is based upon the long-established accounting precept that only *purchased* goodwill should be expressed quantitatively in the accounts.

However, the reader will recognize that this precept, even if valid or useful, is inappropriate when applied in this instance. There has been no purchase of goodwill. The goodwill, if it exists, is an asset of the partnership, a measurement of which has been established independently of the settlement with the retiring partner. Clearly, the partnership did not acquire its own goodwill, nor did it transfer a portion of it to the retiring partner. If the goodwill identifies with Z, no payment would be made therefor, as its value to the partnership would necessarily dissipate with the withdrawal of the retiring partner. Rather, the transaction merely offers evidence, however cogent, as to the existence and amount of partnership goodwill. If the accountant is persuaded that the $10,000 excess payment does, in fact, represent a valid measure of a one-third interest in the unrecorded goodwill—giving due attention to the imponderables of such a calculation—then either the total amount of goodwill ($30,000) should be recorded, or none should be recorded with the bonus method used to record the retirement. It appears inconsistent to recognize the existence of intangibles and then to record but a fraction of their value. If the total amount of goodwill is to be recorded, the following entries should be made:

Method 2 (as modified):

Goodwill	30,000	
X, capital		10,000
Y, capital		10,000
Z, capital		10,000
Z, capital	60,000	
Notes payable to Z		60,000

These two methods may be analyzed as before for equivalence in respect to their effects on the partners' equities. Regardless of the method employed, the interest on the unpaid liability to the retiring partner remains an expense in determining the periodic net income of the partnership.

Death of a Partner

The death of a partner dissolves a partnership under provisions of the Uniform Partnership Act (Section 31). However, modifications of the Act adopted by a number of states permit the partners to prevent dissolution by including a contrary provision in the partnership agreement.

It is important that the partnership agreement specify the procedures to be followed upon the death of a partner whether or not legal dissolution is a consequence of the death. Whether the surviving partners acting separately or the partnership entity purchases the interest of the deceased partner, a determination of the value of this equity at the date of death is an important first consideration. Where the partnership continues as an operating entity under the control of the surviving partners, the agreement may provide that payments for this interest be based upon recorded partnership values, or that a revaluation of assets be made and the adjusted capital interests be based thereon.[4] Where the agreement is silent in respect to payments made for a deceased partner's interest, the amount of settlement is the result of negotiations between the estate of the deceased partner and the surviving partners. The estate is accorded the same status under Section 42 as a retiring partner, viz., the option to receive either interest on an unliquidated capital balance, or profits attributable to the use of this equity.

Once the capital interest of the deceased partner is determined, the remaining partners must agree upon an acceptable means of settlement. Life insurance coverage in respect to individual partners is one commonly employed method of meeting this contingency. Two types of life insurance are often used: (1) cross-insurance and (2) entity insurance. If cross-insurance is utilized, the lives of individual partners are insured by the other partners independently of the partnership. Where this type of coverage exists, the partnership does not incur an expense. If entity insurance is used, the partnership insures the lives of each of the partners, and although nondeductible for income tax purposes, the premium payments represent proper expense charges in determining periodic partnership net income.

If insurance is evaluated as a low-return investment as compared to alternative types of investment and accordingly is rejected as the vehicle to provide a means of settlement, the partners must decide whether to make a liquidating payment in cash or to make distributions of assets in kind. If the partnership is to be terminated, it is probable that distribution will be made in specific assets, although it is unlikely that the assets will be those originally contributed. However, if it is anticipated that partnership operations will continue, a method of installment payments, with interest, is a common method of discharging the obligation to the estate of the deceased partner.

---

[4] Again, the problem of determining the amount of goodwill to be recognized may arise. The argument for recording only the "purchased" goodwill is subject to the same limitation as in the case of a retiring partner.

Legal Status of a Retiring or Deceased Partner

The fact of partnership dissolution does not of itself result in the discharge of individual partners from unpaid partnership debts. However, Section 36 provides that "a partner is discharged from any existing liability upon dissolution of the partnership by an agreement to that effect between himself, the partnership creditors and the person or partnership continuing the business." Assuming proper notice is given past and prospective creditors, the retiring or deceased partner is, at most, liable for only those obligations existing at the date of dissolution.

NOTE

The validity of the rule for determining new capital of a partnership following an expansion in the ownership structure (page 505) is confirmed as follows:

Let $A =$ capital of old partners before investment,
$\quad$ $B =$ tangible assets invested by new partner,
$\quad$ $\alpha =$ percent interest in capital retained by the old partners,
$\quad$ $\beta =$ percent interest in capital acquired by the new partner,
$\quad$ $G =$ goodwill implicit in the transaction,
$\quad$ $C =$ total capital, including goodwill, after the investment,
$\quad$ $D =$ capital of old partners after the investment, and
$\quad$ $E =$ capital of the new partner after the investment.

By definition, the following equations are valid:

$$C = A + B + G,$$
$$C = D + E,$$
$$G > 0 \text{ (the assumption is that goodwill exists)}.$$

Case 1. Goodwill Identified with Existing Partners. This requires that $C = B \div \beta > A \div \alpha$. It is assumed that the old partners possess a yet undetermined amount of goodwill and the following equations are valid:

$$D = A + G = \alpha C,$$
$$E = B = \beta C.$$

Therefore,

$$C = B \div \beta = (A + G) \div \alpha.$$

Since $G > 0$,

$$B \div \beta > A \div \alpha.$$

Case 2. Goodwill Identified with New Partner. This requires that $C = A \div \alpha > B \div \beta$. Again, by the assumptions stated, the following equations are appropriate:

$$D = A = \alpha C,$$
$$E = B + G = \beta C.$$

Therefore,

$$C = A \div \alpha = (B + G) \div \beta.$$

Since G > 0,

$$A \div \alpha > B \div \beta.$$

From the above calculations, it is obvious that *if* goodwill does not exist $(G = 0)$,

$$C = A \div \alpha = B \div \beta,$$

and the amounts of capital computed under each of the alternatives specified by the rule described on page 505 are equal.

QUESTIONS

1. What circumstances or conditions cause a legal dissolution of a partnership?

2. Discuss three alternative explanations and related accounting treatments of the following situation. A new partner is admitted to a partnership on the basis of contributing additional assets. Further, the new partner's agreed upon interest in the previously recorded equity of the partnership plus the tangible assets he contributed is smaller than the value of the assets he contributed.

3. What is the usual accounting procedure for calculating the value of unrecorded intangibles ("goodwill") implied in the transactions surrounding the admission of a new partner?

4. What two conditions are necessary for the bonus method and goodwill method to have equivalent effects on the relative balances in the capital accounts?

5. Partners A and B have equal capital balances and share profits and losses in a 70:30 ratio. Upon admission of C to the partnership, goodwill is recognized and allocated to the capital accounts of A and B. Should the goodwill be allocated on a 50:50 basis or a 70:30 basis? Why?

6. Partners A and B have equal capital balances and share profits and losses in a 70:30 ratio. Upon admission of C to the partnership, C's capital account is credited with a bonus. In charging the bonus to the capital accounts of A and B, on what basis should it be allocated? Why?

7. If a partner sells part of his interest in the partnership to another individual, is the purchase price reflected on the books of the partnership? Why, or why not?

8. What special problems may arise when a new partner acquires a partnership interest directly from one or more partners?

9. Suppose an existing partnership plans to admit a new partner whose profit-and loss-sharing percentage will be different from his percentage interest in

partnership capital. In this instance, explain why the conventional approach to calculating goodwill to be recorded with the new partner's admission might not be appropriate.

10. If goodwill is to be recognized at the time of a partner's retirement, should the partnership recognize the entire amount of goodwill or merely that portion of the intangible associated with the retiring partner? Explain.

11. In the event of a partner's death, is there concurrent dissolution of the partnership or may the enterprise continue in existence?

12. What is the general method for determining the tax basis of a new partner's interest in a partnership?

13. Enumerate several important factors which the accountant should consider in evaluating the appropriateness of recognizing implied goodwill upon the retirement and/or withdrawal of a partner from a partnership.

EXERCISES

Exercise 14-1

Andrey and Coda share profits equally and have equal investments in their partnership. The partnership's net assets are carried on the books at $40,000. Kramer is admitted to the partnership with a one-third interest in profits and net assets. Kramer pays $18,000 cash into the partnership for his interest.

Prepare journal entries to show three possible methods of recording on the partnership books the admission of Kramer. State the conditions under which each method would be appropriate.

(AICPA adapted)

Exercise 14-2

Grey and Danos are partners sharing profits and losses 60:40 respectively. Their capital account balances are: Grey, $42,000, and Danos, $30,000. Journalize the admission of Uecker to the partnership under the following independent conditions:

a. Uecker invests $26,000 for a one-fourth interest in partnership capital. Goodwill implicit in the investment is to be recorded.

b. Uecker invests $16,000 for a one-fifth interest in partnership capital. Total capital after the admission of Uecker is to be $88,000.

c. Uecker purchases one third of the interests of the existing partners, paying $15,000 to each partner. Goodwill implied by the purchase price is to be recorded.

Exercise 14-3

Journalize the admission of Knighton to the partnership of Simmons and Patten in each of the following independent cases. The capital balances of Simmons and Patten are $12,000 and $8,000 respectively; they share profits and losses equally.

a. Knighton is admitted to a one-third interest in capital with a contribution of $10,000.

b. Knighton is admitted to a one-fourth interest in capital with a contribution of $8,000. Total capital of the new partnership is to be $28,000.

c. Knighton is admitted to a one-fifth interest in capital upon contributing $4,000. Total capital of the new partnership is to be $25,000.

d. Knighton is admitted to a one-fourth interest in capital by the purchase of one fourth of the interests of Simmons and Patten for $5,500. Total capital of the new partnership is to be $20,000.

e. Same conditions as in (d), except that the new partnership capital is to be $22,000.

f. Knighton is admitted to a one-third interest in capital upon contributing $7,000, after which each partner is to have an equal capital equity in the new partnership.

g. Knighton is admitted to a one-fifth interest in capital upon contributing $6,000. Total capital of the new partnership is to be $30,000.

Exercise 14–4

Two long-time partners, Zap and Zing, finally decided that their partnership did not have enough zip to compete in the modern world. As a consequence, they are considering the admission of Zow to the partnership. Prior to Zow's entry, the capital interests of Zap and Zing are $24,000 and $36,000, respectively. They share profits and losses in a 30:70 ratio. Several alternative plans for admitting Zow are being considered, each of which is described below:

1. Zow contributes $10,000 cash to the partnership in exchange for a 20 percent interest in capital, profits, and losses.

2. Zow pays $10,000 to the partners in exchange for a 25 percent interest in capital, profits, and losses. Thus, 25 percent of each partner's interest is transferred to Zow. Zap and Zing agree to distribute the $10,000 between them such that Zap receives $4,000 and Zing receives $6,000.

3. Zow contributes $20,000 to the partnership in exchange for a 20 percent interest in profits, losses, and capital.

Required:

For each of the three alternatives (a) present the journal entries to reflect the goodwill method of recording the events; and (b) present the journal entries to reflect the bonus method of recording the events. Label your answers 1–a; 1–b; 2–a; 2–b; 3–a; 3–b.

Exercise 14–5

Sam retired from the Synthetic Partnership on January 1, 1977. In accordance with the provisions of the partnership agreement, Sam was paid $90,000 from the partnership assets in satisfaction of his one-third interest. This amount was based on a formula that was specified in the original partnership agreement. It was determined by such factors as number of years of service to the partnership, capital contributed, and recent years' sales and earnings performance of the partnership. Sam's capital balance on January 1, 1977, was $60,000. Bud and Helen, the other partners, each have one-third interests and $60,000 capital balances. Assume that the tangible assets of the partnership are correctly valued.

Required:

a. Journalize Sam's retirement under each of the three alternative methods.
b. Discuss the relative merits of each method, noting the conditions under which each may draw the greatest support. As a part of your answer, state which method appears least appropriate under the circumstances.

PROBLEMS

Problem 1

Boatsman, Baskin, and Beam are partners. Their profit-sharing ratio and capital balances at December 31, 1977, are as follows:

Partners	Profit-Sharing Ratio	Capital Balance
Boatsman	60%	$97,000
Baskin	30	65,000
Beam	10	38,000

Conroy is admitted to the partnership on January 2, 1978, by investing $45,000 for a 20 percent interest in capital and profits.

Required:

a. Prepare journal entries for each of three alternative methods of recording the admission of the new partner.
b. Assume that Conroy purchased an interest in the partnership ratably from the existing partners. Prepare a schedule of cash transfers to Boatsman, Baskin, and Beam.
c. Under assumption (b), prepare journal entries for each of two alternative methods of recording the admission of Conroy.

Problem 2

Streuling and Wilson are partners in the Sailmaker Company and have capital balances of $64,000 and $56,000 respectively on December 31, 1977. Profits and losses are shared 60:40. Moore is admitted to the partnership on January 2, 1978, by investing $50,000 for a one-fourth interest in capital and profits.

Required:

a. Prepare journal entries to record the admission of Moore under both the bonus and goodwill methods.
b. Assuming the goodwill method is used to record the admission of Moore *and* that subsequently the goodwill is written off, compare the effect of this

treatment on the partners' capitals with that of the bonus method under the following three independent conditions (ignore the effects of other changes in capital):

		Percentage Interest in Profits		
		Streuling	Wilson	Moore
Case 1	....	45%	30%	25%
Case 2	....	50	25	25
Case 3	....	42	28	30

Problem 3   ✓

You have been engaged to prepare financial statements for the partnership of Alexander, Randolph, and Ware as of June 30, 1977. The partnership was formed originally by Alexander and Barnes on July 1, 1976. At that date Barnes contributed $400,000 cash. Alexander contributed land, building, and equipment with market values of $110,000, $520,000, and $185,000, respectively. The land and building were subject to a mortgage securing an 8 percent note (interest rate of similar notes at July 1, 1976). The note is due in quarterly payments of $5,000 plus interest on January 1, April 1, July 1, and October 1 of each year. Alexander made the July 1, 1976 principal and interest payment personally. The partnership then assumed the obligation for the remaining $300,000 balance.

The partnership agreement provided that Alexander had contributed a certain intangible benefit to the partnership due to his many years of business activity in the area to be serviced by the new partnership. The assigned value of this intangible asset plus the net tangible assets he contributed gave Alexander a 60 percent initial capital interest in the partnership. Alexander was designated to receive an annual salary of $24,000 plus an annual bonus of 4 percent of net income after deducting his salary but before deducting interest on partners' capital investments (see below). Both the salary and the bonus are operating expenses of the partnership. Each partner is to receive a 6 percent return on his average capital investment, such interest to be an expense of the partnership. All residual profits or losses are to be shared equally.

On October 1, 1976, Barnes sold his partnership interest and rights as of July 1, 1976, to Ware for $370,000. Alexander agreed to accept Ware as a partner if he would contribute sufficient cash to meet the October 1, 1976 payment on the mortgage. Ware made the payment from personal funds.

On January 1, 1977, Alexander and Ware admitted a new partner, Randolph, who invested $150,000 cash for a 10 percent capital interest based on the initial investments at July 1, 1976, of Alexander and Barnes. At January 1, 1977, the book value of the partnership's assets and liabilities approximated their market values. Randolph contributed no intangible benefit to the partnership. Similar to the other partners, Randolph is to receive a 6 percent return on his average capital investment. His investment also entitled him to 20 percent of the partnership's profits or losses as defined above. However, for the year ended June 30, 1977, Randolph would receive one-half of his pro rata share of the profits or losses.

The accounting records show that on February 1, 1977, Other Miscellaneous Expenses had been charged $3,600 in payment of hospital expenses incurred by Alexander's eight-year-old daughter.

All salary payments to Alexander have been charged to his drawing account. On June 1, 1977, Ware made a $33,000 withdrawal. These are the only transactions recorded in the partners' drawing accounts. Since Ware's withdrawal is not an expense of the partnership, it is understood to be a reduction in his capital investment. The trial balance as of June 30, 1977, is as follows:

	Dr. [Cr.]
Current assets	$ 307,100
Fixed assets, net	1,285,800
Current liabilities	[157,000]
8% mortgage note payable	[290,000]
Alexander, capital	[515,000]
Randolph, capital	[150,000]
Ware, capital	[400,000]
Alexander, drawing	24,000
Randolph, drawing	—
Ware, drawing	33,000
Sales	[872,600]
Cost of sales	695,000
Administrative expenses	16,900
Other miscellaneous expenses	11,100
Interest expense	11,700

Required:

Prepare a workpaper to adjust the net income [loss] and partners' capital accounts for the year ended June 30, 1977, and to close the net income [loss] to the partner capital accounts at June 30, 1977. Amortization of goodwill, if any, is to be over a ten-year period. Use the following column headings and begin with balances per books as shown.

Description	Net Income [Loss] Cr. [Dr.]	Partners' Capital			Other Accounts	
		Alexander Cr. [Dr.]	Randolph Cr. [Dr.]	Ware Cr. [Dr.]	Amount Dr. [Cr.]	Name
Book balances at June 30, 1977	$137,900	$515,000	$150,000	$400,000		

(AICPA adapted)

Problem 4

A, B, and C decide to practice law together as of January 1, 1977. They enter into an agreement under which they share profits and losses in the proportion of 50 percent, 25 percent, and 25 percent, respectively, and agree to contribute $50,000 in cash in these same proportions to provide working capital. They decide to keep their books on a cash basis.

On January 1, 1978, B died and the remaining partners agreed to admit D, giving him a 20 percent share in the profits with a minimum guarantee of

$10,000 per year whether operations are profitable or not. A and C have percentages of 45 and 35 respectively. This partnership is of one year's duration, and at the end of this period C decides to retire but permits the use of his name in future partnerships subject to the payment to him of $5,000 per annum to be treated as an expense of the partnership.

As of January 1, 1979, a partnership is formed in which C's name is utilized in accordance with his proposal and to which E is admitted. The partners' interests in this partnership are as follows: A, 55 percent; D, 30 percent; E, 15 percent.

Since there were no substantial accruals at the end of the year, disbursements for expenses made during any one period were treated as expenses of the then current partnership. These disbursements were $70,000 in 1977, $80,000 in 1978, and $90,000 in 1979.

Receipts of fees were as follows:

	Earned by Partnership		
	No. 1	No. 2	No. 3
1977	$ 80,000		
1978	145,000	$40,000	
1979		50,000	$70,000

Each new partnership agreement provided for the newly created partnership to purchase from the old partnership the $50,000 capital originally paid in by A, B, and C. The agreements also provided that the partners should bear the cost of acquisition of this amount in the proportion which they shared profits (and losses). However, it was agreed that an incoming partner, or one acquiring an increased percentage, need not make his contribution in cash immediately but could have the same charged to his drawing account. All such partners availed themselves of this privilege. Partners selling all or a part of their interest in capital are credited through their drawing accounts and immediately withdraw the amount of such credit. In addition to drawings made under this agreement, the partners or their heirs made cash drawings as follows:

	A	B	C	D	E
1977	$10,500	$27,750	$13,750		
1978	40,000	4,750	5,000	$7,000	
1979	10,000	5,000	15,000	2,500	$5,000

Required:

Prepare schedules or statements showing the details of transactions in the partners' drawing accounts and capital accounts for each of the years involved. These accounts should be in such form that the balance at the end of each year which was available for withdrawal by each partner is shown in that partner's drawing account. The capital accounts are to reflect only the $50,000 original investment.

(AICPA adapted)

Problem 5

Jensen and Bean, equal partners in the Discount Hardware Stores, sold a one-third interest in Store No. 3 to Cottingham, manager of that store, on January 1, 1978. The new partnership will operate as the SuperDis Hardware Company. Jensen and Bean will continue to operate other stores. The balance sheet of Store No. 3 at January 1, 1978, was as follows:

Assets			Equities		
Merchandise		$63,000	Accounts payable		$20,000
Fixtures and equipment ..	$22,000				
Allowance for deprecia-					
tion	10,000	12,000	Capital:		
Prepaid expenses		3,900	Jensen	$30,000	
Utility deposits		1,100	Bean	30,000	60,000
		$80,000			$80,000

Furniture and fixtures, which have an estimated remaining life of five years, were revalued at $18,000, according to the agreement of sale. Each partner contributed $1,000 as working capital, which was credited to his drawing account. The following transactions for the year 1978 were all in cash:

Sales	$620,000
Merchandise purchases	493,000
Salaries and wages (including salary of $9,000 to	
Cottingham, as manager)	77,000
Expenses	25,400
New equipment purchased 7/1/78 (estimated life—	
10 years)	3,000

You are also given the following information:

Merchandise inventory, December 31, 1978	$60,000
Prepaid expenses, December 31, 1978	3,000

The check record was kept open until all 1978 bills were paid before closing the books as of December 31, 1978.

The partnership agreement provides for a salary of $750 monthly to Cottingham. All remaining profits are divided equally.

Partners' drawing accounts each show a net debit balance of $3,000.

	Jensen	Bean
Income from Discount Hardware Stores (all ordinary income)	$55,000	$55,000
Interest income	4,000	3,000
Long-term capital gains [losses]—does not include anything from SuperDis partnership transactions	4,000	[3,000]
	$63,000	$55,000

Required:

a. Prepare a schedule showing the cash payment which Cottingham made to Jensen and Bean.

b. Prepare an income statement of the SuperDis Hardware Company for the year ended December 31, 1978, including a schedule showing the distribution of profit and loss to the partners.

c. Prepare a statement showing the total taxable income of Jensen and of Bean before personal deductions. (Assume their original contributions were equal amounts of cash.)

d. Compute the tax basis of the partners' interests in the new partnership on December 31, 1978.

(AICPA adapted)

Problem 6

Gary and John have been operating a business for several years as partners, during which time they have divided profits equally. They need additional capital to expand their business and have agreed to admit Steve to the partnership as of January 1, 1977, with a one-third interest in profits and in the capital. Steve is to pay cash into the business as additional capital in an amount equal to one half of the combined capital of the present two partners, redetermined as follows:

The average partnership profits, after partners' salaries, for the past two years are to be capitalized at the rate of 10 percent per annum, which will redetermine the aggregate capital of the two present partners. Before such capitalization of profits, the accounts are to be adjusted for errors and omissions.

The business has not followed a strict accrual basis of accounting. As a result the following items have been omitted from the books:

Item	Balance 12/31/74	Balance 12/31/75	Balance 12/31/76
Accrued expenses	$3,201	$2,472	$4,360
Prepaid expenses	1,010	1,226	872
Accrued income	—	250	475

In addition, no provision has been made for loss on uncollectible accounts. It is agreed that a provision of $4,500 is needed as of December 31, 1976, of which $600 is for 1975 accounts. Charge-offs have been made to expense in 1974 and 1973 and prior accounts—$1,200; in 1975 of 1974 accounts—$3,100, and of 1975 accounts—$400; in 1976 of 1975 accounts—$2,280, and of 1976 accounts—$525.

The inventory at December 31, 1976, contains some obsolete goods carried at cost of $4,300. A 20 percent write-down is to be made to reduce these items to their present value.

In 1975 and 1976, salaries of $3,000 for each partner were taken out of the business and charged to expense before determining profits. It has been agreed that the salaries should have been $4,000 each.

The following financial data are available:

Balance Sheet
December 31, 1976

Assets		*Equities*	
Cash	$ 7,000	Accounts payable	$ 43,200
Accounts receivable	42,500	Notes payable	25,000
Notes receivable	6,000	Accumulated depreciation—	
		fixtures	5,300
Merchandise	64,000	Gary, capital	22,000
Store fixtures	12,400	John, capital	36,400
	$131,900		$131,900

	1974	1975	1976
Profit per books	$ 8,364	$ 8,585	$10,497
Gary, capital	20,000	24,000	22,000
John, capital	25,000	33,000	36,400

Required:

Show the computation of the amount that Steve will pay into the partnership, and prepare a balance sheet as it would appear after adjustment for errors and omissions and after redetermination of capital accounts and receipt of Steve's capital contribution as of January 1, 1977.

(AICPA adapted)

Problem 7

The partnership agreement of Jones, McDill, Gilrey, Carter, and Adams contained a buy and sell agreement, among numerous other provisions, which would become operative in case of the death of any partner. Some provisions contained in the buy and sell agreement were as follows:

ARTICLE V. *Buy and Sell Agreement*

1. Purposes of the Buy and Sell Agreement.

(*a*) The partners mutually desire that the business shall be continued by the survivors without interruption or liquidation upon the death of one of the partners.

(*b*) The partners also mutually desire that the deceased partner's estate shall receive the full value of the deceased partner's interest in the partnership and that the estate shall share in the earnings of the partnership until the deceased partner's interest shall be fully purchased by the surviving partners.

2. Purchase and Sale of Deceased Partner's Interest.

(*a*) Upon the death of the partner first to die, the partnership shall continue to operate without dissolution.

(*b*) Upon the decedents' death, the survivors shall purchase and the executor or administrator of the deceased partner's estate shall sell to the surviving partners the deceased partner's interest in the partnership for the price and upon the terms and conditions hereinafter set forth.

(*c*) The deceased partner's estate shall retain the deceased partner's interest until the amount specified in the next paragraph shall be paid in full by the surviving partners.

(*d*) The parties agree that the purchase price for the partnership interest shall be an amount equal to the deceased partner's capital account at the date of death. Said amount shall be paid to the legal representative of decedent as follows:

(i) The first installment of 30 percent of said capital account shall be paid within 60 days from the date of death of the partner or within 30 days from the date on which the personal representative of decedent becomes qualified by law, whichever date is later, and

(ii) The balance shall be due in four equal installments which shall be due and payable annually on the anniversary date of said death.

3. Deceased Partner's Estate's Share of the Earnings.

(*a*) The partners mutually desire that the deceased partner's estate shall be guaranteed a share in the earnings of the partnership over the period said estate retains an interest in the partnership. Said estate shall not be deemed to have an interest in the partnership after the final installment for the deceased partner's capital account is paid even though a portion of the guaranteed payments specified below may be unpaid and may be due and owing.

(*b*) The deceased partner's estate's guaranteed share of the earnings of the partnership shall be determined from two items and shall be paid at different times as follows:

(i) First, interest shall be paid on the unpaid balance of the deceased partner's capital account at the same date the installment on the purchase price is paid. The amount to be paid shall be an amount equal to accrued interest at the rate of 6 percent per annum on the unpaid balance of the purchase price for the deceased partner's capital account.

(ii) Second, the parties agree that the balance of the guaranteed payment from the partnership earnings shall be an amount equal to 25 percent of the deceased partner's share of the aggregate gross receipts of the partnership for the full 36 months preceding the month of the partner's death. Said amount shall be payable in 48 equal monthly installments without interest, and the first payment shall be made within 60 days following the death of the partner or within 30 days from the date on which the personal representative of deceased becomes qualified, whichever date is later; provided, however, that the payments so made under this provision during any 12-month period shall not exceed the highest annual salary on a calendar-year basis received by the partner for the three calendar years immediately preceding the date of his death. In the event that said payment would exceed said salary, then an amount per month shall be paid which does not so exceed said highest monthly salary, and the term over which payments shall be paid to the beneficiary shall be lengthened out beyond the said 48 months in order to complete said payments.

Jones and Adams were both killed simultaneously in an automobile accident on January 10, 1977. The surviving partners notified the executors of both estates that the first payment due under the buy and sell agreement would be paid on March 10, 1977, and that subsequent payments would be paid on the 10th day of each month as due.

The following information was determined from the partnership's records:

Partner	Profit- and Loss- Sharing Ratio	Capital Account on January 10, 1977	Annual Salaries to Partners by Years		
			1974	1975	1976
Jones	30	$25,140	$16,500	$17,000	$17,400
McDill	25	21,970	15,000	15,750	16,500
Gilrey	20	4,780	12,000	13,000	14,000
Carter	15	5,860	9,600	10,800	12,000
Adams	10	2,540	8,400	9,600	10,800

The partnership's gross receipts for the three prior years were:

1974	....	$296,470
1975	....	325,310
1976	....	363,220

Required:

Prepare a schedule of the amounts to be paid to the Jones Estate and to the Adams Estate in March, 1977; December, 1977; and January, 1978. The schedule should identify the amounts attributable to earnings and to interest in the guaranteed payments and to capital. Supporting computations should be in good form.

(AICPA adapted)

Problem 8

Smith and Company is a family partnership engaged in the wholesale trade. It closes its books at December 31. During the year, all transactions are recorded on a cash receipts and disbursements basis. However, at the end of the fiscal year, adjustment is made to what was termed the "inventory account" for all items necessary to reflect operations and financial position on an accrual basis.

Partner E died on October 31, 1977. His will left equal shares in his estate to partners A and C and an outsider, F. For purposes of this problem, assume no probate period and that E's estate was distributed immediately. All remaining partners, together with F, agreed that the business of Smith and Company would continue as a partnership of A, B, C, D, and F, with beginning interest on November 1, 1977, as computed on a proper accrual basis to October 31, and after distribution of E's interest on that date.

Depreciation of fixed assets may be ignored.

Balances as shown by the books of the firm were as follows in the accompanying illustration:

	January 1, 1977	October 31, 1977
Cash	$ 42,000	$ 55,000
Inventory account	195,000	195,000
Fixed assets	60,000	59,000
Accruals	29,000	16,000
Notes payable	100,000	60,000
Partners' equity	168,000	168,000
Sales	...	2,000,000
Purchases	...	1,725,000
Operating expenses	...	210,000

In addition to the above, the following information concerning the inventory account was available:

At January 1, 1977: accounts receivable, $80,000; merchandise, $200,000; freight claims (on incoming merchandise), $2,000; prepaid operating expenses, $10,000; accounts payable, $90,000; allowances due customers, $7,000. At October 31, 1977: accounts receivable, $83,300; merchandise, $221,000; freight claims (on incoming merchandise), $1,500; prepaid operating expenses, $6,000; accounts payable, $85,000; allowances due customers, $8,000.

Partners' equities and profit- and loss-sharing ratio:

	Equities	Profit and Loss Ratio
A	$ 10,500	6.25%
B	52,500	31.25
C	77,000	37.50
D	7,000	12.50
E	21,000	12.50
	$168,000	100.00%

Required:

a. Prepare an income statement for the period January 1 to October 31, 1977.

b. Prepare a statement of financial position on November 1, 1977.

(AICPA adapted)

Problem 9

The trial balance of AB, a partnership, on January 1, 1977 is shown on page 533.

Profits and losses were to be shared equally by A and B.

As of December 31, 1977, C purchased for $125,000 in cash from partners A and B a one-third interest in the partnership; each partner agreed to transfer one third of his individual capital account to C. Prior to C's admission, it was

	Debit	Credit
Cash	$ 70,000	
Accounts receivable	50,000	
Notes receivable	40,000	
Merchandise inventories	35,000	
Land	85,000	
Buildings and equipment—less allowance for depreciation ..	15,000	
Investments—at cost	35,000	
Prepaid insurance	4,500	
Office supplies	3,000	
Bank loans		$ 45,000
Accounts payable		60,000
Accrued taxes		2,500
First-mortgage 7 percent long-term notes		55,000
Capital accounts:		
A		100,000
B		75,000
	$337,500	$337,500

decided that a valuation reserve of $5,000 should be provided with respect to the investments; that an allowance for bad debts should be established in the amount of $10,000; and that the valuation of buildings and equipment should be reduced to $11,000. Profit sharing by C commenced on January 1, 1978.

As of December 31, 1978, D was admitted to a one-fourth interest in the partnership and contributed the following assets from a business previously operated by him as a sole proprietor:

Cash	$80,000
Accounts receivable	70,000
Investments	10,000

The following liabilities incurred by D in his previous business were assumed by the new partnership:

Accounts payable	$20,000
Bank loans	30,000

As an inducement to merge his enterprise with the ABC partnership, D was allowed goodwill of $25,000. Profits were to be shared equally by A, B, C, and D in the new firm, commencing January 1, 1979.

Additional data to be used in the solution of this problem are as follows:

	Year Ended December 31	
	1977	1978
Profit of the firm	$19,000	$27,000
Drawings:		
A	10,000	7,500
B	7,000	6,000
C	—	14,000

For the purposes of simplicity, it is assumed that profits for each year were realized in cash and that the balance sheet of the firm on January 1, 1977, did not change during the two-year period, except as indicated in the terms of this problem.

Required:

a. Prepare an interim work sheet for the two-year period from January 1, 1977, through December 31, 1978.
b. Prepare journal entries to record the admission of C and D, assuming goodwill is implicitly determined.

(AICPA adapted)

15

Partnership Dissolution and Liquidation

INTRODUCTION

The Liquidation Process

THE NATURE of partnership dissolution, viz., "the change in the relation of the partners caused by any partner ceasing to be associated in the carrying on as distinguished from the winding up of the business" (Section 29), was discussed in the previous chapter where attention focused on the continuity of partnership operations. In this chapter, emphasis will be placed upon the accounting problems and procedures involved in the winding up (liquidation) of partnership affairs—that interval of time between legal *dissolution* and effective *termination* of partnership operations.

Accounting Problems in Partnership Liquidation

The basic objectives of the partnership during the liquidation process are to convert the firm's assets to cash with minimum loss in value (*realization* of assets), to discharge valid partnership liabilities, and to distribute cash and any unrealized assets to the individual partners in an equitable manner. The primary objective underlying the accounting function during the liquidation process is to provide information adequate for an equitable disbursement of the partnership assets to creditors and partners, in compliance with the law. The accounting focus is therefore shifted from the measurement of periodic income to the determination of realization gains and losses, the allocation of these gains and losses among the partners, the payment of partnership creditors, and the planning and recording of asset distributions to partners. Careful attention must be given to relevant provisions of the Uniform Partnership Act, the partnership agreement, and in some instances, state and federal insolvency (bankruptcy) statutes. It is especially important that the accounting process be guided primarily by legal rights and obligations.

Basic Dichotomy—Partnership Solvency and Insolvency

Since the liquidation of solvent and insolvent partnerships introduces essentially different problems, each condition will be separately considered. For purposes of the following discussion, a partnership is regarded as insolvent when its recorded assets are of insufficient amount to discharge existing partnership liabilities, i.e., an entity approach to the condition of insolvency. From a purely legal point of view, however, partnership insolvency is defined in terms of the underlying aggregative concept: "The now settled view is that a partnership is insolvent only when the surplus of *individual* assets [of the partners] over *non-partnership debts* is insufficient, together with partnership assets to pay partnership obligations."[1] This more restrictive definition of partnership insolvency need not stultify the value of the entity definition which is used in subsequent discussion. The aggregative (or legal) notion of partnership insolvency will be illustrated as a special condition of entity insolvency, viz., that circumstance where the separate net assets of individual partners are inadequate to discharge the partnership obligations not paid with partnership assets.

In the process of liquidating a partnership which is solvent by the entity definition, two alternative ways of proceeding with the liquidation may be identified. First, under the "simple liquidation" process, all of the partnership assets are realized or converted *before* any distributions are made to the partners. In this case, the accounting treatment is relatively simple. Since the amount of the total liquidation gain or loss is known before asset distributions to partners, the accountant needs only to indicate a distribution of assets which compiles with the order of priority established by existing statutes.

Second, under the "installment payments" approach to liquidation, the partners elect to receive liquidating payments in a series of installments *prior* to the point in time at which partnership assets are completely realized or converted. In this case, the accountant must develop a plan of settlement which will produce the same ultimate distribution as if payments had been deferred until all of the noncash assets were converted.

Following an examination of simple liquidations, the accounting problems associated with installment payments will be analyzed; separate consideration will be given to situations in which there exists one insolvent partner, so long as all are not insolvent. In the final section of this chapter,

---

[1] Reed Rowley, *Rowley on Partnership* (New York: The Bobbs-Merrill Co., Inc., 1960), vol. II, p. 85 (emphasis supplied).

the accounting problems associated with insolvent partnerships will be analyzed. The rights of both partnership creditors and individual creditors will be examined with reference to provisions of the Uniform Partnership Act, the Federal Bankruptcy Act, and selected decisions of the common law.

SIMPLE LIQUIDATION

Basic Distributive Rights

If all of the partnership assets are converted into cash before any distribution is made to creditors or to individual partners, a condition of simple liquidation exists. In this circumstance, the distribution of assets will be made in the order of priority established in the Uniform Partnership Act where that Act is operative. Section 40 (B) of the Act provides:

The liabilities of the partnership shall rank in order of payment, as follows:
- (I)   Those owing to creditors other than partners, *A/P N/P*
- (II)   Those owing to partners other than for capital and profits, *A/P partner N/P Partner*
- (III) Those owing to partners in respect of capital, *Balance on Capital acts*
- (IV)   Those owing to partners in respect of profits. *gains on liquidation*

Since the conversion of all noncash assets precedes the distribution of cash to the partners, the total amount of gain or loss on realization is known at the time of distribution. Unless a specific *liquidation* gain and loss ratio is indicated in the partnership agreement, the gain or loss should be allocated to the partners in the current profit and loss residual ratio, i.e., salary and interest factors are disregarded. This basis for distribution appears equitable, as realization gains or losses frequently reflect, in large part, adjustments of prior years' reported profits, which were distributed on this basis. Additionally, gains or losses which can be attributed to the *fact* of liquidation are in essence components of the overall profitability of the business, and thus should relate to individual partners in the same ratio as normal periodic earnings and losses of the partnership. The position taken by some accountants that liquidation losses are capital losses, and thus distributable in the relative ratios of the partners' capital balances, would appear to have no greater validity in the period of liquidation than during the period of normal operations.

Where current profits are transferred in the closing entry sequence to the partners' capital accounts, priorities (III) and (IV) of Section 40 (B) coalesce. In any event, however, the distinction between capital and profits is of no practical consequence, unless a "deficit" in the profits account is not absorbed by, or offset against, capital balances before distribution of cash to individual partners. Since an "equitable" settlement is the controlling consideration in most partnership law, the existence of a nonabsorbed deficit condition seems unlikely, unless expressly anticipated and provided for in the partnership agreement. Consequently, elements (III) and (IV) will hereafter be considered as one priority status.

The basic rights of creditors and partners in a simple liquidation are illustrated in the paragraphs which follow.

Case 1. The balance sheet of the WaTex Company at the date of dissolution is as follows:

Assets		Equities	
Cash	$10,000	Liabilities	$12,000
Noncash assets	80,000	Capital:	
		Able	31,000
		Holmes	20,000
		Thomas	27,000
	$90,000		$90,000

During liquidation, $50,000 is realized from the conversion of the noncash assets. The partners share profits and losses in the ratio 5:3:2.

Given these data, a *partnership liquidation schedule* may be prepared as in Illustration 15–1.

Illustration 15–1
WATEX COMPANY
Schedule of Partnership Liquidation
Dr. [Cr.]

	Assets			Claimants		
					Residual Equities	
	Cash	Noncash	Priority Claims	Able	Holmes	Thomas
Profit and loss ratio				50%	30%	20%
Preliquidation balances ...	$ 10,000	$ 80,000	$[12,000]	$[31,000]	$[20,000]	$[27,000]
Realization of assets and allocation of loss	50,000	[80,000]		15,000	9,000	6,000
Predistribution balances ..	$ 60,000	$ –0–	$[12,000]	$[16,000]	$[11,000]	$[21,000]
Cash distribution:						
Priority claims	[12,000]		12,000			
Partners' residual equities	[48,000]			16,000	11,000	21,000
Termination of partnership	$ –0–	$ –0–	$ –0–	$ –0–	$ –0–	$ –0–

The schedule of partnership liquidation is the primary historical statement which reflects partnership transactions during the period of liquidation. The schedule indicates the condition of the partnership at the date of dissolution (preliquidation balances), losses sustained in the conversion of noncash assets, the allocation of losses to the partners in their profit and loss ratio, and the distribution of cash in the order of payment specified in Section 40 (B). The same schedular format may be expanded to include other significant events during the liquidation process.

Partners' Debit Balances

In the previous illustration, each of the partners had a sufficiently large credit balance in his capital account to absorb his proportionate share of the realization loss. However, such a favorable circumstance does not always exist. Frequently, an individual partner's share of the realization loss will exceed his capital credit, producing a *debit balance* in his capital account. This capital deficiency creates a valid claim of the partnership against the partner; Section 18 (A) specifies that "each partner . . . must contribute toward the losses, whether of capital or otherwise, sustained by the partnership according to his share in the profits." Additionally, Section 40 (D) provides that "the partners shall contribute, as provided by Section 18 (A), the amount necessary to satisfy the liabilities; but if any, but not all, of the partners are insolvent, or, not being subject to process, refuse to contribute, the other partners shall contribute their share of the liabilities, and, in the relative proportions in which they share the profits, the additional amount necessary to pay the liabilities." Since Section 40 relates to the sequence of distribution of partnership assets in settlement of partnership liabilities, it is important that the term "liability" in this particular usage be fully understood. This section of the Act contemplates that liabilities may be generated either by accumulated losses from operations, realization losses, or the *loss* incurred when a partner with a debit balance in his capital account fails to contribute personal assets sufficient in amount to remove this deficit. In fact, Section 40 (A) defines the assets of a partnership to include contributions due from the partners for this cause;[2] consequently, a partner's failure to contribute to the extent of his capital deficiency is equivalent to a realization loss for the remaining partners. Thus, if an amount equal to a debit balance is not collected from the delinquent partner, it is allocated in total to the remaining partners as if it were a realization loss; the allocation is made in the ratio of the remaining partners' original shares of profits and losses. For example, assume X, Y, and Z share profits and losses in the ratio 5:3:2. If Y should fail to contribute to the partnership the amount of a debit balance in his capital account, X and Z will share this loss (a capital deficiency) in the ratio 5:2, i.e., 5/7 to X and 2/7 to Z; if X should fail to contribute for a preexistent capital deficiency, Y and Z would share this loss in the ratio 3:2, i.e., 3/5 to Y and 2/5 to Z.

---

[2] The discerning reader will note that this provision is consistent with the legal definition of partnership insolvency, whereby insolvency is impossible unless the claims against the individual partners are uncollectible due to a condition of personal insolvency.

The effects of partners' debit balances on the liquidation process and their treatment in the partnership liquidation schedule are illustrated in the following case.

Case 2. The balance sheet of Super Serv Company immediately prior to the liquidation of the partnership is given below:

Assets		*Equities*	
Cash	$ 5,000	Liabilities	$15,000
Noncash assets	45,000	Capital:	
		Johnson	9,000
		Granof	6,000
		Deakin	20,000
	$50,000		$50,000

The partners share profits and losses in the ratio 4:4:2. It is assumed that Johnson and Deakin have personal resources sufficient in amount to "make good" capital debit balances which may be created during the liquidation process. Granof has no available personal assets. The noncash assets of the partnership are realized in the amount of $15,000.

A partnership liquidation schedule based upon these data is shown in Illustration 15–2.

In this instance, Granof's uncollectible debit balance generates an addi-

Illustration 15–2
SUPER SERV COMPANY
Schedule of Partnership Liquidation
Dr. [Cr.]

	Assets		Claimants	Residual Equities		
	Cash	Noncash	Priority Claims	Johnson	Granof	Deakin
Profit and loss ratio				40%	40%	20%
Preliquidation balances	$ 5,000	$ 45,000	$[15,000]	$[9,000]	$[6,000]	$[20,000]
Realization of assets and allocation of loss	15,000	[45,000]		12,000	12,000	6,000
Balances	$ 20,000	$ –0–	$[15,000]	$ 3,000	$ 6,000	$[14,000]
Absorption of Granof's balance (4:2)				4,000	[6,000]	2,000
Balances	$ 20,000	$ –0–	$[15,000]	$ 7,000	$ –0–	$[12,000]
Contribution by Johnson ...	7,000			[7,000]		
Predistribution balances	$ 27,000	$ –0–	$[15,000]	$ –0–	$ –0–	$[12,000]
Cash distribution:						
Priority claims	[15,000]		15,000			
Partners' residual equities .	[12,000]					12,000
Termination of partnership ..	$ –0–	$ –0–	$ –0–	$ –0–	$ –0–	$ –0–

tional "realization loss" to be absorbed by Johnson and Deakin in their relative profit and loss ratio, whereas Johnson contributes personal assets to restore the debit balance in his capital account to zero. It should be noted that if Johnson had failed to contribute personal assets, the partnership would have remained solvent, since cash was otherwise available to discharge liabilities to partnership creditors.

Partners' Loans

In the distribution of partnership assets, the Uniform Partnership Act ranks payments to partners in respect to loans ahead of payments on their capital accounts. However, this priority has functional significance *only* if it is contemplated that payments are to be made to partners with capital deficiencies. And, as a matter of fact, repayment of a partner's loan is not generally made where the partner has a capital deficiency. If in liquidation a partner's capital account has a debit balance, the partner is required by Section 18 of the Act to contribute an amount equal to his debit balance. Of course, the partnership may be unable to collect this amount from the delinquent partner. Under these circumstances, if partnership assets are first distributed to the partner in repayment of his loan, the assets may be permanently lost. In effect, the distribution in repayment of a (deficient) partner's loan increases the partnership losses to be allocated to the remaining (solvent) partners, assuming the deficient partner does not satisfy his obligation. To prevent this sequence of events, the rule of *setoff* has been generally accepted by the courts as a means of achieving an equitable settlement; accordingly, debit balances are offset against partners' loans to the fullest extent possible, *before* any cash distribution is made.[3]

Application of the rule of setoff is illustrated in the following case.

Case 3. The preliquidation balances of the assets and equities of the Austin Appliance Partnership are given below:

Assets		Equities		
Cash	$ 20,000	Liabilities		$ 40,000
Noncash assets	80,000	Partners' loans:		
		Bruns	$ 4,000	
		Jensen	5,000	
		Miles	7,000	16,000
		Partners' capital:		
		Bruns	$10,000	
		Jensen	12,000	
		Miles	16,000	
		Schiff	6,000	44,000
	$100,000			$100,000

---

[3] This general provision may be challenged by the individual creditors of an insolvent partner; in the event of such a challenge, the accountant should advise the withholding of cash in an amount equal to the loan balance pending a final determination of priorities.

The partners share profits and losses in the ratio 3:3:2:2. Bruns, Jensen, and Miles are committed to making contributions for any debit balances which may be created by loss absorption and are assumed to have sufficient personal assets for this purpose; Schiff has only $2,000 of available personal assets. The noncash assets are realized during liquidation for $30,000.

A partnership liquidation schedule for this case is given in Illustration 15–3.

This case illustrates the offset principle as it relates to the loans of two partners (Bruns and Jensen), a partial contribution by Schiff in reduction of a capital deficiency, the absorption of the capital debit residue of Schiff by the remaining partners (Bruns, Jensen, and Miles), and a full contribution by a partner (Bruns) in respect to an existing debit balance. The occurrence of two separate offsets of Jensen's loan against a debit belance in his capital account was merely a consequence of the schedular sequence. If the complete liquidation relationship between Schiff and the partnership (partial contribution and absorption of residue debit balance) had been first established, only one setoff—$3,750 in amount—would have been required in respect to Jensen. Of course, the total effect would remain unchanged.

Liquidation Expenses

In each of the previous cases, the reference to "realization of assets and allocation of loss" indicated the *net* proceeds realized on the disposition of noncash assets. Such a description is appropriate when an item of expense is directly related to the sale of an asset, e.g., commissions on sales. If, however, expenses are incurred during the liquidation process which are not directly associated with specific assets but rather are identifiable only with the liquidation process or period, it may be preferable to separately disclose such expenses in the liquidation schedule. Whatever the treatment, no substantive change will result in the distribution of partnership assets. The "residual" profit and loss ratio properly relates to the allocation of expenses as well as to gains and losses from realization of assets. If one of the partners assumes sole responsibility for managing or directing the liquidation activities and is accorded a specific fee for such service, this cost should be clearly disclosed as a separate liquidation expense, with a corresponding increase in the relevant partner's capital account. Such an assignment discloses more completely the effect of the expense on the liquidation process, and it effectively precludes a premature distribution of cash to this managing partner, a distribution subject to legal challenge should a debit balance ultimately exist in his capital account.

INSTALLMENT (PERIODIC) PAYMENTS

Basic Accounting Problem

Under conditions of simple liquidation, the total gain or loss on the realization of assets, including the effects of liquidation expenses, is known

AUSTIN APPLIANCE PARTNERSHIP
Schedule of Partnership Liquidation
Dr. [Cr.]

	Assets			Claimants						
					Residual Equities					
					Bruns		Jensen		Miles		Schiff
	Cash	Noncash	Priority Claims	Loan	Capital	Loan	Capital	Loan	Capital	Capital
Profit and loss ratio					30%		30%		20%	20%
Preliquidation balances	$ 20,000	$ 80,000	$[40,000]	$[4,000]	$[10,000]	$[5,000]	$[12,000]	$[7,000]	$[16,000]	$[6,000]
Realization of assets and allocation of loss	30,000	[80,000]			15,000		15,000		10,000	10,000
Balances	$ 50,000	$ –0–	$[40,000]	$[4,000]	$ 5,000	$[5,000]	$ 3,000	$[7,000]	$[6,000]	$ 4,000
Offset of loans against debit balances:										
Bruns				4,000	[4,000]					
Jensen						3,000	[3,000]			
Balances	$ 50,000	$ –0–	$[40,000]	$ –0–	$ 1,000	$[2,000]	$ –0–	$[7,000]	$[6,000]	$ 4,000
Contribution by Schiff	2,000									[2,000]
Balances	$ 52,000	$ –0–	$[40,000]	$ –0–	$ 1,000	$[2,000]	$ –0–	$[7,000]	$[6,000]	$ 2,000
Absorption of Schiff's debit balance (3:3:2)					750		750		500	[2,000]
Balances	$ 52,000	$ –0–	$[40,000]	$ –0–	$ 1,750	$[2,000]	$ 750	$[7,000]	$[5,500]	$ –0–
Additional offset against Jensen's loan balance						750	[750]			
Balances	$ 52,000	$ –0–	$[40,000]	$ –0–	$ 1,750	$[1,250]	$ –0–	$[7,000]	$[5,500]	$ –0–
Contribution by Bruns for debit balance	1,750				[1,750]					
Predistribution balances	$ 53,750	$ –0–	$[40,000]	$ –0–	$ –0–	$[1,250]	$ –0–	$[7,000]	$[5,500]	$ –0–
Cash distribution:										
Priority claims	[40,000]		40,000							
Partners' loans	[8,250]					1,250		7,000		
Partner's residual equity	[5,500]								5,500	
Termination of partnership	$ –0–	$ –0–	$ –0–	$ –0–	$ –0–	$ –0–	$ –0–	$ –0–	$ –0–	$ –0–

before distribution of cash is made to individual partners. However, if the liquidation period should extend over a prolonged period of time, it may be appropriate to make partial distributions of cash periodically to the partners *before* all of the assets have been realized, provided certain precautions are taken. In this regard, the accountant often assumes a special fiduciary status with respect to the ultimate claims of both partnership creditors and the individual partners against the available cash accumulation of the partnership. Therefore, he must be particularly circumspect in determining the amount of each installment payment in order to avoid an overdistribution to one or more of the partners. The fiduciary may be held liable for losses which proceed from excessive distributions. Thus, a distribution procedure is needed which will enable the accountant to compute periodic payments that may be made safely without undue risk of personal liability.

As an underlying basis, the accountant first must estimate the *largest potential loss* that may be incurred in future realizations of noncash assets. Since the equities of the partners are based upon the book values of the partnership assets, the total recorded value of the noncash assets approximates the maximum potential loss to the partnership.[4] If the accountant *assumes* the actual incurrence of the maximum potential loss, he may easily compute its hypothetical effect on the individual partners' capital balances. Any debit balance in a partner's capital account that results from this loss allocation process represents still another *potential* loss to the other partners in that it may not be satisfied by contributions of the deficient partner. Accordingly, it should be allocated to the remaining partners—in effect, it is a reallocation of a portion of the maximum potential loss to the partnership. This sequence of hypothetical loss absorptions will result in one or more partners' capital accounts having credit balances which, in total, are equal to the cash available for distribution to partners. Initially, this amount is the total cash less claims of outside creditors. After obligations to creditors are discharged, the residual amount of cash on hand may be distributed in amounts equal to these adjusted credit balances. Then, if the noncash assets in fact prove worthless and if all debit balances are absorbed in sequence, a zero balance will necessarily exist in each of the partners' capital accounts.

Periodic Computation of Safe Payments to Partners

The procedure outlined above, expressed in the form of a *partnership liquidation schedule* and supported by a *calculation of safe installment payments,* is illustrated in Case 4 which follows.

Case 4. On January 1, 19X1, Dahl, Hersey, and Katz agree to dissolve their partnership. Their preliquidation capital balances and percentage interests in profits and losses are:

---

[4] See page 553 for a more precise statement of the maximum potential loss.

Partner	Capital	Ratio
Dahl	$25,000	50%
Hersey	45,000	30
Katz	15,000	20

The partnership has cash of $5,000 and noncash assets of $85,000; liabilities to outside creditors amount to $5,000. The partners elect to make periodic distributions of all accumulated cash at the end of each month during the liquidation process. The following data relate to the realization of assets:

	Book Values	Net Proceeds
January	$25,000	$20,000
February	40,000	20,000
March	10,000	5,000
April	10,000	2,000

The partnership liquidation schedule and the supporting calculation of safe installment payments are shown in Illustrations 15–4 and 15–5. Several important conclusions can be drawn from an analysis of the illustrations in this case:

1. The total cash payments to each partner are equivalent to the amount of a single payment computed under a simple liquidation procedure. This is illustrated as follows:

Simple Liquidation Method

	Dahl	Hersey	Katz
Preliquidation balances	$25,000	$45,000	$15,000
Realization loss ($85,000 − $47,000)	19,000	11,400	7,600
Partners' claims	$ 6,000	$33,600	$ 7,400

Installment Payments Method

	Dahl	Hersey	Katz
January	$ –0–	$20,000	$ –0–
February	2,500	11,500	6,000
March	2,500	1,500	1,000
April	1,000	600	400
Total payments	$ 6,000	$33,600	$ 7,400

Illustration 15–4

DAHL, HERSEY, AND KATZ PARTNERSHIP
Schedule of Partnership Liquidation
Dr. [Cr.]

	Assets		Priority Claims	Claimants — Residual Equities		
	Cash	Noncash		Dahl	Hersey	Katz
Profit and loss ratio				50%	30%	20%
Preliquidation balances	$ 5,000	$ 85,000	$[5,000]	$[25,000]	$[45,000]	$[15,000]
Realization of assets and allocation of loss	20,000	[25,000]		2,500	1,500	1,000
Balances	$ 25,000	$ 60,000	$[5,000]	$[22,500]	$[43,500]	$[14,000]
Payment of liabilities	[5,000]		5,000			
Balances	$ 20,000	$ 60,000	$ –0–	$[22,500]	$[43,500]	$[14,000]
January installment payment (see supporting schedule—Illustration 15–5)	[20,000]				20,000	
Balances	$ –0–	$ 60,000		$[22,500]	$[23,500]	$[14,000]
Realization of assets and allocation of loss	20,000	[40,000]		10,000	6,000	4,000
Balances	$ 20,000	$ 20,000	$ –0–	$[12,500]	$[17,500]	$[10,000]
February installment payment (see supporting schedule—Illustration 15–5)	[20,000]			2,500	11,500	6,000
Balances	$ –0–	$ 20,000		$[10,000]	$ [6,000]	$ [4,000]
Realization of assets and allocation of loss	5,000	[10,000]		2,500	1,500	1,000
Balances	$ 5,000	$ 10,000	$ –0–	$ [7,500]	$ [4,500]	$ [3,000]
March installment payment (see supporting schedule—Illustration 15–5)	[5,000]			2,500	1,500	1,000
Balances	$ –0–	$ 10,000		$ [5,000]	$ [3,000]	$ [2,000]
Realization of assets and allocation of loss	2,000	[10,000]		4,000	2,400	1,600
Balances	$ 2,000	$ –0–		$ [1,000]	$ [600]	$ [400]
Final payment to partners	[2,000]			1,000	600	400
Termination of partnership	$ –0–	$ –0–	$ –0–	$ –0–	$ –0–	$ –0–

Illustration 15–5

DAHL, HERSEY, AND KATZ PARTNERSHIP

Calculation of Safe Installment Payments
Dr. [Cr.]

	Residual Equities		
	Dahl	*Hersey*	*Katz*
Profit and loss ratio	50%	30%	20%
Computation of January installment:			
Predistribution balances	$[22,500]	$[43,500]	$[14,000]
Potential loss—noncash assets—$60,000	30,000	18,000	12,000
Balances	$ 7,500	$[25,500]	$ [2,000]
Potential loss—Dahl's debit balance	[7,500]	4,500	3,000
Balances	$ –0–	$[21,000]	$ 1,000
Potential loss—Katz's debit balance		1,000	[1,000]
Safe payments to partners	$ –0–	$[20,000]	$ –0–
Computation of February installment:			
Predistribution balances	$[12,500]	$[17,500]	$[10,000]
Potential loss—noncash assets—$20,000 ...	10,000	6,000	4,000
Safe payments to partners	$ [2,500]	$[11,500]	$ [6,000]
Computation of March installment:			
Predistribution balances	$ [7,500]	$ [4,500]	$ [3,000]
Potential loss—noncash assets—$10,000 ...	5,000	3,000	2,000
Safe payments to partners	$ [2,500]	$ [1,500]	$ [1,000]

2. The ratio of the partners' capital balances at the end of February exhibits a significant relationship, viz., the ratio of capital balances is equal to the profit and loss ratio. When this condition exists, all subsequent installment distributions are based upon the profit and loss ratio (see March and April installment payments in Illustration 15–4). Future losses, should they occur, are allocated on this basis, and thus the availability of cash for distribution to partners indicates that the total equity of the partners exceeds the total potential loss. The computation of safe payments is, in fact, an iterative process that systematically causes the ratio of partners' equities to converge to the profit and loss ratio as rapidly as can be accomplished by controlling cash distributions to partners. Therefore, after one payment is allocated among two or more partners, subsequent distributions to these partners will be in the same ratio as their relative profit and loss ratio. Additionally, after a payment has been made to all partners, the ratio of the partners' equities will be equal to the profit and loss ratio. This fact is confirmed by the data of Case 4 with the February installment payment. In this case, a supporting calculation to determine safe payments to partners is unnecessary *after* the February distribution.

3. The order of payments in the schedule of partnership liquidation is consistent with the order of priority established in the Uniform Partnership Act, i.e., distributions are first made to creditors; subsequent payments, as cash becomes available, are to partners.

Partners' Loans

It has been noted previously that in partnership liquidation a partner's loan balance should be offset against a debit balance in his capital account; accordingly, liquidating payments are based upon each partner's *total* equity (or net equity in the event of a capital deficit) in the partnership. This principle is equally valid in the case of installment payments made to partners during the period of liquidation. The total equity of each partner (the sum of both loan and capital balances) should be entered in the calculation of safe installment payments. Entering the total equity implicitly recognizes the relevance of setoff in the event a partner's capital balance is completely absorbed in the process of allocating potential losses. In the schedule of partnership liquidation, however, indicated payments to each partner are traditionally reported as first in abatement of loans and second in reduction of capital balances.

The addition of this variable, partners' loans, to a liquidation process involving installment distributions is illustrated in the following case.

Case 5. The partners of the Jackson Company agree to dissolve their partnership on March 31, 19X1. Their preliquidation capital and loan account balances and the profit and loss ratio are:

Partner	Capital	Loan	Ratio
W	$16,000	$4,000	50%
X	29,000	2,000	20
Y	23,000		20
Z	9,000	1,000	10

The partnership has a cash balance of $10,000 and noncash assets of $80,000; obligations to outside creditors amount to $6,000. Available cash is to be distributed at the end of each month during the period of liquidation. Assets are realized as follows:

	Book Values	Net Proceeds
April	$54,000	$30,000
May	24,000	18,000
June	2,000	–0–

Illustration 15–6

JACKSON COMPANY

Schedule of Partnership Liquidation

Dr. [Cr.]

| | Assets | | Claimants | Residual Equities | | | | | | |
	Cash	Noncash	Priority Claims	W Loan	W Capital	X Loan	X Capital	Y Capital	Z Loan	Z Capital
Profit and loss ratio					50%		20%	20%		10%
Preliquidation balances	$ 10,000	$ 80,000	$[6,000]	$[4,000]	$[16,000]	$[2,000]	$[29,000]	$[23,000]	$[1,000]	$[9,000]
Realization of assets and allocation of loss	30,000	[54,000]			12,000		4,800	4,800		2,400
Balances	$ 40,000	$ 26,000	$[6,000]	$[4,000]	$ [4,000]	$[2,000]	$[24,200]	$[18,200]	$[1,000]	$[6,600]
Payment to creditors	[6,000]		6,000							
Balances	$ 34,000	$ 26,000	$ –0–	$[4,000]	$ [4,000]	$[2,000]	$[24,200]	$[18,200]	$[1,000]	$[6,600]
April installment payment (see supporting schedule—Illustration 15–7)	[34,000]					2,000	17,000	11,000	1,000	3,000
Balances	$ –0–	$ 26,000	$ –0–	$[4,000]	$ [4,000]	$ –0–	$ [7,200]	$ [7,200]	$ –0–	$[3,600]
Realization of assets and allocation of loss	18,000	[24,000]			3,000		1,200	1,200		600
Balances	$ 18,000	$ 2,000		$[4,000]	$ [1,000]		$ [6,000]	$ [6,000]		$[3,000]
May installment payment (see supporting schedule—Illustration 15–7)	[18,000]			4,000			5,600	5,600		2,800
Balances	$ –0–	$ 2,000		$ –0–	$ [1,000]		$ [400]	$ [400]		$ [200]
Realization of assets and allocation of loss	–0–	[2,000]			1,000		400	400		200
Termination of partnership	$ –0–	$ –0–	$ –0–	$ –0–	$ –0–	$ –0–	$ –0–	$ –0–	$ –0–	$ –0–

The partnership liquidation schedule is given in Illustration 15–6, and the supporting calculation of safe installment payments is given in illustration 15–7.

Illustration 15–7

JACKSON COMPANY

Calculation of Safe Installment Payments
Dr. [Cr.]

	Residual Equities (Capital and Loan Balances)			
	W	X	Y	Z
Profit and loss ratio	50%	20%	20%	10%
Computation of April installment:				
Predistribution balances .	$[8,000]	$[26,200]	$[18,200]	$[7,600]
Potential loss—noncash assets—$26,000	13,000	5,200	5,200	2,600
Balances	$ 5,000	$[21,000]	$[13,000]	$[5,000]
Potential loss—W's debit balance	[5,000]	2,000	2,000	1,000
Safe payments to partners	$ –0–	$[19,000]	$[11,000]	$[4,000]
Computation of May installment:				
Predistribution balances .	$[5,000]	$ [6,000]	$ [6,000]	$[3,000]
Potential loss—noncash assets—$2,000	1,000	400	400	200
Safe payments to partners	$[4,000]	$ [5,600]	$ [5,600]	$[2,800]

The illustrations for Case 5 accent several concepts previously discussed:

1. Although the total equity (capital and loan balance) of each partner is used in the calculation of safe installment payments, any cash distribution to a partner is assumed to apply first against the partner's loan account, with any remaining payment made against his capital balance.

2. Since installment payments were made to X, Y, and Z in April, the ratio of their *total equities* at the end of April should be equal to their relative profit and loss ratio. This equality is confirmed by the schedule of partnership liquidation (7200:7200:3600 = 20:20:10). The schedule additionally indicates that subsequent distributions to these partners are made in their relative profit and loss ratio (e.g., in May, 1200:1200:600 = 20:20:10). Since an installment payment is made to W in May, all of the partners' equities at May 31 are in their respective profit and loss ratio; subsequent distributions, if any, would be made on the basis of this ratio.

Cash Predistribution Plan

In the partnership liquidation schedule and supporting calculation of safe installment payments, a new and separate calculation is required each time an installment distribution is contemplated—at least until such time as the partners' equities are in their relative profit and loss ratio. Yet, it may be desirable to establish a systematic plan for distributing partnership assets in advance of the start of the liquidation process. Such a cash *predistribution plan* must anticipate the determination of the amount of safe payments to the partners at any point in time.

The following sequence of operations is used in establishing the predetermined order and amount of distribution payments:

1. Using each partner's residual equity (combined capital and loan balances) and percentage interest in profits and losses, compute the partners' *loss-absorption potentials*. The amount of this potential for each partner is the amount of possible loss the partnership may incur before the partner is obliged to contribute new assets to the partnership, i.e., his residual equity divided by his percentage interest in profits and losses.

For example, if Baker and Moore have equities (including loans) of $48,000 and $40,000, respectively, and share profits and losses in the ratio 6:4, a table of loss-absorption potentials may take the following form:

BAKER-MOORE PARTNERSHIP
Loss Absorption Potentials

Partner	Equities	Profit and Loss Ratio	Loss-Absorption Potentials	Order of Equity Absorption
Baker	$48,000	60%	$ 80,000 = ($48,000 ÷ .60)	1
Moore	40,000	40	100,000 = ($40,000 ÷ .40)	2

A loss of $80,000 would totally absorb Baker's equity in the partnership (including any possible offset of a loan balance should one exist), whereas a loss of $100,000 would be required before Moore's total equity would be absorbed.

2. After calculating the loss-absorption potential of each partner, prepare a schedule which assumes potential losses in sequence such that the amount of each assumed loss is sufficient to absorb the equity of exactly one partner, beginning with the partner having the smallest loss-absorption potential. The order of this equity absorption is indicated in the table of loss-absorption potentials, i.e., in the order of ascending amounts of loss-absorption potentials.

If the Baker-Moore Partnership has cash of $7,000, noncash assets of $93,000, and liabilities of $12,000, such a schedule would assume the following form:

BAKER-MOORE PARTNERSHIP

Schedule of Loss Absorption
Dr. [Cr.]

	Assumed Losses	Baker	Moore
Profit and loss ratio		60%	40%
Preliquidation balances		$[48,000]	$[40,000]
Potential loss to absorb Baker's equity	$[80,000]	48,000	32,000
Balances		$ –0–	$ [8,000]
Potential loss to absorb Moore's remaining equity	[8,000]		8,000
Balance			$ –0–

In this simple case the total potential loss is attributed to the degree of realization of noncash assets; therefore, as noted before, the book value of noncash assets is assumed to establish a maximum possible loss. This case illustrates the important principle that after one partner's equity has been totally eliminated, additional losses are absorbed by the remaining partners in their relative profit and loss ratio. Given the assumption that debit balances will *not* be restored to zero by contributions, no benefit is to be derived by allocating subsequent assumed losses to all partners; doing so would simply require a reallocation of the debit balances created in the first allocation. In this example, Moore is the only remaining partner with an equity; consequently he must absorb 100 percent of all additional losses, and a loss of $8,000 would thus completely absorb his $8,000 equity. In the schedule, the sequence progresses until all partners' equities have been reduced to zero, unless the cash on hand exceeds the claims of outside creditors; in this event, the schedule should be continued until a balance remains in but one partner's capital account.

3. Using the above schedule, which indicates the effect of loss absorption on the several equities, construct a predistribution plan indicating in sequence the distribution of cash as it is made available to the partnership. This is accomplished by reverse movement through the loss-absorption schedule, as the continued availability of cash systematically negates the assumption of potential losses:

BAKER-MOORE PARTNERSHIP
Cash Predistribution Plan

		Distributions		
		Priority Claims	Baker	Moore
Preliquidation cash balance	$ 7,000	100%		
Subsequent collections (on realization of noncash assets):				
First	$ 5,000	100%		
Next	8,000			100%
Next	80,000		60%	40
Noncash assets	$93,000			
Any additional cash collected			60	40

It should be observed that any available cash in excess of the $93,000 book value of noncash assets implies a net realization gain, which must be credited to the partners in accordance with the partners' profit- and loss-sharing ratio. The percentages in the schedule may be easily converted to dollar amounts and also included in the cash predistribution plan; however, this translation would not indicate explicitly the proper distribution if only a portion of the indicated cash were made available.

Liquidation Expenses and Unrecorded Liabilities

The total potential loss of a partnership has heretofore been assumed to be equal to the book value of noncash assets. This assumption is true *only* if the assets are determined to be completely worthless, *and* if *additional* expenses are not incurred in the process of liquidation, and if all partnership liabilities have been properly recorded. However, if liquidation expenses, including disposal costs for noncash assets, should exceed the proceeds from asset realization, the actual loss suffered will be greater than the assumed loss. Additionally, unrecorded liabilities to outside creditors may be discovered during the period of liquidation; necessarily, these claims will rank ahead of the residual claims of partners. Therefore, in order to avoid personal liability, the fiduciary should explicitly recognize these items in the liquidation schedule where the amounts are predictable with reasonable accuracy. In the calculation of safe installment payments, provision may be made for estimated future liquidation expenses and unrecorded liabilities by treating them as additions to the potential loss as previously determined. This adjustment has the effect of reserving cash in an amount equal to the total of anticipated liquidation expenses and unrecorded liabilities. In the event a cash predistribution plan is used, adjustments for estimated liquidation expenses and unrecorded liabilities should be indicated by withholding cash available for distribution; the plan will then provide for the distribution of the remaining cash in the prescribed manner.

INSOLVENT PARTNERSHIP

Basic Rights

In an earlier discussion, partnership insolvency was said to exist where recorded partnership assets are insufficient to discharge partnership liabilities. As noted, this definition emphasizes the financial condition of the partnership, viewed as a separate and distinct entity. It thereby ignores the existence and potential value of the partnership claim against the individual partners for debit balances in their capital accounts; at least one such debit balance must exist if partnership liabilities exceed partnership assets. In the discussion to follow, it is initially assumed that the partnership creditors first exhaust partnership assets in discharging partnership liabilities, and thereafter make claims against the partners jointly for any remaining unpaid balances of partnership debts. Two conditions are possible:

1. One or more of the individual partners possesses separate net assets sufficient to meet the claims of the partnership creditors (i.e., legally, the partnership is not insolvent).

2. The partners individually do not have sufficient assets to discharge all existing partnership debts (i.e., the partnership is legally insolvent, and considering the claims of partnership creditors, all of the partners are individually insolvent). Manifestly, the order of distributing the partners' individually owned assets depends upon the relative rights of partnership and individual creditors.

To determine the basic rights of creditors, it is important first to marshal the assets of both the partnership and the several partners. This legal doctrine, *marshaling of assets,* prescribes that partnership assets and individual assets constitute separate pools of resources against which partnership creditors and individual creditors, respectively, have initial and separate recourse. If the partnership is insolvent, partnership assets are completely exhausted in the *partial* settlement of partnership debts. If the partnership is solvent, creditors of individual partners have a claim against the remaining partnership assets to the extent of the partner's residual interest therein. Once individual creditors have satisfied their claims against individual assets, the partnership creditors may recover from the partners' separately owned assets to the extent of their unsatisfied claims, *regardless of the equity status of the partner in the firm* (debit or credit balance). A special point of interest in this allocation process is the definition of individual and partnership assets and liabilities. A difficult and legally unresolved problem relates to a debit balance existing in an insolvent partner's capital account (whether or not the *other* partners are insolvent). Section 40 (i) of the Uniform Partnership Act is explicit on this point:

> Where a partner has become bankrupt or his estate is insolvent the claims against his separate property shall rank in the following order:
> (I)   Those owing to separate creditors,
> (II) Those owing to partnership creditors,
> (III) Those owing to partners by way of contribution.

Under this Act, the obligation to the partnership, and the remaining partners, for a debit balance does not constitute a *separate* or *individual* liability of the insolvent partner. The language of the Federal Bankruptcy Act, which emphasizes the marshaling principle, would also appear to support this position. There exists, however, a possible legal *interpretation* of the "contribution obligation" as constituting an individual liability of the partner. In this regard, the following observations made at the time the Uniform Partnership Act was formulated are relevant:

> It is to be hoped that eventually in all our courts of insolvency the liability of the partner to contribute to the payment of partnership liabilities, correctly described by the Act as a partnership asset, will be treated as on a parity with his other liabilities for purpose of distribution of his insolvent estate.[5]

> This [Section 40 (i)] however introduces several changes into the law as it is established by the weight of authority. A partner who has paid the partnership debts can at present [prior to passage of the Act] prove for contribution against the insolvent partner's estate and share *pari passu* with his other separate creditors.[6]

A contrary opinion is expressed in the following terms:

> It is submitted that the partner, by paying the partnership debts, should be held to have stepped into the right of the partnership creditors against the assets of the insolvent partner. He should not obtain, however, in respect to that estate a better position than the person whose claim he has paid. Indeed, if he were allowed to do so, the rule giving priority to separate creditors on the separate estate would be to that extent nullified.[7]

The first opinion (Crane) appears to support the position that a partner's debit balance in his capital account, particularly if it represents an obligation to a solvent partner who has personally discharged the total claims of partnership creditors, constitutes a separate liability of the insolvent partner. The counterargument, however, focuses on the apparent *equity* of the provision in the Uniform Partnership Act. It may be concluded, therefore, that in those states which have not adopted the Uniform Partnership Act, or in federal bankruptcy cases, it is possible that the individual partner's

---

[5] Judson A. Crane, "The Uniform Partnership Act—A Criticism," *Harvard Law Review,* June 1915, pp. 784–85.

[6] Ibid., p. 786.

[7] William Draper Lewis, "The Uniform Partnership Act," *Harvard Law Review,* January 1916, pp. 307–8.

estate may be prorated among his separate creditors and his obligation to the partnership.[8]

The basic rights of creditors, apropos of the underlying principle in respect to the marshaling of assets, may then be summarized as follows:

1. Partnership creditors should seek the discharge of partnership debts by first exhausting partnership assets (exclusive of contributions of partners) to the extent of their claims.

2. A partner's individual creditors should first seek recourse against his separate assets to the extent of their claims. Under the Uniform Partnership Act, amounts due to the partnership by way of contribution do not constitute individual liabilities; under common law, or in federal bankruptcy cases, the contribution requirement *may* be construed as an individual liability sharing *pari passu* with other individual liabilities.

3. To the extent of their unsatisfied claims, partnership creditors may prove against the residual assets of an individual partner after his separate creditors have been satisfied, regardless of the amount of his residual interest in the partnership.

4. To the extent of their unsatisfied claims, a partner's individual creditors may prove against the *recorded* interest of the individual partner in the residual assets of a solvent partnership.

5. If a partner pays more than his share of partnership liabilities, he has a claim, as measured by the resulting credit balance in his account, against those partners with debit balances (representing their unrequited share of partnership losses).

Accounting Analysis of the Insolvent Partnership

Determination of amounts to be allocated to the various creditor and equity interests will be illustrated under each of the two conditions of insolvency: (1) an insolvent partnership with at least one solvent partner, and (2) an insolvent partnership with all partners insolvent.

Case 6. At Least One Solvent Partner. The trial balance of the ABC Partnership, after realization of assets but before distribution of cash to either creditors or partners, is as follows:

	Debit	Credit
Cash	$20,000	
Liabilities		$30,000
A, capital		10,000
B, capital	5,000	
C, capital	15,000	
	$40,000	$40,000

---

[8] Even other interpretations have been made. In *Robinson* v. *Security Co.,* Ann Cas 1915C, 1170, it was held that a judgment should be rendered "dividing the distributable assets belonging to the estate of each partner ratably among the separate creditors of such partners together with the partnership creditors." Marshaling of assets was not applied even *in form* in this case.

A, B, and C share profits and losses in the ratio 2:4:4. The separate financial status of each individual partner, excluding his interest in, or obligation to, the partnership, is as follows:

	Assets (Realizable Value)	Liabilities
A	$ 5,000	$20,000 - 15
B	6,000	4,000 -2
C	30,000	10,000 - 19

Given these data, it is apparent that both A and B are insolvent. A's individual liabilities exceed his individual assets and his interest in the firm (even assuming his partnership interest is recoverable at book value), and B's obligations to individual creditors ($4,000) and to the partnership ($5,000) exceed his individual assets. It is assumed further that partnership creditors obtain a judgment against C and that he makes full payment of the partnership obligations to its outside creditors, using his separate assets as necessary. Schedules of partnership liquidation and distribution of separate assets of the individual partners under the provisions of the Uniform Partnership Act are given in Illustrations 15–8 and 15–9.

Illustration 15–8

ABC PARTNERSHIP

Schedule of Partnership Liquidation

Dr. [Cr.]

	Assets		Claimants		
				Residual Equities	
	Cash	Priority Claims	A	B	C
Profit and loss ratio			20%	40%	40%
Balances	$ 20,000	$[30,000]	$[10,000]	$ 5,000	$ 15,000
Payment of liabilities	[20,000]	20,000			
Balances	$ –0–	$[10,000]	$[10,000]	$ 5,000	$ 15,000
Establish status of each partner's personal solvency. Record payment of partnership liabilities by C from his separate assets ..		10,000			[10,000]
Balances	$ –0–	$ –0–	$[10,000]	$ 5,000	$ 5,000
Contribution by B	2,000			[2,000]	
Balances	$ 2,000	$ –0–	$[10,000]	$ 3,000	$ 5,000
Allocation of B's debit balance ...			1,000	[3,000]	2,000
Balances	$ 2,000	$ –0–	$ [9,000]	$ –0–	$ 7,000
Contribution by C	7,000				$ [7,000]
Balances	$ 9,000	$ –0–	$ [9,000]	$ –0–	$ –0–
Distribution of cash	[9,000]		9,000		
Termination of partnership	$ –0–	$ –0–	$ –0–	$ –0–	$ –0–

Illustration 15–9

A, B, AND C

Schedule of Distribution of Separate Assets

	A	B	C
Separate assets	$ 5,000	$ 6,000	$ 30,000
Separate liabilities (Rank I)	[20,000]	[4,000]	[10,000]
Separate capital [deficit]	$[15,000]	$ 2,000	$ 20,000
Payment of partnership debts (Rank II)			[10,000]
Separate capital [deficit]	$[15,000]	$ 2,000	$ 10,000
Payment of debt to partnership (Rank III) ...		[2,000]	[7,000]
Separate capital [deficit]	$[15,000]	$ –0–	$ 3,000
Distribution of cash by partnership	9,000		
Separate capital [deficit]	$ [6,000]	$ –0–	$ 3,000
Obligations of B to A and C through the partnership	1,000	[3,000]	2,000
Separate capital [deficit]	$ [5,000]	$[3,000]	$ 5,000

If the Uniform Partnership Act is not controlling in this case *and* if the partners' obligations to the firm are adjudged individual liabilities sharing *pari passu* with other individual obligations, the schedule will be modified only by the amount of B's contribution to the firm (since A, the second insolvent partner, does not have an obligation to contribute to the partnership). The amount of B's contribution is calculated as follows:

	B		
	Liabilities	Ratio of Assets to Liabilities	Asset Settlement
To partnership	$5,000	2/3	$3,334
Separate creditors	4,000	2/3	2,666
	$9,000		$6,000

Under these conditions, A, the only partner with a credit balance, will receive $445 more than under the provisions of the Uniform Partnership Act, C will contribute $889 less to the partnership, and B's personal creditors will receive $1,334 less.

Case 7. All Partners Insolvent. Assume the same facts as in Case 6, except that C has separate assets of $10,000 rather than $30,000. In this circumstance, the partnership is legally insolvent, as it will be shown that there are insufficient partnership assets and net assets of individual partners to make a full settlement with partnership creditors.

Under the provisions of the Uniform Partnership Act, the partnership creditors will receive the $20,000 of partnership cash and the $2,000 excess assets of B (those not required to discharge separate debts), leaving a deficiency in payments to partnership creditors of $8,000. The $22,000 distribution to these creditors will necessarily be made according to priorities established by law.[9]

If the partners' obligations to the partnership are considered separate (individual) liabilities and are accorded the same status as other separate liabilities, the distribution of separate property is calculated as follows:

		B	
	Liabilities	Ratio of Assets to Liabilities	Asset Settlement
To partnership	$5,000	2/3	$3,334
Separate creditors	4,000	2/3	2,666
	$9,000		$6,000

		C	
	Liabilities	Ratio of Assets to Liabilities	Asset Settlement
To partnership	$15,000	2/5	$ 6,000
Separate creditors	10,000	2/5	4,000
	$25,000		$10,000

The allocation of B's separate assets remains unchanged in this case, as there is no adjustment of B's financial status. Consequently, where the partners' obligations to contribute to the firm for debit balances are confirmed legally and given an equal status with their separate liabilities, the partnership creditors will receive an additional $7,334 ($1,334 + $6,000) from the partnership, $1,334 being contributed by B and $6,000 being contributed by C. It should be noted, however, that this calculational technique ignores the subtlety introduced by the inherent variability of the obligation to the partnership when two or more partners are involved, i.e., the undischarged balance must be absorbed by the remaining partners, which accordingly alters the relative ratio of liabilities to separate creditors and to the partnership.

---

[9] These priorities are discussed in Chapter 16.

COMPREHENSIVE ILLUSTRATION

Case 8 illustrates the preparation of a cash predistribution plan, a partnership liquidation schedule, and the related supporting calculations and schedules, given a more complex situation in which four partners decide to liquidate their partnership and one of the four partners is insolvent.

Case 8. The partners of Slippery Walk Company agree to dissolve their partnership on July 1, 19X1, since the operations of the company have met with financial difficulties. The preliquidation capital and loan account balances and profit and loss ratio are:

Dr. [Cr.]

Partner	Capital	Loan	Ratio
James	$[36,000]	$[14,000]	20%
McDonald	[28,000]	4,000 *	20
Pearson	[12,000]	[4,000]	50
Quigley	[30,000]		10

* Loan to McDonald from Slippery Walk Company.

The partners and creditors have agreed that Quigley should oversee the liquidation of the partnership's assets and distribution of cash to creditors and partners. Quigley forecasts that it will take approximately three months to complete the liquidation. The partners request that available cash be distributed at the end of each month, and they inquire of Quigley as to when they should expect to participate in the cash distribution. As a consequence, Quigley wishes to develop a cash predistribution plan. The loss absorption potentials of the partners are calculated as follows:

SLIPPERY WALK COMPANY
Loss Absorption Potentials

Partner	Equities	Loss Ratio	Loss Absorption Potentials	Order of Equity Absorption
James	$50,000	20%	$250,000 = $50,000/.2	3
McDonald ..	24,000	20	120,000 = 24,000/.2	2
Pearson	16,000	50	32,000 = 16,000/.5	1
Quigley	30,000	10	300,000 = 30,000/.1	4

Since the schedule of loss absorption is based upon hypothetical losses rather than actual or expected losses, it can be prepared without considering the actual asset and liability position of the company. This schedule is presented below:

SLIPPERY WALK COMPANY

Schedule of Loss Absorption
Dr. [Cr.]

	Assumed Losses	Partners' Equities			
		James	McDonald	Pearson	Quigley
Profit and loss ratio		20%	20%	50%	10%
Preliquidation balances		$[50,000]	$[24,000]	$[16,000]	$[30,000]
Potential loss to absorb Pearson's equity	$[32,000]	6,400	6,400	16,000	3,200
Balances		$[43,600]	$[17,600]	$ –0–	$[26,800]
Additional loss to absorb McDonald's equity	[44,000]*	17,600	17,600		8,800
Balances		$[26,000]	$ –0–		$[18,000]
Additional loss to absorb James' equity	[39,000]†	26,000			13,000
Balances		$ –0–			$ [5,000]
Additional loss to absorb Quigley's equity	[5,000]				5,000
Balance					$ –0–

* The additional loss necessary to absorb McDonald's equity is based on the assumption that Pearson will not contribute personal assets to cover a debit balance in his capital account. Thus, the additional loss will be shared by James, McDonald, and Quigley in a 20:20:10 ratio. Therefore, the additional loss is calculated as $17,600 ÷ .4 = $44,000.

† The additional loss to absorb James' equity is based on the 20:10 loss ratio between the remaining partners with credit balances, James and Quigley. Thus, it is calculated as $26,000 ÷ ⅔ = $39,000.

On July 1, 19X1, Slippery Walk's assets and liabilities are: cash, $6,000; noncash assets, $244,000; and liabilities, $130,000. The cash predistribution plan is presented below:

SLIPPERY WALK COMPANY

Cash Predistribution Plan

		Distributions			
	Priority Claims	James	McDonald	Pearson	Quigley
Cash distributions:					
First $130,000	100%				
Next 5,000					100%
Next 39,000		66⅔%			33⅓
Next 44,000		40	40%		20
All additional receipts		20	20	50%	10

Quigley anticipates that the realization of noncash assets will follow the pattern below:

July, 19X1 .... $144,000 net cash proceeds
August, 19X1 .... 20,000 net cash proceeds
September, 19X1 .... 20,000 net cash proceeds

Based upon this information and the cash predistribution plan, Quigley is able to answer the partners' and creditors' inquiries as to when they might anticipate receiving cash. Quigley's forecast is based on his plan to retain $10,000 cash at the end of July and $4,000 at the end of August as a reserve for future unrecorded liabilities. By the end of September, Quigley expects that all liquidation expenses and unrecorded liabilities will be known so that a final cash distribution can be made. His forecast is summarized below:

Forecasted Schedule of Payments

Payee	July 31 Payments	August 31 Payments	September 30 Payments
Creditors	$130,000		
James	3,333	$17,333	$11,733
McDonald			6,400
Pearson			
Quigley	6,667	8,667	5,867
Total expected payments	$140,000	$26,000	$24,000
Cash to be held in reserve	$ 10,000	$ 4,000	$ –0–

Importantly, Quigley's forecast is based upon his subjective estimates of when and how much cash will be generated from the liquidation of assets. Actual events may differ substantially from his expectations.

Contrary to the cash predistribution plan and Quigley's forecast of payments, which are *ex ante* statements of what is expected to happen in the future, the schedule of partnership liquidation is a historical document that reports the actual transactions which occur during the liquidation period. The schedule of partnership liquidation for Slippery Walk Company is based upon the following events which took place during the three month liquidation of the company.

	Liquidation of Noncash Assets		
	Discovery of Unrecorded Liabilities	Cash Proceeds Net of Liquidation Expenses	Book Values of Liquidated Assets
During July	–0–	$136,000	$180,000
During August	$8,000	22,000	18,000
During September	–0–	20,000	46,000

Cash disbursements at the end of each month amounted to all available cash balances except for a $10,000 cash reserve at the end of July and a $4,000 cash reserve at the end of August. During the month of August, Pearson contributed $5,000 to the partnership to partially compensate for his capital deficiency. He was unable to make any further contributions.

The schedule of partnership liquidation is presented in Illustration 15–10.

The actual sequence of cash distributions, as presented in Illustration 15–10, is precisely consistent with the cash predistribution plan except for the $8,000 payment for liabilities which were discovered in August, after the cash predistribution plan was prepared. Nevertheless, Pearson's $5,000 contribution of cash to the partnership (in August) potentially could have altered the sequence of payments from that which was indicated by the cash predistribution plan. That plan was constructed on the assumption that none of the partners would be able to make additional investments to cover capital deficiencies. Pearson's $5,000 contribution obviously strengthened his capital position relative to the other partners. Thus, his stronger position would warrant his participation in cash distributions somewhat sooner than was indicated by the cash predistribution plan. However, since the total amount of available cash was not large enough to provide any cash return to Pearson, the actual distribution of cash did in fact conform to the predistribution plan.

The cash predistribution plan is prepared prior to the liquidation period and must be based upon conservative assumptions with respect to future events. Because future events may turn out to be inconsistent with those assumptions and as a precautionary confirmation of the decisions to distribute cash, it is wise to prepare a schedule of safe installment payments in support of each cash distribution. Illustration 15–11 presents this schedule for Slippery Walk Company.

QUESTIONS

1. What are the principal activities of a partnership during the liquidation process?

2. What is the order of priority for the distribution of assets under Section 40 (B) of the Uniform Partnership Act?

3. If after liquidation of the partnership assets, a partner has a debit balance in his capital account, what procedure would be followed if the partner is solvent (i.e., he holds personal assets sufficient to cover the capital deficiency)? What if the partner is insolvent?

4. Explain the rule of "setoff."

5. If one partner is assigned the role of managing the liquidation process and is to be compensated for this service by the partnership, how should the compensation be recorded in the records of the partnership?

6. If installment (periodic) payments are to be made during the course of

Illustration 15-10

SLIPPERY WALK COMPANY

Schedule of Partnership Liquidation

Dr. [Cr.]

	Assets		Priority Claims	Claimants / Residual Equities						
	Cash	Noncash		James Loan	James Capital	McDonald Loan	McDonald Capital	Pearson Loan	Pearson Capital	Quigley Capital
Profit and loss ratio					20%		20%		50%	10%
Preliquidation balances	$ 6,000	$ 244,000	$[130,000]	$[14,000]	$[36,000]	$ 4,000	$[28,000]	$[4,000]	$[12,000]	$[30,000]
Realization of assets and allocation of loss—July	136,000	[180,000]			8,800		8,800		22,000	4,400
Balances	$142,000	$ 64,000	$[130,000]	$[14,000]	$[27,200]	$ 4,000	$[19,200]	$[4,000]	$ 10,000	$[25,600]
Payment of creditors	[130,000]		130,000							
July 31 installment payment	[2,000]									2,000
Balances on July 31	$ 10,000	$ 64,000	$ –0–	$[14,000]	$[27,200]	$ 4,000	$[19,200]	$[4,000]	$ 10,000	$[23,600]
Realization of assets and allocation of gain—August	22,000	[18,000]			[800]		[800]		[2,000]	[400]
Recognition of unrecorded liabilities			[8,000]		1,600		1,600		4,000	800
Contribution by Pearson	5,000								[5,000]	
Balances	$ 37,000	$ 46,000	$[8,000]	$[14,000]	$[26,400]	$ 4,000	$[18,400]	$[4,000]	$ 7,000	$[23,200]
Payment of creditors	[8,000]		8,000							
August 31 installment	[25,000]			14,000	667					10,333
Balances on August 31	$ 4,000	$ 46,000	$ –0–	$ –0–	$[25,733]	$ 4,000	$[18,400]	$[4,000]	$ 7,000	$[12,867]
Realization of assets and allocation of loss—September	20,000	[46,000]			5,200		5,200		13,000	2,600
Offset of loans against capital accounts						[4,000]	4,000	4,000	[4,000]	
Balances	$ 24,000	$ –0–	$ –0–	$ –0–	$[20,533]	$ –0–	$ [9,200]	$ –0–	$ 16,000	$[10,267]
Allocation of Pearson's capital deficiency					6,400		6,400		[16,000]	3,200
Balances	$ 24,000	$ –0–	$ –0–	$ –0–	$[14,133]	$ –0–	$ [2,800]	$ –0–	$ –0–	$ [7,067]
September 30 installment	[24,000]				14,133		2,800			7,067
Termination of partnership	$ –0–	$ –0–	$ –0–	$ –0–	$ –0–	$ –0–	$ –0–	$ –0–	$ –0–	$ –0–

Illustration 15–11

SLIPPERY WALK COMPANY

Schedule of Safe Installment Payments
Dr. [Cr.]

	Partners' Equities			
	James	*McDonald*	*Pearson*	*Quigley*
Profit and loss ratio	20%	20%	50%	10%
Computation of July 31 installment:				
Predistribution balances	$[41,200]	$[15,200]	$ 6,000	$[25,600]
Potential loss, $80,000*	32,000	32,000	[6,000]	16,000
Balances	$ [9,200]	$ 16,800	$ –0–	$ [9,600]
Potential loss, $16,800	11,200	[16,800]		5,600
Balances	$ 2,000	$ –0–		$ [4,000]
Potential loss, $2,000	[2,000]			2,000
Safe payment to partner	$ –0–			$ [2,000]
Computation of August 31 payment:				
Predistribution balances	$[40,400]	$[14,400]	$ 3,000	$[23,200]
Potential loss, $53,000†	21,200	21,200	[3,000]	10,600
Balances	$[19,200]	$ 6,800	$ –0–	$[12,600]
Potential loss, $6,800	4,533	[6,800]		2,267
Safe payments to partners	$[14,667]	$ –0–		$[10,333]

Computation of Sept. 30 payment:
 Predistribution balances constitute safe payments to partners since no potential
 losses exist.

---

 * $64,000 noncash assets + $10,000 reserve for unrecorded liabilities + $6,000 capital
deficiency of Pearson = $80,000.
 † $46,000 noncash assets + $4,000 reserve for unrecorded liabilities + $3,000 capital
deficiency of Pearson = $53,000.

liquidation, what factors might the accountant be concerned with in determining the amounts of cash or other assets to be distributed?

7. Describe the role and usefulness of a schedule of safe (installment) payments.

8. How are loans from partners accounted for in the schedule of partnership liquidation and in the schedule of safe (installment) payments?

9. What hypothetical losses and/or hypothetical cash transfers are recorded in a schedule of partnership liquidation?

10. What is a "cash predistribution plan"? What are "loss-absorption potentials"?

11. To what extent does a cash predistribution plan reflect the actual gains or losses resulting from the liquidation of assets?

12. How should expected liquidation expenses and/or unrecorded liabilities be treated in proceeding with the process of liquidation by installments?

13. What events would cause the safe distribution of cash to differ in sequence from that indicated by a cash predistribution plan?

14. Briefly explain the "marshaling of assets" principle.

EXERCISES

Exercise 15–1

Garner, Louis, and Ramsey are partners in the Cleanall Company and have capital balances on January 1, 1977, of $100,000, $70,000, and $142,000, respectively. After electing to liquidate the business, the partners convert the non-cash assets of $234,000 into $184,000 cash. All the liabilities, totaling $30,000, are paid; and the remaining cash is distributed among the partners. They share profits and losses: Garner, 60 percent; Louis, 30 percent; Ramsey, 10 percent.

Required:

Prepare a partnership liquidation schedule showing how cash is distributed.

Exercise 15–2

The balance sheet of the Manning Company just prior to liquidation is as follows:

Assets $266,000	Accounts payable	$18,000
	Tracey, loan	12,000
	Manning, capital	96,000
	Smith, capital	80,000
	Tracey, capital	60,000

Manning, Smith, and Tracey share profits and losses in the ratio of 3:6:1, respectively.

Required:

Construct a systematic plan showing how cash should be distributed to the various equities as it becomes available during the liquidation process.

Exercise 15–3 ◑

Three partners, Tex, Astro, and Em, have found themselves confronted with most discouraging business results; hence, they have sadly concluded that operations must be terminated and their partnership liquidated. Profits and losses are shared as follows: Tex, 50%; Astro, 30%; Em, 20%. As the accountant placed in charge of this partnership, you have responsibility for the liquidation and distribution of assets. When you assume your responsibilities, the partnership balance sheet is as follows:

Cash	$ 8,000	Liabilities	$10,000
Other assets	82,000	Loan from Tex	6,000
		Tex, capital	6,000
		Astro, capital	34,000
		Em, capital	34,000
Total Assets	$90,000	Total Equities	$90,000

During the first two months of your duties, the following events occur:

1. Assets having a book value of $60,000 are sold for $20,000 cash.
2. Previously unrecorded liabilities of $4,000 are recognized.
3. Before distributing available cash balances to creditors and partners, you conclude that a cash reserve of $1,000 should be set aside for future potential expenses.
4. Remaining cash balances are distributed to creditors and partners.

Required:

Prepare a schedule of partnership liquidation which covers all of the events described above.

Exercise 15–4

Harrison and Lambert are partners sharing profits and losses equally. Prior to the liquidation of their partnership, they had capital balances of $50,000 and $30,000, respectively. During the liquidation process, all of the partnership's assets were sold and sufficient cash was received to pay all partnership creditors except for one in the amount of $16,000. Both partners are personally solvent.

Required:

Calculate how much cash each partner should contribute to the partnership to satisfy the remaining liability and eliminate any claims between the partners.

Exercise 15–5

The Cotton, Miller, and Sterling Partnership is being dissolved. All liabilities have been liquidated. The remaining assets on hand are being realized by a comparatively slow conversion schedule. The following are details of the partners' accounts:

Partner	Capital Account (Original Investment)	Current Account (Undistributed Earnings Net of Drawings)	Loans to Partnership	Profit and Loss Ratio
Cotton	$40,000	$3,000 credit	$30,000	40%
Miller	50,000	4,000 debit		40
Sterling	20,000	2,000 credit	10,000	20

Required:

Prepare a predistribution plan showing how cash payments should be made to the partners as assets are realized.

(AICPA adapted)

Exercise 15–6

Grey, Hill, Lang, and Petersen share profits and losses 40:30:20:10. Their capital and loan account balances are:

	Capital	*Loan*
Grey	$56,000	$14,000
Hill	82,000	4,000
Lang	36,000	
Petersen	24,000	4,000

The partners agree to dissolve their partnership, at which date unpaid liabilities amount to $20,000 and noncash assets total $210,000.

During the first month of liquidation, assets having a book value of $110,000 were sold for $62,000. During the second month, assets recorded at $64,000 were sold for $51,000. During the third month, the remaining unsold assets were determined to be worthless.

Required:

Prepare a schedule of liquidation indicating the cash distribution which is made at the end of each month of the liquidation period.

PROBLEMS

Problem 1

John, Sandra, and Keith, partners in the Quality Photography Company, prepare to liquidate their business. On December 31, 1977, the partnership account balances are:

Cash	$ 5,430	Trade payables	$12,892
Other assets	61,870	Loans from partners:	
		John	8,000
		Sandra	4,000
		Keith	14,000
		Capital balances:	
		John	16,402
		Sandra	1,469
		Keith	10,537
	$67,300		$67,300

John, Sandra, and Keith share profits and losses 50:30:20.

It is agreed that cash made available during liquidation shall be distributed to the partners at the end of each month. However, an amount sufficient to provide for anticipated future expenses and unrecorded liabilities is to be withheld.

A summary of transactions for the three-month liquidation period is as follows:

	Liquidation of Noncash Assets		Liquidation Expenses	Newly Discovered Unrecorded Partnership Liability	Estimated Future Expenses and Unrecorded Liabilities
	Book Value	Cash Realized			
January	$24,700	$20,120	$1,200	$ –0–	$3,000
February	33,170	28,400	1,400	1,550*	800
March	4,000	3,700	200	–0–	–0–

* The partnership bookkeeper failed to record the real property tax liability in December, 1977.

Required:

Prepare a partnership liquidation schedule indicating amounts of periodic cash distributions.

Problem 2

On August 25, 1977, Hobson, Caswell, and Clendinning entered into a partnership agreement to acquire a speculative second mortgage on undeveloped real estate. They invested $111,000, $64,000, and $25,000, respectively. They agreed on a profit and loss ratio of 4:2:1, respectively.

On September 1, 1977, they purchased for $200,000 a mortgage note with an unpaid balance of $240,000. The amount paid included interest accrued from June 30, 1977. The note principal matures at the rate of $4,000 each quarter. Interest at the annual rate of 8 percent computed on the unpaid balance is also due quarterly.

Regular interest and principal payments were received on September 30 and December 31, 1977. A working capital imprest fund of $300 was established, and collection expenses of $140 were paid in December.

In addition to the regular September payment on September 30 the mortgagor made a lump-sum principal reduction payment of $20,000 plus a penalty of 2 percent for prepayment.

Because of the speculative nature of the note, the partners agree to defer recognition of the discount until their cost has been fully recovered.

Required:

a. Assuming that no cash distributions were made to the partners, prepare a schedule computing the cash balance available for distribution to the partners on December 31, 1977.

b. After payment of collection expenses the partners expect to have cash in the total amount of $340,000 available for distribution to themselves for interest and return of principal. They plan to distribute the cash as soon as possible so that they can individually reinvest the cash.

Prepare a schedule as of September 1 showing how the total cash of $340,000 should be distributed to the individual partners by installments as it becomes available.

(AICPA adapted)

Problem 3

You are requested to assist the DEF Partnership in winding up its affairs. Your investigation discloses the following trial balance as of June 30, 1977:

	Debit	Credit
Cash	$ 12,000	
Accounts receivable	44,000	
Inventory	28,000	
Plant and equipment (net)	198,000	
Dickens, loan	24,000	
Fritz, loan	15,000	
Accounts payable		$ 34,000
Dickens, capital		134,000
Ensley, capital		90,000
Fritz, capital		63,000
	$321,000	$321,000

The partners share profits and losses as follows: Dickens, 50 percent; Ensley, 30 percent; and Fritz, 20 percent. They are considering an offer of $200,000 for the accounts receivable, inventory, and plant and equipment as of June 30. The $200,000 would be paid to the partners in installments, the number and amounts of which are to be negotiated.

Required:

Prepare a cash predistribution plan as of June 30, 1977, showing how the $200,000 cash would be distributed as it became available.

(AICPA adapted)

Problem 4

Assume the same facts as in Problem 3, except that the partners have decided to liquidate their partnership instead of accepting the offer of $200,000. Cash is distributed to the partners at the end of each month.

A summary of the liquidation transactions follows:

July:
$ 33,000—collected on accounts receivable; balance is uncollectible.
$ 20,000—received for the entire inventory.
$ 2,000—liquidation expenses paid.
$ 16,000—cash retained in the business at end of the month.

August:
$ 3,000—liquidation expenses paid.
As part payment of his capital, Fritz accepted in item of special equipment that he developed which had a book value of $8,000. The partners agreed that a value of $20,000 should be placed on this item for liquidation purposes.
$ 5,000—cash retained in the business at the end of the month.

September:
$150,000—received on sale of remaining plant and equipment.
$ 2,000—liquidation expenses paid.
No cash retained in the business.

Required:

Prepare a schedule of cash payments as of September 30, 1977, showing how the cash was distributed.

(AICPA adapted)

Problem 5

The partners of the Longhaul Company agreed to dissolve their partnership on March 31, 1977. Their preliquidation capital and loan account balances and the profit and loss ratio were:

Partner	Capital	Loan	Ratio
W	$16,000	$4,000	50%
X	29,000	2,000	20
Y	23,000		20
Z	9,000	1,000	10

The partnership had a cash balance of $10,000 and noncash assets of $80,000; obligations to outside creditors amounted to $6,000. Available cash was to be distributed at the end of each month during the period of liquidation. Assets were realized as follows:

	Book Values	Net Proceeds
April	$54,000	$30,000
May	24,000	18,000
June	2,000	–0–

Required:

a. On the basis of information available on March 31, prepare a plan for the distribution of cash.
b. Prepare a schedule showing how the April and May disbursements of cash were distributed.

Problem 6

Mettlen, Cundiff, Jentz, and Nelson decide to dissolve their partnership. Accordingly, they plan a program of piecemeal conversion of assets in order to minimize liquidation losses. Partners share profits and losses as follows: Mettlen, 40 percent; Cundiff, 35 percent; Jentz, 15 percent; and Nelson, 10 percent. The period of liquidation begins on June 1, 1977, when the trial balance of the partnership is as follows:

	Debit	Credit
Cash	$ 200	
Receivables	25,900	
Inventory, June 1, 1977	42,600	
Equipment (net)	19,800	
Accounts payable		$ 3,000
Mettlen, loan		6,000
Cundiff, loan		10,000
Mettlen, capital		20,000
Cundiff, capital		21,500
Jentz, capital		18,000
Nelson, capital		10,000
	$88,500	$88,500

Required:

a. Prepare a schedule as of June 1, 1977, showing how cash will be distributed among partners as it becomes available.

b. On July 31, 1977, cash of $12,700 is available for payment to creditors and partners. How should it be distributed?

c. Assume that the partnership elects to continue operations rather than suffer liquidation. Subsequent to this decision, the partnership earns profits of $23,625. How should the profits be distributed if, in addition to the afore-mentioned profit-sharing arrangement, it was provided that Nelson receive a bonus of 5 percent of the net income from operations, such bonus to be treated as a partnership expense?

(AICPA adapted)

Problem 7

Ford, Piper, and Taylor are partners in the Taylor Supply Company and share profits and losses 50:30:20. Their capital balances on January 1, 1977, are:

Ford	$ 5,000 debit
Piper	39,000 credit
Taylor	24,000 debit

The partnership liabilities are $15,000. On liquidation, the noncash assets of $18,000 are converted into $4,000 cash. The nonbusiness (personal) assets and liabilities of each partner are:

Partner	Assets	Liabilities
Ford	$13,000	$14,000
Piper	17,000	6,400
Taylor	21,000	3,200

Required:

Prepare a partnership liquidation schedule according to the provisions of—

a. Bankruptcy law.

b. Uniform Partnership Act.

Problem 8

The following trial balance pertains to the Crystal Ball Partnership which is being terminated. Noncash assets have been liquidated but cash has not been distributed to creditors or partners:

	Debit	Credit
Cash	$ 30,000	
Liabilities		$120,000
Mallaro, capital	60,000	
Gilpin, capital		90,000
Kersbergen, capital	120,000	
	$210,000	$210,000

The individual financial status of the partners, excluding their relationships to the partnership are:

	Assets	Liabilities
Mallaro	$120,000	$ 90,000
Gilpin	150,000	300,000
Kersbergen	240,000	90,000

Required:

a. Prepare a schedule of partnership liquidation and a schedule indicating the partners' personal financial status under the provisions of the Uniform Partnership Act.
b. Calculate the amounts the partnership and the creditors of the separate partners would receive if the partners' obligations to the firm were adjudged individual liabilities.

Problem 9

A, B, and C formed the ABC Company, a partnership, with A contributing $12,000 of capital, B contributing $8,000, and C contributing $6,000. In their partnership agreement, A, B, and C provided that the partnership was to exist for 20 years, but the partners made no provision as to the proportions in which profits and losses were to be shared. During the course of operating the partnership, A made a loan of $1,000 to the partnership which has not been repaid, and the partnership also owes outside creditors additional amounts which exceed the value of partnership assets by $3,000.

Required:

a. Under the Uniform Partnership Act, in absence of a specific agreement between the parties, how is the compensation and profit for each partner determined during the course of operating the partnership?
b. Under the Uniform Partnership Act—
   (1) If A wishes to terminate the partnership but B and C do not, does A have the right to withdraw from the partnership? *Explain.*
   (2) If A, B, and C agree to terminate the partnership, how will losses be divided?

c. Discuss—
  (1) The rule of "marshaling of assets."
  (2) The distinction between the "dissolution" of the partnership and the "winding up" of partnership affairs.
d. If D becomes a partner in ABC Company and replaces A, what is D's liability with respect to obligations arising before his admission to the partnership?

(AICPA adapted)

Problem 10

Mathis, Overton, and Downey are partners sharing profits in the ratio of 4:3:2, respectively. The partnership and two of the partners are currently unable to make full payment of their obligations to creditors. The balance sheet of the partnership and an enumeration of the assets and liabilities of the separate partners are as follows:

MOD PARTNERSHIP

Balance Sheet

(Date)

Assets		Equities		
Cash	$ 500	Accounts		
Other assets	60,500	payable		$37,000
		Capital:		
		Mathis	$10,000	
		Overton	6,000	
		Downey	8,000	24,000
	$61,000			$61,000

Assets and Liabilities of Partners M, O, and D

Excluding Partnership Interests

Partner	Cash and Cash Value of Personal Assets	Liabilities
Mathis	$31,000	$20,000
Overton	9,450	11,900
Downey	4,000	5,000

Required:

a. Assuming that "other assets" are converted into $33,500 cash, prepare a partnership liquidation schedule *and* a complementary schedule indicating the distribution of partners' personal assets according to the provisions of the Uniform Partnership Act.
b. Calculate the minimum amount which must be realized from the sale of noncash partnership assets in order that the personal creditors of Overton will receive full settlement of their claims.

(AICPA adapted)

unit four

FIDUCIARY
AND
INSTITUTIONAL
ACCOUNTING

16

Corporate Liquidation and Reorganization

ACCOUNTING PROBLEMS relating to the expansion of corporate business through mergers and acquisitions were considered in Unit One. Based on an assumption of continuity with respect to the operations of a corporate affiliation, Unit Two comprised an extended analysis of consolidated statements. A set of circumstances may exist, however, which calls for a contraction in the scale of business activity, or disinvestment. Financial distress, which is a significant factor in corporate disinvestment, may result from managerial miscalculation, operation malfunction, unfavorable economic influences, competitive market encroachments, and for numerous other reasons. Consequently, it may be useful at this time to examine some of the accounting problems which relate to corporate liquidation and reorganization.

LIQUIDATION

A corporation's existence may be terminated either by *voluntary* or *involuntary* petition. Voluntary dissolution may be initiated by the incorporators in the event that the corporation has not commenced business or issued shares of stock; subsequently, a corporation may be voluntarily dissolved with consent of the shareholders. Involuntary dissolution may be initiated by the corporate shareholders (or directors), by the state, or by creditors.

In respect to action taken by the state, the Business Corporation Act of Texas, for example, provides that a corporation may be involuntarily dissolved as a consequence of any of the following:

(1)   The corporation or its incorporators have failed to comply with a condition precedent to incorporation; or

(2)   The original articles of incorporation or any amendments thereof were procured through fraud; or

(3)   The corporation has continued to transact business beyond the scope of the purpose or purposes of the corporation as expressed in its articles of incorporation; or

(4)   A misrepresentation has been made of any material matter in any application, report, affidavit, or other document submitted by such corporation pursuant to this Act.

(5)   The corporation has failed to file any report within the time required by law, or has failed to pay any fees, franchise taxes or penalties prescribed by law when the same have become due and payable;

(6)   The corporation has failed to maintain a registered agent in this state as required by law; or

(7)   When a corporation is convicted of a felony or when a high managerial agent is convicted of a felony in the conduct of the affairs of the corporation, the Attorney General may file an action to involuntarily dissolve the corporation in a district court of the county in which the registered office of the corporation is situated. . . . The court may dissolve the corporation involuntarily if it is established that:

(*a*)   The corporation, or a high managerial agent acting in behalf of the corporation, has engaged in a persistent course of felonious conduct; and

(*b*)   To prevent future felonious conduct of the same character, the public interest requires such dissolution. [Texas Business Corporation Act, Art. 7.01]

In regard to involuntary dissolution initiated by creditors, the National Bankruptcy Act provides that three or more persons who have provable claims fixed as to liability and liquidated (certain) as to amount, aggregating in total $500 or more, may file a petition in bankruptcy against any qualified debtor, or if the total number of creditors is less than 12, then one such creditor, whose claim is $500 or more, may file [Section 59(b)].

A debtor's financial distress may be produced by, or result in, a condition of *insolvency*. It is important to distinguish between insolvency in the equity sense and its bankruptcy meaning. *Equity insolvency* exists when a debtor is unable to pay his debts as they mature. *Bankruptcy insolvency* is interpreted by the National Bankruptcy Act as a condition where the aggregate of a debtor's property at fair valuation is less than the amount of his existing liabilities [Section 1 (19)]. It is apparent that insolvency in the bankruptcy sense may exist without a condition of equity insolvency, e.g., where there has been a value shrinkage in noncurrent assets without a parallel reduction in the amount of long-term debt. It is perhaps more usual to find the converse—an insolvent debtor in the equity sense who is solvent by the bankruptcy definition.

Early in the history of the United States, the Congress was given constitutional authority to enact uniform bankruptcy laws. The first act was passed in 1800. Other laws were enacted in 1841 and 1867, after the repeal of predecessor statutes. The fourth and final National Bankruptcy Act was passed in 1898. Although the 1898 Act has been frequently amended, it remains currently effective in all states. Perhaps the most significant amendment thereto was the Chandler Act of 1938 which revised and enlarged many provisions of the 1898 statute.[1] The amended federal law currently contains 15 chapters, 7 relating to bankruptcy, 6 pertaining to debtor relief, and 2 which refer to Maritime Commission liens and railroad adjustments.[2] Certain Bankruptcy Rules governing forms, practice, and procedure took effect in October, 1973. To the extent these Rules are in conflict with the National Bankruptcy Act, as amended, the Rules override.

It is important that state *insolvency* legislation and jurisdiction be clearly distinguished from federal *bankruptcy* legislation and jurisdiction. Insolvency laws are the enactments of the several states relating to the equitable distribution of the resources of a distressed debtor, while the National Bankruptcy Act is the controlling federal statute in such proceedings. The federal law is accorded superior constitutional status, and the insolvency laws of the several states must necessarily be consistent therewith. The state statutes remain operative to the extent they do not controvert the federal Act.

Bankruptcy (National Bankruptcy Act)

A business enterprise confronted with financial failure may undertake reorganization or dissolution voluntarily or involuntarily under the aegis of federal or state law. However, an insolvent debtor's action taken under state laws resulting in voluntary or involuntary receivership automatically constitutes an "act of bankruptcy," thereby providing the basis for legal action under the National Bankruptcy Act.

It is the purpose of the National Bankruptcy Act to provide for an orderly and equitable distribution of a bankrupt debtor's property among his creditors; once the bankruptcy proceedings are terminated, the debtor is discharged of most of his unpaid debts (some are not dischargeable), after which he may initiate steps for financial rehabilitation and renew business operations.

---

[1] Currently two bankruptcy bills are pending before Congress. Among the proposed changes are the establishment of independent bankruptcy courts, the creation of a bankruptcy agency, uniform federal exemptions for individuals, and a consolidation of Chapters X and XI into one chapter for reorganizations.

[2] Hereafter, provisions of the National Bankruptcy Act will be cited by section number, enclosed in brackets, following the relevant provisions. The cited sections of the Act may be found under Title 11 of the United States Code Annotated by observing the cross referencing table provided in the U.S.C.A. The reader is referred to the U.S.C.A. for complete statements of the cited sections as well as related interpretations by the courts.

References to the Bankruptcy Rules are cited as Rule, followed by the number of the rule.

Who May Become a Bankrupt.   Any person, except a municipal, rail-road, insurance, or banking corporation or a building and loan associa-tion, is entitled to the benefits of the Act as a voluntary bankrupt. A volun-tary bankrupt initiates his procedure by filing a petition with the United States District Court. According to one bankruptcy authority, voluntary bankruptcies occur more than one hundred times as frequently as involun-tary ones.[3]

Any natural person, except a wage earner or farmer, and any moneyed, business, or commercial corporation, except a building and loan associa-tion, a municipal, railroad, insurance, or banking corporation, owing debts in the amount of $1,000 or over, may be adjudged an involuntary bank-rupt upon default or an impartial trial and shall be subject to the pro-visions and entitled to the benefits of the Act. The status of an alleged bankrupt as a wage earner or farmer shall be determined as of the time of the commission of the act of bankruptcy [Section 4].

Acts of Bankruptcy.   Before creditors can proceed to have a debtor adjudged bankrupt, the debtor must have committed an act of bankruptcy. A debtor has committed an act of bankruptcy if he has:

(1)   concealed, removed, or permitted to be concealed or removed any parts of his property, with intent to hinder, delay, or defraud his creditors or any of them; or

(2)   transferred, while insolvent, any portion of his property to one or more of his creditors with intent to prefer such creditors over his other creditors; or

(3)   suffered or permitted, while insolvent, any creditor to obtain a lien upon any of his property through legal proceedings and not having vacated or discharged such lien within thirty days from the date thereof or at least five days before the date set for any sale or other disposition of such property; or

(4)   made a general assignment for the benefit of his creditors; or

(5)   while insolvent or unable to pay his debts as they mature, procured, permitted, or suffered voluntarily or involuntarily the appointment of a receiver or trustee to take charge of his property; or

(6)   admitted in writing his inability to pay his debts and his willingness to be adjudged a bankrupt [Section 3].

Courts of Bankruptcy.   The District Courts of the United States are bankruptcy courts having exclusive original jurisdiction over bankruptcy matters. These courts conduct equity proceedings and may be referred to as courts of equity. Court officials include the District Judge, an appointed referee, and often a designated trustee (or trustees). A referee is appointed by the judge of the bankruptcy court for a six-year term and is normally authorized to conduct all necessary bankruptcy proceedings. The actions of the referee remain subject to review by the judge, and the referee must

---

[3] David G. Epstein, *Debtor-Creditor Relations In A Nutshell* (St. Paul, Minn.: West Publishing Co., 1973), p. 136.

render reports periodically to the court in respect to his findings of fact and conclusions of law.

The National Bankruptcy Act also creates the office of trustee. At the first meeting of the creditors of the bankrupt, a trustee is appointed. If the creditors fail to select a trustee, the court will make the appointment. Among other duties, trustees will:

(1) collect and reduce to money the property of the bankrupt estates, under the direction of the court, and close up the estates as expeditiously as is compatible with the best interests of the parties in interest;

(2) deposit all money received by them in designated depositories;

(3) account for and pay over to the estates under their control all interest received by them upon funds belonging to such estates;

(4) keep records and accounts showing all amounts and items of property received and from what sources, all amounts expended and for what purposes, and all items of property disposed of;

(5) examine all proofs of claims and object to the allowance of such claims as may be improper;

(6) furnish such information concerning the estates of which they are trustees and their administration as may be requested by parties in interest;

(7) report to the courts in writing the condition of the estates, the amounts of money on hand, and such other details as may be required by the courts, within the first month after their appointment and every two months thereafter, unless otherwise ordered by the court;

(8) make final reports and file final accounts with the courts fifteen days before the days fixed for the final meetings of the creditors; and

(9) lay before the final meetings of the creditors detailed statements of the administration of the estates [Section 47(a)].

When a petition in bankruptcy has been filed in a court of equity, a receiver often is selected to take possession of the debtor's property. His role is essentially that of a custodian. He serves until such time as the petition is either dismissed or a trustee is appointed and qualified. In some instances, the receiver may be continued as trustee.

Liquidation Sequence. Once a distressed debtor has been judicially determined a bankrupt, the progress of dissolution consists of four additional steps: (1) marshaling and protection of the debtor's property, (2) conversion of the noncash assets, (3) equitable distribution of the proceeds from conversion to those creditors having provable claims and in the order of their priority, and (4) formal discharge of the bankrupt debtor.

The trustee or receiver accepts custodial responsibility for the debtor's property for the purpose of preserving and protecting the interests of the several creditors. Legal title to the property vests in the trustee when it is surrendered to his custody. Upon being adjudged a bankrupt, or upon filing a voluntary petition, the debtor has the duty to prepare a schedule showing the amount and kind of his property, the location thereof and its money value, and a list of all his creditors, including all persons asserting contingent, unliquidated, or disputed claims, showing their residence, if known, and the amount due to or claimed by each of them, and the security held by them, if any. At least five days before the first meeting of his creditors the bankrupt must file a statement of his affairs in such form as the Supreme Court may prescribe [Section 7(a)].[4]

A creditor having a claim against a bankrupt estate must present a *proof of claim* within six months after the first creditors' meeting. A proof of claim consists of a statement in writing and signed by a creditor, setting forth the following: the claim; the consideration therefor; whether any, and if so, what securities are held therefor; whether any, and if so, what payments have been made thereon; and that the claim is justly owing from the bankrupt to the creditor [Section 57(a)].

Liabilities Proved and Allowed. Debts of the bankrupt which may be proved and allowed against his estate include, among others, those which are founded upon:

(1)   a fixed liability, as evidenced by a judgment, or an instrument in writing, absolutely owing at the time of the filing of the petition, whether then payable or not;

(2)   an open account, or a contract express or implied;

(3)   provable debts reduced to judgments after the filing of the petition and before the consideration of the bankrupt's application for discharge;

(4)   the right to recover damages in any action for negligence instituted prior to and pending at the time of the filing of the petition in bankruptcy; and

(5)   claims for anticipatory breach of contracts, executory in whole or in part, including unexpired leases of real or personal property [Section 63(a)].

Liabilities Having Priority. Certain classes of a distressed debtor's obligations must be fully satisfied before settlement is made with other creditors. A priority status attaches to the following debts, and distribution is made in the indicated order:

(1)   the actual and necessary costs and expenses of preserving the estate of the bankrupt subsequent to filing the petition, and the filing fees paid by creditors in involuntary cases (administration costs);

(2)   wages, not to exceed $600 to each claimant, which have been earned within three months before the date of the commencement of the proceeding, due to workmen, servants, clerks, or traveling or city salesmen on salary or commission basis, whole or part time, whether or not selling exclusively for the bankrupt;

(3)   taxes legally due and owing by the bankrupt to the United States or any State or any subdivision thereof which are not released by a discharge in bankruptcy; and

(4)   debts other than for taxes owing to any person, including the United States, who by the laws of the United States is entitled to priority, and rent owing to a landlord who is entitled to priority by applicable state law, *provided,*

---

[4] The time was changed by the Bankruptcy Rules to require filing with the petition in the case of voluntary bankruptcy and within ten days after adjudication if involuntary.

however, that such priority for rent to a landlord shall be restricted to the rent which is legally due and owing for the actual use and occupancy of the premises affected, and which accrued within three months before the date of bankruptcy [Section 64(a)].

Setoff or Counterclaim.   In all cases of mutual debts or mutual credits between the estate of a bankrupt and a creditor, one debt is set off against the other, and only the balance is allowed or paid [Section 68].

Discharge of Debtor.   Following the conversion of a debtor's assets and an equitable distribution of the proceeds among his several creditors, the debtor is released from all of his debts provable in bankruptcy. A discharge in the bankruptcy provides an effective release in respect to these debts, *except* such as:

(1)   are due as a tax levied by the United States, or any State, county, district, or municipality;

(2)   are liabilities for obtaining money or property by false pretenses or false representations or for willful and malicious conversion of the property of another; or for willful and malicious injuries to the person or property of another;

(3)   have not been duly scheduled in time for proof and allowance;

(4)   are for wages which have been earned within three months before the commencement of the proceedings in bankruptcy due to workmen, servants, clerks, or traveling or city salesmen, on salary or commission basis, whole or part time, whether or not selling exclusively for the bankrupt; or

(5)   are due for moneys of an employee received or retained by his employer to secure the faithful performance by such employee of the terms of a contract of employment [Section 17].

Assignment for Benefit of Creditors

Liquidation proceedings normally are carried out through formal bankruptcy *or* an informal assignment for the benefit of creditors. The latter proceeding is merely an arrangement whereby the corporate property is transferred to designated assignees (the assignees frequently are also creditors). The assignee compares to a trustee in bankruptcy proceedings. He takes possession of the debtor's assets, converts the noncash asset, makes distributions to creditors with due regard to the priority of their claims, and renders a final accounting upon a closing of the estate. Assignment may be preferred to bankruptcy proceedings in that the debtor has the authority to designate the liquidator (assignee), often enjoys reduced legal expenses, and has fewer constraints as to time in respect to conversion and ultimate distribution. Unlike bankruptcy proceedings, there is no formal discharge of the distressed debtor in an assignment for the benefit of creditors.

Many states have enacted statutes which provide for assignments. An assignment for the benefit of creditors constitutes an act of bankruptcy, however, and the assignee is compelled to surrender custody of the debtor's property should a petition in bankruptcy be filed.

The Statement of Affairs

Previous reference has been made to the importance of filing schedules of assets, liabilities, and exempt property by the bankrupt. Failure to file such reports may result in the debtor's loss of discharge or his suffering of other penalties. Among the reports of special importance is the *statement of affairs*. This statement, which details the realization proceeds expected from the conversion of the debtor's assets juxtaposed against the claims of secured and unsecured creditors, may be especially useful in aiding the debtor in determining the extent of his financial deficiency.[5]

The statement of affairs exhibits some of the properties of the familiar corporate balance sheet; yet, there are significant differences. Most importantly, the underlying assumption of business continuity is rejected in favor of a liquidation emphasis; manifestly, this has implications for the valuation of corporate assets. In general, expected realizable values are substituted for unamortized costs. In order to assign these values to individual assets, however, the "liquidation concept" must be more definitively formulated. For example, anticipated liquidation within 30 days often produces a different estimate of realizable value than a liquidation period of six months. Thus, if the ultimate liquidation period is indefinite, adequate disclosure may be better served by preparing more than one statement under different time assumptions. The classificational format of the balance sheet is essentially an ordered enumeration of assets in relative liquidity sequence, with liabilities grouped in two broad time-oriented classes. In the statement of affairs, however, the assets are classified according to their availability to creditors, viz., those pledged with fully secured creditors, those pledged with partially secured creditors, and those which are free or unencumbered. Similarly, liabilities are classed in terms of their legal preferences, viz., priority claims, obligations which are fully secured, obligations which are partially secured, and unsecured claims. It is evident that the statement of affairs is primarily oriented toward the legal status of claims against the enterprise rather than the cost of future service potentials. As an obvious corollary of this new emphasis, stockholders' equity accounts lose their significance in the statement of affairs. In fact, they are only included in a supporting statement, primarily as an explanation of the current insolvency condition.

Illustrative Problem. Preliminary to the preparation of a statement of affairs, a conventional balance sheet should be prepared, supported by additional supplementary data, including estimates of realization proceeds

---

[5] The Bankruptcy Rules provide for the filing of a schedule of all debts, a schedule of all property at market value, and a statement of affairs (a questionnaire concerning details of the business, as opposed to what accountants refer to as a "statement of affairs"). The schedule of debts contains the following categories: creditors with priority, creditors holding security, creditors having unsecured claims without priority [Rule 108(a) and (b)].

from noncash assets. Other relevant information should also be accumulated in respect to pledged assets and liabilities which are expected to emerge during the course of the liquidation proceedings.

The balance sheet of the Roman Company on March 31, 1977, is as follows:

THE ROMAN COMPANY
Balance Sheet
March 31, 1977

Assets

Cash	$ 1,850
Accounts receivable	21,200
Notes receivable	15,000
Merchandise	41,000
Arco common stock (60 shares at cost)	5,800
Land	6,500
Building (net of depreciation)	92,000
Machinery and equipment (net of depreciation)	43,000
	$226,350

Equities

Bank loan—First State Bank	$ 10,000
Notes payable	70,000
Accounts payable	90,625
Accrued wages	3,775
Accrued interest:	
Bank loan	375
Notes payable	600
Retained earnings [deficit]	[99,025]
Capital stock	150,000
	$226,350

Based upon an estimated interval of time for liquidation, the land is appraised at $7,800 and the building is estimated to have a current market value of $85,000. The machinery and equipment are valueless except as salvage, $8,000. Merchandise has a current salable value of $20,000. On March 31, the Arco common stock is quoted on the security exchange at 110. Receivables are estimated to be collectible according to the following schedule:

Notes receivable	100 percent
Accounts receivable:	
$10,000	100 percent
10,000	70 percent
1,200	Uncollectible

The First State Bank loan is secured by the Arco common stock, and the notes payable are secured by a first mortgage on the land and building.

The statement of affairs of the Roman Company is shown in Illustration 16–1.

Illustration 16–1

THE ROMAN COMPANY

Statement of Affairs
March 31, 1977

Assets

Book Value				Realizable Value
	Assets Pledged with Fully Secured Creditors:			
$ 6,500	Land	$ 7,800		
92,000	Building	85,000	$92,800	
	Notes payable	$70,000		
	Accrued interest	600	70,600	$22,200
	Assets Pledged with Partially Secured Creditors:			
5,800	Arco common stock		$ 6,600	
	Bank loan—First State Bank	$10,000		
	Accrued interest	375	10,375	
	Free Assets:			
1,850	Cash			1,850
15,000	Notes receivable			15,000
21,200	Accounts receivable			17,000
41,000	Merchandise			20,000
43,000	Machinery and equipment			8,000
	Realizable value of uncommitted assets			$84,050
	Liabilities having priority			3,775
	Net free assets			$80,275
	Estimated Deficiency to Unsecured Creditors			14,125
$226,350				$94,400

Equities

Book Value				Unsecured
	Liabilities Having Priority:			
$ 3,775	Accrued wages		$ 3,775	
	Fully Secured Creditors:			
70,000	Notes payable		$70,000	
600	Accrued interest		600	
	Partially Secured Creditors:			
	Bank loan—First State Bank:			
10,000	Principal		$10,000	
375	Accrued interest		375	
			$10,375	
	Arco common stock		6,600	$ 3,775
	Unsecured Creditors:			
90,625	Accounts payable			90,625
	Stockholders' Equity:			
150,000	Capital stock			
[99,025]	Retained earnings [deficit]			
$226,350				$94,400

Illustration 16–2

THE ROMAN COMPANY

Deficiency Account
March 31, 1977

Estimated losses:		Estimated gains:		
Accounts receivable	$ 4,200	Land	$	1,300
Merchandise	21,000	Arco common stock		800
Machinery and equipment ..	35,000	Capital stock		150,000
Building	7,000	Retained earnings [deficit] ..		[99,025]
		Estimated deficiency to un-		
		secured creditors		14,125
	$67,200		$	67,200

A *deficiency account* (Illustration 16–2) frequently is appended to the statement of affairs and provides supporting detail in respect to estimated gains and losses on realization, the algebraic sum of which, when added to the total stockholders' equity reflected in the balance sheet, explains the impairment of capital—the estimated deficiency to unsecured creditors.

Statement Annotations

Assets Pledged with Fully Secured Creditors. In this category are listed those assets having a fair valuation equal to, or in excess of, the debts for which they have been pledged as collateral.

Assets Pledged with Partially Secured Creditors. Under this heading are listed those assets having a fair valuation less than the amount of the debts for which they have been pledged to secure.

Free (or Uncommitted) Assets. These assets are unencumbered and are not otherwise identified with a specific liability. This includes that portion of assets pledged with fully secured creditors in excess of the amount of the related liability.

Liabilities Having Priority. These are debts which, by statute— Section 64(a)—must be liquidated before uncommitted assets are available for the payment of unsecured debts.

Fully Secured Liabilities. These are liabilities which are protected by the pledge of specific assets which are expected to realize at least as much as the amount of the related obligations.

Partially Secured Liabilities. These liabilities represent obligations of the debtor for which specific assets have been pledged, the estimated value of which is less than the related obligation. The amount of these liabilities not covered by secured assets reverts to the status of unsecured claims.

Unsecured Liabilities. These debts have no designated legal priority, and no specific property is available as collateral to insure their payment.

Stockholders' Equity. The balances of capital stock and retained earnings are entered only in the "book value" column in the statement of affairs. However, they are included in the deficiency account, indicating thereby the extent to which estimated gains and losses on realization can be absorbed by the existing stockholders' equity.

Special Problems

Reserves. Accountants are encouraged to limit use of the word "reserve" and to adopt more descriptive and more meaningful terminology. Notwithstanding the fact of poor terminological identification, these items must nonetheless be properly classified in the statement of affairs. When the term is used to describe a valuation account, the balance should be deducted from the related asset, with the "net" value of the asset extended to the book value column in the statement of affairs. In the case of liability "reserves," credit balances should be classified in a manner consistent with the priority and security provisions cited earlier. Indeed, such items in the liability category frequently have a priority status, such as "Reserve for Federal Income Taxes." Appropriations of retained earnings, or "surplus reserves," are elements of the stockholders' equity and should be so reported.

Contingent Liabilities. Since contingent liabilities, as such, have no place in the statement of affairs, their probable status by the end of the liquidation period must be ascertained and correctly described. For example, notes receivable which have been discounted, for which there is little likelihood of dishonor, should be omitted from the statement of affairs. In respect to those notes for which dishonor is likely, however, the face amount of the notes should be reported as a liability on the credit side of the statement and extended to the "unsecured" column.

Other "contingent" liabilities should be similarly reported in the statement of affairs as unsecured claims to the extent there is a reasonable probability that such an obligation will, in fact, exist within the period during which a claim may be filed.

Accrued Interest. Accrued interest receivable or payable should be added to the obligation to which it relates. In the event a note receivable is pledged to secure a debt, the interest accrued thereon is usually considered as additional security and is reported as a complement of the note. Similarly, accrued interest on notes payable should be associated with the related notes.

Prepaid Insurance. The appropriate treatment in the statement of affairs of unexpired premiums on insurance depends upon the circumstances of each case. Although there may be a determinable cash surrender value of an insurance policy, it is not available except upon cancellation of the policy; further, the cash surrender value may expire before the expected date at which liquidation will be completed. Accordingly, unless such cancellation is expected, it is usual to report unexpired premiums only in terms of book value, without an anticipation of any realizable value.

Discount on Capital Stock. In the event capital stock is sold at a discount, creditors often have a claim against the shareholders in the amount of the unpaid discount. If it is probable that the discount is recoverable from existing shareholders, i.e., it has a cash realizable value, then it is appropriate to report this value as an unencumbered asset, but only to the extent of the creditors' deficiency. However, because there may exist reasonable doubt as to the accuracy of other realizable values, it may be expedient to evaluate the discount at its total collectible amount— whether or not necessary to cover a creditor deficiency.

Extended Usefulness of the Statement of Affairs

The statement of affairs presently occupies a relatively unimportant position in the catalogue of accounting reports. Its status is at least partially related to the essentially ex post facto nature of the statement. It may, in fact, be categorized as a financial autopsy, as it reflects the undesirable financial circumstance which then exists, with an analysis of the individual value losses generating the impairment of capital.

It is not inconceivable, however, that the concepts embodied in the statement of affairs might be usefully employed in the forward planning of management. For example, in preparing financial statements for short-term credit purposes, the concept of value is often more significant than that of unexpired costs. Rather than modify or provide interpretive elaboration of the conventional balance sheet to reflect such value adjustments, such as lower of cost or market in respect to inventories—an essentially inconsistent position when related to the going-concern assumption—the accountant might profitably extend the use of the statement of affairs. With an accepted emphasis on realizable asset values and the legal status of debts, this statement may be a valuable tool for financial analysis and interpretation. By recognizing the need for unique financial statements for various special purposes, balance sheet concepts may be more easily integrated with the income determination objective without undesirable exceptions.

REORGANIZATION

As an alternative to liquidation, a distressed debtor may attempt to rehabilitate a financially floundering business through reorganization. Usually, the value of business resources to a going concern is greater than the realization proceeds which derive from forced liquidation. A debtor contemplating some form of continuity of corporate life, instead of immediate dissolution, has recourse to both judicial and nonjudicial remedies. Among the latter are agreements executed by the creditors to extend the settlement period, composition agreements, voluntary assignments for the benefit of creditors, and creditor management committees. Judicial remedies usually involve the creation of an equity receivership or formal reorganization under Chapter X or Chapter XI of the National Bankruptcy Act. Proceedings under Chapters X and XI are referred to as rehabilitative actions, whereas the other forms of relief discussed earlier are called "straight bankruptcies."

Nonjudicial Remedies

Extending the Settlement Period. Where the debtor's distress is clearly temporary in nature, it may be expedient—and advantageous— for his creditors to merely extend the period for the payment of outstanding obligations. This arrangement allows the debtor to continue management of the business, wherein he may be expected to convert such assets, without pain of forced liquidation, as will produce realization proceeds sufficient to liquidate existing debts. Such an agreement is often effective where the scale of business is small and there are relatively few creditors.

Composition Settlement. A settlement by composition refers to an arrangement, contractually entered into by the debtor and his creditors *and* between the several creditors, in which the creditors agree to accept less than original contract amounts in full payment of their claims. These settlements, which originate with the debtor, provide for ratable distribution of the debtor's assets in full discharge of his obligations. Usually, in circumstances where composition settlements are employed, the debtor is insolvent within the bankruptcy meaning of this expression.

If there is a small number of dissenting creditors, a composition may nonetheless be executed if the assenting creditors allow full, or some preferred, payment of the obligations of the dissenting group. Throughout the proceedings, the debtor must remain completely candid in respect to disclosing his total assets; he must demonstrate no unauthorized preference for any creditor. The means of payment are usually cash and/or notes. Such an arrangement frequently is favored by the creditors in that it often prevents costly delays in final debt retirement.

Voluntary Assignment for the Benefit of Creditors. An insolvent debtor may elect to convey his property by assignment to a trustee or assignee for the benefit of his creditors. The purpose of such assignment is to enable the debtor's representative to convert the property, as may be necessary, and to distribute the proceeds ratably among the creditors. If contractually agreed to by the several creditors, the assignment may result in the debtor's discharge from his debts. Should there remain any undistributed assets, they are returned by the trustee to the debtor. A voluntary assignment for the creditors' benefit constitutes an act of bankruptcy.

Creditor Management Committee. The creditor management committee is a form of debtor-creditor alliance which provides for creditor committee management of the debtor's business for the purposes of rehabilitation, reorganization, or eventual liquidation. The control of the business rests with the committee, which may elect to contribute new capital if it appears financially and operationally feasible. Frequently, it is necessary to make use of an extension of the settlement period as a vehicle of financial revival. Properties are normally returned to the debtor when obligations have been discharged or otherwise provided for.

Judicial Remedies

Should the debtor prefer to employ legal remedies instead of the non-judicial remedies outlined above, he may elect to enter a petition for equity receivership, or he may initiate reorganization proceedings under the debtor relief provisions of the National Bankruptcy Act.

Equity Receivership. Receivership for insolvent debtors may be a consequence of voluntary or involuntary petition. A court of equity having jurisdiction over such proceedings may be either a federal or state tribunal. A receiver is appointed by the court to receive custody of the debtor's property in order to prevent unwarranted attachments of the assets to the detriment of the creditors and the business. Normally the receiver operates the business with a view to rehabilitation, or failing that, an orderly liquidation. The receiver continues as the administrative and operating head of the business pending adoption of a plan of reorganization. If the terms of the proposed reorganization are not agreeable to dissenting creditors, it may become necessary to either "buy them off" or proceed with a judicial sale. In the event of sale, the proceeds of realization are equitably distributed to the recalcitrant creditors. Because the judicial sale is often costly and dilatory, and in order to safeguard minority interests, the court may establish an "upset" price below which bids are not accepted.

Equity receiverships which relate to large corporations are normally within the jurisdiction of the federal courts. However, because this type of litigation has generally proven to be unusually long and expensive, federal equity receiverships are not utilized as often as in the past; rather, distressed debtors are more frequently electing the debtor relief provisions of the National Bankruptcy Act.

Chapter X (National Bankruptcy Act). A petition for reorganization under Chapter X of the National Bankruptcy Act is filed in a United States District Court. The petition may be voluntarily initiated by the debtor corporation, or involuntarily filed by three or more creditors, or an indenture trustee acting in their behalf, whose liquidated (certain) claims aggregate $500 or more. This petition may be filed either before or after an adjudication in bankruptcy. Upon approval of the petition, the judge will either appoint a disinterested trustee, or continue the debtor in possession of the business assets. In the event that the debtor's liabilities exceed $250,000, a trustee *must* be appointed.

Upon appointment, the trustee will take title to the debtor's assets and endeavor to continue without interruption the normal operations of the business. Frequently, he will retain the operating personnel of the debtor. Upon appointment and qualification, the trustee, together with his other responsibilities:

(1)   shall, if the judge shall so direct, investigate the acts, conduct, property, liabilities, and financial condition of the debtor, the operation of its business and the desirability of the continuance thereof, and any other matter relevant to the proceeding or to the formulation of a plan, and report thereon to the judge;

(2)   shall report to the judge any facts ascertained by him pertaining to fraud, misconduct, mismanagement and irregularities, and to any causes of action available to the estate;

(3)   shall, at the earliest date practicable, prepare and submit a brief statement of his investigation of the property, liabilities, and financial condition of the debtor, the operation of its business and the desirability of the continuance thereof, in such form and manner as the judge may direct, to the creditors, stockholders, indenture trustees, the Securities and Exchange Commission, and such other persons as the judge may designate; and

(4)   shall give notice to the creditors and stockholders that they may submit to him suggestions for the formulation of a plan, or proposals in the form of plans, within a time therein named [Section 167].

Once a plan of reorganization has been prepared and filed with the court, all interested parties—including creditors and shareholders—are heard concerning any objections they may choose to interpose. The plan must in all respects be fair and equitable, preserving the previous priorities of the various interested parties. Additionally, the plan must be feasible. The debtor corporation to be reorganized must demonstrate the existence of sufficient working capital, sound credit potential, earnings of sufficient amount to meet fixed charges, and financially sound capitalization. Necessarily, there must be additional evidence of good management. The fairness and feasibility of the plan is clearly a function of the financial adjustments included therein. These may include capital restructuring, debt abatement or elimination, and a modification of interest rates. With respect to the valuation of assets of the debtor corporation in the reorganization process, the significant values are those which are expected to be realized on the basis of a going concern. These values often, although not inevitably, coincide with current market values.

If the debt is at least three million dollars, the Securities and Exchange Commission must issue an advisory report on the plan prior to court approval. Once the plan has been approved, it is presented to the creditors and shareholders for ratification. Before final confirmation, the plan must be formally agreed to in writing by those creditors holding two thirds in dollar amount of each class of claims filed and allowed. Solvent firms must receive the approval of the majority of each class of stock also. The reorganized debtor corporation continues thereafter with a new corporate life, subject only to such obligations as are imposed by the plan.

According to one authority, reorganizations under Chapter X are much less common than under Chapter XI.[6] However, many commentators contend that a firm must choose Chapter X when the reorganization plan will give rise to more than a minor adjustment of a large amount of publicly held debt.[7]

Chapter XI (National Bankruptcy Act). Unlike Chapter X, which is an option for corporations only, Chapter XI is available to any form of business. Only a debtor may initiate proceedings under Chapter XI. General creditors are the only parties affected by a Chapter XI reorganization whereas under Chapter X general and secured creditors and stockholders may be affected. Unlike in Chapter X where a court-appointed trustee controls the company, under Chapter XI the debtor company continues to control operations while it is working out a plan for paying its debts. However, the referee has the discretion to appoint a receiver to operate the business.[8]

The debtor's first step is to file a voluntary petition along with schedules and a statement of affairs [Rules 11–3 and 11–11]. The Court schedules a meeting of the creditors, and at this meeting the creditors may elect a creditors' committee [Rules 11–25(a) and 11–27(a)].

At their first meeting the creditors may examine the debtor on such matters as reasons for its financial difficulty and anticipated changes in the operation of its business. Among the duties of the creditors' committee are to consider whether the debtor's proposed plan is in the creditors' best interests and to report to the creditors on the progress of the proceeding. The committee may employ an auditor to render assistance.

The creditors' proposed plan must be approved in writing by a majority in number and amount of each class of creditors with filed and allowable claims. After acceptance of the plan has been attained, the court appoints an agent to distribute the funds.

During the rehabilitation period financial statements are prepared by accountants, one group representing the debtor and one the creditors. Since the purpose of Chapter XI is to rehabilitate rather than to liquidate, the statements are not prepared on the basis of liquidation values, but

---

[6] Epstein, *Debtor-Creditor Relations,* p. 272.

[7] Ibid., p. 283.

[8] In October 1975, W. T. Grant Co. filed a Chapter XI bankruptcy petition. Efforts of a stockholders' organization to have the proceedings converted to Chapter X were unsuccessful. In February, 1976 Grant's Creditors' Committee voted to seek to have the firm adjudicated a bankrupt, and that month a Bankruptcy Judge authorized liquidation. In April 1976 the firm was formally adjudged bankrupt. And so ended the saga of one firm's attempt at rehabilitation. Some others have been more successful.

rather somewhere between a going concern basis and a liquidation basis. The debtor's accountant is likely to prepare projections of results of operations and cash flow for the rehabilitation period. Accountants for the creditors may draw up a pro-forma balance sheet giving affect to the proposed plan of arrangement.

RECEIVERS' ACCOUNTS

In the event that a fiduciary assumes responsibility for the management of a distressed business, the appropriate scope of the system of accounts to be maintained must be established. Where a receiver is appointed by a court of equity, legal title to the assets of the debtor is usually conveyed to the receiver, who is then accountable to the court of his appointment, to the creditors, and to other interested parties. The receiver may elect to open new books of account, or he may continue the old books. The books of the distressed debtor are occasionally continued primarily for reasons of simplicity in record-keeping. Frequently, however, it may be desirable in an equity receivership to open new books to facilitate distinguishing between those obligations of the debtor which existed prior to the appointment of the receiver and those created after his appointment.

In the event that a separate set of accounts is maintained by the receiver, it is important to determine specifically which of the debtor's assets are to be conveyed to the receiver. His accountability necessarily relates only to those assets designated by the order of his appointment. The debts preexistent to the receivership usually remain in the debtor's books, although their liquidation frequently is the responsibility of the receiver. For this reason, the receiver should clearly identify "new" and "old" debts; similarly, a distinction should be made between the "old" assets, and those newly acquired during receivership. This is particularly important in respect to receivables. Receivable balances existing previous to the appointment of a receiver are the responsibility of the fiduciary only in respect to collection; accountability in respect to balances created subsequent to the receiver's appointment extends both to the prudence of granting credit and also to the effectiveness in account collection. Procedural details in accounting for an equity receivership are described in the illustrative example to follow.

Illustrative Problem. The account balances of the Insolvo Company on March 31, 1977, are:

Cash	$ 600
Accounts receivable	4,000
Notes receivable	5,800
Merchandise	18,000
Long-lived assets	24,000
Other assets	2,600
	$55,000

Allowance for doubtful accounts	$ 400
Accumulated depreciation	2,000
Accounts payable	21,000
Capital stock	40,000
Retained earnings [deficit]	[8,400]
	$55,000

A petition for equity receivership was filed by the Insolvo Company, and Charles Louis was appointed receiver to assume management responsibility on April 1. For the period April 1 through August 31, the following transactions were completed:

(1) All corporate assets were transferred to the receiver; existing debts of the Insolvo Company were continued in the corporate books of account; new accounts were opened by the receiver in respect to the transferred assets.

(2) Credit purchases of merchandise were $40,000.

(3) Credit sales amounted to $69,000; cash sales were $4,000.

(4) Collections of cash were made on:

Notes receivable	$ 4,800
Accounts receivable (old)	2,100
Accounts receivable (new)	51,000

(5) Payments were made by the receiver as follows:

Accounts payable (old)	$16,000
Accounts payable (new)	34,000
Operating expenses	2,500
Receiver's expenses	1,000

(6) Adjustments recorded on August 31 by the receiver were:

Depreciation (5 months)	$1,200
Estimated doubtful accounts:	
Accounts receivable (old)	950
Accounts receivable (new)	1,600
Accounts written off:	
Accounts receivable (old)	400
Notes receivable	1,000

(7) Closing entries were made by both the receiver and the Insolvo Company on August 31; unsold merchandise on this date was $16,000.

Entries for these transactions are journalized in Illustration 16–3.

A working paper which combines the accounts of the corporation and the receiver (before giving effect to closing entries) for the purpose of preparing conventional financial statements is shown in Illustration 16–4. The formal statements may be easily extracted therefrom.

Illustration 16–3

Receiver's Books

(1) Cash 600
    Accounts receivable (old) 4,000
    Notes receivable 5,800
    Merchandise, April 1 18,000
    Long-lived assets 24,000
    Other assets 2,600
        Allowance for doubtful accounts (old) ... 400
        Accumulated depreciation ... 2,000
        Insolvo Company—in receivership ... 52,600

(2) Purchases 40,000
        Accounts payable (new) 40,000

(3) Cash 4,000
    Accounts receivable (new) 69,000
        Sales 73,000

(4) Cash 57,900
        Notes receivable 4,800
        Accounts receivable (old) ... 2,100
        Accounts receivable (new) ... 51,000

(5) Accounts payable (new) 34,000
    Insolvo Company—in receivership ... 16,000
    Operating expenses 2,500
    Receiver's expenses 1,000
        Cash 53,500

Corporation's Books

(1) Charles Louis, receiver 52,600
    Allowance for doubtful accounts ... 400
    Accumulated depreciation 2,000
        Cash 600
        Accounts receivable 4,000
        Notes receivable 5,800
        Merchandise 18,000
        Long-lived assets 24,000
        Other assets 2,600

(2) No entry.

(3) No entry.

(4) No entry.

(5) Accounts payable 16,000
        Charles Louis, receiver ... 16,000

(6) Depreciation expense 1,200
    Bad debts expense 2,550
        Accumulated depreciation 1,200
        Allowance for doubtful accounts (old) .. 950
        Allowance for doubtful accounts (new) .. 1,600

    Bad debts expense 1,000
    Allowance for doubtful accounts (old) 400
        Notes receivable 1,000
        Accounts receivable (old) 400

(7) Sales 73,000
    Merchandise, August 31 16,000
        Merchandise, April 1 18,000
        Purchases 40,000
        Operating expenses 2,500
        Receiver's expenses 1,000
        Bad debts expense 3,550
        Depreciation expense 1,200
        Income summary 22,750

    Income summary 22,750
        Insolvo Company—in receivership 22,750

(6) No entry.

(7) Charles Louis, receiver 22,750
        Income summary 22,750

    Income summary 22,750
        Retained earnings 22,750

Illustration 16–4

THE INSOLVO COMPANY—IN RECEIVERSHIP

Combined Account Working Paper
For Five Months Ended August 31, 1977

	Receiver's Accounts	Insolvo Accounts	Eliminations Dr.	Eliminations Cr.	Income Statement	Balance Sheet
Cash	9,000					9,000
Accounts receivable (old)	1,500					1,500
Accounts receivable (new)	18,000					18,000
Merchandise, April 1	18,000				18,000	
Long-lived assets	24,000					24,000
Other assets	2,600					2,600
Purchases	40,000				40,000	
Operating expenses	2,500				2,500	
Receiver's expenses	1,000				1,000	
Depreciation expense	1,200				1,200	
Bad debts expense	3,550				3,550	
Charles Louis, receiver		36,600		(1) 36,600		
	121,350	36,600				
Merchandise, August 31	16,000					16,000
Net income					22,750	
					89,000	71,100
Allowance for doubtful accounts (old)	950					950
Allowance for doubtful accounts (new)	1,600					1,600
Accumulated depreciation	3,200					3,200
Accounts payable (old)		5,000				5,000
Accounts payable (new)	6,000					6,000
Capital stock		40,000				40,000
Retained earnings [deficit]		[8,400]				[8,400]
Sales	73,000				73,000	
Insolvo Company—in receivership	36,600		(1) 36,600			
	121,350	36,600				
Merchandise, August 31	16,000				16,000	
Net income						22,750
			36,600	36,600	89,000	71,100

In the event that the receivership is terminated on August 31, a return of the corporate management to Insolvo officials by Charles Louis would be recorded by an entry in the books of the receiver as follows:

The Insolvo Company—in receivership	59,350	
Allowance for doubtful accounts (old)	950	
Allowance for doubtful accounts (new)	1,600	
Accumulated depreciation	3,200	
Accounts payable (new)	6,000	
Cash		9,000
Accounts receivable (old)		1,500
Accounts receivable (new)		18,000
Merchandise		16,000
Long-lived assets		24,000
Other assets		2,600

The contra entry in the Insolvo Company books is:

Cash	9,000	
Accounts receivable	19,500	
Merchandise	16,000	
Long-lived assets	24,000	
Other assets	2,600	
Allowance for doubtful accounts		2,550
Accumulated depreciation		3,200
Accounts payable		6,000
Charles Louis, receiver		59,350

REALIZATION AND LIQUIDATION ACCOUNT

Conventional financial statements often reflect only an ancillary objective of a fiduciary; it may be more important to summarize periodically the liquidation and distribution activities of the fiduciary. A special report which accommodates this objective is the *realization and liquidation account*. The reference to *account* in the title of the report accents the traditional format of the statement. Other arrangements of the account information have been suggested and are referred to subsequently in this chapter.

The realization and liquidation account is essentially a statement of accountability, reflecting the activities of the fiduciary—either a receiver or a trustee—in converting the debtor's noncash assets and proceeding with the orderly distribution of the proceeds in settlement of the debtor's several liabilities. To this report is normally appended the fiduciary's cash account. The orthodox report form consists essentially of three principal divisions. These basic segments are outlined as follows:

Assets

Assets to be realized	xxx	Assets realized (conversion proceeds)	xxx
Assets acquired (or discovered)	xxx	Assets not realized	xxx

Liabilities

Liabilities liquidated	xxx	Liabilities to be liquidated	xxx
Liabilities not liquidated	xxx	Liabilities incurred	xxx

Revenues and Expenses; Gains and Losses

Supplementary charges	xxx	Supplementary credits	xxx

A summation of the debits in the three statement categories juxtaposed against the summation of credits will disclose an imbalance, which may be described as the net gain or loss for the liquidation period.

Using the data for the receivership previously discussed, the conventional realization and liquidation account takes the form shown in Illustration 16–5. The receiver's Cash account is given following:

Cash

(1) Balance, March 31	600	(5) Accounts payable (old)	16,000
(3) Sales	4,000	(5) Accounts payable (new)	34,000
(4) Accounts receivable (old)	2,100	(5) Operating expenses	2,500
(4) Accounts receivable (new)	51,000	(5) Receiver's expenses	1,000
(4) Notes receivable	4,800	Balance, August 31	9,000
	62,500		62,500
Balance, August 31	9,000		

The Insolvo Company's stockholders' equity accounts are:

Capital Stock

		(1) Balance, March 31	40,000

Retained Earnings

(1) Balance, March 31	8,400	Net income (April 1 to August 31)	22,750

The use of the numeric codes to identify contra elements in the realization and liquidation account indicates that the statement may be easily prepared by entering the transactions of the fiduciary directly into the relevant statement categories. This connective notation would not, however, appear in the formal report.

Illustration 16–5

THE INSOLVO COMPANY
CHARLES LOUIS—RECEIVER

Realization and Liquidation Account
April 1, 1977 to August 31, 1977

Assets to Be Realized:				
(1) Accounts receivable (old)	4,000			
Less: Allowance for doubtful accounts (old)	400	3,600		
(1) Notes receivable		5,800		
(1) Merchandise		18,000		
(1) Long-lived assets	24,000			
Less: Accumulated depreciation	2,000	22,000		
(1) Other assets		2,600		
Assets Acquired:				
(3) Accounts receivable (new)		69,000		
Supplementary charges:				
(2) Purchases		40,000		
(5) Operating expenses		2,500		
(5) Receiver's expenses		1,000		
Liabilities Liquidated:				
(5) Accounts payable (old)		16,000		
(5) Accounts payable (new)		34,000		
Liabilities Not Liquidated:				
Accounts payable (old)		5,000		
Accounts payable (new)		6,000		
Net Income		22,750		
		248,250		

Liabilities to Be Liquidated:				
(1) Accounts payable (old)				21,000
Liabilities Incurred:				
(2) Accounts payable (new)				40,000
Supplementary Credits:				
(2) Sales				73,000
Assets Realized:				
(4) Accounts receivable (old)				2,100
(4) Accounts receivable (new)				51,000
(4) Notes receivable				4,800
Assets Not Realized:				
Accounts receivable (old)		1,500		
Less: Allowance for doubtful accounts (old)		950		550
Accounts receivable (new)		18,000		
Less: Allowance for doubtful accounts (new)		1,600		16,400
Merchandise				16,000
Long-lived assets		24,000		
Less: Accumulated depreciation		3,200		20,800
Other assets				2,600
				248,250

Statement Annotations

Assets to Be Realized. Included in this category are the *carrying values* of all assets of the debtor at the date of the fiduciary's appointment (or at the beginning of the current period if the statement is not a cumulative record of fiduciary activities).

Assets Acquired. These are additional assets which are acquired (or discovered) during the period of fiduciary accountability.

Assets Realized. This description reflects the extent of conversion of noncash assets, with the *realization proceeds* therefrom the appropriate value measure.

Assets Not Realized. This summarizes the assets on hand at the date of the preparation of the statement, usually valued at the same amount indicated in the original accountability (assets to be realized or assets acquired).

Liabilities to Be Liquidated. These obligations of the debtor are those existing at the date of appointment of the fiduciary (or the beginning of the current period if the statement is not a cumulative record of fiduciary activities).

Liabilities Incurred. These liabilities are the additional obligations assumed by the fiduciary during the period of his accountability.

Liabilities Liquidated. These are the debt cancellations during the period, identified by creditor class.

Liabilities Not Liquidated. These are the unpaid claims existing at the end of the period to which the statement refers.

Supplementary Charges. For the most part these are the expenses incurred during the period of receivership, although they do not include asset expirations or specific losses on the conversion of noncash assets.

Supplementary Credits. These credits include revenues earned during the period, other than amortization of deferred income items; specific gains on the conversion of noncash assets are not included.

Special Problems

The reader will observe that the net income (or loss) for the period is the algebraic sum of the debit and credit balances in the above 10 categories. Additionally, it is important to note that because asset credits are expressed in terms of realization proceeds, net income (or loss) is partially explained in terms of the changes in asset categories as well as by the supplementary charges and credits for the period.

Sales and Purchases. The fiduciary may record merchandise purchased as either "assets acquired," or as "supplementary charges." Similarly, sales may be recorded as either "assets realized," or as "supplementary credits." If operating transactions are relatively numerous, the supplementary charge-credit categories are preferred.

Cash Discounts. The fiduciary may choose between one of two alternative methods in recording cash discounts in respect to receivables and payables. For accounts payable, the amount of the obligation net of discounts and allowances may be debited to "liabilities liquidated" when payment is made. Although the discount and allowance variance between "liabilities to be liquidated" and "liabilities liquidated" is not specifically identified by this treatment, the variance nonetheless enters the calculation of realization gain or loss, as there will be no remaining balance in "liabilities not liquidated."

If the fiduciary should elect to debit "liabilities liquidated" with the invoice billing (gross) when payment is made, then a contra credit equal to the amount of discounts and allowances will appear as a "supplementary credit." This purchase discount and allowance credit is again a factor in the calculation of realization gain or loss, although in this instance it is separately identified.

A parallel accounting treatment may be applied to receivable balances and related sales discounts and allowances.

Depreciation and Uncollectibles. Depreciation expense and estimated bad debts usually are not separately identified in the realization and liquidation account. They are reflected, however, in the estimated period-end balances in the accumulated depreciation and allowance for uncollectibles accounts, which are reported contra in "assets not realized." The expenses are thus factors in the calculation of net income or loss for the period.

Accruals. Where the amounts of accrued income items in the "assets to be realized" category are subsequently realized at larger amounts, two alternative accounting treatments are available. The accountant may credit "assets realized" with the amount accrued at the start of the period, crediting the additional amount collected to "supplementary credits." Or, the increase in the amount of the accrual since the start of the period may be entered as accrued interest in "assets acquired," with a contra credit to "supplementary credits." The subsequent collection may then be recorded by a credit to "assets realized." Comparable treatment may be accorded accrued expenses.

Favorable or Unfavorable Settlement of Liabilities. In the event that the creditors agree to accept less than face value for their obligations, the settlement discount should be preferably reported as a "supplementary credit," with the total amount of the canceled obligation reported as "liabilities liquidated." In the event a premium payment is required in order to liquidate an overdue indebtedness, accounting treatment would parallel that for a discount settlement; accordingly, the amount of the premium should be entered as a "supplementary charge."

In measuring gain or loss on the favorable settlement of liabilities, recognition must also be given to the reasonableness of the interest rate on the new debt. *FASB Interpretation No. 2, "Imputing Interest on Debt*

Arrangements Made Under the Federal Bankruptcy Act," states in this regard:

APB Opinion No. 21 applies to notes issued by a debtor in a reorganization, arrangement, or under other provisions of the Federal Bankruptcy Act. A note issued under such circumstances in exchange (in whole or in part) for an existing note or notes shall be considered a "note exchanged for property" for purposes of applying *APB Opinion No. 21*. In addition, an existing note shall be considered as originating in a reorganization, arrangement, or under other provisions of the Federal Bankruptcy Act and therefore as being a new note if its original terms are modified, altered, or otherwise changed as a part of the agreement with creditors. Accordingly, interest shall be imputed by applying *APB Opinion No. 21* if the new note does not specify interest or specifies an interest rate which is unreasonable in the particular circumstances.

Illustrative Problem—Alternative Statement Form

When continuing the business operations is a significant part of the trustee's responsibilities, the conventional account form of the realization and liquidation statement is often restructured in a columnar format with emphasis on both operating results and liquidation activities. This is illustrated below.

Account balances of the Crescent Company on May 1, 1977, were as follows:

Cash	$ 900	Allowance for doubtful	
		accounts	$ 700
Notes receivable	8,000	Accumulated depreciation	1,400
Accounts receivable	14,000	Accounts payable	26,000
Merchandise	26,000	Capital stock	40,000
Equipment	8,600	Retained earnings [deficit]	[10,600]
	$57,500		$ 57,500

The creditors of the Crescent Company selected a trustee, Paul Martin, to operate the business until conditions warranted its return to the corporate management. Transactions from May 1 through November 1, 1977, were:

(1)   Additional equipment was discovered, value $1,100.
(2)   Merchandise was purchased on account, $50,000.
(3)   Sales were: credit, $84,000; cash, $10,500.
(4)   Collections were made as follows: notes receivable, $7,000; accounts receivable (old), $9,200; accounts receivable (new), $74,000.
(5)   Payments made by the fiduciary were: accounts payable (old), $21,000; accounts payable (new), $16,000; operating expenses, $9,000; ABC 5 percent bonds, $1,600; trustee's expenses, $5,000. Discounts taken on accounts payable (old) were $400; on accounts payable (new), $360.

(6)   Accounts receivable (old) written off were $550; the remaining balance of notes receivable was considered uncollectible.

(7)   November 1, 1977, adjustments are required in respect to—

Taxes accrued since May 1 .... $800
Depreciation, May 1 to November 1 940
Estimated uncollectible accounts (required balances in allowance accounts):
   Old accounts 600
   New accounts 780

(8)   Merchandise inventory on November 1 was $24,000. Management of the business was returned to officers of the Crescent Company on November 1.

The statement of realization, liquidation, and operations is shown in Illustration 16–6. Although the inclusion of the corporation equity accounts implies that the receiver is using the "old" books, only minor modifications are required to reflect the accounts in a "new" set of books established by the receiver. Additionally, more formal summaries of results of operations and realization and liquidation proceedings may be prepared from this detailed statement of the trustee's activities.

QUESTIONS

1.   Who may initiate a petition for the *voluntary* dissolution of a corporation? The *involuntary* dissolution of a corporation?

2.   List three "acts of bankruptcy." Why is the committing of such an act significant?

3.   What is the liquidation sequence once a debtor has been judicially determined a bankrupt?

4.   Certain classes of a distressed debtor's liabilities must be fully satisfied before other creditors can receive a settlement. What are they?

5.   What is a "statement of affairs"? What distinguishes this statement from the conventional balance sheet?

6.   How should contingent liabilities be reported in the statement of affairs?

7.   Can you project an extension in the usefulness of a statement of affairs for financially prospering enterprises—the going concerns?

8.   Briefly describe what is meant by an "equity receivership."

9.   What unique classification and descriptive distinctions should be made in the set of accounts that are prepared to record the actions of the receiver in a reorganization?

10.   What purpose is served by the preparation of the realization and liquidation account? In outline, cite the several categories found in the realization and liquidation account.

Illustration 16–6

THE CRESCENT COMPANY—IN RECEIVERSHIP
PAUL MARTIN, TRUSTEE

Realization, Liquidation, and Operations
For Six Months Ended November 1, 1977

Debits	Balances, May 1	Transactions and Adjustments — Debit	Transactions and Adjustments — Credit	Profit and Loss — Realization and Liquidation Dr. [Cr.]	Profit and Loss — Trading Dr. [Cr.]	Balances, November 1
Cash	900	(3) 10,500 (4) 90,200	(5) 52,600			49,000
Assets to be realized:						
Notes receivable	8,000		(4) 7,000	1,000		–0–
Accounts receivable (old)	14,000		(4) 9,200 (6) 550			4,250
Allowance for doubtful accounts (old)	[700]	(6) 550	(7) 450			[600]
Merchandise, May 1	26,000		(8) 26,000			–0–
Equipment	8,600					8,600
Accumulated depreciation	[1,400]		(7) 940			[2,340]
Assets discovered:						
Equipment		(1) 1,100				1,100
Assets acquired:						
Accounts receivable (new)		(3) 84,000	(4) 74,000			10,000
Allowance for doubtful accounts (new)			(7) 780			[780]
ABC bonds		(5) 1,600				1,600
Merchandise, November 1		(8) 24,000				24,000
	55,400					94,830

Credits

Liabilities to be liquidated:						
Accounts payable (old)	26,000	(5) 21,400				4,600
Liabilities incurred:						
Accounts payable (new)		(5) 16,360	(2) 50,000			33,640
Accrued taxes			(7) 800			800
Stockholders' equity:						
Capital stock	40,000		(1) 1,100			40,000
Deficit	[10,600]					[9,500]
Supplementary charges:						
Purchases of merchandise		(2) 50,000			50,000	
Trustee's expenses		(5) 5,000		5,000		
Operating expenses		(5) 9,000			9,000	
Taxes		(7) 800			800	
Depreciation		(7) 940			940	
Bad debts expense		(7) 780			780	
Loss on realization of accounts receivable (old)		(7) 450		450		
Merchandise, May 1		(8) 26,000			26,000	
Supplementary credits:						
Merchandise, November 1			(8) 24,000		[24,000]	
Sales of merchandise			(3) 94,500		[94,500]	
Discount on purchases			(5) 760		[760]	
Loss on realization				6,450		[6,450]
Profit on trading					[31,740]	31,740
	55,400	342,680	342,680	6,450		94,830

EXERCISES

Exercise 16–1

An accountant is often confronted with problems relating to bankruptcy proceedings. The following items relate to pertinent points of law with which he should be familiar. Determine whether each legal conclusion is true or false according to bankruptcy law. For items which are false, explain why they are false.

a. Insolvency in the bankruptcy sense is a financial status in which the aggregate fair value of the assets of an entity is not sufficient to pay outstanding liabilities.
b. A preference in bankruptcy prefers one creditor over the others.
c. Acts of Bankruptcy include concealing, mutilating or falsifying books of account in contemplation of bankruptcy.
d. The Federal Bankruptcy Act specifically grants the Federal District Courts exclusive original jurisdiction over bankruptcy proceedings.
e. The filing of a voluntary petition in bankruptcy does not automatically operate as an adjudication or determination that the petitioner is bankrupt.
f. An involuntary petition in bankruptcy may be filed only if the debtor has committed an act of bankruptcy.

(AICPA adapted)

Exercise 16–2

Refer to the introductory facts and instructions of Exercise 16–1 to solve this problem.

a. The federal Bankruptcy Act considers a partnership as an entity separate from the partners.
b. Federal, state and local taxes are discharged by bankruptcy.
c. Insolvency in the bankruptcy sense is the same as insolvency in the equity sense.
d. A trustee in a bankruptcy proceeding is usually elected by the creditors.
e. A priority in a bankruptcy proceeding is given for administration costs including accountants' and attorneys' fees.
f. A referee in a bankruptcy proceeding is elected by a majority of the creditors having provable claims.

(AICPA adapted)

Exercise 16–3

Each of the following relates to points of bankruptcy law. Select the one BEST answer for each of the following items.

1. A voluntary petition in bankruptcy may
   a. Not be filed by a person who has income in excess of $10,000 per year.
   b. Not be filed by a self-employed professional.
   c. Be filed only if insolvency, in the bankruptcy sense, is at least $1,500.
   d. Be filed by an individual who is solvent in the bankruptcy sense.

2. Of the following items, the highest priority for payment in full before general creditors' claims in a bankruptcy proceeding is assigned to
    a. Wages, in a limited amount, if earned within three months preceding bankruptcy.
    b. Wages owed to an insolvent employee.
    c. Administration costs of bankruptcy.
    d. Unpaid federal income taxes.

3. Under Chapter XI of the Bankruptcy Act, a plan to be accepted and confirmed by the Court
    a. Must be accepted by all creditors.
    b. May be approved by a majority of creditors by number.
    c. May be approved by one-third of the creditors by number if their claims equal two-thirds of provable claims.
    d. Requires approval of a majority both as to number of creditors and amount of claims of creditors where claims have been proved and allowed.

4. Insolvency in the bankruptcy sense
    a. Is the same as insolvency in the equity sense.
    b. Must be present if the debtor seeks to file a voluntary petition in bankruptcy.
    c. Is normally easier to establish than insolvency in the equity sense.
    d. Is a financial status in which the liabilities exceed the aggregate fair value of the assets.

(AICPA adapted)

Exercise 16–4

Each of the following relates to points of bankruptcy law. Select the one BEST answer for each of the following items.

1. Which of the following statements *best* describes a composition agreement unanimously agreed to by all creditors?
    a. It provides for the appointment of a receiver to take over and operate the debtor's business.
    b. It is subject to approval by a federal district court judge.
    c. It provides for a discharge of the debts included in the composition agreement upon performance by the debtor.
    d. It binds only those creditors who do *not* subsequently withdraw from the agreement prior to its consummation.

2. Dexter had assets of $80,000 and liabilities of $100,000, all unsecured. He owed $25,000 to each of the following: Petrie, Dey, Mabley, and Norris. Petrie, Dey, and Mabley agreed with each other and with Dexter to accept 70 cents on the dollar in immediate satisfaction of their debts. Under these circumstances
    a. The agreement is void for lack of consideration.
    b. The agreement would *not* constitute an act of bankruptcy.
    c. Norris would be bound by the agreement.
    d. The agreement described is an assignment for the benefit of creditors.

3. Ted Dolson has filed a voluntary petition in bankruptcy. His assets are listed as $4,200 and his liabilities $18,750. His creditors include (1) three employees who have *not* been paid wages for six weeks at $100 per week per employee, (2) the United States government for $6,900 in back income and social security taxes, (3) his former wife for back alimony payments of $3,000, and (4) suppliers for goods purchased on open account for $7,050. In this situation

    a. All the debts in question are dischargeable in bankruptcy.

    b. Claims must be filed within three months of the filing of the petition in bankruptcy.

    c. The wage earners have the first priority after administration costs.

    d. The United States government claim will take precedence over the security interests of secured creditors.

(AICPA adapted)

Exercise 16–5

For several years Martin supplied raw materials to Western, Inc., who processed the goods into a finished product for sale to retail customers.

Martin supplied goods to Western on credit terms, and to secure his claim for unpaid goods, Martin obtained and properly perfected a "floating lien" on all of the goods sold to Western.

Six months ago Martin heard that Western, Inc., was in financial difficulty and stopped selling goods to the firm. Martin was not paid by Western for several shipments of goods and heard that recently Western made a general assignment for the benefit of its creditors. Also Martin heard that a group of Western's creditors may attempt to place Western into bankruptcy.

Required:

a. Has Western committed an "act of bankruptcy"? Explain.

b. Is the commission of an "act of bankruptcy" necessary to become a voluntary bankrupt? Explain.

c. Under what circumstances may Western's creditors proceed to have Western adjudicated an involuntary bankrupt?

d. Assume that Western's creditors may proceed to have it adjudicated an involuntary bankrupt. What action would they have to take in order to commence a bankruptcy proceeding?

e. Will the number of creditors required to commence an involuntary bankruptcy proceeding vary depending upon the number of Western's creditors? Explain.

f. How will Martin be treated in the bankruptcy proceedings if Western is adjudicated a bankrupt? Explain.

(AICPA adapted)

Exercise 16–6

You are to determine whether each of the legal conclusions is true or false according to the general principles of bankruptcy law.

a. In order for a person to be adjudged a bankrupt under the Bankruptcy Act—
   (1) He must owe debts totaling more than $2,000.
   (2) There must be at least three creditors.
   (3) A petition in bankruptcy must be filed by a majority of creditors.
   (4) The creditor must agree to the commencement of bankruptcy proceedings.
   (5) A petition in bankruptcy must be filed.
b. Acts of bankruptcy include a debtor—
   (6) Making a fraudulent conveyance.
   (7) Intentionally making a preference.
   (8) Making a general assignment for the benefit of creditors.
   (9) Orally admitting his willingness to be adjudged a bankrupt.
   (10) Requesting the appointment of a receiver immediately before becoming insolvent.
c. Bankruptcy proceedings may be instituted against any person or corporation, including—
   (11) A married woman.
   (12) A municipal corporation.
   (13) A banking corporation.
   (14) A building and loan corporation.
   (15) A partnership.
d. Classes of claims which have priority under the provisions of the Bankruptcy Act include—
   (16) Expenses of bankruptcy administration.
   (17) Wages earned within one year before the date of bankruptcy.
   (18) Debts of less than $50.
   (19) Taxes.
   (20) Claims of creditors which are outstanding for more than three years.
e. Debts discharged by completion of bankruptcy proceedings and discharge of the debtor include—
   (21) Contract obligations which are not due until three years following the act of bankruptcy.
   (22) Trade accounts payable.
   (23) Taxes.
   (24) Debts incurred within one month after the bankrupt's discharge.
   (25) A debt arising from the commission of a willful injury.

(AICPA adapted)

Exercise 16–7

In the course of examining the financial statements of Superior Systems, Inc., the financial vice president discloses that the corporation has a serious collection problem with one of its customers, Vizar Components, Inc. Vizar is approximately $10,000 in arrears; its checks have been returned for insufficient funds. Other creditors have similar claims against Vizar.

You have also learned that the principal creditors, including Superior, have held a meeting to consider possible alternative courses of action. During the meeting, an examination of the financial statements of Vizar revealed that it was in a difficult current position, but that it had sufficient assets to meet liabilities in the event of a bankruptcy proceeding. The meeting also revealed that Vizar's problems had built up over the past two years due to poor management. The company appears to have significant potential to return to profitability if properly managed.

Required:

a. What are the chief objections to proceeding against Vizar in bankruptcy? Explain.
b. What are the viable alternatives to a bankruptcy proceeding? Explain.

(AICPA adapted)

Exercise 16–8

During the examination of the financial statements of Delta Corporation, you note that as of September 30, 1978:

1. Current liabilities exceed current assets.
2. Total assets substantially exceed total liabilities.
3. Cash position is poor and current payables are considerably in arrears.
4. Trade and secured creditors are pressing for payment and several lawsuits have been commenced againt Delta.

Further investigation reveals the following:

1. On August 31, 1978, Delta made a $1,000 payment to Oliveros on a $20,000 mortgage indebtedness over one year in arrears. The fair-market value of the mortgaged property is $35,000.
2. On September 20, 1978, a trade creditor, Miller, obtained a judgment against Delta which under applicable law constitutes a lien on Delta's real property.
3. On September 22, 1978, Delta paid a substantial amount to Helms, a supplier, on an account over one year old.
4. On September 27, 1978, Delta executed and delivered a financing statement to Honea, a vendor, from whom Delta had purchased some new machinery six months earlier. Honea duly filed and perfected the financing statement.

Required:

a. As of September 30, 1978, did any of the above transactions legally constitute acts of bankruptcy? Explain.
b. As of September 30, 1978, could the creditors of Delta file an involuntary petition in bankruptcy against Delta if a sufficient number of them having a sufficient amount of claims decide to do so? Explain.
c. Independent of your answers to parts *a* and *b,* assume the same facts set out above except that Delta's total liabilities exceed total assets and that on October 2, 1978, Delta filed a voluntary petition in bankruptcy, and a Trustee has been appointed.
   (1)   What are the rights, if any, of the Trustee against each of the creditors involved in the four transactions stated in the problem? Explain.

(2)   What are the general requirements for creditors to be entitled to vote on and participate in a bankruptcy proceeding? Explain for each of the four creditors involved whether he meets these requirements. Why?

(AICPA adapted)

PROBLEMS

Problem 1

I. M. Train, toy manufacturer, on October 31, 1977, prepared the following enumeration of resources and creditor claims:

Resources:
Petty cash, $250, including expense vouchers for $119.
Cash, $2,615.
Accounts receivable, $3,680, of which $3,380, are believed to be collectible.
Toy materials and supplies, $12,000; estimated market value, $8,400.
Toys in process, $8,100; estimated market value, $2,000.
Building, $20,000; estimated market value, $9,000.
Display equipment, $11,800; estimated market value, $8,200.
Claims:
Accounts payable:

Gem Supply Company	$ 2,800
Ornamental Trinkets, Inc.	6,300
R. M. Brown	15,000
A. K. Moyer	1,700

Notes payable:
American State Bank, $20,000. The display equipment is pledged as collateral.
Texas Finance Company, $15,000. Unsecured notes receivable, $10,000, and warehouse receipts for finished goods are pledged as collateral. The finished goods (manufactured toys) have a book value of $8,000 and an estimated current value of $7,500. The notes receivable are estimated to be fully collectible.
Accrued wages, $1,750.

Required:

a.   Prepare a statement of affairs as of October 31, 1977.
b.   Prepare a schedule of payments to creditors on this date, indicating whether the amount of the settlement is a full or partial liquidation.

Problem 2

A receiver was appointed on September 30, 1977, for Green, Inc. On this date, the following balance sheet accounts are available:

Assets

Petty cash		$ 120
Cash in bank		2,400
Accounts receivable	$32,000	
Notes receivable	20,000	$52,000
Allowance for bad debts	340	51,660
Accrued interest, notes receivable		600
Merchandise		29,200
Prepaid insurance		240
Prepaid advertising		190
Building	$80,000	
Accumulated depreciation	21,000	59,000
Furniture and fixtures	$ 7,200	
Accumulated depreciation	1,600	5,600
Organization costs		1,740
Goodwill		4,000
		$154,750

Equities

Accrued wages	$ 2,800	
Accrued property taxes	1,810	
Accounts payable	79,800	
Notes payable	15,000	
Accrued interest payable	150	$ 99,560
Contributed capital:		
Common stock	$70,000	
Premium	2,000	
	$72,000	
Retained earnings:		
Deficit	16,810	55,190
		$154,750

It is estimated that conversion of assets will realize cash in the following amounts:

Notes receivable (with accrued interest)	$19,100
Accounts receivable	25,000
Merchandise	19,000
Building	25,000
Furniture and fixtures	2,000

Notes payable of $10,000 are secured by merchandise, the book value of which is $20,000. Notes payable of $5,000 are secured by the furniture and equipment. Interest expense is allocable ratably to all outstanding notes payable.

Required:

a. Prepare a statement of affairs as of September 30.
b. Prepare a supporting deficiency account or report on this date.

Problem 3

The Machine Manufacturing Company has been forced into bankruptcy as of April 30, 1977. The following list of account balances was prepared by the company bookkeeper as of April 30, 1977:

Cash	$ 2,700
Accounts receivable	39,350
Notes receivable	18,500
Inventories:	
Raw materials	19,600
Work in process	35,100
Finished machines	12,000
Supplies	6,450
Tools	14,700
Prepaid expenses	950
Plant and property:	
Land	20,000
Buildings	75,000
Machinery	80,900
	$325,250

Note payable to the First Bank	$ 15,000
Notes payable to suppliers	51,250
Accounts payable	52,000
Accrued salaries and wages	8,850
Accrued property taxes	2,900
Employees' taxes withheld	1,150
Accrued wage taxes	600
Accrued interest on bonds	1,800
First-mortgage bonds payable	90,000
Accumulated depreciation—buildings	33,750
Accumulated depreciation—machinery	32,100
Common stock ($100 par value)	75,000
Deficit	[39,150]
	$325,250

Additional Information:

a. Of the total accounts receivable $10,300 are believed to be good. The other accounts are doubtful, but it seems probable that 20 percent finally can be collected.

b. A total of $15,000 of the notes receivable have been pledged to secure the note payable to the First Bank. All except $2,500 of these appear to be good. Interest of $800 is accrued on the $12,500 of good notes pledged and $300 is accrued on the $15,000 payable to the bank. The remaining notes are not considered collectible.

c. The finished machines are expected to be sold for one-third above their cost, but expenses in disposing of them will equal 20 percent of their sales price. Work in process can be completed at an additional cost of $15,400, of which $3,700 would be material used from the raw material inventory. The work in process, when completed, will probably sell for $40,000, and costs of sale will be 20 percent of sales price. The raw material not used will realize $8,000. Most of the value of tools consists of special items. After completion of work in process, the tools should sell for $3,000. The supply

inventory which will not be needed to complete work should sell for $1,000.
d.   Land and buildings are mortgaged as security for bonds. They have an appraised value of $95,000. The company recently purchased $20,000 of machinery on a conditional sales contract. It still owes $12,000 principal on this contract which is included in the notes payable. These machines, having a current used value of $10,000, are repossessed. The Machine Manufacturing Company remains liable for the unpaid obligation. Depreciation taken on these machines amounts to $1,800. The remaining machinery is believed to be salable at $10,000, but costs of selling it may be $1,000.

Required:

a.   Prepare a statement showing the estimated deficiency to unsecured creditors, indicating clearly the causes of the deficiency. You need not consider any expenses of liquidation which are not stated in the information given.
b.   Compute the percentage of probable payments to unsecured creditors.

(AICPA adapted)

Problem 4

The financial condition of the Rawley Manufacturing Corporation was very unstable, although it had unimpaired contributed capital in the amount of $60,000 and accumulated earnings of $8,522. This condition was attributable to a deficiency of quick assets: cash, $265, and trade receivables, $4,062. Its current obligations to trade creditors amounted to $25,289. Other assets were raw materials, $16,000; work in process, $34,400; finished goods, $5,700; machinery and dies, $33,384. In order to continue operations, it was necessary to obtain sufficient cash to meet current payrolls and to pay miscellaneous expenses.

At a meeting of the principal creditors, it was decided to advance $6,000 to the Rawley Manufacturing Corporation to enable it to meet obligations presently due; additionally, it was decided to permit continuance of operations until the present in-process stock could be completed and sold. These operations were to be conducted by a trustee appointed by the creditors.

Transactions completed during the trusteeship were cash disbursements for labor, $16,625; for expenses, $4,530; and for additional dies, $750; raw materials purchased on account, $6,300; sales on account, $72,300; loss on collection of old accounts, $380; expenses incurred, on account, $15,000. Unliquidated account balances at the termination of the trusteeship period were as follows: accounts receivable (new), $3,382; accounts payable (new), $89; raw materials, $2,000; finished goods, $30,000; and machinery and dies, $34,134.

Required:

Prepare in orthodox form a statement of realization and liquidation with supporting schedules. Ignore the effects of depreciation in the determination of operating profit.

Problem 5

Using the data of Problem 4, prepare *in columnar form* a realization and liquidation statement. Ignore the effects of depreciation in the determination of operating profit.

Problem 6

The Hardhyt Corporation is in financial difficulty because of a deficiency in sales volume. Its stockholders and principal creditors want an estimate of the financial results of the liquidation of the assets and liabilities and the dissolution of the corporation. The corporation's trial balance follows:

HARDHYT CORPORATION

Postclosing Trial Balance
December 31, 1977

Cash	$ 1,000	
Accounts receivable	20,500	
Allowance for bad debts		$ 350
Inventories	40,000	
Supplies inventory	3,000	
Downhill Railroad 5 percent bonds	5,000	
Accrued bond interest receivable	750	
Advertising	6,000	
Land	4,000	
Building	30,000	
Accumulated depreciation—building		5,000
Machinery and equipment	46,000	
Accumulated depreciation—machinery and equipment		8,000
Accounts payable		26,000
Notes payable—bank		25,000
Notes payable—officers		20,000
Payroll taxes payable		800
Wages payable		1,500
Mortgage payable		42,000
Mortgage interest payable		500
Capital stock		50,000
Retained earnings	29,100	
Reserve for product guarantees		6,200
	$185,350	$185,350

The following information has been collected in anticipation of a meeting of the stockholders and principal creditors to be held on January 2, 1978.

a. Cash includes a $300 protested check from a customer. The customer stated that he would have funds to honor the check in about two weeks.

b. Accounts receivable include accounts totaling $10,000 that are fully collectible and have been assigned to the bank in connection with the notes payable. Included in the unassigned receivables is an uncollectible account of $150. The Allowance for Bad Debts account of $350 now on the books will adequately provide for other doubtful accounts.

c. Purchase orders totaling $9,000 are on hand for the corporation's products. Inventory with a book value of $6,000 can be processed at an additional cost of $400 to fill these orders. The balance of the inventory, which includes obsolete materials with a book value of $1,200, can be sold for $10,500.

d. In transit at December 31 but not recorded on the books was a shipment of defective merchandise being returned by a customer. Mr. Hardhyt, president of the corporation, had authorized the return and the refund of the purchase price of $250 after the merchandise had been inspected. Other than this return Mr. Hardhyt knows of no other defective merchandise that would bear upon the appropriated Reserve for Product Guarantees account. The merchandise being returned has no salvage value.

e. The Supplies Inventory is comprised of advertising literature, brochures, and other sales aids. These could not be replaced for less than $3,700.

f. The Downhill Railroad bonds are recorded at face value. They were purchased in 1974 for $600, and the adjustment to face value was credited to Retained Earnings. At December 31, 1977, the bonds were quoted at 18.

g. The Advertising account represents the future benefits of a 1977 advertising campaign. Ten percent of certain advertising expenditures were placed in the account. Mr. Hardhyt stated that this was too conservative and that 20 percent would result in a more realistic measure of the market that was created.

h. The land and building are in a downtown area. A firm offer of $50,000 has been received for the land which would be used as a parking lot; the building would be razed at a cost of $12,000 to the buyer. Another offer of $40,000 was received for the real estate which the bidder stated would be used for manufacturing that would probably employ some Hardhyt employees.

i. The highest of the offers received from used machinery dealers was $18,000 for all of the machinery and equipment.

j. One creditor, whose account for $1,000 is included in the accounts payable, confirmed in writing that he would accept 90 cents on the dollar if the corporation paid him by January 10.

k. Wages payable include year-end adjustments of $325 payable to certain factory employees for their overtime during the busy season.

l. The mortgage payable is secured by the land and building. The last two monthly principal payments of $200 each were not made.

m. Estimated liquidation expenses amount to $3,200.

n. For income tax purposes the corporation has the following net operating loss carry-overs (the tax rate is 50 percent):

$$
\begin{array}{ll}
1975 \ldots\ldots\ldots\ldots & \$10,000 \\
1976 \ldots\ldots\ldots\ldots & 12,000 \\
1977 \ldots\ldots\ldots\ldots & 8,000 \\
\end{array}
$$

Required:

a. Prepare a statement of affairs. Assets should be classified according to their availability for secured and unsecured creditors, and liabilities should be classified according to their legal priority and secured status. The statement should have the following column headings:

For Assets:	For Liabilities and Capital:
Book Value	Book Value
Assets	Liabilities and Capital
Appraised Value	Amount Unsecured
Estimated Amount Available	
Loss or Gain on Realization	

b. Prepare a schedule indicating the estimated settlement per dollar of unsecured liabilities.

(AICPA adapted)

Problem 7

The Boutique Company was unable to meet its obligations. As a result, John Nunn was appointed receiver on February 5, 1977. The following accounts were taken from the books as of that date:

Cash	$ 560
Accounts receivable	6,210
Merchandise	16,536
Prepayment of expenses	704
Fixtures	12,942
	$36,952

Accounts payable	$16,100
Notes payable	3,500
Accrued wages, taxes, etc	1,200
Accrued rent	600
Accumulated depreciation	3,803
Capital stock	10,000
Retained earnings	1,749
	$36,952

In the period from February 5, to April 30, 1977, the receiver's actions resulted in the following:

a. An audit of the accounts receivable disclosed that there were an additional $237 of accounts receivable which had not been brought on the books.
b. Merchandise costing $7,500 was sold for cash.
c. A portion of the fixtures, which cost $5,376 and had accumulated depreciation of $942, was sold.
d. Accounts receivable totaling $1,882 were collected. Other accounts amounting to $741 have been determined to be worthless.
e. Claims have been approved and paid for $1,010 of the wages and taxes which were accrued at February 5. Wage claims for $125 which were unrecorded on February 5 have also been approved and paid. Other claims have not yet been paid.
f. Expenses for wages and supplies used in liquidating the business to April 30 amounted to $1,300. Fees for the receiver need not be considered.
g. Rent under leases has continued to accrue in the amount of $900. Interest of $70 has accrued on notes payable.
h. Cash receipts and cash disbursements show the following:

Cash receipts:
Collection of accounts	$1,882
Sales of merchandise	8,300
Sale of fixtures	1,000

Cash disbursements:
Accrued wages and taxes	1,135
Expenses of the receivership	1,300

Required:

Prepare a formal statement of realization and liquidation and related gain and loss account for the period ended April 30, 1977.

(AICPA adapted)

Problem 8

JONES, INC.

Balance Sheet, as of March 31, 1977
(Prepared by the Company's Bookkeeper)

Assets

Current Assets:

Cash		$ 2,000	
Notes receivable	$ 4,640		
Less: Notes receivable discounted	4,640		
Accounts receivable		4,000	
U.S. Treasury bonds		10,000	
Inventories:			
Finished goods	$15,000		
Work in process	4,500		
Raw materials	6,000	25,500	
Total Current Assets			$ 41,500

Other Assets:

Subscriptions to capital stock			12,500
Investments			2,300
Property and equipment:			
Real estate		$45,000	
Factory equipment		24,000	
		$69,000	
Less: Accumulated depreciation		20,000	49,000
Total Assets			$105,300

Liabilities

Current Liabilities:

Notes payable:			
To Manufacturers' Trust Co.	$10,000		
To Alex Smith	25,000	$35,000	
Accounts payable		24,000	
Accrued liabilities:			
Salaries and wages	$ 992		
Property taxes	460	1,452	
Total Current Liabilities			$ 60,452

Long-Term Liabilities:

First mortgage on real estate		$15,000	
Second mortgage on real estate		20,000	35,000
Total Liabilities			$ 95,452

Capital

Capital stock—authorized, subscribed and issued, 500 shares, par $100 per share		$50,000	
Less: Deficit		[40,152]	9,848
Total Liabilities and Capital			$105,300

An analysis of the company's accounts disclosed the following:

a. Jones, Inc., started business April 1, 1966, with authorized capital of $50,000, represented by shares of $100 par value each. Of the 500 authorized shares, 375 were fully paid at par and 125 were subscribed at par, payment to be made on call.

b. The Manufacturers' Trust Company holds $10,000 of U.S. Treasury bonds as security for its $10,000 loan; it also holds the first mortgage of $15,000 on the company's real estate, interest on which is paid through March 31, 1977.

c. The real estate includes land, which cost $5,000, and a building erected thereon at a cost of $40,000. Of the accumulated depreciation, $5,000 is applicable to the building and $15,000 to the factory equipment. The realizable value of the real estate is estimated to be $30,000.

d. The note payable to Alex Smith is secured by a chattel mortgage on factory equipment and the inventories. Interest on the note has been paid through March 31, 1977.

e. Alex Smith holds the second mortgage on the real estate.

f. The notes receivable, $4,640, which were discounted, though not yet due, are deemed uncollectible.

g. Of the $4,000 of accounts receivable, $2,000 are considered good; of the remaining $2,000 it is expected that one half will be uncollectible.

h. Inventories are valued at cost; finished goods are expected to yield 110 percent of cost. Goods in process cost $4,500 and have a realizable value, if scrapped, of $900. It is estimated, however, that the work in process can be completed into finished goods by the use of $1,200 of raw material and an expenditure of $1,400 for labor and other costs. The raw material deteriorates rapidly, and is estimated to realize only 25 percent of cost.

i. The factory equipment, which cost $24,000 on April 1, 1972, is considered to have a realizable value of $5,000 at March 31, 1977.

j. The subscription to the capital stock for 125 shares at par, is due from Wyman Jones, president of the company, and is fully collectible.

k. Investments include 15 shares (a 1 percent interest) of the common stock of the Bourbon Company, acquired at a cost of $1,500, but with a market value of $3,390 at March 31, 1977; and 20 shares of treasury stock for which the company paid $800.

l. No expenses of liquidation nor accruals not specifically mentioned need be considered.

The committee has called for payment of the capital stock subscription and has decided to have the goods in process converted into finished goods, which are expected to realize 110 percent of cost. Completion of goods in process can be done so quickly that no further expenses than those mentioned above will be incurred.

Required:

a. Prepare a statement of affairs on March 31, 1977.

b. Prepare a supporting deficiency account detailing estimated gains and losses.

c. Calculate amounts and settlement percentages for each class of creditors.

(AICPA adapted)

Problem 9

The Neversink Corporation advises you that it is facing bankruptcy proceedings. As the company's CPA you are aware of its condition.

The balance sheet of the Neversink Corporation at June 30, 1977, and supplementary data are presented below:

Assets

Cash	$ 2,000
Accounts receivable, less allowance for bad debts	70,000
Inventory, raw material	40,000
Inventory, finished goods	60,000
Marketable securities	20,000
Land	13,000
Buildings, less allowance for depreciation	90,000
Machinery, less allowance for depreciation	120,000
Goodwill	20,000
Prepaid expenses	5,000
Total Assets	$440,000

Liabilities and Capital

Accounts payable	$ 80,000
Notes payable	135,000
Accrued wages	15,000
Mortgages payable	130,000
Common stock	100,000
Retained earnings [deficit]	[20,000]
Total Liabilities and Capital	$440,000

Supplementary Data:

a. Cash includes a $500 travel advance which has been expended.

b. Accounts receivable of $40,000 have been pledged in support of bank loans of $30,000. Credit balances of $5,000 are netted in the accounts receivable total.

c. Marketable securities consisted of government bonds costing $10,000 and 500 shares of Bartlett Company stock. The market value of the bonds is $10,000 and the stock is quoted at $18 per share. The bonds have accrued interest due of $200. The securities are collateral for a $20,000 bank loan.

d. Appraised value of raw materials is $30,000 and finished goods is $50,000. For an additional cost of $10,000, the raw materials would realize $70,000 as finished goods.

e. The appraised value of fixed assets is: land, $25,000; buildings, $110,000; machinery, $75,000.

f. Prepaid expenses will be exhausted during the liquidation period.

g. Accounts payable include $15,000 of withheld payroll taxes and $6,000 of obligations to creditors who had been assured by the president they would be paid. There are unrecorded employer's payroll taxes in the amount of $500.

h. Wages payable are not subject to any limitations under bankruptcy laws.

i. Mortgages payable consist of $100,000 on land and buildings, and a $30,000 chattel mortgage on machinery. Total unrecorded accrued interest on these mortgages amounted to $2,400.

j.   Estimated legal fees and expenses in connection with the liquidation are $10,000.

k.   Probable judgment on a pending damage suit is $50,000.

l.   You have not rendered an invoice for $5,000 for last year's audit, and you estimate a $1,000 fee for liquidation stock.

Required:

a.   Prepare a statement of affairs.

b.   Compute the estimated settlement per dollar of unsecured liabilities.

(AICPA adapted)

Problem 10

The Martin Manufacturing Company cannot meet its obligations, and a receiver is appointed on April 28, 1977. The books are closed on that date and the following trial balance drawn off:

Cash	$	800
Receivables		1,400
Finished goods		100,000
Materials and supplies		15,000
Goods on consignment (out)		220,000
Employee's bonds		4,700
Unexpired insurance		800
Machinery and equipment		507,300
		$850,000

Accounts payable	$110,000
Bank overdraft	1,000
Bank loans	105,000
Smith and Company	250,000
Acceptances	23,000
Collateral notes payable	4,700
Lease—machinery	30,000
Accrued interest on lease	2,000
City taxes accrued	4,000
Mortgage on machinery	100,000
Accrued interest on mortgage	3,000
Accumulated depreciation	7,300
Capital stock—preferred	100,000
Capital stock—common	100,000
Retained earnings	10,000
	$850,000

On November 20, 1977, the receiver, having disposed of all assets except $400 accounts receivable which he considers doubtful calls upon you to prepare an interim statement for the information of shareholders and creditors. An examination of the company's and the receiver's books and records discloses the following:

a. Cash receipts:

Collection of accounts receivable	$ 1,000
Rebate upon cancellation of all insurance	100
Proceeds from surrender of insurance policy on life of manager	1,000
Sales of finished goods during receivership	75,000
Rent of sublet portion of building	1,000
Unclaimed wages	500
Interest on bank account	200
Sale of all goods and supplies on hand after operations were discontinued	25,000
Sale of all machinery and equipment owned	200,000
	$303,800

b. Cash disbursements:

City taxes	$ 4,000
Interest on city taxes	400
Mortgage	100,000
Interest on mortgage	5,000
Labor, materials, and other operating and general expenses during receivership	61,000
	$170,400

c. Of the stocks on hand on April 28, finished goods costing $60,000 were sold during the receivership operations and $9,000 materials and supplies were used.

d. The accounts payable are understated by $10,000 and include an item of $5,000 which is in dispute.

e. The merchandise on consignment was pledged as collateral for the advances by Smith & Company and was accepted by them in part payment of these advances at full book value.

f. The collateral notes payable were for accommodation of employees and were secured by deposit of bonds. The notes were paid by the employees and the bonds returned to them.

g. The lease covered machinery worth $30,000 used by the company under a lease agreement. It was returned by the receiver and was accepted in full satisfaction of this agreement and all interest accrued.

h. Claims were filed for all liabilities except an item of $7,000 accounts payable.

i. Receiver's fees need not be considered.

Required:

Prepare a columnar statement showing the realization of assets, liquidation of liabilities, and operations during the receivership; also indicate amounts of unsecured creditors' claims and available assets on November 20, 1977.

(AICPA adapted)

Problem 11

The stockholders of the Agriculture Equipment Company, vendors of horse-drawn machinery, resolved at their meeting of June 13, 1977, to liquidate as of

August 31, 1977. The May 31, 1977, financial statement on which the stock-holders predicated their decision to liquidate follows:

AGRICULTURE EQUIPMENT COMPANY
Balance Sheet
As of May 31, 1977

Assets

Cash	$ 36,750
Accounts receivable	33,500
Inventory	120,250
Total Current Assets	$190,500
Furniture, fixtures, trucks, etc., less accumulated depreciation	20,500
Land and building, less accumulated depreciation	30,000
Total Assets	$241,000

Equities

Accounts payable, including taxes		$ 15,600
Interest accrued on mortgage		250
Accrued payroll		450
Total Current Liabilities		$ 16,300
6% mortgage due January 1, 1979		10,000
Capital stock, 4,200 shares, par value $50		210,000
Retained earnings—balance at January 1, 1977	$24,050	
Less loss for 5 mos. to May 31, 1977	19,350	
Balance		4,700
Total Equities		$241,000

According to the stockholders' resolution of June 13, the liquidation is to be effected by the directors (who, being principal stockholders, serve without compensation) as follows:

"The $15,000 cash bid of a local real estate operator for the equity in the land and building is to be accepted immediately, the purchaser to assume the outstanding mortgage of $10,000 and to pay all expenses of title search, closing, etc. Title is to pass as of June 30, 1977, and Agriculture Equipment Company is to pay mortgage interest accrued to that date. Insurance and taxes prepaid prior to June 30, 1977, are to be absorbed by vendor.

"All merchandise on hand is to be offered for sale at 80 percent of regular sales prices, such special sale to be conducted from June 17 to June 26 (both dates inclusive). These sales are to be on a strictly cash basis and to be final—no returns permitted.

"An auction is to be conducted on June 29 on the company's premises and is to include all merchandise not disposed of during the previous 10-day sale. All furniture, fixtures, and trucks and other equipment are also to be auctioned at this time. All sales made at such auction are to be strictly cash and final.

"Any merchandise still remaining unsold after the auction is to be advertised daily in newspapers of neighboring communities and disposed of at best prices obtainable.

"All employees, except the manager-bookkeeper, are to be given immediate notice of their release, at the close of business on June 30, and to be paid up to July 31. The manager-bookkeeper is to be given immediate notice of his release effective August 31, 1977, on which date he will be paid his salary for the four months ending December 31.

"A liquidating dividend (final) is to be paid on September 2, 1977, to all stockholders of record as of August 31, 1977."

Sales of merchandise to regular customers on credit for the period from June 1 to 16 inclusive amounted to $9,500 and were merged with the liquidation sales. All merchandise unsold after the auction was finally disposed of in August.

Depreciation subsequent to May 31, 1977, may be ignored.

Following is a summary of the cash transactions for the three months ended August 31, 1977:

Cash Transactions

		Dr.	Cr.
June	Cash sales—regular	$ 5,850	
	Accounts receivable collections	23,500	
	Cash sales (special 20% discount)	47,350	
	Cash received from auction sales:		
	Merchandise	31,500	
	Furniture, fixtures, and trucks	8,250	
	Auctioneer's commission and expenses		$ 2,850
	Interest on mortgage paid to May 31		300
	Proceeds from sale of land and building	15,000	
	Officers and office salaries (including separation payments and $450 accrued payroll)		5,550
	Accounts payable		15,600
July	Accounts receivable collections	1,250	
	Postauction sales:		
	Merchandise	3,500	
	Furniture, fixtures, and trucks	2,300	
	Salary of manager-bookkeeper for July		400
Aug.	Accounts receivable collections (final)	3,700	
	Collection agency fees		375
	Salary of manager-bookkeeper (including separation payment)		2,000
	Legal fees and expenses re liquidation		675
		$142,200	$27,750

Required:

Prepare from the foregoing information:

a.   A columnar working sheet showing the postings of cash transactions, the adjustments, losses of realization and expenses of liquidation, and the cash available for final distribution.

b.   A statement showing the amount of cash to be distributed as a liquidating dividend to each of the following stockholders:

A	1,600 shares
B	1,200 shares
C	900 shares
D	360 shares
E	140 shares
Total	4,200 shares

(AICPA adapted)

17

Accounting for Estates and Trusts

ADMINISTRATION BY A FIDUCIARY

Introduction

A *fiduciary* is a person to whom is entrusted the property of another for safekeeping, management, and/or distribution, and who is accountable therefor to various interested parties. Either an individual or a corporation may serve in this capacity. The importance of the fiduciary relationship has been indicated previously in references to receivers and trustees for financially distressed businesses. The fiduciary occupies an equally important role in respect to the administration of estates and trusts.

Upon the death of an individual (the *decedent*), it is necessary that a personal representative of the deceased assume custody and control of his estate. In the event that the decedent has executed a valid will in which is indicated his choice of a representative, his wishes will normally control. In such a circumstance, the decedent is said to have died *testate*, he is referred to as the *testator*, and when confirmed by court appointment, his representative is known as the *executor*. Should the decedent fail to execute a valid will, he is said to have died *intestate*, and his representative selected by the court is known as an *administrator*. If there exists a will, the last expressions of the decedent contained therein usually will govern the distribution of his estate; if no will exists, or if the will is determined to be invalid, the various state *laws of descent and distribution* will control the disposition of the decedent's estate. The laws of descent control the disposition of real property; the laws of distribution regulate the disposition of personal property.

The administration of estates normally comes within the purview of courts referred to as *probate, surrogate, orphan's,* or *county* courts. Before a will can become an effective instrument of fiduciary authority, it must be *admitted to probate.* To probate a will is to prove its validity, i.e., to prove that it was executed by a competent decedent without duress or other improper influence, and that it represents the last expressions of the decedent concerning the disposition of his property. Witnesses to the signing of the will may be called upon to testify as to these and other matters and the genuineness of the various signatures. Once the will is admitted to probate, the court may then proceed to the appointment of an executor. If the person named in the will is able and willing to serve, he is usually confirmed by the court and is issued *letters testamentary,* which are the evidence of his formal authority to assume the role of fiduciary. If an administrator is appointed, he is similarly issued *letters of administration* empowering him to act as fiduciary.

Role of the Fiduciary in Estate Administration

While one is not bound to accept appointment as a fiduciary, once it has been accepted there is a commitment to faithfully discharge the obligations of that trust. The fiduciary must first seek out and take possession of the property of the deceased; he is then charged with exercising reasonable prudence in respect to the care and management of the property. Consequently, he is required to keep estate resources invested to the extent that investments may profitably be made; to liquidate all just debts of the decedent, including estate and inheritance taxes; and to distribute the decedent's property according to the provisions of the will or in the manner prescribed by law.

Real property of the testator usually passes directly by *devise* to *devisees* identified in the will, legal title vesting in the latter at the date of the decedent's death. However, since the fiduciary is frequently called upon to include both real and personal property in various reports required by governmental agencies, including those submitted for federal estate and state inheritance tax purposes, it may be desirable to include real property in the inventory of the decedent's assets. While the fiduciary has no accountability with respect thereto, he may petition the court to allow the sale of such property in order to meet the obligations of the decedent when personal property is clearly inadequate for this purpose.

Inventory of Assets

The fiduciary is required to submit a complete inventory of the properties of the decedent to the court of his appointment. This inventory should contain a full and complete description of all assets which are entrusted to the care and management of the fiduciary. Some of the assets may have no apparent value; yet, for reasons of completeness in the enumeration, such items should be detailed, with an indication of no value. Among the assets often included in an estate inventory are bank balances, valuables in locked depositories, corporate and government securities, advances to legatees, accrued interest, dividends receivable, accounts and other receivables, judgments payable to the estate, and interests in jointly owned property. The proceeds from a life insurance policy for which the estate is the indicated beneficiary are properly included as an estate asset; in the event that other beneficiaries are specified, payment is made directly to those named, and the relevant insurance contracts are excluded from the estate inventory. Where the estate includes a partnership interest, this property right must be disclosed and evaluated. Liquidation of the partnership may be necessary unless continuity is provided for and assured by the decedent's will or the partnership agreement. If liquidation is not required, valuation problems are likely to arise unless a means of arriving at a value of the partnership interest is specified in the partnership agreement or in a buy-sell agreement.

The assignment of value to estate assets is the primary responsibility of the fiduciary, although he may be aided by court-appointed appraisers. For example, the Texas Probate Code provides:

Within ninety days after his qualification, unless a longer time shall be granted by the court, the representative shall file with the clerk of court a verified, full and detailed inventory, in one written instrument, of all the property of such estate which has come to his possession or knowledge, which inventory shall include:

(a)   all real property of the estate situated in the State of Texas;

(b)   all personal property of the estate wherever situated.

The representative shall set out in the inventory his appraisement of the fair market value of each item thereof as of the date of death in the case of grant of letters testamentary or of administration or as of the date of grant of letters of guardianship, as the case may be; provided that if the court shall appoint an appraiser or appraisers of the estate, the representative shall determine the fair market value of each item of the inventory with the assistance of such appraiser or appraisers and shall set out in the inventory such appraisement. The inventory shall specify what portion of the property, if any, is separate property and what portion, if any, is community property. If any property is owned in common with others, the interest owned by the estate shall be shown, together with the names and relationship, if known, of co-owners. Such inventory, when approved by the court and duly filed with the clerk of court, shall constitute for all purposes the inventory and appraisement of the estate referred to in this Code. The court for good cause shown may require the filing of the inventory and appraisement at a time prior to ninety days after the qualification of the representative [Section 250].

The statutes of the various states often provide that in addition to real property, specific items of personalty pass directly to the distributees. These items may include specified household effects, clothing of the decedent, and other personal effects which are considered of special value to the surviving spouse and/or minor children. Legal title to all personal property not so exempted vests in the fiduciary. Only those items of personalty for which the fiduciary assumes legal responsibility are included in the inventory of assets.

When assets are discovered subsequent to the filing of the inventory, it is appropriate that the fiduciary file a supplemental report, enumerating these additions. The sum of the original and supplemental listings comprises the *corpus,* or the *principal,* of the estate at date of the decedent's death.

Claims against the Estate

The fiduciary is obliged in most states to give public notice to those having claims against the estate of the decedent requesting them to make a presentment of these claims within a specified period of time. Presentment may be made either to the fiduciary or to the court. The fiduciary must necessarily determine the validity of the claims, rejecting those considered to be invalid; in this connection, he is required to exhaust all appropriate legal defenses, including the statute of limitations and the statute of frauds. The length of time allowed for creditors to file a claim against the estate varies among the several states; a period frequently prescribed is one year from the date of the publication of the first notice. In many states this period has been shortened to six months or less.

Once the validity of claims has been confirmed, the fiduciary must establish the *sequence of paying* the various obligations and proceed with their settlement. In the event the estate is solvent, the order of settlement may not be especially important. However, for insolvent estates, the statues provide the priority sequence which the fiduciary must follow if he is to avoid personal liability for improper distribution. The following order of payment is fairly typical:

1. Funeral and administration expenses.
2. Debts which are secured by a lien on the decendent's property.
3. Taxes, including estate and inheritance taxes.
4. Judgments in force which are a lien against property of the decedent at time of death.
5. Provable debts against the estate.
6. Wages due domestics or other employees.
7. Sustenance payments to the widow for a specified period of time.

The Texas Probate Code provides for the following priorities in respect to the claims against the estates of decedents:

Class 1. Funeral expenses and expenses of last sickness for a reasonable amount to be approved by the court, not to exceed one thousand dollars, any excess to be classified and paid as other unsecured claims.
Class 2. Expenses of administration and expenses incurred in the preservation, safe-keeping, and management of the estate.

Class 3. Claims secured by mortgage or other liens so far as the same can be paid out of the proceeds of the property subject to such mortgage or other lien, and when more than one mortgage or lien shall exist upon the same property, the oldest shall be first paid; but no preference shall be given to such mortgage or lien.

Class 4. All other claims legally exhibited within six months after the original grant of letters testamentary or of administration.

Class 5. All claims legally exhibited after the lapse of six months from the original grant of letters testamentary or of administration [Section 322].

Where the decedent's estate is small, the involvements of estate administration may be reduced somewhat. The Model Small Estates Act provides for the following simplified procedure:

Summary Administration of Small Estates. If it shall appear at the time of the appointment of a personal representative or at any time subsequent thereto by an allegation in the petition for the appointment of the personal representative, by a separate affidavit or otherwise, that the value of the entire estate, less liens and encumbrances, does not exceed [$10,000], the court in its discretion may authorize a summary administration of the estate in any one or more of the following respects:

(1) By ordering that notice be given to creditors to present their claims within [three (3) months] after the first publication of such notice or be barred as in other cases;

(2) By dispensing with notice by publication in any or all subsequent portions of such proceeding and ordering that notice be given by posting or mailing in lieu of publication;

(3) By appointing but one appraiser for valuing the assets of the estate;

(4) By dispensing entirely with the appointment of an appraiser, if the value of the estate is readily determinable, and by authorizing the personal representative alone to appraise the estate;

(5) By exercising its discretion in fixing the amount of the bond of the personal representative, or dispensing with such bond, but in the absence of special circumstances, the bond shall be fixed in the amount of the value of any part of the estate which the court can determine from examination that the personal representative could easily convert during the period of administration plus the value of the gross annual income of the estate;

(6) By conferring upon the personal representative full power to sell, lease for periods not exceeding one year, mortgage, assign, transfer or convey any property of the estate upon such terms and conditions and for such considerations as he may determine, without any other order or confirmation of the court; or

(7) By ordering final distribution of the estate at any time after the expiration of such [three (3) months'] period after the first publication of notice to creditors.

In any such case creditors not presenting their claims within the time stated in the notice to creditors shall be barred as in other cases. No error in the statement of the value of the estate or the subsequent discovery of additional assets shall affect the validity of any order directing the summary administration of the estate or any order or proceeding in connection with the administration of the estate. Any person dealing with a personal representative upon whom powers have been conferred as herein prescribed shall be entitled to rely fully upon the powers so conferred upon him, but such personal representative in exercising any such powers shall be held accountable to the estate and shall make a final report and account of his administration to be settled by the court as in other cases [Model Small Estates Act, Section 11, 9C, U.L.A., 1967 edition].[1]

Bequests of Personal Property

A testator's bequest of personal property is referred to as a *legacy;* the recipient is called a *legatee.* Legacies are classified as specific, demonstrative, general, and residual.

1. A *specific* legacy is a bequest of personal property which is specifically identified in the will; it normally consists of such items as clothing, ornaments, furniture, securities, and other personal effects.
2. A *demonstrative* legacy is a testamentary bequest payable out of a designated fund or specified asset accumulation. Gifts of cash payable out of a designated bank account and the bequest of a quantity of grain from a specified granary are examples of demonstrative legacies.
3. A *general* legacy, unlike a demonstrative legacy, is a bequest of money or other property without special designation as to source.
4. A *residual* legacy is the terminal distribution of personal property after all debts have been paid and all other legacies distributed or otherwise provided for. A residual legatee receives the residue of the estate.

Legacies are distributed in the priority outlined above; in the event there is insufficient property to satisfy all legacies, they will be abated or scaled down in the reverse of this order. A legacy may not always be paid, even though there exists a solvent estate; in such an instance, the default is termed a "failure" of a legacy. Failure may exist where the legatee has died previous to the testator's death, the property has undergone deterioration or has suffered destruction, or there exist provisions in the will which controvert public policy.

The statutes of many states provide for bequests by *advancement* where the decedent dies intestate. Should the decedent during his lifetime make a gift of property to individuals (usually children or lineal descendents) who would otherwise be entitled to inherit a part of the estate of the donor upon his death, the bequest may be regarded as an advancement in anticipation of the advancee's intestate share. However, all gratuitous *inter vivos* transfers before death are regarded as absolute gifts, not advancements, unless contrary intent can be demonstrated.

---

[1] Uniform Laws and Model Acts are promulgated by the National Conference of Commissioners on Uniform State Laws. Such laws may be adopted by the various state legislatures verbatim, in modified form, or not at all.

Role of the Fiduciary in Trust Administration

Provision may be made by a testate decedent that property comprising his estate, or a part thereof, shall be placed in trust. A *trust* is an arrangement whereby title to property is transferred to a *trustee,* either an individual or corporation, who holds or manages the property for the benefit of others. While there are various types of trusts, two classes predominate— living trusts and testamentary trusts. *Living trusts, or trusts inter vivos,* are created and become operative during the lifetime of the creator. A *testamentary trust* is created by provision in the will of the testator. In the event the trustee is also specified in the will, he becomes a *testamentary trustee.*

A trust is created or established by a *donor, trustor,* or *founder;* those expected to derive benefit therefrom are *beneficiaries.* The trust agreement may provide that the principal of the trust shall eventually be distributed to one beneficiary while income is to be currently awarded another. However, the principal and income beneficiary may be the same person; for example, the income only of a trust may be distributed to a beneficiary until he attains his majority, after which the principal is conveyed to him. The income beneficiary is called a *cestui que trust.* If he receives income for life, he is referred to as a *life tenant.* The recipient of the principal of the trust is termed a *remainderman.* If the beneficiary has the ability to designate who will receive the income or the principal at some later date, he is referred to as having a *power of appointment.*

A trustee normally has only such authority as is conveyed to him by the trust instrument. This authority usually includes:

1. The incurrence of those costs and expenses necessary to the preservation of the trust principal.
2. The sale, exchange, or improvements in respect to existing realty.
3. The settlement, totally or by compromise, of claims against the trust estate.
4. The making of new investments and disposition of existing investments.
5. The distribution of property to distributees as provided in the trust agreement.
6. The making of advances to beneficiaries.
7. The payment to or expending of income for the benefit of minors.

A testamentary trustee does not accept an accountability as a fiduciary until trust property is conveyed to him. Legal title to real property customarily vests in the trustee upon the decedent's death; title to personal property, however, passes to the trustee with the transfer of property. The trustee is charged with exercising that degree of care in respect to trust property as he would exercise as a reasonably prudent businessman acting in his own self-interest. The creator of a trust may, by provision in the trust instrument, reserve unto himself the right to relieve the trustee from duties and liabilities otherwise imposed upon him; similarly, by express provision in the trust instrument, the creator of the trust may add to or impose new duties, restrictions, privileges, and powers upon the trustee. The trustee may also be relieved of his duties by a court of competent jurisdiction. The Uniform Trusts Act specifically provides that such a court may, for cause shown and upon notice to the beneficiaries, relieve a trustee from any or all of the duties and restrictions which would otherwise be imposed upon him [Uniform Trusts Act, Section 19, 9C, U.L.A., 1967 edition].

The trustee should weigh carefully the desirability of investing uncommitted cash accumulations in income-producing assets, subject to existing statutory constraints. Where there is reasonable doubt as to the propriety of a proposed course of action in respect to investments, the trustee should seek the opinion of legal counsel; he is usually allowed a reasonable period of time in which to make such investments without penalty for uninvested funds. He is under a special duty to keep separate the trust assets from his own property, unless a contrary provision exists in the trust instrument. In the event of loss which may arise from commingling of trust and other properties, courts have held the trustee guilty of a breach of trust.

DUAL BASES OF ACCOUNTABILITY

Principal (Corpus) and Income Distinguished

It is especially important that the fiduciary carefully identify those elements which comprise the principal of an estate or trust and those which make up its income. A testator's direction that the principal and income from an estate shall be distributed to different beneficiaries accents the importance of this distinction. The distinction between principal and income can also be important in the computation of income taxes. The principal-income distinction is difficult to make, and often subtle, because of the diverse provisions of state statutes and the special characteristics of the elements themselves. The decedent may expressly indicate, either in the will or in the trust indenture, the criteria to be used in making the identification; where no such provision exists, the courts must necessarily look to the statutes for distinguishing characteristics. It is important that accounting records be established and maintained by the fiduciary in such manner as to preserve this distinction.

The Revised Uniform Principal and Income Act[2] provides that in the absence of any contrary terms in the trust instrument, principal and income shall be defined as follows:

(a)   Income is the return in money or property derived from the use of principal, including return received as
(1)   rent of real or personal property, including sums received for cancellation or renewal of a lease;

---

[2] This statute has been adopted in 20 states.

(2)   interest on money lent, including sums received as consideration for the privilege of prepayment of principal except as provided in section 7 on bond premium and bond discount;

(3)   income earned during administration of a decedent's estate as provided in section 5;

(4)   corporate distributions as provided in section 6;

(5)   accrued increment on bonds or other obligations issued at discount as provided in section 7;

(6)   receipts from business and farming operations as provided in section 8;

(7)   receipts from disposition of natural resources as provided in sections 9 and 10;

(8)   receipts from other principal subject to depletion as provided in section 11;

(9)   receipts from disposition of underproductive property as provided in section 12.

(b)   Principal is the property which has been set aside by the owner or the person legally empowered so that it is held in trust eventually to be delivered to a remainderman while the return or use of the principal is in the meantime taken or received by or held for accumulation for an income beneficiary. Principal includes

(1)   consideration received by the trustee on the sale or other transfer of principal or on repayment of a loan or as a refund or replacement or change in the form of principal;

(2)   proceeds of property taken on eminent domain proceedings;

(3)   proceeds of insurance upon property forming part of the principal except proceeds of insurance upon a separate interest of an income beneficiary;

(4)   stock dividends, receipts on liquidation of a corporation, and other corporate distributions as provided in section 6;

(5)   receipts from the disposition of corporate securities as provided in section 7;

(6)   royalties and other receipts from disposition of natural resources as provided in sections 9 and 10;

(7)   receipts from other principal subject to depletion as provided in section 11;

(8)   any profit resulting from any change in the form of principal except as provided in section 12 on underproductive property;

(9)   receipts from disposition of underproductive property as provided in section 12;

(10)   any allowances for depreciation established under sections 8 and 13(a)(2).

(c)   After determining income and principal in accordance with the terms of the trust instrument or of this Act, the trustee shall charge to income or principal expenses and other charges as provided in section 13 [Revised Uniform Principal and Income Act, Section 3, 7 U.L.A.].

In respect to charges against and credits to income and principal, the Revised Uniform Principal and Income Act contains the following general provisions:

(a) Unless the will otherwise provides and subject to subsection (b), all expenses incurred in connection with the settlement of a decedent's estate, including debts, funeral expenses, estate taxes, interest and penalties concerning taxes, family allowances, fees of attorneys and personal representatives, and court costs shall be charged against the principal of the estate.

(b) Unless the will otherwise provides, income from the assets of a decedent's estate after the death of the testator and before distribution, including income from property used to discharge liabilities, shall be determined in accordance with the rules applicable to a trustee under this Act and distributed as follows:

(1) to specific legatees and devisees, the income from the property bequeathed or devised to them respectively, less taxes, ordinary repairs, and other expenses of management and operation of the property, and an appropriate portion of the interest accrued since the death of the testator and of taxes imposed on income (excluding taxes on capital gains) which accrue during the period of administration;

(2) to all other legatees and devisees, except legatees of pecuniary bequests not in trust, the balance of the income, less the balance of taxes, ordinary repairs, and other expenses of management and operation of all property from which the estate is entitled to income, interest accrued since the death of the testator, and taxes imposed on income (excluding taxes on capital gains) which accrue during the period of administration, in proportion to their respective interests in the undistributed assets of the estate computed at times of distribution on the basis of inventory value.

(c) Income received by a trustee under subsection (b) shall be treated as income of the trust [Revised Uniform Principal and Income Act, Section 5, 7, U.L.A.].

There are a number of circumstances for which the above generalizations are not completely descriptive. They are discussed in the following section.

Special Problems

Accrued Items.   Accruals of income at the date of the decedent's death are normally regarded as components of estate principal; such accruals often consist of interest on receivable or investment balances. Interest on these assets earned during tenancy is regarded as income of the estate. In respect to savings accounts and time deposits, accrued interest is regarded as either principal or income depending upon when the interest credit is made available to the depositor. Accrued interest payable normally follows the same classification rules with respect to income or principal as does interest receivable, i.e., interest accrued to the date of the testator's death is a debt of the estate and accordingly chargeable to principal when disbursed; interest paid or incurred subsequently is ordinarily chargeable to income.

In most states, rents receivable at the date of the decedent's death are includible in the principal of the estate; the amount of rent earned during tenancy is regarded as income. Similarly, rent expense payable at date of death is a charge against the estate principal, while accruals thereafter are charges against income.

It is assumed that taxes on real property of the testator customarily do not accrue. The tax expense rather is regarded as relating to the period when the tax becomes a lien on the assessed property. Where the lien becomes effective before the decedent's death, the tax expense is chargeable to the principal of the estate; where the lien becomes effective subsequent to the decedent's death, the expense is a charge against income. As indicated earlier, estate taxes are levied against and payable out of the principal assets of the estate. Income taxes, however, must be identified with the elements making up the taxable base. The amount of income tax which relates to gains or losses on the conversion of principal assets is chargeable to principal; the amount levied on normal operating net income during the administration of the estate is chargeable against income. Income taxes for a fractional period prior to the decedent's death are payable out of the principal of the estate.

Dividends Received.   Corporate dividends are not generally accounted for on an accrual basis. Ordinary cash dividends declared prior to the decedent's death are a part of the principal of the estate; declarations subsequent to death usually represent income of the estate. In some states, the significant identifying date is the date of record. In respect to dividends which are declared and received during tenancy, the statutes of the several states are not wholly agreed as to the most appropriate accounting classification. Some follow the Massachusetts rule, which generally provides that all cash dividends, whatever their magnitude and from whatever source, are to be regarded as income accruing to the income beneficiary; stock dividends, however, are regarded as additions to principal. In application of this rule, the *form* of the dividend controls. Other states follow the Pennsylvania rule which emphasizes the *source* of the declaration. If it is determined that the dividend is payable out of earnings accumulated prior to the creation of the trust estate, all dividends—whether in cash or shares of stock—are regarded as belonging to principal. However, if it is established that only those earnings accumulated subsequent to the formation of the trust estate are declared as dividends, the receipt (including the market value of stock dividends) is accorded the status of income. The distinction is frequently implemented in terms of whether the dividend is ordinary or extraordinary. Where dividends relate partially to earnings accumulated prior to the creation of the trust estate and partially subsequent thereto, the fiduciary may apportion the receipt as between income and principal. In this allocation, reliance is usually placed on the relative book values of the corporate stock at the date of the decedent's death and at the date of dividend payment. If the book value after the dividend payment is less than the book value at date of the decedent's death, an amount equivalent to the reduction in value shall be credited to principal with the residual amount of the receipt regarded as income. Stock dividends are accorded parallel treatment, although the allocation is made in terms of shares of stock.

Stock rights which are a part of the decedent's estate at death, or which are acquired subsequently in respect to corporate securities belonging to the deceased at date of death, are elements of principal; accordingly, proceeds from the sale of such rights, reflecting conversion gains and losses, are also regarded as principal.

In respect to corporate distributions, the underlying emphasis of the Massachusetts rule is clearly reflected in the Revised Uniform Principal and Income Act:

(a) Corporate distributions of shares of the distributing corporation, including distributions in the form of a stock split or stock dividend, are principal. A right to subscribe to shares or other securities issued by the distributing corporation accruing to stockholders on account of their stock ownership and the proceeds of any sale of the right are principal.

(b) Except to the extent that the corporation indicates that some part of a corporate distribution is a settlement of preferred or guaranteed dividends accrued since the trustee became a stockholder or is in lieu of an ordinary cash dividend, a corporate distribution is principal if the distribution is pursuant to

(1) a call of shares;

(2) a merger, consolidation, reorganization, or other plan by which assets of the corporation are acquired by another corporation; or

(3) a total or partial liquidation of the corporation, including any distribution which the corporation indicates is a distribution in total or partial liquidation or any distribution of assets, other than cash, pursuant to a court decree or final administrative order by a government agency ordering distribution of the particular assets.

(c) Distributions made from ordinary income by a regulated investment company or by a trust qualifying and electing to be taxed under federal law as a real estate investment trust are income. All other distributions made by the company or trust, including distributions from capital gains, depreciation, or depletion, whether in the form of cash or an option to take new stock or cash or an option to purchase additional shares, are principal.

(d) Except as provided in subsections (a), (b), and (c), all corporate distributions are income, including cash dividends, distributions of or rights to subscribe to shares or securities or obligations of corporations other than the distributing corporation, and the proceeds of the rights or property distributions. Except as provided in subsections (b) and (c), if the distributing corporation gives a stockholder an option to receive a distribution either in cash or in its own shares, the distribution chosen is income.

(e) The trustee may rely upon any statement of the distributing corporation as to any fact relevant under any provision of this Act concerning the source or character of dividends or distributions of corporate assets [Revised Uniform Principal and Income Act, Section 6, 7, U.L.A.].

These provisions, particularly subsection (e), extend the "form" test of the Massachusetts rule to include a "source" test in certain instances. However, this latter criterion logically does not include ordinary stock dividends, as in the Pennsylvania rule.

In most states, the courts have held that dividends payable from sources other than earnings relate to principal. Script and property dividends are accorded treatment equivalent to cash dividends. Liquidating dividends are accounted for by the fiduciary as in a commercial enterprise, i.e., they are regarded as a return of capital and are accordingly classified as adjustments of principal.

Partnership Earnings. It is normally assumed that partnership profits do not accrue. Partnership net income is determined as a consequence of, and concurrent with, a formal closing of the partnership books. Where the partnership books are closed upon the death of a partner, the calculated share of profits assigned to the deceased partner for the fractional period previous to the date of death is normally regarded as principal of his estate. In the event the partners, pursuant to provisions of the partnership agreement, elect not to close the partnership books until a date subsequent to the testator's death, there is no evident consensus among accountants as to the disposition of partnership earnings for the interval between the last closing date prior to the decedents' death and the subsequent closing date. Should the partnership agreement provide for interest on partners' capitals, such interest prior to the decedent's death is includible in principal; that which accrues during the subsequent period is income.

Depreciation and Maintenance. Depreciation (or value exhaustion) may or may not be chargeable against the income of an estate or trust during a period of tenancy. This question depends upon the testator's intentions, as indicated in the will or trust instrument, in respect to preserving the principal of the estate intact. In the absence of any indication of the testator's intent, state law controls.

Expenditures for repairs, and other maintenance outlays, the effect of which is to materially improve or enhance the value of estate or trust properties follow traditional rules of capitalization, i.e., they are normally chargeable to principal. However, those expenditures the benefits of which merely preserve the normal operating efficiency of the depreciable assets are regarded as income charges. Where the benefits relate partially to principal and partially to income, an apportionment of the expenditure should be made, based upon estimates of measurable benefit.

In the event that trust estate properties consist of wasting assets, i.e., mineral deposits, timber, etc., the wishes of the testator or state law will also control in respect to charges for depletion.[3] If there is persuasive evidence that the testator intended to preserve for the remainderman the undiminished value of the original property, the fiduciary should withhold for the remainderman income in an amount equal to the value exhaustion for depletion. However, if the evidence indicates that income, without reduc-

---

[3] For example, the Revised Uniform Principal and Income Act provides that with respect to receipts for royalties for mineral interests, 27.5 percent of gross receipts (but not to exceed 50 percent of net receipts before deducting depletion) is to be added to principal as a depletion allowance [Revised Uniform Principal and Income Act, Section 9, 7, U.L.A.].

tion in amount for depletion, should accrue to the benefit of the income beneficiary, the principal should be reduced accordingly by the amount of cumulative depletion allowances.

Discount/Premium on Bond Investments. Corporate bonds held by the decedent are usually evaluated in terms of prices established by exchange quotations or over-the-counter trading at the date of the decedent's death. To the extent that premiums or discounts are reflected in these quotations, a question exists as to subsequent amortization by the fiduciary. A position often taken is that no provision should be made for the amortization of premium or the accumulation of discount. According to this view, principal is not regarded as having been affected so long as the estate consists of the specific assets inventoried, and the periodic interest receipts are classified as estate income. Consequently, the act of disposing of the bonds becomes the critical point for recognizing the increase or impairment in the value of estate corpus.

In respect to bonds *acquired by the fiduciary during tenancy,* however, premiums are customarily amortized while discounts are not amortized. This convention in respect to amortization is manifestly inconsistent with the treatment of premiums or discounts on bond investments included in the original estate inventory. Of course, the wishes of the testator will prevail should they indicate otherwise. In recording amortization, it is important to recognize that brokerage expenses and transfer fees are elements of investment cost. As in the case of securities existing at date of death, gains and losses on the conversion of subsequently acquired investments are regarded as principal.

Expenses. Those expenses which are clearly identifiable with the conservation, management, and distribution of the principal of the trust-estate are appropriate charges against principal; however, income of the trust-estate must bear the charges for expenses which pertain to the earning of income during a period of tenancy. The Revised Uniform Principal and Income Act enumerates various expense items to be charged either against income or against principal.

(a) The following charges shall be made against income:

(1) ordinary expenses incurred in connection with the administration, management, or preservation of the trust property, including regularly recurring taxes assessed against any portion of the principal, water rates, premiums on insurance taken upon the interests of the income beneficiary, remainderman, or trustee, interest paid by the trustee, and ordinary repairs;

(2) a reasonable allowance for depreciation on property subject to depreciation under generally accepted accounting principles, but no allowance shall be made for depreciation of that portion of any real property used by a beneficiary as a residence or for depreciation of any property held by the trustee on the effective date of this Act for which the trustee is not then making an allowance for depreciation;

(3) one-half of court costs, attorney's fees, and other fees on periodic judicial accounting, unless the court directs otherwise;

(4) court costs, attorney's fees, and other fees on other accountings or judicial proceedings if the matter primarily concerns the income interest, unless the court directs otherwise;

(5) one-half of the trustee's regular compensation, whether based on a percentage of principal or income, and all expenses reasonably incurred for current management of principal and application of income;

(6) any tax levied upon receipts defined as income under this Act or the trust instrument and payable by the trustee.

(b) If charges against income are of unusual amount, the trustee may by means of reserves or other reasonable means charge them over a reasonable period of time and withhold from distribution sufficient sums to regularize distributions.

(c) The following charges shall be made against principal:

(1) trustee's compensation not chargeable to income under subsections (a) (4) and (a) (5), special compensation of trustees, expenses reasonably incurred in connection with principal, court costs and attorney's fees primarily concerning matters of principal, and trustee's compensation computed on principal as an acceptance, distribution, or termination fee;

(2) charges not provided for in subsection (a), including the cost of investing and reinvesting principal, the payments on principal of an indebtedness (including a mortgage amortized by periodic payments of principal), expenses for preparation of property for rental or sale, and, unless the court directs otherwise, expenses incurred in maintaining or defending any action to construe the trust or protect it or the property or assure the title of any trust property;

(3) extraordinary repairs or expenses incurred in making a capital improvement to principal, including special assessments, but, a trustee may establish an allowance for depreciation out of income to the extent permitted by subsection (a) (2) and by section 8;

(4) any tax levied upon profit, gain, or other receipts allocated to principal notwithstanding denomination of the tax as an income tax by the taxing authority;

(5) if an estate or inheritance tax is levied in respect of a trust in which both an income beneficiary and a remainderman have an interest, any amount apportioned to the trust, including interest and penalties, even though the income beneficiary also has rights in the principal [Revised Uniform Principal and Income Act, Section 13, 7, U.L.A.].

FIDUCIARY ACCOUNTS AND REPORTS

Fiduciary accounting accents the importance of delegated authority. The accounts of the fiduciary should clearly disclose the measure of his accountability and the extent to which it has been discharged. This emphasis on accountability compels a change in the fundamental accounting equation, which is modified as follows:

$$\text{Estate (Trust) Assets} = \text{Accountability}$$

It is evident that this accountability is stated in terms of total assets, without deducting the amount of existing claims against the estate or trust. A fiduciary is responsible for all of the assets entrusted to him; payment of existing claims is one way that a fiduciary discharges that responsibility.

The accounts and reports of the fiduciary should be kept in such form and detail as to sharply focus upon the *dual* responsibility of the fiduciary —in respect to income *and* in respect to principal. While the statutes of the various states provide important criteria for making this distinction, in many instances they do not prescribe the exact form and content of the fiduciary's accounts and reports.

Accounting Procedures and Entry Sequence for an Estate

Once the inventory of the decedent's assets has been filed, books of the estate should be opened in which are debited the accounts for assets enumerated in the inventory with a contra credit to Estate Principal, or Estate Corpus. Separate accounts should be provided for cash which is includable in the principal of the estate and cash which accumulates during tenancy and otherwise qualifies as estate income. The valuations assigned the various noncash assets are those indicated in the inventory. The Estate Principal, or Estate Corpus, account is credited with the gross amount of the inventory and represents the *initial* accountability of the fiduciary. In the event that other assets are discovered subsequent to the filing of the inventory, accounts should be opened for such assets with appropriate credits to Assets Subsequently Discovered. This account is a suspended credit to Estate Principal, to which it is closed at the end of the fiduciary accounting period.

Liabilities of the decedent are not recorded by the fiduciary until paid. Upon payment, an account—Debts of the Decedent Paid—is debited for the liquidation settlement. This transaction represents a reduction in the accountability of the fiduciary; accordingly, Debts of the Decedent Paid is essentially a suspended debit to Estate Principal. In respect to both assets and liabilities, the amount of account detail (and the necessity for subsidiary records) will be governed by the magnitude and diversity of assets in, and the number of claimants against, estate properties.

Gains or losses on the conversion of principal assets increase or decrease the accountability of the fiduciary in respect to the principal of the estate. Gain on Realization should be credited for conversion gains, and Loss on Realization should be debited for conversion losses; both accounts are closed to Estate Principal at the end of the accounting period. The increased (decreased) accountability of the fiduciary as a consequence of his profitable (unprofitable) employment of estate assets is not an attempt to measure net income; rather, it reflects a dominant stewardship orientation, the historical prototype of which is found in the master-slave relationship of Roman times. In this era, the slave was charged with funds entrusted to him by his master and with the increase attributable to fortunate investments; subsequently, he was discharged of his accountability to the extent of his repayment of resources advanced or accumulated or by other disposition as directed by the master. Most economic theories of income and asset valuation manifestly are not relevant to this type of fiduciary relationship. Correspondingly, the objectives of income determination and of stewardship reporting are essentially contradictory and are not accommodated by a single theoretical framework.

In addition to paying the debts of the decedent, the accountability of the fiduciary is further decreased by disbursements for funeral and administration expenses. A single Funeral and Administration Expenses account may be used for these outlays, or it may be desirable to identify the various expenses separately. Where a single account is used, its inclusions usually consist of expenses of last illness, funeral expenses, payments to the executor or trustee for administrative services to conserve the estate principal, accountant's, attorney's, and appraiser's fees, and court costs. The fiduciary's accountability in respect to principal is also decreased by the payment of estate taxes and the distribution of legacies. If a legacy involves the distribution of specific assets, the valuation assigned the distributed assets is the carrying value (accountability basis) of each asset, regardless of its current market value. This procedure is consistent with a stewardship, or accountability, objective. Where there are relatively few legatees, a single account—Legacies—may be sufficient; however, if the number of legatees is large, it may be desirable to use a separate account for each legatee. Where state inheritance taxes are to be charged against the legatees' accounts, or where it is necessary to reduce the legacies, it is especially important that separate accounts be maintained.

In respect to the fiduciary's accountability as to income, it is conventional to open an Income account to which are credited the various items of income for the estate. One account may be used for this purpose, or where there are numerous sources of income, several accounts which are descriptive as to source may be appropriate. Similarly, expenses incurred which are chargeable to such income should be debited to an Expenses–Income account or to several expense accounts detailing the nature of the expense. It is important that account designations clearly indicate an identification with either income or principal, where the conventional terminology does not convey the fact of this association. Distributions to income beneficiaries are usually charged to a Distribution to Income Beneficiary account, with the name of the indicated donee often appended.

Illustrative Problem

The following is a simplified case illustration of estate-trust accounting. William Archer died on June 1, 1978. His will, admitted to probate on June 10, 1978, provided that Andrew Archer, Sr., son of the decedent, be appointed executor. The will also provided that specific legacies of $2,500 cash be awarded to Andrew Jr. and Mark, grandsons of the decedent; $12,000 and the decedent's personal automobile to Andrew Sr.; personal effects and estate income to the widow, Alice; and the remainder of the estate property, after payment of debts and expenses and distribution of legacies, to be placed in trust. The income from the trust is to be paid to the widow during her lifetime, with the principal to be distributed equally to Andrew Jr. and Mark upon the widow's death.

Andrew Archer, Sr., filed the following inventory with the probate court on June 25:

Cash in bank	$ 28,000
Personal effects	750
Life insurance policies payable to the estate	30,000
1,000 shares of Edens Company $50 par value common stock—at market	49,000
500 shares of Cincy, Inc., 6 percent, $30 par value preferred stock—at market	15,000
20 Burnett Corporation 5 percent 30-year $1,000 bonds (interest payable March 1 and September 1)	19,600
Automobile	2,600
Dividend receivable (declared May 15, payable July 15, Edens Company common)	1,500
Interest receivable (Burnett Corporation bonds)	250
	$146,700

On the same date, the fiduciary opened accounts for the estate of William Archer and recorded the inventory as follows:

June 25	Cash—principal	28,000	
	Personal effects	750	
	Life insurance	30,000	
	Edens Company common stock	49,000	
	Cincy, Inc. preferred stock	15,000	
	Burnett Corporation bonds	19,600	
	Automobile	2,600	
	Dividend receivable	1,500	
	Interest receivable	250	
	Estate principal		146,700

Transactions and entries of the fiduciary in the period following were:

June 28   Public notice was given that creditors of the estate of the decedent should make a presentment of their claims.

July 15   Paid funeral expenses, $1,400.

Funeral and administration expenses	1,400	
Cash—principal		1,400

July 16   Collected dividends on Edens stock.

Cash principal	1,500	
Dividend receivable		1,500

July 20   Undeposited cash, $1,200, discovered among the decedent's personal belongings.

Cash—principal	1,200	
Assets subsequently discovered		1,200

July   31   Received payment on insurance policies.

Cash—principal 30,000
    Life insurance   30,000

Aug.   15   Sold 100 shares of Cincy, Inc., stock for $4,000.

Cash—principal 4,000
    Cincy, Inc., preferred stock   3,000
    Gain on realization   1,000

Sept.   1   Collected interest on Burnett Corporation bonds.

Cash—principal   250
Cash—income   250
    Interest receivable   250
    Income   250

Sept.   15   Paid debts of the decedent, $2,950.

Debts of the decedent paid 2,950
    Cash—principal   2,950

Oct.   1   Paid cash legacies provided for in the will.

Legacy—Andrew Archer, Sr. 12,000
Legacy—Andrew Archer, Jr. 2,500
Legacy—Mark Archer 2,500
    Cash—principal   17,000

Oct.   3   Delivered automobile (current market value, $1,800) to An-
drew Archer, Sr.

Legacy—Andrew Archer, Sr. 2,600
    Automobile   2,600

Oct.   3   Delivered decedent's personal effects to widow.

Legacy—Alice Archer   750
    Personal effects   750

Oct.   10   Collected cash dividend of $1,000 on Edens Company common
stock.

Cash—income   1,000
    Income   1,000

Oct.   15   Paid attorney's fees, $1,000, and other administrative expenses,
$2,500. Of the latter, $200 relates to income.

Funeral and administration expenses 3,300
Expenses—income   200
    Cash—principal   3,300
    Cash—income   200

Oct.   30   Three percent semiannual dividend declared on Cincy, Inc.,
preferred stock.

Dividend receivable 360
    Income   360

Nov. 1 Income of the estate in the amount of $500 is distributed to the widow.

Distribution to income beneficiary—Alice Archer	500	
Cash—income		500

Nov. 5 Two hundred shares of Edens Company common stock were sold for $9,000.

Cash—principal	9,000	
Loss on realization	800	
Edens Company common stock		9,800

Dec. 1 $250 interest accrued on Burnett Corporation bonds to December 1.

Interest receivable	250	
Income		250

Dec. 1 The executor rendered an accountability report to the probate court.

Charge and Discharge Statement

A report detailing the particulars of estate administration should be prepared and submitted periodically to the court of appropriate jurisdiction. Such a report is the charge and discharge statement. It may be regarded as an interim or a final statement of the fiduciary's accountability, depending upon the period of time normal to the completion of the settlement of the estate. The general form of the statement is normally prescribed by the statutes of the various states; however, there is no apparent consensus as to a single most desirable form. The two-division statement to be illustrated in the following pages is generally descriptive of many of the reports presently in use.

The charge and discharge statement is a classified enumeration of the estate resources for which the fiduciary is accountable, and a description of the manner in which he has discharged his accountability during the period of his administration. His responsibilities for principal and income are separately reported. In respect to *principal,* the report indicates those asset categories for which the fiduciary *charges* himself, or has accepted a custodial responsibility. They include:

1. Assets enumerated in the inventory.
2. Assets subsequently discovered.
3. Gains recognized on the conversion or other disposition of principal assets.

There follows the discharge of the fiduciary's accountability, i.e., the offered justification for which the fiduciary *credits* himself. These credits include:

1. Payment of funeral and administration expenses.
2. Debts of the decedent paid.
3. Estate and inheritance taxes paid.
4. Payment or distribution of legacies.
5. Losses realized on conversion or other disposition of principal assets.

To the extent that there remains an undistributed asset accumulation, as would exist in respect to an interim report, or in a final report preceding the transfer of assets to a testamentary trust, these accounts should be enumerated with assigned valuations.

In respect to income, the fiduciary *charges* himself for income earned since the date of the decedent's death. Items of income, if significant, should be identified as to source. Dispositions of income for which the fiduciary customarily *credits* himself include:

1. Expenses which are chargeable to such income.
2. Payments or other distributions to income beneficiaries.

Some accountants prefer to prepare separate reports for income and principal; their contents would necessarily be the same as the categories described above for a two-division statement.

Using the data of the estate of William Archer, a charge and discharge statement as of December 1 would assume the form shown in Illustration 17–1. This statement is a summary report and where necessary should be supported by schedules providing informative details with respect to each of the major categories. If subsequent reports are necessary, they are prepared on a cumulative basis and will continue to disclose fully the fiduciary's activities during the period of his accountability.

Closing Entries

When activities of estate administration are concluded, a final report is rendered, after which the fiduciary closes the accounts of the estate. In respect to principal, this involves closing to Estate Principal those relevant accounts created during the administration representing increases or decreases in the fiduciary's accountability. Accordingly, Assets Subsequently Discovered, Gains and Losses on Realization, Debts of the Decedent Paid, Legacies Paid or Distributed, and Funeral and Administration Expenses are closed to Estate Principal. Similarly, the accounts which are chargeable to income should be closed thereunto. They include Expenses—Income and Distributions to Income Beneficiary. Unless assets remain for some ultimate disposition, these entries should reduce all accounts to zero balances.

Illustration 17–1

ESTATE OF WILLIAM ARCHER
ANDREW ARCHER, SR., EXECUTOR

Charge and Discharge Statement
June 1, 1978, to December 1, 1978

As to Principal

I charge myself with:

Assets per inventory		$146,700
Assets subsequently discovered		1,200
Gain on realization		1,000
Total		$148,900

I credit myself with:

Funeral and administration expenses	$ 4,700	
Debts of decedent paid	2,950	
Legacies paid or distributed:		
Andrew Archer, Sr.	14,600	
Andrew Archer, Jr.	2,500	
Mark Archer	2,500	
Alice Archer	750	
Loss on realization	800	28,800
Balance as to principal		$120,100

Which includes:

Cash	$ 49,300
Edens Company common stock	39,200
Cincy, Inc., preferred stock	12,000
Burnett Corporation bonds	19,600
Total	$120,100

As to Income

I charge myself with:

Income collected or accrued		$ 1,860

I credit myself with:

Expenses chargeable to income	$ 200	
Distribution to income beneficiary	500	700
Balance as to income		$ 1,160

Which includes:

Cash	$ 550
Dividend receivable	360
Interest receivable	250
Total	$ 1,160

Properties Transferred to Trustee

In the illustration begun earlier in this chapter, provision was made for the transfer of estate properties to a trustee, *after* the fiduciary's payment of debts of the decedent and expenses of administration and the payment and/or delivery of legacies. If it is assumed that the transfer of properties is made concurrent with the rendering of the charge and discharge statement on December 1, 1978, the following entries are required to close the books of the estate and to open the trust accounts:

Executor's Books

Dec. 1	Assets subsequently discovered	1,200	
	Gain on realization	1,000	
	Estate principal		2,200
Dec. 1	Estate principal	28,800	
	Debts of the decedent paid		2,950
	Funeral and administration expenses		4,700
	Legacy—Andrew Archer, Sr.		14,600
	Legacy—Andrew Archer, Jr.		2,500
	Legacy—Mark Archer		2,500
	Legacy—Alice Archer		750
	Loss on realization		800
Dec. 1	Income	700	
	Expenses—income		200
	Distribution to income beneficiary		500
Dec. 1	Estate principal	120,100	
	Income	1,160	
	K. L. Mantle, trustee		121,260
Dec. 1	K. L. Mantle, trustee	120,100	
	Cash—principal		49,300
	Edens Company common stock		39,200
	Cincy, Inc., preferred stock		12,000
	Burnett Corporation bonds		19,600
Dec. 1	K. L. Mantle, trustee	1,160	
	Cash—income		550
	Dividend receivable		360
	Interest receivable		250

Trustee's Books

Dec. 1	Cash—principal	49,300	
	Edens Company common stock	39,200	
	Cincy, Inc., preferred stock	12,000	
	Burnett Corporation bonds	19,600	
	Trust principal		120,100
Dec. 1	Cash—income	550	
	Dividend receivable	360	
	Interest receivable	250	
	Income		1,160

The trustee normally accepts fiduciary responsibility concurrent with the transfer of trust property to him. All accrued income prior to the creation of a living trust is includable as trust principal; income earned thereafter is distributable to income beneficiaries. In respect to testamentary trusts, however, the trust usually becomes effective at date of death and income earned thereafter is trust income, notwithstanding a delay in the transfer of trust properties to the trustee.

The trustee's accounting essentially parallels that of the executor. The Trust Principal and Income accounts are the summary accounts of the trustee, indicating his separate accountability as to both principal and income.

The trustee should render periodic reports of his stewardship to the court recounting the activities of his trust administration. As in the case of estates, the content of such statements depends upon the statutory provisions of the relevant state. The Uniform Trustees Accounting Act suggests that interim reports contain:

(a) the period which the account covers;

(b) the names and addresses of the living beneficiaries known to the trustee, with a statement as to those known to be minors or under legally declared disability; and a description of any possible unborn or unascertained beneficiaries; and the name of the surety or sureties on the trustee's bond with the amount of such bond;

(c) in a separate schedule the trust principal on hand at the beginning of the accounting period and the then status of its investment; the investments received from the settlor and still held; additions to trust principal during the accounting period with the dates and sources of acquisition; investments collected, sold or charged off during the accounting period, with the consequent loss or gain and whether credited to principal or income; investments made during the accounting period, with the date, source and cost of each; deductions from principal during the accounting period, with the date and purpose of each; and trust principal on hand at the end of the accounting period, how invested, and the estimated market value of each investment;

(d) in a separate schedule the trust income on hand at the beginning of the accounting period, and in what form held; trust income received during the accounting period, when, and from what source; trust income paid out during the accounting period, when, to whom, and for what purpose; trust income on hand at the end of the accounting period, and how invested;

(e) that neither any seller of, nor buyer from, the trustee of trust property during the accounting period was at the time of such sale or purchase (1) in the case of a corporate trustee, an affiliate, or any officer, employee, or nominee of the trustee or of an affiliate; or was (2) in the case of a non-corporate trustee a relative, partner, employer, employee, or business associate; but none of the provisions of this subsection shall apply to purchases and sales made by brokers for the trustee or to stock exchanges;

(f) a statement of unpaid claims with the reason for failure to pay them, including a statement as to whether any estate or inheritance taxes have become due with regard to the trust property, and if due, whether paid;

(g) a brief summary of the account;

(h) such other facts as the court may by rule or court order require.

Within thirty days after the end of each yearly period thereafter during the life of the trust the testamentary trustee then in office shall file with the same court an intermediate account under oath showing corresponding facts regarding the current accounting period [Section 3, Uniform Trustees Accounting Act, 9C, U.L.A., 1967 edition].

As to the final accounting, the Act provides:

Within [   ] days after the termination of every testamentary trust the trustee, and in the case of the transfer of the trusteeship due to the death, resignation, removal, dissolution, merger or consolidation of a sole trustee, the successor in interest of the old trustee, shall file with the [probate court of the county where the will was admitted to probate] a final account under oath, showing for the period since the filing of the last account the facts required by Section 3 regarding intermediate accountings and in case of termination of the trust the distribution of the trust property which the accountant proposes to make [Section 4, Uniform Trustees Accounting Act, 9C, U.L.A., 1967 edition].

QUESTIONS

1. Briefly describe the responsibilities of a fiduciary (executor, administrator) in the administration of an estate.
2. What types of assets are frequently excluded from the fiduciary's inventory of assets?
3. What is a typical *sequence of payment* for the various estate obligations?
4. The fiduciary must distinguish in his records between the principal (corpus) and the income of an estate or trust. Why?
5. As a general rule, how are accruals of income and expense identified with the principal and with the income of an estate?
6. Should depreciation be charged against the principal or income of an estate?
7. What is the fundamental equation for fiduciary accounting? For what reason is this expression stated in terms of claims against the estate or trust?
8. Once an inventory of the decedent's assets has been filed, what accounts should be opened by the executor (administrator) in which to record the transactions for the estate?
9. What is the *charge and discharge statement?* What information does it provide?

EXERCISES

Exercise 17–1

Read the introductory facts below and then denote whether each of the sentences below is true or false according to the general principles of trust law, such as the Revised Uniform Principal and Income Act. If an answer is false, explain why it is false.

Accountant Smathers is Trustee of a testamentary trust established by Parker's will. The corpus of the trust consists of "blue chip" securities and a large office building subject to a mortgage. The will provides that trust income is to be paid to Parker's wife during her lifetime, that the Trust will terminate on her death, and that the corpus is then to be distributed to the Brookdale School for Boys.

a. If Smathers receives a cash dividend on one of the Trust securities, he may not use it to purchase additional securities for the trust corpus without compensating Parker's wife.
b. If Smathers receives a 5 percent stock dividend, he should distribute it to Mrs. Parker.
c. The cost of insurance on the office building should be deducted by Smathers from the income paid to Mrs. Parker.

d. Monthly principal payments to amortize the mortgage are deducted from Mrs. Parker's income.

e. Proceeds from fire insurance on the office building would be a part of the corpus.

(AICPA adapted)

Exercise 17–2

Refer to the facts and the instructions of 17–1 above to answer the following true-false questions.

a. The cost of exercising stock warrants is chargeable to trust income.

b. The Brookdale School is the remainderman of the trust created under Parker's will.

c. The beneficiaries of the trust have an equitable interest in the trust income and corpus.

d. The beneficiaries of the trust would have standing in court to proceed against the trustee for waste of the corpus.

e. If Mrs. Parker and the Brookdale School agree to terminate the trust and divide the corpus, Smathers would have to comply with their wishes.

(AICPA adapted)

Exercise 17–3

Lloyd Carlisle died on January 18, 1978. His will was admitted to probate on February 5, and Arthur Waddell was appointed executor of the estate. The following transactions relate to the executorial period, February 6 through July 1, 1978:

a. Waddell filed the following inventory of Carlisle's assets with the court:

Cash on deposit, Second National Bank	$ 5,690
Undeposited currency	220
Common stock, Stuchell Corporation:	
1,000 shares (par, $10) @ $27	27,000
6%, 20-year Harley Company debentures:	
10 bonds @ $200	2,000
Automobile	4,300
Household furnishings	1,950
Life insurance, payable to the estate	10,000
Dividends receivable, Stuchell stock:	
Dividend declared January 15, 1978	800
Interest receivable:	
Harley Company bonds (January 1 and July 1)	
January 1 to January 18	6

b. Funeral expenses of $934 were paid by Waddell.

c. Six $1,200 Arnheim, Inc., bonds, 5 percent November 1 and May 1, were discovered upon search of the decedent's personal belongings.

d. The life insurance policy was collected.

e. Notice was published for the presentment of claims against the estate, after which debts of the decedent amounting to $1,450, were validated and paid.
f. The dividend on Stuchell stock was collected.
g. All of the common stock of the Stuchell Corporation was sold for cash, $24,600.
h. Executorial fees were paid Waddell in the amount of $2,100.
i. The May 1 interest collection was made on Arnheim, Inc., bonds.
j. The automobile was sold for $3,100 cash.
k. According to the conditions of the will, a cash legacy was paid to Mary Carlisle, the widow, in amount of $10,000.
l. The July 1 interest collection was made on Harley Company debentures.
m. All income earned to July 1 was distributed to the widow; all other assets remaining in the estate were distributed equally to Tom and Larry Carlisle, sons of the decedent.

Required:

a. Journalize the above transactions on the books of Arthur Waddell, executor.
b. Make closing entries on July 1 to close the executor's books.

Exercise 17–4

Albert Sims, attorney-at-law, died on July 1, 1978. His partner, Henry Creek, was appointed executor of his estate and filed with the probate court on July 18 the following inventory of assets of the deceased:

Deposit balance, First State Bank	$ 4,800
4% RX bonds, interest payable April 1 and October 1 (par, $40,000)	32,200
Accrued interest on RX bonds	400
6% cumulative Cleburne, Inc., preferred stock, 200 shares (par, $35,000)	19,300
100 shares of Bancroft-Benson no-par common stock	4,200
Value of properties established by court-appointed appraisers:	
Office building of the law partnership (separately owned by Simon)	46,000
Automobile	2,200
	$109,100

An additional 200 shares of Bancroft-Benson were discovered by the executor on September 1.

The office building was sold on September 14 to Bruegman and Sons, realtors, for $41,000; the 300 shares of Bancroft-Benson were sold on September 21 for $13,100. On October 1 interest was collected on the RX bonds.

During the three months ended October 1, 1978, the executor made the following payments:

Funeral expenses	$ 2,500
Administrative expenses	1,900
Debts of the decedent	15,500

The will of the deceased provides that legacies and income be distributed as follows:

> To widow, Mary:
> Cash, $17,000.
> Cleburne stock.
> Income of estate.
>
> To son, Arnold:
> Cash, $10,000.
> Automobile.
>
> To son, Charles:
> Cash, $10,000.
> RX bonds.
> The residue.

Required:

a. Prepare the executor's journal entries for estate transactions for the quarter ended October 1, 1978.
b. Journalize the distribution of income and the distribution of legacies on October 2; making closing entries for the estate.

Exercise 17–5

William Fess was named executor of the estate of Huey Howard, who died on March 13, 1978. On December 31, 1978, the executor prepared the following trial balance:

ESTATE OF HUEY HOWARD

Trial Balance

December 31, 1978

Investments:		
Stocks	$18,500	
Bonds	42,000	
Accrued interest receivable	75	
Cash—principal	10,850	
Cash—income	2,125	
Household effects	2,375	
Loss on realization	650	
Gain on realization		$ 1,200
Assets subsequently discovered		5,520
Debts of decedent paid	5,600	
Funeral expenses	950	
Administration expenses	2,570	
Estate corpus		79,275
Income		3,575
Expenses—income	380	
Distribution to income beneficiary	995	
Legacy—Arnold Howard	2,500	
	$89,570	$89,570

Required:

Prepare a charge and discharge statement for the estate of Huey Howard.

Exercise 17–6

Alex Dunn, Jr., died on January 15, 1978; his records disclose the following estate:

Cash in bank	$ 3,750
6% note receivable, including $50 accrued interest	5,050
Stocks	50,000
Dividends declared on stocks	600
6% mortgage receivable, including $100 accrued interest	20,100
Real estate—apartment house	35,000
Household effects	8,250
Dividend receivable from Alex Dunn, Sr., trust fund	250,000
Total	$372,750

On July 1, 1953, the late Alex Dunn, Sr., created a trust fund, with his son, Alex Dunn, Jr., as life tenant, and his grandson as remainderman. The assets in the fund consist solely of the outstanding capital stock of Dunn, Inc., namely, 2,000 shares of $100 par each. At the creation of the trust, the book—as well as the market—value of these shares was $400,000 and at December 31, 1977, was $500,000. On January 2, 1978, Dunn, Inc., declared a 125 percent cash dividend payable February 2, 1978, to shareholders of record January 12, 1978.

The executor's transactions from January 15, to 31, 1978, were as follows:

Cash receipts:

Jan. 20	Dividends	$ 1,500.00
25	6% notes receivable	5,000.00
	Interest accrued on note	58.33
	Stocks sold, inventoried at $22,500	20,000.00
	6% mortgage sold	20,100.00
	Interest accrued on mortgage	133.33
28	Sale of assets not inventoried	250.00
29	Real estate sold	30,000.00
		$77,041.66

Cash disbursements:

Jan. 20	Funeral expenses	$ 750.00
23	Decedent's debts	8,000.00
25	Decedent's bequests	10,000.00
31	Distribution of income to widow	500.00
		$19,250.00

Required:

Prepare a charge and discharge statement for the executor for the period from January 15 to January 31, 1978.

(AICPA adapted)

PROBLEMS

Problem 1

Cal Chase, partner in Chase-Dacey Farm Implements, died on March 31, 1978. Nat Dacey was named executor of his partner's estate which consisted of the following:

Cash	$ 25,100
Livestock	48,000
Ranch land and improvements including farm buildings, fencing, etc.—at appraised valuation	31,600
4% Gantry Company debentures, interest January 1 and July 1 (par, $60,000)	52,000
Interest receivable—Gantry Company debentures	600
150 shares Collegaire common stock (par, $30,000)	26,000
One-half interest in Chase-Dacey partnership—at appraised valuation	84,000
	$267,300

Legacies are to be distributed as follows:

a. Livestock and ranch properties to the widow, Shirley, together with the deceased's partnership interest in Chase-Dacey Farm Implements.
b. $30,000 par value of Gantry Company debentures to son, Richard.
c. Collegaire common stock to Fabens Military Academy.
d. Residual estate, after payments of funeral and administrative expenses, debts of decedent and other specific bequests, to the widow. Income of the estate, excluding partnership net income, is to be distributed as collected to the son, Richard. The interest of the deceased in partnership net income was 50 percent and is bequeathed to the widow.

Transactions of the executor were:

Apr. 2   Filed the March 31 inventory of the deceased.
     15   Paid funeral and administrative expenses, $6,200.
     30   Sold $30,000 par value of Gantry Company debentures for $23,500 and accrued interest.
     30   Distributed estate income.
May 1   Paid debts of decedent, $9,400.
     10   Paid federal estate and state inheritance taxes, $28,700.
     20   Dividends declared on Collegaire stock on April 14 were received, $600.
     21   Distributed estate income.
July 1   Collected interest on Gantry Company debentures.
      1   Partnership profits for the second quarter of 1978 are reported to be $7,000.
      1   Distributed estate income, legacies, and residual estate properties as provided in the will.

Required:

a. Prepare entries on the books of the executor through July 1, 1978.
b. Journalize entries to close the books of the estate.

Problem 2

Arthur Taine died in an accident on May 31, 1978. His will, dated February 28, 1965, provided that all just debts and expenses be paid and that his property be disposed of as follows:

Personal residence—devised to Bertha Taine, widow.
United States Treasury bonds and Puritan Company stock—to be placed in trust. All income to go to Bertha Taine during her lifetime, with right of appointment upon her death.
Seneca Company mortgage notes—bequeathed to Elaine Taine Langer, daughter.
Cash—a bequest of $10,000 to David Taine, son.
Remainder of estate—to be divided equally between the two children, Elaine Taine Langer and David Taine.

The will further provided that during the administration period Bertha Taine was to be paid $300 a month out of estate income, calculated and reported on a cash basis. David Taine was named as executor and trustee.

An inventory of the decedent's property was prepared. The fair market value of all items as of the date of death was determined. The preliminary inventory, before the computation of any appropriate income accruals on inventory items, follows:

Personal residence property	$ 45,000
Jewelry—diamond ring	9,600
York Life Insurance Company—term life insurance policy on life of Arthur Taine:	
Beneficiary—Bertha Taine, widow	120,000
Granite Trust Company—3% savings bank account, Arthur Taine, in trust for Philip Langer (grandchild), interest credited January 1 and July 1; balance May 31, 1978	400
Fidelity National Bank—checking account; balance May 31, 1978	143,000
$100,000 United States Treasury bonds, 3%, 2004, interest payable March 1 and September 1	100,000
800 shares Puritan Company common stock	64,000
700 shares Meta Mfg. Company common stock	70,000
$9,700 Seneca Company first-mortgage notes, 6%, 1982, interest payable May 31 and November 30	9,900

The executor opened an estate bank account to which he transferred the decedent's checking account balance. Other deposits, through July 1, 1979, were as follows:

Interest collected on bonds:	
$100,000 United States Treasury:	
September 1, 1978	$ 1,500
March 1, 1979	1,500
Dividends received on stock:	
800 shares Puritan Company:	
June 15, 1978, declared May 7, 1978 payable to holders of record as of May 27, 1978	800
September 15, 1978	800
December 15, 1978	1,200
March 15, 1979	800
June 15, 1979	800
Net proceeds of June 19, 1978, sale of 700 shares of Meta Mfg. Company	68,810

Payments were made from the estate's checking account through July 1, 1979 for the following:

Funeral expenses	$ 2,000
Assessments for additional 1976 federal and state income taxes ($1,700) plus interest ($110) to May 31, 1978	1,810
1978 income taxes of Arthur Taine for the period January 1, 1978, through May 31, 1978, in excess of amounts paid by the decedent on declarations of estimated tax	9,100
Federal and state fiduciary income taxes, fiscal years ending June 30, 1978 ($75), and June 30, 1979 ($1,400)	1,475
Federal and state estate taxes	58,000
Monthly payments to Bertha Taine: 13 payments of $300	3,900
Attorney's and accountant's fees	25,000

The executor waived his commission. However, he desired to receive his father's diamond ring in lieu of the $10,000 specific legacy. All parties agreed to this in writing, and the court's approval was secured. All other specific legacies were delivered by July 15, 1978.

Required:

Prepare a charge and discharge statement as to principal and income, and its supporting schedules, to accompany the attorney's formal court accounting on behalf of the executor of the estate of Arthur Taine for the period from May 31, 1978, through July 1, 1979. The following supporting schedules should be included:

1. Original Capital of Estate.
2. Gain on Disposal of Estate Assets.
3. Loss on Disposal of Estate Assets.
4. Funeral, Administration, and Other Expenses.
5. Debts of Decedent Paid.
6. Legacies Paid or Delivered.
7. Assets (Corpus) on Hand, July 1, 1979.
8. Proposed Plan of Distribution of Estate Assets.
9. Income Collected.
10. Distribution of Income.

(AICPA adapted)

Problem 3

Using the data of Problem 4, Chapter 16, prepare a charge and discharge statement for the trustee for the interim period of operations and partial liquidation of the Rawley Manufacturing Corporation.

Problem 4

The will of E. M. Dodd, who died on December 31, 1972, provided cash bequests of $40,000 to Mrs. Dodd and $15,000 each to two children, the residuary estate to be divided equally among the three beneficiaries. Mrs. Dodd was appointed executrix and trustee without fees or other emoluments.

By court order Mrs. Dodd was to receive a family allowance of $4,000 a month, commencing January 1, 1973, payable from income or from any cash principal available if the income should be inadequate. The estate never had enough cash available to pay the full allowance nor could any part of the cash bequests be paid. Accordingly a considerable liability to Mrs. Dodd had accumulated toward the end of 1978 for the unpaid portion of the family allowance, as shown by the following trial balance of the estate ledger at December 31 of that year:

Cash	$ 200	
Securities	20,000	
Building A	200,000	
Accumulated depreciation		$ 36,000
Building B	160,000	
Accumulated depreciation		38,400
Mortgage—building B		32,000
Revolving fund—building A	1,800	
Revolving fund—building B	2,400	
Mrs. E. M. Dodd—family allowance		288,000
Mrs. E. M. Dodd—paid on account	178,000	
Estate corpus		168,000
	$562,400	$562,400

The balance in the estate corpus account was made up as follows:

Appraisal of assets	$365,000
Deduct—funeral expenses, etc.	15,000
	$350,000
Add—income:	
Dividends received	6,000
Rentals, after deducting expenses and mortgage interest to date	100,000
	$456,000
Deduct—family allowance	288,000
Balance	168,000

For want of cash the beneficiaries decided to settle all liabilities by transfer of property, and they requested their attorney to petition the court for approval of the following agreement to take effect as of December 31, 1978:

> The building B and its revolving fund are to be conveyed to Mrs. Dodd subject to the mortgage. In turn she agrees to waive all her claims against the estate for expenditures not refunded to her, including one of $5,000 for estate income taxes paid by her and not collected from the estate, and in addition to pay attorney's fees of $6,000 for the estate. Furthermore, all beneficiaries agree to have the family allowance discontinued after December 31, 1978, and also to waive their claims to the cash bequests.

The court gave its approval to the agreement and ordered an intermediary accounting by the trustee as of December 31, 1978.

Required:

Based upon the above information, prepare:

a.   Columnar work sheet showing the trial balance before and after adjustment.

b.   Statement of Mrs. Dodd's account.

c. Trustee's intermediary accounting in the form of a charge and discharge statement.

(AICPA adapted)

Problem 5

James Roe died on December 31, 1978, and left an estate that was to be divided equally among his four children, all legally of age:

> Mary Roe Powell
> Albert Roe
> Edward Roe
> Ethel Roe

All funeral expenses, doctor's bills, and other liabilities, including all death duties and estate taxes, were to be paid by the Cohasset Trust Company from a fund that had been provided by the deceased during his lifetime and was on deposit with the trust company. Any balance remaining in this fund, after all payments had been made, was to be retained by the trust company in payment for its services. The trust company agreed to accept that balance in full settlement.

Two trusts will ultimately be set up—one for Mary and the other for Ethel. The eldest son, Albert, was appointed sole executor and trustee of the estate and of the trusts to be created. The principal of each trust was to remain intact during the beneficiary's lifetime, but each beneficiary had the right of appointment (by this right each daughter could direct to whom the principal of her trust should be paid at her death). The two sons, Albert and Edward, were each to receive their one-quarter share without any restrictions. The net income from the estate was to be distributed semiannually.

The inventory of the estate consisted of—

Cash in bank	$ 100,000
$400,000, 3⅜% municipal bonds at market value	400,000
20,000 shares of no-par value stock of Roe Manufacturing Company, appraised at	5,400,000
1,000 shares Cohasset Trust Company stock of $100 par, market value $300 per share	300,000
Waterfront property at Cohasset Bay, appraised at	800,000
	$7,000,000

The heirs decided to leave the estate undivided for the present under the trusteeship of Albert Roe who, with his brother Edward and his brother-in-law John Powell, continued the management of the Roe Manufacturing Company.

The coupons of the municipal bonds were payable on June 30 and December 31. The Roe Manufacturing Company continued to pay each month a dividend of 50 cents per share and the Cohasset Trust Company paid a dividend of $12.50 per share, both on June 1 and December 1. No income was received from the Cohasset Bay property.

On July 1, 1979, Ethel Roe was killed in an automobile accident. By the terms of her will, appointing Albert Roe executor, she left $500,000 in specific bequests, the balance of her estate to be equally divided among her brothers and sister. The estate of Ethel Roe consisted solely of her interest in the estate of her father, with the exception of cash in bank which was just enough to pay burial costs, death duties, and all other liabilities.

The executor of the estate of James Roe, with the consent of the court and of the other heirs, decided to advance to the estate of Ethel Roe the $500,000 required to pay the specific bequests and to charge the amount against her share in the estate of James Roe. It was likewise decided to grant the requests of Albert Roe for an advance of $200,000 and of Edward Roe for an advance of $100,000 against their shares in the latter estate. Both agreed to interest charges on these advances from July 1, 1979, at a reasonable rate that would also be fair to the Mary Roe Powell trust, but no interest would be charged on the $500,000 advanced to the estate of Ethel Roe.

In order to provide the necessary cash funds on August 1, 1979, the $400,000 municipal bonds and the 1,000 shares Cohasset Trust Company stock were sold respectively for $420,000 and $320,000 net after broker's commissions, taxes, and other selling expenses, and on that date the above advances were made.

No change in the executorship and trusteeship of Albert Roe was to take place on account of Ethel Roe's death, but with the consent of the court and of the heirs, her remaining interest in her father's estate was to be divided as of the date of her death in accordance with the terms of her will.

The trustee paid the following expenses in 1979:

> Incidental expenses for the year applicable in equal amounts to
> the six months before and after the death of Ethel Roe ...... $ 1,290
> Taxes on real estate, payable in June and December 18,000

Trustee's commissions at the legal rates for "receiving and paying out" as follows:

> 5% on the first .... $ 2,000
> 2½% on the next 20,000
> 1½% on the next 28,000
> 2% on the balance.

One half of these rates is for receiving and one half for paying. The same rates apply to principal and to income cash. These commissions are paid June 30 and December 31.

Required:

a. Prepare a columnar work sheet to which the transactions in the six months before and after division of the Ethel Roe estate are posted so as to produce the balance sheets of the estate of James Roe immediately after the division of the estate of Ethel Roe on July 1, 1979, and on December 31, 1979. Show the calculation of the rate of interest charged to Albert and Edward Roe and give the reason why the use of that rate should be considered fair to the Mary Roe Powell trust.

b. Prepare the trustee's intermediary accounting as at December 31, 1979, in the form of a charge and discharge statement, showing the payments to each beneficiary.

(AICPA adapted)

18

Principles of
Governmental
Accounting

THE PRINCIPAL ORIENTATION of current accounting research is the development of an internally consistent and articulated accounting theory for profit-oriented commercial enterprises. There is, however, a parallel need —equally compelling—for analysis and methodological refinement in other accounting domains. In this chapter, the underlying concepts of governmental accounting will be outlined briefly; procedural detail is presented only in digest or summary form. For a more complete discussion, the reader is referred to texts devoted exclusively to this subject.

BASIC CONCEPTS OF GOVERNMENTAL ACCOUNTING

Several fundamental propositions which relate to governmental accounting *generally* will be discussed before attention is directed to more specific accounting relationships. Following an exploratory treatment of the fundamental notion of funds, the reader is introduced briefly to the related concepts of expendable and nonexpendable funds, budgeting and budgetary accounting, encumbrances and obligations, appropriations, and apportionments and allotments.

The Nature of Funds

Every accounting system must incorporate some type of *unit* concept which provides a basis for deciding fundamental questions such as: What economic events should be recorded by the system and what events should be disregarded? In regard to accounting for profit-oriented businesses, the accounting unit is generally described as an *entity*. Thus, partnerships, corporations, and corporate affiliations are typical examples of accounting entities. In governmental accounting, the primary accounting unit is referred to as a *fund*. The National Committee on Governmental Accounting defined a *fund* and pointed out its significance in the following terms:

Governmental accounting systems should be organized and operated on a fund basis. A fund is defined as an independent fiscal and accounting entity with a self-balancing set of accounts recording cash and/or other resources together with all related liabilities, obligations, reserves, and equities which are segregated for the purpose of carrying on specific activities or attaining certain objectives in accordance with special regulations, restrictions, or limitations.[1]

This definition emphasizes the separate and distinct character of a fund. *Specific* activities or objectives are attributable to a fund; the fiscal and accounting unit is *independent;* the set of accounts is *self-balancing;* the resources and related liabilities are segregated. However, this should not be misinterpreted as an implication that one governmental organization represents one fund. Many governmental organizations, e.g., a city, include many separately identifiable activities, each of which may justify the creation of a separate fund. Obviously, the number of funds which may be identified will depend, in part, upon the size and operational spectrum of the governmental entity.

Although the concept of separate funds in governmental accounting essentially reflects the impact of inherent legal restrictions, Professor William J. Vatter foresees a much broader application and has accordingly generalized the fund concept.[2] Professor Vatter observes that some economic unit must always serve as an accounting frame of reference. Choice of the optimum unit is, therefore, an especially important first step in the accounting process. In the fund theory of accounting, it is proposed that such a unit should be devoid of personal implications, as are alleged to exist in the proprietary and entity theories; at the same time, the unit must be adequately defined with a clear specification of its boundaries. The principal emphasis of the fund theory is that it focuses on a specified area of operations, a center of interest, which significantly does not depend upon legal or other forms of personality. The fund configuration is that of a unit of activity to which a collection of assets relates. Since the operations of the fund entail acquisition and disposition of various kinds of assets, the fund accounts must include a record of the restrictions or limitations on the use of these assets, i.e., a unique form of equity. Some types of asset receipts carry no special restrictions other than those implicit in the definition of the fund. Such an asset inflow should be recorded in special accounts as

[1] National Committee on Governmental Accounting, Municipal Finance Officers Association of the United States and Canada, *Governmental Accounting, Auditing, and Financial Reporting* (Chicago, 1968), pp. 6–7.

[2] William J. Vatter, *The Fund Theory of Accounting and Its Implications for Financial Reports* (Chicago: The University of Chicago Press, 1947), p. 12.

revenue. Since the operations of the fund also involve the release of services in order to achieve the objectives of the fund, expense accounts must be provided. This collection (or system) of accounts reflects the essence of the fund, encompassing the operational concepts of assets, specific restrictions on assets, revenue and expense, and fund surplus (balance of unrestricted assets). The use of funds in governmental accounting conforms closely with this theoretical structure. Additionally, while the business entity is presently conceived to be the nucleus for commercial accounting, Vatter argues that the fund may be a more appropriate and efficient unit of account.

Expendable and Nonexpendable Funds

An expendable fund is an aggregation of resources which are totally available for expenditure in achieving the objectives of the fund. Revenues for such a fund may derive from taxes, fees, special assessments, proceeds of bond issues, or interfund transfers. Fund *expenses* include those expenditures required for services, supplies, *and equipment*. Since existing fixed assets represent prior expenditures of a fund, they are, perforce, *excluded* from an enumeration of resources of an expendable fund. The appropriateness of this approach to the concept of fund resources will be examined subsequently in more detail.

A nonexpendable fund requires that the principal or capital balance of the fund be preserved intact. A revolving fund which is expected to generate revenues sufficient in amount to cover operating expenses of the fund, without dilution of principal, is an example of a nonexpendable fund. Additionally, a trust fund which permits the expenditure of income only is a nonexpendable fund. The expendable fund will be emphasized in this chapter, with only brief mention made of nonexpendable funds.

The Budget and Budgetary Accounting

The operations of expendable revenue funds, which encompass the principal recurring activities of a governmental body, are normally controlled by a system of budgets and budgetary accounting. The objectives of a governmental budget for an expendable fund are usually a combination of both planning and control. Initially, the governmental budget is an estimate of anticipated expenditures during a given period or for a specified purpose, with proposed methods of financing the budget objectives—i.e., a planning budget. Once approved, however, the estimated expenditures are translated into expenditure authorizations, which represent specific legislative or higher administrative approved amounts. Thus, the budget (as modified) becomes a relatively inflexible control device which operationally prohibits unfavorable variances from budgetary estimates. Consequently, rather than serving as a useful guide or standard by which to measure efficient performance, the governmental budget is often a rigid instrument of control, expressed in the form of legal ceilings for the amount of expenditures.

Although budgets are widely used in commercial accounting to facilitate planning and control, they generally are not recorded in the accounts. In governmental accounting, on the other hand, the authorized budget is formally recognized in special *budgetary accounts*. In effect, each fund has a self-balancing, independent set of budgetary accounts which are used to accumulate and preserve budgetary information, i.e., estimated revenues and authorized expenditures. These accounts constitute a formal record of the financial plan. In contrast to the budgetary accounts, different accounts are used to record actual transactions; these are generally referred to as *proprietary accounts*. Significantly, the balance in a given proprietary account, e.g., Revenues, can be compared with its corresponding budgetary account, Estimated Revenues, to evaluate how closely actual operations have conformed to what was budgeted. Indeed, subsequent analysis will show how corresponding budgetary and proprietary accounts are closed in one entry, thereby leaving a permanent record of the difference between budgeted and actual data.

Even though expenditures are initially restricted by the creation of different funds, a formal budget is necessary to indicate amounts to be spent for each activity financed by the individual funds. In the absence of economic competition and the discipline of the profit motive, the government must place greater reliance on budgets and budgetary control as an effective means of controlling expenditures. It is obvious, however, that budgetary control limits only the amount of the total expenditures for each program; without further analyses and additional controls, this technique fails to measure the type of efficiency indicated by a comparison of "standard costs" of program accomplishments with actual costs.

Encumbrances and Obligations

A system of *encumbrances* is a means of restricting or reserving available spending authority pending the recording of actual liabilities and/or expenditures. As purchase orders and other commitments for expenditures are approved, the authority to make expenditures is restricted so as to ensure the future availability of assets to pay for the approved expenditures. Until the actual expenditure has been determined and charged against the spending authority of the fund, the encumbered portion of available funds may not be used for purposes other than those contemplated at the time resources are thus restricted. If it is then determined that an excessive amount of resources has been encumbered, the difference between the amount of the original encumbrance and the amount of the actual liability may be re-encumbered for other purposes. Budgetary control is accordingly exercised by application of the encumbrance concept concurrent with the execution of bilateral agreements, i.e., at the time of commitment (executory contract stage), rather than at the time of the receipt of goods or the rendering of services.

In federal governmental accounting, a system of *obligations* is used to accomplish essentially the same objectives as encumbrances in state and local governmental accounting. The Unliquidated Obligations account is a budgetary account which refers to a reservation of available funds to meet specific commitments. Thus, the term "obligation" in federal governmental accounting is operationally equivalent to the term "encumbrance" in state and local governmental accounting.

Appropriations

An appropriation is a formal authorization to a governmental unit or agency to commit not more than a stated amount of fund resources for specified entity purposes, usually within a given period of time. The appropriation is the source of available spending authority, or available funds, referred to above. The authorization has two principal objectives: (1) to provide an upper limit on amounts that may be encumbered, or obligated, and (2) to authorize payments to be made to liquidate obligations when the amounts are confirmed and actual liabilities are established, either during the appropriation period or in a subsequent period. An appropriation normally expires at the end of the budget period, and an unobligated (unencumbered) balance is usually withdrawn or canceled. Most of the activities of federal governmental agencies are financed through direct appropriations by the Congress to draw on the General Fund of the United States Treasury, whereas agencies of state or local governments receive their spending authority primarily from state legislatures or municipal councils.

Professor Vatter argues that the concepts of appropriations and encumbrances have special implications for the "equities" concept in accounting. He states:

The treatment of encumbrances and appropriations in fund accounting suggests that "equities"—or whatever the items on the right-hand side of the balance sheet may be called—are not mere legal liabilities. Rather, these items seem to be viewed clearly as restrictions against the fund of assets, and they serve to earmark portions of the aggregate assets in the fund for specific purposes or to state just what specific provisions must be borne in mind in the management of the assets of the fund.[3]

Allotments and Apportionments

Allotments (state and local) and apportionments (federal) are methods of allocating appropriations over the budget period. They represent a partial release of a unit's appropriation for a given subinterval of time by the legislative or administrative body, and operate as a form of expenditure control. This type of control is designed to prevent overexpenditure in the

---

[3] Ibid., p. 41.

early part of the budget period; the hope is to eliminate the need for deficiency appropriations that might otherwise develop at the end of the period.

Where the number of administrative levels within a governmental entity is large, both of these terms may be used to indicate the allocation process at different levels. For example, in the federal government, the Congress *appropriates* a certain amount of spending authority; the Budget Director thereafter *apportions* elements of this authority over the budget period to various agencies, e.g., the Department of Defense; finally, the Department of the Army receives period *allocations* from the Defense Department, which it then *allots* for the same time period to lower command (administrative) units for ultimate use in program implementation. Notwithstanding this seeming confusion of terms, the basic objective of apportionments and/or allotments remains invariant, viz., partial periodic releases of spending authority over the budgetary period.

STATE AND LOCAL GOVERNMENTAL UNITS

The financial management of both state and local governmental units requires essentially the same type of information and reports; each is subject to comparable legal constraints. Consequently, the basic account structure described following generally applies to either type of entity.

The accounting principles which relate to state and local governments, and derivative procedures and systems, were effectively summarized in 1968 by the National Committee on Governmental Accounting (see Appendix to this chapter).[4] These principles reflect the basic objectives of governmental accounting, viz., (1) assistance in, and validation of, compliance with appropriate statutory provisions, and (2) disclosure of the financial condition and operations of the governmental unit. The principal differences in accounting for profit-oriented enterprises and institutional entities are largely attributable to the overriding importance of legal requirements in respect to the latter type of entity.

The number and the type of separate funds included in an efficient accounting system depend upon relevant statutory provisions and the amount of effective control exercised through the financial management of resources. It is important to note, however, that an excessive number of funds frequently introduces an undesirable inflexibility into the financial system. In the discussion to follow, the basic characteristics of the principal funds of a conventional governmental unit or subdivision will be emphasized; some attention is given to procedural detail. Skill in manual record-keeping for the various funds, a facility which frequently accents their

---

[4] National Committee on Governmental Accounting, *op. cit.* This analysis of applicable principles and procedures is a revised edition of two earlier documents: *Municipal Accounting and Auditing,* originally published in 1951; and *A Standard Classification of Municipal Accounts,* published in 1953.

inherent interrelationships, may be gained by the reader in working the problems provided at the end of the chapter.

Although the nature of the accounting entities for "general fixed assets" and "general long-term debt" is not, in fact, consonant with the concept of a fund, these separate, self-balancing sets of accounts are conventional inclusions in a governmental accounting system, and thus are discussed with the traditional funds.

General Fund

The General Fund, or General Revenue Fund, is used to account for all revenues, and the activities financed by these revenues, which are not reflected in a special fund. In terms of scope, most of the current operations of the governmental unit are financed by the General Fund. Accordingly, a variety of sources provide revenue for, and a wide range of activities are financed by, this omnibus fund.

The principal revenue sources of the General Fund of a municipality include such items as property taxes, licenses, fines, penalties, and other fees. Conventional expenditure classifications include the functions provided by the fire, police, and sanitation departments, and administrative or clerical activities. Some capital outlays also are directly financed by the General Fund. An additional classification indicating the purpose of the outlay, e.g., wages, supplies, etc., will often support these primary (functional) expenditure summaries.

In accounting for the General Fund, account recognition should be given to the approval of the budget. This is effected by formally journalizing the budgetary accounts, viz., the Estimated Revenues for the period, the Appropriations (authorized expenditures) which operate as a control on actual expenditures for the period, and the increment (decrement) to Fund Balance[5] for the budgeted surplus (deficit). Such an entry may take the following form:

Estimated revenues	200,000	
Appropriations		198,000
Fund balance		2,000

These data reflect a budget which anticipates a $2,000 surplus, i.e., an excess of estimated revenues over authorized expenditures. Although it may not be immediately clear why estimated revenues are entered as debits and appropriations (the authority to incur expenses) are entered as credits, subsequent analysis of the closing entries will clarify the appropriateness of this entry. Additionally, this summary entry for the budgetary accounts anticipates the use of subsidiary ledgers in which are accumulated relevant data indicating the sources of estimated revenues, and the functional al-

---

[5] A frequently used, alternative title for the Fund Balance account is Unappropriated Surplus. Fund Balance, however, is the terminology recommended by the National Committee on Governmental Accounting.

locations of authorized expenditures. Other data may also be provided in these subsidiary accounts as necessary.

The recording of receivables generated by earned revenues and their subsequent collection is not significantly different from commercial accounting procedures. Property taxes—a principal source of General Fund revenue—are recorded at the time of assessment (essentially an accrual accounting basis). Concurrently, an allowance for estimated uncollectible accounts is established. This entry is of the following form:

```
Taxes receivable ...............................  150,000
     Allowance for uncollectible accounts ............        10,000
     Revenues ....................................       140,000
```

At the time any portion of the tax levy becomes delinquent, it is transferred to Taxes Receivable—Delinquent, and the related allowance account is reclassified accordingly. If the receivable balance is ultimately collected, the allowance is closed to the Fund Balance account. Other revenues, such as licenses and fee, are conventionally recorded, on a cash basis, in the same Revenues account. This proprietary account for revenues actually earned is usually supported by detailed source data in the same subsidiary ledger which is used for estimated revenues. Thus, both estimated and actual revenues, classified by source, are juxtaposed in the same subsidiary revenue ledger. Certain unrestricted receipts which are not budgeted, such as the proceeds from the sale of fixed assets, frequently accrue to the benefit of the General Fund. However, these receipts are normally entered in a separate account, Surplus Receipts, to distinguish them from currently budgeted revenues.

In governmental accounting, proper budgetary control requires the use of an encumbrance system in which a record of future commitments is established as soon as orders are placed or contracts are issued. When the actual liability is determined, the entry for the encumbrance is reversed and the actual liability is recorded. On this date, an authorized expenditure of an appropriated fund is assumed to have occurred, although actual cash disbursements may be deferred. Appropriations for salaries and wages, bond interest, and other recurring expenditures often are not encumbered but are recorded concurrent with the liquidating payment. Typical entries to record an encumbrance and to record the subsequent reversal and related expenditure (here for an amount less than that anticipated) are as follows:

```
Encumbrances ......................................  11,000
     Reserve for encumbrances ......................        11,000

Appropriation expenditures ..........................  10,500
     Vouchers (accounts) payable ...................        10,500

Reserve for encumbrances ..........................  11,000
     Encumbrances ..................................        11,000
```

Although precautions may be taken to insure that encumbrances are sufficient in amount to cover related subsequent expenditures, it is not unlikely that the appropriation expenditure may exceed the encumbrance. In any event, the amount encumbered is merely reversed, and the actual liability and expenditure recorded.

If an expenditure does not represent a claim against an individual, an organizational entity, or some other fund, it is recorded merely as an Appropriation Expenditure, or as a direct charge against Fund Balance if it were not previously budgeted. Accordingly, the purchase of a fixed asset with General Fund resources is accounted for not unlike a current "expense."

As in the case of Revenues, Encumbrances and Appropriation Expenditures are summary accounts. Consequently, these planned and actual expenditures, classified according to function, are also entered in an appropriation subsidiary ledger. This accumulation of detailed operating expenditures, by functions, is particularly important, since comparison of these totals (past and future expenditures) with the amounts appropriated discloses the degree of compliance with budgetary restrictions. Within each functional category, more refined classifications may be indicated, or coded, as is additionally required by legislative or administrative bodies.

At the end of the fiscal period, the budgetary and operating accounts are closed, and residual balances are transferred to Fund Balance. Given a circumstance where estimated revenues exceed actual revenues and where appropriations exceed expenditures and encumbrances, the following closing entries are illustrative:

Revenues	199,000	
Fund balance	1,000	
Estimated revenues		200,000
Appropriations	198,000	
Appropriation expenditures		180,000
Encumbrances		15,000
Fund balance		3,000

The closing entry sequence, with each corresponding set of budgetary and proprietary accounts being closed in a separate entry, results in separate debits and/or credits to the Fund Balance, each of which indicates the difference between budgeted and actual data. A $4,000 credit balance remains in the Fund Balance account:

Budgeted surplus	$2,000
Excess of appropriations over appropriation expenditures and encumbrances	3,000
	$5,000
Less: Excess of estimated revenues over actual revenues	1,000
Fund Balance	$4,000

The balance in this budgetary account (Fund Balance) approximates the "actual" surplus from the operations of the current period, calculated as follows:

Actual revenues	$199,000
Actual expenditures	180,000
	$ 19,000
Encumbrances (estimated amount of future expenditures)	15,000
Surplus from current operations	$ 4,000

It is well to note, however, that the possible difference between the amounts encumbered and the subsequent actual liabilities is essentially analogous to errors in estimated expense accruals in respect to profit-motivated commercial enterprises.

The Reserve for Encumbrances account is not closed at the end of the fiscal period, since it represents commitments made which are not as yet firmly established as determinable liabilities. In the following period, this reserve is often reclassified as Reserve for Encumbrances—Prior Year. Thereafter, a distinction is made between those expenditures which relate to current year's encumbrances and those which relate to prior years' encumbrances; expenditures associated with prior years' appropriations are charged directly against the Reserve for Encumbrances—Prior Year, or recorded in Appropriation Expenditures—Prior Year, which is closed against the corresponding reserve at the end of the period. It is this "real account" property that makes the Reserve for Encumbrances especially useful. Within a given period, it serves no special purpose, as the "nominal" budgetary accounts, Encumbrances and Appropriation Expenditures, effectively measure the use of available funds. However, since the unexpended and unencumbered portion of a current appropriation usually lapses at the end of the fiscal period, as indicated by the illustrative closing entry, the authority to expend funds from prior years' appropriations is reflected in the Reserve for Encumbrances account balance. Significantly, however, since a liability does not then exist, this account is normally included with Fund Balance (unappropriated surplus) in the enumeration of fund equities to indicate the amount of the total surplus of the governmental entity at the end of the fiscal period.

Where fund assets are segregated for a specified purpose or usage, it is often desirable to adjust the Fund Balance account by creating a reserve account balance equal in amount to the asset. If, for example, a $1,000 debit balance exists in Petty Cash, a reserve could be set up as follows:

Fund balance	1,000	
Reserve for petty cash		1,000

As a consequence of such an entry, the Fund Balance account would indicate only the unappropriated resources (or deficit) available for subsequent appropriations. If the asset cost were originally recorded as a debit to Appropriation Expenditures, such as occurs with the purchase of supplies, the entry above would be modified to record the asset, i.e., substitute the asset account for Fund Balance. The closure of Appropriation Expenditures will then accomplish the desired reduction in Fund Balance.

The General Fund frequently engages in transactions with other funds of the governmental unit. For example, Debt Service Fund contributions are frequently financed by the General Fund; additionally, the General Fund may contribute the initial capital necessary to create an Intragovernmental Service Fund; also, unappropriated surpluses of other funds are frequently transferred to the General Fund by the legislative body. As indicated by the nature of the transaction, either a debtor-creditor relationship should be recorded, or the Fund Balance account should be adjusted for the receipt or expenditure.

The catalog of financial statements for the General Fund usually includes (1) a balance sheet, (2) a statement analyzing the changes in Fund Balance, (3) a statement comparing actual revenues with estimated revenues, and (4) a statement comparing appropriations with expenditures and encumbrances. The balance sheet is relatively conventional; however, the equity section normally carries the descriptive caption, "Reserves and Fund Balance," or alternatively, "Reserves and Surplus." Also, as previously noted, fixed assets are usually excluded from the enumeration of fund assets. The analysis of changes in Fund Balance relates to both the budgetary and proprietary operations of the General Fund, and thus reflects the overall results of the governmental unit's operations of the period. The statement of appropriations, expenditures, and encumbrances reflects the extent to which departments have complied with legal constraints in respect to amounts authorized.

Special Revenue Funds

Special Revenue Funds are sometimes established to account for revenues from specific tax assessments or other special sources which are to be used to finance specified activities. They are usually provided for by statute or charter. Typical activities include the operations of public parks and schools which are administered by special boards or commissions. The number of special revenue funds utilized should be kept to a minimum, however, since the usual activities of these funds often may be satisfactorily financed and managed through the General Fund, thereby eliminating unnecessary confusion in the financial reports and minimizing rigidities in the financial structure which hinder planning.

Once created, however, each Special Revenue Fund should be accounted for as a separate entity. Resources are restricted to the activities anticipated by the creating authority and should not be diverted to other uses. The operation of a Special Revenue Fund is usually controlled by the general budget of the governmental unit, and thus requires both budgetary and proprietary accounts. The accounting sequence for such a fund and the periodic financial statements are essentially the same as those prepared for the General Fund.

Illustrative Entries. The following entries are among the more common entries of a special revenue fund. Assume that a city finances a research library by levying a special property tax. In addition, $10,000 is provided annually from the General Fund to supplement operational expenses. An entry to record the budget would be as follows:

Estimated revenues	80,000	
Appropriations		77,000
Fund balance		3,000

If taxes levied amount to $80,000, and none are deemed to be uncollectible, an entry as follows would be made:

Taxes receivable	80,000	
Revenues		80,000

The entry to record the amount receivable from the General Fund is:

Due from General Fund	10,000	
Revenues		10,000

When the library staff orders books estimated to cost $26,000, the entry is as follows:

Encumbrances	26,000	
Reserve for encumbrances		26,000

Because of unexpected price changes, the books actually cost $27,500. The following entry is made to record receipt of the books:

Appropriation expenditures	27,500	
Vouchers payable		27,500
Reserve for encumbrances	26,000	
Encumbrances		26,000

The closing entries take the same form as those of the General Fund.

Intragovernmental Service Funds

Intragovernmental Service Funds, sometimes referred to as revolving funds or working capital funds, are established to finance activities of a manufacturing or service nature—e.g., shops and garages, central purchases, and stores departments. These functional unit subdivisions provide services primarily for the benefit of other departments of the governmental unit and are to be distinguished from activities financed primarily from the sale of products or services to the public; the latter are typically accounted for by Enterprise Funds.

An Intragovernmental Service Fund may be initially established and financed by advances from the General Fund, by the sale of bonds, or by resources contributed by two or more funds. This initial contribution may be reported as Capital, or Contributions from the X Fund. The fund operates, and is accounted for, in much the same manner as a commercial business enterprise, except that its objective is to earn sufficient revenues to absorb operating costs rather than to maximize profits.

Cost accounting records aid in establishing prices for services performed by Intragovernmental Service Funds for other departments. Necessarily, the total expenditures of such a fund are limited to the amounts which various departments are authorized to spend for its services. Consequently, it is unnecessary for a legislative body to restrict its expenditures through appropriations. A formal plan or legal budget is not required, and budgetary accounts such as those typically used in other funds to indicate compliance with statutory provisions are unnecessary.

Fixed assets which are acquired by an Intragovernmental Service Fund are recorded as assets of the fund, as depreciation thereon must be provided for and included in the pricing base if the fund is to be kept intact.

The financial statements required for adequate reporting of an Intragovernmental Service Fund include a balance sheet and a statement of operations. The forms of these statements essentially parallel those of conventional statements for a commercial enterprise engaged in a similar activity.

Illustrative Entries.   The following entries are among the more common entries of an intragovernmental service fund. Assume that a city decides to acquire and to issue all supplies centrally. The following entry illustrates the receipt of $80,000 cash and $12,600 of supplies from the General Fund.

Cash	80,000	
Inventory of supplies	12,600	
Contribution from General Fund		92,600

Part of the cash is used to purchase a warehouse costing $50,000 (with $10,000 of this amount allocated to land) and a delivery truck costing $12,000. The purchase is recorded as follows:

Land	10,000	
Building	40,000	
Delivery truck	12,000	
Cash		62,000

The following entries journalize the issuance of supplies costing $6,000 to the General Fund (at a mark-up of 25% on cost) and the later collection of the amount due:

Cost of supplies issued	6,000	
Inventory of supplies		6,000
Due from General Fund	7,500	
Billings to departments		7,500
Cash	7,500	
Due from General Fund		7,500

The following entry records the purchase of supplies costing $14,500 on credit:

Inventory of supplies	14,500	
Vouchers payable		14,500

Depreciation is recorded on the buildings and the truck as follows:

```
Warehousing expense ..............................   5,000
Delivery expense ..................................   3,000
    Accumulated depreciation—buildings  ..............          5,000
    Accumulated depreciation—delivery equipment ......          3,000
```

At year end all revenue and expense accounts are closed and the excess of billings over costs is recorded as a credit to Retained Earnings.

Special Assessment Funds

Special Assessment Funds are used primarily to finance permanent improvements or services, such as sidewalks or road construction, which are to be paid for wholly, or in part, from special tax levies against the benefited properties. Improvements or services of this type are to be distinguished from those which benefit the entire community and are paid for from general revenues or through the issuance of general obligation bonds. For each special assessment project, a new fund is created. If the improvements are initially to be financed by bond issues (pending receipt of assessments), the bond proceeds are accounted for by this fund, as well as the assessments ultimately collected, which are then used to pay the bond interest and principal.

The legislative authorization for a Special Assessment Fund, unlike the fiscal period appropriations in respect to the General Fund, relates specifically to a single project, whatever may be the time required for its completion. Each project, and thus each fund, requires separate accounting and reporting. Both budgetary and proprietary accounts are used, as well as appropriation and encumbrance procedures. Initially, upon creation of the fund, Improvements Authorized is debited and Appropriations credited; when the assessments are levied, an appropriate receivables account is debited, and Improvements Authorized is credited. Since the costs of improvements constructed are recorded as expenditures of the fund and thereafter closed to the Appropriations account, no record is made in the fund of the investment in fixed assets. However, upon the completion of the project, an entry is made in the General Fixed Assets group of accounts (to be discussed later) in which the total cost of the improvements constructed is debited to relevant asset accounts; contra credits are made to an investment account. Fund Balance is credited for interest on the assessments and is debited for interest payments on outstanding bonds.

The recommended financial statements for a Special Assessment Fund include a balance sheet, a statement of cash receipts and disbursements, and a statement comparing expenditures and encumbrances with appropriations.

Illustrative Entries. The following entries concerning the construction of sidewalks in a new subdivision of a city are among the more common entries of a Special Assessment Fund.

The following entry records the authorization of the construction of sidewalks costing $85,000:

Improvements authorized 85,000
    Appropriations   85,000

A temporary loan of $40,000 from the General Fund to finance some costs is recorded as follows:

Cash 40,000
    Due to General Fund   40,000

If property owners in the subdivision are assessed $85,000, due currently, for the sidewalks, the following entry would be made:

Assessments receivable—current 85,000
    Improvements authorized   85,000

The receipt of and subsequent payment of a bill for $38,000 from a contractor, previously encumbered for $35,000, are recorded as follows:

Reserve for encumbrances 35,000
    Encumbrances   35,000

Expenditures 38,000
    Contracts payable   38,000

Contracts payable 38,000
    Cash   38,000

If the cost of the sidewalks is exactly $85,000, the following closing entry is made at the time of the completion of the construction:

Appropriations 85,000
    Expenditures   85,000

In addition, the sidewalks are included among the assets of the General Fixed Assets group of accounts.

Capital Projects Funds

In 1968 the National Committee on Governmental Accounting recommended that Capital Projects Funds be established as a replacement and expansion of the more traditional Bond Funds. Bond Funds are used to account for the proceeds of general bond issuances, except for those which relate to and are accounted for by Special Assessment Funds and Enterprise Funds. Capital Projects Funds, on the other hand, give recognition to the fact that many major capital projects are now financed by a variety of sources in addition to bond issuances. Excluding the capital additions of Special Assessment and Enterprise Funds, Capital Projects Funds are designed to account for the *receipt* and *expenditure* of all resources used for the acquisition of major, long-term capital additions and improvements.

Following a memorandum recording of a capital project authorization, assets are generally recorded with debits to descriptive receivable accounts or cash and corresponding credits to Appropriations, if desired, or Fund Balance. Normal encumbrance procedures and accounts are employed in regard to fund disbursements. Once the acquisition or construction is completed, the capital outlays are recorded in the General Fixed Assets group of accounts and the Capital Projects Fund is closed. If a bond issuance were the means of financing, provision is usually made to retire these bonds either from the Debt Service Fund or from the General Fund. The bonds are not typically recorded as a liability of the Capital Projects Fund. After the closing of the Appropriation and Expenditure accounts, as well as premiums and/or discounts on any bonds issued, any remaining Fund Balance in the Capital Projects Fund is transferred to an appropriate fund. If bonds were issued to finance the capital project, the balance should be transferred to the fund from which resources are to be provided for bond retirement, e.g., the Debt Service Fund. Otherwise, the transfer generally is to the General Fund.

Statements which disclose the financial condition and operations of a Capital Projects Fund include a balance sheet, an analysis of changes in the fund balance, and a statement of estimated and actual revenue.

Illustrative Entries. The construction of a new city hall will be used to provide examples of the more common entries of a Capital Projects Fund. Assume that a $4,000,000 bond issue for the construction is approved by the voters. No entry is necessary to record the authorization of the bond issue. The sale of the bonds at par is recorded as follows:

Cash	4,000,000	
Appropriations		4,000,000

An architect is engaged at a price of $120,000 to prepare plans for the city hall. His fee is recorded as follows:

Encumbrances	120,000	
Reserve for encumbrances		120,000

The payment of the architect's fee is recorded with the following entries:

Reserve for encumbrances	120,000	
Encumbrances		120,000
Expenditures	120,000	
Cash		120,000

Entries like the three immediately above would be used to record the amounts charged by the contractor. (Assume this amount is $3,800,000.) Upon completion of the project, a closing entry as follows would be made:

Appropriations	4,000,000	
Expenditures		3,920,000
Fund balance		80,000

The unexpended cash is transferred to the Debt Service Fund, and the following entry made:

Fund balance	80,000	
Cash		80,000

The new city hall building is included among the assets of the General Fixed Assets group of accounts.

Debt Service Funds

If long-term debt is to be repaid from the resources of Special Assessment Funds or is issued to support the activities of Enterprise Funds, those designated funds generally account for the servicing of the debt. Regarding other long-term, governmental debt, Debt Service Funds are established to account for payments of interest, principal, and other related charges.

Budgetary accounts are employed to record contributions and earnings necessary to service the debt. Similarly, the Appropriations account is credited for the debt-servicing payments that must be made during the period. Contributions to the fund are credited to revenues, and cash payments for interest, debt retirements, and fiscal agent service costs are debited to Expenditures. In the case of term bonds, the Debt Service Fund accumulates investments until the maturity date of the bonds, at which time its aggregate resources should be at least equal in amount to the maturity value of the bonds. The bonds are not recorded as liabilities of the Debt Service Fund until they mature, at which time the bond liability is credited and Expenditures is debited. Expenditures is closed, as is also Appropriations, to Fund Balance; and the bond liability is paid for with the cash realized from investments of the Debt Service Fund.

The financial statements that must be prepared to adequately disclose the financial position and operations of a Debt Service Fund include a balance sheet and a statement of revenues, expenditures and fund balances. Interim financial statements which facilitate the management of the fund include comparisons between budgeted and actual revenues, and between budgeted and actual expenditures.

Illustrative Entries.   The following entries are among the more common entries of a Debt Service Fund. Assume that on January 1, 1977, 6% bonds payable with a face value of $100,000 will mature. Interest at 6% will fall due on January 1 and July 1, 1977 with respect to the $1,000,000 of bonds maturing in later years.

The entry to record the budget is:

Estimated revenues	166,000	
Appropriations		166,000

The following entry records a transfer from the General Fund to service the debt:

Cash	166,000	
Revenues		166,000

On January 1 the entries below are made to record the entry for the liability and the subsequent payment:

Expenditures	136,000	
Bonds payable		100,000
Interest payable		36,000

Bonds payable	100,000	
Interest payable	36,000	
Cash		136,000

The July 1 $30,000 liability and payment are recorded in a like manner. At year end the closing entry is:

Revenues	166,000	
Appropriations	166,000	
Expenditures		166,000
Estimated revenues		166,000

Trust and Agency Funds

Trust and Agency Funds are created to account for money and property received and held by a governmental unit as trustee, or agent, for individuals or other government units. Separate accounts should be established and maintained for the transactions and balances of each Trust or Agency Fund. With the exception of Pension Funds, budgetary accounts are not required in accounting for this type of fund. Agency Funds are used primarily to account for money collected for some other entity. The accounting procedures significantly parallel those found in nongovernmental fiduciary accounting. Where the corpus of a trust fund is nonexpendable, a distinction between principal and income should be carefully preserved.

Financial statements for Trust and Agency Funds normally include a balance sheet, a statement of cash receipts and disbursements, and a statement showing changes in fund reserves or balances.

Illustrative Entries—Trust Funds. The following entries are among the common entries of a nonexpendable trust fund in which no principal may be expended.

The receipt of a $500,000 cash gift from a wealthy citizen would be recorded:

| Cash | 500,000 | |
| Endowment principal fund balance | | 500,000 |

The entry to record the investment of the cash would be as follows:

| Investments | 500,000 | |
| Cash | | 500,000 |

Earnings of the trust fund are to be expended on native trees and shrubs to be planted on city-owned land. Earnings of the fund are recorded:

| Cash | 30,000 | |
| Interest revenue | | 30,000 |

| Interest revenue | 30,000 | |
| Due to Endowment Earnings Fund | | 30,000 |

The entry to record the transfer to the Endowment Earnings Fund is:

```
Due to Endowment Earnings Fund ...................    30,000
    Cash .......................................                30,000
```

All of the above entries are recorded in the Endowment Principal Fund. The remaining entries illustrated are recorded in the Endowment Earnings Fund.

```
Due from Endowment Principal Fund ................    30,000
    Revenues .....................................                30,000
Cash ..............................................    30,000
    Due from Endowment Principal Fund ............                30,000
Expenditures .....................................    29,750
    Cash ........................................                29,750
```

The excess of revenues over expenditures is closed to the fund balance.

Illustrative Entries—Agency Funds. The following entries appear frequently in an Agency Fund. Assume that the city collects some property taxes on behalf of a separate school district. The following entry would be made to record the amount to be collected and remitted to the school district:

```
Taxes receivable for other funds and units .............    480,000
    Tax agency fund balance ......................                480,000
```

The collection and subsequent remittance of the school district taxes are recorded by the following entries:

```
Cash ..............................................    480,000
    Taxes receivable for other funds and units ........                480,000
Tax agency fund balance .........................    480,000
    Cash ........................................                480,000
```

Enterprise Funds

Enterprise Funds exist primarily to finance services rendered to the public. They are typically self-supporting and include such activities as electric, gas, or water utilities, air terminal service, and public housing. The accounting for such funds follows the basic pattern of accounting for a commercial business enterprise. Budgets are frequently prepared, and expenditures are not controlled by means of restrictive appropriations.

Fixed assets acquired and used by Enterprise Funds should be capitalized and carried in the enumeration of fund assets; their costs should be systematically allocated (charged to expense) over their estimated lives.

Financial statements of Enterprise Funds are analogous to those prepared for private enterprises. In the case of an Enterprise Fund balance sheet, fixed assets are typically listed first in the enumeration of assets, and bonds payable rank first in the order of fund liabilities. This variant from the conventional balance sheet classification sequence is adopted to accent the dominant long-term character of the funds.

Illustrative Entries. The following entries concerning the operation of a bus service by a city are among the more common entries of an Enterprise Fund.

A summary entry recording the bus service revenue for the year would be as follows:

```
Cash .......................................  2,200,000
    Bus service revenue .......................          2,200,000
```

The following entry records the purchase of buses on credit:

```
Buses in service ..............................   230,000
    Vouchers payable ..........................             230,000
```

Depreciation and other operating expenses are recorded in the same manner as for commercial organizations. At year end the nominal accounts are closed to retained earnings.

If one-fourth of the net income for the year is required to be transferred to the General Fund as of March 1 of the succeeding year, and net income is $120,000, the following entry would be made:

```
Retained earnings ...........................    30,000
    Due to General Fund ......................              30,000
```

General Fixed Assets—A Self-Balancing Group of Accounts

The accounts for Enterprise Funds, Intragovernmental Service Funds, and Trust Funds include fixed assets which are the property of these funds. Other fixed assets of the governmental unit, however, are grouped in a general category—General Fixed Assets. These assets are frequently acquired using the proceeds of general obligation bonds, i.e., they are financed from Capital Projects Funds; they may also be purchased out of general revenues, financed from special assessments, or acquired by gift. Since they are not properly regarded as assets of the acquiring fund, the cost is recorded as an Appropriation Expenditure. Accordingly, this class of fixed assets is carried in a separate, self-balancing set of accounts.

Fixed assets should be valued at original cost, or, if acquired by gift, at appraised valuation at date of receipt; the contra credit(s) is made to one or more investment accounts. The investment accounts are designed to disclose the sources of the resources used to acquire the fixed assets, e.g., general fund revenues, general obligation bonds, federal grants, etc. Since general fixed assets are assumed to be nonproductive of taxes or other general revenues, depreciation is not usually recorded in the general accounting records. This failure to record cost expiration is a significant point of departure from profit-oriented enterprise accounting, wherein depreciation is an important factor in net income determination. Any disposition of fixed assets is recorded by reversing the entry of acquisition.

The balance sheet of the General Fixed Asset group should disclose both the amount of fixed assets, classified by type, and the corresponding investment accounts indicating the source of the asset acquisitions. In addition, a statement of the changes in general fixed assets for the period, classified by source, function, and activity, may be useful.

Illustrative Entries. The following entries are among the more common entries of the General Fixed Assets group of accounts.

The sidewalks financed by special assessments and discussed on page 676 would be recorded as follows:

```
Improvements other than buildings ................     85,000
     Investment in general fixed assets—
       Special Assessments Fund—property
       owner assessments ........................               85,000
```

The above entry may be made in memorandum form only as it is financed entirely by the property owners.

The city hall completed and financed by a bond issue, discussed on page 677, would be recorded as follows:

```
Buildings  ....................................... 3,920,000
     Investment in general fixed assets—
       Capital Projects Fund—bond issue ..........           3,920,000
```

The following entry is recorded upon the receipt of a gift of land (for use in any manner desired) valued at $55,000 from an anonymous citizen:

```
Land .........................................     55,000
     Investment in general fixed assets—
       General Fund—donations .................               55,000
```

General Long-Term Debt—A Self-Balancing Group of Accounts

The amount of unmatured bonds which are payable from general revenues should be carried in a separate and independent self-balancing group of accounts. The General Long-Term Debt accounts should reflect the present value of principal and interest payable in the future; this present value is often represented as the principal amount of the bonds. Prior to 1968, the National Committee on Government Accounting recommended that the *total* amount of principal *and* interest to be paid in future years should be shown in the Long-Term Debt accounts. This practice continues to be employed in many systems. Contra accounts (debit) indicate the amount of resources currently available as well as the amounts yet to be provided for the retirement of these unmatured bonds.

This collection of accounts is neither used to account for the proceeds from the sale of bonds, nor for the payment of principal and interest thereon. Rather, it is merely used to record the amount of outstanding bonded debt of the governmental unit at a specific point in time. There is, however, a relationship between this group of accounts and other funds. At the time bonds are issued (the proceeds of which are generally accounted for through a Capital Projects Fund), a credit entry is made in the General Long-Term Debt account group to record the liability created by the issue. The offsetting debit is to an account entitled Amount to Be Provided for Payment of Principal. Annual increases in the balance of Debt Service

Funds should be reflected in this group of accounts to the extent that these investment amounts are specifically designated for payment of the liabilities. If the Debt Service Fund accumulation relates only to bond principal, Amount in Debt Service Fund is debited and Amount to Be Provided for Payment of Principal is credited. As liquidating payments are applied in reduction of bond principal out of the Debt Service Fund resources, the originating entry to record the liability is reversed to the extent of debt abatement and the appropriate contra accounts are credited. As observed earlier, a bond liability may also be accounted for in a Special Assessment Fund or in an Enterprise Fund; in such instances, these bonds may not be included in the General Long-Term Debt group of accounts, as they refer to specific commitments of other funds. However, if the bonds are general obligation bonds, thereby affecting the general credit of the governmental unit, the bonds should be included in the General Long-Term Debt group of accounts as well as the accounts of the specific fund to which they relate.

For reporting purposes, a statement of general long-term debt should be prepared indicating the amount of bonds payable in future years and the amount presently available and to be provided for their retirement.

Illustrative Entries. The following entries are among the more common entries of the General Long-Term Debt group of accounts.

The following entry is made to record the issuance of $4,000,000 of bonds, the proceeds of which were used to construct a new city hall, as described on page 677.

Amount to be provided for payment of term bonds .. 4,000,000
    Term bonds payable   4,000,000

On page 678 an entry illustrated the transfer from the General Fund to the Debt Service Fund of $166,000 to be used to pay interest and to retire $100,000 of serial bonds. This transaction calls for the following entry in the General Long-Term Debt group of amounts:

Amount available in Debt Service Fund
    for payment of regular serial bonds   100,000
        Amount to be provided for payment
        of regular serial bonds   100,000

The above results in a reduction in the amount "to be provided."

The redemption of the bonds results in the journalizing of:

Regular serial bonds payable   100,000
    Amount available in Debt Service Fund
    for payment of regular serial bonds   100,000

Summary

This description of funds and the related two groups of self-balancing accounts has necessarily been abbreviated. The authors have sought merely to accent the outstanding characteristics of each fund. Although some mention was made of the use of subsidiary ledgers in reference to the operation of the General Fund, it should be recognized that these data provide basic information for all of the funds. Hopefully, the most prominent characteristics of local and state accounting have been exposed, even though in broad outline.

FEDERAL GOVERNMENT

Introduction

Accounting in the federal government began with an Act of Congress in 1789 which established the United States Treasury. For 130 years, the Treasury maintained the government's accounts. During this period, however, the federal government's accounting methods remained essentially unchanged, with a predominant emphasis upon compiling evidence to determine whether or not a specific governmental agency's transactions complied with its appropriations and other Congressional directives.

The first substantial effort directed toward accounting reform was the enactment of the Budget and Accounting Act of 1921. This Act was the first law to give expression to the concept of the Presidential Budget; in this regard, provision was made for the creation of the administrative office of the Bureau of the Budget. Additionally, the General Accounting Office, a legislative agency, was established with a Comptroller General as its principal officer. Various proposals have been made during the past two decades for improving accounting in the federal government, including the recommendations of the first and second Hoover Commission reports (1949 and 1955). Particularly significant legislative responses were the Budget and Accounting Procedures Act of 1950 and Public Law 863 (1956); the latter Act contains many of the proposals of the second Hoover Report, including the provision for accrual accounting in agency systems.

Currently, the executive branch of the federal government is charged with the development of accounting systems and procedures, limited only by the outline of basic principles and standards established by the Comptroller General. The governmental agency is regarded as the fundamental accounting entity, and its executive head assumes responsibility for agency activities, including accounting. It is therefore inappropriate to speak of *the* accounting system of the federal government. Federal governmental accounting is essentially a collection of the separate accounting systems of its many agencies and the Treasury Department. The accounts of each agency are ordinarily maintained on a decentralized basis; the Treasury Department, as the central fiscal agent of the federal government, is responsible for integrating, or consolidating, the separate accounts of the various agencies.

Basic Objectives

The objectives of accounting in the federal government, as set out in Section 111 of the Budget and Accounting Procedures Act of 1950, may be briefly summarized as follows:

Accounting in the Federal government must provide (1) full disclosure of the results of financial operations, (2) adequate financial information needed in the management of operations and the formulation and execution of the budget, (3) effective control over income, expenditures, funds, property, and other assets, and (4) evidence that financial transactions have been consummated in accordance with laws, regulations, or other legal requirements.[6]

These objectives are comparable to those of commercial enterprise accounting, with two significant exceptions. The strong, even dominating, emphasis that there must be accumulated evidence indicating that financial transactions of a governmental agency accord with legal requirements is one basic difference; the other exception relates to the relative lack of emphasis in governmental accounting on measuring the economic progress of the accounting entity over a period of time. Progress is not measured in governmental entities in terms of monetary or economic increments which are beneficial to owners or investors; rather, the financial activities of such entities accent the importance of administering and expending resources in the most appropriate manner for the attainment of service objectives. Where the "results of operations" are expressed primarily in terms of the degree of attainment of social or service goals, the primary function of accounting becomes one of reporting effectively on how resources are acquired, administered, and used in attainment of these goals.

As a general rule, the governmental accounting process has not included attempts to measure "outputs" or the degree of attainment of social or service goals. However, considerable effort has been concentrated in recent years on the development and implementation of budgeting systems which incorporate such measurements. These Planning-Programming-Budgeting Systems require a careful analysis of "program structures," which involves the identification of general objectives, the refinement of general objectives into a detailed outline of subobjectives, and the classification of governmental expenditures in terms of specific programs that are planned to accomplish specific subobjectives. Following the analysis of program structures, special emphasis is placed upon cost-effectiveness analyses which utilize "benefit" measures to the extent possible. The ultimate goal of these studies is to provide the decision makers with significant information as to the comparative effectiveness of alternative governmental programs.

Basic Accounting Procedures

In 1948, the Accounting Systems Division of the General Accounting Office was established. The objective of this division, later subsumed under

---

[6] Adapted from Sec. 111, P. L. 864, 81st Congress, 64 Stat. 832.

the office of the Comptroller General, was to establish accounting principles and standards of general applicability to governmental units and to assist agencies in the structuring of accounting systems. These objectives have been aided in their implementation by the issuance of three types of memoranda having general application:

1. GAO General Regulations. These are mandatory for all agencies of the government, and are generally procedural in nature.
2. Accounting Systems Memoranda. Less formal devices than the Regulations, these memoranda make interim changes in the former and are usually concerned with individual problems.
3. Accounting Principles Memoranda. These are general statements having broad application which purport to establish the underlying foundation on which federal government accounting is to be based.

In accounting for federal governmental agencies and their subunits, the use of budgetary accounts essentially parallels their use by state and local governments. In other respects, the accounting process more closely resembles commercial enterprise accounting. The basic reporting entity in federal governmental accounting is the executive agency, which is an independent reporting unit. Periodically the Treasury Department consolidates the reports of the various agencies. Prior to 1968, the overall financial plans and reports for the federal government were summarized in three partially complementary and partially competing budgets: (1) the administrative budget; (2) the consolidated cash budget; and (3) the national income accounts budget. In 1967, the President's Commission on Budget Concepts recommended "that a unified summary budget statement be used to replace the present three or more competing concepts. . . ."[7] As a consequence, the unified budget is now the primary summary statement of the federal government, supported, of course, by a variety of more detailed statements and analyses. The unified budget is comprised of four basic sections: budget appropriations; budget receipts, expenditures, and lending; means of financing; and outstanding federal securities and federal loans at the end of the year.

Most operations of the federal government are financed and controlled by a General Fund of the Treasury Department; however, there exist a number of trust funds, for which the beneficiaries are individuals or foreign governments. The General Fund accommodates within its accounts structure a large number of agency funds which are created by Congress by appropriation for administrative purposes. Each of these funds identifies with an agency or department of the federal government. An outline of these fund relationships is:

---

[7] *Report of the President's Commission on Budget Concepts* (Washington, D.C.: U.S. Government Printing Office, 1967), p. 6.

General Fund of the Treasury
    Expendable funds of the agencies
        General appropriated funds
        Special appropriated funds
    Revolving funds of the agencies
        Government corporations
        Non-incorporated activities
Trust and Deposit Funds[8]

An expendable fund is one which is available for making expenditures for designated purposes; necessarily, it does not include fixed assets. A revolving fund is a self-sustaining fund which in the long run is expected to generate revenues equivalent in amount to its operating expenses. A separate set of budgetary accounts for each fund is desirable, but this need not imply a physical separation of resources or the keeping of separate accounting records for each fund.

The proprietary accounts of some governmental agencies are currently maintained on a cash basis, notwithstanding the passage, in 1956, of Public Law 863, which made the conversion to accrual accounting mandatory for all agencies. The conversion to an accrual basis is being carried out to a significant degree, however, following the 1967 recommendations of the President's Commission on Budget Concepts.

Property accounting in the federal government is the responsibility of that executive agency which acquires, uses, and disposes of expendable materials, supplies, and fixed assets. Accounting Principles Memoradum No. 1 provides that the accountable value of acquired property is its original cost, or, if cost is not available, the appraised valuation at date of acquisition. In respect to depreciation of fixed assets, the criterion of "usefulness" is recommended. The Memorandum recommends the recording of depreciation for those agencies, and in respect to those projects, in which fixed assets represent a significant portion of the resources employed, such as transportation facilities, public utilities, and construction agencies. Depreciation should also be provided where costs are important determinants of price, and in those circumstances where the activity of the agency involves program use (as contrasted with administrative use) of fixed assets. Depreciation is not ordinarily recorded where fixed assets are relatively unimportant in discharging the routine functions of the agency.

Federal Agency Accounting—An Illustrative Example

The basic concepts which underlie the accounting system of an agency of the federal government will be briefly illustrated in the following para-

---

[8] Howard W. Bordner, "Appropriations and Funds," *The Federal Accountant*, December 1957, p. 12.

graphs, although an explanation of many of the administrative details and methodological subtleties are omitted.

The agency is assumed to be financed initially, and primarily, by appropriations of the federal government. Once the appropriation is established by an enactment of the Congress, the agency records this fact as follows:

```
Fund balances with U.S. Treasury ................... 225,000
    Unapportioned appropriations ..................          225,000
```

This entry reflects the availability of funds on the books of the Treasury for discharging agency functions during the current period.

Although funds have been appropriated to the agency, final authority to use these funds depends upon action by the executive budget office. Although this apportionment may be scheduled for release periodically over the fiscal period, it will be here assumed that $210,000 is apportioned for immediate use. The agency records this event in the following manner with the entry:

```
Unapportioned appropriations ....................... 210,000
    Unallotted apportionments ....................          210,000
```

This reflects the extent to which Treasury funds may be expended through an authorized disbursing agent. The $15,000 reservation of appropriated funds by the budget office may be subsequently apportioned to the agency, or it may be used for other authorized purposes—including a planned saving by the executive branch of the federal government.

If the agency head subsequently allots $200,000 to agency divisions and subdivisions, against which they may make commitments during the year, the following entry is made:

```
Unallotted apportionments ......................... 200,000
    Unobligated allotments .......................          200,000
```

The effect of this entry is to reserve $10,000 of the total spending authority of the agency for unexpected requirements—an internal administrative control through financial management. Actually only a portion of the agency's spending authority is usually made available to operating units periodically (quarterly) during the year in order to prevent a unit's overspending during the first months of the fiscal year. The Unobligated Allotments account is, of course, supported by a collection of detailed, subsidiary allotment accounts.

Orders are placed for equipment in the amount of $50,000 and supplies in the amount of $40,000:

```
Unobligated allotments ............................. 90,000
    Unliquidated obligations .......................          90,000
```

This entry essentially parallels the encumbrance process for local and state governmental units, with the term "obligations" substituted for "encumbrances."

The equipment, cost $51,000, and supplies, cost $38,000, are received by the agency:

```
Unliquidated obligations ...........................  90,000
    Unobligated allotments .........................           90,000
Fixed assets ......................................  51,000
Inventories .......................................  38,000
    Accounts payable ..............................           89,000

Unobligated allotments ............................  89,000
    Expended appropriations ........................           89,000
```

In this entry sequence, the obligation entry is reversed, and the assets and liabilities are recorded. Additionally, the Unobligated Allotments is reduced by the amount of confirmed expenditures. Thus, the Unobligated Allotments account continues to reflect the available obligational authority.

Salaries of $100,000 are approved for payment without prior obligation:

```
Salaries ..........................................  100,000
    Accounts payable ..............................           100,000

Unobligated allotments ............................  100,000
    Expended appropriations ........................           100,000
```

The recorded liabilities are certified for payment by a disbursing agent of the Treasury:

```
Accounts payable ..................................  189,000
    Fund balances with U.S. Treasury ..............           189,000
```

An additional allotment of $5,000 is made to one of the agency divisions; supplies in the amount of $4,900 are ordered by the division:

```
Unallotted apportionments .........................  5,000
    Unobligated allotments ........................           5,000

Unobligated allotments ............................  4,900
    Unliquidated obligations ......................           4,900
```

At the end of the fiscal period, there exist accrued salaries of $7,000; additionally, it is determined that supplies in the amount of $30,000 have been consumed during the period.

```
Salaries ..........................................  7,000
    Accrued salaries ..............................           7,000

Unobligated allotments ............................  7,000
    Expended appropriations ........................           7,000

Operating expenses ................................  30,000
    Inventories ...................................           30,000
```

No adjustment of the budgetary accounts is required in respect to the consumption of supplies, as obligational authority was expended at the time the supplies were received. (The assumption is made that depreciation on fixed assets is not to be recorded; if depreciation were recorded, the entry would parallel that for the recognition of expense for materials consumed.)

At the end of the fiscal year, the agency trial balance is as follows:

Fund balances with		Accrued salaries	$ 7,000
U.S. Treasury	$ 36,000	Unobligated allotments	4,100
Inventories	8,000	Unallotted apportionments	5,000
Fixed assets	51,000	Unapportioned appropriations	15,000
Salaries	107,000	Unliquidated obligations	4,900
Operating expenses	30,000	Expended appropriations	196,000
	$232,000		$232,000

The period-end closing entries for the agency are:

Unobligated allotments	4,100	
Unallotted apportionments	5,000	
Unapportioned appropriations	15,000	
Fund Balances with U.S. Treasury		24,100
Expended appropriations	196,000	
Salaries		107,000
Operating expenses		30,000
Invested capital		59,000

The first entry above reflects the expiration of obligational authority at the end of the fiscal year, leaving a fund balance with the U.S. Treasury of $11,900—equal in amount to the accrued liability of $7,000 and the unliquidated obligation (comparable to a Reserve for Encumbrances) of $4,900. The second entry closes current expenses and expended appropriations, with the difference of $59,000 representing the increase in net assets during the period (inventory of $8,000 and fixed assets of $51,000). This increment in Invested Capital is, of course, distorted to the extent of unrecorded depreciation on the fixed assets.

An unclassified statement of financial position at the end of the period would assume the following form:

AN AGENCY FINANCED FROM APPROPRIATIONS
Statement of Financial Position
June 30, 1977

Assets

Fund balances with U.S. Treasury	$11,900
Inventories	8,000
Fixed assets	51,000
	$70,900

Liabilities, Unliquidated
Obligations, and Invested Capital

Accrued salaries	$ 7,000
Unliquidated obligations	4,900
Invested capital	59,000
	$70,900

In addition to the statement of financial position, other statements often prepared by an agency include analyses of changes in invested capital, the status of appropriations, and reconciliation of program costs with obligations.

In this illustrative example, many types of recurring transactions have been omitted. Rather, emphasis has focused on the summary effect of transactions and the complemetary nature of budgetary (control) and proprietary accounts of a federal governmental agency.

REGULATORY ACCOUNTING

Frequently, because of a condition of limited competition (or no competition) in a given industry, regulatory agencies are established to protect the public from unwarranted abuses and discrimination, while concurrently assuring the regulated industry of receiving a fair return on its investment. In respect to public utilities, the regulating agency operates primarily as a guardian of the public in its role as consumer. Other commissions and agencies emphasize the public as an investor. For example, the Securities and Exchange Commission is especially concerned with the form and content of published financial statements, in order that there may be a full and complete disclosure to investors of all material facts concerning securities publicly offered for sale. Manifestly, regulatory accounting relates principally to the accumulation of those data, and in such form, as will enable the regulating agency to accomplish its service function to the public.

Five regulatory agencies (Interstate Commerce Commission, Federal Power Commission, Federal Communications Commission, Federal Maritime Commission, Civil Aeronautics Board) are presently authorized to prescribe uniform systems of accounts for industries subject to their jurisdiction. Others, such as the Federal Trade Commission and the Rural Electrification Administration, prescribe reporting rules but not complete accounting systems. The authority of the Securities and Exchange Commission over accounting practice is expressed in very general terms; however, it is implemented by regulations which often specify the form and content of financial statements.

Prescribed Accounts and Reports

The uniform systems of accounts, cited above, are typically described in terms of charts of accounts, accompanied by detailed explanations of the composition of the individual accounts. While the installation of the accounting system remains the primary responsibility of the regulated company, the latter must usually file a copy of its manual or chart of accounts with the relevant commission, and report any subsequent changes thereto. Periodic financial reports are also required of the regulated company, and its accounts are usually subject to a periodic audit by the staff of the regulatory commission.

Among the activities often performed by a regulatory commission in respect to accounting and reporting systems are the following.[9]

---

9 "Federal Communications Accounting Explained" (Government and Industry Section) *The Federal Accountant,* June 1963.

1.   Prescribe a uniform system of accounts with which regulated companies must comply.
2.   Issue rulings and interpretative elaborations periodically in respect to various procedures outlined in the system.
3.   Give notice of approval before specified types of accounting transactions are completed.
4.   Review the financial statements of regulated companies on a continuing basis.

It is evident that the authority of the regulatory commission in recording and reporting requirements often extends beyond the prescription of uniform accounts. In addition to the activities cited above, the commission will often formulate rules for the valuation of plant and other properties, establish regulations as to the retention of records, engage in analyses to develop the cost of performing specific services, and set depreciation rates.

Theoretical Framework

Regulatory accounting has developed largely through trial and error. The proliferation of independent agencies, the desire for autonomy, and the resulting lack of communication between agencies have all impeded the development of a common underlying theoretical framework in regulatory accounting.

Because of the importance of rate regulation, public utility accounting manifestly emphasizes the rate base and operating income. Rate making consists of compiling the various cost elements to provide the relevant service, which include operating expenses, depreciation, depletion and amortization, taxes, and the allowable return on the rate base. This summation of costs should be equivalent to the revenues required by the utility; accordingly, it is used in establishing the rate for consumers. The rate base includes the cost of plant devoted to the particular service, reduced by accrued depreciation, and increased by an allowance for working capital.

The emphasis on operating income has generated the concept of "above- or below-the-line" revenues and expenses. "Above-the-line" items consist of all revenues and expenses that relate directly to regulated services, and thus enter into the computation of operating income, while other items not so defined are accounted for "below-the-line." In this context, net operating income is the amount returned on the rate base. It is therefore evident that the problems of regulatory accounting relate primarily to a determination of the proper inclusions in operating income and the appropriate components of the rate base.

In spite of the heterogeneity implicit in the various agency systems, there are nonetheless some fundamental propositions to which all generally subscribe. They include the *standard of reasonableness* and the concept of *original cost*. The *standard of reasonableness* is defined as the right of a commission or agency to pass upon the justice and fairness of charges to the accounts of the regulated enterprise; additionally, it provides a rationale for determining the amount of operating expenses to be charged to consumers (by inclusion in the rate base).[10] Consequently, the level of costs incurred, or allowed, in providing the service should not exceed that level which would prevail were the enterprise not protected by monopolistic privilege. The *original cost* concept relates to fixed assets acquired by a regulated company, and in general, accents the importance of cost to the owner who first dedicated the properties to public service. For newly created assets, this measurement is comparable to cost valuation in conventional accounting. Any excess of acquisition cost over original cost is recorded in a separate account by the regulated company, to be disposed of subsequently as directed by the regulatory commission. Depreciation is normally computed on original cost, on the basis that charges to expense in a regulated company should relate to actual costs first incurred, without inflation by amounts added by subsequent transfers. Regulatory systems of accounts usually reject "goodwill" and "going value" as amortizable parts of the cost of acquisition.

GOVERNMENTAL ACCOUNTING SYSTEMS RECONSIDERED

Federal and Nonfederal Systems Compared

Federal governmental accounting exists in an environmental setting, and is sustained by a type of authority which is substantially different from that of state and local governmental accounting. The federal government carries on a wide variety of activities, all of which are subject, in respect to accounting principles and standards, to supervision and control by the Comptroller General. Accounting functions are accordingly closely coordinated. At the state and local levels, on the other hand, the accounting function is carried on within autonomous units or subdivisions, each of which is relatively free to elect its own system of accounts. Improvement and consistency at the state and local level depend upon the ability of an organization, without significant formal authority, to provoke wide acceptance and use of what it believes to be sound accounting principles.

Although each federal appropriation is assumed to create a fund, the operations of which must accommodate to legal constraints, the reporting entity remains the agency. In state and local governmental accounting, however, each fund is a separate entity having its own set of accounts. Individual appropriations do not establish funds; rather, they represent authorizations and limitations on expenditures for a specific purpose in respect to an existing fund. In both instances, however, the fund concept operates as an instrument of control.

In respect to fixed assets, state and local governments frequently use a

---

[10] Hussein A. Sharaf, "An Evaluation of the Regulative Aspects of Accounting Requirements for Public Utilities in the United States" (Ph.D. dissertation, The University of Illinois, 1959), p. 7.

single group of self-balancing accounts for all fixed assets, with the exception of those included in revolving-type funds such as Enterprise Funds. In the federal government, each agency is regarded as a separate operating entity which controls and accounts for specific fixed assets. For this reason, the recording of depreciation is perhaps more widely accepted within the federal system than in state and local governments.

Governmental and Commercial Accounting Compared

Because governmental accounting is not a homogeneous function, it is difficult to contrast in any meaningful manner governmental accounting taken as a whole with accounting for commercial enterprises. Yet, there are certain fundamental differences. Governmental accounting emphasizes the fund as a nucleus of accounting activity, as compared to the operating entity in commercial accounting. The related technique of recording outstanding purchase orders or contractual commitments by the use of an encumbrance or obligation system significantly departs from accounting for commercial business enterprises. This practice, which accents the equity side of the balance sheet, emphasizes restrictions upon assets, rather than the reporting of legal liabilities only. With respect to operations, governmental activity is in most instances nonprofit oriented, while the motivation to maximize wealth is an overriding business objective which underlies commercial accounting. Nonetheless, concepts of revenue are similar in both systems, and concepts of expense differ materially only in respect to depreciation and amortization.

APPENDIX: SUMMARY OF RECOMMENDED ACCOUNTING PRINCIPLES (NATIONAL COMMITTEE ON GOVERNMENTAL ACCOUNTING)[11]

1. *Legal Compliance and Financial Operations.* A governmental accounting system must make it possible: (*a*) to show that all applicable legal provisions have been complied with; and (*b*) to determine fairly and with full disclosure the financial position and results of financial operations of the constituent funds and self-balancing account groups of the governmental unit.

2. *Conflicts between Accounting Principles and Legal Provisions.* If there is a conflict between legal provisions and generally accepted accounting principles applicable to governmental units, legal provisions must take precedence. Insofar as possible, however, the governmental accounting system should make possible the full disclosure and fair presentation of

---

[11] National Committee on Governmental Accounting, Municipal Finance Officers Association of the United States and Canada, *Governmental Accounting, Auditing, and Financial Reporting* (Chicago, 1968), pp. 3–14.

financial position and operating results in accordance with generally accepted principles of accounting applicable to governmental units.

3. *The Budget and Budgetary Accounting.* An annual budget should be adopted by every governmental unit, whether required by law or not, and the accounting system should provide budgetary control over general governmental revenues and expenditures.

4. *Fund Accounting.* Governmental accounting systems should be organized and operated on a fund basis. A fund is defined as an independent fiscal and accounting entity with a self-balancing set of accounts recording cash and/or other resources together with all related liabilities, obligations, reserves, and equities which are segregated for the purpose of carrying on specific activities or attaining certain objectives in accordance with special regulations, restrictions, or limitations.

5. *Types of Funds.* The following types of funds are recognized and should be used in accounting for governmental financial operations as indicated.

(1) The General Fund to account for all financial transactions not properly accounted for in another fund;

(2) Special Revenue Funds to account for the proceeds of specific revenue sources (other than special assessments) or to finance specified activities as required by law or administrative regulation;

(3) Debt Service Funds to account for the payment of interest and principal on long-term debt other than special assessment and revenue bonds;

(4) Capital Projects Funds to account for the receipt and disbursement of moneys used for the acquisition of capital facilities other than those financed by special assessment and enterprise funds;

(5) Enterprise Funds to account for the financing of services to the general public where all or most of the costs involved are paid in the form of charges by users of such services;

(6) Trust and Agency Funds to account for assets held by a governmental unit as trustee or agent for individuals, private organizations, and other governmental units;

(7) Intragovernmental Service Funds to account for the financing of special activities and services performed by a designated organization unit within a governmental jurisdiction for other organization units within the same governmental jurisdiction;

(8) Special Assessment Funds to account for special assessments levied to finance public improvements or services deemed to benefit the properties against which the assessments are levied.

6. *Number of Funds.* Every governmental unit should establish and maintain those funds required by law and sound financial administration. Since numerous funds make for inflexibility, undue complexity, and unnecessary expense in both the accounting system and the over-all financial

administration, however, only the minimum number of funds consistent with legal and operating requirements should be established.

7. *Fund Accounts.* A complete self-balancing group of accounts should be established and maintained for each fund. This group should include all general ledger accounts and subsidiary records necessary to reflect compliance with legal provisions and to set forth the financial position and the results of financial operations of the fund. A clear distinction should be made between the accounts relating to current assets and liabilities and those relating to fixed assets and liabilities. With the exception of Intragovernmental Service Funds, Enterprise Funds, and certain Trust Funds, fixed assets should not be accounted for in the same fund with the current assets, but should be set up in a separate, self-balancing group of accounts called the General Fixed Asset Group of Accounts. Similarly, except in Special Assessment, Enterprise, and certain Trust Funds, long-term liabilities should not be carried with the current liabilities of any fund, but should be set up in a separate, self-balancing group of accounts known as the General Long-term Debt Group of Accounts.

8. *Valuation of Fixed Assets.* The fixed asset accounts should be maintained on the basis of original cost, or the estimated cost if the original cost is not available, or, in the case of gifts, the appraised value at the time received.

9. *Depreciation.* Depreciation on general fixed assets should not be recorded in the general accounting records. Depreciation charges on such assets may be computed for unit cost purposes, provided such charges are recorded only in memorandum form and do not appear in the fund accounts.

10. *Basis of Accounting.* The accrual basis of accounting is recommended for Enterprise, Trust, Capital Projects, Special Assessment, and Intragovernmental Service Funds. For the General, Special Revenue, and Debt Service Funds, the modified accrual basis of accounting is recommended. The modified accrual basis of accounting is defined as that method of accounting in which expenditures other than accrued interest on general long-term debt are recorded at the time liabilities are incurred and revenues are recorded when received in cash, except for material or available revenues which should be accrued to reflect properly the taxes levied and the revenues earned.

11. *Classification of Accounts.* Governmental revenues should be classified by fund and source. Expenditures should be classified by fund, function, organization unit, activity, character, and principal classes of objects in accordance with standard recognized classification.

12. *Common Terminology and Classification.* A common terminology and classification should be used consistently throughout the budget, the accounts, and the financial reports.

13. *Financial Reporting.* Financial statements and reports showing the current condition of budgetary and proprietary accounts should be pre-

pared periodically to control financial operations. At the close of each fiscal year, a comprehensive annual financial report covering all funds and financial operations of the governmental unit should be prepared and published.

QUESTIONS

1. What is a "fund" in a governmental accounting context?
2. Distinguish between *expendable* and *nonexpendable* funds.
3. What are the primary objectives of a governmental budget for an expendable fund?
4. Distinguish between *budgetary* and *proprietary* accounts.
5. What is the purpose of a system of encumbrances? How does it differ from a system of obligations?
6. Describe the function of the General Fund or General Revenue Fund.
7. What kinds of statements are used to report the activities of the General Fund?
8. Characterize and distinguish between an agency *expendable* fund and an agency *revolving* fund.
9. Describe the principal differences between federal governmental and state or local governmental accounting.

EXERCISES

Exercise 18–1

Select the best answer for each of the following.

1. The operations of a public library receiving the majority of its support from property taxes levied for that purpose should be accounted for in

   a. The general fund.
   b. A special revenue fund.
   c. An enterprise fund.
   d. An intragovernmental service fund.
   e. None of the above.

2. The liability for general obligation bonds issued for the benefit of a municipal electric company and serviced by its earnings should be recorded in
   a. An enterprise fund.
   b. The general fund.
   c. An enterprise fund and the general long-term debt group.
   d. An enterprise fund and disclosed in a footnote in the statement of general long-term debt.
   e. None of the above.

3. The proceeds of a federal grant made to assist in financing the future construction of an adult training center should be recorded in
   a. The general fund.
   b. A special revenue fund.

      c. A capital projects fund.

      d. A special assessment fund.

      e. None of the above.

4. The receipts from a special tax levy to retire and pay interest on general obligation bonds issued to finance the construction of a new city hall should be recorded in a

      a. Debt service fund.

      b. Capital projects fund.

      c. Revolving interest fund.

      d. Special revenue fund.

      e. None of the above.

5. The operations of a municipal swimming pool receiving the majority of its support from charges to users should be accounted for in

      a. A special revenue fund.

      b. The general fund.

      c. An intragovernmental service fund.

      d. An enterprise fund.

      e. None of the above.

6. The fixed assets of a central purchasing and stores department organized to serve all municipal departments should be recorded in

      a. An enterprise fund and the general fixed assets group

      b. An enterprise fund.

      c. The general fixed assets group.

      d. The general fund.

      e. None of the above.

7. The monthly remittance to an insurance company of the lump sum of hospital-surgical insurance premiums collected as payroll deductions from employees should be recorded in

      a. The general fund.

      b. An agency fund.

      c. A special revenue fund.

      d. An intragovernmental service fund.

      e. None of the above.

8. Several years ago a city provided for the establishment of a sinking fund to retire an issue of general obligation bonds. This year the city made a $50,000 contribution to the sinking fund from general revenues and realized $15,000 in revenue from securities in the sinking fund. The bonds due this year were retired. These transactions require accounting recognition in

      a. The general fund.

      b. A debt service fund and the general long-term debt group of accounts.

      c. A debt service fund, the general fund and the general long-term debt group of accounts.

      d. A capital projects fund, a debt service fund, the general fund and the general long-term debt group of accounts.

      e. None of the above.

                         (AICPA adapted)

Exercise 18–2

Select the best answer for each of the following.

1. A city realized large capital gains and losses on securities in its library endowment fund. In the absence of specific instructions from the donor or state statutory requirements, the general rule of law holds that these amounts should be charged or credited to
   a. General fund income.
   b. General fund principal. 679
   c. Trust fund income.
   d. Trust fund principal.
   e. None of the above.

2. The activities of a central motor pool which provides and services vehicles for the use of municipal employees on official business should be accounted for in
   a. An agency fund.
   b. The general fund.
   c. An intragovernmental service fund. 673
   d. A special revenue fund.
   e. None of the above.

3. A transaction in which a municipal electric utility paid $150,000 out of its earnings for new equipment requires accounting recognition in
   a. An enterprise fund.
   b. The general fund. 680
   c. The general fund and the general fixed assets group of accounts.
   d. An enterprise fund and the general fixed assets group of accounts.
   e. None of the above.

4. In order to provide for the retirement of general obligation bonds, a city invests a portion of its general revenue receipts in marketable securities. This investment activity should be accounted for in
   a. A trust fund.
   b. The enterprise fund.
   c. A special assessment fund. 678
   d. A special revenue fund.
   e. None of the above.

5. The activities of a municipal employee retirement plan which is financed by equal employer and employee contributions should be accounted for in
   a. An agency fund.
   b. An intragovernmental service fund.
   c. A special assessment fund.
   d. A trust fund. 679
   e. None of the above.

6. A city collects property taxes for the benefit of the local sanitary, park and school districts and periodically remits collections to these units. This activity should be accounted for in
   a. An agency fund.
   b. The general fund. 680

   c.   An intragovernmental service fund.
   d.   A special assessment fund.
   e.   None of the above.

7. A transaction in which a municipal electric utility issues bonds (to be repaid from its own operations) requires accounting recognition in
   a.   The general fund.
   b.   A debt service fund.
   c.   Enterprise and debt service funds.
   d.   An enterprise fund, a debt service fund and the general long-term debt group of accounts.
   e.   None of the above.

8. A transaction in which a municipality issued general obligation serial bonds to finance the construction of a fire station requires accounting recognition in the
   a.   General fund.
   b.   Capital projects and general funds.
   c.   Capital projects fund and the general long-term debt group of accounts.
   d.   General fund and the general long-term debt group of accounts.
   e.   None of the above.

9. Expenditures of $200,000 were made during the year on the fire station in item 8. This transaction requires accounting recognition in the
   a.   General fund.
   b.   Capital projects fund and the general fixed assets group of accounts.
   c.   Capital projects fund and the general long-term debt group of accounts.
   d.   General fund and the general fixed assets group of accounts.
   e.   None of the above.

                                                                (AICPA adapted)

Exercise 18–3

   The statements below are based on the information from the following journal entries. Select the best answer for each statement.

   The following related entries were recorded in sequence in the general fund of a municipality:

1. Encumbrances	$12,000	
Reserve for encumbrances		$12,000
2. Reserve for encumbrances	12,000	
Encumbrances		12,000
3. Expenditures	12,350	
Vouchers payable		12,350

1. The sequence of entries indicates that
   a.   An adverse event was foreseen and a reserve of $12,000 was created; later the reserve was cancelled and a liability for the item was acknowledged.
   b.   An order was placed for goods or services estimated to cost $12,000; the actual cost was $12,350 for which a liability was acknowledged upon receipt.

  c. Encumbrances were anticipated but later failed to materialize and were reversed. A liability of $12,350 was incurred.

  d. The first entry was erroneous and was reversed; a liability of $12,350 was acknowledged.

2. Entries similar to those for the general fund may also appear on the books of the municipality's

  a. General fixed-assets group.

  b. General bonded-debt group.

  c. Trust fund.

  d. Special-revenue fund.

3. Assuming appropriate governmental accounting principles were followed, the entries

  a. Occurred in the same fiscal period.

  b. Did **not** occur in the same fiscal period.

  c. Could have occurred in the same fiscal period, but it is impossible to be sure of this.

  d. Reflect the equivalent of a "prior period adjustment" had the entity concerned been one operated for profit.

4. Immediately after entry number one was recorded, the municipality had a balanced general fund budget for all transactions. What would be the effect of recording entries two and three?

  a. **Not** change the balanced condition of the budget.

  b. Cause the municipality to show a surplus.

  c. Cause the municipality to show a deficit.

  d. **Not** affect the current budget but would affect the budget of the following fiscal period.

                (AICPA adapted)

Exercise 18–4

  The following items pertain to state and local governmental units. Select the best answer for each.

1. What type of account is used to earmark the fund balance to liquidate the contingent obligations of goods ordered but **not** yet received?

  a. Appropriations.

  b. Encumbrances.

  c. Obligations.

  d. Reserve for encumbrances.

2. Premiums received on general obligation bonds are generally transferred to what fund or group of accounts?

  a. Debt service.

  b. General long-term debt.

  c. General.

  d. Special revenue.

3. Self-supporting activities that are provided on a user charge basis are accounted for in what fund?

  a. Agency.

  b. Enterprise.

  c. Intragovernmental service.

  d. Special revenue.

4. A city should record depreciation as an expense in its

  a. General fund and enterprise fund.

  b. Intragovernmental service fund and general fixed-assets group of accounts.

  c. Enterprise fund and intragovernmental service fund.

  d. Enterprise fund and capital-projects fund.

               (AICPA adapted)

Exercise 18–5

  The following items pertain to state and local governmental units. Select the best answer for each.

1. Authority granted by a legislative body to make expenditures and to incur obligations during a fiscal year is the definition of an

  a. Appropriation.

  b. Authorization.

  c. Encumbrance.

  d. Expenditure.

2. An account for expenditures does **not** appear in which fund?

  a. Capital projects.

  b. Enterprise.

  c. Special assessment.

  d. Special revenue.

3. Part of the general obligation bond proceeds from a new issuance was used to pay for the cost of a new city hall as soon as construction was completed. The remainder of the proceeds was transferred to repay the debt. Entries are needed to record these transactions in the

  a. General fund and general long-term debt group of accounts.

  b. General fund, general long-term debt group of accounts, and debt-service fund.

  c. Trust fund, debt-service fund, and general fixed-assets group of accounts.

  d. General long-term debt group of accounts, debt-service fund, general fixed-assets group of accounts, and capital-projects fund.

4. Cash secured from property tax revenue was transferred for the eventual payment of principal and interest on general obligation bonds. The bonds had been issued when land had been acquired several years ago for a city park. Upon the transfer, an entry would **not** be made in which of the following?

  a. Debt-service fund.

  b. General fixed-assets group of accounts.

  c. General long-term debt group of accounts.

  d. General fund.

5. Equipment in general governmental service that had been constructed ten years before by a capital-projects fund was sold. The receipts were accounted for as unrestricted revenue. Entries are necessary in the
   a. General fund and capital-projects fund.
   b. General fund and general fixed-assets group of accounts.
   c. General fund, capital-projects fund, and enterprise fund.
   d. General fund, capital-projects fund, and general fixed-assets group of accounts.

   (AICPA adapted)

Exercise 18–6

The following statements refer to transactions of Brockton City. Select the best answer for each of the following items.

1. In preparing the general-fund budget of Brockton City for the forthcoming fiscal year the city council appropriated a sum greater than expected revenues. This action of the council will result in
   a. A cash overdraft during that fiscal year.
   b. An increase in encumbrances by the end of that fiscal year.
   c. A decrease in the fund balance.
   d. A necessity for compensatory offsetting action in the debt-service fund.

2. Brockton City's water utility, which is an enterprise fund, submits a bill for $9,000 to the general fund for water service supplied to city departments and agencies. Submission of this bill would result in
   a. Creation of balances which will be eliminated on the city's combined balance sheet.
   b. Recognition of revenue by the water-utility fund and of an expenditure by the general fund.
   c. Recognition of an encumbrance by both the water-utility fund and the general fund.
   d. Creation of a balance which will be eliminated on the city's combined statement of changes in fund balances.

3. Brockton City's water utility, which is an enterprise fund, transferred land and a building to the general city administration for public use at **no** charge to the city. The land was carried on the water-utility books at $4,000 and the building at a cost of $30,000 on which $23,000 depreciation had been recorded. In the year of the transfer what would be the effect of the transaction?
   a. Reduce retained earnings of the water utility by $11,000 and increase the fund balance of the general fund by $11,000.
   b. Reduce retained earnings of the water utility by $11,000 and increase the total assets in the general fixed-assets group by $11,000.
   c. Reduce retained earnings of the water utility by $11,000 and increase the total assets in the general fixed-assets group by $34,000.
   d. Have **no** effect on a combined balance sheet for the city.

4. Brockton City has approved a special-assessment project in accordance with applicable laws. Total assessments of $500,000, including 10% for the city's share of the cost, have been levied. The levy will be collected from

property owners in ten equal annual installments commencing with the current year. Recognition of the approval and levy will result in entries of

a. $500,000 in the special-assessment fund and $50,000 in the general fund.

b. $450,000 in the special-assessment fund and $50,000 in the general fund.

c. $50,000 in the special-assessment fund and $50,000 in the general fund.

d. $50,000 in the special-assessment fund and **no** entry in the general fund.

5. What would be the effect on the general-fund balance in the current fiscal year of recording a $15,000 purchase for a new fire truck out of general-fund resources, for which a $14,600 encumbrance had been recorded in the general fund in the previous fiscal year?

a. Reduce the general-fund balance $15,000.

b. Reduce the general-fund balance $14,600.

c. Reduce the general-fund balance $400.

d. Have **no** effect on the general-fund balance.

6. Brockton City's debt-service fund (for term bonds) recorded required additions and required earnings for the current fiscal year of $15,000 and $7,000, respectively. The actual revenues and interest earnings were $16,000 and $6,500, respectively. What are the necessary entries to record the year's actual additions and earnings in the debt-service fund and in the general long-term-debt group, respectively?

a. $22,500 and $22,000.

b. $22,000 and $22,000.

c. $22,500 and $22,500.

d. $22,500 and **no** entry.

7. Brockton City serves as collecting agency for the local independent school district and for a local water district. For this purpose, Brockton has created a single agency fund and charges the other entities a fee of 1% of the gross amounts collected. (The service fee is treated as general-fund revenue.) During the latest fiscal year a gross amount of $268,000 was collected for the independent school district and $80,000 for the water district. As a consequence of the foregoing, Brockton's general fund should

a. Recognize receipts of $348,000.

b. Recognize receipts of $344,520.

c. Record revenue of $3,480.

d. Record encumbrances of $344,520.

8. When Brockton City realized $1,020,000 from the sale of a $1,000,000 bond issue, the entry in its capital-project fund was

Cash $1,020,000
  Revenues $1,000,000
  Premium on bonds   20,000

Recording the transaction in this manner indicates that

a. The $20,000 **cannot** be used for the designated purpose of the fund but must be transferred to another fund.

   b.   The full $1,020,000 can be used by the capital-project fund to accomplish its purpose.
   c.   The nominal rate of interest on the bonds is below the market rate for bonds of such term and risk.
   d.   A safety factor is being set aside to cover possible contract defaults on the construction.

9. What will be the balance-sheet effect of recording $50,000 of depreciation in the accounts of a utility, an enterprise fund, owned by Brockton City?
   a.   Reduce total assets of the utility fund and the general fixed-assets group by $50,000.
   b.   Reduce total assets of the utility fund by $50,000 but have **no** effect on the general fixed-assets group.
   c.   Reduce total assets of the general fixed-assets group by $50,000 but have **no** effect on assets of the utility fund.
   d.   Have **no** effect on total assets of either the utility fund or the general fixed-assets group.

(AICPA adapted)

Exercise 18–7

   William Bates is executive vice-president of Mavis Industries, Inc., a publicly held industrial corporation. Bates has just been elected to the city council of Gotham City. Prior to assuming office as a city councilman, he asks you as his CPA to explain the major differences that exist in accounting and financial reporting for a large city when compared to a large industrial corporation.

Required:

a.   Describe the major differences that exist in the purpose of accounting and financial reporting and in the types of financial reports of a large city when compared to a large industrial corporation.
b.   Why are inventories often ignored in accounting for local governmental units? Explain.
c.   Under what circumstances should depreciation be recognized in accounting for local governmental units? Explain.

(AICPA adapted)

Exercise 18–8

a.   Reference is frequently made in governmental accounting to "budgetary" and "proprietary" accounts. Define these expressions as they relate to the governmental entity. Do budgetary accounts have a parallel in commercial enterprise accounting? Does the budget occupy the same role in both accounting systems?
b.   The concept of a "fund" is inherent in governmental accounting systems. Discuss the nature of this concept, and distinguish the unique characteristics of the various equities which are implicit therein.

PROBLEMS

Problem 1

The following account balances were included in the January 1, 1977, trial balance of the General Fund of the City of Tallwood:

Reserve for encumbrances—prior year $20,000
Unappropriated surplus 42,000

During the 1977 fiscal year, the General Fund engaged in the following transactions:

a. The budget for the 1977 fiscal year was adopted, with estimated revenues of $300,000 and appropriations of $293,000.
b. The general tax levy for the year was $250,000; estimated uncollectible accounts amount to $10,000.
c. Wages and salaries in the amount of $90,000 were approved for payment. (These expenditures were processed without prior encumbrance.)
d. Supplies ordered in 1976 were received at a cost of $21,000. This closes all purchase orders from the prior year.
e. Negotiations for the purchase of a building were completed, the construction cost of which was estimated to be $150,000.
f. Payment was made for the approved vouchers in (c) and (d) above.
g. Revenue from licenses and fees in the amount of $55,000 was collected.
h. Collections of current taxes in the amount of $200,000 were received.
i. The purchase of the building in (e) above was approved for payment, the settlement price being $140,000.
j. $10,000 was received from the sale of fixed assets.
k. An invoice of $20,000 was received for gas and electricity from the appropriate municipal subdivision.
l. Orders were placed for supplies in the amount of $60,000.

Required:

a. Prepare journal entries to record these 1977 transactions of the General Fund, and indicate what other funds, if any, are affected.
b. Prepare closing entries for the General Fund.
c. Prepare an analysis of Fund Balance for 1977.

Problem 2

The Sleepy Haven Township's adjusted trial balance for the General Fund at the close of its fiscal year ending June 30, 1978, is shown following:

SLEEPY HAVEN TOWNSHIP
General Fund Trial Balance
June 30, 1978

Cash	$ 1,100	
Taxes receivable—current (Note 1)	8,200	
Allowance for uncollectible taxes—current		$ 150
Taxes receivable—delinquent	2,500	
Allowance for uncollectible taxes—delinquent		1,650
Miscellaneous accounts receivable	4,000	
Allowance for uncollectible accounts		400
Due from Intragovernmental Service Fund	5,000	
Appropriation expenditures (Note 2)	75,500	
Encumbrances	3,700	
Revenues (Note 3)		6,000
Due to Enterprise Fund		1,000
Vouchers payable		2,000
Reserve for encumbrances—prior year		4,400
Reserve for encumbrances		3,700
Surplus receipts (Note 4)		700
Appropriations		72,000
Fund balance		8.000
	$100,000	$100,000

Note 1: The current tax roll and miscellaneous accounts receivable, recorded on the accrual basis as sources of revenue, amounted to $50,000 and $20,000 respectively. These items have been recorded on the books subject to a 2 percent provision for uncollectible accounts.

Note 2: Includes $4,250 paid during the fiscal year in settlement of all purchase orders outstanding at the beginning of the fiscal year.

Note 3: Represents the difference between the budgeted (estimated) revenues of $70,000 and the actual revenues realized during the fiscal year.

Note 4: Represents the proceeds from sale of equipment damaged by fire.

Required:

a. Prepare in columnar form an Analysis of Changes in Fund Balance for the year ending June 30, 1978, with column headings: "Estimated," "Actual," and "Excess or Deficiency of Actual Compared with Estimated."

b. Prepare a General Fund balance sheet at June 30, 1978.

(AICPA adapted)

Problem 3

The following balances relate to the General Fund of the City of Valhalla on July 1, 1978:

Cash	$ 28,500	Vouchers payable	$12.000
Taxes receivable—delinquent	31,200	Reserve for encumbrances	14,000
Allowance for uncollectible taxes		Reserve for materials and	
receivable—delinquent	[2,800]	supplies	5,300
Materials and supplies	5,300	Fund balance	30,900
	$ 62,200		$62,200

During the fiscal year ended June 30, 1979, the following transactions were completed:

a. The annual budget was adopted by the City Council; it provided for estimated revenues of $325,000 and appropriations of $330,000.

b. The current year's tax bill was levied in the amount of $300,000, of which $14,000 of receivable balances were estimated to be uncollectible.

c. Vouchers were approved in respect to all encumbrances of July 1, 1978. Orders for new equipment were placed in the amount of $28,000.

d. Receivables for delinquent taxes were collected, $23,000, with interest and penalties of $460.

e. Cash of $10,000 was advanced to the General Fund by the Debt Service Fund.

f. The equipment ordered in (c) was vouchered for $30,000.

g. Vouchers were approved for wages and salaries, $225,000.

h. Vouchers were approved for the purchase of materials and supplies, $65,000.

i. Collections of $274,000 were made in respect to current year tax assessments; unpaid receivable balances were transferred to the Taxes Receivable —Delinquent account.

j. Additional collections for the issuance of licenses and permits amounted to $33,000.

k. Vouchers were paid, $330,000.

l. Orders were placed for additional materials and supplies in the amount of $20,000. Supplies on hand on June 30, 1979, were $12,000.

Required:

a. Prepare journal entries for the General Fund for the transactions enumerated above.

b. Journalize closing entries for the General Fund for the fiscal year ended June 30, 1979.

c. Prepare a balance sheet for the General Fund as of June 30, 1979.

Problem 4

The Town of Sargentville uses budgetary accounts and maintains accounts for each of the following types of funds:

Symbol	Fund
A	Capital Projects Fund
B	General Long-Term Debt
C	General Fund
D	Property Accounts (General Fixed Assets)
E	Debt Service Fund
F	Special Assessment Fund
G	Special Revenue Fund
H	Trust and Agency Fund
S	Enterprise Fund
T	Intragovernmental Service Fund

The chart of accounts of the *General Fund* follows:

Symbol	Account
1	Appropriations
2	Cash
3	Due from other funds
4	Due to other funds
5	Encumbrances
6	Expenditures
7	Reserve for encumbrances
8	Revenues
9	Revenues (estimated)
10	Surplus receipts
11	Fund balance
12	1977 taxes receivable
13	Vouchers payable

The following transactions were among those occurring during 1977:

a. The 1977 budget was approved. It provided for $520,000 of General Fund revenue and $205,000 of school fund revenue.

b. The budgeted appropriations for the General Fund amounted to $516,000.

c. An advance of $10,000 was made from the General Fund to a fund for the operation of a central printing service used by all departments of the municipal government. (This had not been budgeted and is not expected to be repaid.)

d. Taxes for General Fund revenues were levied, totaling $490,000.

e. Contractors were paid $200,000 for the construction of an office building. The payment was from proceeds of a general bond issue of 1976.

f. Bonds of a general issue, previously authorized, were sold at par for $60,000 cash.

g. Orders were placed for supplies to be used by the Health Department—estimated cost, $7,500.

h. Vouchers approved for payment of salaries of town officers in the amount of $11,200. (No encumbrances are recorded for wages and salaries.)

i. The supplies ordered in (g) were received and vouchers were approved for the invoice price of $7,480.

j. Fire equipment was purchased for $12,500 and the voucher approved.

k. A payment of $5,000 was made by the General Fund to a fund for eventual redemption of general obligation bonds.

l. Of the taxes levied in (d), $210,000 were collected.

m. Taxes amounting to $1,240, written off as uncollectible in 1974, were collected. No amount was in the budget for such collections.

n. $1,000 of the advance made in (c) was returned because it was not needed.

o. Supplies for general administrative use were requisitioned from the store's fund. A charge of $1,220 is made for the supplies.

p. The General Fund advanced $30,000 cash to provide temporary working capital for a fund out of which payment will be made for a new sewerage installation. Eventual financing will be by means of assessments on property holders on the basis of benefits received.

q. Equipment from the Highway Department was sold for $7,000 cash. This sale was not included in the budget and depreciation is not funded.

r. The town received a cash bequest of $75,000 for the establishment of a Scholarship Fund.

s. Previously approved and entered vouchers for payment of Police Department salaries of $6,200 and for the transfer of $500 to the Police Pension Fund were paid.

t. Receipts from licenses and fees amounted to $16,000.

Required:

Prepare a table indicating for each transaction, by means of the appropriate numerals, the account debited and the account credited in the General Fund. If a transaction requires an entry in any fund(s) other than the General Fund, indicate the fund(s) affected by appropriate notation.

(AICPA adapted)

Problem 5

The following transactions represent practical situations frequently encountered in accounting for municipal governments. Each transaction is independent of the others.

1. The city council of Bernardville adopted a budget for the general operations of the government during the new fiscal year. Revenues were estimated at $695,000. Legal authorizations for budgeted expenditures were $650,000.

2. Taxes of $160,000 were levied for the special revenue fund of Millstown. One percent was estimated to be uncollectible.

3. *a.* On July 25, 1977, office supplies estimated to cost $2,390 were ordered for the city manager's office of Bullersville. Bullersville, which operates on the calendar year, does not maintain an inventory of such supplies.

   b. The supplies ordered July 25 were received on August 9, 1977, accompanied by an invoice for $2,500.

4. On October 10, 1977, the general fund of Washingtonville repaid to the utility fund a loan of $1,000 plus $40 interest. The loan had been made earlier in the fiscal year.

5. A prominent citizen died and left ten acres of undeveloped land to Harper City for a future school site. The donor's cost of the land was $55,000. The fair value of the land was $85,000.

6. *a.* On March 6, 1977, Dahlstrom City issued 4% special assessment bonds payable March 6, 1983, at face value of $90,000. Interest is payable annually. Dahlstrom City, which operates on the calendar year, will use the proceeds to finance a curbing project.

   b. On October 29, 1977, the full $84,000 cost of the completed curbing project was accrued. Also, appropriate closing entries were made with regard to the project.

7. *a.* Conrad Thamm, a citizen of Basking Knoll, donated common stock valued at $22,000 to the city under a trust agreement. Under the terms of the agreement, the principal amount is to be kept intact; use of

revenue from the stock is restricted to financing academic college scholarships for needy students.

    b. On December 14, 1977, dividends of $1,100 were received on the stock donated by Mr. Thamm.

8. *a.* On February 23, 1977, the town of Lincoln, which operates on the calendar year, issued 4% general obligation bonds with a face value of $300,000 payable February 23, 1987, to finance the construction of an addition to the city hall. Total proceeds were $308,000.

    b. On December 31, 1977, the addition to the city hall was officially approved, the full cost of $297,000 was paid to the contractor, and appropriate closing entries were made with regard to the project. (Assume that no entries have been made with regard to the project since February 23, 1977.)

Required:

For each transaction, prepare the necessary journal entries for *all* of the funds and groups of accounts involved. *No explanation of the journal entries is required.* Use the following headings for your workpaper.

Trans- action Number	Journal Entries	Dr.	Cr.	Fund or Group of Accounts

In the far right column, indicate in which fund or group of accounts each entry is to be made, using the coding below:

Funds:

General	G
Special revenue	SR
Capital projects	CP
Debt service	DS
Special assessments	SA
Enterprise	E
Intragovernmental service	IS
Trust and agency	TA

Groups of accounts:

General fixed assets	GFA
General long-term debt	LTD

(AICPA adapted)

Problem 6

The City of Bel Air entered into the following transactions during the year 1977:

    a. A bond issue was authorized by vote to provide funds for the construction of a new municipal building which it was estimated would cost $500,000. The bonds were to be paid in 10 equal installments from a Debt Service Fund, payments being due March 1 of each year. Any balance of the Capital Projects Fund is to be transferred directly to the Debt Service Fund.

b. An advance of $40,000 was received from the General Fund to underwrite a deposit on the land contract of $60,000. The deposit was made.

c. Bonds of $450,000 were sold for cash at 102. It was decided not to sell all of the bonds because the cost of the land was less than was expected.

d. Contracts amounting to $380,000 were let to Michela and Company, the lowest bidder, for the construction of the municipal building.

e. The temporary advance from the General Fund was repaid and the balance on the land contract was paid.

f. Based on the architect's certificate, warrants were issued for $320,000 for the work completed to date.

g. Warrants paid in cash by the treasurer amounted to $310,000.

h. Due to changes in the plans the contract with Michela and Company was revised to $440,000; the remainder of the bonds were sold at 101.

i. Before the end of the year the building had been completed and additional warrants amounting to $115,000 were issued to the contractor in final payment for the work. All warrants were paid by the treasurer.

Required:

a. Record the above transactions in Capital Projects Fund T-accounts. Designate the entries in the T-accounts by the numbers which identify the data.

b. Prepare applicable fund balance sheets as of December 31, 1977, considering only the proceeds and expenditures from capital projects fund transactions.

(AICPA adapted)

Problem 7

The Cobleskill City Council passed a resolution requiring a yearly cash budget by fund for the City beginning with its fiscal year ending September 30, 1977. The City's financial director has prepared a list of expected cash receipts and disbursements, but he is having difficulty subdividing them by fund. The list follows:

Cash receipts
Taxes:

General property	$ 685,000
School	421,000
Franchise	223,000
	1,329,000

Licenses and permits:

Business licenses	41,000
Automobile inspection permits	24,000
Building permits	18,000
	83,000

Intergovernmental revenue:

Sales tax	1,012,000
Federal grants	128,000
State motor vehicle tax	83,500
State gasoline tax	52,000
State alcoholic beverage licenses	16,000
	1,291,500

Charges for services:
Sanitation fees .... $ 121,000
Sewer connection fees   71,000
Library revenues   13,000
Park revenues   2,500
                                                  207,500

Bond issues:
Civic center   347,000
General obligation   200,000
Sewer   153,000
Library   120,000
                                                  820,000

Other:
Proceeds from the sale of investments 312,000
Sewer assessments   50,000
Rental revenue   48,000
Interest revenue   15,000
                                                  425,000
                                               $4,156,000

Cash disbursements
General government .... $ 671,000
Public safety   516,000
Schools   458,000
Sanitation   131,000
Library   28,000
Rental property   17,500
Parks   17,000
                                                 1,838,500

Debt service:
General obligation bonds   618,000
Street construction bonds   327,000
School bonds   119,000
Sewage disposal plant bonds   37,200
                                                 1,101,200

Investments   358,000

State portion of sales tax   860,200

Capital expenditures:
Sewer construction (assessed area)   114,100
Civic center construction   73,000
Library construction   36,000
                                                   223,100
                                               $4,381,000

The financial director provides you with the following additional information:

1. A bond issue was authorized in 1976 for the construction of a civic center. The debt is to be paid from future civic center revenues and general property taxes.

2. A bond issue was authorized in 1976 for additions to the library. The debt is to be paid from general property taxes.

3. General obligation bonds are paid from general property taxes collected by the general fund.

4. Ten percent (10%) of the total annual school taxes represents an individually voted tax for payment of bonds the proceeds of which were used for school construction.

5. In 1974, a wealthy citizen donated rental property to the City. Net income from the property is to be used to assist in operating the library. The net cash increase attributable to the property is transferred to the library on September 30 of each year.

6. All sales taxes are collected by the City; the state receives 85% of these taxes. The state's portion is remitted at the end of each month.

7. Payment of the street construction bonds is to be made from assessments previously collected from the respective property owners. The proceeds from the assessments were invested and the principal of $312,000 will earn $15,000 interest during the coming year.

8. In 1976, a special assessment in the amount of $203,000 was made on certain property owners for sewer construction. During fiscal 1977, $50,000 of this assessment is expected to be collected. The remainder of the sewer cost is to be paid from a $153,000 bond issue to be sold in fiscal 1977. Future special-assessment collections will be used to pay principal and interest on the bonds.

9. All sewer and sanitation services are provided by a separate enterprise fund.

10. The federal grant is for fiscal 1977 school operations.

11. The proceeds remaining at the end of the year from the sale of civic center and library bonds are to be invested.

Required:

Prepare a budget of cash receipts and disbursements by fund for the year ending September 30, 1977. All interfund transfers of cash are to be included.

(AICPA adapted)

Problem 8

You were engaged to examine the financial statements of the Mayfair School District for the year ended June 30, 1977, and were furnished the General Fund trial balance which appears below.

MAYFAIR SCHOOL DISTRICT

General Fund Trial Balance
June 30, 1977

	Debit	Credit
Cash	$ 47,250	
Taxes receivable—current year	31,800	
Estimated losses—current year taxes		$ 1,800
Temporary investments	11,300	
Inventory of supplies	11,450	
Buildings	1,300,000	
Estimated revenues	1,007,000	
Appropriations—operating expenses		850,000
Appropriations—other expenditures		150,000
State grant revenue		300,000
Bonds payable		1,000,000
Vouchers payable		10,200
Due to Intragovernmental Service Fund		950
Operating expenses:		
Administration	24,950	
Instruction	601,800	
Other	221,450	
Transfer to Debt Service Fund (principal and interest)	130,000	
Capital outlays (equipment)	22,000	
Revenues from tax levy, licenses, and fines		1,008,200
General fund balance		87,850
Total	$3,409,000	$3,409,000

Your examination disclosed the following information:

a.   The recorded estimate of losses for the current year taxes receivable was considered to be sufficient.

b.   The local government unit gave the school district 20 acres of land to be used for a new grade school and a community playground. The unrecorded estimated value of the land donated was $50,000. In addition a state grant of $300,000 was received and the full amount was used in payment of contracts pertaining to the construction of the grade school. Purchases of classroom and playground equipment costing $22,000 were paid from general funds.

c.   Five years ago a 4 percent, 10-year, sinking fund bond issue in the amount of $1,000,000 for constructing school buildings was made and is outstanding. Interest on the issue is payable at maturity. Budgetary requirements of an annual contribution of $130,000 ($90,000 principal and $40,000 interest) and accumulated earnings to date aggregating $15,000 were accounted for in separate Debt Service Fund accounts.

d.   Outstanding purchase orders for operating expenses not recorded in the accounts at year-end were as follows:

Administration	$1,000
Instruction	1,200
Other	600
Total	$2,800

e. The school district operated a central machine shop. Billings amounting to $950 were properly recorded in the accounts of the General Fund but not in the Intragovernmental Service Fund.

Required:

a. Prepare the formal adjusting and closing entries for the General Fund.
b. The foregoing information disclosed by your examination was recorded only in the General Fund. Prepare the formal adjusting journal entries for the (1) General Fixed Asset Group, (2) General Long-Term Debt, and (3) Intragovernmental Service Fund, to correct the failure to record the relevant transactions of 1977 and previous years.

(AICPA adapted)

Problem 9

The City of Happy Hollow has engaged you to examine its financial statements for the year ended December 31, 1977. The City was incorporated as a municipality and began operations on January 1, 1977. You find that a budget was approved by the City Council and was recorded, but that all transactions have been recorded on the cash basis. The bookkeeper has provided an Operating Fund trial balance. Additional information is given below:

1. Examination of the appropriation-expenditure ledger revealed the following information:

	Budgeted	Actual
Personal services	$ 45,000	$38,500
Supplies	19,000	11,000
Equipment	38,000	23,000
Totals	$102,000	$72,500

2. Supplies and equipment in the amounts of $4,000 and $10,000 respectively, had been received, but the vouchers had not been paid at December 31.
3. At December 31, outstanding purchase orders for supplies and equipment not yet received were $1,200 and $3,800, respectively.
4. The inventory of supplies on December 31 was $1,700 by physical count. The decision was made to record the inventory of supplies. A city ordinance requires that expenditures are to be based on purchases, not on the basis of usage.
5. Examination of the revenue subsidiary ledger revealed the following information:

	Budgeted	Actual
Property taxes	$102,600	$ 96,000
Licenses	7,400	7,900
Fines	4,100	4,500
Totals	$114,100	$108,400

It was estimated that 5% of the property taxes would not be collected. Accordingly, property taxes were levied in an amount so that collections would yield the budgeted amount of $102,600.

6. On November 1, 1977, Happy Hollow issued 8% General Obligation Term Bonds with $200,000 face value for a premium of $3,000. Interest is payable each May 1 and November 1 until the maturity date of November 1, 1991. The city council ordered that the cash from the bond premium be set aside and restricted for the eventual retirement of the debt principal. The bonds were issued to finance the construction of a city hall, but no contracts had been let as of December 31.

Required:

a. Complete the worksheet on page 718, showing adjustments and distributions to the proper funds or groups of accounts in conformity with generally accepted accounting principles applicable to governmental entities. (Formal adjusting entries are not required.)
b. Identify the financial statements that should be prepared for the General Fund. (You are not required to prepare these statements.)
c. Draft formal closing entries for the General Fund.

(AICPA adapted)

Problem 10

The Intergalaxy Division, an agency of the federal government, was established on July 1, 1977. The activities of the agency will be financed by annual appropriations.

During the fiscal year ended June 30, 1978, the following transactions, in sequence, were completed:

a. An appropriation of $500,000 was approved by Congress for the Intergalaxy Division.
b. The Budget Office apportioned $450,000 to the agency.
c. The agency director allotted $440,000 to operating units for carrying out assigned projects.
d. An order was placed in the amount of $200,000 for equipment to monitor planned space flights.
e. Salaries of $125,000 were approved for payment without prior obligation.
f. Supplies of $80,000 were ordered.
g. The equipment, cost $200,000, and supplies, cost $78,000, were received.
h. The recorded liabilities were certified for payment by a disbursing agent of the Treasury.
i. Upon request by the Intergalaxy Division, the Budget Office apportioned an additional $45,000 to the agency. Concurrently, the agency director allotted an additional $54,000 to operating unit subdivisions.
j. A research contract for $85,000 was granted to Space University.
k. Services of $25,000 were received under the research contract; the remaining services are to be received in the next fiscal period.
l. On June 30, 1978, accrued salaries of $4,000 and depreciation of $20,000 were recorded; additionally, it was determined that the inventory of supplies amounted to $10,000.

CITY OF HAPPY HOLLOW
Worksheet to Correct Trial Balance
December 31, 1977

	Operating Fund Trial Balance	Adjustments		General Fund	Debt Service Fund	Capital Projects Fund	General Fixed Assets	General Long-Term Debt
		Debit	Credit					
Debits								
Cash	$238,900							
Expenditures	72,500							
Estimated revenues	114,100							
Equipment								
Encumbrances								
Inventory of supplies								
Taxes receivable—current								
Amount to be provided for the payment of term bonds								
Amount available in debt service fund—term bonds								
	$425,500							
Credits								
Appropriations	$102,000							
Revenues	108,400							
Bonds payable	200,000							
Premium on bonds payable	3,000							
Fund balance	12,100							
Vouchers payable								
Investment in general fixed assets—general fund revenue								
Reserve for encumbrances								
Reserve for inventory of supplies								
Estimated uncollectible current taxes								
	$425,500							

Required:

a. Prepare journal entries to record the above transactions.
b. Prepare a preclosing trial balance for the agency.
c. Prepare closing entries.
d. Prepare a statement of financial position at June 30, 1978.

Problem 11

Regulatory accounting underlies the delicate process of harmonizing the sometimes divergent interests of government, private enterprise, and the public. In view of its manifest importance, the theoretical framework for regulatory accounting should consistently and completely facilitate the objectives of the regulating agencies.

Required:

a. What are the primary objectives of regulatory bodies?
b. What basic accounting criteria, or standards, are relevant to the regulation of public utilities?
c. Among the propositions applicable to the valuation of fixed assets, it is usually pointed out that public utilities have traditionally capitalized the interest charges on funds borrowed to finance the construction of plant and equipment. Explain the significance of this position, and relate it, if possible, to the basic accounting standards in (*b*) above.

Problem 12

The City of Larkspur provides electric energy for its citizens through an operating department. All transactions of the Electric Department are recorded in a self-sustaining fund supported by revenue from the sales of energy. Plant expansion is financed by the issuance of bonds which are repaid out of revenues.

All cash of the Electric Department is held by the City Treasurer. Receipts from customers and others are deposited in the Treasurer's account. Disbursements are made by drawing warrants on the Treasurer.

The following is the postclosing trial balance of the department as of June 30, 1977:

Cash on deposit with City Treasurer	$ 2,250,000	
Due from customers	2,120,000	
Other current assets	130,000	
Construction in progress	500,000	
Land	5,000,000	
Electric plant	*50,000,000	
Accumulated depreciation—electric plant		$10,000,000
Accounts payable and accrued liabilities		3,270,000
5% electric revenue bonds		20,000,000
Accumulated earnings		26,730,000
	$60,000,000	$60,000,000

* The plant is being depreciated on the basis of a 50-year composite life.

During the year ended June 30, 1978, the department had the following transactions:

a. Sales of electric energy—$10,700,000.
b. Purchases of fuel and operating supplies (on account)—$2,950,000.
c. Construction of miscellaneous system improvements (financed from operations)—$750,000.
d. Fuel consumed—$2,790,000.
e. Miscellaneous plant additions and improvements placed in service—$1,000,000 (depreciate ½ year).
f. Wages and salaries paid—$4,280,000.
g. Sale on December 31, 1977, of 20-year 5 percent electric revenue bonds, with interest payable semiannually—$5,000,000.
h. Expenditures out of bond proceeds for construction of Larkspur Steam Plant Unit No. 1 and control house—$2,800,000.
i. Operating materials and supplies consumed—$150,000.
j. Payments received from customers—$10,500,000.
k. Expenditures out of bond proceeds for construction of Larkspur Steam Plant Unit No. 2—$2,200,000.
l. Warrants drawn on City Treasurer in settlement of accounts payable—$3,045,000.
m. Larkspur Steam Plant placed in service June 30, 1978.

Required:

A worksheet for the Revenue Fund of the Electric Department showing:

a. The balance sheet amounts at June 30, 1977.
b. The transactions for the year.
c. The balance sheet amounts at June 30, 1978.
d. The sources and applications of funds during the year.

(AICPA adapted)

Problem 13

The following information pertains to the operations of the General Fund of the X County. Functions of this county government include operating the county jail and caring for the county courts.

Funds to finance the operations are provided from a levy of county taxes against the various towns of the county, from the state distribution of unincorporated business taxes, from board of jail prisoners assessed against the towns and against the state, and from interest on savings accounts.

The balances in the accounts of the fund on January 1, 1977, were as follows:

Cash in savings accounts	$ 60,650
Cash in checking accounts	41,380
Cash on hand (undeposited prisoners' board receipts)	320
Inventory of jail supplies	3,070
Due from towns and state for board of prisoners	3,550
General Fund balance	108,970

The budget for the year 1977 as adopted by the county commissioners provided for the following items of revenue and expenditure:

(1) Town and county taxes $20,000
(2) Jail operating costs 55,500
(3) Court operating costs 7,500
(4) Unincorporated business tax 18,000
(5) Board of prisoners (revenue) 5,000
(6) Commissioners' salaries and expenses 8,000
(7) Interest on savings 1,000
(8) Miscellaneous expenses 1,000

General Fund balance was appropriated in sufficient amount to balance the budget. At December 31, 1977, the jail supply inventory amounted to $5,120, cash of $380 was on hand, and $1,325 of prisoners' board bills were unpaid. The following items represent all of the transactions which occurred during the year, with all current bills vouchered and paid by December 31, 1977:

Item (1) was transacted exactly as budgeted.
Item (2) cash expenditures amounted to $55,230
Item (3) amounted to 7,110
Item (4) amounted to 18,070
Item (5) billings amounted to 4,550
Item (6) amounted to 6,670
Item (7) amounted to 1,050
Item (8) amounted to 2,310

During the year, $25,000 was transferred from the savings accounts to the checking accounts.

Required:

From the above information, prepare a worksheet providing columns to show:

a. The transactions for the year.
b. Variances between budgeted and actual revenues and expenditures for the year.
c. Balance sheet of the General Fund, December 31, 1977.

(AICPA adapted)

unit five

SPECIAL SALES CONTRACTS

19

Accounting for
Installment Sales
and Consignments

A. INSTALLMENT SALES

Nature of Installment Sales

THE INSTALLMENT sales contract is a special type of credit arrangement which provides for a schedule of predetermined, periodic collections from the sale of real estate, merchandise, or other personal property. In respect to the usual credit sale, the collection interval is comparatively short and title passes unconditionally to the buyer concurrent with the completion of the sale; however, installment sales contracts are more frequently characterized by (1) a cash down payment at the date of sale followed by periodic (frequently equal) payments over a relatively long period of time, and (2) a transfer of title which remains conditional until the debt is fully discharged.

In view of the typically long collection period, and the concomitant increase in risk, a variety of contractual arrangements are used to provide some additional measure of protection to the seller. Many of these agreements involve some form of title retention by the seller. In other types of agreements, title passes to the purchaser under a mortgage or lien arrangement. Such contracts enable the vendor to reclaim possession of transferred property in those instances where the purchaser is in default.

Despite these safeguards, losses from installment sales tend to be significantly larger than those from short-term credit sales. This may be attributed, in part, to such unique variables as the extended collection period, the relatively small value of many items of repossessed merchandise (whether due to physical deterioration, obsolescence, or depreciation), increased collection expenses, and necessary costs of repossession. Accordingly, the accountant must carefully appraise the measurement of net income where the amount of revenue from installment sales contracts is significant.

Criteria for Gross Profit Recognition

The accounting process of measuring net income from installment sales should theoretically follow the conventional treatment for ordinary credit sales, i.e., by relating gross sales of an accounting period with costs and expenses which appertain thereto. In this reckoning, provision must necessarily be made for the accrual of certain costs expected to be incurred in the future (e.g., those associated with collection) and for estimated losses due to uncollectible receivables. However, because of the prolonged period for liquidating receivable balances, losses in respect thereto are frequently large, and realistic estimates of other costs (or expenses) which relate to installment sales are often difficult to determine.

For these and other reasons, special methods of accounting for installment sales which accent cash collections have been developed. Among the various proposed income determination concepts, each of which focuses primarily on the recognition of gross profit, are the following:

1. Gross profit (sales less cost of goods sold) is not given account recognition until collections are equivalent in amount to the cost of the transferred property; all subsequent receipts are then recorded as realized gross profit. This deferral of gross profit until cost is totally recovered appeals to accounting conservatism. Perhaps a circumstance involving a one-time installment sale with an unusually high degree of risk may justify the application of this method; however, it appears to be an overly cautious criterion for income recognition when applied to a business regularly engaged in installment sales transactions.

2. Collections of receivable balances are first recognized as elements of gross profit; subsequent collections are accounted for as a return of cost. This approach essentially controverts the reason for a unique income determination concept, as the timing of revenue recognition closely parallels the preferred theoretical treatment for regular sales; consequently, it has gained very little support.

3. Each collection is regarded as a partial recovery of cost and a partial realization of gross profit, in the same proporation that these two elements are present in the original selling price. This treatment is known as the *installment sales method*. The frequency of its use derives importantly from the fact that it is approved for income tax purposes. Apropos of Section 453(a) of the Internal Revenue Code, "a person who regularly sells or otherwise disposes of personal property on the installment plan may return as income therefrom in any taxable year that proportion of the installment payments actually received in that year which the gross profit, realized or to be realized when payment is completed, bears to the total contract price." This treatment is also extended to the sale of realty in Section 453(b).

Although the installment sales method (and occasionally the cost recovery method) of recognizing income on installment sales contracts had been used for financial reporting purposes for many years, the Accounting Principles Board severely restricted the method's general acceptability in 1966 with the issuance of *APB Opinion 10*, "Omnibus Opinion— 1966." In this opinion, the Board stated:

Chapter 1A of ARB No. 43, paragraph 1, states that "Profit is deemed to be realized when a sale in the ordinary course of business is effected, unless the circumstances are such that the collection of the sales price is not reasonably assured." The Board reaffirms this statement; it believes that revenues should ordinarily be accounted for at the time a transaction is completed, with appropriate provision for uncollectible accounts. Accordingly, it concludes that, in the absence of the circumstances referred to above, the installment method of recognizing revenue is not acceptable.

A footnote to the final statement amplified the qualification:

The Board recognizes that there are exceptional cases where receivables are collectible over an extended period of time and, because of the terms of the transactions or other conditions, there is no reasonable basis for estimating the degree of collectibility. When such circumstances exist, and as long as they exist, either the installment method or the cost recovery method of accounting may be used. (Under the cost recovery method, equal amounts of revenue and expense are recognized as collections are made until all costs have been recovered, postponing any recognition of profit until that time.)

Thus, the Board left open the possibility that the installment sales method might be acceptable, but the use of the term "exceptional cases" suggested that such instances would be rare.

Following the promulgation of this Opinion, several sensational cases involving overstatement of income during the early years of long-term sales contracts occurred, generally in the real estate industry. As a consequence, in 1973 two *AICPA Industry Accounting Guides* ("Accounting for Retail Land Sales" and "Accounting for Profit Recognition on Sales of Real Estate") were issued. These guides dealt with a number of problems relating to revenue and income recognition on long-term (and often complex) sales contracts, but among other recommendations, the installment sales method was resurrected from the "exceptional cases" category. Accordingly, the method must at present be regarded as a generally accepted accounting practice; its applicability still, however, depends upon the existence of circumstances where the collectibility of the sales price cannot be reasonably estimated.

The Installment Sales Method

With respect to regular sales, revenue is realized (or confirmed) upon completion of the sale transaction; accordingly, it is recognized in the accounting period when title transfers to the buyer. This identification of revenue with the period of sale appears reasonable in view of the fact that there is either an immediate recovery of the total sales price, or collection is made within a relatively short period of time. However, in the case of installment sales, the collection period is frequently an extended interval and the probability of loss because of uncollectible receivables is significantly greater than for regular sales; for this reason, attention is diverted from the date of sale to the process of collection. Under the installment sales method, revenue, or more precisely gross profit, is considered realized (confirmed) in the period of collection rather than in the period of sale. The amount of gross profit recognized in a given period depends upon the relevant gross profit rate and the collected amount of installment receivables.

To illustrate, assume an installment sale of property, the cost of which was $3,000, was made on December 31, 1976, for $5,000, with a cash down payment of $1,000 and 40 monthly payments of $100 scheduled thereafter. The total gross profit to the seller was $2,000 (40 percent of the selling price). Under the installment sales method, annual realized gross profit is recognized according to the following table:

Year	Cash Collected	Gross Profit Realized	
		Computations	Amount
1976	$1,000	$1,000/$5,000 × $2,000	$ 400
1977	1,200	1,200/ 5,000 × 2,000	480
1978	1,200	1,200/ 5,000 × 2,000	480
1979	1,200	1,200/ 5,000 × 2,000	480
1980	400	400/ 5,000 × 2,000	160
Totals	$5,000		$2,000

The deferral of gross profit recognition, which is the essence of the installment sales method, compels the accountant to examine the consistency of the treatment of related expenses. It is evident that the deferral of gross profit, in effect, constitutes a delayed recognition of both sales revenue *and* cost of goods sold. Significantly, however, other operating expenses—some of which relate directly to installment selling, such as distribution costs, collection expenses, and other administrative overhead—are accounted for as period costs. Accordingly, the matching of revenue from installment sales relates only to those product costs incident to, and directly associated with, the acquisition or manufacture of merchandise; the matching process in this application does not extend to other operating expenses. Adovcates for the nondeferral of these expenses frequently argue (1) that conservatism is best served by this treatment, (2) that such expenses often have only a tenuous relationship to either the sales or collection patterns, (3) that realistic measurements for accruals are frequently difficult to estimate with dependable accuracy, and (4) that this method accords with income tax provisions. However, these arguments, at best, merely reflect pragmatic constraints on the more consistent, and preferable, bases of associating costs and revenues. Where the installment sales method is used, it would appear that the materiality doctrine is the only meaningful basis for a nondeferral of many conventional operating expenses.

The treatment of bad debt losses poses a special problem. The installment sales method is predicated upon somewhat uncertain collection prospects, and accordingly defers the recognition of profit. Additionally, it is frequently assumed that the repossession privilege affords the vendor an opportunity to recover the amount of uncollectible installment receivables, at least to the extent of the unrecovered costs of the reclaimed merchandise which are implicit in these balances. Under these circumstances, it would appear that provision for estimated bad debt losses is not required. However, when it becomes evident that the value of repossessed merchandise fails to compensate for corresponding losses of uncollectible accounts (viz., unrecovered cost and previously recognized gross profit), estimates of these losses should be made in the same manner as for other credit sales. Since the cost of the merchandise transferred at date of sale is often the principal component of the ultimate loss, the provision for bad debts is properly reported in the period of sale.

Interest on Unpaid Installment Receivable Balances

Because the collection period for installment sales is often prolonged and may involve large amounts of unliquidated receivable balances, interest is often explicitly charged on these unpaid balances. Where this condition prevails, each installment collection consists of (1) amounts applied in liquidation of the unpaid principal (receivable) balance and (2) interest income. The installment contract may expressly provide for an allocation of the scheduled payments, detailing that portion of each collection which shall relate to the debt principal and interest.

The interest requirement may follow one of several common patterns. These include the following:

1. Cash payments of equal amount are made each period. Each successive installment collection includes an *increased* reduction of principal and a corresponding *decrease* in interest. This is the conventional method of payment on installment sales contracts and will be illustrated subsequently.
2. Interest is charged on the receivable balance unpaid at the beginning of each period. Normally, where this approach is followed, there is a constant reduction of principal in each successive period. Also, the amount of cash received decreases with each collection as a consequence of a decreasing amount of interest.

The first approach is illustrated using the following data:

Installment sale made on January 1, 1976 .... $2,500.00
Cash down payment 500.00
Annual installment collection for 4 consecutive years (including 5
   percent interest) *564.02

 * Computation of equal periodic payment:
     Periodic payment = original unpaid receivable balance
                         ÷ present value of an annuity of $1 for 4 periods at 5%
                       = $2,000 ÷ 3.5459505
                       = $564.02.

Table of Entries for Periodic Collections

Date	Cash (Debit)	Interest Earned (Credit)	Installment Accounts Receivable (Credit)	Unpaid Balance
1/1/76				$2,500.00
1/1/76	$500.00		$500.00	2,000.00
1/1/77	564.02	(a) $100.00	464.02	1,535.98
1/1/78	564.02	(b) 76.80	487.22	1,048.76
1/1/79	564.02	(c) 52.44	511.58	537.18
1/1/80	*564.04	(d) 26.86	537.18	–0–

   (a) $2,000.00 × 5% = $100.00.
   (b) $1,535.98 × 5% = $ 76.80.
   (c) $1,048.76 × 5% = $ 52.44.
   (d) $ 537.18 × 5% = $ 26.86.
   * Adjusted to reflect the requirements of the terminal payment.

Although no further detailed illustrations are offered at this time, the second interest pattern described is illustrated subsequently with a journal entry sequence for the sale of realty on an installment basis.

If the installment sales contract does not provide for interest, or if the stated interest rate is less than the prevailing current rate for debts with similar terms, security, and risk, *APB Opinion 21,* "Interest on Receivables and Payables," requires the recognition of imputed interest. In this circumstance, the stated receivable would be adjusted downward by a "valuation discount," and based upon this discounted value and the scheduled periodic payments, the installment sale would be handled in the same manner as is illustrated in the previous example.[1]

Accounting Procedures for the Installment Sales Method

Various accounting procedures may be used to record transactions using the installment sales method. The sequence of entries described and il-

---

[1] Since the installment sales method tends to recognize income evenly over the life of the contract, the AICPA Committee on Land Development Companies in "Accounting for Retail Land Sales" recommended that imputed interest be ignored (in the interest of simplicity) when the installment sales method is applied.

lustrated in the following pages is essentially a distillate of current accounting practice.

Although there are no substantive differences in the several applications of this income concept, it is convenient to consider separately two basic types of property transfers, with their attendant procedural details:

1. Installment sales of items other than regular merchandise—realty and casual sales of personal property (see Illustration 19–1).
2. Installment sales of conventional merchandise (see Illustration 19–3).

Entries for Installment Sale of Realty (and Other Casual Sales). The following installment sale transaction is assumed to occur on January 31, 1977.

Sales of realty (Plot 9)	$100,000
Cost of the realty	70,000
Gross profit on sale (30 percent of the sales price)	$ 30,000
Expenses of sale	$ 2,000
Collection schedule:	
Cash down payment at date of sale	20,000
Note secured by a mortgage lien on the realty. Liquidation is to be made by eight annual payments of $10,000. Six percent interest is payable each January 31 on the unpaid balance at the beginning of the year.	80,000

In order to emphasize the special effect of the installment sales method on revenue recognition from the sale of realty, entries which indicate the recognition of gross profit under the installment method (i.e., ratably over the periods in which collections are made) are juxtaposed against entries determining net income by the conventional accrual method (i.e., in the period of sale) for a two-year period in Illustration 19–1. A comparative

Illustration 19–1

	Accrual Method (Gross Profit Recognized in Period of Sale)		*Installment Sales Method (Gross Profit Recognized with the Progress of Collection)*	
(1) January 31, 1977. Sale of Plot 9, cost $70,000, for $100,000, and collection of cash down payment of $20,000 (gross profit rate = 30%).				
Cash 20,000		20,000		
Note receivable 80,000		80,000		
Real estate (Plot 9)	70,000		70,000	
Gain on sale of realty	30,000			
Deferred gross profit on sale of realty			30,000	
(2) January 31, 1977. Payment of expenses related to sale.				
Expenses of realty sales 2,000		2,000		
Cash	2,000		2,000	

Illustration 19–1 (continued)

	Accrual Method (Gross Profit Recognized in Period of Sale)		Installment Sales Method (Gross Profit Recognized with the Progress of Collection)
(3) December 31, 1977. Realized gross profit on installment basis: $20,000 × 30% = $6,000.			
Deferred gross profit on sale of realty			6,000
Realized gross profit on sale of realty			6,000
(4) December 31, 1977. Accrued interest income on note receivable for 11 months: $80,000 × 6% × 11/12 = $4,400.			
Interest receivable	4,400		4,400
Interest earned		4,400	4,400
(5) December 31, 1977. Year-end closing.			
Gain on sale of realty	30,000		
Realized gross profit on sale of reality ...			6,000
Interest earned	4,400		4,400
Expenses of realty sales		2,000	2,000
Income summary		32,400	8,400
(6) January 1, 1978. Reversal of entry (4).			
Interest earned	4,400		4,400
Interest receivable		4,400	4,400
(7) January 31, 1978. Receipt of first installment on note receivable and interest of $4,800 ($80,000 × 6%).			
Cash	14,800		14,800
Note receivable		10,000	10,000
Interest earned		4,800	4,800
(8) December 31, 1978. Gross profit on installment basis: $10,000 × 30% = $3,000.			
Deferred gross profit on sale of reality ...			3,000
Realized gross profit on sale of realty			3,000
(9) December 31, 1978. Accrued interest income on note receivable for 11 months: $70,000 × 6% × 11/12 = $3,850.			
Interest receivable	3,850		3,850
Interest earned		3,850	3,850
(10) December 31, 1978. Year-end closing.			
Realized gross profit on sale of realty ...			3,000
Interest earned	4,250		4,250
Income summary		4,250	7,250

analysis of the annual amounts of recognized gross profit over the total time interval is given in Illustration 19–2.

Illustration 19–2

ACCRUAL AND INSTALLMENT METHODS COMPARED

Year	Collections	Uncollected Balance at Year-End	Recognized (Realized) Gross Profit on Sale of Realty		Deferred Gross Profit at Year-End	
			Accrual Method	Installment Method	Accrual Method	Installment Method
1977	$ 20,000	$80,000	$30,000	$ 6,000	–0–	$24,000
1978	10,000	70,000	–0–	3,000	–0–	21,000
1979	10,000	60,000	–0–	3,000	–0–	18,000
1980	10,000	50,000	–0–	3,000	–0–	15,000
1981	10,000	40,000	–0–	3,000	–0–	12,000
1982	10,000	30,000	–0–	3,000	–0–	9,000
1983	10,000	20,000	–0–	3,000	–0–	6,000
1984	10,000	10,000	–0–	3,000	–0–	3,000
1985	10,000	–0–	–0–	3,000	–0–	–0–
Totals	$100,000		$30,000	$30,000		

Note: Interest earned and period costs are accorded equivalent treatment under both methods, and thus are excluded from this analysis.

Entries for Installment Sale of Merchandise. In application of the installment sales method to a merchandising operation, it is important that the accounting system be modified sufficiently to accommodate the necessary account detail and additional procedures. This involves many considerations, among which are the following:

1. Sales, accounts receivable, and cost of sales should be given separate account designations identifying them as either "regular" or "installment."
2. It may be convenient to maintain separate installment receivable accounts by year of sale.
3. The journalizing process should accent gross profit deferral, either at the date of sale or in the period-end closing process. The latter is clearly preferable when installment sales represent a large amount of the total revenue; additionally, it is the only feasible method when the periodic inventory method is used.
4. Gross profit should, as indicated before, be periodically recognized in proportion to the current collections of installment accounts receivable; this recognition becomes an essential part of the sequence of adjusting entries.

Recording procedures are also influenced, at least partially, by the method of inventory accounting used. In Illustration 19–3, we assume perpetual inventory records are maintained.

Assume the following data relate to the XY Corporation:

Sales:	1977	1978
Regular	$200,000	$220,000
Installment	100,000	110,000
Merchandise inventory, January 1	10,000	20,000
Merchandise inventory, December 31	20,000	15,000
Purchases	185,000	189,900
Cost of sales:		
Regular	115,000	130,000
Installment	60,000	64,900
Selling expenses	50,000	65,000
Provision for doubtful accounts (regular sales)	1,000	1,100
Collections on account:		
Installment accounts receivable—1977	30,000	40,000
Installment accounts receivable—1978		50,000
Accounts receivable (regular)	180,000	230,000

These data are recorded in summary form for each of the two years in Illustration 19–3. Although the comparative interperiod effect of electing the installment sales method is not again calculated, it remains essentially consistent with the results derived in Illustration 19–2. Since sales of

Illustration 19–3

(1) January–December, 1977. Regular and installment sales in 1977.

Accounts receivable (regular)	200,000	
Installment accounts receivable—1977	100,000	
Sales (regular)		200,000
Installment sales		100,000

(2) January–December, 1977. Purchases of merchandise in 1977.

Merchandise inventory	185,000	
Accounts payable (cash)		185,000

(3) January–December, 1977. Selling expenses and provision for doubtful accounts during 1977.

Selling expenses	50,000	
Estimated loss on doubtful accounts	1,000	
Accounts payable (cash)		50,000
Allowance for doubtful accounts		1,000

(4) January–December, 1977. Collection of receivables during 1977.

Cash	210,000	
Accounts receivable (regular)		180,000
Installment accounts receivable—1977		30,000

(5) January–December, 1977. Determination of cost of sales for 1977.

Cost of sales (regular)	115,000	
Cost of installment sales	60,000	
Merchandise inventory		175,000

(6) December 31, 1977. Determination of 1977 deferred gross profit on installment sales. Gross profit rate = $40,000 ÷ $100,000 = 40%.

Illustration 19–3 (*continued*)

Installment sales	100,000	
Cost of installment sales		60,000
Deferred gross profit on installment sales—1977		40,000

(7) December 31, 1977. Realized gross profit in 1977 on installment sales.

Year of Sale	Gross Profit Rate	Collections	Realized Gross Profit
1977	40%	$30,000	$12,000

Deferred gross profit on installment sales—1977	12,000	
Realized gross profit on installment sales		12,000

(8) December 31, 1977. Year-end closing for realized gross profit.

Realized gross profit on installment sales	12,000	
Income summary		12,000

(9) December 31,1977. Year-end closing for other nominal accounts.

Sales (regular)	200,000	
Cost of sales (regular)		115,000
Estimated loss on doubtful accounts		1,000
Selling expenses		50,000
Income summary		34,000
Income summary	46,000	
Retained earnings		46,000

(10) January–December, 1978. Regular and installment sales in 1978.

Accounts receivable (regular)	220,000	
Installment accounts receivable—1978	110,000	
Sales (regular)		220,000
Installment sales		110,000

(11) January–December, 1978. Purchases of merchandise in 1978.

Merchandise inventory	189,900	
Accounts payable (cash)		189,900

(12) January–December, 1978. Selling expenses and provision for doubtful accounts during 1978.

Selling expenses	65,000	
Estimated loss on doubtful accounts	1,100	
Accounts payable (cash)		65,000
Allowance for doubtful accounts		1,100

(13) January–December, 1978. Collection of receivables during 1978.

Cash	320,000	
Accounts receivable (regular)		230,000
Installment accounts receivable—1977		40,000
Installment accounts receivable—1978		50,000

(14) January–December, 1978. Determination of cost of sales for 1978.

Illustration 19–3 (*continued*)

Cost of sales (regular)	130,000	
Cost of installment sales	64,900	
Merchandise inventory		194,900

(15) December 31, 1978. Determination of 1978 deferred gross profit on installment sales. Gross profit rate = $45,100 ÷ $110,000 = 41%.

Installment sales	110,000	
Cost of installment sales		64,900
Deferred gross profit on installment sales—1978		45,100

(16) December 31, 1978. Realized gross profit in 1978 on installment sales.

Year of Sale	Gross Profit Rate	Collec- tions	Realized Gross Profit
1977	40%	$40,000	$16,000
1978	41	50,000	20,500

Deferred gross profit on installment sales—1977	16,000	
Deferred gross profit on installment sales—1978	20,500	
Realized gross profit on installment sales		36,500

(17) December 31, 1978. Year-end closing for realized gross profit.

Realized gross profit on installment sales	36,500	
Income summary		36,500

(18) December 31, 1978. Year-end closing for other nominal accounts.

Sales (regular)	220,000	
Cost of sales (regular)		130,000
Estimated loss on doubtful accounts		1,100
Selling expenses		65,000
Income summary		23,900
Income summary	60,400	
Retained earnings		60,400

merchandise on the installment basis often extend over many periods of business operations, however, calculations of net income under the conventional accrual method and the installment sales method will eventually tend to converge.

If the periodic inventory method is used, the determination of cost of sales cannot be made until the end of the period. Further, it may be necessary to use some estimating procedure to allocate the total cost of sales between regular and installment sales.

Financial Statement Presentation

Transactions involving installment sales introduce several problems in respect to informative reporting. As with other special types of transactions, adequacy of disclosure is a compelling consideration. Significantly, however, informative reporting may be accomplished in a number of ways. The preferable statement format will depend upon the characteristics of each particular situation. For this reason, various alternative approaches are illustrated in the following pages using the data contained in Illustration 19–3.

Income Statement. With respect to the income statement, the degree of detail to be reported frequently will vary, depending upon the magnitude of installment sales revenues in relation to total sales. For example, if installment sales are relatively insignificant in amount, the type of presentation in Illustration 19–4 may be appropriate.

Illustration 19–4

THE XY CORPORATION

Income Statement
For Year Ended December 31, 1978
(Installment Sales Are Not Significant in Amount)

Sales	$220,000
Cost of goods sold	130,000
Gross profit	$ 90,000
Realized gross profit on installment sales	36,500
Total gross profit	$126,500
Expenses	66,100
Net Income	$ 60,400

Alternatively, should installment sales represent a material segment of the total revenues of a business enterprise, additional detail may be required for a full and informative disclosure. In this event, the accountant may elect one of two basic approaches, viz.:

1. The presentation of details concerning installment transactions may be integrated, but separately identified, in the income statement, supported as necessary with appropriate footnotes (see Illustration 19–5).
2. The presentation of details concerning installment transactions may be principally disclosed in one or more separate schedules which support a summarized income statement (see Illustrations 19–6 and 19–7).

Many other variants on these illustrative statement forms are available. One principle, however, that is common to all of the above illustrations is the reporting of the *total* sales in the year that the installment sales contract is signed, with deferral of the gross profit to future periods. This principle has traditionally been adhered to in practice, and it was further supported in "Accounting for Retail Land Sales." However, when installment

Illustration 19–5

THE XY CORPORATION

**Income Statement
For Year Ended December 31, 1978
(Installment Sales Are Significant in Amount)**

			Sales	
		Total	*Regular*	*Installment*
Sales		$330,000	$220,000	$110,000
Cost of goods sold:				
Merchandise inventory				
January 1	$ 20,000			
Purchases	189,900			
	$209,900			
Merchandise inventory,				
December 31	15,000			
Total		194,900	130,000	64,900
Accrual-basis gross profit on 1978 sales		$135,100	$ 90,000	$ 45,100
Less: Gross profit to be deferred on 1978				
installment sales		24,600		24,600
		$110,500		$ 20,500
Add: Realized gross profit in 1978 on				
installment sales of prior year—1977		16,000		16,000
Total gross profit realized in 1978 on				
installment sales (Note 1)				$ 36,500
Total realized gross profit		$126,500		
Expenses (detailed)		66,100		
Net Income		$ 60,400		

Note 1: Approximately one third of the sales of the XY Corporation are represented by installment sales, for which the average collection period is three years. Gross profit on these sales is deferred until realized (or confirmed) through collection of receivable balances. This procedure is used for both financial accounting and income tax purposes.

sales are a significant portion of a firm's total business, one may reasonably question this reporting of the total revenue in the year of sale. To the extent that the revenue of a firm is an important variable in the analysis of its financial prospects, this practice introduces a certain amount of distortion. An alternative that is presently receiving consideration by accounting policy-makers and practitioners is to defer revenue recognition as well as profit recognition. Thus, for a firm that has a gross profit rate of 40 percent and deferred gross profit of $40,000, application of this alternative would result in the deferral of revenue of $100,000 and related costs of $60,000, instead of merely deferring the net amount of $40,000. In succeeding periods, revenue would be recognized in the amount of cash collections, and the related deferred costs (at the rate of 60 percent) would be matched thereagainst.

Illustration 19–6

THE XY CORPORATION

Income Statement
For Year Ended December 31, 1978
(Installment Sales Are Significant in Amount)

Sales		$220,000
Cost of goods sold:		
Merchandise inventory, January 1, 1978	$ 20,000	
Purchases	189,900	
	$209,900	
Less: Shipment of merchandise on installment		
basis—1978 (Schedule 1)	64,900	
	$145,000	
Less: Merchandise inventory, December 31,		
1978	15,000	130,000
Gross profit on regular sales		$ 90,000
Add: Realized gross profit on installment sales		
(Schedule 1)		36,500
Total gross profit		$126,500
Expenses (detailed)		66,100
Net Income		$ 60,400

Illustration 19–7

SCHEDULE 1

THE XY CORPORATION

Calculation of Realized Gross Profit on Installment Sales
For Year Ended December 31, 1978

Realized gross profit on 1978 installment sales:		
Installment sales—1978	$110,000	
Cost of installment sales—1978	64,900	
Gross profit on installment sales—1978		
(41% of sales)	$ 45,100	
Collections on 1978 installment sales	$ 50,000	
Rate of gross profit in 1978	41%	
Gross profit realized in 1978 on 1978 sales		$20,500
Realized gross profit on 1977 installment sales:		
Collections on 1977 installment sales in 1978	$ 40,000	
Rate of gross profit in 1977	40%	
Gross profit realized in 1978 on 1977 sales		16,000
Total gross profit realized in 1978 (Note 1)		$36,500

Note 1: Gross profit on installment sales is regarded as realized in the accounting period in which installment accounts receivable are collected.

Balance Sheet. With respect to balance sheet presentation, installment accounts receivable from the sale of merchandise are usually classified as current assets and shown as follows:

Assets

Current Assets:

Notes receivable	$25,000	
Accounts receivable	60,000	
	$85,000	
Less: Allowance for doubtful accounts	5,000	$ 80,000
Installment accounts receivable:		
From 1977 sales	$50,000	
From 1978 sales	90,000	140,000

This treatment accords with the accepted notion of current assets as consisting of "cash and other assets that are reasonably expected to be realized in cash or sold or consumed during the normal operating cycle of the business."[2] Installment transactions generate an operating cycle, at least for one segment of the enterprise's operations, which by definition includes the *collection* of these accounts. On the other hand, it would be difficult to justify this classification for an installment contract, or contracts, resulting from a transaction which is unrelated to normal operations (e.g., the infrequent sale of land held either for expansion or investment); consequently, receivable balances which derive from such a source should be reported in the "investments" or the "other assets" section of the balance sheet.

The balance of Deferred Gross Profit on Installment Sales at the end of an accounting period has been reported in various sections of the balance sheet. Some companies have included it with other deferred credits, between the liability and the stockholders' equity sections. Others have included it in the liability section. And still other companies have reported the balance as a valuation adjustment of the related receivable. In "Accounting for Retail Land Sales," the AICPA committee prescribed the last alternative, i.e., reporting the deferred profit as a deduction from the receivable. Since application of the installment sales method is particularly significant in this industry, and also because this particular *Industry Accounting Guide* was approved by the Accounting Principles Board, one might reasonably conclude that current practice in general would tend to favor this alternative.

Defaults and Repossessions

If one who has purchased goods on an installment contract defaults in any of the scheduled payments, the vendor may repossess or reclaim the units sold to satisfy the residual indebtedness. Normally, the goods repossessed are subsequently resold, either in their reclaimed condition or after costs have been incurred to restore them to a more marketable state. Default and repossession requires that the vendor (1) record the repossessed

---

[2] Section 1027.25, *APB Accounting Principles—Current Text.*

item in an appropriate inventory account at its market value at date of repossession; (2) eliminate, or remove, the uncollected receivable balance of the defaulted account; (3) write off the amount of deferred gross profit implicit in the above receivable balance; and (4) enter the resulting gain or loss on repossession.

Assume the following data in respect to a default and concurrent repossession on April 15, 1977:

```
Installment accounts receivable—1975 ................. $1,000
Deferred gross profit on installment sales—1975
    (gross profit rate 30 percent of selling price) .........   300
Estimated market value of item repossessed in its
    reclaimed condition .............................   600
```

The entry for repossession on April 15, 1977, is made as follows:

```
Inventory of repossessed merchandise ...................... 600
Deferred gross profit on installment sales—1975 ............. 300
Loss on defaults (repossessions) ......................... 100
    Installment accounts receivable—1975 ................         1,000
```

Costs of restoration which relate to repossessed merchandise should be accounted for as a cost increment to the Inventory of Repossessed Merchandise account; resale of repossessed merchandise should be accounted for in the conventional manner for regular or installment sales transactions.

With respect to the valuation of repossessed merchandise (or other property), the above entry assumes that *fair market value* in present condition at date of repossession is appropriate. This value is the estimated cash purchase price of the repossessed units as established in the local used-goods, or wholesale, market. Subsequent calculations of net income for the used-goods department of the business are then relatively reliable indexes of operating efficiency. Arguments are also made for other valuation bases, including:

1. The value of repossessed property should be the *book value* of the unliquidated indebtedness, i.e., the uncollected balance of the relevant installment account receivable reduced by the amount of deferred gross profit which relates thereto. Clearly, the actual value of repossessed goods may have little relationship to the book value of the indebtedness. The seller is compelled to reclaim the merchandise to minimize a potential loss; the magnitude of that loss should be determined preferably by a comparison of the used-goods replacement cost of the item repossessed and the book value of the indebtedness. Accordingly, the residual net book value of uncollected receivables has gained comparatively little support as a valuation basis for repossessed merchandise.
2. No value should be assigned to the repossessed asset; rather, a loss at date of repossession should be recognized in the amount of the book

value of the indebtedness. Upon resale of the repossessed item, the total sales price is regarded as revenue. This treatment, which fails to ascribe *any* value to repossessed property, can be justified only on the grounds of conservatism; consequently, it is seldom used in accounting practice.

As a consequence of the above considerations, the use of the used-goods replacement cost value as an inventory valuation basis for repossessed goods is generally subscribed to by most accountants.

The above entry for the repossession of goods on defaulted contracts assumes a relatively simple circumstance with complete knowledge of all relevant data. In the case of a one-time sale of realty, this condition is often satisfied. However, in regard to the sale of merchandise in the normal course of business, more careful consideration should be given to the timing of the repossession. If the default and repossession occur in an accounting period subsequent to the period of sale, the applicable gross profit rate is established, and a certain proportion of the total gross profit has been previously recognized in the accounts. Consequently, the repossession entry may be recorded as illustrated earlier, wherein the debit to Deferred Gross Profit is based upon the amount of unrealized gross profit implicit in the uncollectible balance; this requires a subsequent recognition, in the normal period-end closing process, of realized gross profit on collections during the current year prior to the default. Alternatively, the debit to Deferred Gross Profit may be based upon the balance of the receivable at the beginning of the period. This type of entry denies the existence of realized gross profit on current period collections prior to the default, and reduces the repossession loss by the same amount. In effect, this represents a movement in the direction of the concept of total cost recovery prior to the recognition of any gross profit; it approximates the *ex post facto* analysis of "bad debt" losses as the sum of unrecovered cost— calculated as the difference between merchandise cost and total collections on account—plus previously recognized gross profit. However, since the method is retroactively applied only to the beginning of the period, the measurement of repossession loss still includes a composite of the two factors.

If the repossession of merchandise occurs in the period of sale, the gross profit rate (a composite) is not yet determinable. Therefore, recording the repossession must necessarily be accomplished in two steps. On the date of repossession, one may conceive of the original transaction as essentially abrogated and reverse the original entry of sale; to the extent of prior collections on the account, a value is established in a special nominal account—Revenue from Defaulting Customers. Additionally, the repossessed merchandise is recorded in an appropriate account, with a corresponding credit to Loss on Repossessions. When the average gross profit rate for the period is established, the cost of installment sales which are currently in default is closed to the Loss on Repossessions account. If these two nominal accounts are subsequently combined, there results a correct measure of the unrecovered cost. Alternatively, only the repossession may be recorded on the date of default, with a credit to Loss on Repossessions. After the gross profit rate is established at the end of the period, the receivable and the associated deferred gross profit may be written off to Loss on Repossessions, and gross profit realized on collections received prior to default. In essence, these methods reflect the same two basic concepts which are applicable to repossessions in accounting periods subsequent to the period of sale.

The balance in the Repossessed Merchandise Inventory account is usually reported on the balance sheet as a current asset; gain or loss on repossessions is reported variously in the income statement either as an adjustment to realized gross profit on installment sales, as a separately identified item of gain or loss, or as an addition to (or deduction from), the loss on doubtful accounts. Alternatively, if a provision has been previously made for losses on doubtful accounts which included an allowance for installment sales, the loss on repossessions may be charged to Allowance for Doubtful Accounts.

B. ACCOUNTING FOR CONSIGNMENTS

Nature of Consignments

A consignment is a conveyance of the custody of goods from the owner, designated the *consignor,* to one who acts as his agent, designated the *consignee.* The agent, who is often locationally more accessible to available markets than is the consignor, undertakes to sell the consigned merchandise for the owner under a commission arrangement. Viewed legally, the transfer of the custody of goods is a bailment; accordingly, the laws of agency control in respect to determining the rights and responsibilities of each party (the consignor as principal, the consignee as agent). In respect to the consignor, the transaction for the transfer of goods is often described as a *consignment out;* to the consignee, the receipt of these goods is frequently termed a *consignment in.*

The basic distinction between a sale and a consignment relates to the passage of legal title. In a transaction of sale, legal title vests in the buyer concurrent with the delivery of goods—either to the buyer or to a common carrier. Notwithstanding the fact that there is also a change in the custody of goods in a consignment transaction, legal title continues to identify with the consignor until the relevant goods are sold by the consignee to a third party. Legal title thus passes directly from the consignor to the ultimate transferee, the buyer, when the sale is completed.

In recognition of the unique characteristics of consignment transactions, the following fundamental criteria are appropriate guidelines for accounting procedures:

1. Since title to consigned goods continues to vest in the consignor, such goods should be reported in the inventory of the consignor and excluded from the inventory of the consignee.
2. Goods on consignment do not create revenue, or satisfy the revenue realization criterion, for either the consignor or consignee until they are sold to a third party.
3. The consignor is accountable as owner for all costs incurred which directly related to the goods from date of shipment to the date of sale by the consignee, except as may otherwise be provided by specific contractual agreement between the parties.
4. The consignee, in his capacity as a bailee, is charged with the exercise of due care with respect to the goods held on consignment; accordingly, it may be appropriate to maintain a notational or memorandum record of consigned goods awaiting sale.

Several reasons why a consignment arrangement may be advantageous to both the consignor and the consignee are recounted as follows: *First,* it may be an appropriate vehicle for enlarging channels of distribution for new products, particularly where the demand for these products is uncertain. Additionally, if the goods are high unit-cost items and if the risks of obsolescence and price change are great, retailers may hesitate to purchase such goods; yet, they may be willing to display and to sell them on the condition that the consignor carry the burden of inventory investment and risk. *Second,* there is an obvious investment advantage to the consignee, since he is not compelled to make a commitment of funds in advance of ultimate sale. *Third,* in respect to the consignor, the retention of legal title should serve to reduce his credit risk. In the event of the legal dissolution of the consignee enterprise, creditors of the consignee may not attach these goods as would be possible if the goods were *sold* on credit. *Fourth,* the consignor establishes and continues to retain control over the selling price of consigned merchandise; the exercise of this authority is seldom possible when the goods are sold to the retailer. Notwithstanding these apparent advantages to the consignor and consignee, there has been a noticeable decrease in the use of consignments in recent years, primarily due, no doubt, to improvements in the distribution function generally and to more liberal return privileges on sales contracts.

Rights and Responsibilities Relating to Consignments

Consignment provisions should be outlined clearly in a written contract executed by the consignor and the consignee, dealing with such matters as commissions, allowable terms of sale, responsibility for the collection of accounts receivable and losses from uncollectible accounts, expenses of the consignee in respect to the receipt, maintenance, and sale of consigned merchandise, remittances to the consignor, care and protection of the consigned goods, and the nature and time schedule for reports to be rendered by the consignee. In respect to other matters not specifically referred to in the consignment agreement, the laws of bailment and agency establish the rights and responsibilities of the parties. Since these rights and responsibilities are reciprocally related, i.e., a right of the consignee translates as a responsibility of the consignor, the primary provisions relating to the consignee only are enumerated as follows:

1. *Rights of the consignee:*
    a. The right to compensation for selling the consigned goods and reimbursement for necessary expenses connected therewith. The commission (or other form of reimbursement) to be allowed the consignee is normally a negotiated value between the parties. Reimbursement for necessary expenses often covers such expenditures as freight, insurance, storage, and the usual warranty costs.
    b. The right to make the usual, but not extraordinary, warranties in respect to the quality of merchandise; the consignor is then bound by such warranties.
    c. The right to extend credit for the sale of consigned merchandise in terms consistent with those which are conventional in business enterprises selling similar goods; the consignor may limit this right by express agreement. The receivables from the sale of consigned merchandise (and any related bad debt losses) are those of the consignor. If the consignee, by contractual agreement, assumes responsibility for the collection of these receivables, he is called a *del credere agent,* and is normally allowed extra compensation for the additional risk assumed.
2. *Responsibilities of the consignee:*
    a. To care for and protect the goods held on consignment in a prudent and responsible manner.
    b. To exert reasonable efforts to sell the goods in compliance with the terms of the consignment contract. In granting credit (if this is not denied by the contract), the consignee must exercise a degree of prudence consonant with the credit standards of similar types of business enterprises. The goods should be sold at prices specified by the consignor and in the absence of specification, at a price that appears to represent the best interests of the consignor. Similarly, the consignee should exercise reasonable diligence in the collection of receivables.
    c. To keep the consignor's goods separate and apart from other goods in order to assure their easy identification. This requirement normally presumes physical separation; however, in the event this proves to be impractical, the consignee should maintain accounting records in sufficient detail to permit identification of consigned goods. A collateral obligation, although related to the

separation of consigned merchandise, is the responsibility to preserve the separateness of consignment transactions in the accounting records; sales, reimbursable expenses, inventory, and accounts receivable from consignments all must be clearly designated in order that the interests of the consignor may be distinguished and protected.

d. To render periodic reports and to make liquidating settlements in respect to consignment transactions (goods received, sold, and on hand) as specified in the consignment contract. The contract may require monthly, weekly, or even daily reports to the consignor. The periodic report is typically referred to as an *account sales*. It should specify the goods received on consignment, those sold, relevant expenses, the amount due the consignor, and the amount remitted. A representative form of an account sales is shown in Illustration 19–8.

ACCOUNTING BY THE CONSIGNEE

Since legal title to consigned goods does not vest in the consignee, formal inclusion of these units in the inventory of the consignee is unwarranted and incorrect. However, as previously noted, the consignee will usually find it desirable to use various memoranda to record merchandise held on consignment, detailing both the kind and quantity of consigned units.

In respect to transactions involving the sale of consigned merchandise and related expenses, it is customary to record the revelant data in a special summary Consignment In account. This account is credited with the proceeds from the sale of consigned merchandise and is debited for reimbursable expenses incurred in connection therewith and for commissions earned by the consignee. Consequently, the Consignment In account is essentially a reflection of a bilateral debtor-creditor relationship. If the account indicates a residual credit balance, it is evident that an indebtedness flows from the consignee to the consignor; alternatively, should a debit balance exist, the receivable indicates an indebtedness payable to the consignee.

The Consignment In account may be supported by subsidiary records, depending upon the need for additional account detail. The data usually contained in the summary account and the related subsidiary records are the basic source information for the *account sales,* which is fundamentally a classified enumeration of all transactions between the consignor and the consignee, concluding with the calculation of their reciprocal debtor-creditor status. Where transactions are executed with several consignors, it is appropriate that an account sales should be submitted to each; accordingly, it may also be desirable to establish a separate Consignment In account for each consignor. In the event the number of consignors is un-

Illustration 19–8

ACCOUNT SALES

Matthewson Retailers
Houston, Texas
(Consignee)

		No. J-4
		March 31, 1977
		Date

Sold for Account and Risk of (consignor):
Jackson Manufacturing Company
231 Makin Street
Moline, Illinois   61265

Account sales of:
Color Television Sets (Model AK-320)

Date	Explanation	Quantity	Amount
March 1	Balance on hand (carried forward)	–0–	$ –0–
March 1–31	Received	15	
	TOTAL	15	$ –0–
March 1–31	Sales:		
	TV Sets (AK-320) @ $400 each	10	4,000
	GROSS		$4,000
	Charges:		
	Warranty adjustments (on sets sold)	$ 20	
	Local freight (on 15 sets)	15	
	Commissions (20%)	800	835
	NET		$3,165
March 31	Remittance enclosed		$3,165
March 31	Balances	5	$ –0–

usually large, these separate accounts logically comprise the subsidiary records.

Illustrative Entries

Following are the entries made by a consignee (Matthewson Retailers) for certain typical consignment transactions (the data used are the March transactions reported in the account sales in Illustration 19–8):

1. To record the receipt of 15 color TV sets from the Jackson Manufacturing Company.

Prepare a memorandum entering thereon the fact of the receipt of the consigned goods, the name of the consignor, the quantity of units ordered and received, and the storage or display location.

2. To record drayage (local transportation) on the 15 TV sets delivered to Matthewson Retailers.

Consignment in—Jackson Manufacturing Company   15
    Cash   15

3. To record the sale of 10 TV sets @ $400 each.

Cash (or Accounts receivable—consignment sales) 4,000
    Consignment In—Jackson Manufacturing Company   4,000

4. To record the outlay for warranty adjustments on TV sets sold during March.

Consignment in—Jackson Manufacturing Company   20
    Cash   20

5. To record the 20 percent commission earned on the March sales of TV sets.

Consignment in—Jackson Manufacturing Company   800
    Commissions earned—consignment sales   800

6. To record the remittance to accompany the March 31 account sales forwarded to the consignor.

Consignment in—Jackson Manufacturing Company 3,165
    Cash   3,165

After the above entries are posted, the Consignment In account will appear as follows:

Consignment In—Jackson Manufacturing Company

March 1–31	Drayage	15	March 1–31	Ten TV sets	
	Warranty			sold	4,000
	adjustments	20			
	Commission	800			
March 31	Cash remitted	3,165			
		4,000			4,000

Modifications of Entries and Account Structure

On some occasions the consignee may remit cash to the consignor in advance of the sale of any of the consigned goods; such an advance should be debited to the Consignment In account (or a special receivable account) and should be used to abate subsequent remittances to the consignor. Additionally, if the consignor assumes the responsibility for credit sales (i.e., the consignee is not a *del credere agent*), the remittance accompanying the account sales may consist of both cash and transferred open accounts. Of course, if the ultimate purchasers of consigned goods remit directly to the consignor, it is probable that the account sales will reflect an amount due to the consignee.

Should there be but one monthly consignment transaction, or several transactions involving the same type of merchandise, there is little need for subsidiary account detail. Procedural variations may be required, however, to accommodate special or unique consignment arrangements. For example, if a second shipment of consigned merchandise of a different type is received from the Jackson Company, e.g., 20 black and white TV sets (Model SS-100), a more formal set of unit inventory records may be required. Additionally, the accumulation of cost and revenue data may be reflected in more detailed records as follows:

Controlling account: Consignment In Control—Jackson Manufacturing Company
Subsidiary accounts: Consignment In—Jackson Manufacturing Company
                        (Model AK-320)
                        Consignment In—Jackson Manufacturing Company
                        (Model SS-100)

This type of account structure would facilitate the preparation of a *control account sales,* expressed in dollars only, supported by *subsidiary account sales* for each type of merchandise expressed in both units and dollar amounts.

Financial Statement Presentation

In the income statement of the consignee, the *commissions earned* should be reported as an item of operating income. A balance in the Consignment In account represents either a debt to or receivable from the consignor, and should be reported in the balance sheet as a current asset if a debit balance and as a current liability if a credit balance. Consignment In account balances which relate to different consignors should not, however, be offset; rather, the sum of the debit balances should be reported as an asset and the sum of the credit balances should be reported separately as a liability.

ACCOUNTING BY THE CONSIGNOR

The specific accounting procedures for the consignor depend upon the following two circumstances: (1) consignment transactions may be recorded in separate accounts, or merely entered in standard account classifications which accommodate both consignment and nonconsignment transactions; and (2) perpetual or periodic inventory methods may be used in the existing accounting system of the consignor. Whatever the basic format elected by the consignor, he must maintain a record, or set of records, reflecting consigned units shipped, sales of consigned goods and related expenses, and the status of his accountability with each consignee.

Consignment Out Account

In the event consignment transactions are commingled with other operating data, no unique accounting problems are presented. If it is desired to separate the regular and consignment sales, however, a special account, *Consignment Out,* is created in which are summarized the basic data concerning consignment transactions. The normal inclusions in the account are revealed as follows:

Consignment Out—(Name of Consignee)

Cost of goods shipped on consignment	Sales of consigned goods as reported by consignee on account sales
Expenses related to consignment, incurred by consignor	
Expenses related to consignment, incurred and reported by the consignee on the account sales	
Commissions earned on consigned goods sold by the consignee and reported on the account sales	
Debit (credit) adjustment to yield the correct end-of-period account balance —the cost of the inventory of goods held on consignment, and other deferred costs which relate thereto	

During the accounting period, the Consignment Out account effectively operates as a summary account in respect to all consignment transactions. At the end of the period, however, it is conventionally adjusted such that the residual balance represents the sum of the cost of unsold consigned goods and relevant deferred expenses. The relevant deferred expenses— including those of both the consignor and the consignee—may then be reallocated and separately identified as Deferred Consignment Costs in the accounts and/or balance sheet of the consignor. These capitalizable outlays include all expenditures incurred to place the goods in position for sale, e.g., freight charges, drayage costs, and shipping insurance; they do not include expenditures for advertising, commissions, or other direct selling costs.

Illustrative Entries—Perpetual Inventory

Illustration 19–9 presents in tabular form the entries made by the consignor (Jackson Manufacturing Company) for the transactions relative to the consignment arrangement reflected in the account sales in Illustration 19–8; additionally, the necessary period-end adjustments are illustrated. Entries are given under two assumptions: (1) a separate set of accounts is used for consignment sales and regular sales, and (2) one set of accounts is used for *both* regular and consignment sales. Under each assumption, a perpetual inventory system is used.

At the end of the period (the month of March), the Consignment Out account will appear as follows:

Consignment Out—Matthewson Retailers

Shipped 15 TV sets (Model AK-320)		2,250	Sale of 10 TV sets (Model AK-320)	4,000
Consignor's expenditures:				
Crating costs	45			
Freight-out	60	105		
Consignee's expenditures:				
Warranty adjustments	20			
Local freight	15			
Commissions	800	835		
Period-end adjustment (consignment profit)		1,600	Balance carried forward	790
		4,790		4,790
April 1 inventory—5 TV sets (Model AK-320) @ $158		790		

The assignment of costs for purposes of inventory valuation and the determination of profit on consignment sales is analyzed in detail in Illustration 19–10.

Inventoriable and Noninventoriable Costs

In respect to the tabular calculation in Illustration 19–10, it is important to note the fundamental distinction between inventoriable costs and noninventoriable costs. The inventoriable costs include the original merchandise costs and subsequent value increments; to the extent that these costs attach to unsold units, they are properly deferred to future periods to be matched against related revenues. Packing, freight, and drayage paid by the consignee are illustrative of expenditures usually regarded as increasing the value of the consigned units.

Contrariwise, the noninventoriable costs are those expenditures that fail to add value to the unsold consigned units, and are accordingly charged to expense in the period of outlay. In addition to the normal selling expenses of the consignee, there are frequently other, sometimes unusual, expendi-

Illustration 19-9

JOURNAL ENTRIES BY CONSIGNOR

(Perpetual Inventory Method)

	Separate Accounts Used for Consignment Transactions		Regular Accounts Used for Consignment Transactions	
(1) To record cost of 15 TV sets shipped on consignment, at $150 per set:				
	Consignment out—Matthewson Retailers 2,250		Merchandise on consignment 2,250	
	Inventory	2,250	Inventory	2,250
(2) To record crating costs, $45, incurred by the consignor on the above shipment:				
	Consignment out—Matthewson Retailers ... 45		Deferred consignment costs 45	
	Cash	45	Cash	45
(3) To record $60 freight paid by the consignor on the shipment in (1):				
	Consignment out—Matthewson Retailers 60		Deferred consignment costs 60	
	Cash	60	Cash	60
(4) To record transaction details reported in the account sales (Illustration 19-8):				
	Cash 3,165		Cash 3,165	
	Consignment out—Matthewson Retailers 835		Warranty expense 20	
	Consignment out—Matthewson Retailers	4,000	Deferred consignment costs 15	
			Commissions 800	
			Sales	4,000

Warranty adjustments (on sets sold) .... $ 20
Drayage on 15 sets 15
Commissions on sets sold 800
    $835

(5) To adjust the balance in the Consignment Out account to the end-of-the-period capitalizable costs in respect to unsold goods, and to recognize profit on consignment sales:

Consignment out—Matthewson Retailers 1,600
    Consignment profit 1,600

Inventoriable costs related to 15 sets:

Inventory value when shipped	$2,250	
Packing expense	45	
Freight-out	60	
Local freight—consignee	15	
Total	$2,370	
Unit cost ($2,370 ÷ 15)		$ 158
Inventory valuation ($158 × 5)		$ 790
Preadjustment *Credit* balance in Consignment Out account		810
Debit adjustment		$1,600

To adjust inventory account for the end-of-the period cost of goods held by the consignee:

*Cost of sales 1,580
    Merchandise on consignment 1,500
    Deferred consignment costs 80

(6) To close:

Consignment profit 1,600
    Income summary 1,600

Sales 4,000
    Cost of sales 1,580
    Warranty expense 20
    Commissions 800
    Income summary 1,600

* The expired portion of deferred consignment costs, $80, may be identified as a separate expense in this entry.

Illustration 19–10

	Consigned Merchandise			Inventory		Profit and Loss		
	Units	Total Cost	Unit Cost	Units	Valuation	Units	Costs	Amounts
Sales (10 units @ $400)								$4,000
Inventoriable costs:								
Incurred by consignor:								
Merchandise cost when shipped	15	$2,250	$150	5	$750	10	1,500	
Packing expense	15	45	3	5	15	10	30	
Freight-out	15	60	4	5	20	10	40	
Incurred by consignee:								
Local freight	15	15	1	5	5	10	10	1,580
								$2,420
Selling expenses incurred by consignee:								
Warranty adjustments							$ 20	
Commissions							800	820
Profit on consignment sales			$158					$1,600
Inventory valuation				5	$790			

tures which are generally regarded as noninventoriable costs. In respect to transshipments of consigned goods, the ultimate valuation of the inventory should reflect costs of transporation which are not in excess of those normally incurred by direct shipment from the consignor; any additional transportation cost should be regarded as a current expense. Similarly, in the event that a portion of unsold consigned goods are returned to the consignor, they should be restored to the inventory account at their original acquisition cost, and the incremental expenditures, to the extent they are not recoverable from the consignee, should be reported as current expenses. Expenditures for repairs and other charges in respect to the care and safety of consigned goods are usually accounted for as period costs, and accordingly charged to expense in the period in which they are incurred.

Deferred Consignment Costs

It has been previously noted that there are several alternative methods of recording and disclosing the inventoriable value increments incurred in the consignment expenditures. The entries in Illustration 19–9 harmonize with the concepts of asset valuation and the matching of revenues and expenses under both assumptions; however, many variations are possible.

Even where the Consignment Out account is used to accumulate the inventoriable costs associated with the consignment arrangement, the consignor may elect to separately identify the additional value increments. These amounts are easily calculated by using the transaction details such as are depicted in Illustration 19–10. In the event that a Deferred Consignment Costs account is to be used in conjunction with a Consignment Out account, Entry No. 5 in Illustration 19–9 would be modified as follows:

Deferred consignment costs (5 units @ $8)	40	
Consignment out—Matthewson Retailers	1,560	
Consignment profit		1,600

The total capitalized value of consignment costs, as before, would consist of—

Inventory of Goods on Consignment:	
Consignment out—Matthewson	
Retailers (5 units @ $150)	$750
Deferred consignment costs	40
Total	$790

The balance in the Deferred Consignment Costs account would remain $40 until the end of the succeeding accounting period, at which time it would require additional adjustment. Alternatively, the Deferred Consignment Costs account may be debited for each relevant cost when incurred, as in the procedure where "regular" accounts are used for both consignment and nonconsignment transactions. This procedure seems unnecessary, however, in view of the existence of the specially created Consignment Out account and the procedure outlined above for periodically identifying, by adjustment, the deferred consignment costs.

In those circumstances where separate accounts are not maintained, the entries in Illustration 19–9 may also be modified. In particular, the packing and freight expenditures may be charged directly to their standard expense classifications. If this practice were followed, the individual expense accounts would have to be adjusted at the end of the period to give effect to the $40 cost deferment in respect to unsold goods. In the opinion of the authors, the previously illustrated technique is preferable. If practical considerations compel the use of normal expense classifications, then materiality—a practical doctrine—may also indicate that it is unnecessary to defer the additional inventoriable expenditures.

Modification of Entries for Periodic Inventory Method

The entries in Illustration 19–9 assume that a perpetual inventory is maintained by the consignor. In the event that the periodic inventory method is followed, only minor modifications of the entries in this illustration are required.

When consignment transactions are recorded separately, Entry No. 1 takes the following form:

```
Consignment out—Matthewson Retailers ................. 2,250
    Consigned shipments ............................        2,250
```

The Consigned Shipments account is essentially a suspense credit to Purchases, and is created primarily to effect dollar control (necessarily at standard or estimated cost) in respect to current shipments. No other changes are required except to close this account to Purchases at the end of the accounting period.

If the "regular" accounts are used to record consignment transactions, the changes are equally minor. Only a memorandum record is usually made of the shipment (Entry No. 1). Subsequent transactions are recorded as before. In the closing sequence, a Merchandise on Consignment account is created with a balance of $750, and the Deferred Consignment Costs account is adjusted to yield a residual balance of $40.

Financial Statement Presentation

In some cases the consignee may remit more or less than the amount due the consignor as reported on the account sales. If more is remitted than is due (or an advance is made), the excess remittance should be credited to a separate account, Payable to Consignee, rather than to the Consignment Out account. The balance in this account is properly reported as a current liability in the balance sheet of the consignor, as in most instances, it will be abated, or eliminated by offset, as amounts due are reported on subsequent account sales. If an advance is more permanent in nature, it should, of course, be reported as a long-term liability.

Where the consignee remits less than the reported amount due, the deficiency should be debited by the consignor to an asset account, Due from Consignee, and reported as a receivable under the current asset caption in the balance sheet. For example, if Matthewson Retailers (Illustration 19–9) remitted only $2,165 with the account sales, the consignor's entry to record the receipt would be as follows:

Cash	2,165	
Due from consignee—Matthewson Retailers	1,000	
Consignment out—Matthewson Retailers	835	
Consignment out—Matthewson Retailers		4,000

If, however, the $1,000 differential consists of trade accounts receivable transferred to the consignor by the consignee, the above entry should be modified to reflect this circumstance.

The balance in the Consignment Out account, after adjustment at the end of the accounting period, should be reported on the balance sheet of the consignor as follows:

Current Assets:
  Inventories:
    Merchandise on hand $12,500
    Consigned merchandise 790 $13,290

In the event a Deferred Consignment Costs account is used, it should be classified as a current asset—either in the inventory or prepaid expense category.

With respect to the income statement, the operating data for consignment transactions are often merged with other reported revenues and costs. However, a more prominent form of disclosure, and one that is especially appropriate if consignment sales are significant in respect to total revenues, is given in Illustration 19–11.

Illustration 19–11

THE BISHOP WHOLESALE CORPORATION
Income Statement
For Year Ended December 31, 1977

	Con-signment Sales	Regular Sales	Total
Sales	$40,000	$100,000	$140,000
Cost of sales	24,000	58,000	82,000
Gross profit on sales	$16,000	$ 42,000	$ 58,000
Operating expenses:			
Selling expenses	$ 8,000	$ 14,000	$ 22,000
Administrative expenses		25,000	25,000
Total operating expenses	$ 8,000	$ 39,000	$ 47,000
Net Income	$ 8,000	$ 3,000	$ 11,000

A word of caution should be sounded in respect to the above type of presentation. The reported profit on consignment sales may be overstated, perhaps significantly, in view of the fact that the administrative costs are totally charged against the regular sales. Even if management desires to analyze the consignment transactions on a direct cost, or contribution margin basis, this reporting implicitly assumes that *all* administrative costs are rigidly fixed or otherwise unrelated to the consignment activity. Preferably, some effort should be made to allocate these costs, both on direct and absorption cost bases, in order to generate useful indexes for each revenue-producing activity.

QUESTIONS

1. Distinguish between installment sales and regular credit sales. Do the differences between these types of credit arrangement generate different bases for the recognition of gross profit?

2. Why do credit losses on installment sales transactions tend to be larger than those from other forms of credit sales?

3. What underlying process is involved in the "installment sales method" of revenue recognition?

4. What special problem do bad debt losses present with respect to installment sales? How is this difficulty resolved under the "installment sales method"?

5. To what extent are variations in the form and content of income statements introduced by the presence of installment sales which are material in amount?

6. List several different balance sheet classifications for "Deferred Gross Profit on Installment Sales." Which classification is most widely accepted?

7. What steps must a vendor take to record a default and repossession of goods which have been sold on an installment basis?

8. What elections are available to the accountant in recording the valuation of repossessed merchandise? Which method is most frequently used?

9. Outline the procedural sequence for recording the repossession of merchandise *in the period of sale*. In periods *subsequent to* the period of sale.

10. How is the Loss (Gain) on Repossessions reported in the income statement?

11. What is a consignment? Who are the parties to this business transaction?

12. Distinguish between a sale and a consignment.

13. How should one account for inventory of consigned merchandise?

14. Do goods "sold" on consignment satisfy the revenue realization criterion? Explain.

15. In the absence of limiting arrangements, which party in the consignment is generally responsible for costs incurred which relate directly to the goods from date of shipment to the date of sale?

16. Under what circumstances would a consignment arrangement produce advantage to both the consignee and the consignor?

17. What is an "account sales" and what information does it normally include?

18. What data are recorded in the "Consignment In" account on the consignee's books? How is the balance (debit or credit) of this account presented on the balance sheet of the consignee?

19. How is the "Consignment Out" account balance reported on the balance sheet of the consignor?

20. What accounts arise as a result of the consignee remitting more or less than the amount due the consignor as reported on the account sales? How are these accounts classified on the balance sheet of the consignor?

EXERCISES

Exercise 19–1

CMPW Corporation, which began business on January 1, 1977, appropriately uses the installment-sales method of reporting for accounting purposes. The following data were obtained for the years 1977 and 1978:

	1977	1978
Installment sales	$350,000	$420,000
Cost of installment sales	280,000	315,000
General and administrative expenses	35,000	42,000
Cash collections on installment sales of:		
1977	150,000	125,000
1978	—	200,000

Select the *best* answer for each of the following questions.

1. What should the balance in the deferred-gross-profit control account be on December 31, 1978?
    a. $53,000
    b. $70,000
    c. $95,000
    d. $105,000

2. A 1977 sale resulted in a default early in 1979. At the date of default, the balance of the installment receivable was $6,000, and the repossessed merchandise had a fair value of $4,100. Assuming the repossessed merchandise is to be recorded at fair value, the gain or loss on repossession should be:

    a. $0
    b. A $700 loss
    c. A $4,100 gain
    d. A $4,800 loss

    (AICPA adapted)

Exercise 19–2

The Nielsen Realty Company sold a plot of real estate for $80,000 designated as the Hudson Addition. The property originally cost $25,000, and $35,000 was subsequently spent for grading, drainage, and other similar costs. Expenses incident to sale were $6,000. The terms of the sale were: 20 percent down payment and a note specifying five annual payments (at year-end) including a constant reduction in principal *and* 6 percent interest per annum on the unpaid balance at the start of each year.

Required:

a. Prepare a schedule of payments.
b. Prepare journal entries through the second installment assuming the installment sales method is used.
c. Indicate how the amounts relating to the second period should be reported on the income statement and balance sheet.

Exercise 19–3

The following is the preclosing trial balance of the Paulson Company on December 31, 1977:

Cash	$100,000	
Installment accounts receivable—1976	40,000	
Installment accounts receivable—1977	60,000	
Installment sales		$100,000
Cost of installment sales	70,000	
Deferred gross profit—1976		30,000
Capital stock		80,000
Retained earnings		60,000
	$270,000	$270,000

Required:

a. Prepare journal entries on December 31, 1977, to record the gross profit realized in 1977 and complete the closing of the accounts. The rate of gross profit on sales in 1976 was 25 percent.
b. On February 10, 1978, a customer defaults on his payments and the merchandise is repossessed. Prepare the journal entry for the repossession given the following information:

Original sale	$500
Date of sale	July, 1976
Collections to date	$300
Estimated market value of	
repossessed goods	$100

Exercise 19–4

On October 1, 1977, the Wiedner Company sold a television set costing $400 to Purmer for $600. Purmer made a down payment of $150 and agreed to pay $25 the first of each month for 18 months thereafter.

The first two installments due on November 1 and December 1, 1977, were paid. In 1978, five payments were made by Purmer, who then defaulted on the balance of his payments. The set was repossessed on November 1, 1978. The company closes its books on December 31.

Required:

a. Give three different amounts that might be shown as realized gross profit for 1977 and indicate the circumstances under which each of these amounts would be acceptable.

b. Assuming that the repossessed television set has a wholesale value of $50 and a retail value of $75, prepare a journal entry to record the repossession under the "installment method" of accounting. Explain fully the reasoning applicable to your entry.

(AICPA adapted)

Exercise 19–5

On April 1, 1977, the DFP Department Store sold an item of furniture which cost $160, for $280. A down payment of $30 was made with the provision that additional payments of $25 be made monthly thereafter. Interest was to be charged the customer at a monthly rate of 1 percent on the unpaid contract balance; the monthly remittance was to apply first to the accrued interest and the balance to the principal.

After completing four monthly payments, the customer defaulted and the furniture was reclaimed; the replacement value of the furniture (used) was estimated to be $75.

The DFP Department Store maintains a perpetual inventory with respect to major appliances and furniture.

Required:

Make all journal entries for the installment sale, from April 1, 1977, through September 1, 1977.

Exercise 19–6

Yurkovich Sales Corporation sells goods and accounts for such sales on the installment basis. At the end of each year it takes up gross profit on the basis of the year(s) of collection rather than the year of sale; accordingly, each collection consists of cost and gross profit elements.

The balances of the control accounts for Installment Accounts Receivable at the beginning and end of 1977 were:

	January 1, 1977	December 31, 1977
Installment accounts receivable—1975	$ 24,020	–0–
Installment accounts receivable—1976	344,460	$ 67,440
Installment accounts receivable—1977		410,090

As collections are made, the company debits Cash and credits Installment Accounts Receivable. During 1977, upon default in payment by customers, the company repossessed merchandise having an estimated wholesale value of $1,400. The sales had been made in 1976 for $5,400, and $3,200 had been collected prior to default. The company recorded the default and repossession by a debit to Inventory of Repossessed Merchandise and a credit to Installment Accounts Receivable—1976 for the uncollected receivable balance.

The company's sales and cost of sales for the three years involved are summarized below:

	1975	1976	1977
Net sales	$380,000	$432,000	$602,000
Cost of sales	247,000	285,120	379,260

Required:

a. Prepare journal entries to record at December 31, 1977, the recognition of profits and any other adjustments arising from the above data. Give complete explanations in support of your entries.

b. Give one acceptable alternate method of handling the repossession and discuss the relative merits of it as compared to the method you used in *a*.

(AICPA adapted)

Exercise 19–7

Prepare all journal entries relating to the following transactions for the Cazel Office Supply Company, consignor:

a. A consignment of 100 secretarial desks is sent to the Jones Company (a *del credere* agent). The cost of each desk is $62, and each is marked to sell for $100.

b. $150 freight on the above shipment is paid by the consignor.

c. The following account sales is received by the Cazel Office Supply Company at the end of the fiscal year:

Desks received	100		
Unsold desks	25		
Desks sold	75 @ $100		$7,500
Less:			
Commission		$750	
Advertising		100	850
Amount remitted			$6,650

Exercise 19–8

In March, 1977, the Vashik Company shipped 600 cartons of Polish sausage on consignment for sale to Overmeyer and Associates, total cost $4,200. Packing and shipping costs, paid by Vashik Company, amounted to $265. The shipment was recorded as follows:

Overmeyer and Associates	6,000	
Transportation out	265	
Merchandise		4,200
Cash		265
Profit on consigned shipment		1,800

On December 28, 1977, the following account sales prepared by Overmeyer and Associates was received by the Vashik Company:

Sales (400 units @ $10)		$4,000
Costs and expenses:		
Insurance to December 31, 1977	$220	
Drayage	50	
Commission	400	670
Check enclosed		$3,330

The account sales was recorded by the Vashik Company with a debit to Cash and a credit to Overmeyer and Associates for $3,330.

On February 28, 1978, a second account sales was received by the consignor, although it has not yet been recorded, detailing the following:

Sales (150 units @ $10)		$1,500
Costs and expenses:		
Insurance to February 28, 1978	$ 40	
Commission	150	190
Balance due		$1,310

The Vashik Company closes its books December 31.

Required:

Make any appropriate entries to adjust and correct the books of the Vashik Company through February 28, 1978, reflecting consignment profit realized to this date.

Exercise 19–9

The four journal entries which are shown below were used by a consignee to record the transactions arising out of a consignment of merchandise to him.

March 27, 1977

Consignment in	24	
Cash		24

April 25, 1977

Cash	800	
Consignment in		800

April 25, 1977

Consignment in	200	
Commission earned		200

May 5, 1977

Consignment in	576	
Cash		576

Required:

a. Describe fully the transactions which were recorded by the journal entries.
b. Prepare journal entries to record the consignment transactions *on the books of the consignor.* Assume that the consigned goods cost $400 and that the consignor keeps perpetual inventory records.
c. State how the facts should be presented on balance sheets of both the con-

signee and consignor as of April 30, 1977. Explain your reasons for such presentation.

(AICPA adapted)

Exercise 19–10

Sommerfeld, Inc., shipped 200 Super-X appliances to Jones Bros., retail distributors, for sale on a 15 percent *del credere* commission basis. The cost of each appliance was $83, with an additional payment of $2 per unit to crate and ship to the consignee. It was agreed that Sommerfeld would draw a sight draft on the consignee for 60 percent of the cost of the appliances, the advance to be recovered periodically by monthly deductions (based on units sold) from the remittances which accompany the account sales. All expenses of the consignee are deducted monthly as incurred.

The following account sales was rendered by the consignee at the conclusion of the first month's operations:

Sales of Super-X appliances (60 units @ $100)		$6,000
Deductions for:		
Expenses paid by the consignee	$310	
Advance	?	
Commission	900	?
Remittance to consignor		$?

Required:

a. Give all entries on the books of the consignee.
b. Give entries for the month's transactions in the consignor's books assuming the use of a perpetual inventory and with the further assumption that consignment transactions are recorded separately.

PROBLEMS

Problem 1

A specialty appliance distributor selling on the installment basis was organized as a retail sales outlet on January 1, 1974. Reorganization was begun, however, after three and one-half years operations, on July 1, 1977. Operating data for this interim period was summarized following:

Year	Sales	Cost of Sales	Expenses*
1974	$ 60,000	$36,000	$15,000
1975	100,000	61,000	16,000
1976	120,000	75,600	17,500
1977	70,000	32,900	14,000

* Excludes gains or losses from defaulted accounts.

Year of Sale	Collections				Accounts Defaulted		
	1974	1975	1976	1977	1975	1976	1977
1974	$40,000	$19,000			$1,000		
1975		80,000	$ 18,000			$2,000	
1976			100,000	$15,000			$5,000
1977				68,000			2,000

Repossessed merchandise is assumed to have no value.

Required:

Prepare an analysis of net income for each year (or fractional year) contrasting the differences when—

a. Net income is computed using the installment method of accounting for sales revenue.

b. Net income is computed on the assumption that revenue is recognized at the time of sale, and bad debts are charged to expense as they occur.

Problem 2

The Little Bit Sales Company balance sheet on January 1, 1977, reported the following:

Cash	$ 20,000	Accounts payable	$ 30,000
Merchandise inventory	120,000	Deferred gross profit on installment sales—1975	12,000
Accounts receivable (regular)	11,000	Deferred gross profit on installment sales—1976	29,400
Allowance for doubtful accounts	[1,000]	Capital stock	203,000
Installment accounts receivable—1975	30,000	Retained earnings	75,600
Installment accounts receivable—1976	70,000		
Various assets	100,000		
	$350,000		$350,000

Transactions during 1977 were (summarized):

Sales:
Regular (on credit)	$300,000
Installment	100,000
Purchases of merchandise (cash)	238,000
Ending inventory (periodic basis)	130,000
Cost of installment sales	57,000
Selling expenses	105,000
Allowance for doubtful accounts	¼ of 1% of regular sales

Collections on installment receivables:
1975 accounts	$ 20,000
1976 accounts	40,000
1977 accounts	55,000
Regular accounts	280,000

Required:

a. Compute gross profit rates for 1975, 1976, and 1977.
b. Prepare journal entries for 1977, including adjusting and closing entries at December 31.
c. Prepare an income statement for 1977.
d. Prepare a balance sheet as of December 31, 1977.

Problem 3

The Thomas Appliance Store started business on January 1, 1977. Separate accounts were set up for installment and cash sales, but no perpetual inventory record was maintained. On the installment sales, a down payment of one third was required, with the balance payable in 18 equal monthly installments. A Deferred Gross Profit account was created at each year-end in respect to the current year's installment sales. When contracts were defaulted, the unpaid balances were charged to Bad Debt Expense, and sales of repossessed merchandise were credited to this account. The expense account was adjusted at the year-end to reflect the actual loss.

A summary of the transactions of the Thomas Appliance Store for 1977 and 1978 follows:

	1977	1978
Sales:		
New merchandise for cash	$ 21,348	$ 29,180
New merchandise on installment (including one-third cash down payment)	188,652	265,320
Sales of repossessed merchandise	600	700
Purchases	154,000	173,585
Physical inventories at December 31:		
New merchandise at cost	36,400	48,010
Repossessions at realizable (market) value	150	160
Unpaid balances of installment contracts defaulted:		
1977 sales	2,865	3,725
1978 sales		3,010
Cash collections on installment contracts, exclusive of down payments:		
1977 sales	42,943	61,385
1978 sales		55,960

Required:

a. Compute the gross profit rates for the years 1977 and 1978.
b. In T-account form, reproduce the ledger accounts for installment accounts receivable.
c. Calculate the net loss on defaulted accounts for the year 1977; it is assumed that realizable value is an appropriate value basis for repossessed merchandise.
d. Prepare a schedule showing the realized gross profit for the year 1978 that would be reported on the income statement.

(AICPA adapted)

Problem 4

The LVP Appliance Company started business on January 1, 1977. Separate accounts were established for installment and cash sales, but no perpetual inventory record was maintained.

On installment sales, the price was 106 percent of the cash sale price. A standard installment contract was used whereby a down payment of one fourth of the installment price was required, with the balance payable in 15 equal monthly installments. (The interest charge per month is 1 percent of the unpaid cash sale price equivalent at each installment.)

Installments receivable and installment sales were recorded at the contract price. When contracts were defaulted, the unpaid balances were charged to bad debt expense. Sales of default merchandise were credited to bad debt expense.

```
Sales:
    Cash sales ............................ $126,000
    Installment sales ......................  265,000
    Repossessed sales ......................      230
Inventory, January 1, 1977:
    Merchandise inventory ..................   58,060
Purchases, 1977:
    New merchandise ........................  209,300
Inventories, physical, December 31, 1977:
    New merchandise ........................   33,300
    Repossessed inventory ..................      180
Cash collections on installment contracts, 1977:
    Down payments ..........................   66,250
    Subsequent installments ................   79,341
        (Average six monthly installments on all con-
        tracts except on defaulted contracts)
```

Five contracts totaling $1,060 were defaulted in each case after three monthly installments were paid.

Interest should be recognized in the period earned.

Required:

a. A computation of the gross profit rate for 1977.
b. A schedule showing, by payment, for the first seven months: the cash sale price equivalent, the contract balance, the amount of interest earned, and the cash collected on a $1,060 installment sale contract.
c. A computation of the net gain or loss on defaulted contracts during 1977.
d. A computation of the realized gross profit for 1977.

(AICPA adapted)

Problem 5

The Ashton Corporation ships goods on consignment to Hubbard Distributors, a consignee. The consignment contract provides that the consignor shall bear all expenses of the consignee which relate to the consignments; an agency commission of 30 percent of all consignment sales shall be paid to the consignee. The consignee is required to render an account sales at each year-end and to remit all cash due plus a $5,000 advance because of the existence of a considerable quantity of unsold merchandise. The accounts of the Ashton Corporation showed the following balances at December 31, 1977 (end of the accounting period):

Cash	$ 60,000	
Accounts receivable (net)	180,000	
Plant and equipment (net)	250,000	
Accounts payable		$ 80,000
Advance from consignee		5,000
Merchandise inventory (regular)	140,000	
Consignment out (valuation of goods on consignment at December 31, 1977, exclusive of deferred shipping costs)	30,000	
Deferred shipping costs—goods on consignment (paid by consignor)	2,000	
Commission on consignment sales	30,000	
Deferred shipping costs—goods on consignment (paid by consignee)	1,000	
Advertising costs (paid by consignee)	13,000	
Sales, regular		800,000
Sales, consignment		100,000
Cost of goods sold, regular	320,000	
Cost of goods sold, consignment	40,000	
Selling expenses	190,000	
Administrative expenses	150,000	
Capital stock		400,000
Retained earnings (January 1, 1977)		21,000
	$1,406,000	$1,406,000

Assume an income tax rate of 52 percent and that 20 percent of the tax liability is paid at the year's end; income taxes are not reflected by the above balances.

Required:

Based upon the above data prepare an income statement for 1977, reporting consignment transactions separately, and a balance sheet as of December 31, 1977.

Problem 6

Transactions are executed between a consignor and consignee under provisions of a contract stipulating that (a) the consignor will reimburse the consignee for all costs related to piano consignments except advertising costs, which are to be borne 60 percent by the consignor and 40 percent by the consignee; (b) the consignee's commission will be 20 percent of sales; and (c) receivables arising from consignment sales are to be carried on the books of the consignor.

Inventoriable expenditures incurred in addition to merchandise cost at shipment date are carried in a deferred cost account by the consignor. Both parties close their books at calendar year-end.

The transactions during the first accounting period were:

a. The consignor shipped 10 pianos to the consignee, cost $300 each, to sell at $700.

b. The consignor paid $150 for crating, freight, and insurance on the 10 pianos shipped on consignment.

c. The consignee paid $50 drayage upon receiving the above shipment of 10 pianos.

d. The consignee sold three pianos for $500 cash down payment (per piano), the balance to be paid at the end of 12 months.

e. The consignee paid $300 advertising costs relating to the pianos.

f. The consignee sold five pianos for cash at the agreed price.

g. The consignee submitted an account sales and remitted the cash due on the eight pianos sold. No collections had been made on the receivables.

h. The books were adjusted and closed.

Required:

a. Prepare all entries for the period (including any memorandum entries) on the books of both the consignor and the consignee as indicated by the above information. Assume that both parties utilize perpetual inventory procedures and that consignment transactions are recorded separately.

b. Prepare the account sales.

Problem 7

The Caps Manufacturing Company and Marks Retailers entered into a consignment agreement whereby the latter would sell sets of Columbian silverware on a consignment basis. The terms of the agreement provided that Marks would receive a commission of 25 percent on sales price and bill Caps for all expenses except 10 percent of advertising expenditures. Both firms close their books on December 31. Marks agreed to render an account sales at each year's end and remit all cash then due. Caps utilizes perpetual inventory procedures; both firms keep consignments separate from other merchandise transactions. Transactions were:

a. November 15, 1977. Caps shipped goods on assignment, 100 sets to sell at $30, cost $12 per set. Packing and freight costs, $200, were paid by the consignor.

b. December 31, 1977. An account sales was rendered by the consignee, reporting no sales but expenditures of $100 for local freight and $50 for advertising.

c. January–April, 1978. Consignee sold 90 sets at the agreed sales price.

d. April 30, 1978. Caps shipped goods on consignment, 200 sets to sell at $31, cost $13 per set. Packaging and freight costs, $400, were paid by the consignor.

e. April 30, 1978. Consignee paid $200 for local freight on the above shipment.

f. May, 1978. Consignee paid $300 for advertising, all of which related to consigned merchandise.

g. May–December, 1978. Consignee sold 110 sets at the agreed sales prices, which include the remainder of the sets from the first shipment.

h. December 31, 1978. An account sales was prepared; the required remittance was made.

Required:

a. Prepare an account sales and give all entries on the books of the consignee for 1977 and 1978.

b. Give all entries on the books of the consignor for 1977 and 1978.

Problem 8

The Franklin Manufacturing Company closes its books annually on December 31. In making an investigation of the accounts of the company in respect to 1977, you discover the following facts:

a. During November and December, the company shipped stoves to two dealers, A and B, on a consignment basis. The consignment agreements provided that the stoves were to be sold by the consignee at a list price of $180 each. The consignee was to be allowed a 25 percent commission on each sale and was to be reimbursed for all expenses paid in connection with the stoves. Sales on account are at the risk of the consignee.

b. At the time of shipment, the consignor debited Trade Accounts Receivable and credited Sales $120 for each stove, this being the usual sale price received by the consignor on the basis of which a gross profit of 20 percent on cost is realized.

c. All cash received from these two consignees was credited to Trade Accounts Receivable. No other entries have been made in respect to these accounts.

d. Information as to all of the transactions with the consignees is given following:

    (1)   Stoves shipped out: to A—100, to B—40.

    (2)   Stoves unsold by consignees as of 12/31/77: A—35, B—25.

    (3)   Crating and shipping cost to consignor—$84.

    (4)   Freight paid by consignees: A—$130; B—$100.

    (5)   Cash advanced by A at date of receipt of the first 100 stoves—$4,000. Cash subsequently remitted by A—$5,395.

    (6)   Cash remitted by B—$575.

Required:

a. Show, by entries in T-accounts, transactions completed and adjustments required by the Franklin Company.

b. Prepare a trial balance of the accounts affected by these transactions and adjustments.

(AICPA adapted)

appendix

Compound
Interest Tables

Table A
(Amount of 1: $(1 + i)^n$)

	6%	7%	8%	9%	10%	11%	12%	13%	14%	15%
1	1.060000	1.070000	1.080000	1.090000	1.100000	1.110000	1.120000	1.130000	1.140000	1.150000
2	1.123600	1.144900	1.166400	1.188100	1.210000	1.232100	1.254400	1.276900	1.299600	1.322500
3	1.191016	1.225043	1.259712	1.295029	1.331000	1.367631	1.404928	1.442897	1.481544	1.520875
4	1.262477	1.310796	1.360489	1.411582	1.464100	1.518070	1.573519	1.630474	1.688960	1.749006
5	1.338226	1.402552	1.469328	1.538624	1.610510	1.685058	1.762342	1.842435	1.925415	2.011357
6	1.418519	1.500730	1.586874	1.677100	1.771561	1.870415	1.973823	2.081952	2.194973	2.313061
7	1.503630	1.605781	1.713824	1.828039	1.948717	2.076160	2.210681	2.352605	2.502269	2.660020
8	1.593848	1.718186	1.850930	1.992563	2.143589	2.304538	2.475963	2.658444	2.852586	3.059023
9	1.689479	1.838459	1.999005	2.171893	2.357948	2.558037	2.773079	3.004042	3.251949	3.517876
10	1.790848	1.967151	2.158925	2.367364	2.593742	2.839421	3.105848	3.394567	3.707221	4.045558
11	1.898299	2.104852	2.331639	2.580426	2.853117	3.151757	3.478550	3.835861	4.226232	4.652391
12	2.012196	2.252192	2.518170	2.812665	3.138428	3.498451	3.895976	4.334523	4.817905	5.350250
13	2.132928	2.409845	2.719624	3.065805	3.452271	3.883280	4.363493	4.898011	5.492411	6.152788
14	2.260904	2.578534	2.937194	3.341727	3.797498	4.310441	4.887112	5.534753	6.261349	7.075706
15	2.396558	2.759032	3.172169	3.642482	4.177248	4.784589	5.473566	6.254270	7.137938	8.137062
16	2.540352	2.952164	3.425943	3.970306	4.594973	5.310894	6.130394	7.067326	8.137249	9.357621
17	2.692773	3.158815	3.700018	4.327633	5.054470	5.895093	6.866041	7.986078	9.276464	10.761264
18	2.854339	3.379932	3.996019	4.717120	5.559917	6.543553	7.689966	9.024268	10.575169	12.375454
19	3.025600	3.616528	4.315701	5.141661	6.115909	7.263344	8.612762	10.197423	12.055693	14.231772
20	3.207135	3.869684	4.660957	5.604411	6.727500	8.062312	9.646293	11.523088	13.743490	16.366537
21	3.399564	4.140562	5.033834	6.108808	7.400250	8.949166	10.803848	13.021089	15.667578	18.821518
22	3.603537	4.430402	5.436540	6.658600	8.140275	9.933574	12.100310	14.713831	17.861039	21.644746
23	3.819750	4.740530	5.871464	7.257874	8.954302	11.026267	13.552347	16.626629	20.361585	24.891458
24	4.048935	5.072367	6.341181	7.911083	9.849733	12.239157	15.178629	18.788091	23.212207	28.625176
25	4.291871	5.427433	6.848475	8.623081	10.834706	13.585464	17.000064	21.230542	26.461916	32.918953

Table B

(Present Value of 1):$(1 + i)^{-n}$

	6%	7%	8%	9%	10%	11%	12%	13%	14%	15%
1	0.943396	0.934579	0.925926	0.917431	0.909091	0.900901	0.892857	0.884956	0.877193	0.869565
2	0.889996	0.873439	0.857339	0.841680	0.826446	0.811622	0.797194	0.783147	0.769468	0.756144
3	0.839619	0.816298	0.793832	0.772183	0.751315	0.731191	0.711780	0.693050	0.674972	0.657516
4	0.792094	0.762895	0.735030	0.708425	0.683013	0.658731	0.635518	0.613319	0.592080	0.571753
5	0.747258	0.712986	0.680583	0.649931	0.620921	0.593451	0.567427	0.542760	0.519369	0.497177
6	0.704961	0.666342	0.630170	0.596267	0.564474	0.534641	0.506631	0.480319	0.455587	0.432328
7	0.665057	0.622750	0.583490	0.547034	0.513158	0.481658	0.452349	0.425061	0.399637	0.375937
8	0.627412	0.582009	0.540269	0.501866	0.466507	0.433926	0.403883	0.376160	0.350559	0.326902
9	0.591898	0.543934	0.500249	0.460428	0.424098	0.390925	0.360610	0.332885	0.307508	0.284262
10	0.558395	0.508349	0.463193	0.422411	0.385543	0.352184	0.321973	0.294588	0.269744	0.247185
11	0.526788	0.475093	0.428883	0.387533	0.350494	0.317283	0.287476	0.260698	0.236617	0.214943
12	0.496969	0.444012	0.397114	0.355535	0.318631	0.285841	0.256675	0.230706	0.207559	0.186907
13	0.468839	0.414964	0.367698	0.326179	0.289664	0.257514	0.229174	0.204165	0.182069	0.162528
14	0.442301	0.387817	0.340461	0.299246	0.263331	0.231995	0.204620	0.180677	0.159710	0.141329
15	0.417265	0.362446	0.315242	0.274538	0.239392	0.209004	0.182696	0.159891	0.140096	0.122894
16	0.393646	0.338735	0.291890	0.251870	0.217629	0.188292	0.163122	0.141496	0.122892	0.106865
17	0.371364	0.316574	0.270269	0.231073	0.197845	0.169633	0.145644	0.125218	0.107800	0.092926
18	0.350344	0.295864	0.250249	0.211994	0.179859	0.152822	0.130040	0.110812	0.094561	0.080805
19	0.330513	0.276508	0.231712	0.194490	0.163508	0.137678	0.116107	0.098064	0.082948	0.070265
20	0.311805	0.258419	0.214548	0.178431	0.148644	0.124034	0.103667	0.086782	0.072762	0.061100
21	0.294155	0.241513	0.198656	0.163698	0.135131	0.111742	0.092560	0.076798	0.063826	0.053131
22	0.277505	0.225713	0.183941	0.150182	0.122846	0.100669	0.082643	0.067963	0.055988	0.046201
23	0.261797	0.210947	0.170315	0.137781	0.111678	0.090693	0.073788	0.060144	0.049112	0.040174
24	0.246979	0.197147	0.157699	0.126405	0.101526	0.081705	0.065882	0.053225	0.043081	0.034934
25	0.232999	0.184249	0.146018	0.115968	0.092296	0.073608	0.058823	0.047102	0.037790	0.030378

Table C
(Amount of Annuity of 1): $[(1 + i)^n - 1]/i$

	6%	7%	8%	9%	10%	11%	12%	13%	14%	15%
1	1.000000	1.000000	1.000000	1.000000	1.000000	1.000000	1.000000	1.000000	1.000000	1.000000
2	2.060000	2.070000	2.080000	2.090000	2.100000	2.110000	2.120000	2.130000	2.140000	2.150000
3	3.183600	3.214900	3.246400	3.278100	3.310000	3.342100	3.374400	3.406900	3.439600	3.472500
4	4.374616	4.439943	4.506112	4.573129	4.641000	4.709731	4.779328	4.849797	4.921144	4.993375
5	5.637093	5.750739	5.866601	5.984711	6.105100	6.227801	6.352847	6.480271	6.610104	6.742381
6	6.975319	7.153291	7.335929	7.523335	7.715610	7.912860	8.115189	8.322706	8.535519	8.753738
7	8.393838	8.654021	8.922803	9.200435	9.487171	9.783274	10.089012	10.404658	10.730491	11.066799
8	9.897468	10.259803	10.636628	11.028474	11.435888	11.859434	12.299693	12.757263	13.232760	13.726819
9	11.491316	11.977989	12.487558	13.021036	13.579477	14.163972	14.775656	15.415707	16.085347	16.785842
10	13.180795	13.816448	14.486562	15.192930	15.937425	16.722009	17.548735	18.419749	19.337295	20.303718
11	14.971643	15.783599	16.645487	17.560293	18.531167	19.561430	20.654583	21.814317	23.044516	24.349276
12	16.869941	17.888451	18.977126	20.140720	21.384284	22.713187	24.133133	25.650178	27.270749	29.001667
13	18.882138	20.140643	21.495297	22.953385	24.522712	26.211638	28.029109	29.984701	32.088654	34.351917
14	21.015066	22.550488	24.214920	26.019189	27.974983	30.094918	32.392602	34.882712	37.581065	40.504705
15	23.275970	25.129022	27.152114	29.360916	31.772482	34.405359	37.279715	40.417464	43.842414	47.580411
16	25.672528	27.888054	30.324283	33.003399	35.949730	39.189948	42.753280	46.671735	50.980352	55.717472
17	28.212880	30.840217	33.750226	36.973705	40.544703	44.500843	48.883674	53.739060	59.117601	65.075093
18	30.905653	33.999033	37.450244	41.301338	45.599173	50.395936	55.749715	61.725138	68.394066	75.836357
19	33.759992	37.378965	41.446263	46.018458	51.159090	56.939488	63.439681	70.749406	78.969235	88.211811
20	36.785591	40.995492	45.761964	51.160120	57.274999	64.202832	72.052442	80.946829	91.024928	102.443583
21	39.992727	44.865177	50.422921	56.764530	64.002499	72.265144	81.698736	92.469917	104.768418	118.810120
22	43.392290	49.005739	55.456755	62.873338	71.402749	81.214309	92.502584	105.491006	120.435996	137.631638
23	46.995828	53.436141	60.893296	69.531939	79.543024	91.147884	104.602894	120.204837	138.297035	159.276384
24	50.815577	58.176671	66.764759	76.789813	88.497327	102.174151	118.155241	136.831465	158.658620	184.167841
25	54.864512	63.249038	73.105940	84.700896	98.347059	114.413307	133.333870	155.619556	181.870827	212.793017

Table D
(Present Value of Annuity of 1): $[1 - (1 + i)^{-n}]/i$

	6%	7%	8%	9%	10%	11%	12%	13%	14%	15%
1	0.943396	0.934579	0.925926	0.917431	0.909091	0.900901	0.892857	0.684956	0.877193	0.869565
2	1.833393	1.808018	1.783265	1.759111	1.735537	1.712523	1.690051	1.668102	1.646661	1.625709
3	2.673012	2.624316	2.577097	2.531295	2.486852	2.443715	2.401831	2.561153	2.321632	2.283225
4	3.465106	3.387211	3.312127	3.239720	3.169865	3.102446	3.037349	2.974471	2.913712	2.854978
5	4.212364	4.100197	3.992710	3.889651	3.790787	3.695897	3.604776	3.517231	3.433081	3.352155
6	4.917324	4.766540	4.622880	4.485919	4.355261	4.230538	4.111407	3.997550	3.888668	3.784483
7	5.582381	5.389289	5.206370	5.032953	4.868419	4.712196	4.563757	4.422610	4.288305	4.160420
8	6.209794	5.971299	5.746639	5.534819	5.334926	5.146123	4.967640	4.798770	4.638864	4.487322
9	6.801692	6.515232	6.246888	5.995247	5.759024	5.537048	5.328250	5.131655	4.946372	4.771584
10	7.360087	7.023582	6.710081	6.417658	6.144567	5.889232	5.650223	5.426243	5.216116	5.018769
11	7.886875	7.498674	7.138964	6.805191	6.495061	6.206515	5.937699	5.686941	5.452733	5.233712
12	8.383844	7.942686	7.536078	7.160725	6.813692	6.492356	6.194374	5.917647	5.660292	5.420619
13	8.852683	8.357651	7.903776	7.486904	7.103356	6.749870	6.423548	6.121812	5.842362	5.583147
14	9.294984	8.745468	8.244237	7.786150	7.366687	6.981865	6.628168	6.302488	6.002072	5.724476
15	9.712249	9.107914	8.559479	8.060688	7.606080	7.190870	6.810864	6.462379	6.142168	5.847370
16	10.105895	9.446649	8.851369	8.312558	7.823709	7.379162	6.973986	6.603875	6.265060	5.954235
17	10.477260	9.763223	9.121638	8.543631	8.021553	7.548794	7.119630	6.729093	6.372859	6.047161
18	10.827603	10.059087	9.371887	8.755625	8.201412	7.701617	7.249670	6.839905	6.467420	6.127966
19	11.158116	10.335595	9.603599	8.950115	8.364920	7.839294	7.365777	6.937969	6.550620	6.198231
20	11.469921	10.594014	9.818147	9.128546	8.513564	7.963328	7.469444	7.024752	6.623131	6.259331
21	11.764077	10.835527	10.016803	9.292244	8.648694	8.075070	7.562003	7.101550	6.686957	6.312462
22	12.041582	11.061240	10.200744	9.442425	8.771540	8.175739	7.644646	7.169513	6.742944	6.358663
23	12.303379	11.272187	10.371059	9.580207	8.883218	8.266432	7.718434	7.229658	6.792056	6.398837
24	12.550358	11.469334	10.528758	9.706612	8.984744	8.348137	7.784316	7.282883	6.835137	6.433771
25	12.783356	11.653583	10.674776	9.822580	9.077040	8.421745	7.843139	7.329985	6.872927	6.464149

INDEX

Index

This book has been set in 10 and 9 point Times Roman, leaded 2 points. Unit numbers are in 24 point Craw Modern; unit titles are in 18 point Craw Modern. Chapter numbers are in 48 point Craw Modern; chapter titles are in 18 point Craw Modern. The size of the type page is 27 by 46½ picas.